Governance of Arctic Shipping

Publications on Ocean Development

A SERIES OF STUDIES ON THE INTERNATIONAL, LEGAL, INSTITUTIONAL, AND POLICY ASPECTS OF OCEAN DEVELOPMENT

General Editors

Robin Churchill
Alex Oude Elferink

VOLUME 84

The titles published in this series are listed at *brill.com/pood*

Governance of Arctic Shipping

Balancing Rights and Interests of Arctic States and User States

Edited by

Robert C. Beckman
Tore Henriksen
Kristine Dalaker Kraabel
Erik J. Molenaar
J. Ashley Roach

BRILL
NIJHOFF

LEIDEN | BOSTON

Library of Congress Cataloging-in-Publication Data

Names: Beckman, Robert C. (Law teacher), editor. | Henriksen, Tore, 1964– editor. | Kraabel, Kristine Dalaker. | Molenaar, Erik Jaap, editor. | Roach, J. Ashley, editor. | National University of Singapore. Centre for International Law, sponsoring body. | K.G. Jebsen Centre for the Law of the Sea, sponsoring body.
Title: Governance of Arctic shipping : balancing rights and interests of Arctic states and user states / edited by Robert C. Beckman, Tore Henriksen, Kristine Dalaker Kraabel, Erik J. Molenaar, J. Ashley Roach.
Description: Leiden ; Boston : Brill Nijhoff, 2017. | Series: Publications on ocean development, ISSN 0924-1922 ; volume 84 | "This book arose out of a discussion between the Centre for International Law (CIL) of the National University of Singapore and the K.G. Jebsen Centre for the Law of the Sea (JCLOS) at UiT The Arctic University of Norway, in Tromso. CIL and JCLOS decided to organise jointly an international conference in Singapore in December 2015 to examine the governance of Arctic shipping."—ECIP foreword. | Includes bibliographical references and index.
Identifiers: LCCN 2017028544 (print) | LCCN 2017031463 (ebook) | ISBN 9789004339385 (E-book) | ISBN 9789004339378 (hardback : alk. paper)
Subjects: LCSH: Arctic Ocean—Navigation—Law and legislation—Congresses. | Maritime law—Arctic regions—Congresses.
Classification: LCC KZA1667 (ebook) | LCC KZA1667 .G68 2017 (print) | DDC 343.09/62091632—dc23
LC record available at https://lccn.loc.gov/2017028544

Typeface for the Latin, Greek, and Cyrillic scripts: "Brill". See and download: brill.com/brill-typeface.

ISSN 0924-1922
ISBN 978-90-04-33937-8 (hardback)
ISBN 978-90-04-33938-5 (e-book)

This book is printed on acid-free paper and produced in a sustainable manner.

Contents

Foreword

The focus of this book is on the governance of Arctic shipping. The sub-theme is the need to balance the rights and interests of the Arctic States, user States and other stakeholders in developing cooperative mechanisms on the governance of Arctic shipping as the amount of shipping in the Arctic increases due to the receding sea ice.

I will first provide some background on the legal regime governing the Arctic for readers who are not familiar with the Arctic and/or the international law of the sea.

The Arctic Ocean is part of our global commons. The 1982 United Nations Convention on the Law of the Sea (UNCLOS) governs the Arctic Ocean as it does all the other oceans and seas of the world. In a speech I was privileged to make on 10 December 1982 as President of the Third United Nations Conference on the Law of the Sea, I described UNCLOS as a 'constitution for the oceans'. As a result, maritime claims by the littoral States in the Arctic Ocean must be consistent with the regimes set out in UNCLOS on internal waters, territorial sea, contiguous zone, exclusive economic zone and continental shelf. The rights of coastal States and user States in these maritime zones are prescribed in UNCLOS. In other words, the international law applicable to the Arctic Ocean is UNCLOS. All the Arctic States, including the United States, accept this proposition.

UNCLOS has, however, taken into account the special environmental characteristics of the Arctic. Although Article 234 of UNCLOS on Ice-Covered Areas does not mention the Arctic, it was negotiated by Canada, the United States and the former Soviet Union, to apply to the Arctic. Article 234 empowers coastal States to adopt and enforce non-discriminatory laws and regulations for the prevention, reduction and control of marine pollution from vessels in ice-covered areas within the limits of their exclusive economic zone.

My second point is that on all matters relating to international shipping, UNCLOS refers to the International Maritime Organization (IMO) as the competent international organisation. The increased presence of vessels in the Arctic has raised concerns about whether current international rules and standards are sufficient for guiding vessels in this hostile and remote environment. Responding to these concerns, the IMO has developed special regulations for ships operating in polar waters and incorporated them into several existing IMO Conventions, including the International Convention for the Safety of Life at Sea (SOLAS) and the International Convention for the Prevention of Pollution from Ships (MARPOL). These provisions are known as the Polar Code, and they entered into force on 1 January 2017. Additional amendments to the International Convention on Standards of Training, Certification and Watchkeeping for Seafarers (STCW) will enter into force on 1 July 2018.

The Arctic Council has played an important role in the governance of Arctic shipping and in protecting the marine environment in Arctic waters. The Council is an inter-governmental forum established by the eight Arctic States in 1996. The purpose of the Council is to foster cooperation and coordination among the Arctic States, 'with the involvement of the Arctic indigenous communities and other Arctic inhabitants' as well as contributions from invited experts and observers. In 2013, Singapore was accepted as one of the twelve non-Arctic State observers, together with important East Asian States, namely China, Japan and the Republic of Korea.

This book arose out of a discussion between the Centre for International Law (CIL) of the National University of Singapore and the K.G. Jebsen Centre for the Law of the Sea (JCLOS) at UiT The Arctic University of Norway, in Tromsø. CIL and JCLOS decided to organise jointly an international conference in Singapore in December 2015 to examine the governance of Arctic shipping. It was agreed that academics would be invited to present papers on the governance of Arctic shipping, and that the authors would include academics from the Arctic States as well as from four of the Asian States that are observers at the Arctic Council—China, Japan, Korea and Singapore. It was also agreed that a representative of the IMO should be invited, as well as a representative of the Arctic indigenous peoples.

The main objective of the Conference was to increase understanding among the Arctic States, user States and other stakeholders concerning the issues that must be addressed if the amount of shipping in the Arctic increases due to the receding sea ice. The presentations at the Conference helped stakeholders understand how other stakeholders viewed the issues, and provoked a lively discussion and exchange of views. After the Conference, the members of the editorial committee from JCLOS and CIL asked the authors to revise their papers to take into account the discussions at the Conference as well as suggestions of the editors.

The Chapters in this book are organised as follows. Chapters 1 to 3 provide the background necessary for readers to understand the legal and institutional issues concerning the governance of shipping in the Arctic. In Chapter 1, Lawson W Brigham provides an overview of the changing maritime Arctic and new marine operations. In Chapter 2, Erik J Molenaar provides an overview of the legal and institutional framework governing Arctic shipping, with special attention to the Arctic Council. In Chapter 3, Dalee S Dorough outlines the rights, interests and role of the Arctic Council Permanent Participants.

Chapters 4 and 5 are devoted to the role of the IMO. In Chapter 4, Aldo Chircop analyses the IMO and UNCLOS and their role in the governance of

Arctic shipping. Finally, in Chapter 5, J Ashley Roach explains the Polar Code and its adequacy.

Chapters 6 to 8 examine the rights, interests, positions and practice on Arctic shipping from the perspective of the Arctic coastal States. Jan J Solski analyses Russia, Donald R Rothwell analyses Canada and the United States, and Tore Henriksen analyses Norway, Denmark (on behalf of Greenland) and Iceland.

Chapters 9 to 11 examine the rights, interests, positions and practice on Arctic shipping from the perspective of user States, with special reference to Asian flag States. In Chapter 9, Deukhoon (Peter) Han and Sung-Woo Lee examine the issues from the perspective of Asian flag States generally, and the Republic of Korea in particular. In Chapter 10, Guifang (Julia) Xue and Yu Long examine how the principles of equal treatment and non-discrimination apply to Arctic shipping. In Chapter 11, Kentaro Nishimoto examines the rights and interests of Japan in regard to Arctic shipping.

Chapters 12 and 13 examine whether lessons learned with respect to the governance of shipping in Southeast Asia may be relevant to the governance of Arctic shipping. In Chapter 12, Robert C Beckman and Sun Zhen examine the cooperative mechanism for the Straits of Malacca and Singapore. In Chapter 13, Captain M Segar examines the Singapore experience in oil spill preparedness and response.

The Conclusions are set out in the Chapter 14. In this Chapter, the editors summarise some of the major findings in the previous Chapters and make recommendations on the future governance of Arctic shipping. The recommendations are a result of discussions among the editors during and after the Conference on the future governance of Arctic shipping. These discussions focused in particular on the issue of whether some features of the Cooperative Mechanism for the Straits of Malacca and Singapore could serve as a model for establishing cooperative mechanisms on shipping in the Arctic. As will be seen in the concluding Chapter, the editors believe that there are indeed some lessons from Southeast Asia that could be used as a model for establishing cooperative mechanisms in the Arctic. Because I played a role in negotiating the cooperative mechanism for the Straits of Malacca and Singapore, I am especially pleased with these conclusions.

Finally, I would like to congratulate the editors from JCLOS and CIL for what I believe will be an important contribution to the governance of Arctic shipping. It is also my hope this book will lead to further collaborations and research between JCLOS and CIL.

Tommy T B Koh
Chairman, Governing Board, CIL

Acknowledgements

The editors are grateful to all the authors for their contributions to this book. We would like to record our special thanks to Glen Jeffries, Research Assistant at the K.G. Jebsen Centre for the Law of the Sea (JCLOS), UiT The Arctic University of Norway, Tromsø, for his excellent work and invaluable support with the preparation of the manuscript, specifically with regard to checking the online references and creating the List of Abbreviations. We would also like to express our gratitude to Brill Publishing for their cooperation and support on this project.

List of Figures

List of Abbreviations

AARI	Russian Federation Arctic and Antarctic Research Institute
ACAP	Arctic Contaminants Action Program, Arctic Council Working Group
ACGF	Arctic Coast Guard Forum
ACIA	Arctic Climate Impact Assessment
ACS	Arctic Council System
AEC	Arctic Economic Council
AEPS	Arctic Environmental Protection Strategy
AIS	Automatic Identification System
AMAP	Arctic Monitoring and Assessment Program, Arctic Council Working Group
AMSA	Arctic Marine Shipping Assessment
ANSR	Administration of the Northern Sea Route
AORF	Arctic Offshore Regulators Forum
APM	Associated Protective Measure (IMO)
Arctic Five	Canada, Denmark, Norway, the Russian Federation and the United States
Arctic States	Canada, Denmark, Finland, Iceland, Norway, Sweden, the Russian Federation and the United States
ARHC	Arctic Regional Hydrographic Commission
ASEAN	Association of Southeast Asian Nations
ASNA	Arctic Slope Native Association
ATBA	Area to be avoided (IMO)
AWPPA	Arctic Waters Pollution Prevention Act
BWM	Ballast Water Management
CAFF	Conservation of Arctic Flora and Fauna, Arctic Council Working Group
CAO	Code of Administrative Offences of the Russian Federation
CCC	Sub-Committee on Carriage of Cargoes and Containers (IMO)
CDEM	Construction, design, equipment and manning
CEDAW	Convention on the Elimination of All Forms of Discrimination Against Women
CLCS	Commission on the Limits of the Continental Shelf
CNIIMF	Central Marine Research and Design Institute
COLREG	Convention on the International Regulations for Preventing Collisions at Sea
CSA	Shipping Act of Canada

DE	Sub-Committee on Ship Design and Equipment (IMO)
DNV	Det Norske Veritas
ECA	Emission control area
EEA	European Economic Area
EEZ	Exclusive Economic Zone
EFZ	Exclusive Fishery Zone
EOC	Singapore Emergency Operations Committee
EPPR	Emergency Preparedness, Prevention and Response, Arctic Council Working Group
EU	European Union
FAL	Facilitation Committee (IMO)
FNI	Fridtjof Nansen Institute
FPZ	Fisheries Protection Zone
FSB	Federal Security Service of the Russian Federation
FSI	Sub-Committee on Flag State Implementation (IMO)
GAIRAS	Generally accepted international rules and standards
GATT	General Agreement on Tariffs and Trade
GMDSS	Global Maritime Distress and Safety System
GT	Gross tonnage
HFO	Heavy Fuel Oil
HTW	Sub-Committee on Human Element, Training and Watchkeeping (IMO)
IACS	International Association of Classification Societies
IAEA	International Atomic Energy Agency
IALA	International Association of Marine Aids to Navigation and Lighthouse Authorities
ICAO	International Civil Aviation Organization
ICC	Inuit Circumpolar Council
ICERD	International Convention on the Elimination of All Forms of Racial Discrimination
ICS	International Chamber of Shipping
IGC Code	International Code for the Construction and Equipment of Ships Carrying Liquefied Gases in Bulk
IHO	International Hydrographic Organization
III	Sub-Committee on Implementation of IMO Instruments (IMO)
III Code	IMO Instruments Implementation Code
ILA	International Law Association
ILO	International Labour Organization
IMCO	Inter-governmental Maritime Consultative Organization
IMO	International Maritime Organization

INSROP	International Northern Sea Route Programme
IOC	Intergovernmental Oceanographic Commission
ISPS Code	International Ship and Port Facility Security Code
IUCN	International Union for the Conservation of Nature
IWC	International Whaling Commission
JAMSTEC	Japan Agency for Marine-Earth Science and Technology
JCAR	Japan Consortium for Arctic Environmental Research
LEG	Legal Committee (IMO)
LNG	Liquefied natural gas
MARPOL	International Convention for the Prevention of Pollution from Ships
MEPA	Greenland Marine Environmental Protection Act
MEPC	Marine Environment Protection Committee (IMO)
MoD	Russian Federation Ministry of Defence
MoH	Russian Federation Marine Operation Headquarters
MPA	Marine protected area; Maritime and Port Authority of Singapore[1]
MSC	Maritime Safety Committee (IMO)
NCSR	Sub-Committee on Navigation, Communications and Search and Rescue (IMO)
NEAFC	North-East Atlantic Fisheries Commission
NGO	Non-governmental organisation
nm	nautical mile(s)
NORDREG	Northern Canada Vessel Traffic Services Zone Regulations
NEP	Northeast Passage
NSR	Northern Sea Route
NWP	Northwest Passage
OPRC	International Convention on Oil Pollution Preparedness, Response and Cooperation
PAME	Protection of the Arctic Marine Environment, Arctic Council Working Group
Paris MoU	Paris Memorandum of Understanding on Port State Control
PPR	Sub-Committee on Pollution Prevention and Response (IMO)
PPSA	Singapore Prevention of Pollution of the Sea Act
PSSA	Particularly Sensitive Sea Area (IMO)
Polar Code	International Code for Ships Operating in Polar Waters
PSC	Port State Control
RFB	Regional Fishery Body
RFMA	Regional Fisheries Management Arrangement
RFMO	Regional Fisheries Management Organization

1 Chapter 13 of this Volume only.

SAO	Senior Arctic Officials (Arctic Council)
SAR	Search and Rescue
SCTF	Enhancing Scientific Cooperation in the Arctic Task Force (Arctic Council)
SDC	Sub-Committee on Ship Design and Construction (IMO)
SDWG	Sustainable Development Arctic Council Working Group
SOLAS	International Convention for the Safety of Life at Sea
SOMS	Straits of Malacca and Singapore
SOR	Ship and Ocean Foundation
SRS	Ship reporting system
SSA	Greenland Safety at Sea Act
SSSA	Norwegian Ship Safety and Security Act
STCW	International Convention on Standards of Training, Certification and Watchkeeping for Seafarers
TCC	Technical Cooperation Committee (IMO)
TFAMC	Task Force on Arctic Marine Cooperation
TFOPP	Task Force on Arctic Marine Oil Pollution Prevention
TSCZ	1958 Convention on the Territorial Sea and the Contiguous Zone
TSS	Traffic separation scheme
TTEG	Tripartite Technical Expert Group on Safety of Navigation in the Straits of Malacca and Singapore
UNCITRAL	United Nations Commission on International Trade Law
UNCLOS	United Nations Convention on the Law of the Sea
UNCTAD	United Nations Conference on Trade and Development
UN Declaration	United Nations Declaration on the Rights of Indigenous Peoples (also referred to as UNDRIP)
UNEP	United Nations Environment Programme
UNESCO	United Nations Educational, Scientific and Cultural Organization
UNGA	United Nations General Assembly
UNTS	United Nations Treaty Series
VHF	Very high frequency
VLCC	Very large crude carriers
VTS	Vessel Traffic Services
WCO	World Customs Organization
WMO	World Meteorological Organization
WTO	World Trade Organization
WWF	World Wide Fund for Nature
WWNWS	World Wide Navigational Warning Service

List of Contributors

Robert C Beckman

is the Head of the Ocean Law and Policy programme and the former Director of the Centre for International Law (CIL), a university-level research centre at the National University of Singapore (NUS). He is also an Associate Professor at the NUS Faculty of Law, an Adjunct Senior Fellow at the S Rajaratnam School of International Studies (RSIS), Nanyang Technological University, and a member of the National Executive Committee of CSCAP Singapore. Since 2009, he has lectured in the summer programme at the Rhodes Academy of Oceans Law and Policy in Rhodes, Greece, and he is a member of the Governing Board for the Rhodes Academy. He also lectures in the International Maritime Boundary Workshops organised by CIL. He has published widely on ocean law and policy issues.

Lawson W Brigham

is Distinguished Professor of Geography & Arctic Policy at the University of Alaska Fairbanks, a Fellow at the US Coast Guard Academy's Center for Arctic Studies and Policy, and a Senior Fellow at the Institute of the North. Dr Brigham was a career US Coast Guard officer and he commanded four Coast Guard cutters including the icebreaker *Polar Sea* on Arctic & Antarctic expeditions. During 2004–09, he was chair of the Arctic Council's Arctic Marine Shipping Assessment and Vice Chair of the Council's working group on Protection of the Arctic Marine Environment. Dr Brigham has been a research fellow at Woods Hole Oceanographic Institution, a faculty member of the US Coast Guard Academy and the Naval Postgraduate School, and Alaska Director of the US Arctic Research Commission. He is a graduate of the US Coast Guard Academy (BS), a US Naval War College distinguished graduate, and holds graduate degrees from Rensselaer Polytechnic Institute (MS) and Cambridge University (MPhil & PhD). His research interests have focused on the Russian maritime Arctic, Arctic climate change, polar marine transportation, and polar geopolitics. Dr Brigham was a 2008 signer of the American Geographical Society's Flier's and Explorer's Globe, the Society's historic globe of exploration, in recognition of *Polar Sea*'s 1994 voyages becoming the first ship in history to reach the extreme ends of the global ocean. Dr Brigham is a member of the World Economic Forum's Global Agenda Council on the Arctic, and was elected to the Norwegian Scientific Academy for Polar Research.

Aldo Chircop

(JSD, Dalhousie 1988) is Professor of Law and Canada Research Chair (Tier I) in Maritime Law & Policy at Dalhousie University. He is based at the Marine & Environmental Law Institute (MELAW, Schulich School of Law) and is faculty at the International Development Studies Programme and Research Fellow at the Centre for Foreign Policy Studies, both at the Faculty of Arts and Social Sciences. In 1988–1992, he held directorships of the Mediterranean Institute (University of Malta) and International Ocean Institute and was legal advisor on Malta's delegation to the Preparatory Commission established by the UN Convention on the Law of the Sea. On joining Dalhousie in 1992, he was Director of the Marine Affairs Program. In 2003–2005, he was Canadian Chair in Marine Environmental Protection at the IMO's World Maritime University, Sweden. Dr Chircop has published extensively in the law of the sea, maritime law and coastal management fields. He is co-editor of the *Ocean Yearbook* (Martinus Nijhoff Publishers). His co-authored work *Maritime Law* (with Gold & Kindred; Toronto: Irwin Law, 2003) received a national prize at the Canadian Bar Association in 2005. His research focuses on interstitial issues of the international law of the sea and maritime law, in particular the regulation of polar shipping, use of maritime regulatory tools for marine spatial planning and conservation, and development of Canadian maritime law. Dr Chircop is a member of the Nova Scotia bar and Chair of the International Working Group on Polar Shipping of the Comité Maritime International.

Dalee S Dorough

(Inuit-Alaska) specialises in public international law, international human rights law, Indigenous human rights standards, political and legal relations between nation-states and Indigenous peoples, and Alaska Natives. She is an Associate Professor of Political Science at University of Alaska Anchorage, responsible for the sub-field of International Relations. Active for decades at the UN, ILO, OAS, and other international fora, she is also an Expert Member of the UN Permanent Forum on Indigenous Issues. She holds a PhD from the University of British Columbia, Faculty of Law (2002) and a Master of Arts in Law & Diplomacy from The Fletcher School at Tufts University (1991).

Recent publications include: 'The Revision of ILO Convention No. 107: A Subjective Assessment' and 'Conference Remarks', in D S Dorough, R Dunbar Ortiz, G Alfredsson, P Wille and L Swepston, eds, *Indigenous Peoples' Rights in International Law: Emergence and Application—A Book in Honor of Asbjorn Eide at Eighty* (Copenhagen: Galdu and International Work Group on Indigenous

Affairs, 2015); 'Indigenous Peoples' Right to Self-Determination and Other Rights Related to Access to Justice: Normative Framework', Wilton Littlechild and Elsa Stamatopoulou, eds, *Indigenous Peoples' Access To Justice, Including Truth And Reconciliation Processes*, (New York: Columbia University Academic Commons, 2014), electronic format: http://dx.doi.org/10.7916/D8GT5M1F; and 'Reflections on the UN Declaration on the Rights of Indigenous Peoples: An Arctic Perspective', in Steven Allen and Alexandra Xanthaki, eds, *Reflections on the UN Declaration on the Rights of Indigenous Peoples* (Oxford: Hart Publishing, 2011), pp 507–33.

Deukhoon (Peter) Han
is a Senior Researcher at the Korea Maritime Institute (KMI). Before he joined KMI, he was a practicing attorney in the areas of international trade, contracts, and maritime affairs in Los Angeles, USA. He was a judicial clerk for the Kansas District Court of Shawnee County. After he joined KMI in 2011, he has served as a legal researcher on KMI's international research team. His research areas are extensive. He is interested in international law, international commercial law, shipping law and North-South Korean maritime law. Currently, he is researching the impact of the Trans-Pacific Partnership (TPP) on the Korean Fisheries Subsidies regime. He is a frequent adviser to the Korean Ministry on the legal review of MOUs, and legal issues such as FAO Port State Measures Agreement. He represented the Republic of Korea in the 11th ICSP meeting of the UN Fish Stocks Agreement and the 67th and 68th Sessions of the UN informal consultation meetings on a sustainable fisheries resolution. He is a member of the New York Bar and District of Columbia Bar. He has written on maritime and fisheries issues including two recent publications: 'A Study on International Community's legislation and legal cases on IUU activities' (*Korea Business Law Association Journal*, 2014) and 'A study on comparative legal research on North-South Korea's maritime legal system and policy tasks for its integration' (*KMI*, 2015).

Tore Henriksen
is the Director of the KG Jebsen Centre for the Law of the Sea (JCLOS), UiT The Arctic University of Norway, Tromsø. He is also Professor at the Faculty of Law, where he has taught for almost 20 years and also served as its Dean. Professor Henriksen is an expert on law of the sea issues. He established and was director of the LLM programme on the Law of the Sea at the University of Tromsø. Professor Henriksen has been a visiting fellow at the Lauterpacht Centre for International Law, University of Cambridge and the Max Planck Institute for Comparative Public Law and International Law, University of Heidelberg. He

has written particularly on issues concerning international fisheries law. In recent years he has been the leader of an interdisciplinary research project on Arctic shipping and has contributed his own research to the project.

Kristine Dalaker Kraabel

is a PhD Research Fellow at the KG Jebsen Centre for the Law of the Sea (JCLOS), UiT The Arctic University of Norway, Tromsø. Her research focus includes ocean law and policy issues, specifically the conservation and sustainable use of marine biological diversity of areas beyond national jurisdiction. The working title of her PhD thesis is 'The Conservation and Sustainable Use of Marine Biodiversity in Areas Beyond National Jurisdiction: A Legal Analytical Model for Determining the Necessary Institutional Arrangements'. Kristine is the former Associate Director of the Centre for International Law (CIL) at the National University of Singapore, where she assisted the CIL Director with administration and special projects and supported the CIL research staff with all aspects of editing and publication. She completed her Bachelor of Arts at Westhampton College at the University of Richmond, where she majored in Political Science and Economics, and her Juris Doctor at the University of Richmond School of Law.

Sung-Woo Lee

is a Director General at the Port & Logistics Division of the Korea Maritime Institute, a public think-tank in Korea specialising in the area of maritime transport and international logistics. He has been involved in various governmental projects, many of which are associated with shipping management, dryport planning, and port logistics park development. He received his PhD from the University of Seoul. He was previously affiliated with the Centre of Urban Planning and Environmental Management at the University of Hong Kong as a visiting professor. His interests include managerial and strategic aspects of international logistics and maritime transport, the possibility of an Arctic logistics system and port-city interaction and globalisation. He is a member and associate editor of the International Association of Maritime Economists. He is also an advisor to the Korean government and other governments on issues related to logistics. He is also working to support the 'Eurasia Initiative' policy of the Korean government in terms of logistics.

Yu Long

is a PhD Candidate at the KoGuan Law School at Shanghai Jiaotong University. He also works as a Research Assistant at the Center for Rule of Ocean Law Studies focusing on the law of the sea issues in general and Arctic law and policy, specifically with regard to the legal framework for balancing rights and interests of Arctic States and other States.

Erik J Molenaar
has been with the Netherlands Institute for the Law of the Sea (NILOS) at Utrecht University since 1994 and currently holds the position of Deputy Director. In 2006, he also became employed by UiT The Arctic University of Norway, where he currently is a Professor with the KG Jebsen Centre for the Law of the Sea (JCLOS). After having completed his PhD on 'Coastal State Jurisdiction over Vessel-Source Pollution' (1998) and his tasks as assistant rapporteur to the International Law Association (ILA)'s Committee on Coastal State Jurisdiction Relating to Marine Pollution, he broadened his research field with international fisheries law and the international law relating to the Antarctic and Arctic. In addition to fundamental research, he has also provided juridical advice to, inter alia, various shipping and fishing companies, Netherlands and Norwegian Ministries, the European Parliament, the European Commission, UNEP and the FAO. His research has led to his participation in various diplomatic conferences and other intergovernmental meetings, including the annual meetings of several regional fisheries management organisations. Since late 2013, his research has a specific focus on participation, allocation and the ecosystem approach to polar fisheries.

Kentaro Nishimoto
is an Associate Professor at the School of Law, Tohoku University, Japan. He obtained his doctorate from the University of Tokyo in 2011, with a thesis on 'Territoriality and Functionality in the Historical Formation of the Modern Law of the Sea'. He teaches public international law at Tohoku University, and also teaches a course on the law of the sea at the Graduate School of Public Policy at the University of Tokyo. He serves on a number of government committees and expert groups in Japan, such as the Advisory Board on the Extension of the Continental Shelf at the Headquarters for Ocean Policy. His current research focuses on the legal regime of the outer continental shelf, settlement of maritime disputes in Asia, marine biological diversity beyond areas of national jurisdiction, and legal issues concerning the Arctic. His recent publications on the Arctic include: 'The Status of the Maritime Area around the Svalbard Islands in International Law', in *Governing the Arctic Ocean* (Toshindo, 2013) (in Japanese) and 'Coastal States' Regulation and the Regime of the International Straits in the Arctic Sea Route', in *International Straits* (Toshindo, 2015) (in Japanese).

J Ashley Roach

Captain, JAGC, US Navy (retired) was attorney adviser in the Office of the Legal Adviser, US Department of State, from 1988 until he retired at the end of January 2009. He was responsible for law of the sea matters. He is Visiting Senior Principal Research Fellow at the Centre for International Law, National University of Singapore. He has taught, advised and published extensively on national maritime claims and other law of the sea issues, including the Arctic, island disputes, and piracy and armed robbery at sea. He has negotiated, and participated in the negotiation of, numerous international agreements involving law of the sea issues. He received his LLM (highest honors in public international law and comparative law) from the George Washington University School of Law in 1971 and his JD from the University of Pennsylvania Law School in 1963.

Donald R Rothwell

is Professor of International Law, and Deputy Dean at the ANU College of Law, Australian National University where he has taught since July 2006. His research has a specific focus on law of the sea, law of the polar regions, and implementation of international law within Australia as reflected in over 200 articles, book chapters and notes in international and Australian publications. Rothwell has authored, co-authored or edited 21 books including most recently Rothwell, Oude Elferink, Scott and Stephens (eds), *The Oxford Handbook of the Law of the Sea* (OUP, 2015); Molenaar, Oude Elferink, and Rothwell (eds), *The Law of the Sea and the Polar Regions: Interactions between Global and Regional Regimes* (Martinus Nijhoff, 2013), and *Law of the Sea* (Edward Elgar, 2013).

Major career works include *The International Law of the Sea* (Hart, 1st 2010; 2nd 2015) with Stephens, and *The Polar Regions and the Development of International Law* (CUP, 1996). Rothwell is also Co-Editor of the *Australian Year Book of International Law*. Since 2012, he has been Rapporteur of the International Law Association (ILA) Committee on 'Baselines under the International Law of the Sea'. Rothwell was previously Challis Professor of International Law and Director of the Sydney Centre for International and Global Law, University of Sydney (2004–2006), where he had taught since 1988. He has acted as a consultant or been a member of expert groups for UNEP, UNDP, IUCN, the Australian Government, and acted as advisor to the International Fund for Animal Welfare (IFAW).

Captain M Segar

is the Assistant Chief Executive (Operations) of the Maritime and Port Authority of Singapore (MPA).

He holds a Master (Foreign-going) Certificate of Competency and a Master of Science (Maritime Administration & Environmental Protection) from the World Maritime University, Malmo (Sweden). Prior to his current appointment in MPA, he was a Port of Singapore Authority (PSA) sponsored student and after his sailing career, he worked with the Port of Singapore Authority as a Harbour Pilot (1 Jan 1990 to 1 Feb 1996). He then joined MPA as a Marine Officer and was subsequently promoted as the Port Master, MPA (Jan 2001 to Jul 2008). He was awarded the Public Administration Medal (Bronze) in 1998; the Commendation Medal during the Severe Acute Respiratory Syndrome (SARS) outbreak in 2003; and the Public Administration Medal (Silver) in 2010.

In his current capacity as the Assistant Chief Executive (Operations), Captain Segar oversees operational matters pertaining to the smooth and safe running of the Port of Singapore, so as to ensure that the world's busiest port remains safe, secure and efficient, thereby facilitating the development and promotion of Singapore as a hub port and international maritime centre. Captain Segar also oversees the administration of Singapore's responsibilities as a Flag State, Port State and Coastal State, and the use of technology to enhance Singapore's operations.

Jan J Solski

is a PhD Research Fellow at the KG Jebsen Centre for the Law of the Sea (JCLOS), UiT The Arctic University of Norway, Tromsø. His research focuses on the international law of the sea, and specifically on Russian practice in regulating navigation on the Northern Sea Route. The working title of his PhD thesis is 'Russian Coastal State Jurisdiction over Commercial Vessels Navigating the Northern Sea Route'. Jan holds academic degrees from universities in Poland and Norway, including a bachelor's and a master's degree in Russian and English Studies from the the Adam Mickiewicz University in Poznań; a master's degree in Law from the European School of Law and Administration in Warsaw; and a Master of Laws in the Law of the Sea from the University of Tromsø. As part of his research activity he has participated in the 2012 Summer Academy at the International Tribunal for the Law of the Sea in Hamburg and the 2013 NVP-Nansen summer school 'Shipping in Arctic Water: the interaction of sea ice, ship technology, climate change, economy and other operational conditions' in Longyearbyen, Svalbard. Jan has presented his research at numerous conferences in Finland, Norway and Russia and published his work in academic and popular journals.

Sun Zhen
is a member of the Ocean Law and Policy team at the Centre for International Law at the National University of Singapore where she focuses on legal issues in the Arctic and the regulation of international shipping by the International Maritime Organization. Her other research interests include maritime security, the protection of submarine cables, jurisdictional conflicts within the law of the sea and international dispute resolution. Zhen received her LLB from the Hainan University Law School, an LLM in International Law from the China University of Political Science and Law, a further LLM (Distinction) in International Law from the University of Edinburgh, and a PhD from the University of Cambridge, United Kingdom. She is admitted to the bar in the People's Republic of China.

Guifang (Julia) Xue
is Chair Professor of KoGuan Law School, Shanghai Jiao Tong University where she serves as Executive Director to the Research Base on National Marine Rights and Strategy and Center for Polar and Deep Ocean Development. Before she shifted her base to Shanghai in June 2013, she had served since 2005 as the Director for the Law of the Sea Institute, Ocean University of China (OUC). Besides day-to-day functions of the Institute for the Law of the Sea and the Law School, she was responsible for funding applications and project operations, and chaired commissioned projects for drafting or revising laws and regulations related to marine affairs. In OUC, she also chaired the Department of International Law, School of Law and Political Science, in which her responsibilities included course designation and theses examination for postgraduate students.

She has extensive research experience in the areas related to the United Nations Convention on the Law of the Sea. She looks at issues related to the practice of China on its marine legislation, ocean management, and international cooperation, and has published widely on related issues. She is also active in academic activities in the national and international arenas. She hosts courses on International Law of the Sea, the UNCLOS & International Fisheries Agreements, and Law of the Sea and Marine Affairs. She is also involved in training courses on these matters.

PART 1

Background and Context

CHAPTER 1

The Changing Maritime Arctic and New Marine Operations

*Lawson W Brigham**

1 Introduction

Great change has come to the maritime Arctic early in the 21st century. Globalisation of the Arctic—the linkage of the vast natural resources of the region, such as hydrocarbons and mineral wealth, to global markets—is underway. Exploration and development of regional natural resources represents a new era in the Arctic's connections to a future global economy. Global climate change, manifested in transformational changes in Arctic sea ice extent and thickness, is also a major change agent that has significant implications for expanded marine access and navigation seasons in Arctic coastal regions as well as the Central Arctic Ocean. In addition to these economic and climatic change forces, the voices of the Arctic indigenous peoples who have lived in the region for millennia are being heard in international forums such as the Arctic Council and within the Arctic States. The Arctic States are challenged to protect their Arctic peoples in the face of these historic changes and provide for measures of economic stability, while developing the region in sustainable ways. Simultaneously, the process of the delineation of the outer continental shelf in the Arctic Ocean is underway as stipulated in Article 76 of the United Nations Convention on the Law of the Sea (UNCLOS). In the midst of this complex set of interacting drivers is the evolving process for developing a set of regulatory measures to enhance Arctic marine safety and environmental protection. Achieving realistic, workable measures for governance will require broad engagement and close cooperation among the Arctic States, non-Arctic States, Arctic indigenous peoples, and many stakeholders and actors in the global maritime industry. The host of players involved in this process will have to be sensitive to the basic navigational rights, duties and freedoms; the environmental security issues facing the region; and the sustainable development challenges of expanded Arctic marine operations.

* The research and writing of this Chapter was supported by US National Science Foundation grant award 1263678 to the University of Alaska Fairbanks.

 | DOI 10.1163/9789004339385_002

From a marine navigation perspective the Arctic Ocean, smallest of our planet's oceans, has always been a relatively isolated, remote environment that remains ice-covered most of the year. It is a 'Mediterranean Sea' nearly enclosed by the North American, Eurasian and Greenlandic land masses with openings to the Atlantic Ocean near Greenland and Svalbard and a shallow opening to the Pacific Ocean through the Bering Strait.[1] Very cold air masses from these surrounding large, continental land areas influence every aspect of the physical environment. Figure 1.1 illustrates the confining nature of the Arctic Ocean's geography that restricts the movement of deep water, heat and sea ice into and out of the ocean. Also included on the map is the 500-metre bathymetric contour, which shows the breadth of the continental shelves to the north of Eurasia (along the Russian maritime Arctic), the widest and largest shelves of the global ocean. The complex physical geography of the ocean—shallow coastal seas, narrow straits, large archipelagoes (the Canadian Arctic Archipelago and archipelagoes of the Siberian islands north of Russia)—and cold, high-latitude climatology have shaped the maritime history of the Arctic and will continue to frame future Arctic marine use and the governance of the region.

In addition, Figure 1.1 delineates a large marine area in the Central Arctic Ocean that is largely in deep waters of the basin. This region is created by the five Arctic Ocean coastal States—Canada, Denmark/Greenland, Norway, Russia and the United States—exercising their rights and claiming Exclusive Economic Zones (EEZs) out 200 nautical miles (nm) from their respective coastlines. The resulting enclosed area is the international high seas of the Arctic Ocean defined by UNCLOS and is outside the national jurisdiction of the coastal States; the water column of this marine area is not part of their internal waters, territorial sea or EEZ. Notably, in July 2015 the five Arctic Ocean coastal States signed a declaration concerning the prevention of unregulated high seas fishing in the Central Arctic Ocean.[2] Since there is no current commercial fishing in this region, this action is following a precautionary approach. An effort is currently underway to have additional Arctic States and non-Arctic fishing nations sign an agreement to limit future, unregulated fishing at the top of the world. This same marine area is also tied to the ongoing process of delineation of the outer continental shelves of the Arctic Ocean coastal States, a process allowed under Article 76 of UNCLOS. Scientific surveys have in recent

1 Lawson W Brigham, 'Arctic Ocean' in John B Hattendorf (ed), *The Oxford Encyclopedia of Maritime History* (Oxford University Press, 2007) 135–143, at 135.

2 Declaration Concerning the Prevention of Unregulated High Sea Fisheries in the Central Arctic Ocean, signed 16 July 2015 in Oslo, Norway by Canada, Denmark, Norway, Russia and the United States.

FIGURE 1.1 *Central Arctic Ocean region*

summers been conducted by icebreakers to this remote region to support the extended seabed claims of the coastal States.

This introductory Chapter provides background and context for the discussions in the Chapters that follow. One focus is on current Arctic marine traffic and defining what is meant by 'Arctic shipping'. A second theme is the role of the Arctic Council in addressing marine safety and environmental protection issues, and a summary of outcomes and recommendations of the Council's Arctic Marine Shipping Assessment (AMSA) conducted between 2004 and 2009. Included is a section on the key drivers and uncertainties of future Arctic navigation that were identified by the AMSA scenarios creation process. Arctic sea ice changes are also presented as well as a brief discussion on the challenges of projecting future Arctic marine traffic that is related less to the retreat of sea ice and more to global shipping economics and commodities prices. An overview and short history of the development of the International Maritime Organization's Polar Code rounds out this introduction, as the new Code is a historic governance regime for polar waters.

2 The Arctic States—Marine Operations and Cooperation

Geographically and politically there are eight Arctic States—Canada, Denmark, Finland, Iceland, Norway, Sweden, Russia and the United States—that have sovereign territory on or above the Arctic Circle. All are key maritime states with commercial ships engaged in Arctic and global marine operations. All eight are also active and influential members of the International Maritime Organization (IMO) and the International Hydrographic Organization (IHO). Two of the maritime states, Finland and Sweden, do not border on the Arctic Ocean, but both have significant winter operations in the seasonally ice-covered Baltic Sea. One might question whether Iceland is an Arctic State, but its northern border intersects with the Arctic Circle and when it extends its EEZ out 200 nm to the north, it clearly meets the criteria. Figure 1.2 shows the relative position and size of the Arctic State sovereign territories, with Russia encompassing more than half of the coastal area. The map also illustrates two major Arctic marine routes: Russia's Northern Sea Route (NSR), which is defined in federal law as the set of routes between Kara Gate (the southern tip of Nova Zemlya) and the Bering Strait; and the Northwest Passage (NWP), the set of waterways through the straits of the Canadian Arctic Archipelago that link Baffin Bay in the east to the Bering Strait in the west. Additional key marine routes are indicated in the Barents Sea, around the east and west coast of Greenland, to Svalbard, into Canada's Hudson Bay, and through the Bering Strait and across the Bering Sea (into the Pacific).

Table 1.1 includes select Arctic marine transportation traffic data for the Central Arctic Ocean, NWP and NSR. Early in the 21st century there have been a (remarkable) 120 voyages by icebreakers to the North Pole for science and tourism; however, only one of these voyages was conducted in spring during a time of maximum thickness of Arctic sea ice and all the remaining voyages were conducted at the height of summer and minimum sea ice conditions.[3]

Data for complete voyages of the NWP indicate that only 236 such voyages from the first by the Norwegian explorer Roald Amundsen aboard *Gjoa*

3 The Soviet nuclear icebreaker *Sibir* operated in the Central Arctic Ocean from 8 May through 19 June 1987. North Pole Drift Station 27 was evacuated on 18–20 May 1987 and the North Pole was reached on 25 May 1987.

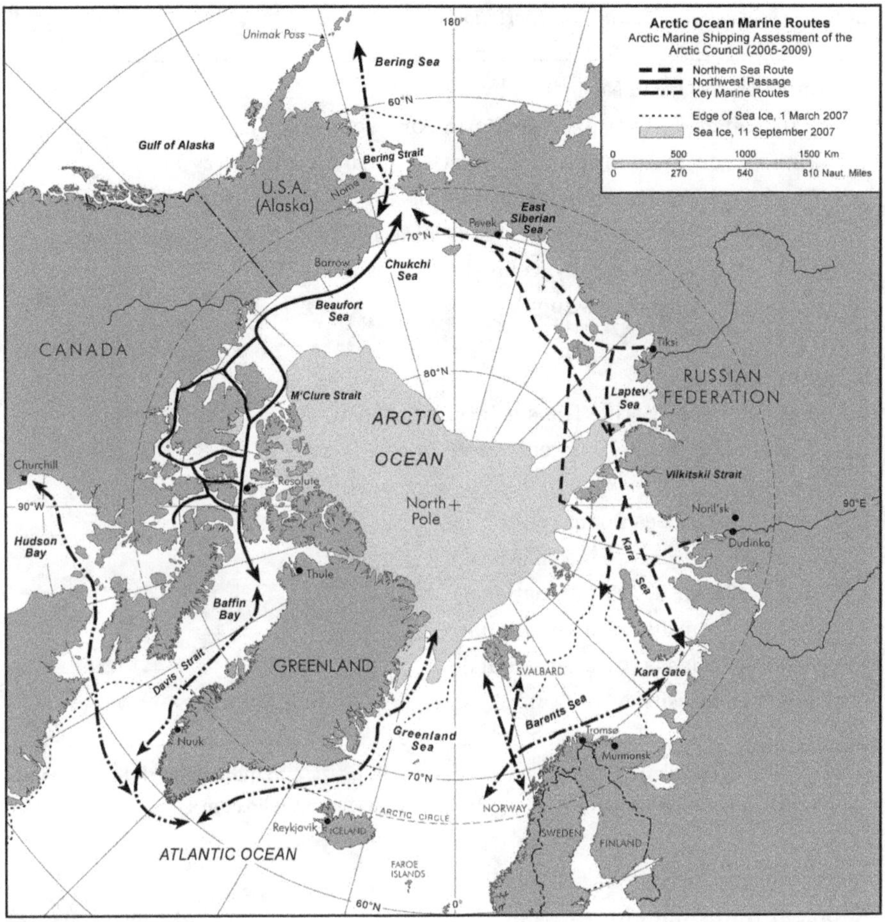

FIGURE 1.2 *Arctic Ocean marine routes*

in 1903–06 until the end of the summer navigation season in 2015.[4] In recent decades, a majority of the voyages have been by adventurers aboard small powered vessels and sailing yachts; a small minority of successful voyages have been completed by commercial carriers, icebreakers, and small cruise ships. However, these numbers relate solely to the trans-Arctic voyages using the full NWP and do not consider the more than 100 sailings of commercial ships and icebreakers supporting the summer sealift of supplies to Arctic communities using the many waterways throughout the Canadian Arctic Archipelago.

4 NWP data provided by Robert K Headland, Scott Polar Research Institute, Cambridge University, United Kingdom.

TABLE 1.1 *Key Arctic marine transportation data*

A. Central Arctic Ocean Navigation by Icebreaker[a]

- 120 Icebreaker Transits to the North Pole (1977–2015) (Russia 100; Sweden 7; Germany 5; USA 4; Canada 3; Norway 1)
- Single Late Winter/Spring (Non-summer) Transit to the North Pole (Soviet Nuclear Icebreaker *Sibir* 8 May to 19 June 1987)
- 7 Trans-Arctic Voyages by Icebreaker via the North Pole (1991, 1994, 1996 and 2005)

B. Northwest Passage[b]

- 236 Complete Marine Transits (ocean to ocean) Through the Canadian Archipelago by 176 Different Vessels (1906–2015)

C. Recent Northern Sea Route Traffic[c]

- 2011: 41 transits (16 international)
- 2012: 46 transits (27 international)
- 2013: 71 transits (28 international)
- 2014: 53 transits (31 international)
- 2015: 18 transits

SOURCES: [a]R. K. Headland, Scott Polar Research Institute, UK and the author. [b]R.K. Headland [c]Northern Sea Route Information Office, Murmansk (www.arctic-lio.com).

A look at traffic data for the NSR indicates a very high level of marine use, especially during the era of the Soviet Union. Table 1.2 shows high levels of ship traffic with 331 ships on 1306 voyages during a peak year of 1987 (cargo carried was a high of 6.6 million tons).[5] Most of this marine traffic (ice-capable cargo ships supported by a large fleet of icebreakers) was linked to Soviet development of Arctic natural resources so that the USSR could remain independent of international commodities markets and trading. Nothing compares today to this level of activity as indicated by the recent NSR data for 2011–2015 in Table 1.2. Due to the difficult economic conditions of the Russian Federation during the last decade of the 20th century, marine traffic and cargo carried decreased along the NSR. Since 2011, there has been a resurgence of interest in

5 Lawson W Brigham and Ben Ellis, 'Arctic Marine Transport Workshop Report' (Scott Polar Research Institute, Cambridge University, 28–30 September 2004) at A-17.

TABLE 1.2 *Arctic shipping data for the Northern Sea Route, 1985–2003*

Year	Total Amount of Cargo*	# Ships	# Voyages
1985	6161	296	1115
1986	6455	312	1224
1987	6579	331	1306
1988	6295	296	1016
1989	5823	273	928
1990	5510	252	886
1991	4804	243	811
1992	3909	206	606
1993	3016	117	463
1994	2300	153	315
1995	2362	134	309
1996	1642	75	234
1997	1945	70	220
1998	1458	51	152
1999	1580	49	155
2000	1587	52	169
2001	1800	60	194
2002	1600	47	170
2003	1700	47	160

*Cargo in thousands of tons
SOURCE: V. Mikhailichenko in Brigham, L. and B. Ellis (2004). Arctic Marine Transport Workshop (28–30 September) Report. Institute of the North and U.S. Arctic Research Commission.

re-establishing the NSR as a robust national Arctic waterway to facilitate the movement of Russian Arctic natural resources to international markets.

The Arctic States have had close cooperation during the past two decades, and arguably have enhanced regional stability, primarily by the establishment of the Arctic Council through the 1996 Ottawa Declaration.[6] The Council, an intergovernmental forum and consensus body, focuses in particular on environmental protection and sustainable development. Not discussed in the Arctic

6 Declaration of the Establishment of the Arctic Council, signed 19 September 1996 in Ottawa, Canada by the eight Arctic States.

Council are fisheries issues (left to regional fisheries management bodies), whaling issues (left to the domain of the International Whaling Commission), and military-security issues. Thus, the primary focus of the Council is on the environment, people and sustainability. The only voting members are the eight Arctic States, led by a chair rotating every two years with consensus required to take action on all initiatives, such as the projects of the working groups and task forces. Six Arctic indigenous groups, named the Permanent Participants, have their own delegations (although they are also citizens of an Arctic State) and sit with the Arctic State representatives at all Council meetings (e.g., of the Arctic Ministers and Senior Arctic Officials). The formal inclusion of indigenous representatives in this international forum is a unique and pioneering effort to recognise and respect the values and cultural heritage of the Arctic indigenous peoples (For further discussion, see Chapter 3 of this Volume). The observers of the Arctic Council are organised in three categories. As of June 2017 these are: non-Arctic States (13); intergovernmental and inter-parliamentary organisations (13); and nongovernmental organisations (13). The primary role of these observer groups is to observe the Council's work and obtain an informed view of Arctic affairs; they can also contribute their expertise to the working groups and task forces.[7]

It is important to note that the substantive work of the Council is conducted in six working groups and additional task forces as needed. The working groups on Protection of the Arctic Marine Environment (PAME), and Emergency Prevention, Preparedness and Response (EPPR) have had particular relevance to issues of Arctic marine operations and shipping. Key assessment reports issued by the Council and produced by its working groups include: the Arctic Climate Impact Assessment (2004), the Arctic Human Development Report (2004), the Arctic Oil and Gas Assessment (2008), the Arctic Marine Shipping Assessment (2009), and the Arctic Biodiversity Assessment (2013). As of March 2017, the Arctic Council had a number of special groups working on issues related to future Arctic marine operations and shipping: the Task Force on Arctic Marine Cooperation (2015), the Task Force on Arctic Telecommunications Infrastructure (2015), the Scientific Cooperation Task Force (2013), the Ecosystems-Based Management Expert group (2011), and the Expert Group in support of implementation of the framework for action on Black carbon and Methane (2015).[8] All of this important work will have future influences on the

7 For information on the Arctic Council, the role of observers and to review the Observers Manual, see https://www.arctic-council.org, accessed 15 March 2017.

8 *Ibid.*

evolving governance structures that will enhance Arctic marine safety and environmental protection.

3 What is Arctic Shipping?

The term 'Arctic shipping' has many different meanings for a host of stakeholders and the global media. Many believe Arctic shipping relates to trans-Arctic voyages by perhaps container ships or tankers on new global trade routes through and across the Arctic Ocean. However, this is a narrow definition and the same ships could be on destinational voyages where a ship sails out of the Arctic after performing a marine operation (such as delivering a cargo) or loading an Arctic natural resource destined to a global market. A more holistic approach to a general definition is to include all vessels (100 tons or more) that are operating anywhere in Arctic waters: the type of vessels, the activity they are undertaking, and the cargo they might be carrying. Such an approach would include: bulk carriers, container ships, liquefied natural gas (LNG) carriers, offshore oil and gas service and supply ships, passenger ships, icebreakers, ferries, government vessels, tugs and barges, fishing vessels, and perhaps large private pleasure craft. The Arctic Council's AMSA used this approach in its marine traffic data gathering in an effort to include all vessels that could discharge into Arctic marine waters and release emissions into the lower atmosphere.[9] A follow-on Arctic Council study conducted by the PAME Working Group, *The Arctic Ocean Review*, used 'Arctic marine operations and shipping' to denote a broad approach to the global maritime industry's operating in the Arctic marine environment.[10] For this volume on Arctic maritime legal issues and governance, 'Arctic marine operations and shipping' is a useful and inclusive definition that is not constrained by a focus on trans-Arctic navigation.

4 Arctic Sea Ice Changes and Impacts

Arctic sea ice is undergoing profound changes early in the 21st century—thinning, extent reduction in all seasons, and a reduction in the area of multiyear

9 Arctic Council, *Arctic Marine Shipping Assessment 2009 Report* (Arctic Council, 2009) (AMSA Report) 70–91.

10 Arctic Ocean Review Project Final Report Phase II 2011–2013 (AOR II) (15 May 2013) 1–100, at 32, accessed 15 March 2017 at http://www.pame.is/index.php/projects/arctic-marine-shipping/the-arctic-ocean-review-aor.

ice. Since 1979 and the advent of routine satellite coverage (by passive microwave sensors), the decline of sea ice extent at the summer minimum has been approximately 13 per cent per decade.[11] The summer minima of Arctic sea ice area during 2007 to 2015 have remarkably been the nine lowest of the satellite period (since 1979). The same satellite sensors have recorded an approximate 2.7 per cent decrease in winter Arctic sea ice extent.[12] A report by the US National Snow and Ice Data Center noted that January 2016's Arctic sea ice extent was the lowest in the satellite record; this extent averaged 13.53 million square kilometres, an area 1.04 million square kilometres *below* the 1981 to 2010 average.[13] It is likely these trends will continue under warming air temperatures, warming surface waters, and increasing areas of water (darker ocean waters) open to solar radiation. The uncertainty of the future is highlighted by the fact the observed sea ice extent is declining faster than global climate models predict.

This extraordinary transformation of the Arctic's sea ice cover has important, obvious implications for Arctic marine navigation: the changes provide for greater marine access throughout the region and potentially longer seasons of navigation along such waterways as the NSR in the Russian Arctic and the NWP through the Canadian Arctic Archipelago. However, one of the critical factors for current and future marine operations is that the Arctic Ocean is not ice-free year round, but it is ice-covered fully or partially in autumn, winter and spring through the century. Thus, ice-class ships will be required for much of the year for safety and operational reliability when any sea ice is present. Global climate model simulations of Arctic sea ice also indicate that a disappearance of old or multi-year sea ice may occur in summer sometime before mid-century. At that historic point during a future summer, the Arctic Ocean for a short period would be entirely ice-free with no sea ice surviving into the next season. After this event, only seasonal (first year) sea ice would cover a future Arctic Ocean in all seasons, very likely making it more navigable. It is also highly plausible that the future sea ice cover will be more mobile under the influence of regional winds, a key factor making the ease of ship navigation less certain.

---

11 Martin O Jeffries, James E Overland and Donald K Perovich, 'The Arctic Shifts to a New Normal' (2013) *Physics Today* 35–40, at 36.

12 Donald J Cavalieri and Claire L Parkinson, 'Arctic Sea Ice Variability and Trends, 1979–2010' (2012) *The Cryosphere* 881–889.

13 National Snow and Ice Data Center Report, 'Arctic Sea Ice Hits New Record Low for January' (2016) *Eco* at 12.

5 Arctic Council's Arctic Marine Shipping Assessment

The Arctic Council released in April 2009 a key report that relates directly to current and future Arctic marine use. AMSA followed the Council's Arctic Climate Impact Assessment and Arctic Marine Strategic Plan; both were released in 2004 and noted future increases in Arctic marine operations. The AMSA 2009 Report is not only a comprehensive assessment of current and future Arctic marine operations, but a policy document of the Council since the seventeen AMSA recommendations were negotiated and consensus reached by the eight Arctic States.[14] AMSA, led by Canada, Finland, and the United States during 2005–2009, was conducted under PAME. AMSA was a broad assessment of Arctic marine activity, including indigenous marine use, with a clear focus on marine safety and environmental protection challenges, consistent with the Arctic Council's charter mandates on environmental protection and sustainable development. To support the AMSA research, thirteen major workshops were held on a broad range of themes: scenarios of future Arctic navigation, environmental impacts, marine infrastructure, Arctic marine incidents, Arctic indigenous use, marine insurance, maritime industry stakeholders, and AMSA integration. Fourteen AMSA town hall meetings were held in Arctic communities to hear directly the concerns and interests of indigenous residents.[15] A baseline database of Arctic marine activity was developed from marine traffic information provided by each of the Arctic States. This strategy was used to ensure that the traffic data was the official national Arctic shipping data for what each state designated as their Arctic region. An estimated 6000 vessels were found to operate in the Arctic marine environment during 2004; fishing vessels made up slightly less than half the total and bulk carriers twenty per cent of the total.[16] Importantly, the database identified areas of high concentration of Arctic marine traffic, such as the Norwegian coast, northwest Russia, the west coast of Greenland (in summer) and the North Pacific Great Circle Route through Alaska's Aleutian Islands.[17]

The AMSA 2009 Report contained ninety-six findings under key themes including: marine geography, Arctic climate change and sea ice, the history of Arctic marine transportation, law of the sea and governance of the maritime Arctic, the AMSA traffic database, scenarios and future marine uses, indigenous issues and the human dimension, environmental considerations and impacts,

14 AMSA Report, *supra* note 9 at 6–7.

15 *Ibid.* at 122–133.

16 *Ibid.* at 72.

17 *Ibid.* at 73–75.

and Arctic marine infrastructure requirements and gaps. Selected and fundamental findings include:

- UNCLOS sets the fundamental legal framework for Arctic Ocean governance and the regulation of shipping and marine activities according to maritime zones of jurisdiction.
- Article 234 of UNCLOS provides the coastal States with the right to adopt and enforce non-discriminatory laws and regulations for the prevention, reduction and control of marine pollution in *ice-covered waters*.
- The IMO is the appropriate body for the Arctic States to turn to regarding all issues related to Arctic maritime safety, security and environmental protection. All eight Arctic States are active and influential IMO members.
- As of 2009, there were no special or mandatory IMO safety and environmental standards for ships operating in Arctic waters.
- The most significant threat of ships to the Arctic marine environment is the release of oil from accidental or illegal discharge.
- Although profound changes in the Arctic's sea ice cover are occurring, the continued presence of sea ice in autumn, winter and spring means the region is ice-covered for most of the year, not ice-free. This has significant implications for new regulatory requirements for Arctic ships.
- The key drivers and uncertainties of future Arctic navigation and increased Arctic marine activity are natural resource development and levels of regional trade.
- A large number of uncertainties influence the future of Arctic marine activity, including the legal and governance situation, Arctic State cooperation, climate change variability, an Arctic marine disaster, new resource discoveries, oil prices and other resource commodity pricing, multiple use conflicts, insurance industry roles, new international ship rules and regulations, radical change changes in global trade and more.
- Marine shipping is one of many factors affecting Arctic communities, directly and indirectly. The variety of shipping activities and the range of social, cultural and economic conditions in Arctic communities mean that shipping can have many effects, both positive and negative.
- AMSA town hall meetings indicated that, from an environmental perspective, shipping is viewed as a potential disruption to marine species. Oil spills are one of the largest concerns of the coastal communities. Hunters are also concerned about the impacts of ships on the animals and on their hunting practices.
- Nearly all current Arctic marine traffic is destinational and not trans-Arctic voyaging.

- There is a general lack of marine infrastructure throughout the Arctic, except for the coasts of Iceland, Norway and northwest Russia. For example, the operational network of meteorological and oceanographic observations in the Arctic, essential for accurate weather and wave forecasting for safe navigation, is extremely sparse. Also, significant portions of the primary Arctic shipping routes do not have adequate hydrographic data, and therefore charts, to support safe navigation.[18]

TABLE 1.3 *Recommendations of the Arctic Marine Shipping Assessment*[a]

I ~ Enhancing Arctic Marine Safety
A. Linking with International Organizations*
B. IMO Measures for Arctic Shipping*
C. Uniformity of Arctic Shipping Governance
D. Strengthening Passenger Ship Safety in Arctic Waters
E. Arctic Search & Rescue Instrument*

II ~ Protecting Arctic People and the Environment
A. Survey of Arctic Indigenous Marine Use*
B. Engagement with Arctic Communities*
C. Areas of Heightened Ecological and Cultural Significance*
D. Specially Designated Arctic Marine Areas
E. Protection from Invasive Species
F. Oil Spill Prevention*
G. Addressing Impacts on Marine Mammals*
H. Reducing Air Emissions

III ~ Building the Arctic Marine Infrastructure
A. Addressing the Infrastructure Deficit
B. Arctic Marine Traffic Systems*
C. Circumpolar Environmental Response Capacity*
D. Investing in Hydrographic, Meteorological & Oceanographic Data.

*Key Implementation Progress Made Since April 2009. AMSA Release.
[a]Arctic Council. Arctic Marine Shipping Assessment 2009 Report.

18 *Ibid.* at 154–187.

The seventeen recommendations of AMSA, negotiated and approved by the Arctic State ministers in April 2009, are listed in Table 1.3. The three inter-related themes—Enhancing Arctic Marine Safety, Protecting Arctic People and the Environment, and Building the Arctic Marine Infrastructure—will require close international cooperation, not only among the Arctic States, but between the Arctic States and all maritime nations at the IMO and other international forums. The huge deficit in Arctic marine infrastructure will require careful long-term planning and large investments from a host of public and private sources. Significant progress has been made in implementing a number of key AMSA recommendations. The Arctic States at the Arctic Council ministerial meeting in Nuuk, Greenland on 12 May 2011 signed a binding Arctic search and rescue (SAR) agreement, importantly identifying what Arctic SAR regions would be coordinated by each Arctic State.[19] Responding to the AMSA recommendation (III.C.) for enhancing environmental response, the Arctic States in May 2013 signed a second binding instrument, the *Agreement on Cooperation on Marine Oil Pollution Preparedness and Response in the Arctic*.[20] In response to linking Arctic issues with international bodies, the Arctic States have worked more closely together on Arctic issues at the IMO, the IHO (which established an Arctic Regional Hydrographic Commission) and the World Meteorological Organization. At the IMO, the Arctic States were proactive in pushing for mandatory ship rules and regulations that have been negotiated and approved as the IMO Polar Code. Three working groups of the Arctic Council (Arctic Monitoring and Assessment Programme, Conservation of Arctic Flora and Fauna, and Sustainable Development Working Group), responding to AMSA recommendation II.C., produced in 2013 a comprehensive report (and atlas) titled *Identification of Arctic marine areas of heightened ecological and cultural significance*.[21] This report documents Arctic marine areas that would be sensitive or vulnerable to marine operations, such as oil spills and physical disturbances (noise and ship strikes). During 2014–2015 under the leadership of Norway and Russia, the Arctic Council supported a Task Force on Marine Oil Pollution Prevention that developed a set of key recommendations (in response to AMSA II.F.). The Arctic Council has also encouraged

19 The Arctic States used the Arctic Council process and structure to negotiate the Arctic SAR Agreement. An unofficial map indicated the areas of SAR coordination responsibilities for each of the eight Arctic States.

20 Agreement on Cooperation on Marine Oil Pollution Preparedness and Response in the Arctic, signed 15 May 2013 in Kiruna, Sweden by the Arctic States.

21 'Identification of Arctic marine areas of heightened ecological and cultural significance: Arctic Marine Shipping Assessment (AMSA) IIc'. AMAP/CAFF/SDWG (2013) *Arctic Monitoring and Assessment Programme, Arctic Council.*

the International Whaling Commission (IWC); and a workshop was held in Anchorage, Alaska in March 2014 to discuss the current and future impacts of Arctic marine operations on cetaceans (in response to AMSA II.G.).[22] AMSA called for the development of a comprehensive Arctic marine traffic awareness system (AMSA III.B.) and significant regional progress has been made using new Automatic Identification System (AIS) monitoring and tracking of marine activity by satellite and land-based receivers. The continual improvement of national monitoring systems and Arctic State sharing of real-time marine traffic information can reduce the risks of marine accidents, facilitate response, and provide awareness of user conflict or overlap in regional Arctic seas.

In summary, AMSA is an influential assessment for the Arctic States and a message to a wider globe about measures to protect Arctic people and the environment in an era of increasing marine use in the Arctic Ocean. The AMSA effort can be understood from three perspectives. First, AMSA is a *baseline assessment* of Arctic marine activity (from the 2004 AMSA database) as a historic snapshot of Arctic marine use. Second, AMSA is a *strategic guide* for a host of Arctic and non-Arctic owners, stakeholders and actors. And third, arguably the most important, AMSA is a *policy document* of the Arctic Council since the 2009 report was negotiated and consensus reached for its recommendations by the eight Arctic States.

6 Drivers of Arctic Marine Navigation

One of the major tasks of the AMSA team was to determine the many uncertainties and key driving forces that might shape the future of Arctic navigation out to 2050. A scenarios-based approach was used to determine these factors and create a set of plausible futures for the maritime Arctic. The AMSA scenarios participants identified 120 factors or driving forces that could be influential.[23] The most highly influential factors included: the importance of a stable legal regime (UNCLOS); world trade patterns and radical changes in global trade dynamics; global oil prices; the safety of other global maritime routes (including catastrophic loss of the Suez or Panama canals); rapid climate change and climate changes that are more disruptive sooner than anticipated; a major Arctic shipping disaster; limited windows of Arctic operations (seasonal impacts on shipping economics); the marine insurance industry; transit fees on Arctic routes; new Arctic resource discoveries; conflicts between indigenous uses and

22 'Report of the IWC Workshop on Impacts of Increased Marine Activities on Cetaceans in the Arctic' (IWC Workshop, Anchorage, Alaska USA, 6–7 March 2014).

23 AMSA Report, *supra* note 9 at 93.

commercial navigation; escalation of Arctic maritime disputes; global shifts to nuclear energy; Arctic maritime enforcement; China, Japan and Korea becoming active Arctic maritime nations; and global (IMO) agreements on Arctic ship construction rules and standards.

The diversity of these forces or uncertainties highlight the complexity and global connections that can influence future Arctic marine use. For example, global oil price stability was determined to be a major factor and during the conduct of AMSA oil prices fluctuated from a high of US$147 per barrel to a low of US$55 per barrel. This was deemed a huge factor for future Arctic onshore and offshore hydrocarbon development (and indirectly impacted the levels of marine support and transportation systems). In the AMSA scenarios process, three criteria were used to select two key factors for the scenarios matrix: the degree of plausibility, relevance to Arctic and maritime affairs, and being at the right threshold of the many factors considered.[24] Two factors stood out under this evaluation: *resources and trade* (the level of demand for Arctic natural resources and trade); and *governance* (the degree of relative stability of rules and standards for marine use both within the Arctic and internationally).[25] These two primary factors anchored the axes of uncertainty of the AMSA scenarios matrix that was used to develop a set of four plausible futures for Arctic navigation. It is important to note that climate change and Arctic sea ice retreat were considered significant factors; the profound changes in Arctic sea ice provide for improved Arctic marine access and potentially longer seasons of navigation. However, the economic factors of Arctic natural resource development, connections to global markets, and global commodities prices were deemed primary drivers of Arctic marine operations and shipping. Maritime governance was considered equally key in the form of a stable, operating system of legal and regulatory measures that would be reinforced by broad international cooperation. The importance of the AMSA scenarios effort cannot be underestimated. The process facilitated new and unconstrained thinking, and was a valuable futures tool to handle the complexity of Arctic maritime use. Most critically, the scenarios creation effort assisted in the identification of the major uncertainties or drivers of future Arctic navigation, many of the key risks involved, and the connections of the Arctic to the global economy.

24 *Ibid.* at 96–97.

25 *Ibid.* at 94–95.

7 Evolution of the IMO Polar Code

A historic, new regulatory regime in the polar regions was established when the IMO Polar Code for ships operating in polar waters came into force on 1 January 2017. The Polar Code creates binding or mandatory standards for new and existing commercial vessels and passenger ships of 500 tons or more operating in Arctic and Antarctic waters.[26] The Polar Code has evolved in a long process since 1993 as indicated in the key dates and milestones of Table 1.4. Initially, the IMO promulgated voluntary guidelines for ships operating in Arctic ice-covered waters; by 2009, the voluntary guidelines were adjusted to include ships operating in all polar waters. This change was made to reflect that not all ships would be operating in sea ice, since both marine regions are experiencing broad areas of ice-free conditions during the summer months. The Polar Code is applicable in all Antarctic waters south of 60 degrees south (northern boundary of the Antarctic Treaty). In the Bering Sea, the Polar Code boundary is 60 degrees north; in the North Atlantic, the boundary has been adjusted to reflect the region's warmer waters: running south of Greenland, northeast along the east coast of Greenland, north of Iceland and to the Russian Arctic coast in the Barents Sea. All of Iceland, northern (mainland) Norway and Russia's Kola Peninsula are outside the Polar Code area since they are ice-free year-round.[27]

The Polar Code at its core addresses marine safety and environmental protection challenges for ships operating in remote, cold environments where marine infrastructure is limited or non-existent. The main objective of this IMO effort was to develop a uniform, nondiscriminatory set of rules and regulations that would result in a level playing field for all polar marine operators. However, the Polar Code was never designed to be a new, separate IMO convention but rather a set of amendments to existing IMO instruments, including the International Convention for the Safety of Life at Sea (SOLAS),[28] the International Convention for the Prevention of Pollution from Ships

26 *International Code for Ships Operating in Polar Waters* (Polar Code) applies to commercial carriers and passenger ships 500 tons or more; not included under the Code are fishing vessels and other smaller vessels. For a consolidated online edition of the Polar Code, see International Code for Ships Operating in Polar Waters, accessed 15 March 2017 at http://www.imo.org/en/MediaCentre/HotTopics/polar/Documents/POLAR%20CODE%20TEXT%20AS%20ADOPTED.pdf.

27 *Ibid.* at 8, for illustrated maps of the application of the Polar Code to Antarctic and Arctic waters.

28 International Convention for the Safety of Life at Sea, adopted 1 November 1974, 1184 UNTS 2 (entered into force 25 May 1980), as amended (SOLAS).

TABLE 1.4 *Key dates in the development of the IMO Polar Code*

- 1993 ~ IMO Polar Code Outside Working Group established.
- 1998 ~ Draft Polar Code sent to IMO.
- 2002 ~ IMO voluntary *Guidelines for Ship's Operating in Arctic Ice-Covered Waters.*
- 2004–2009 ~ Conduct of the Arctic Council's Arctic Marine Shipping Assessment; Arctic States call for mandatory application of the *Guidelines* and augmentation of the IMO Conventions for ships operating in polar waters.
- 2006–2008 ~ International Association of Classification Societies (IACS) Unified Requirements for Polar Class Ships adopted.
- 2009 ~ IMO Voluntary and Updated *Guidelines for Ships Operating in Polar Waters.*
- 2010 ~ IMO Working Group on mandatory polar ship requirements established.
- 2014 (November) ~ IMO Marine Safety Committee adopts Polar Code SOLAS[a] amendments.
- 2015 (May) ~ IMO Marine Environmental Protection Committee adopts Polar Code environmental provisions and MARPOL[b] amendments.
- 2017 (1 January) ~ IMO Polar Code enters into force (also for newly built ships).
- 2018 (1 January) ~ IMO Polar Code enter into force for old ships.
- 2018 (1 July) ~ IMO Polar Code STCW[c] training requirements enter into force.

[a]International Convention for the Safety at Life at Sea; [b]International Convention for the Prevention of Pollution from Ships (1973 modified in 1978); [c]International Convention on Standards of Training, Certification and Watchkeeping for Seafarers.

(MARPOL),[29] and the International Convention on Standards of Training, Certification and Watchkeeping for Seafarers (STCW).[30] Ships certified under the Polar Code are now required to have a Polar Ship Certificate issued

29 International Convention for the Prevention of Pollution from Ships, adopted 2 November 1973, 1340 UNTS 184 as amended by Protocol of 1978 Relating to the International Convention for the Prevention of Pollution from Ships of 1973, 17 February 1978, 1340 UNTS 61 (both entered into force 2 October 1983), as further amended (MARPOL).

30 International Convention on Standards of Training, Certification and Watchkeeping for Seafarers, adopted 7 July 1978, 1361 UNTS 2 (entered into force 28 April 1984), as amended (STCW), and the Seafarers' Training, Certification and Watchkeeping (STCW) Code, IMO Doc MSC 96/3/2, 4 November 2015, prepared for adoption by MSC 97 to be convened on 21–25 November 2016 in accordance with the STCW Convention, Art XII(1)(a)(iv), with an expected entry into force on 1 July 2018; Lawson W Brigham, 'IMO Polar Code for Ships Operating in Polar Waters' (2015) *ACCESS Policy Brief Number 4* (Arctic Climate Change Economy and Society) 1.

by the flag State and also carry a Polar Water Operational Manual, which will be unique to a given ship indicating special operational capabilities and limitations. The Polar Ship Certificate will include information on ice class (PC-1 highest to PC-7 lowest); polar ship category (A-operation in medium first-year ice; B-operation in thin first-year ice; and C-operations in open water or in ice conditions less than type A and B); operational limitations; and required additional safety, communications equipment. MARPOL has been amended to include no discharge of oil and oily mixtures in polar waters (Annex I); no discharge of noxious liquid substances (Annex II); and restrictions on discharges of sewage (Annex IV) and garbage/food waste (Annex V) in polar waters.[31] The critical experience, training and certification of polar ship's officer and crew are being developed under the IMO's Subcommittee on Human Element, Training and Watchkeeping, and these new rules will be mandatory on 1 July 2018.

Full implementation of the IMO Polar Code presents a host of policy and practical challenges. A process for gaining a Polar Ship Certificate by the flag States should be operational by 1 January 2017. The ship classification societies and marine insurance industry, using a set of uniform, international rules and regulations, will be key players in evaluating the risks of ships operating in polar waters and assisting the flag States in implementing elements of the Polar Code. The ship classification societies will certify that polar class ships meet the new rules, and the insurance industry will insure only ships that meet the new Polar Code standards. Enforcement of the Polar Code is the responsibility of the flag States. However, port States, particularly those in or near the Arctic, have enforcement roles when ships are operating in Arctic waters. The global maritime industry is challenged to implement two key requirements in a timely fashion: the Polar Water Operational Manual, specific to a given ship that will operate in polar waters; and developing qualified polar mariners from a very small pool of experienced and trained operators. Finally, the Arctic States have a leadership responsibility in the Code's implementation, having called for mandatory polar ship rules in AMSA, and having been active together at IMO in the long negotiations for international safety and environmental regulations for polar ships.

31 The MARPOL Amendments (for oil, noxious liquid substances, sewage and garbage) to the Polar Code will treat Arctic marine waters as if they were Special Areas, joining other marine regions for added protection (such as the Southern Ocean, Baltic Sea, Black Sea and Mediterranean Sea).

8 Challenges of Arctic Shipping Forecasts and Projections

The complexity of Arctic navigation was highlighted by the AMSA scenarios process. Notably, the range of drivers and uncertainties make *accurate* forecasting or projecting future Arctic marine operations highly challenging, if not unattainable. What is most problematic are attempts to determine Arctic traffic based solely on changes of Arctic marine access and the physical changes of Arctic sea ice, profound as they are. Much research also tends to focus on trans-Arctic navigation, with reference to the shorter distances of Arctic voyages, rather than destinational voyages that AMSA indicated are predominant today and likely into future decades. Several studies have analysed and quantified Arctic marine access for the entire Arctic Ocean and Russia's NSR.[32] These are quite useful for strategic planning as they utilise defined Polar Class ships sailing on potential routes through sea ice simulations in the Arctic Ocean. The outcomes of such studies can indicate what is physically plausible for Arctic navigation and what might be feasible, in extended navigation seasons. However, Arctic ship traffic is primarily related to Arctic natural resource development and constrained by the general economics influencing the global maritime enterprise (for container shipping: multi-ports on a given voyage, schedule reliability, just-in-time cargoes, short Arctic seasons, and other economic constraints). The Arctic voyaging of ships such as tankers, bulk carriers, and LNG carriers is influenced by global commodities prices and demand. The same can be said for the fleets (and numbers) of support ships and drill ships that are coupled to the uncertainties of the oil and gas industries. Also, the cruise ship industry is constrained by a relatively short summer season where ice-free conditions are prevailing and daylight is at summer maximum in high latitudes. In summary, projecting the levels of future Arctic marine traffic requires factoring in: the quantification of Arctic marine access (and length of the navigation season for select Polar Class ships); global commodities pricing and the rates of Arctic natural resource development; and a deep understanding of global shipping economics, particularly for container shipping. Another key factor for all types of future Arctic marine operations will be the presence and adequacy of marine infrastructure for safety, security, efficiency and economic viability.

32 Scott R Stephenson, Lawson W Brigham, and Laurence C Smith, 'Marine Accessibility along Russia's Northern Sea Route' (2014) *Polar Geography* 111–133, at 116; Scott R Stephenson, Laurence C Smith, Lawson W Brigham, and John A Agnew, 'Projected 21st Century Changes to Arctic Marine Access' (2013) *Climatic Change* 885–899.

9 Conclusions and the Future

Arctic natural resource development and greater marine access created by Arctic sea ice retreat in an era of anthropogenic climate change are influencing increases in Arctic marine use. It is highly plausible in future decades that the Arctic will be more integrated with the global economy and marine transportation systems will link valuable Arctic commodities to global markets. However, uncertainty remains regarding how existing global trade routes might be influenced by longer navigation seasons in the Arctic Ocean. One option has Arctic routes evolving as *seasonal supplements* to the Suez Canal and other global routes, but not themselves becoming major shipping routes due to the enduring presence of Arctic sea ice in autumn, winter and spring.

The Arctic Council's AMSA will remain as a key policy framework for issues related to marine safety, environmental protection and Arctic marine infrastructure. Pursuing the implementation of AMSA's 17 recommendations will require sustained cooperation among the eight Arctic States and agreement at the IMO (and other international forums, such as the IHO) with a host of non-Arctic States whose flagged ships may use the Arctic Ocean. One of the most critical issues will be addressing the continuing lack of marine infrastructure. This challenge will require large public and private investments, and potential public-private partnerships.

While the new IMO Polar Code is a historic, framework agreement by the maritime states, and key element of Arctic Ocean governance, it is only the beginning of a long process to further protect Arctic peoples and the Arctic marine environment in an era of increasing marine operations. The Polar Code does not address such issues as black carbon from ship emissions, heavy fuel use by ships in the Arctic, and ballast water discharge, but these challenges will likely be addressed at the IMO in the future. It also does not address the huge Arctic marine infrastructure gap. Some will likely push for designation of the whole Arctic Ocean as an IMO Particularly Sensitive Sea Area (PSSA), for the entire region to become an IMO emission control area, and for the designation of marine protected areas. More Arctic commercial ship operations will also place a premium on ship monitoring and tracking, and marine traffic data sharing among the Arctic States. A binding agreement on information transfer (in near real-time) of Arctic traffic data may likely be developed among the Arctic State coast guards and maritime authorities. Future Arctic marine operations and shipping should not be a cause of instability and Arctic State friction, so long as there is a stable, rules-based system of governance under UNCLOS. The legal framework for future Arctic maritime governance is the subject of this volume and that framework should provide regional stability for international cooperation and safe use of the Arctic Ocean throughout the 21st century.

CHAPTER 2

The Arctic, the Arctic Council, and the Law of the Sea

*Erik J Molenaar**

1 Introduction

The international community's interest in the Arctic increased spectacularly in the period between 2004 and 2008. Prior to that, international cooperation on the (marine) Arctic mainly involved Arctic States, and regional cooperation occurred largely by means of non-legally binding instruments and informal fora, rather than through legally binding instruments and intergovernmental organisations. The launch of the Arctic Climate Impact Assessment (ACIA)[1] in 2004 contributed to broadening recognition within the international community that climate change is largely driven by anthropogenic pollution. This recognition grew even more after the dramatic Arctic sea-ice loss in 2007,[2] which spread a sense of alarm and urgency within the international community.

Another game changer was the Russian Federation's planting of its flag on the geographical North Pole's deep seabed in 2007, during the gathering of data on the outer limits of its continental shelf. The Russian Federation's flag planting triggered a number of reactions and counter-reactions. The first of these was the incorrect perception by many—e.g., media, academics, environmental non-governmental organisations (NGOs) and the European Parliament—that the flag planting heralded the last land-grab on earth and a resource bonanza that was unchecked due to an international law vacuum. This incorrect perception was then followed by the incorrect assumption that it would be logical

---

* Email: e.j.molenaar@uu.nl. The author is very grateful for assistance and/or comments received from Bob Beckman, Tore Henriksen, Henning Dobson Fugleberg Knudsen, Amy Merten, Alex Oude Elferink, Ashley Roach, Jan Solski and Jorden Splinter on an earlier version. All Arctic Council documents are available at http://www.arctic-council.org/index.php/en/.

1 ACIA Overview Report and the Scientific Report, accessed 15 March 2017 at http://www.amap.no/arctic-climate-impact-assessment-acia.

2 See information accessed 15 March 2017 at http://nsidc.org/.

 | DOI 10.1163/9789004339385_003

to fill this vacuum by a treaty modelled on the Antarctic Treaty,[3] and calls to that effect.[4]

By means of the 2008 Ilulissat Declaration,[5] the Arctic Ocean coastal States—Canada, Denmark/Greenland, Norway, the Russian Federation, and the United States (also the 'Arctic Five')—dismissed the perception of the Arctic (Ocean) as an international law vacuum governed by a 'first-come, first-served' attitude with all the associated risks of conflicts, 'boom-and-bust' resource exploitation, and other forms of impacts on the environment and its biodiversity. The Arctic Five recalled that 'an extensive international legal framework applies to the Arctic Ocean', namely 'the law of the sea'. In fact, all global instruments apply in principle also to the entire marine Arctic and Arctic Ocean, however defined, and so does the competence of the global bodies established by these instruments. The global component of the international law of the sea is merely one domain of this global framework.

The international law of the sea is made up of a multitude of global, (sub-) regional and bilateral instruments and bodies, acts adopted by such bodies, and rules from other sources, including customary international law. The 1982 United Nations Convention on the Law of the Sea (UNCLOS)[6] and its two Implementation Agreements—the Part XI Deep Seabed Mining Agreement[7] and the Fish Stocks Agreement[8]—function as the cornerstone of the international law of the sea.[9]

3 Antarctic Treaty, adopted 1 December 1959, 402 UNTS 71 (entered into force 23 June 1961).

4 See, *inter alia*, the EP's Resolution on 'Arctic governance' (*Official Journal* 2010, C 9/7; Doc P6_TA(2008)0474) para 15.

5 Ilulissat Declaration, Arctic Ocean Conference of 28 May 2008, 48 ILM 362.

6 United Nations Convention on the Law of the Sea, adopted 10 December 1982, 1833 UNTS 3 (entered into force 16 November 1994).

7 Agreement relating to the Implementation of Part XI of the United Nations Convention on the Law of the Sea of 10 December 1982, adopted 28 July 1994, 1836 UNTS 42 (entered into force 28 July 1996).

8 Agreement for the Implementation of the Provisions of the United Nations Convention on the Law of the Sea of 10 December 1982 relating to the Conservation and Management of Straddling Fish Stocks and Highly Migratory Fish Stocks, adopted 4 August 1995, 2167 UNTS 3 (entered into force 11 December 2001).

9 The envisaged Implementation Agreement on marine biodiversity in areas beyond national jurisdiction (see United Nations General Assembly Resolution 69/292, 6 July 2015, which established a Preparatory Committee (PrepCom) as a further step in the so-called 'BBNJ Process' (biodiversity in areas beyond national jurisdiction)) will eventually be part of this cornerstone as well.

The remainder of this Chapter continues with section 2 'Maritime Zones, Boundaries and Limits in the Marine Arctic', followed by section 3 'International Disputes Relevant to the Marine Arctic', section 4 'The International Legal Framework for the Marine Arctic' and section 5 'The Arctic Council'. The Chapter finishes with section 6 'Conclusions'.

2 Maritime Zones, Boundaries and Limits in the Marine Arctic

2.1 *Maritime Zones*

At present, there are no generally accepted geographical definitions for the terms 'Arctic', 'marine Arctic', 'Arctic Ocean' and 'Central Arctic Ocean'. For the purpose of this Chapter, the term 'marine Arctic' corresponds to the marine waters included within the boundary agreed by the Arctic Council's Conservation of Arctic Flora and Fauna (CAFF) working group (see Figure 2.1 below). The 'Arctic Ocean' is defined in this Chapter as the marine waters north of the Bering Strait, Greenland, Svalbard, and Franz Josef Land, thus excluding the Barents Sea.

As Iceland is located in the marine Arctic as defined in this Chapter, it qualifies as an 'Arctic coastal State'. The Arctic Five obviously also qualify as such. These six States plus Finland and Sweden are 'Arctic States' on account of their membership in the Arctic Council.

The UNCLOS recognises the following distinct maritime zones: internal waters, archipelagic waters, the territorial sea, the contiguous zone, the exclusive economic zone (EEZ), the continental shelf, the high seas and the Area (the international deep seabed). Except for archipelagic waters, all these also occur in the marine Arctic. Terms such as the 'Canadian Arctic Archipelago' and the 'Spitsbergen/Svalbard Archipelago'—even if used by Canada and Norway—do not imply that these States qualify—or claim to qualify—as archipelagic States in the domain of the international law of the sea.[10]

There are four high seas pockets in the marine Arctic, namely the so-called 'Banana Hole' in the Norwegian Sea, the so-called 'Loophole' in the Barents Sea, the so-called 'Donut Hole' in the central Bering Sea, and the 'high seas of the central Arctic Ocean'[11] (see Figure 2.2). While it seems likely that the

---

10 UNCLOS, *supra* note 6, Art 46.

11 This is the terminology used by the Arctic Five in their 'Declaration Concerning the Prevention of Unregulated High Seas Fishing in the Central Arctic Ocean', Oslo, 16 July 2015, accessed 15 March 2017 at https://www.regjeringen.no/en/aktuelt/fishing-arctic-ocean/id2427705/, as well as by the 'Five-Plus-Five' in their subsequent meetings on high

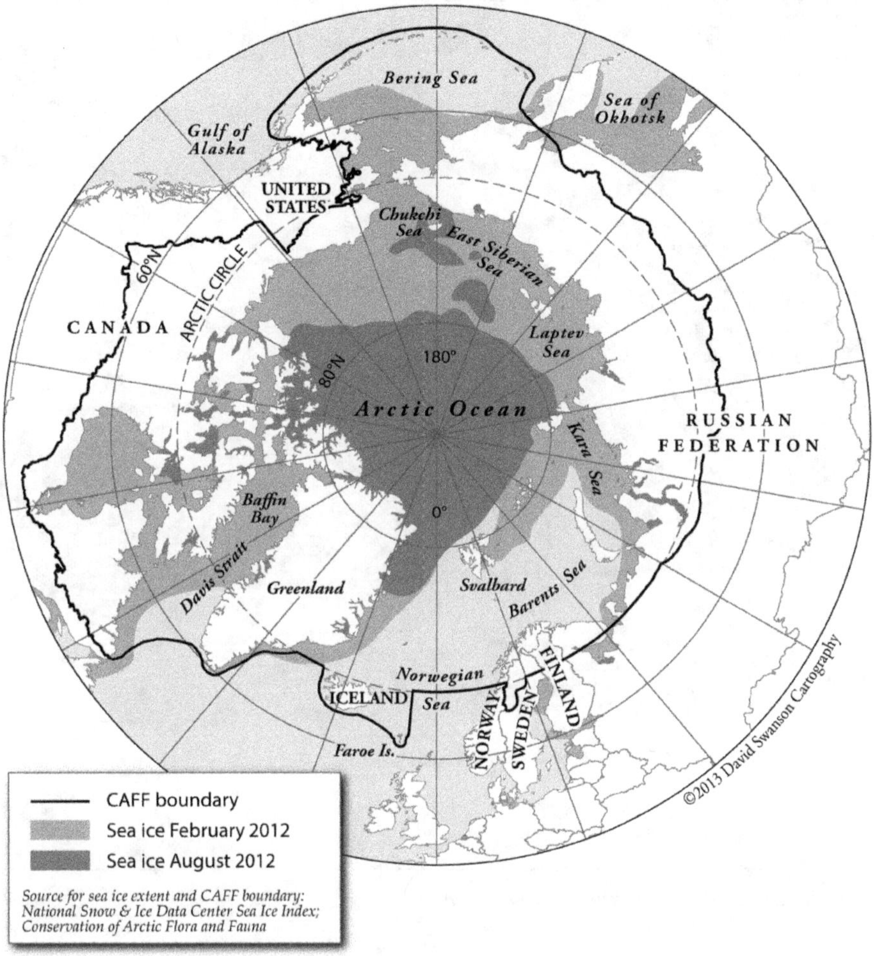

FIGURE 2.1 *The Arctic region: general overview*[12]

marine Arctic will have at least one pocket of the Area—the deep seabed beyond the continental shelves of coastal States[13]—more clarity on this will take

seas fishing in the central Arctic Ocean, see e.g., http://www.dfo-mpo.gc.ca/international/media/statement-declaration-eng.htm, accessed 15 March 2017. See also the use of 'Central Arctic Ocean' by Denmark, Iceland and Norway in the context of the OSPAR Commission's consideration of an Arctic Ice High Seas MPA' (marine protected area; see *infra* note 177 and accompanying text).

12 Map prepared by David Swanson and reproduced here with his permission.

13 UNCLOS, *supra* note 6, Art 1(1)(1).

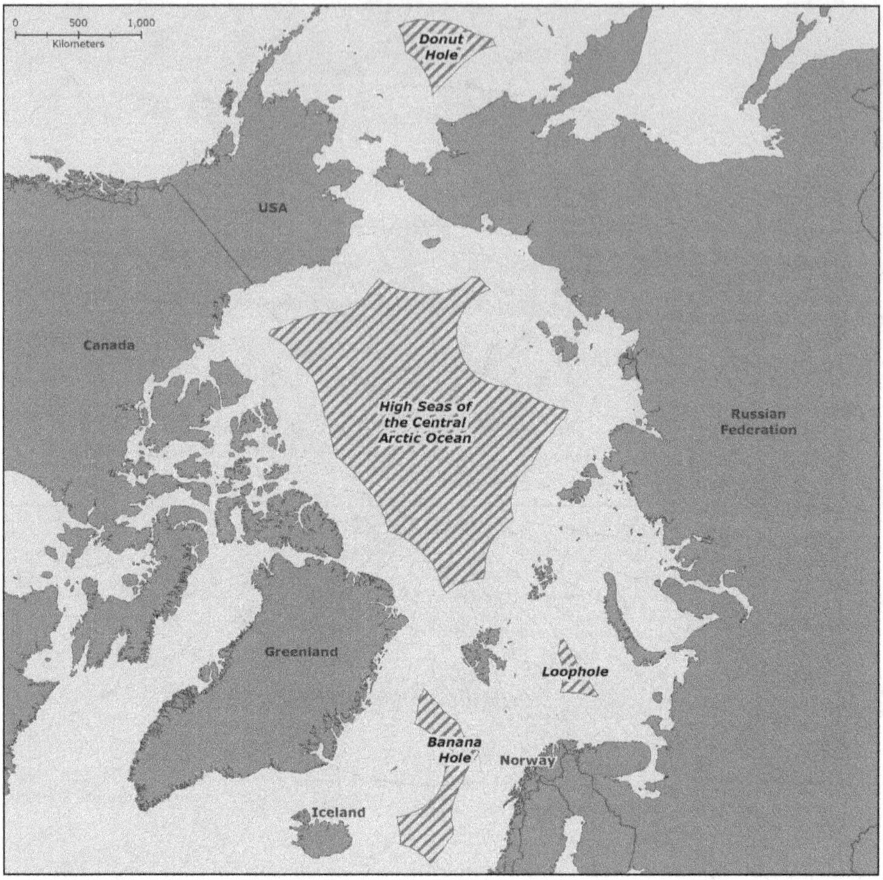

FIGURE 2.2 *High seas pockets in the marine Arctic*[14]

a considerable number of years, *inter alia,* due to the heavy workload of the Commission on the Limits of the Continental Shelf (CLCS) in processing submissions by coastal States.

Arctic coastal States have also established maritime zones that are not explicitly recognised by UNCLOS but are not inconsistent with it either. Examples include 'territorial waters', which comprise both (marine) internal waters and the territorial sea,[15] and 200 nautical mile (nm) maritime zones derived

14 Map used with permission of the Pew Charitable Trusts.

15 E.g., Act No 57, 27 June 2003, on Norway's Territorial Waters and Contiguous Zone. Note also that the concept of territorial waters is used in Article 2 of the 1920 Spitsbergen Treaty (Treaty concerning the Archipelago of Spitsbergen, adopted 9 February 1920, 2 LNTS (entered into force 14 August 1925)).

from the EEZ, in which a coastal State only claims some of the sovereign rights and jurisdiction to which it is entitled pursuant to Article 56 of UNCLOS—for instance, the Fishery Zone (a *de facto* exclusive fishery zone (EFZ)) established by Norway around the island of Jan Mayen.[16] The consistency of EFZs with international law is based on their incorporation into customary international law—probably already in the early 1970s—and the principle of *in maiore stat minus* (who can do more can also do less).

The Fisheries Protection Zone (FPZ) established by Norway around Svalbard in 1977[17] is derived from an EFZ and relied on the EFZ's status as customary international law at the time of its establishment. Rather than designating an EFZ or even an EEZ, however, Norway opted for an FPZ to take account of the diverging views among States on the geographical scope of the Spitsbergen Treaty[18] (see section 3 below).

UNCLOS also recognises the existence of so-called 'historic bays' and 'historic titles' in Articles 10(6), 15 and 298(1)(a)(i). These are part of a coastal State's internal waters—or in exceptional circumstances its territorial sea[19]—provided the requirements under international law on acquisition of title to territory—i.e., effective occupation demonstrated by continuous and peaceful display of State authority in conjunction with explicit recognition or acquiescence by the international community—are met.[20] As examined in Chapters 6 and 7 of this Volume, both the Russian Federation and Canada have claims to historic bays or historic waters located within the marine Arctic.

Chapter 6 on the Russian Federation also examines Russia's reliance on the sector principle or theory in the Arctic, which may have had some relevance for its maritime boundaries with Norway and the United States.[21] So far, however,

16 Regulations of 23 May 1980, No 4, 'establishing the fishing zone around Jan Mayen. Delegation of authority'.

17 Regulations of 3 June 1977, No 6, 'relating to a fisheries protection zone around Svalbard', as amended.

18 *Supra* note 15.

19 *Continental Shelf* (Tunisia/Libyan Arab Jamahiriya) case, Judgment of 24 February 1982, ICJ Rep 1982, at 18, para 100.

20 See also PCA Case No 2013–19 in the Matter of an Arbitration before 'An Arbitral Tribunal Constituted under Annex VII to the 1982 United Nations Convention on the Law of the Sea between the Republic of the Philippines and the People's Republic of China' (*South China Sea* case); Award on Jurisdiction and Admissibility, 29 October 2015, paras 398–399; Award on Merits, 12 July 2016, para 214.

21 Alex G Oude Elferink, 'Does Recent Practice of the Russian Federation Point to an Arctic Sunset for the Sector Principle?' in Suzanne Lalonde and Ted McDorman (eds), *International Law and Politics of the Arctic Ocean; Essays in Honour of Donat Pharand* (Brill/Nijhoff, 2015) 269–290.

Russia has not explicitly exercised coastal State jurisdiction based on the sector principle or theory and has also been in compliance with the rules and procedures on the outer limits of coastal State maritime zones laid down in UNCLOS. It will be interesting to see, however, if this remains unchanged with regard to the Russian Federation's future actions concerning its still unfinished procedure before the CLCS in relation to the geographical North Pole.

Finally, reference can be made to the practice of Norway, the Russian Federation and the United States relating to so-called 'grey areas'. These areas—which are not maritime zones proper—are located within 200 nm from the baselines of one State but situated on the other State's side of the maritime boundary. The EEZ-derived sovereign rights and jurisdiction in these areas have been ceded by the former State to the latter State by means of treaties.[22]

2.2 *Maritime Boundaries and Limits*

Various boundaries in the marine Arctic are still under negotiation, namely between Canada and Denmark/Greenland in the Lincoln Sea, and between Canada and the United States in the Beaufort Sea. Also, while boundary negotiations between the Russian Federation and the United States led to the adoption of a bilateral boundary treaty, it has only been ratified by the United States.[23]

As regards the continental shelf beyond 200 nm in the marine Arctic, the submissions by Denmark, Iceland and Norway have so far led to positive recommendations. The Russian Federation made a revised submission in respect of the Arctic Ocean in August 2015 and Denmark made a submission in respect of the Northern Continental Shelf of Greenland in December 2014. Canada made a submission in respect of the Atlantic Ocean in December 2014, while informing the CLCS that a submission in respect of the Arctic Ocean will be

---

22 For a discussion, see Erik J Molenaar, 'New Maritime Zones and the Law of the Sea' in H Ringbom (ed), *Jurisdiction over Ships—Post-UNCLOS Developments in the Law of the Sea* (Brill/Nijhoff, 2015) 249–277, at 271–274.

23 The treaty is nevertheless provisionally applied. See Robin R Churchill, 'Claims to Maritime Zones in the Arctic—Law of the Sea Normality or Polar Pecularity?' in Alex G Oude Elferink and Donald R Rothwell (eds), *The Law of the Sea and Polar Maritime Delimitation and Jurisdiction* (Martinus Nijhoff Publishers, 2001) 105–124; Tore Henriksen and Geir Ulfstein, 'Maritime Delimitation in the Arctic: The Barents Sea Treaty' (2011) 42 *Ocean Development & International Law* 1–21; and Michael Byers, *International Law and the Arctic* (Cambridge University Press, 2013) at 28–91.

made at a later date.[24] It remains to be seen if the United States may—as a non-party to UNCLOS—still have the opportunity to make submissions to the CLCS. If the recommendations of the CLCS reveal an overlap between continental shelf entitlements—as is highly likely—bilateral, trilateral or perhaps even multilateral negotiations will be needed to agree on maritime boundaries relating to the outer continental shelf.[25] As completion of the procedures involving the CLCS is expected to take a considerable number of years, clarity on the location of such boundaries will only materialise in the more distant future.

This overview of the maritime zones, boundaries and limits in the marine Arctic clearly illustrates that—apart from the FPZ around Svalbard—it is not significantly different from most other marine regions and Oceans. Only the Southern Ocean around the Antarctic continent stands apart, due to the disagreement on sovereignty over Antarctic land territory.

3 International Disputes Relevant to the Marine Arctic

The Arctic and the Antarctic are both polar regions, but are fundamentally different from the perspective of international law. The Arctic is not subject to a disagreement on sovereignty over territory that is even remotely similar to the disagreement that exists in the Antarctic. The only dispute on title to land territory in the Arctic is that between Canada and Denmark/Greenland with regard to the tiny Hans Island in the Nares Strait.[26] News reports in April 2012 suggested that the dispute would soon be resolved by means of dividing the

24 For more information, see http://www.un.org/depts/los/clcs_new/commission_submissions.htm, accessed 15 March 2017.

25 See Alex G Oude Elferink, 'The Delimitation of the Continental Shelf Beyond 200 Nautical Miles in the Arctic Ocean: Recent Developments, Applicable Law and Possible Outcomes' in Myron H Nordquist, John N Moore and Ronán Long (eds) *Challenges of the Changing Arctic. Continental Shelf, Navigation, and Fisheries* (Brill/Nijhoff, 2016) 53–80; Byers, *supra* note 23 at 92–127.

26 See Byers, *supra* note 23 at 10–16; the Joint Statement by the then Canadian Minister of Foreign Affairs Pettigrew and then Danish Minister of Foreign Affairs Møller made in New York on 19 September 2005, accessed 15 March 2017 at https://www.canada.ca/en/news.html); and the short article by Poul Erik Dam Kristensen, then Ambassador of Denmark to Canada, published in the *Ottawa Citizen* on 28 July 2005, which places the dispute in the proper perspective of the positive, on-going cooperation between the two States.

island in two,[27] but at the time of writing this had not (yet) happened. Shared sovereignty by means of a condominium would be an alternative option.[28] It may well be that resolution of the dispute can only be accomplished in conjunction with agreement on maritime delimitation in the Lincoln Sea and the Arctic Ocean.

Various other Arctic-specific international law of the sea disputes exist as well. First, the disagreements on the legal status of the Northwest Passage and other waters within the Canadian Arctic Archipelago, waters within the Northern Sea Route, and the consistency of associated straight baselines with international law. These disputes are examined in Chapters 6 and 7 of this Volume.

Second, the disagreement between Norway and several other parties to the Spitsbergen Treaty on the treaty's geographical scope of application (see above). Norway takes the position that the Treaty, and thereby its key provisions on equal access and non-discrimination, do not apply seaward of the outer limit of the territorial sea. A number of other parties to the Treaty, however, take the view that the Treaty applies to all maritime zones generated by Svalbard.[29] In view of these different positions, Norway established an FPZ off Svalbard—while insisting on its right to establish an EEZ (or EFZ)—and allows a limited number of parties to the Treaty to fish in the FPZ, based largely on historic track records.[30] The relevance of the Spitsbergen Treaty for international merchant shipping and its regulation by Norway is examined in Chapter 8 of this Volume.

4 The International Legal Framework for the Marine Arctic

4.1 *Introduction*

As noted in section 1, UNCLOS and its two Implementation Agreements function as the cornerstone of the international law of the sea. They are supplemented by a multitude of global, (sub-)regional and bilateral instruments and

27 Paul Russell, 'If Hans Island falls, a piece of Canada will be lost' *National* Post, 11 April 2012, accessed 15 March 2017 at http://news.nationalpost.com/full-comment/todays-letters-if-hans-island-falls-a-piece-of-canada-will-be-lost.

28 See Byers, *supra* note 23; Bob Weber, 'Turn Hans Island into a condo to solve long-running Canada-Denmark dispute, academics suggest' *National Post,* 12 November 2015, accessed 15 March 2017 at http://news.nationalpost.com/news/canada/turns-hans-island-into-a-condo-academics-suggest-to-solve-long-running-canada-denmark-dispute.

29 For a discussion, see Erik J Molenaar, 'Fisheries Regulation in the Maritime Zones of Svalbard' (2012) 27 *International Journal of Marine and Coastal Law* 3–58.

30 *Ibid.*

bodies, acts adopted by such bodies, and rules from other sources, including customary international law. This domain is so extensive that even a concise overview cannot possibly be provided here.[31]

A crucial distinction in this domain is that between its global component on the one hand, and its regional, sub-regional and bilateral component on the other. Global instruments apply in principle also to the entire marine Arctic and so does the competence of the bodies established by these instruments (if any). Conversely, the geographical scope of (sub-)regional and bilateral instruments and their bodies' competence (if any) is inherently limited and is commonly explicitly specified.[32] Participation in these instruments and bodies as well as their relationships and compatibility with global and other (sub-) regional and bilateral instruments and their bodies, is therefore of obvious significance.

The (sub-)regional and bilateral component of the international legal framework of the marine Arctic is highly fragmented and complex. This is partly caused by the fact that the marine Arctic comprises not only the Arctic Ocean but also parts of the North Atlantic and the North Pacific Oceans (see Figure 2.2 above). Moreover, while the Arctic Council's substantive mandate is almost unlimited,[33] and the Council is at present generally accepted to be the principal intergovernmental body for Arctic cooperation, its Members do not intend the Council to eventually replace or subsume all pre-existing (sub-) regional or bilateral instruments and bodies, or to preclude new (sub-)regional or bilateral instruments and bodies from being created. Examples in this regard are instruments and bodies relating to the conservation and management of marine mammals[34] and fish stocks, for instance the 1973 Agreement on the Conservation of Polar Bears[35] and its Meetings of Parties (MOPs),[36] and

31 For an overview, see *The Arctic Ocean Review Phase I Report* (2009–2011), available at http://www.pame.is/, accessed 15 March 2017. See also Erik J Molenaar, Alex G Oude Elferink and Donald R Rothwell, *The Law of the Sea and the Polar Regions: Interactions between Global and Regional Regimes* (Martinus Nijhoff Publishers, 2013).

32 Notable exceptions are the Arctic Council (see *infra* note 93 and accompanying text) and the Joint Norwegian-Russian Fisheries Commission.

33 See *infra* note 92 and accompanying text.

34 Evan T Bloom, 'Establishment of the Arctic Council', 93 *American Journal of International Law* 712–722 (1999) 719–720, expects that the Arctic States will continue to avoid dealing with marine mammal issues due to the many associated sensitivities.

35 Agreement on the Conservation of Polar Bears, adopted 15 November 1973, 13 ILM 13 (entered into force 26 May 1976).

36 For information, see http://pbsg.npolar.no/en/meetings/index1.html, accessed 15 March 2017.

the regional fisheries management arrangement (RFMA) on high seas fishing in the central Arctic Ocean that is the likely outcome of the 'Five-Plus-Five' meetings that commenced in December 2015.[37] The point of departure is that these instruments and bodies will continue to exist formally on a stand-alone basis alongside the Arctic Council.

4.2 *The Global Component Relating to International Merchant Shipping*

Regulation of international merchant shipping is predominantly carried out by global bodies, of which the International Maritime Organization (IMO) is unquestionably the most prominent. The pre-eminence of global bodies is a direct consequence of the global nature of international merchant shipping and the interest of the international community in globally uniform minimum regulation. This interest and the pre-eminence of global bodies are safeguarded in several ways by UNCLOS, whose framework on navigation can be regarded as generally accepted on account of the near-universal participation in UNCLOS[38] and the fact that non-parties to UNCLOS do not have significant objections to this framework.

As explained in Chapter 4 of this Volume, UNCLOS recognises the various navigational rights and freedoms of flag States and connects flag and coastal State jurisdiction over international merchant shipping in most instances by so-called 'rules of reference' to the substantive rules and standards adopted within the IMO. So-called 'generally accepted international rules and standards' (GAIRAS) constitute a mandatory minimum for flag State jurisdiction and an optional maximum for coastal State jurisdiction.[39] UNCLOS nevertheless contains a few exceptions which entitle coastal States to impose more stringent rules and standards on transiting foreign vessels. The principal exception is laid down in Article 234 entitled 'Ice-covered areas' and provides:

> Coastal States have the right to adopt and enforce non-discriminatory laws and regulations for the prevention, reduction and control of marine pollution from vessels in ice-covered areas within the limits of the

---

37 For a discussion, see Erik J Molenaar, 'The December 2015 Washington Meeting on High Seas Fishing in the Central Arctic Ocean', post dated 5 February 2016 for *The JCLOS Blog*, accessed 15 March 2017 at http://site.uit.no/jclos/.

38 For information on the status of participation in UNCLOS, see http://www.un.org/depts/los, accessed 15 March 2017.

39 The Award on the Merits in the *South China Sea* case, *supra* note 20 at para 1083, also recognises the so-called 'indirectly binding effect' of UNCLOS for parties to UNCLOS that are not also directly bound to particular GAIRAS.

> exclusive economic zone, where particularly severe climatic conditions and the presence of ice covering such areas for most of the year create obstructions or exceptional hazards to navigation, and pollution of the marine environment could cause major harm to or irreversible disturbance of the ecological balance. Such laws and regulations shall have due regard to navigation and the protection and preservation of the marine environment based on the best available scientific evidence.

Article 234 was included in UNCLOS as a result of the efforts of Canada in particular, which sought to ensure that its 1970 Arctic Waters Pollution Prevention Act (AWPPA) and underlying regulations and orders would no longer be regarded as inconsistent with international law. The negotiations on Article 234 were predominantly conducted by Canada, the then Soviet Union, and the United States, and were closely connected to what eventually became Article 211(6), which enables coastal States to impose tailor-made rules and standards in designated areas of their EEZs.[40] This negotiation history does not mean, however, that any common interpretation that these three States may have with respect to Article 234, would necessarily be opposable to other parties to UNCLOS; whether flag or coastal States.

While Article 234 contains a number of ambiguities—not unlike many other provisions in UNCLOS, and in fact many other treaties—its key purpose is to provide a coastal State with broader prescriptive and enforcement jurisdiction in ice-covered areas than it would normally have in its maritime zones. In particular, in contrast with Article 211(6), Article 234 does not envisage a role for a 'competent international organization' such as the IMO in case the coastal State takes the view that more stringent standards than GAIRAS are needed.

As Article 234 indicates, jurisdiction is subject to several restrictions and can only be exercised for a specific purpose. One such restriction follows from the words 'for most of the year'. Decreasing ice-coverage will mean that Article 234 can gradually be relied on in fewer areas. At the time of writing, Canada, Denmark (in relation to Greenland), Norway (in relation to Svalbard), the Russian Federation, and the United States would be entitled to exercise jurisdiction pursuant to Article 234. Chapters 6 to 8 of this Volume examine which of these States have also actually made use of this entitlement. Whereas

---

40 Among the extensive body of literature on Article 234, see in particular Donald McRae, 'The Negotiation of Article 234' in Franklyn Griffiths (ed) *Politics of the Northwest Passage* (McGill-Queen's University Press, 1987) 98–114; and Kirstin Bartenstein, 'The "Arctic Exception" in the Law of the Sea Convention: A Contribution to Safer Navigation in the Northwest Passage?' (2011) 42 *Ocean Development & International Law* 22–52.

nothing in Article 234 or elsewhere in UNCLOS explicitly excludes its application to waters off the Antarctic continent, this is precluded at present and for the foreseeable future due to the fundamental disagreement on title to territory in Antarctica and the consequential absence of universally recognised coastal States in Antarctica.

As regards the phrase 'within the limits of the exclusive economic zone', it is submitted that the better interpretation is that this merely indicates the outer limits of the EEZ, and does not exclude the territorial sea.[41] This interpretation is consistent with a key feature of the international law of the sea, namely more comprehensive State authority in coastal State maritime zones closer to the coast compared to more distant coastal State maritime zones. Moreover, foreign vessels will in most—if not all—scenarios have to pass through an EEZ before or after navigating through a territorial sea. A requirement to comply with unilateral so-called 'static' (i.e., continuously applicable) standards—i.e., construction, design, equipment and manning (CDEM) standards—while navigating in an EEZ, implies that these will also be complied with during navigation in the adjacent territorial sea. Finally, within their territorial seas, Article 21(2) of UNCLOS provides coastal States at any rate with a separate exception to impose unilateral standards other than CDEM standards (e.g., discharge and navigation standards).

The purpose for which jurisdiction can be exercised pursuant to Article 234 is 'the prevention, reduction and control of marine pollution from vessels'. Even though 'navigation' is mentioned twice in Article 234, it does not explicitly grant jurisdiction for the purpose of ensuring maritime safety. It is nevertheless submitted that Article 234 allows regulations that have environmental protection as a primary purpose and maritime safety as a secondary purpose as well as regulations for which both purposes are more or less equally important.[42]

UNCLOS does not explicitly address the scenario of waters that are both ice-covered and subject to the regime of transit passage, but many commentators argue that the inclusion of the stand-alone Article 234 in the separate Section

41 Bartenstein, *supra* note 40 at 29, eventually favours a literal interpretation, thus excluding the territorial sea.

42 See also paragraph 5 of the Preamble to the International Code for Ships Operating in Polar Waters (Polar Code; IMO Doc MEPC 68/21/Add.1, 5 June 2015, Annex 10), which stipulates: 'The relationship between the additional safety measures and the protection of the environment is acknowledged as any safety measure taken to reduce the probability of an accident, will largely benefit the environment'.

8 of Part XII supports the dominance of Article 234 over transit passage.[43] The International Chamber of Shipping (ICS) supported the opposite view in 2014.[44] Chapters 6 to 11 of this Volume will examine the positions that Arctic coastal States and user States may have in this regard.

4.3 *Regional Cooperation and the Law of the Sea*

UNCLOS and the Fish Stocks Agreement are in many ways framework conventions and do not contain the substantive (material) standards that are necessary for actual regulation, for instance safety standards to deal with cases like the sinking of the *Titanic* or conservation and management measures to prevent overfishing of target species or by-catch of non-target species. Regulation by States individually cannot provide effective solutions for human activities with an inherent or potential transboundary dimension, and multilateral cooperation at the appropriate level is therefore essential.

Which level of regulation—bilateral, (sub-)regional or global—is appropriate, depends mainly on the activity itself. If activities or their impacts are not confined to a particular region—for instance international merchant shipping and activities that produce greenhouse gases—they are often best regulated at the global level. Regional regulation can, for example, be necessary due to the spatial distribution of particular species or habitats, or the spatial reach of land-based and/or marine pollution. Enclosed or semi-enclosed seas, like the Black and Mediterranean Seas, are obvious candidates for regional approaches, as is also reflected in Article 123 of UNCLOS. Regional regulation may also be able to create a level playing field and regional uniformity, which could, *inter alia*, be attractive to companies that operate in multiple jurisdictions or consider doing so.

Regional regulation has disadvantages as well. Often, regulation can only be applied on an *inter se* basis—as between the regional States—due to the *pacta tertiis* principle. States that have not consented to such regulation therefore enjoy 'free rider' benefits. The *pacta tertiis* problem can manifest itself in various ways, for instance by vessels of third States that operate in the region itself or by transboundary impacts from outside the region. More stringent

43 E.g., Kari Hakapää, *Marine Pollution in International Law. Material Obligations and Jurisdiction*, (Suomalainen Tiedeakatemia, 1981) 258; McRae, *supra* note 40 at 110; and Donat Pharand, 'The Arctic Waters and the Northwest Passage: A Final Revisit' (2007) 78 *Ocean Development & International Law* 3–69, at 29.

44 *Arctic Shipping. Position Paper*, ICS, 2014, at para 4, accessed 15 March 2017 at www.ics-shipping.org.

regional regulation can also create competitive disadvantages in comparison with other regions.

UNCLOS encourages or imposes (qualified) obligations to cooperate at the regional level.[45] A similar approach is pursued by various global organisations and their instruments that are part of the global framework of the law of the sea. As a consequence, regional cooperation exists, *inter alia*, in the following fields:[46]

1. *Merchant shipping*: see next subsection;
2. *Pollution incidents*: including but not limited to incidents relating to merchant shipping—whether by means of monitoring, control and surveillance,[47] or contingency planning, preparedness and response (e.g., the Arctic MOSPA[48] and its MOPS);
3. *Search and rescue*: including but not limited to incidents relating to merchant shipping—for instance through the Arctic SAR Agreement[49] and its MOPS;
4. *Marine environmental protection*: in particular through Regional Seas programmes—the majority of which are supported or coordinated by the United Nations Environment Programme (UNEP)[50]—and large marine

---

45 E.g., Part V (Arts 63–67) and Part XII (Arts 198–200).

46 For a more comprehensive overview, see Erik J Molenaar, 'Current and Prospective Roles of the Arctic Council System within the Context of the Law of the Sea' (2012) 27 *International Journal of Marine and Coastal Law* 553 at 558–565.

47 For instance, by means of the Bonn Agreement (Agreement for Cooperation in Dealing with Pollution of the North Sea by Oil and Other Harmful Substances, adopted 13 September 1983, *OJ* 1984, L 188/9, as amended (entered into force 1 September 1989)), or in the framework of the Helsinki Commission (HELCOM; operating pursuant to the 1992 Helsinki Convention (Convention on the Protection of the Marine Environment of the Baltic Sea Area, signed 9 April 1992, 2099 UNTS 197, as amended (entered into force 17 January 2000)). See in particular the HELCOM Response Working Group and its Informal Working Group on Aerial Surveillance, see information at http://www.helcom.fi/helcom-at-work/groups/response/iwgas, accessed 15 March 2017.

48 Agreement on Cooperation on Marine Oil Pollution Preparedness and Response in the Arctic, adopted 15 May 2013 (entered into force 25 March 2016), accessed 15 March 2017 at http://www.arctic-council.org/index.php/en/our-work/agreements.

49 Agreement on Cooperation in Aeronautical and Maritime Search and Rescue in the Arctic, adopted 12 May 2011, 50 ILM 1119 (entered into force 19 January 2013).

50 See http://www.unep.org/regionalseas/, accessed 15 March 2017.

ecosystem (LME) mechanisms, many of which are supported by the Global Environment Facility (GEF)[51];[52]

5. *Conservation and management of marine living resources*: including through regional fisheries management organisations (RFMOs) and RFMAs, other types of regional fisheries bodies (RFBs; including those (also) dealing with marine mammals)[53] as well as regional bodies exclusively aimed at the conservation of marine species; and
6. *Marine scientific research*, for example through the International Council for the Exploration of the Sea (ICES), the North Pacific Marine Sciences Organization (PICES), and the Arctic Scientific Cooperation Agreement[54] that was negotiated under the auspices of the Arctic Council at the time of writing.

Owing to the large number and considerable diversity of these regional bodies and their instruments, it is not possible to provide even a concise overview of their key features and differences; not even those relating to the marine Arctic.[55] One aspect is nevertheless worth singling out: as a general rule, the States participating as full members in these regional regimes do so in their capacity as a coastal State. There are two exceptions to this general rule: the instruments of the Antarctic Treaty System, and RFMOs or RFMAs whose regulatory areas consist partially or entirely of high seas. The former exception is directly linked to the agreement to disagree on the question of sovereignty over land territory in Antarctica, and the latter is a result of the freedom of high seas fishing. The Arctic Council is not covered by these two exceptions. As discussed in section 5, only regional States can be Members of the Council and this is in principle consistent with international law.

---

51 See, *inter alia*, http://www.lme.noaa.gov/ and http://iwlearn.net/, both accessed 15 March 2017.

52 For an overview, see Julien Rochette, Raphaël Billé, Petra Drankier, Erik Molenaar and Lucien Chabason, 'Regional Oceans Governance Mechanisms: A Review' (2015) 60 *Marine Policy* 9–19.

53 See the RFBs-list, accessed 15 March 2017 at http://www.fao.org/fishery/rsn/en; Rochette et al., *supra* note 52.

54 Agreement on Enhancing International Arctic Scientific Cooperation, Fairbanks, 11 May 2017. Not in force; accessed at 19 June 2017 at http://www.arctic-council.org/index.php/en/our-work/agreements.

55 For some literature, see *supra* note 31.

4.4 *Regional Cooperation Relating to Merchant Shipping*

4.4.1 Regulation

As concluded above, UNCLOS does not require or encourage regional regulation in the domain of merchant shipping, as this would undermine UNCLOS's objective of globally uniform minimum standards and the related primacy of the IMO. This notwithstanding, UNCLOS explicitly allows unilateral prescription by coastal States in some scenarios—one of which is Article 234—and implicitly by port and flag States more generally. Nothing in UNCLOS prevents coastal, port or flag States from exercising these rights collectively at the regional level. The legality of regional residual port State prescriptive jurisdiction is in fact acknowledged by Article 211(3) of UNCLOS, which merely requires regional States to give due publicity to such action.

Moreover, IMO practices and several of its instruments explicitly acknowledge a State's residual prescriptive jurisdiction in its capacity as a port State,[56] as a coastal State (e.g., in relation to ballast water exchange and anchoring) or in all three capacities (i.e., as a flag, port or coastal State), provided such exercise is consistent with international law.[57] It is nevertheless understandable that the official position by IMO Members on regional regulation is that this should be avoided in view of the risk it poses to the IMO's authority and the desirability of globally uniform minimum standards.[58] As such a risk is in principle not posed

56 E.g., Regulation 21(8)(2) of Annex I to MARPOL 73/78 (International Convention for the Prevention of Pollution from Ships, adopted 2 November 1973 (as modified by the 1978 Protocol adopted on 1 June 1978 and the 1997 Protocol adopted on 26 September 1997), 1340 UNTS 61, and as regularly amended. Entry into force varies for each Annex. At the time of writing Annexes I–VI were all in force).

57 E.g., Article 1(3) of the AFS Convention (International Convention on the Control of Harmful Anti-fouling Systems on Ships, adopted 5 October 2001 (entered into force 17 September 2008), IMO Doc AFS/CONF/26, 18 October 2001); Article 2(3) of the BWM Convention (International Convention for the Control and Management of Ships' Ballast Water and Sediments, adopted 13 February 2004 (scheduled to enter into force on 8 September 2017), IMO Doc BWM/CONF/36, 16 February 2004; Reg XI-2/2(4) of SOLAS 74 (International Convention for the Safety of Life at Sea, adopted 1 November 1974, 1184 UNTS 277 (entered into force 25 May 1980), with protocols and regularly amended) and para B/4.34 of the International Ship and Port Facility Security Code (ISPS Code; IMO Doc SOLAS/CONF.5/34, of 17 December 2002).

58 See e.g., IMO Assembly Resolution A.1097(29), 1 December 2015, 'Strategic Plan for the Organization (for the six-year period 2016–2021)' at para 2.3, which reads—in part—that the challenge for IMO is to 'provide an effective and efficient response to shipping trends, developments and incidents, and in so doing, stave off regional or unilateral tendencies which conflict with the Organization's regulatory framework'. See also Olav S Stokke, 'Regime interplay in Arctic shipping governance: explaining regional niche selection' (2013) 13 *International Environmental Agreements: Politics, Law and Economics* 65–85.

by (anticipatory) regional implementation of IMO instruments in a manner that respects the *pacta tertiis* principle, however, this is explicitly allowed or even encouraged. This has for instance led the Arctic Council to pursue regional implementation of the IMO's SAR Convention[59] by means of the Arctic SAR Agreement[60] and regional implementation of the IMO's OPRC 90[61] and Intervention Convention[62] by means of the Arctic MOSPA.[63] Another example is the anticipatory—but recommendatory—regional implementation of aspects of the BWM Convention[64] pursued jointly by the Members of the OSPAR Commission,[65] HELCOM[66] and the parties to the Barcelona Convention[67].[68]

These instances of (anticipatory) regional implementation do not affect other States: the first two instances because they only implement and operationalise coastal State obligations and the last because it is pursued exclusively on a flag State basis (even though within a specified geographical area).[69]

59 International Convention on Maritime Search and Rescue, adopted 27 April 1979, 1405 UNTS 118 (entered into force 22 June 1985) as amended.

60 See *supra* note 49.

61 International Convention on Oil Pollution Preparedness, Response and Cooperation, adopted 30 November 1990, 1891 UNTS 77 (entered into force 13 May 1995).

62 International Convention relating to Intervention on the High Seas in Cases of Oil Pollution Casualties, adopted 29 November 1969, 970 UNTS 211 (entered into force 6 May 1975).

63 See *supra* note 48.

64 See *supra* note 57.

65 Established by the OSPAR Convention (Convention for the Protection of the Marine Environment of the North-East Atlantic, adopted 22 September 1992 (entered into force 25 March 1998), 2345 UNTS 67, as amended. Annex V 'On the Protection and Conservation of the Ecosystems and Biological Diversity of the Maritime Area', adopted 23 September 1998 (entered in force 30 August 2000) as amended, consolidated text available at www.ospar.org.

66 See *supra* note 47.

67 Convention for the Protection of the Marine Environment and the Coastal Region of the Mediterranean, adopted 10 June 1995 (entered into force 9 July 2004) accessed 15 March 2017 at http://web.unep.org/unepmap/.

68 Joint Notice to Shipping from the Contracting Parties of the Barcelona Convention, OSPAR and HELCOM on: 'General Guidance on the Voluntary Interim Application of the D1 Ballast Water Exchange Standard by Vessels Operating between the Mediterranean Sea and the North-East Atlantic and/or the Baltic Sea' (Annex 17 to 2012 OSPAR Summary Record).

69 See the acknowledgment of the IMO's primacy in Article 4(2) of Annex V to the OSPAR Convention, *supra* note 65, as well as the more general requirement for consistency with international law included in Article 6 of the Barcelona Convention, *supra* note 67.

Another example of a flag State approach is Annex IV on 'Prevention of Marine Pollution' of the Protocol on Environmental Protection to the Antarctic Treaty.[70]

There are in fact very few examples of regional exercises of residual coastal or port State prescriptive jurisdiction that affect third States. The main exception is the European Union (EU), which has exercised residual jurisdiction in a (*de facto*) port, coastal and flag State capacity.[71] In addition, various regulations in Annex IV to the Helsinki Convention[72] constitute residual prescriptive jurisdiction in all three capacities as well.[73]

4.4.2 Enforcement

As regional cooperation and coordination on enforcement does not undermine globally uniform minimum standards, it is not prohibited or constrained by UNCLOS. Whereas UNCLOS does not encourage such regional action either, the 1991 IMO Assembly Resolution A.682(17) 'Regional Co-operation in the Control of Ships and Discharges' *did*, and triggered the creation of a global network of regional arrangements on port State control (PSC) modelled on the then already almost decade-old Paris MOU.[74] These regional PSC Arrangements for merchant shipping were established to enhance compliance with internationally agreed standards by means of commitments to carry out harmonised and coordinated inspections and to take predominantly corrective enforcement action (i.e., detention for the purpose of rectification). The instruments in which these internationally agreed standards are contained are commonly referred to as the 'relevant instruments', and include the main IMO instruments. A participating Maritime Authority will only apply relevant instruments that are not just in force generally but also for that Maritime Authority.[75] Some applicability gaps can therefore be expected.

---

70 Annexes I–IV, adopted 4 October 1991 (entered into force 14 January 1998) accessed 15 March 2017 at http://www.ats.aq.

71 See, inter alia, Henrik Ringbom, The EU Maritime Safety Policy and International Law (Martinus Nijhoff Publishers, 2008); and Veronica Frank, The European Community and Marine Environmental Protection in the International Law of the Sea. Implementing Global Obligations at the Regional Level (Martinus Nijhoff Publishers, 2007) 227–257.

72 See *supra* note 47.

73 In particular Regulations 4–6, some of which are based on EU enactments.

74 Memorandum of Understanding on Port State Control, adopted 26 January 1982 (in effect 1 July 1982), as regularly amended, consolidated version accessed 15 March 2017 at https://www.parismou.org/. This Chapter uses the version including the 39th amendment, in effect 1 July 2016.

75 *Ibid.*, Sec 2.3.

The Arrangements are non-legally binding and—rather than States as such—Maritime Authorities are parties to them.[76] Saving-clauses have nevertheless been incorporated in the Arrangements to ensure that nothing in them affects residual port State jurisdiction, which includes the right to take more onerous enforcement measures.[77]

The expansion in participation in the Paris MOU and the creation and expansion of eight new arrangements since then,[78] means that almost complete global coverage has now been achieved.[79] While the Arctic Ocean/region and the Southern Ocean/Antarctic region constitute gaps in global coverage, this does not necessarily mean that these gaps require the establishment of new regional PSC Arrangements.[80]

Whereas regional PSC Arrangements are primarily aimed at addressing non-compliance by ships, account can also be taken of the performance of the flag States of these ships. The Paris MOU, for instance, not only requires its Maritime Authorities to detain a ship to ensure that deficiencies are rectified, but also to refuse a ship access to port following multiple detentions.[81] Refusal of access to port depends among other things on whether or not the flag State appears on the annual grey or black lists.[82]

Finally, mention should be made of the following regional mechanisms aimed at enforcement of vessel-source pollution violations:

1. The North Sea Network of Investigators and Prosecutors (NSN), which is a body established in 2002 by the OSPAR Commission in order to facilitate

---

76 Erik J Molenaar, 'Port State Jurisdiction: Toward Comprehensive, Mandatory and Global Coverage' (2007) 38 *Ocean Development & International Law* 225 at 227.

77 E.g., Paris MOU, *supra* note 74, Secs 1.7 and 9.1.

78 I.e., Asia and the Pacific (Tokyo MOU); Latin America (Acuerdo de Viña del Mar); Caribbean (Caribbean MOU); West and Central Africa (Abuja MOU); the Black Sea region (Black Sea MOU); the Mediterranean (Mediterranean MOU); the Indian Ocean (Indian Ocean MOU); and the Arab States of the Gulf (Riyadh MOU).

79 See the information at http://www.imo.org/en/OurWork/MSAS/Pages/PortStateControl.aspx, accessed 15 March 2017.

80 As regards the Arctic region, see Erik J Molenaar, 'Options for Regional Regulation of Merchant Shipping Outside IMO, with Particular Reference to the Arctic Region' (2014) 45 *Ocean Development & International Law* 272 at 284–287. The Paris MOU's Port State Control Committee adopted PSC inspection guidelines on the Polar Code at its 2016 Annual Meeting and forwarded them to the Secretariat of the Tokyo MOU for information.

81 See Paris MOU, *supra* note 74, Secs 3.4–3.13.

82 *Ibid.*, Sec 4. See the 2015 Paris MOU Annual Report, accessed 15 March 2017 at https://www.parismou.org/).

enforcement of international regulation of vessel-source pollution in the North Sea, in close cooperation with the Bonn Agreement;[83]

2. The efforts of HELCOM towards harmonised and effective cooperation on enforcement of vessel-source pollution violations;[84] and
3. The efforts of the EU, including on penalties for vessel-source pollution offences[85] and the establishment of the European Maritime Safety Agency (EMSA), tasked among other things with operating various information systems, thereby reinforcing and supporting the enforcement capability of EU Member States in their capacities as port and coastal States.[86]

4.4.3 Other Domains of Cooperation

Regional cooperation relating to merchant shipping may also relate to other domains than regulation and enforcement. Some examples are:

1. The extensive cooperation between strait States and user States with respect to the Straits of Malacca and Singapore examined in Chapter 12;
2. Cooperation relating to hydrography, which safeguards safe shipping as well as the scientific basis for regulation by other bodies. As regards the Arctic, reference can be made to the Arctic Regional Hydrographic Commission (ARHC) established in October 2010;[87] and
3. Cooperation between coast guards, which commonly extends beyond issues of merchant shipping. As regards the Arctic, mention can be made

83 See information at http://www.ospar.org/about/international-cooperation/north-sea-network, accessed 31 December 2016.

84 E.g., HELCOM Recommendations 19/14, 26 March 1998, and 19/16, 24 March 1998, accessed 15 March 2017 at http://www.helcom.fi/.

85 Directive 2005/35/EC, 7 September 2005, 'on ship-source pollution and on the introduction of penalties, including criminal penalties, for pollution offenses', *OJ* 2005, L 255/11, as amended.

86 See information at http://www.emsa.europa.eu/, accessed 15 March 2017; and Markku Mylly, 'EMSA's Role in Making the Maritime Regulatory System Work: Supporting Compliance through Monitoring and Enforcement' in Marta Chantal Ribiero and Erik J Molenaar (eds), *Maritime Safety and Environmental Protection in Europe. Multiple Layers in Regulation and Compliance* (Gráfica Ediliber, 2015) 175–203, accessed 15 March 2017 at http://www.marsafenet.org/scientific-publications/.

87 For information, see www.iho.int/srv1/index.php?option=com_content&view=article&id=435&Itemid=690&lang=en, accessed 15 March 2017.

of the establishment of the Arctic Coast Guard Forum (ACGF) by 'Agencies Representing Coast Guard Functions' of all Arctic States in October 2015.[88]

5 The Arctic Council

5.1 *Introduction*

The Arctic Council was established in 1996 as a high-level intergovernmental forum by the Ottawa Declaration.[89] The choice for a non-legally binding instrument is a clear indication that the Council was not intended to be an intergovernmental organisation. Canada in particular advocated in the mid-1990s that the Council should be an intergovernmental organisation,[90] but the United States especially could not be convinced.

The Council's mandate broadened pre-existing cooperation under the 1991 Arctic Environmental Protection Strategy (AEPS)[91] to:

> promoting cooperation, coordination and interaction among the Arctic States, with the involvement of the Arctic indigenous peoples and other Arctic inhabitants on common Arctic issues, in particular issues of sustainable development and environmental protection in the Arctic.[92]

88 The ACGF was established pursuant to the 'Joint Statement of the Intent to Further Develop Multilateral Cooperation of Agencies Representing Coast Guard Functions', adopted on 30 October 2015 (on file with author). At the very end, the ACGF Joint Statement approves the ACGF Terms of Reference (ACGF Terms of Reference (on file with author)) 'as the foundation upon which to build the multilateral cooperation mechanism in the Arctic region'. See also Andreas Østhagen, 'The Arctic Coast Guard Forum: Big Tasks, Small Solutions', accessed 15 March 2017 at http://www.thearcticinstitute.org/the-arctic-coast-guard-forum-big-tasks/.

89 'Declaration on the Establishment of the Arctic Council, Ottawa, 19 September 1996'. For a general discussion on the Arctic Council, see Piotr Graczyk and Timo Koivurova, 'The Arctic Council' in Leif C Jensen and Geir Hønneland (eds), *Handbook of the Politics of the Arctic* (Edward Elgar Publishing, 2015) 298–327.

90 Donald R Rothwell, *The Polar Regions and the Development of International Law* (Cambridge University Press, 1996) at 243; and Yoshinobu Takei, 'The Role of the Arctic Council from an International Law Perspective: Past, Present and Future' (2015) VI *Yearbook of Polar Law* 349–374.

91 Adopted 14 June 1991, 30 ILM 1624 (1991).

92 Ottawa Declaration, *supra* note 89, Art 1(a).

While the substantive mandate of the Council thus relates in particular to sustainable development and environmental protection, it is otherwise only subject to the restriction of 'common Arctic issues'. A footnote to Article 1 specifies, however, that the Council 'should not deal with matters related to military security'. The use of the voluntary term 'should'—which is appropriate for a non-legally binding instrument—nevertheless indicates that the Council could deal with such matters anyway, provided there is consensus to do so. In fact, as the Ottawa Declaration is not legally binding, it does not pose much of an obstacle to the Members if they would wish to go even beyond the already very broad mandate of the Council.

The Ottawa Declaration does not specify the geographical mandate of the Arctic Council and, as indicated earlier, there is no generally accepted geographical definition of the term 'Arctic'. Accordingly, different components and outputs of the Arctic Council can have different geographical scopes.[93] This is by no means unique; a similar approach has been pursued in the Antarctic Treaty System, where the spatial scope of the CAMLR Convention[94] includes a more northerly marine area that is not included in the spatial scope of the Antarctic Treaty.[95]

The Arctic Council has three categories of participation: Members, Permanent Participants and Observers. All eight Arctic States are Members; in fact—as noted above—they are Arctic States on account of their establishment of the Council and its predecessor, the AEPS.[96] As neither the Ottawa Declaration nor the Council's Rules of Procedure[97] entitle non-Arctic States or entities to become Members, the Council is essentially 'closed'. This is in principle consistent with international law. In view of the Council's current mandate and main approaches, current international law does not provide non-Arctic States and entities with a clearly applicable and unqualified entitlement to become a Member. The situation would, for example, be different if the Council were to engage in regulation that interferes with rights of third States or entities (e.g., the freedoms of fishing and navigation on the high seas)

93 E.g., Arctic SAR Agreement, *supra* note 49, Art 3(1) and Annex, para (1); Arctic MOSPA, *supra* note 48, Art 3(1) and (2); and Arctic Scientific Cooperation Agreement, *supra* note 54, Art 1 and Annex 1.

94 Convention on the Conservation of Antarctic Marine Living Resources, adopted 20 May 1980, 1329 UNTS 47 (entered into force 7 April 1982) Art 1.

95 Art IV.

96 See also Art 1 of the Arctic Council Rules of Procedure (most recent version adopted by the Kiruna Ministerial Meeting (2013)).

97 See *supra* note 96.

in a manner that would be inconsistent with the *pacta tertiis* principle (e.g., by means of at-sea high seas enforcement).[98]

There are currently six Permanent Participants, namely the Arctic Athabaskan Council (AAC), the Aleut International Association (AIA), the Gwich'in Council International (GCI), the Inuit Circumpolar Council (ICC), the Russian Arctic Indigenous Peoples of the North (RAIPON) and the Saami Council. Article 2 of the Ottawa Declaration opens the door to new Permanent Participants, provided that one of the two criteria included in Article 2 is met and that the number of Permanent Participants remains smaller than the number of Members. This means that there is at present room for one more Permanent Participant. Chapter 3 of this Volume provides an in-depth examination of the interests and roles of the Permanent Participants in relation to Arctic shipping.

Subsection 5.2 devotes more in-depth attention to the third participatory category in the Arctic Council: Observers.

Decision-making within the Council occurs by consensus among the Members.[99] While the Permanent Participants are not entitled to participate in formal decision-making, they have considerable influence in the decision-formation phase prior to formal decision-making, due to the purposes for which the category of Permanent Participants was created, namely 'active participation and full consultation with the Arctic indigenous representatives within the Arctic Council'.[100] Finally, as the Council is 'merely' a high-level intergovernmental forum, it cannot adopt legally binding decisions or instruments. The legally binding Arctic SAR Agreement and the Arctic MOSPA were negotiated within Task Forces established by the Council, and thereby under its auspices. However, their formal adoption and signature took place by ad-hoc diplomatic conferences held in conjunction with the Nuuk (2011) and Kiruna (2013) Ministerial Meetings. This has given rise to the concept of the ACS discussed in subsection 5.4. The 2017 Ministerial Meeting is intended to be used for the signature of the Arctic Scientific Cooperation Agreement that was negotiated within the Scientific Cooperation Task Force (SCTF) at the time of writing.

The operation of the Arctic Council revolves around the bi-annual Ministerial Meetings where, *inter alia*, the Council's output is formally approved or endorsed, new projects and future work plans are adopted, and

98 See Molenaar, *supra* note 46 at 565–568.

99 Article 7 of the Ottawa Declaration and Rules 7 and 8 of the Arctic Council Rules of Procedure.

100 Rule 5 of the Arctic Council Rules of Procedure.

other important decisions, for instance on applications for Observer status, are made. The Council is formally led by a bi-annual rotating chairmanship—held by the United States between 2015 and 2017—and assisted by the Arctic Council Secretariat—based in Tromsø, Norway—led by its Director. The Chair is not only responsible for preparing for the next Ministerial Meeting—in particular to ensure that targets agreed at the previous Ministerial Meeting are met—but also for the Senior Arctic Officials (SAOs) meetings generally held twice each year, as well as the day-to-day operation of the Council.[101]

Most of the substantive work of the Council takes place within its six 'permanent' Working Groups, namely:

1. Arctic Contaminants Action Program (ACAP);
2. Arctic Monitoring and Assessment Programme (AMAP);
3. Conservation of Arctic Flora and Fauna (CAFF);
4. Emergency Prevention, Preparedness and Response (EPPR);
5. Protection of the Arctic Marine Environment (PAME); and
6. Sustainable Development Working Group (SDWG).

Besides establishing additional 'permanent' working groups, the Council can also establish bodies with a limited period of operation, namely Task Forces or other subsidiary bodies (e.g., Expert Groups).[102] As noted above, three legally binding instruments have been negotiated within such Task Forces.

5.2 *Arctic Council Observers*

The status of Observer with the Arctic Council is available for three categories of entities, namely (a) non-Arctic States; (b) inter-governmental and inter-parliamentary organisations, global and regional; and (c) NGOs.[103] As at 19 June 2017, there were a total of 39 Observers; with 13 in category (a), 13 in category (b) and 13 in category (c).[104] Table 2.1 below provides an overview of the non-Arctic States that held, or had applied for, Observer status at the time of writing. In the context of this Volume, it is worth highlighting that the four most important Asian shipping States—China, Japan, Korea (ROK) and Singapore—all had Observer status at the time of writing.

---

101 The Arctic Council Rules of Procedure, which were last revised in 2013, envisage no role for Deputy Ministers' Meetings. Two such Meetings have been held so far, in May 2010 and in May 2012. See Graczyk and Koivurova, *supra* note 89 at 308.

102 Rule 28 of the Arctic Council Rules of Procedure.

103 Article 3 of the Ottawa Declaration and Rule 36 of the Arctic Council Rules of Procedure.

104 The information was accessed 19 June 2017 at http://arctic-council.org/index.php/en/about-us/arctic-council/observers.

The 2015 Iqaluit Ministerial Meeting deferred a decision on all then pending applications for Observer status 'with the goal of deciding on them' at the upcoming 2017 Fairbanks Ministerial Meeting.[105] This seemed to a considerable extent due to diverging positions on how to deal with the EU application. The EU applied for category (b) Observer status prior to the 2009 Tromsø Ministerial Meeting, but a final decision on its application is still forthcoming. The lack of consensus for approving the EU's application was initially caused by its (consideration of) restrictions on the import of seal products and subsequently (also) by its sanctions on the Russian Federation following Russia's annexation of Crimea in early 2014 and the subsequent events in eastern Ukraine.

TABLE 2.1 *Arctic Council Observer States*[106]

Alphabetical list of Observers			Chronological list of Observers		
State	**Year appl.**	**Year adm.**	**State**	**Year appl.**	**Year adm.**
China	2009	2013	Germany	–[a]	1998[b]
France	2000	2000	Netherlands	–[a]	1998[b]
Germany	–[a]	1998[b]	Poland	–[a]	1998[b]
Greece	2014	–[c]	United Kingdom	–[a]	1998[b]
India	2012	2013	France	2000	2000
Italy	2009	2013	Spain	2006	2006
Japan	2009[b]	2013	China	2009	2013
Korea (ROK)	2009	2013	Italy	2009	2013
Mongolia	2013	–[c]	Japan	2009[b]	2013
Netherlands	–[a]	1998[b]	Korea (ROK)	2009	2013
Poland	1996	1998[b]	Singapore	2011	2013
Singapore	2011	2013	India	2012	2013
Spain	–[a]	2006	Switzerland	2014	2017
Switzerland	2014	2017	Mongolia	2013	–[c]
Turkey	2013	–[c]	Turkey	2013	–[c]
United Kingdom	–[a]	1998[b]	Greece	2014	–[c]

a continuation of accredited observer status under the AEPS.

b also present at the ceremony for the signature of the 1996 Ottawa Declaration.

c application rejected prior to the 2017 Fairbanks Ministerial Meeting.

105 'Iqaluit Declaration 2015. On the occasion of the Ninth Ministerial Meeting of the Arctic Council', adopted 24 April 2015, para 51.

106 Status as of 19 June 2017 based on information provided by the Arctic Council Secretariat.

During the period 1996–2009, interest in category (a) Observer status with the Arctic Council was relatively minor. Four of the six Observers (Germany, the Netherlands, Poland and the United Kingdom) had already participated as accredited observers with the AEPS and only two new applications were made (France and Spain) during this period. Judging by the lack of procedural consistency on the continuation or re-accreditation of Observer status in this period,[107] the Arctic States and Permanent Participants did not really consider Observer status to be an important issue. This changed profoundly in the run-up to the 2009 Tromsø Ministerial Meeting when, triggered by the events in 2007–2008 described in section 1, the Arctic States and Permanent Participants were confronted with applications by, *inter alia*, China, the EU, Italy and Korea.

The inability to reach consensus on these applications in 2009 was caused by a number of factors. Prominent among these was the then already ongoing debate on the strengthening or reform of the Council, including on the role therein for non-Arctic States and entities. Concerns existed that premature steps could prejudice progress. Moreover, as regards China and the EU, there were concerns that participation by these large global players might lead to the subordination of Permanent Participants to Observers within the Council. Arctic States and Permanent Participants are also likely to have had concerns on the geopolitical implications of the involvement of these two large global players as well as others that might follow in their footsteps, and a scenario where Arctic States would be outnumbered by non-Arctic States and entities. Strong sentiments and anxieties about changes to the *status quo* and about who 'belongs' in the Arctic and who does not, are likely to have played a role as well. This was in particular relevant for the EU application, as the EU considered imposing import restrictions on seal products at the time, thereby upsetting several Arctic States and Permanent Participants. Many of the concerns that existed in 2009 are equally, or even more, relevant today.

The 2011 Nuuk Ministerial Meeting adopted the so-called 'Nuuk Observer Rules' and decided that these would be applied to the pending applications,[108] thereby deferring a substantive decision to 2013. The Task Force for Institutional Issues (TFII) established in 2011 was, *inter alia*, charged with amending the original (1998) Arctic Council Rules of Procedure[109] to ensure the integration

107 See Molenaar, *supra* note 46 at 581–584.

108 2011 Nuuk Declaration, at page 2, referring to Annex 1 to Report of the May 2011 SAOs Meeting, entitled 'Framework for Strengthening the Arctic Council', containing a section entitled 'The criteria for admitting observers and role for their participation in the Arctic Council'.

109 1998 Iqaluit Declaration. The Rules of Procedure are contained in Annex 1 to the Report of the September 1998 SAOs Meeting (on file with author).

of the Nuuk Observer Rules, and—at a later stage—with drafting an 'Observer manual'. The amended Rules of Procedure and the 'Observer Manual for Subsidiary Bodies' were eventually adopted in 2013[110] and applied to most of the then pending applications. The amendments relate in particular to Rules 37 and 38 as well as Annex 2. They comprise, *inter alia*, abolishment of the status of *ad hoc* Observer, formalisation of the review process, clarity on re-accreditation, continuation and associated decision-making, and a list of seven broad, cumulative criteria for admission.

Amended Rules 37 and 38 read as follows:

> 37. Once observer status has been granted, Observers shall be invited to the meetings and other activities of the Arctic Council unless SAOs decide otherwise. Observer status shall continue for such time as consensus exists among Ministers. Any Observer that engages in activities which are at odds with the Council's Declaration or these Rules of Procedure shall have its status as an Observer suspended.
>
> 38. The primary role of Observers is to observe the work of the Arctic Council. Observers contribute through their engagement in the Arctic Council primarily at the level of working groups. In meetings of the Arctic Council's subsidiary bodies to which Observers have been invited to participate, Observers may, at the discretion of the Chair, make statements after Arctic States and Permanent Participants, present written statements, submit relevant documents and provide views on the issues under discussion. Observers may also submit written statements at Ministerial meetings.
>
> Observers may propose projects through an Arctic State or a Permanent Participant but the total financial contributions from all Observers to any given project may not exceed the financing from Arctic States, unless otherwise decided by the SAOs.

The second sentence of Rule 37 clarifies that Observer status can be discontinued (suspended) at any time at the initiative of the Foreign Affairs Minister of one single Arctic State. So far, however, this has never actually happened; also not before 2013. There have so far nevertheless been at least three instances in which applications for *ad hoc* Observer status have been rejected, namely by

110 2013 Kiruna Declaration, at page 6. An Addendum to the Observer Manual was adopted in October 2015 (Report of the October 2015 SAOs Meeting, at page 24). The consolidated version of the Observer Manual is available at https://oaarchive.arctic-council.org/handle/11374/939, accessed 15 March 2017.

Greenpeace International (2009 and 2011)[111] and by the International Fund for Animal Welfare (IFAW) sometime earlier.[112] Greenpeace International applied once again prior to the 2013 Kiruna Ministerial Meeting but no decision on its application and those of several other NGOs and intergovernmental organisations has been made so far.[113] At the time of writing, the Arctic Council was also reviewing all existing Observers in preparation for a formal decision on their re-accreditation at the 2017 Fairbanks Ministerial Meeting.

The balance between the rights and obligations of Observers—in particular non-Arctic States—has been a sensitive issue for a number of years. This may in part be caused by insufficient awareness among non-Arctic State Observers that current international law does not provide them with a clearly applicable and unqualified entitlement to participate in the Council; let alone a right to become a Member (see previous subsection). Some non-Arctic State Observers are nevertheless dissatisfied with their limited rights pursuant to Rules 37 and 38 and the rather broad and cumulative admission criteria laid down in paragraph 6 of Annex 2 to the Rules of Procedure.

None of the three treaties that have so far been negotiated under the auspices of the Arctic Council provide for accession by non-Arctic States and entities, regardless of them having Observer status. As regards the Arctic SAR Agreement and the Arctic MOSPA this is also understandable, as an entitlement under international law for them to accede cannot be readily identified. The Arctic Scientific Cooperation Agreement is a somewhat different case due to all States' entitlements on marine scientific research pursuant to UNCLOS.[114] However, as the geographical scope of the Arctic Scientific Cooperation Agreement includes both land territory, coastal State maritime

111 Molenaar, *supra* note 46 at 582.

112 Piotr Graczyk, 'Observers in the Arctic Council—Evolution and Prospects' (2011) 3 *Yearbook of Polar Law* 575 at 605, n 137.

113 Graczyk and Koivurova, *supra* note 89 at 320.

114 See the Preamble and Article 6(2) of the Arctic Scientific Cooperation Agreement, and the frequent references to consistency with international law in Articles 6(1), 10 and 16. The Preamble also recognises 'the significant scientific expertise and invaluable contributions to scientific activities being made by non-Parties and specifically by the Arctic Council Permanent Participants and Arctic Council Observers'. Article 17 of the Arctic Scientific Cooperation Agreement is also very different from the virtually identical provisions included in Article 18 of the Arctic SAR Agreement and Article 17 of the Arctic MOSPA. Earlier drafts of the former were amended in response to interventions from category (a) Observers. The final version contains the phrase 'obligations of the Parties under agreements with non-Parties' and thereby implicitly the rights of non-Parties.

zones and areas beyond national jurisdiction,[115] it is still permissible to limit participation to Arctic States.

This distinction between the Arctic SAR Agreement and the Arctic MOSPA on the one hand, and the Arctic Scientific Cooperation Agreement on the other, may also explain—in part—why the formers' negotiation-processes did not involve non-Arctic State Observers—even though some explicitly requested this[116]—while the latter's negotiation-process was open to all categories of Observers, and several non-Arctic States also exercised this entitlement. But broader support for transparency and inclusiveness is likely to have been another reason for the broader participation in the third negotiation-process.

For the sake of completeness, it should be mentioned that none of the three new Arctic bodies established in 2014 and 2015 (see subsection 5.4) entitle non-Arctic States to become (full) Members, with only the AORF providing observer status to petroleum safety regulatory agencies from non-Arctic States (regardless of their having Observer status with the Arctic Council).[117]

In addition to broadening participation in the negotiation of the Arctic Scientific Cooperation Agreement, the Arctic Council has actively explored other opportunities for participation by Observers in Arctic Council activities[118] and various formats to enable dialogue with Observers.[119]

5.3 *The Roles of the Arctic Council*

An appropriate point of departure for an analysis of the roles of the Arctic Council is the Council's mandate as laid down in the Ottawa Declaration. Whereas paragraph (a) of Article 1—cited above in full—lists 'cooperation, coordination and interaction', its paragraphs (b) and (c) mention the Council's role in overseeing and coordinating its Working Groups, and paragraph (d) reads 'disseminate information, encourage education and promote interest in Arctic-related issues'.

The Arctic Council's role in monitoring and assessment is probably what the Council is known best for. For the purpose of this Volume, reference can be

115 Arctic Scientific Cooperation Agreement, *supra* note 54, Annex 1.

116 See Molenaar, *supra* note 46 at 575–577.

117 AORF Terms of Reference, Art III(1)(b).

118 E.g., participation by Observers in the June 2016 tabletop exercise on the Arctic MOSPA (EPPR Working Group Report to the October 2016 SAOs Meeting, at 1). See also the document 'Opportunities for Observer Engagement in AC Working Group Activities' (Doc ACOSUS202).

119 E.g., the 'Special Session on Observer Engagement' prior to the October 2016 SAOs Meeting.

made to the Arctic Marine Shipping Assessment (AMSA).[120] However, the AMSA was in fact more than an assessment as it contained negotiated policy recommendations.[121] The Council's role in providing non-legally binding policy and regulatory guidance has gradually become stronger and more prominent, culminating in such outputs as policy statements, 'regulatory' guidelines,[122] recommendations, and best practices.[123] The non-legally binding status of these outputs is a consequence of the fact that the Council is a high-level intergovernmental forum. In case legally binding output was desirable, however, the Council resorted to its so-called 'decision-shaping' role. A good example in this regard is IMO's decision to commence negotiations on a legally binding Polar Code in response to a proposal by three Arctic Council Members,[124] based on a recommendation agreed within the AMSA.[125]

However, the Council did not confine itself to a decision-shaping role with two other AMSA recommendations, namely in relation to search and rescue, and preparedness and response to oil pollution incidents.[126] In both cases, it decided to take action to ensure regional implementation of global instruments—namely the ICAO Convention[127] and the IMO's SAR Convention, OPRC 90 and Intervention Convention—by commencing negotiations for pan-Arctic instruments under its auspices.

---

120 The 2009 AMSA Report is available at http://www.pame.is/, accessed 15 March 2017.

121 Graczyk and Koivurova, *supra* note 89 at 312, refer to the AMSA as the principal example of 'second-generation' assessments.

122 E.g., the Arctic Offshore Oil and Gas Guidelines, last updated in 2009, accessed 15 March 2017 at http://www.pame.is/.

123 See, e.g., the section 'A strong Arctic Council' in the 'Vision for the Arctic' adopted at the 2013 Kiruna Ministerial Meeting, which reads, in part: 'we will continue our work to strengthen the Arctic Council to meet new challenges and opportunities for cooperation, and pursue opportunities to expand the Arctic Council's roles from policy-shaping into policy-making'.

124 IMO Doc MSC 86/23/9, 24 February 2009, submitted by Denmark, Norway and the United States.

125 See Recommendation I(B), 2009 AMSA Report, *supra* note 120 at 6. For some other examples, see Terry Fenge, 'Canada and the Arctic Council: Our Turn to Conduct the Arctic Orchestra' (2012) April *Policy Options* 54–58 at 55.

126 *Ibid.*, Recommendations I(E) and III(C).

127 Convention on International Civil Aviation, adopted 7 December 1944, 15 UNTS 295 (entered into force 4 April 1947).

5.4 *The Arctic Council System* (ACS)

This author introduced the concept of the ACS some years ago to clarify that legally binding instruments such as the Arctic SAR Agreement and the Arctic MOSPA—and their institutional components—can be part of the Council's output even though they are not formally adopted by it due to the fact that the Council is a high-level intergovernmental forum.[128] Whereas the concept of the Antarctic Treaty System (ATS) has been formally recognised by the Antarctic Treaty Consultative Parties, the concept of the ACS has not been formally recognised by the Council's Members and Permanent Participants. In fact, the acronym ACS is currently widely used to denote the Arctic Council Secretariat.[129]

The ACS concept consists of two basic components. The first component is made up of the Council's constitutive instrument, other Ministerial Declarations, other instruments adopted by the Arctic Council, and the Council's institutional structure. The second component consists of legally binding instruments negotiated under the Council's auspices and their institutional components. The Arctic SAR Agreement and the Arctic MOSPA as well as their MOPs[130] belong to this category, and so will the future Arctic Scientific Cooperation Agreement and its MOPs.[131]

The linkage between the Council and this second component is not confined to the instruments' mere negotiation under the Council's auspices, but also comprises a considerable and increasing extent of substantive and institutional integration. This relates in particular to the role of the EPPR Working Group under the Arctic MOSPA as well as the Arctic SAR Agreement. As regards the former, not only was EPPR closely involved during its negotiation—in particular by developing its Appendix IV 'Operational Guidelines'—but in 2013 it was also tasked to ensure that Appendix IV remains up to date.[132] Among the implementation activities undertaken by EPPR are those developed by its Exercise Design Team (EDT), for instance:

---

128 Molenaar, *supra* note 46.

129 The acronym ATS is occasionally also used to denote the Antarctic Treaty Secretariat.

130 Articles 10 and 14, respectively.

131 Article 12 of the Agreement, *supra* note 54, entitled 'Review of this Agreement', envisages meetings of the Parties. Takei, *supra* note 90 at 356–359, discusses Russian proposals for a legally binding instrument on search and rescue between the Arctic Council Members during 2003–2005.

132 Report of the October 2013 SAOs Meeting, at 11. Article 20(1) of the Arctic MOSPA stipulates that its Appendices are not legally binding.

1. A workshop aimed, among other things, identifying the highest risk Arctic spill scenarios (September 2015);[133]
2. A 'Connectivity Test' of competent authorities listed in the Operational Guidelines (January 2016);[134] and
3. The second functional table-top exercise (13 June 2016), which led to the adoption of an After Action Report, whose recommendations will be addressed by the recently established Marine Environmental Response Experts Group.[135]

As regards EPPR's role vis-à-vis the Arctic SAR Agreement, EPPR's mandate was broadened in 2015 to include search and rescue, and to ensure follow-up in relation to the Arctic SAR Agreement.[136] The October 2015 Arctic Zephyr Tabletop Exercise identified shortcomings on cooperation and coordination in the context of the Arctic SAR Agreement, and made recommendations to address them.[137] In December 2015, EPPR established a SAR Expert Group—led by Norway—which had its 2nd Meeting in June 2016.[138]

This significant substantive and institutional integration of EPPR with the Arctic SAR Agreement and the Arctic MOSPA raises the question of what role remains for the MOPs envisaged under Article 10 of the Arctic SAR Agreement and Article 14(1) of the Arctic MOSPA. At the time of writing, no such MOPs have been convened. As regards the Arctic MOSPA, however, this is expected to change soon, as its Article 14(1) reads, in part:

> The Parties shall meet no later than one year after the entry into force of this Agreement, as convened by the depositary, and from then on as decided by the Parties. [...] Parties may elect to convene such meetings in conjunction with meetings of the Arctic Council.[139]

133 'Background Paper: 2nd Functional Exercise of the MOSPA Agreement' to the March 2016 SAOs Meeting (Doc ACSAOUS202).

134 *Ibid.*

135 EPPR Working Group Report to the October 2016 SAOs Meeting, at 1.

136 Report of the March 2015 SAOs Meeting, at 17–18 (Doc ACSAO-CA04; and Report of the April 2015 SAOs Meeting, at 26 and 28.

137 Presentation by Amy Merten, Chair of the EPPR Working Group, at the March 2016 SAOs Meeting (slides 4–8).

138 EPPR Working Group Report to the October 2016 SAOs Meeting, at 1.

139 The wording of Article 10 of the Arctic SAR Agreement is markedly different, however, as it reads, in part: 'The Parties shall meet on a regular basis in order to consider and resolve issues regarding practical cooperation'.

In light of the Agreement's entry into force on 25 March 2016, the depositary (Norway) was consulting with the SAOs of the other Contracting Parties on when and how to organise the 1st MOP.[140]

The situation with the Arctic Scientific Cooperation Agreement is somewhat different, as none of the existing Arctic Council bodies is an obvious candidate to perform an implementation or other role under this Agreement. Its Article 12(1) contains wording that is virtually identical to that in Article 14(1) of the Arctic MOSPA cited above, but also adds: 'including inviting Arctic Council Permanent Participants and Arctic Council Observers to observe and provide information'. It is submitted that this advances integration with the Arctic Council even further.

Three other Arctic bodies have been established in recent years: the Arctic Economic Council (AEC), the Arctic Offshore Regulators Forum (AORF) and the Arctic Coast Guard Forum (ACGF). While none of them has been formally established by the Council or pursuant to a legally binding instrument negotiated under the Council's auspices, all have linkages with the Council.[141]

The AEC was established in September 2014, six months after the Arctic Council's Task Force to Facilitate the Creation of a Circumpolar Business Forum (TFCBF) completed its work by presenting its report to the March 2014 SOAs Meeting, and the SAOs approved the document 'Facilitating the Creation of the Arctic Economic Council'.[142] At the 2016 Annual AEC Meeting, the delegates adopted the AEC's Rules of Procedure, its Strategic Plan for the years 2016–2018, the various Membership Dues & Classes, and its Membership Application Process.[143] These indicate, *inter alia*, that: the AEC is an independent business NGO governed by Norwegian law; whose business representatives are nominated by Arctic States and Permanent Participants (so-called 'Legacy Members'); whose Executive Committee's Chair will in principle have

140 Information provided by a Norwegian official to the author on 23 November 2016.

141 At the March 2015 SAOs Meeting, the United States proposed the establishment of a body like the AORF (Report of the March 2015 SAOs Meeting, at 9). The Report also notes: 'The U.S. proposed to help clarify the relationship between the AC and this proposed regulators' forum as well as other forums operating outside the Arctic Council (for example, the Arctic Economic Council, Arctic Coast Guard Forum and Arctic Regional Hydrographic Commission)'. However, such a clarification has so far not materialised, whether in the AORF Terms of Reference or otherwise. An earlier proposal for a body like the AORF was made at least as early as October 2013 during an Arctic Offshore Regulator's Meeting, using the International Regulators' Forum as a model (Arctic Offshore Regulator's Meeting, Stavanger, Norway, 31 October 2013. Minutes of Meeting are on file with author).

142 Report of the March 2014 SAOs Meeting, at 6 and Annex.

143 Accessed 15 March 2017 at http://arcticeconomiccouncil.com/.

the nationality of the Arctic State chairing the Arctic Council; and which offers 'non-voting membership' to so-called 'Southern Partners'.[144] One of the four AEC working groups is entitled 'Maritime transportation infrastructure'.

The AORF was established at its inaugural meeting on 30 April and 1 May 2015 and builds on the efforts of the Arctic Council's Task Force on Arctic Marine Oil Pollution Prevention (TFOPP), whose 'Framework Plan for Cooperation on Prevention of Oil Pollution from Petroleum and Maritime Activities in the Marine Areas of the Arctic' (Framework Plan) was accepted by the SAOs in March 2015.[145] The Framework Plan contains several general provisions relating to implementation by national authorities as well as cooperation among national regulators,[146] but no institutional component.

The AORF's Terms of Reference specify that it is an intergovernmental forum with membership limited to Arctic States, represented by their offshore petroleum regulatory agencies.[147] Instead of referring to the Framework Plan, Article II(2)(a) of the AORF Terms of Reference specifies that one of the objectives of the AORF is furthering the recommendations of the TFOPP 'to enhance the capacity of Arctic offshore petroleum safety regulators to prevent marine oil pollution through regular exchanges of knowledge and experience'. The composition of the AORF Management Committee is coordinated with the chairmanship of the Arctic Council.[148] Rather than mentioning particular Arctic Council bodies, Article II(1)(c) of the AORF Terms of Reference stipulates that the AORF 'may collaborate with the Arctic Council and other international fora, as appropriate'. The PAME and EPPR Working Groups would nevertheless be of principal importance.

In contrast with the AEC and the AORF, the establishment of the ACGF in October 2015 did not follow preparatory work by an Arctic Council body, whether a Task Force or some other body. The ACGF is an independent, intergovernmental forum whose memberships consists of 'Agencies Representing Coast Guard Functions' of the Arctic States aimed, among others, at supporting 'agreements between Arctic States, such as those made under the auspices

144 Sections 2.9, 4.1(v) and 7.2(i) of the AEC Rules of Procedure and the document 'Membership Dues & Classes'.

145 Report of the March 2015 SAOs Meeting, at 9. The text of the Framework Plan is included in the April 2015 SAOs Report to Ministers, at 110–117.

146 Framework Plan, *supra* note 145, Arts 1.6.1 and 2.3(a).

147 AORF Terms of Reference', Arts II(1)(a) and III(1)(a), accessed 15 March 2017 at https://www.bsee.gov/what-we-do/international-engagement/forums.

148 *Ibid.*, Arts IV(2) and V(1).

of the Arctic Council, related to coast guard functions'.[149] Rather than merely complementing the Council or the ACS, such support can be regarded as implementation of the Arctic SAR Agreement and the Arctic MOSPA. In light of the exclusion of 'matters related to military security' of the Council's mandate, it is worth noting that neither the ACGF Joint Statement nor the ACGF Terms of Reference[150] use the word 'military' in conjunction with 'security'. As six of the eight participating Agencies have a military or semi-military character,[151] however, it may ultimately also serve as a cooperative mechanism to fill this gap in the Council's mandate. A significant extent of institutional integration between the ACGF and the Arctic Council exists as well. The ACGF will be led by a Chair that rotates in tandem with the chairmanship of the Arctic Council,[152] and there is ample evidence of increasingly close cooperation and coordination with the EPPR Working Group.[153]

The brief analysis of these three recently established Arctic bodies reveals a varying extent of integration—substantively as well as institutionally—with the Arctic Council and the ACS. The ACGF appears to be the most integrated and the AEC the least.[154] However, none of the bodies are part of the Council because they were not formally established by the Council. Also, none were established pursuant to a legally binding instrument negotiated under the Council's auspices. For the time being, the latter criterion is an objective and useful criterion for determining whether or not a body belongs to the ACS.

Leaving definitional issues aside, however, it would be quite understandable if the establishment of three new Arctic bodies within such a short time-span would be regarded as institutional proliferation. Increased efforts on institutional coordination and cooperation seem at any rate justified. The Arctic Council's 2016 Guidelines for Relationships with Outside Bodies[155] may be of some help in this regard.

---

149 ACGF Joint Statement, *supra* note 88, and ACGF Terms of Reference, *supra* note 88 at (i) and (xxii).

150 *Supra* note 88.

151 Østhagen, *supra* note 88.

152 *Ibid.* at (v).

153 See, for instance, EPPR Progress Report to the March 2016 SAOs Meeting, at 2.

154 At the October 2016 SAOs Meeting, only a few Arctic States were interested in formalising the relationship between the Arctic Council and the AEC. Report of the October 2016 SAOs Meeting, at 24.

155 As adopted by the March 2016 SAOs Meeting.

5.5 *The Future Evolution of the Arctic Council and the* ACS *in the Context of International Law*

The Arctic Council is at present generally accepted by the international community as the principal intergovernmental body for Arctic cooperation. The Council's primacy in this regard is, *inter alia*, underscored by the significant interest of non-Arctic States in obtaining Observer status with the Council; in particular since 2008 (see subsection 5.2 above). Milestones of the Council's pathway to primacy are its contribution to the 2004 ACIA—which broadened recognition within the international community that climate change is largely driven by anthropogenic pollution—and its 2009 AMSA Report, which delivers on the need to address inadequacies in the international governance and regulatory regime of the marine Arctic in light of climate change.

The main challenge to the Council's crystallising primacy was—arguably—posed by the high-level cooperation between the Arctic Five following the Russian Federation's planting of its flag on the geographical North Pole's deep seabed in 2007. The convening of the May 2008 Ilulissat ministerial (foreign affairs) meeting and the adoption of its declaration were criticised by the Arctic Council's other three Members and its permanent participants for undermining the Arctic Council.[156] The Arctic Five nevertheless convened once again at ministerial (foreign affairs) level in March 2010, in Chelsea, Canada. At that meeting, however, the US Secretary of State Clinton expressed doubts and concerns over the appropriateness of ministerial (foreign affairs) meetings of the Arctic Five,[157] and no such further meetings have since taken place. The high-level participation at the Arctic Council's 2011 Nuuk Ministerial Meeting—in particular by the United States, which was represented not only by Secretary of State Clinton but also by the Secretary of the Interior Salazar—was another clear sign of the Arctic Five's full support for the Arctic Council.

The 2008 Ilulissat Declaration not only emphasised the applicability of the international law of the sea to the Arctic Ocean, but also observed that the Arctic Five saw 'no need to develop a new comprehensive international legal regime to govern the Arctic Ocean'. This responded to proposals such as those of the World Wide Fund for Nature (WWF) for a 'regional agreement on the management and conservation of the Arctic marine environment' early in

156 See e.g., Report of the April 2010 SAOs Meeting, at para 20; and 'A Parliamentary Resolution on Iceland's Arctic Policy', approved by the Althingi at its 139th legislative session, on 28 March 2011 (on file with author), at Principle No 1 (including Commentary, at 4–6).

157 Torbjørn Pedersen, 'Debates over the Role of the Arctic Council' (2012) 43 *Ocean Development & International Law* 146 at 152.

2008.[158] Another—but very different—proposal was that by the European Parliament in its Resolution of 9 October 2008 on 'Arctic governance' for a 'treaty for the protection of the Arctic, having as its inspiration the Antarctic Treaty, as supplemented by the Madrid Protocol signed in 1991'.[159] The United States dismissed this idea in its Arctic Region Policy as 'not appropriate or necessary'.[160] A further, more elaborate proposal by WWF for a regional framework instrument for the marine Arctic, launched in early 2010,[161] could not attract sufficient support either.

Rather than a comprehensive reform or overhaul, the Council eventually decided on a two-tiered approach of adaptation, namely by strengthening the Arctic Council as such[162]—for instance by the establishment of the Arctic Council Secretariat and the use of assessed contributions—and by the ACS concept. It is submitted that the establishment of the Arctic Council Secretariat did not transform the Council's pre-existing status as a high-level intergovernmental forum into that of an intergovernmental organisation.[163] However, determining this status is admittedly not a straightforward matter due to the absence of a generally accepted definition of 'intergovernmental organization'.[164] The establishment of a permanent secretariat is nevertheless not a decisive factor. This is, *inter alia*, illustrated by the establishment of the

---

158 Rob Huebert and Brooks B Yeager, *A New Sea. The Need for a Regional Agreement on the Management and Conservation of the Arctic Marine Environment* (WWF, 2008) accessed 15 March 2017 at wwf.panda.org/arctic.

159 *Supra* note 4.

160 National Security Presidential Directive/NSPD-66 & Homeland Security Presidential Directive/HSPD-25, 9 January 2009, at Sec III(C)(3), accessed 15 March 2017 at https://fas.org/irp/offdocs/nspd/nspd-66.htm.

161 Timo Koivurova and Erik J Molenaar, *International Governance and Regulation of the Marine Arctic.* (WWF, 2010) accessed 15 March 2017 at www.panda.org/arctic. The 3rd Report in this publication is entitled *A Proposal for a Legally Binding Instrument.*

162 'Strengthening the Arctic Council' is a separate section in the 2013 (Kiruna) and 2015 (Iqaluit) Ministerial Declarations and has been a standing agenda item for SAOs Meetings in recent years.

163 Takei, *supra* note 90 at 353–355. Contra Byers, *supra* note 23 at 9.

164 As the definition agreed by the International Law Commission in 2003 ('Report of the International Law Commission. Fifty-fifth Session' (5 May–6 June and 7 July–8 August 2003) *General Assembly Official Records* 58th Session Supp 10), at 38) was developed in the context of the issue of international responsibility of international organisations, some commentators regard it as inadequate. See Kirsten Schmalenbach, 'International Organizations or Institutions, General Aspects', *Max Planck Encyclopedia of Public International Law* (December 2006) at para 3; and Robin R Churchill and Geir Ulfstein, 'Autonomous Institutional Arrangements in Multilateral Environmental Agreements:

Antarctic Treaty Secretariat in 2004, which was not regarded as having transformed the Antarctic Treaty's decision-making body—the Antarctic Treaty Consultative Meeting—into an intergovernmental organisation. The status of an intergovernmental body is above all determined by the positions of relevant States in this regard. It is in this light sufficient to observe that there are no indications that any of the Arctic Council Members regard the Council at present as an intergovernmental organisation.

The question nevertheless remains whether the current institutional set-up of the Council will be sufficient to address future challenges and ambitions. While support for re-establishing the Council pursuant to a treaty has in the recent past also been expressed by Arctic Council participants—namely by Finland[165] and the Conference & Standing Committee of Parliamentarians of the Arctic Region[166]—the required consensus among the Arctic Council Members to commence such negotiations is not even remotely in sight. A key concern of the Permanent Participants is the risk of losing the very influential participatory status they currently have in the Arctic Council. As international law is inherently dynamic, however, nothing fundamental prevents the Arctic States from progressively developing international law by giving Arctic indigenous peoples a similar participatory status under a treaty.[167]

At the time of writing, discussions on the development of an Arctic Council Strategic Plan and within the Task Force on Arctic Marine Cooperation (TFAMC) indicated that there is a quite minimal appetite for institutional change. As regards the Arctic Council Strategic Plan, delegations at the October 2016 SAOs

---

A Little-Noticed Phenomenon in International Law' (2000) 94 *American Journal of International Law* 623–659, at 632–633.

165 *Finland's Strategy for the Arctic Region 2013* (adopted by Government Resolution on 23 August 2013; Prime Minister's Office Publications No 16/2013) at 44. See Page Wilson, 'An Arctic Council Treaty? Finland's Bold Move', *Arctic Yearbook* 2014, Commentaries, Sec 18, accessed 15 March 2017 at http://www.arcticyearbook.com.

166 See Paragraph 1 of the Conference Statement adopted at the Arctic Parliamentarians' 10th Conference in 2012, which is based on the Report entitled 'Arctic Governance in an Evolving Arctic Region' drawn up by the Standing Committee of Parliamentarians of the Arctic Region. However, the 11th Conference Statement (2014) does not re-affirm such support, with Paragraph 16 merely asking key decision-making authorities to 'Explore new areas for legally binding agreements between the Arctic countries'. The 12th Conference Statement (2016) no longer makes any reference to the issue. All documents accessed 15 March 2017 at http://www.arcticparl.org/.

167 See also the subsection 'International Indigenous Human Rights Standards' in Chapter 3 of this Volume.

Meeting did not seem interested in considering the Council's structure or its relationship to external bodies.[168]

The TFAMC has a mandate to 'assess future needs for a regional seas program or other mechanism, as appropriate, for increased cooperation in Arctic marine areas'.[169] In its report to the 2017 Ministerial Meeting, the TFAMC must identify 'future needs for strengthened cooperation for Arctic marine areas, as well as whether the Council should begin negotiations on a cooperation mechanism for Arctic marine areas—ideally naming the specific mechanism—and/or any other recommendations it may deem appropriate'.[170] At the time of writing, the TFAMC had met four times and appeared to have reached preliminary agreement on the envisaged cooperative mechanism's functions (e.g., furthering implementation of an ecosystem approach to oceans management as well as implementation of the Arctic Council's marine 'output' more in general), but not on its form. While wide support existed for establishing a new body in which 'senior marine managers' would participate, there seemed to be only minimal support to establish this body under a legally binding instrument and empower it to adopt legally binding decisions.[171]

In particular, the Russian Federation seemed to have serious concerns relating to any initiative that could potentially lead to restrictions on economic development in the 'Russian Arctic'. It is important not to lose sight of geographical considerations in this regard. Arguably, about half of the Arctic is Russian and the same could be said of that part of the marine Arctic that consists of coastal State maritime zones. If the TFAMC would opt for something modelled on the OSPAR Commission[172]—and assuming that the OSPAR Commission would not relinquish its competence in the Atlantic sector of the Arctic Ocean[173]—more than half of the remaining marine area would consist

168 Report of the October 2016 SAOs Meeting, at 19; 'Towards an Arctic Council Strategic Plan—Discussion Paper' (Doc ACSAOUS203).

169 2015 Iqaluit Declaration, *supra* note 105 at 5. The Terms of Reference of the TFAMC are included in the Report of the April 2015 Iqaluit SAOs Meeting, at 77–78.

170 TFAMC Terms of Reference, *supra* note 169 at 77.

171 Report of the October 2016 SAOs Meeting, at 21–22.

172 Established by the Convention for the Protection of the Marine Environment of the North-East Atlantic, adopted 22 September 1992, 2345 UNTS 67 (entered into force 25 March 1998) as amended. Annex V 'On the Protection and Conservation of the Ecosystems and Biological Diversity of the Maritime Area,' adopted 23 September 1998 (entered into force 30 August 2000) as amended. Consolidated text accessed 15 March 2017 at http://www.ospar.org/.

173 Similarly, the North-East Atlantic Fisheries Commission (NEAFC) can be assumed not to be willing to relinquish its competence in the Atlantic sector in deference of a

of the Russia's maritime zones. In addition, four Members have no coastal State maritime zones in the remaining area at all, namely Finland, Iceland, Norway and Sweden. It is therefore not difficult to imagine that ambitious and 'costly' proposals by these four could be perceived by the Russian Federation as insincere and unbalanced, as they impose no burden on them and a very heavy burden on the Russian Federation. Finally, it should not be forgotten that—despite encouragement[174]—the Russian Federation has not become a Member of the OSPAR Commission, even though the OSPAR Maritime Area overlaps with Russia's maritime zones.

The pace and direction of progress within the TFAMC is also influenced by the pace and direction of progress within the PrepCom of the BBNJ Process.[175] Some, if not all, Arctic States are likely to proceed cautiously in both processes in order to ensure coherence between their positions and thereby avoid compromising their positions and interests.

Recent developments in the OSPAR Commission relating to a proposal for an OSPAR 'Arctic Ice High Seas MPA' in OSPAR Region I (Arctic Waters) should be highlighted as well. At the meeting of the OSPAR Commission's Biodiversity Committee in early 2016, the Kingdom of Denmark objected to further consideration of this proposal within the OSPAR Commission, *inter alia,* referring to the on-going work of the Arctic Council's TFAMC as well as the overlap between the proposed MPA and areas included in the Kingdom of Denmark's submission to the CLCS.[176] Subsequently, Iceland and Norway sided with the Kingdom of Denmark, jointly taking the view that area-based management measures in the 'Central Arctic Ocean' are better left to the Arctic Council, *inter alia,* due to participation of all relevant coastal States in that body.[177] It

---

future RFMO/A established as a follow-up of the on-going 'Five-plus-Five' meeting. See Molenaar, *supra* note 37 and accompanying text.

174 Olav S Stokke, 'A Legal Regime for the Arctic? Interplay with the Law of the Sea Convention', (2007) 31 *Marine Policy* 402–408, at 406.

175 *Supra* note 9.

176 Summary Record of the 16th BDC Meeting (2016; Doc BDC 16/9/1-E) at para 5.13. The proposal is contained in Doc BDC 16/05/04 Rev.1.

177 Summary Record of the 16th OSPAR Commission Meeting (2016; Doc OSPAR 16/20/1-E) at para 6.27(c), which also mentions that the three States had made a similar statement at HOD 16. It is not clear if, in response to the lack of consensus among OSPAR Members, qualified majority voting was considered or proposed. Article 13(1) of the OSPAR Convention stipulates that decisions and recommendations are adopted by 'unanimous vote' and, in case unanimity is not attainable, decisions and recommendations can be adopted by a 'three-quarters majority vote'. Decision-making in the OSPAR Commission occurs in practice by consensus, however, and qualified majority voting is resorted to

is submitted that these three Arctic States thereby implicitly assert the Arctic Council's primacy over the OSPAR Commission as regards area-based management measures in the overlap-area between OSPAR Region I and the area they refer to as the 'Central Arctic Ocean'. However, the Arctic Council's output on area-based management has so far[178] been fundamentally different from that of the OSPAR Commission, notably due to the former's lack of multilateral designation and adoption of associated restrictions on human activities. One of the concrete implications of the abovementioned primacy-assertion is therefore that adoption of area-based management measures in the overlap-area between OSPAR Region I and the 'Central Arctic Ocean' that are both multilateral and multi-sectoral cannot be expected in the near future.

6 Conclusions

As was pointed out early on in this Chapter, the global component of the law of the sea also applies to the marine Arctic. The same is in fact true for global instruments and bodies that belong to other domains of international law. While a legal vacuum therefore does not exist at the global level, in view of the current and projected impacts of climate change, the marine Arctic evidently needs tailor-made implementation of these global instruments, including by regional bodies such as the Arctic Council.

Except for the tiny Hans Island—which is claimed by Canada as well as Denmark/Greenland—there are no disputes on title to territory in the Arctic. As nothing remotely similar to the fundamental disagreement on title to territory in Antarctic exists in the Arctic, the Antarctic Treaty is clearly not a suitable model for the Arctic.

Apart from archipelagic waters, all the generally accepted maritime zones also occur in the marine Arctic. This, and the absence of significant disputes on title to territory, means that, from a law of the sea perspective, the marine Arctic is not really different from other marine regions and Oceans, with the notable exception of Article 234 of UNCLOS. It is submitted that this general conclusion is not affected by Arctic-specific practices (e.g., the Fisheries Protection

only rarely. See 'List of Decisions, Recommendations and Other Agreements Applicable within the Framework of the OSPAR Convention—Update 2016', accessed 15 March 2017 at http://www.ospar.org/convention/agreements.

178 This consists above all of the 'Framework for a Pan-Arctic Network of Marine Protected Areas', adopted by the PAME Working Group in April 2015, accessed 15 March 2017 at http://www.pame.is/index.php/document-library/pame-reports.

Zone established by Norway around Svalbard, and the Russian Federation's ambiguous—but also unpredictable—reliance on the sector theory), Arctic-specific disputes (e.g., on straight baselines, historic title or waters, the regime of navigation in (parts of) the Northwest Passage and the Northern Sea Route, and the geographical scope of the Spitsbergen Treaty) or the unresolved maritime boundaries and limits in the marine Arctic.

The global component of the international law relating to international merchant shipping also applies to the marine Arctic. UNCLOS is the cornerstone of this global component, and recognises or establishes the navigational rights and freedoms of flag States, the jurisdictional balance on navigation between flag, coastal and port States, and IMO's key role in ensuring globally uniform minimum regulation. However, whereas IMO's primacy in the international regulation of international merchant shipping is generally accepted, regional action relating to merchant shipping can still be useful or desirable, and is not necessarily inconsistent with UNCLOS. Cases in point are the Arctic SAR Agreement and the Arctic MOSPA negotiated under the Arctic Council's auspices to ensure regional implementation of IMO instruments. Other domains for which regional action would not lead to incompatibility or conflict with IMO output include monitoring, surveillance, inspection, and enforcement as well as the international law of the sea (e.g., resolving disputes or furthering implementation).

The pace in which the Arctic Council has evolved since its establishment in 1996 is significant. Milestones in this evolution were the establishment of the Arctic Council Secretariat and the *de facto* creation of what this author has called the concept of the Arctic Council System (ACS). The ACS concept consists of two basic components. The first is made up of the Council's constitutive instrument, other Ministerial Declarations, other instruments adopted by the Arctic Council and the Council's institutional structure. The second component consists of legally binding instruments negotiated under the Council's auspices and their institutional components. The linkage between the two components comprises a considerable and increasing extent of substantive and institutional integration. This relates in particular to the role of the EPPR Working Group.

In 2014 and 2015, the Arctic's institutional complexity increased further by the establishment of three new bodies, namely the AEC, the AORF and the ACGF. While none of these has been formally established by the Council or pursuant to a legally binding instrument negotiated under its auspices, all three have different extents of integration—substantively as well as institutionally—with the Arctic Council and the broader ACS. Rather than forming part of the Council or the broader ACS, however, they could be regarded as belonging to a new, more peripheral category of Arctic cooperative mechanisms. The establishment of these new bodies may well be regarded as institutional proliferation, and require at any rate increased efforts on institutional coordination and cooperation. The Arctic Council's 2016 Guidelines for Relationships with Outside Bodies may be helpful in this regard.

Even though the Arctic Council's substantive mandate is almost unlimited, but at present significantly under-utilised, more optimal use and associated institutional change is in principle constrained by existing (sub-)regional or bilateral instruments and bodies. As a general rule,[179] it can be assumed that the Arctic States have no desire to replace or subsume existing (sub-)regional or bilateral instruments and bodies, or to preclude new (sub-)regional or bilateral instruments and bodies from being created. Pertinent examples are instruments and bodies relating to the conservation and management of marine mammals and fish stocks, for instance the currently on-going Five-plus-Five process on international regulation of high seas fishing in the central Arctic Ocean. In view of the widening acceptance of ecosystem-based ocean management, however, one would expect increasingly closer coordination and cooperation between the Arctic Council and these formally stand-alone instruments and bodies.

Further evolution of the Council and the broader ACS seems inevitable, but the timeframe in which this is to occur is very uncertain. One wildcard in this regard is the commencement of the United States' Trump Administration in January 2017. While the broader ACS will at any rate expand further with the envisaged adoption of the Arctic Scientific Cooperation Agreement in conjunction with the Arctic Council's Ministerial Meeting in 2017, the discussions on the Arctic Council Strategic Plan and the slow progress in the TFAMC towards the end of 2016, suggest that further evolution will occur later rather than sooner.

---

179 While the Kingdom of Denmark, Iceland and Norway have implicitly asserted that the Arctic Council has primacy over the OSPAR Commission as regards area-based management measures in the overlap-area between OSPAR Region I and the area they refer to as the 'Central Arctic Ocean', it is too early to assess if this amounts to an exception to this general rule.

CHAPTER 3

The Rights, Interests and Role of the Arctic Council Permanent Participants

Dalee S Dorough

1 Introduction: Arctic Indigenous Peoples

1.1 *Introduction*

> Inuit are a *maritime people*: our entire culture and identity is based on free movement over the sea and sea ice. We rely on free movement, first and foremost, in order to eat, since so much of our diet is derived from hunting. This mobility is also essential in trade, communication, in obtaining supplies for traditional clothing and art, as well as to maintain pride in our rich cultural heritage. In order to take advantage of the sea ice our communities are predominantly coastal and, in some cases, travel by sea is the only means of moving in or out of our homes.[1]

There are approximately 370 million Indigenous peoples across the globe, ranging from the Aboriginal peoples of Australia to the Maori of New Zealand to the San people of South Africa to the Ainu of Japan. In addition, there are numerous diverse Indigenous communities throughout North, Central and

1 Inuit Circumpolar Council, *The Sea Ice Never Stops: Circumpolar Inuit Reflections on Sea Ice Use and Shipping in Inuit Nunaat*, December 2014 at iii [emphasis added], accessed 21 March 2017 at http://www.inuitcircumpolar.com/uploads/3/0/5/4/30542564/sea_ice_never_stops_-_final.pdf. See also File Number: 36692, Supreme Court of Canada (on appeal from the Federal Court of Appeal) between Hamlet of Clyde River, Nammautaq Hunters & Trappers Organization, and Jerry Natanine, Mayor of Clyde River, Appellants (Plaintiffs/Respondents) and TGS-NOPEC Geophysical Company ASA (TGS), Petroleum Geo-Services, Inc. (PGS), Multi Klient Investment AS (MKI), and the Attorney General of Canada, Respondent (Defendant/Appellant) and Senator Charlie Watt, Rosemarie Kuptana, Peter Ittinuar and Tagak Curley, Proposed Interveners, at page 9, paragraph 24 by Senator Charlie Watt and at pages 56–57 wherein Rosemarie Kuptana states, 'Inuit are a marine people and the entire Arctic is our homeland—Inuit *Nunangat*—including the use and occupation of the sea-ice. As such, we are dependent upon the marine mammals and fish in the Inuit Sea.' Documents can be found at http://www.scc-csc.ca/case-dossier/info/mal-mdaa-eng.aspx?cas=36692, accessed 21 March 2017.

 | DOI 10.1163/9789004339385_004

South America as well as those across the vast region of Asia. At present, there is no formal definition of the term Indigenous peoples. However, the United Nations has developed an informal working definition that includes the following criteria:

> Indigenous communities, peoples and nations are those which, having a historical continuity with pre-invasion and pre-colonial societies that developed on their territories, consider themselves distinct from other sectors of the societies now prevailing on those territories, or parts of them. They form at present non-dominant sectors of society and are determined to preserve, develop and transmit to future generations their ancestral territories, and their ethnic identity, as the basis of their continued existence as peoples, in accordance with their own cultural patterns, social institutions and legal system.[2]

As a dimension of the right to self-determination, self-identification is a crucial element of defining who is an Indigenous people, as affirmed in Article 33[3] of the United Nations Declaration on the Rights of Indigenous Peoples (UN Declaration),[4] which specifically relates to the Arctic Indigenous peoples, including Inuit (and their relations, the Yup'ik). Inuit number approximately 160,000 throughout the Russian Far East, Alaska, Canada and Greenland. This number does not include the Athabaskan of the interior and the Aleut peoples of the Pribilof Islands and the Aleutian Chain, which reside in the sub-Arctic region of Alaska.

In addition, the far north of Scandinavia is populated by the Sami of northern Norway, Sweden, Finland, and the nearby parts of the Russian Federation territory. The 'small nations' of the Russian north are included in this classification as well. There is an extraordinarily diverse range of peoples in this 'small nations' category, which was designed entirely by the national government of

2 *Study of the Problem of Discrimination Against Indigenous Populations*, Final report submitted by the Special Rapporteur, Mr José Martínez Cobo, accessed 21 March 2017 at http://www.un.org/esa/socdev/unpfii/documents/MCS_v_en.pdf. The whole of this voluminous study can be found at http://undesadspd.org/IndigenousPeoples/LibraryDocuments/Mart%C3%ADnezCoboStudy.aspx, accessed 21 March 2017.

3 United Nations Declaration on the Rights of Indigenous Peoples, GA Res 61/295, UN Doc A/RES/61/295 (13 September 2007). Article 33 states, '1. Indigenous peoples have the right to determine their own identity or membership in accordance with their customs and traditions. This does not impair the right of indigenous individuals to obtain citizenship of the States in which they live. 2. Indigenous peoples have the right to determine the structures and to select the membership of their institutions in accordance with their own procedures'.

4 *Ibid.*

the Russian Federation.[5] The numerical designation of 'small nations' does not fully correspond with UN's informal working definition[6] nor does it take into account the distinct status and ways of life—as reflected in Article 33 of the UN Declaration—of the Indigenous peoples throughout the vast Russian Arctic territory.

Like Indigenous peoples in other parts of the world, the Arctic Indigenous peoples have made significant strides in favour of promoting and protecting their lives and homelands at the local, regional, national and international level. Therefore, from a historical perspective and relevant to the present discussion, it is important to address the crucial Arctic-specific political and legal work of the Inuit, dating as far back as the 1950s,[7] to guarantee the sustainable

---

5 As reflected on the website of the Arctic Council, 'RAIPON represents 41 groups of Indigenous peoples of the North, Siberia and the Far East. The total number of people is more than 270 thousand and they live in 60 % of the whole territory of the Russian Federation from Murmansk to Kamchatka'. See http://www.arctic-council.org/index.php/en/about-us/permanent-participants/raipon, accessed 21 March 2017.

6 'Study of the problem of discrimination against indigenous populations', UN Sub-Commission on the Prevention of Discrimination and the Protection of Minorities, by Special Rapporteur, Mr José Martinez Cobo, UN Doc E/CN.4/Sub.2/1986/7 (1986), Indigenous peoples may be identified as follows: 'Indigenous communities, peoples and nations are those which, having a historical continuity with pre-invasion and pre-colonial societies that developed on their territories, consider themselves distinct from other sectors of the societies now prevailing in those territories, or parts of them. They form at present non-dominant sectors of society and are determined to preserve, develop and transmit to future generations their ancestral territories, and their ethnic identity, as the basis of their continued existence as peoples, in accordance with their own cultural patterns, social institutions and legal systems. This historical continuity may consist of the continuation, for an extended period reaching into the present, of one or more of the following factors: Occupation of ancestral lands, or at least of part of them; Common ancestry with the original occupants of these lands; Culture in general, or in specific manifestations (such as religion, living under a tribal system, membership of an indigenous community, dress, means of livelihood, lifestyle, etc.); Language (whether used as the only language, as mother-tongue, as the habitual means of communication at home or in the family, or as the main, preferred, habitual, general or normal language); Residence in certain parts of the country, or in certain regions of the world; Other relevant factors'.

7 Norman Chance, 'Project Chariot: The Nuclear Legacy of Cape Thompson', accessed 21 March 2017 at http://arcticcircle.uconn.edu/SEEJ/chariotseej.html. Chance researched and provided a case study on the so-called 'peaceful uses' of radioactive material in the Arctic: 'Not surprisingly, assurances that Chariot would not be a hazard to the subsistence way of life of the Point Hope Inupiat were sharply rejected by the village council. Immediately following the close of the meeting, the council voted unanimously to oppose detonation of the bomb. As Foote summarized the results of the meeting in his report of the event: The net result of the first official presentation of Project Chariot to the people of Point Hope was to produce a profound lack of confidence in the sincerity of the AEC'.

development of their territory within the circumpolar Arctic. Though there is an enormous diversity in/among Arctic Indigenous peoples and communities, the author is most familiar with the diplomacy demonstrated by Inuit throughout a wide variety of international and inter-governmental developments, including the Arctic Council. Furthermore, the Inuit, as a coastal and maritime people, in contrast to that of the other Permanent Participants of the Arctic Council, have had a more active and sustained role in matters concerning the Arctic Ocean and coastal seas due to their reliance upon these life-giving forces and the need to be responsive to related potential threats. Therefore, this Chapter will focus upon the concerns of the Inuit in relation to Arctic shipping and its potential impact on their cultural values and unique homelands.

1.2 *Inuit of the Arctic Circumpolar Region*

Long before the Arctic became a vogue research topic, Inuit turned their attention toward the objective of ensuring that they would become primary actors in the development of Arctic policy and the political discourse concerning this distinct part of the world. Much of this focused work began in 1959 when the United States Alaska Statehood Act was adopted[8] and state government land selections triggered encroachments onto Inupiat territory above the Arctic Circle. In 1966, the Arctic Slope Native Association (ASNA) was organised for the purpose of pursuing explicit recognition of the Inupiat right to self-determination and their collective rights to lands, territories and resources.[9]

This political organising was propelled even further by the 1967 discovery of oil on the North Slope of Alaska. The ASNA maintained their legal agenda through the filing of the 1971 *Edwardsen v. Morton*[10] case, asserting that the US Department of Interior failed to safeguard Inupiat rights when the state of Alaska and the oil industry trespassed onto their sovereign homelands. With incredible foresight as to the dramatic changes that the Inupiat of the North Slope would see, the late Eben Hopson[11] undertook the organisation of the

8 Alaska Statehood Act, 72 Stat 339, Public Law 85–508, 85th Congress, HR 7999, July 7, 1958, provided for the declaration of the State of Alaska as a State of the United States of American and its admission into the Union.

9 Creation of ASNA on 15 January 1966, in Barrow, Alaska in order to 'claim 56 million acres of land in the Arctic, having the natural boundaries of the Brooks Range going south, and going west to the Chukchi Sea, the Beaufort Sea and the demarcation line'. See http://www.asrc.com/About/History/Pages/Pre-ANCSA.aspx, accessed 21 March 2017.

10 *Edwardsen v Morton*, 369 F Supp 1359 (DC, 1973). See also David S Case and David A Voluck (eds), *Alaska Natives and American Laws*, 3d ed (University of Alaska Press, 2012) 75–80.

11 See background and history of Eben Hopson, first Mayor of the North Slope Borough, memorialised by Jon Buchholdt, an early advisor to Hopson, accessed 21 March 2017 at http://www.ebenhopson.com/SecondOpeningPage.htm.

North Slope Borough (under state law) in 1972[12] and began making preparations for the creation of the Inuit Circumpolar Council (ICC).[13] Many of today's Arctic enthusiasts are wholly ignorant of the Arctic Coastal Zone Management newsletter—the North Slope Borough's early publication—and the ICC's early work explicitly devoted to Arctic policy and its development. Indeed, at the founding meeting of the ICC in June of 1977 at Barrow, Eben Hopson's words spoke volumes about intellectual property, sustainable development, resource rights and management, cultural rights and the distinct status of the Inupiat:

> Our language contains the memory of four thousand years of human survival through the conservation and good managing of our Arctic wealth.... Our language contains the intricate knowledge of the ice that we have seen no others demonstrate.[14]

Furthermore, at the 1977 organising conference, Inuit identified the need for a comprehensive Arctic Policy written from an Inuit perspective. Inuit leaders throughout Alaska, Canada and Greenland have worked throughout the life of the ICC to draft and adopt a set of comprehensive principles for an Arctic

12 See generally the web site of the North Slope Borough, accessed 21 March 2017 at http://www.north-slope.org/. See also Gunnar Knapp and Thomas A Morehouse, 'Alaska's North Slope Borough Revisited', prepared for submission to *Polar Record* (University of Alaska Anchorage, Institute of Social and Economic Research, January 1991) 2–4.

13 Author was a direct participant in this work. In addition, see generally http://www.inuitcircumpolar.com/icc-international.html, accessed 21 March 2017. The Inuit of the Arctic circumpolar region organised themselves internationally through the Inuit Circumpolar Conference (ICC) founded in 1977 in Barrow, Alaska. The goals of the ICC are: To strengthen unity among Inuit of the Circumpolar region; To promote Inuit rights and interests on the international level; To ensure and further develop Inuit culture and society for both the present and future generations; To seek full and active participation in the political, economic, and social development in our homelands; To develop and encourage long-term policies which safeguard the Arctic environment; and To work for international recognition of the human rights of all Indigenous Peoples. The organisation has an internationally elected President and an Executive Council with two elected Inuit from each of the four regions. The ICC gained United Nations Non-Governmental Organization (NGO) status in 1983 and has been active in the UN's work as a leading and well-respected indigenous NGO. See generally Dalee Sambo, 'Inuit Assert Control Over Arctic,' *Arctic Policy Review* (July/August 1977), Arctic Coastal Zone Management Newsletter (August 1983); Aqqaluk Lynge, *Inuit* (Attuakkiorfik, 1992).

14 Opening Statement of Eben Hopson, 13 June 1977, Barrow, Alaska at the founding meeting of the then Inuit Circumpolar Conference. Hopson, accessed 21 March 2017 at http://www.ebenhopson.com/icc/ICCKeynote.html.

Policy.[15] These Arctic Policy principles have been complemented by a number of declarations, including one on Arctic sovereignty[16] and another on resource development.[17]

In addition to the focus upon Arctic Policy principles, the ICC initiated a range of working groups and commissions to address an array of concerns, from language preservation to Arctic transportation to communications and many other foci of direct relevance to improving the quality of life for Inuit scattered across the Arctic circumpolar region. One such commission focused upon environmental protection of Inuit and their Arctic territory.[18] Early engagement in the Working Group on Arctic International Relations led to discussions about formalising a circumpolar wide regional body to focus specifically on environmental protection.[19]

In 1983, through the International Union for the Conservation of Nature (IUCN)'s Environmental Commission, the ICC became actively involved in the redrafting of the World Conservation Strategy and the work of the IUCN more in general. This marked the first direct involvement of Indigenous peoples within the IUCN and an opportunity to bring the Arctic Indigenous world perspective into a global conservation strategy. Unfortunately, the animal rights movement

---

15 *Principles and Elements for a Comprehensive Arctic Policy,* Inuit Circumpolar Conference (McGill University, 1992) and revised edition entitled *Inuit Arctic Policy*, Inuit Circumpolar Council (Nuuk, Greenland, 2014).

16 A Circumpolar Inuit Declaration on Sovereignty in the Arctic, April 2009, on file with author. See also http://www.inuitcircumpolar.com/sovereignty-in-the-arctic.html, accessed 21 March 2017.

17 A Circumpolar Inuit Declaration on Resource Development Principles in Inuit Nunaat, 2011, on file with author. See also http://www.inuitcircumpolar.com/resource-development-principles-in-inuit-nunaat.html, accessed 21 March 2017.

18 ICC Environmental Commission, chaired by Greenlandic Inuk, Finn Lynge, who was also Greenland's representative to the European Parliament.

19 The author was a member of the Working Group on Arctic International Relations along with other academics, government diplomats, scientists from both government and non-government institutions and non-Indigenous environmental NGOs. See also Working Group on the North and Canada's International Relations (1988), The North and Canada's International Relations, Ottawa: Canadian Arctic Resources Committee; Oran R Young, 'The Age of the Arctic' *Foreign Policy* 61 (Winter 1985–1986) 160–79; Oran R Young 'The Political Dynamics of International Regions: The Arctic as a Multiple-Use Region', ch 5 (1992) [Prepared under the sponsorship of the MacArthur Foundation to draw lessons from the work of the Working Group on Arctic International Relations. An earlier version of the essay was presented at the conference 'Arctic Perspectives: The Changing Role of the United States in the Circumpolar North', Fairbanks, 12–14 August 1992]; Oran R Young, 'The Work of the Working Group on Arctic International Relations' *Northern Notes IV* (December 1996).

within the IUCN created an extremely hostile reception for Inuit, especially in relation to the ancient practice of bowhead whaling.[20] Nevertheless, the ICC received the Global 500 Award from the United Nations Environment Program,[21] which was humbly accepted by then ICC President Mary Simon, who later became the first Canadian Ambassador for Circumpolar Affairs as well as to the Kingdom of Denmark.

One priority initiative was ICC's direct involvement with human rights standard-setting exercises in a variety of inter-governmental fora ranging from the International Labour Organization (ILO) and the United Nations, to the Organization of American States, the UN Educational, Scientific and Cultural Organization (UNESCO) and other institutions. The acknowledgement of Inuit as a distinct voice and contributor to international relations was afforded by confirmation of Non-Governmental Organization (NGO) status to the ICC by the UN Economic and Social Council in 1983.[22] This status provided access to and direct participation of the ICC representatives at all UN meetings of concern to Inuit.[23]

1.3 *International Indigenous Human Rights Standards*

To be sure, one of the most important results of Inuit engagement with the United Nations was the adoption of the UN Declaration in 2007.[24] The UN Declaration is a comprehensive international human rights instrument that affirms the distinct status and human rights of the world's Indigenous peoples, including those within the Arctic circumpolar region. Article 43 affirms that the

---

20 Finn Lynge, translated by Marianne Stenbaek, *Arctic Wars, Animal Rights, Endangered Peoples* (University Press of New England, 1992).

21 Jason Dittmer and Fiona McConnell, *Diplomatic Cultures and International Politics: Translations, Spaces and Alternatives* (Routledge, 2016).

22 At the time Hans-Pavia Rosing, President of ICC, stated, 'This is a great achievement for such a relatively young organization and provides the ICC with an important forum to present our views and exchange ideas ... We take this acceptance of our NGO application as recognition by the United Nations of the important role Inuit can play in promoting the objectives of the U.S. and in assisting the international community in developing a greater awareness of and sensitivity to the Arctic region, its environment and its inhabitants'. Prior to this designation, ICC had participated in, and contributed to, various specialised agencies of UNESCO.

23 NGO Status provided the ICC formal and special consultative status with UN ECOSOC and its agencies, committees, and commissions, as well as with the UN Secretariat. See Resolution 83–13 Addressing Inuit Circumpolar Conference Consultative Status to the United Nations at http://www.inuitcircumpolar.com/resolutions.html, accessed 21 March 2017.

24 UN Declaration, *supra* note 3.

norms embraced by the UN Declaration constitute 'the minimum standards for the survival, dignity and well-being of the indigenous peoples of the world'.

Among other interrelated human rights, the operative provisions of the UN Declaration affirm that Indigenous peoples have the right to self-determination as well as 'the right to the lands, territories and resources which they have traditionally owned, occupied or otherwise used or acquired.'[25] Also, protection of environmental integrity, the right to culture, subsistence, and a host of many other rights are explicitly affirmed in the UN Declaration. Furthermore, UN Member States' support for this human rights instrument has been reiterated on three occasions since its adoption, including in the September 2014 Outcome Document adopted through a high-level plenary session of the General Assembly known as the World Conference on Indigenous Peoples.[26]

Furthermore, the ILO revision of their Convention 107, which resulted in ILO Convention No. 169 on Indigenous and Tribal Peoples (ILO C169), is relevant not only due to its ratification by Denmark and Norway, but also because it is now regarded by the ILO and others as a necessary interpretative document in the framework of Indigenous human rights. Specifically, the ILO has pronounced that

> With the adoption of the UN Declaration, the international normative framework regulating the protection of the rights of indigenous peoples has been firmly strengthened. The ILO [C169] is fully compatible with the UN Declaration on the Rights of Indigenous Peoples and *the two instruments are mutually reinforcing*. The two instruments provide the solid framework for promoting indigenous peoples' rights and addressing the existing implementation gaps at all levels ...[27]

Unfortunately, States were on such a rampage to diminish the right of Indigenous peoples to self-determination that it had a residual effect on the

25 *Ibid.*, Art 26(1).

26 Outcome document of the high-level plenary meeting of the General Assembly known as the World Conference on Indigenous Peoples, Resolution adopted by the General Assembly on 22 September 2014, UN Doc A/RES/69/2 (2014). See also General Assembly, Rights of indigenous peoples, UN Doc. A/RES/71/178 (19 December 2016), preamble: "Reaffirming the United Nations Declaration on the Rights of Indigenous Peoples, which addresses their individual and collective rights"; and General Assembly, Rights of indigenous peoples, UN Doc. A/RES/70/232 (23 December 2015), preamble.

27 See UN-Indigenous Peoples' Partnership (UNIPP), 'For democratic governance, human rights and equality', Multi-Donor Trust Fund, Terms of Reference ILO, OHCHR, UNDP, Framework Document (UNIPP, 2010) 4 [emphasis added].

drafting of the Ottawa Declaration, by which the Arctic Council was established in 1996.[28] The Ottawa Declaration includes a footnote associated with the term 'peoples', which reads as follows: 'The use of the term "peoples" shall not be construed as having any implications as regard the rights which may attach to the term under international law'. However, scholars and practitioners have rightly commented on this unusual dynamic and affirmed that the term 'peoples' within the ILO in particular, has no legal or political impact in its interpretation in light of its use in international law and the right to self-determination of peoples.[29] It is critical to underscore the fact that Indigenous peoples' representatives and UN Member States, in the course of the negotiations of the UN Declaration squarely dealt with the collective, political right to self-determination, which is recognised as the pre-requisite to the exercise and enjoyment of all other human rights. In this way, the legal effect of the adoption of the UN Declaration and the fact that it and ILO C169 must now be read as 'mutually reinforcing', the term 'peoples' is no longer neutral but rather affirms the right to self-determination of Indigenous peoples.[30] And, again, that this right is the same right enunciated as a principle in Article 1(2) of the UN Charter[31] and a right of all peoples in the twin Articles 1 of the International Covenants.[32] It is therefore submitted that the footnote within the Ottawa

28 Declaration on the Establishment of the Arctic Council, Joint Communique of the Governments of the Arctic Countries on the Establishment of the Arctic Council, Ottawa, Canada, 19 September 1996, commonly referred to as the 'Ottawa Declaration'.

29 Lee Swepston, 'A New Step in International Law on Indigenous and Tribal Peoples: ILO Convention No. 169 of 1989' 15 *Oklahoma City University Law Review* (1989) at 677; Lee Swepston, 'The Indigenous and Tribal Peoples Convention (No 169): Eight Years After Adoption' in Cynthia Price Cohen (ed) *Human Rights of Indigenous Peoples* (Transnational Publishers, 1998) at 17: 'What does this mean for self-determination? In itself, it means nothing in the context of deciding what "self-determination" actually implies. ... The Convention takes no position whatsoever on the question of political autonomy outside the boundaries of existing States; this is a question for the United Nations in a larger political context'. Further at 22: Another criticism is that Article 1(3) somehow limits the rights of indigenous peoples to self-determination. Again, this patently is not so. Convention No. 169 simply refers the decision on the content of this right to the United Nations, where it rightly belongs'.

30 UN Declaration, *supra* note 3, Art 3: 'Indigenous peoples have the right to self-determination. By virtue of that right they freely determine their political status and freely pursue their economic, social and cultural development'.

31 Charter of the United Nations, 26 June 1945, 1 UTS at xvi.

32 International Covenant on Civil and Political Rights, adopted 16 December 1966, 999 UTS 171 (entered into force 23 March 1976); International Covenant on Economic, Social and Cultural Rights, adopted 16 December 1966, 993 UTS 3 (entered into force 3 January 1976).

Declaration is now obsolete and should no longer become a factor or argument to reduce or diminish the right of Arctic Indigenous peoples to have an equal seat at the table of the Arctic Council, especially in light of possible future dialogue to reform or restructure the Arctic Council on the basis of a legally binding treaty.

It should be iterated that specific rights to lands, territories and resources have been recognised for some Indigenous peoples in the Arctic region. For example, the 1971 Alaska Native Claims Settlement Act transferred right and title of 44 million acres of lands, territories and resources, including surface and subsurface, to Alaska Natives.[33] Throughout the Canadian Arctic, a range of comprehensive land claims agreements have been negotiated with the Inuit, culminating in the transferal of right and title to lands, territories and resources.[34] These land claims treaties also affirmed hunting, fishing and gathering rights, and management and co-management of resources. Significantly, in the Labrador Inuit Land Claims Agreement,[35] Inuit rights to the 12-nautical mile territorial sea, consistent with UNCLOS[36] are affirmed and elaborated upon. In regard to the 'Zone', the Nunatsiavut Government is responsible for the Inuit domestic harvest and the Government of Canada maintains responsibility for management of the fisheries, including quotas, and international shipping. However, if there are changes to existing laws, marine transportation routes or if new and different environmental guidelines are proposed, the

33 Alaska Native Claims Settlement Act, 85 Stat 688, Public Law 92–203, HR 10367, 18 December 1971 (codified as amended at 43 USCA §§ 1601–1629a (2004)).

34 James Bay and Northern Quebec Agreement, 1975; Inuvialuit Final Agreement, 1984; Nunavut, 1999; Labrador Inuit Land Claims Agreement by referendum in December 2004.

35 See Land Claims Agreement Between the Inuit of Labrador and Her Majesty the Queen in Right of Newfoundland and Labrador and Her Majesty the Queen in Right of Canada, accessed 21 March 2017 at https://www.aadnc-aandc.gc.ca/eng/1293647179208/1293647660333; see also Labrador Inuit Land Claims Agreement Annual Report—1 December 2005 to 31 March 2007 '1.2.3 Ocean Management The Labrador Inuit Settlement Area includes an adjacent ocean zone extending to the limit of Canada's territorial sea. Any major initiatives to establish marine management plans or to develop non-renewable resources in the Zone require prior consultation with the Nunatsiavut Government. Major developments in the Zone also require the negotiation of Inuit Impacts and Benefits Agreements'. The comprehensive agreement also addresses navigation, fisheries, Inuit harvesting rights, marine protected areas, petroleum development as well as benefit sharing and the overall requirement to consult the Nunatsiavut Government in relation to any and all impacts related to the Settlement area. See https://www.aadnc-aandc.gc.ca/eng/1328023902556/1328024079372#key12, accessed 21 March 2017.

36 United Nations Convention on the Law of the Sea, adopted 10 December 1982, 1833 UNTS 3 (entered into force 16 November 1994) (UNCLOS).

Government of Canada must first consult with Inuit. And, a joint management committee may be established for activities within this Zone.[37]

Furthermore, each of the modern day treaties negotiated with the Inuit are protected by Section 35 of the Canadian Constitution.[38] Though each agreement is not perfect and difficulties in implementation have emerged, it is highly significant that the collective rights to lands, territories and resources of Arctic Indigenous peoples have been affirmed. In addition, the Greenland Government was originally initiated as home rule government in 1979 largely on the basis of the need to address the Inuit's right to self-determination.[39] Therefore, it is even more important that Arctic States as well as other States respect and recognise the political, economic, social and cultural rights of Arctic Indigenous peoples and fully take into account the status, rights and responsibilities of these distinct Indigenous governments and entities.

In regard to the UN Declaration's status, though the whole of the instrument is not legally binding, there are a range of important provisions that create Member State obligations due to their status as norms of customary international law. According to the International Law Association (ILA) Committee on Rights of Indigenous Peoples (ILA Committee) and its expert commentary on the UN Declaration, 'the relevant areas of indigenous peoples' rights with respect to which the discourse on customary international law arises are self-determination; autonomy or self-government; cultural rights and identity; land rights as well as reparation, redress and remedies'.[40] However, like the

37 Labrador Inuit Land Claims Agreement, *supra* note 34. 'Major developments in the Zone also require the negotiation of Inuit Impacts and Benefits Agreements'. The comprehensive agreement also addresses navigation, fisheries, Inuit harvesting rights, marine protected areas, petroleum development as well as benefit sharing and the overall requirement to consult the Nunatsiavut Government in relation to any and all impacts related to the Settlement area.

38 Constitution Act, 1982, Section 35 provides '(1) The existing aboriginal and treaty rights of the aboriginal peoples of Canada are hereby recognized and affirmed; (2) in this Act, "Aboriginal Peoples of Canada" includes the Indian, Inuit and Métis peoples of Canada; (3) for greater certainty, in subsection (1) "treaty rights" includes rights that now exist by way of land claims agreements or may be so acquired; and (4) notwithstanding any other provision of this Act, the aboriginal and treaty rights referred to in subsection (1) are guaranteed equally to male and female persons'.

39 Home Rule Act, 1979. Recent developments are reflected in the Act on Greenland Self-Government, Act No 473 of 12 June 2009 (English translation) at http://naalakkersuisut.gl/~/media/Nanoq/Files/Attached%20Files/Engelske-tekster/Act%20on%20Greenland.pdf, accessed 21 March 2017.

40 International Law Association, The Hague Conference (2010), Interim Report of the Committee on Rights of Indigenous Peoples, 43. accessed 21 March 2017 at http://www.ila-hq.org/en/committees/index.cfm/cid/1024.

interrelated, interdependent, indivisible and interconnected nature of human rights, the ILA Committee recognised that 'it would be inappropriate to deal with these areas separately … the rights just listed are all strictly interrelated … to the extent that the change of one of its elements affects the whole.'[41]

Today, with new opportunities and the reality of climate change, the previous neglect of and disregard for the Inuit and the Arctic circumpolar region overall has been overshadowed and overtaken by extraordinary enthusiasm as well as economic power and influence from all quarters of the non-Inuit world. The offshore oil and gas industry, mining interests, environmentalists, social scientists, and a diverse array of governmental and non-governmental organisations and other entities from across the globe have all set their sights on the Arctic.

President Obama's August 2015 visit to Alaska is but one example. He forthrightly centered on the need for State policy makers to integrate climate change into all areas of public policy making.[42] And, today, rather than incrementalism, Arctic Indigenous peoples are experiencing more dramatic change over a shorter period of time.

Because of these increasing external pressures and the fundamental international human rights developments toward safeguarding Indigenous peoples from compounding adverse effects on their Arctic homelands and coastal areas, it is crucial to provide an Arctic Council[43] Permanent Participant perspective about Arctic shipping and its potential impact on their territories. In particular, the international human rights standards that have emerged following entry into force of UNCLOS must serve as constructive benchmarks for determining the shortcomings of the UNCLOS provisions and other international treaties, agreements and other constructive arrangements. Far too often, parties of UNCLOS and others have focused upon the provisions concerning maritime boundaries and limits in the context of the Commission on the Limits of the Continental Shelf while paying little to no attention to the other important chapters of this treaty, and in particular the provisions related to protection of the marine environment, the sustainable use and conservation of marine living resources and ice-covered areas.

As Eben Hopson noted in 1977, 'uniform recognition'[44] of the rights and status of Arctic Indigenous peoples is needed. Though the UN Declaration has

41 *Ibid.*

42 Remarks by President Barack Obama at the GLACIER Conference, Anchorage, Alaska, Dena'ina Civic and Convention Center, accessed 21 March 2017 at https://www.whitehouse.gov/the-press-office/2015/09/01/remarks-president-glacier-conference-anchorage-ak.

43 Ottawa Declaration, *supra* note 28.

44 Hopson, *supra* note 11.

affirmed a comprehensive array of individual and collective human rights of Indigenous peoples, respect for and recognition of such rights throughout the circumpolar Arctic remains outstanding and uneven. This is especially true for the so-called small nations of the North within the Russian Federation as well as the Sami of northern Norway, Sweden, Finland and the Russian Federation.

For Inuit, a critical element is the need to recognise the profound relationship that they have with the Arctic Ocean coastal areas and their respective lands, territories and resources. In this context, the term 'territories' should be regarded as comprehensive and inclusive of the coastal land areas, shore fast sea ice, offshore areas of the ocean itself, including the seabed, which have been traditionally used for millennia as the source of sustenance in the way of whales, seals, walrus, migratory birds and other marine life.

2 Arctic Council Permanent Participants

In regard to the Arctic Council, recognising that the Arctic is in fact the homeland of Indigenous peoples, the Arctic States[45] ensured that the Indigenous peoples concerned were pivotal actors in the future agenda items within the purview of the Arctic Council established in 1996.[46]

> Out of a total of 4 million inhabitants of the Arctic, approximately 500,000 belong to indigenous peoples. Indigenous peoples' organizations have been granted Permanent Participants status in the Arctic Council. The Permanent Participants have full consultation rights in connection with the Council's negotiations and decisions. The Permanent Participants represent a unique feature of the Arctic Council, and they make valuable contributions to its activities in all areas.[47]

Indeed, organisations such as the ICC participated in the earliest ministerial meetings that ultimately outlined the purpose and mandate of this high-level inter-governmental forum. Originally, Permanent Participant status

45 Canada, Denmark, Finland, Iceland, Norway, the Russian Federation, Sweden and the United States as reflected in the Ottawa Declaration, 1996, *supra* note 28.

46 Ottawa Declaration, *supra* note 28.

47 See http://www.arctic-council.org/index.php/en/about-us/permanent-participants, accessed 21 March 2017.

was accorded to the ICC, the Sami Council[48] and the Russian Association of Indigenous Peoples of the North (otherwise referred to as RAIPON).[49] Later and consistent with the provisions of the Ottawa Declaration, the Gwich'in Council International,[50] the Aleut International Association,[51] and the Arctic Athabaskan Council[52] were accorded Permanent Participant status.[53]

---

48 The Saami Council is a voluntary Saami organisation (a non–governmental organisation), with Saami member organisations in Finland, Russia, Norway and Sweden. Since its foundation in 1956 the Saami Council has actively dealt with Saami policy tasks. See generally http://www.saamicouncil.net/?deptid=1116, accessed 21 March 2017.

49 Arctic Council web site, accessed 21 March 2017 at http://www.arctic-council.org/index.php/en/about-us/permanent-participants/raipon: 'The purpose of RAIPON is to protect indigenous peoples' human rights, defend their legal interests, assist in solving environmental, social, economic, cultural and educational issues, and to promote their right to self-governance. RAIPON works with the State Duma and the Government of the Russian Federation regarding legislation related to indigenous peoples' issues'.

50 See generally http://www.gwichin.org/, accessed 21 March 2017: 'The Gwich'in Council International (GCI) was established as a non-profit organization in 1999 by the Gwich'in Tribal Council in Inuvik, Northwest Territories, to ensure all regions of the Gwich'in Nation in the Northwest Territories, Yukon and Alaska are represented at the Arctic Council, as well as to play an active and significant role in the development of policies that relate to the Circumpolar Arctic.... In total, the Gwich'in Council International founding members represent approximately 9,000 indigenous peoples of Gwich'in descent'.

51 See http://aleut-international.org/, accessed 21 March 2017: 'The organization was formed to address environmental and cultural concerns of the extended Aleut family whose well-being has been connected to the rich resources of the Bering Sea for millennia.... The need to understand global processes, such as transboundary contaminants transport, the impacts of climate change, and the effects of commercial fisheries on the ecosystem of the Bering Sea to name a few, was an impetus in joining in the work of international fora where AIA is actively pursuing collaboration with governments, scientists, and other organizations in developing programs and policies that could improve the wellbeing of the Aleut people and their environment. AIA was admitted as a permanent participant of the Arctic Council in 1998 and was granted Special Consultative Status by the Economic and Social Council of the United Nations in 2004'.

52 See http://www.arcticathabaskancouncil.com/aac/?q=about, accessed 21 March 2017: 'The Arctic Athabaskan Council (AAC) is an international treaty organization established to defend the rights and further the interests internationally of American and Canadian Athabaskan member First Nation governments in the eight-nation Arctic Council and other international fora. AAC is an authorized "Permanent Participant" in the Arctic Council. In addition, AAC seeks to foster a greater understanding of the shared heritage of Athabaskan peoples of Arctic North America'.

53 In the event of newly composed Arctic Indigenous peoples' organisations, Article 2 of the Ottawa Declaration provides: 'Permanent participation is equally open to other Arctic organizations of indigenous peoples with majority Arctic indigenous constituency,

In regard to the Arctic Council and its activities, some important ongoing initiatives have had a positive and direct impact upon the presence, role and rights of its Permanent Participants. The fact that Indigenous peoples, through their Permanent Participant status, have been able to effectively occupy both an intellectual and political space within this inter-governmental regime in order to comprehensively promote and protect their rights and interests, is highly significant.

2.1 *Role and Influence of the Permanent Participants*

When the eight circumpolar Arctic States were drafting the Arctic Council's original Rules of Procedure,[54] the author argued that Indigenous peoples should have equal status to that of Member States, including voting rights.[55] However, this proposal was not aggressively pursued by Inuit leadership at the time. Though Permanent Participant representatives do not have the formal right to vote, they have extraordinary influence over all issues for consideration due to the consensus decision-making approach of the Arctic Council.[56] In addition, according to the Rules of Procedure, they are consulted on a wide range of matters, including the agenda, location of meetings, selection of representatives for purposes of Senior Arctic Official meetings, etc.[57] So, for all intents and purposes, the Permanent Participants have an 'equal' seat at the table and have substantial influence over the matters before the Arctic Council. It is also important to acknowledge that organisations such as the ICC enjoy an esteemed reputation within the Arctic Council due to their constructive

---

representing: 1. a single indigenous people resident in more than one Arctic State; or 2. more than one Arctic indigenous people resident in a single Arctic State. The determination that such an organization has met this criterion is to be made by decision of the Council. The number of Permanent Participants should at any time be less than the number of members'.

54 Arctic Council Rules of Procedure as adopted by the Arctic Council at the First Arctic Council Ministerial Meeting Iqaluit, Canada, 17–18 September 1998, and Revised by the Arctic Council at the Eighth Arctic Council Ministerial Meeting Kiruna, Sweden, 15 May 2013, accessed 21 March 2017 at https://oaarchive.arctic-council.org/bitstream/handle/11374/940/2015-09-01_Rules_of_Procedure_website_version.pdf?sequence=1.

55 Dalee S Dorough, 'Indigenous Peoples and the Law of the Sea: the Need for an Arctic Perspective' in Davor Vidas and Willy Østreng (eds) *Order for the Oceans at the Turn of the Century* (Kluwer Law International, 1999) 407–426, at 424.

56 Ottawa Declaration, *supra* note 28, Arctic Council, Rules of Procedure, Part II, General Provisions, para 8.

57 *Ibid.*, paras 15 and 21.

engagement, display of diplomacy and willingness to collaborate and cooperate with all other stakeholders, including Member States.[58]

The Arctic Council's emphasis on sustainable development and environmental protection, in their broadest terms, are in alignment with the objectives of most, if not all, of the Permanent Participants. Generally, the Arctic Council's diverse array of working groups and research activities intersect in multiple ways with the purposes and principles of Permanent Participants. It is also crucial to recognise the binding agreements that have emerged within the context of the Arctic Council, which the Permanent Participants should have been able to have greater input and influence upon in light of their status within the organisation and their corresponding regional governments, which control the very limited Arctic infrastructure as well as means to respond. This is a compelling argument that the Permanent Participants could have made in relation to the Agreement on Cooperation on Aeronautical and Maritime Search and Rescue in the Arctic as well as the Agreement on Cooperation on Marine Oil Pollution Preparedness and Response in the Arctic.[59] In addition, there are ongoing negotiations on the Agreement on Enhancing International Arctic Scientific Cooperation, which is envisaged to be signed at the 2017 Arctic Council Ministerial Meeting. Here again, in light of the rights, role and responsibilities of Arctic Indigenous peoples and the need for greater respect for and recognition of Indigenous knowledge, the Permanent Participants should be at the front and center of this emerging agreement.[60]

---

58 See Gary N Wilson, 'Inuit diplomacy in the circumpolar north' *Canadian Foreign Policy Journal*, Volume 13, Issue 3, 2007; Olav S Stokke and Geir Hønneland (eds), *International Cooperation and Arctic Governance: Regime Effectiveness and Northern Region Building*, (Routledge, 2006) 175.

59 See respectively Arctic Council Agreement on Cooperation on Aeronautical and Maritime Search and Rescue in the Arctic, at https://oaarchive.arctic-council.org/handle/11374/531 and Agreement on Cooperation on Marine Oil Pollution Preparedness and Response in the Arctic at http://www.arctic-council.org/index.php/en/our-work/agreements, both accessed 21 March 2017.

60 See generally information on the Scientific Cooperation Task Force of the Arctic Council at http://www.arctic-council.org/index.php/en/our-work2/8-news-and-events/360-sctf-copenhagen, accessed 21 March 2017.

3 Arctic Shipping: Concerns of the Permanent Participants

3.1 *Introduction*

In regard to a number of recent Arctic Council initiatives relevant to their purposes and principles, the adoption of a range of recommendations made in the 2009 Arctic Marine Shipping Assessment report are important and topical. These recommendations highlight the need for safeguarding, *inter alia*, cultural uses and the Arctic Ocean environment from the impacts of marine shipping. They also call for substantive collaboration with the International Whaling Commission and the International Maritime Organization (IMO) in order to achieve a range of objectives.

In addition, when the United States recently assumed chairmanship of the Arctic Council, it announced its desire to highlight Arctic Marine Protected Areas (cultural significance) and Arctic Marine Cooperation[61] (including research) under the broad theme of 'Arctic Ocean Safety, Security & Stewardship'.[62] The ICC representatives have stated that they welcome these initiatives,

61 The 2015–2017 Arctic Council work plan during the US Chairmanship contains initiatives aimed at promoting Arctic Ocean safety, security, and stewardship, improving economic and living conditions throughout the Arctic and addressing the impacts of climate change. At page 4 of this document: 'Arctic Marine Cooperation: Arctic Council Ministers established the Task Force on Arctic Marine Cooperation to "assess future needs for a regional seas program or other mechanism, as appropriate, for increased cooperation in Arctic marine areas." Looking ahead to the future of the Arctic Ocean, the Task Force is assessing the needs for international cooperation to meet these future challenges and opportunities. Based on this needs assessment, the Task Force will make recommendations for new mechanisms for international cooperation, as appropriate, to meet these future needs' (TFAMC), accessed 21 March 2017 at http://www.state.gov/documents/organization/249166.pdf.

62 Remarks of John Kerry, Secretary of State, at the Legislative Assembly of Nunavut, Iqaluit, Canada, 24 April 2015: 'Another effort that's critical to ensuring the stewardship of the Arctic Ocean is continuing the Council's work on developing a pan-Arctic network of marine protected areas. As the ice continues to melt, navigability of the Arctic Ocean is expanding. And while there are benefits to that—and there are some—increased human traffic also means that even more maritime ecosystems will be at risk of being either disturbed or even destroyed. Creating a network of marine protected areas throughout the region will help us safeguard areas that are particularly significant both culturally and ecologically. And we can also create a regional seas program for the Arctic, something that nations have done in other parts of the world to improve cooperation on marine science and share best practices.' Available at https://oaarchive.arctic-council.org/bitstream/handle/11374/913/ACMMCA09_Iqaluit_2015_US_Remarks_on_US_Chairmanship.pdf?sequence=1&isAllowed=y, accessed 21 March 2017.

however, with some caveats.[63] Nevertheless, both topics are relevant to the exercise and enjoyment of Indigenous human rights and the management, safeguarding and harvesting of marine mammals—especially to guarantee that Inuit are able 'to maintain and develop their political, economic and social systems or institutions, to be secure in the enjoyment of their own means of subsistence and development'.[64] For reasons unclear to Inuit, to date the Arctic Council has avoided dealing with the management and conservation of marine mammals in a comprehensive, circumpolar wide fashion. Potentially, this is due to the plethora of marine mammal organisations in Alaska, the numerous regimes created by the various land claims agreements in Canada and conditions in Greenland. It may also be due to the potential for creating conflicts amongst the Arctic States and their respective existing and future activities and use of the Arctic Ocean.

It is important to note that the current US Chairmanship of the Arctic Council indicated, in the context of a question related to the future of the Arctic Council, that the unique and positive feature of Permanent Participants must be maintained.[65] In this regard, he further stated that there were no formal discussions about the potential for the restructuring of the Arctic Council under a legally binding treaty and quipped by sharing an American colloquialism: 'if it ain't broken, don't fix it'.

And, certainly, the Arctic Council provides the world community with an important starting point in terms of a region-specific regime to monitor impacts on the Arctic Ocean and the lands of the coastal States. However, in my view, the Arctic Council does not go far enough in light of the political and international Indigenous human rights developments, the expansion of interests, and the urgent issues facing Arctic Indigenous inhabitants and each coastal State.

A renewed agenda and potentially a more robust international regime is needed to take into account the dramatic changes impacting this fragile ecosystem, the homelands and coastal seas of the Arctic Indigenous peoples. At present, there are few precedents for equal representation of Indigenous peoples within an inter-governmental structure. One possible model is the UN Permanent Forum on Indigenous Issues, comprised of eight-member State

63 Dialogue with James Stotts, ICC President for Alaska, 13 October 2015.

64 UN Declaration, *supra* note 3, Art 20.

65 David Balton, Chairperson of the Arctic Council, under US Chairmanship, Arctic Science Summit Week News briefings News / World News, 18 March 2016 5:00 PM ADT at http://www.alaskapublic.org/2016/03/18/arctic-council-meeting-ends-climate-change-among-topics/, accessed 21 March 2017.

elected experts and eight Indigenous nominated experts that sit in equity. The international human rights developments as well as the extensive rights affirmed in the various specific agreements in Alaska, Canada and Greenland militate in favour of an equal or upgraded status for Arctic Indigenous peoples, especially in the event that the Arctic Council moves towards organisation under a legally binding treaty.[66]

Like many of the issues facing all Arctic Indigenous peoples and States, even the single issue of ice free navigation of the Arctic Ocean itself necessitates a comprehensive response and a possible new regime that will effectively involve Indigenous peoples as well as other stakeholders, such as non-Arctic States, environmental organisations, scientific researchers, etc. Any such regime must include Indigenous peoples and must afford them full recognition of and respect for their fundamental human rights. And, the rights and interests of the Permanent Participants must take priority over the economic interests of States centred far from the North Pole and the Arctic Ocean.

As mentioned above, on 31 August 2015 in Alaska, President Barack Obama offered closing remarks to the GLACIER conference,[67] which involved ministers from over 20 countries and other high-level participants. He emphasised the need for urgent, collective action to curb the adverse impacts of climate change and repeatedly referenced Indigenous communities that have and will continue to feel these impacts firsthand.

---

66 Valur Ingimundarson, 'The Arctic Governance System: The Dynamics of Intergovernmental Bargaining and Institutional Integration' (presented at 30–31 January 2016 Democracy in the West Nordic--The role of national parliaments in Arctic governance, Grindavik, Iceland) at 8: 'I do not see why the current role of the Permanent Participants cannot be retained—or even expanded to the status of equal partners—under a more formal mechanism even if it were negotiated by states. The Inuit Circumpolar Council and other indigenous organizations are among those that have made the case for shared sovereignty. It could be done on the basis of the rights of indigenous peoples for self-determination, which are rooted in international law. Further, in the past, the Arctic states themselves have not always behaved as role models and treated the indigenous peoples as real partners. The temporary suspension of the operations of [RAIPON] is a case in point. The Greenlandic government's boycott of the Arctic Council, for it was not given full access to the Kiruna meeting shows that a tension exists between the Arctic states and the indigenous peoples. In a post-colonial age, increased global interest in the Arctic is impossible to reconcile with the exclusion of the indigenous peoples from Arctic decision-making'.

67 US Department of State, Conference on Global Leadership in the Arctic: Cooperation, Innovation, Engagement and Resilience, August 30–31, 2015, Alaska, background information at https://2009-2017.state.gov/e/oes/glacier/index.htm, accessed 21 March 2017.

3.2 *Climate Change*

Arctic Indigenous communities have felt the dramatic and direct impacts of climate change.[68] They also know that they will begin to feel even greater impacts from increased Arctic shipping. In particular, our North Slope and northwest Inupiat and Siberian Yupik whaling communities, where the existence and stability of sea ice is crucial to the survival of both humans and marine mammals, are witnessing changing ice conditions and more rapid disappearance of sea ice.[69] For example, Inuit are concerned about the bowhead whale migration, the safety of whaling crews and the conclusion of successful whale hunts in both the spring and fall. Furthermore, directly related to whaling and other marine mammal hunts, little discussion and no concrete decisions have been made about the effect and impact that shipping has on ice stability and consistency. As a result of transit through once solid ice, Arctic ice is becoming fractured and older, multi-year ice is fast disappearing.[70]

3.3 *Changing Ice Conditions*

These changing ice conditions may be accelerated by the presence of icebreakers, which intentionally disrupt the sea ice. One resulting outcome is the triggering of 'earlier than normal breakups' that thereby 'damage Inuit transportation corridors'. As has already been observed, Inuit hunters have identified that in 'transitional ice areas, passing ships can be even more dangerous'. For example, 'hunters pursue bears and other game on ice floes and vessels moving between the hunters and the land could unwittingly separate those floes and strand the hunters' causing life threatening conditions for Inuit.[71]

---

68 'Impact of climate change mitigation measures on Indigenous peoples and on their territories and lands', UN Doc E/C.19/2008/10, Study submitted by Victoria Tauli-Corpuz and Aqqaluk Lynge at the Seventh Session of the Permanent Forum on Indigenous Issues, 19 March 2008, accessed 21 March 2017 at http://www.un.org/esa/socdev/unpfii/documents/E_C19_2008_10.pdf.

69 Julie Raymond-Yakoubiana, Yury Khokhlovb and Anastasiya Yarzutkina, 'Indigenous Knowledge and Use of Bering Strait Region: Ocean Currents' Final report to the National Park Service, Shared Beringian Heritage Program for Cooperative Agreement H99111100026 (Kawerak, Inc, 2014) at 31: 'Changes in ice conditions are among the biggest changes noted by local experts. All three communities experience later freeze-up and earlier break-up of ice' and further at 32: 'Experts have also noted that the ice is thinner, which contribute to earlier break-up'.

70 Communications with Duane Smith, ICC President for Canada, 20 November 2015; Indigenous Knowledge and Use of Bering Strait Region: Ocean Currents, *supra* note 69 at 32–33: 'Another change is the absence of older, thicker ice … older ice no longer arrives.'

71 *Sea Ice Never Stops, supra* note 1 at 29.

3.4 *Coastal Erosion*

In addition, severe coastal erosion[72] is taking place and impacting more and more coastal communities as well as those on river watersheds and deltas. The dramatic weather changes present greater risks for hunters both on land and at sea, where conditions are now either unknown or becoming more dramatic and fast changing. Furthermore, Permanent Participants have expressed concern about the passage of vessels, vessel speeds and the need for speed limits in areas where the coastline is susceptible to erosion or disruption due to waves not to mention disruption of migration routes and adverse impacts on habitat. One response has been the establishment of the Arctic Waterways Safety Committee by a series of northern and northwestern Alaska Native communities, with the objective of implementation of the 'lawful best practices to ensure a safe, efficient, and predictable operating environment for all Arctic waterway users.'[73]

Many Inuit communities are experiencing reduced biodiversity and/or invasion of species as a result of increased shipping. All of these conditions are a threat to Indigenous human development as distinct cultures. The matter of prey depletion is one result of 'expansion of industrial scale commercial bottom trawl fishing into the northern Bering Sea and has alarmed the Tribes in the Bering Strait region'.[74]

Again, when both climate change-induced conditions are compounded with the potential adverse impacts of increased Arctic shipping, it is not yet

---

72 Robin Bronen, 'Climate-Induced Displacement of Alaska Native Communities' *Brookings LSE—Internal Displacement Project,* 30 January 2013) on file with author and at https://www.brookings.edu/wp-content/uploads/2016/06/30-climate-alaska-bronen-paper.pdf, accessed 21 March 2017.

73 Arctic Waterways Safety Committee: 'The purpose of the Arctic Waterways Safety Committee is to bring together local marine interests in the Alaskan Arctic in a single forum, and to act collectively on behalf of those interests to develop best practices to ensure a safe, efficient, and predictable operating environment for all current and future users of the waterways'. Representatives of the Alaska Beluga Whale Committee; Alaska Eskimo Whaling Commission; Alaska Nanuuq Commission; Eskimo Walrus Commission; Ice Seal Committee; Oil & Gas Tugs (Barges & Cargo); Mining; Fishing; Alaska Marine Pilots; Municipality of Nome; Northwest Arctic Borough; North Slope Borough; Regional Tribal Organization (Kawerak, Maniilaq, or ICAS; and Passenger Vessel Sector are engaged in this innovative approach to monitoring coastal waterways and the impacts of Arctic shipping and marine transportation). See http://www.arcticwaterways.org/, accessed 21 March 2017.

74 *Sea Ice Never Stops, supra* note 1 at 34, reprinting of Kawerak, Inc., Case Study: Ice Seal and Walrus Project.

known how devastating both may be on the communities represented by the Permanent Participants.

3.5 *Tourism and Lack of Infrastructure*

Increased marine shipping activity has also literally taken some Inuit communities by surprise[75] and they too, may bring severe impacts. In this regard, the ICC has identified concerns related to cruise ships and the tourism industry that disrupt traditional economic and other activities from not only the presence, noise and disruption of ice conditions but also due to the desire of tourists to view the Arctic environment, seabird colonies as well as marine mammals distinct to Arctic coastal communities.[76] Furthermore, Inuit are worried about the safety and security risks associated with cruise ships, holding dozens or even hundreds of passengers, entering their homeland with ever-increasing regularity,[77] especially in light of the fact that they do not have the ways and means to respond to an emergency in the event that there is an accident of life threatening condition.

In regard to infrastructure alone, along the coast of the Bering Sea, Chukchi and Beaufort Sea of Alaska, there are only few deepwater ports. In fact, in recent interviews of US state government representatives, they have identified the fact that issues such as 'power cost equalization, public safety, education and the necessary things that are constitutionally mandated' require immediate attention because the associated infrastructure for these matters are next to non-existent in the Arctic.[78] These same leaders underscored the need for

---

75 George Bryson, 'How'd these Germans get to Alaska? They took the fabled Northwest Passage' *Anchorage Daily News* (15 August 2008) reprinted by then parent company McClatchey DC at http://www.mcclatchydc.com/news/nation-world/national/article24495799.html#storylink=cpy, accessed 21 March 2017. See also Brady Dennis and Chris Mooney, 'Luxury cruise ship sets sail for the Arctic from Seward', *The Washington Post* (17 August 2016) accessed 21 March 2017 at http://www.adn.com/arctic/2016/08/16/luxury-cruise-ship-sets-sail-for-the-arctic/.

76 *Sea Ice Never Stops, supra* note 1 at 29.

77 *Ibid.* at 32.

78 Shady Oliver, 'Interview: Lt. Gov. Mallott shares Arctic priorities' *Alaska Dispatch News* (28 February 2016) accessed 21 March 2017 at http://www.adn.com/article/20160228/interview-lt-gov-mallott-shares-arctic-priorities; Shady Oliver, 'Interview: Sen. Donny Olson's Arctic priorities for 2016' *Alaska Dispatch News* (21 February 2016) accessed 21 March 2017 at http://www.adn.com/article/20160221/interview-sen-donny-olsons-arctic-priorities-2016; Shady Oliver, 'Interview: Barrow's Rep. Ben Nageak talks Arctic issues' *Alaska Dispatch News* (16 February 2016) accessed 21 March 2017 at http://www.adn.com/article/20160216/interview-barrows-rep-ben-nageak-talks-arctic-issues; Shady Oliver, 'Interview: Gov. Walker

a deepwater port on Alaska's northwest coast as well as other infrastructure needs related to Internet, roads, and non-renewable resource development.[79]

3.6 *Impacts on Marine Mammals and Habitat*

Marine mammals that the Inuit have relied on for thousands of years are extremely vulnerable to increased shipping. 'Vessel noise alone can impact the movement of marine animals, thus affecting community hunting. Marine mammals have very sensitive hearing and equate noise with danger ... displacing them from important habitat and hunting areas'.[80] For example, bowhead and other whales rely heavily on their hearing and are adept at using their voices to navigate in complete darkness through ice. Furthermore, Inuit fishers have reported significant decreases in sea life when seismic ships pass through an area, which also impacts on calving grounds.[81] In addition, northwestern Inuit communities recognise that the 'Bering Strait is a bottleneck for an assortment of marine mammal migration paths' and have expressed concern about impacts of vessel traffic on migrating marine mammals.[82] Though important IMO guidelines concerning noise from commercial shipping[83] exist, who will enforce such guidelines to ensure that such disruption and adverse impact is minimised?

3.7 *Operational and Accidental Pollution by Vessels*

Sewage and grey water discharge can also create problems in public health and can kill aquatic life, as can jettisoned solid waste and garbage.[84] Bilge water, which is often mixed with oil leaked from a ship's engine, can likewise harm

---

outlines Arctic priorities' *Alaska Dispatch News* (6 February 2016) accessed 21 March 2017 at http://www.adn.com/article/20160206/interview-gov-walker-outlines-arctic-priorities.

79 *Ibid.*

80 *Sea Ice Never Stops, supra* note 1 at 34, reprinting of Kawerak, Inc, Case Study: Ice Seal and Walrus Project. See also Affidavit of Tagak Curley, *supra* note 1 at 118, specifically at para 11, where he states: 'Marine mammals are extremely sensitive to development. The Arctic, and its marine areas in particular, are very fragile. Once marine wildlife is disturbed, it is altered permanently. If there is no set of rules that honour the long tradition of respecting wildlife and protecting the traditional hunt, it will be lost forever'.

81 *Sea Ice Never Stops, supra* note 1 at 32. See also Affidavit of Senator Charlie Watt, *supra* note 1 at 9, para 26, specifically addressing seismic testing and impacts on marine mammals.

82 Indigenous Knowledge and Use of Bering Strait Region: Ocean Currents, *supra* note 69 at 5.

83 See IMO Doc MEPC.1/Circ.833, of 7 April 2014, 'Guidelines for the reduction of underwater noise from commercial shipping to address adverse impacts on marine life'.

84 *Sea Ice Never Stops, supra* note 1 at 30.

marine life and damage the fragile northern environment. At present, little to no infrastructure and in particular, port reception facilities, exist in the Arctic to handle the disposal of grey water and waste by these ships.[85] Though there is a dire need for infrastructure in the Arctic, Inuit remain concerned about the siting and construction of ports without their collaboration, consultation and consent as these plans could have direct impacts on the integrity of their subsistence hunting, fishing and other marine activities. Furthermore, the discharge of ballast water and shipborne pollutants into Arctic waters and the local ecosystem are not only forms of pollution but also may introduce invasive alien species and thereby lead to significant and irreversible ecosystem changes. And, though there may be strict controls for exhaust emissions of oceangoing vessels in other marine regions, at present, there are no specific measures to ban or limit the burn off of high-sulphur fuels in the Arctic. The various forms of contamination, whether from airborne or other sources of pollution, presents 'a serious public health threat for families' dependent on marine foods.'[86]

In regard to the vessels themselves, collisions between Inuit hunters and their crafts as well as collisions with larger ships transiting the area, may leave small, sometimes traditional crafts, vulnerable in already hazardous cold climate, Arctic water conditions. Though national legislation in Canada and the Russian Federation and possibly other flag States address vessel classifications as well as the IMO Polar Code and the associated IACS Unified Requirements for Polar Ships, at present, who has the capacity to actively police the Arctic Ocean to ensure that any ships traversing into or through the Arctic have the proper classification to meet the needs for ice capability? Any such ships should have reinforced hulls, initial containment capability and they should adhere to the numerous Arctic Council emergency guidelines for oil spill response or emergency response.[87]

Furthermore, vessels entering Arctic waters may not always be prepared for the rigours of northern operations and sea ice infested waters.[88]

---

85 *Ibid.* at 32.

86 *Ibid.* at 35.

87 See specifics of Arctic Council Agreement on Cooperation on Marine Oil Pollution Preparedness and Response in the Arctic at http://www.arctic-council.org/index.php/en/our-work/agreements, accessed 21 March 2017.

88 Jeremy Kasper, assistant research professor at UAF, explained 'Ice moves in ways that we still can't fully predict'. Colleague Geophysicist Andy Mahoney, assistant research professor at University of Alaska Fairbanks, wrote 'The forces involved in this can be tremendous. It's the wind acting on the ice sometimes over hundreds of kilometers and it can generate a lot of surface stress on the ice that can push two ice floes together with an almost

Additionally, as noted above, disaster response capabilities are limited as there is no infrastructure to even resupply these ships or handle disposal of grey water and other human waste not to mention the hardware to respond to the safety and security concerns related to the influx of visitors on ships, which may endanger not only the environment but themselves.[89] And, though discharge and disposal may take place elsewhere, there is potential for the ocean currents to carry or transport such waste and pollution discharge from other regions to Arctic waters.[90]

In 1989, in the south central region of Alaska, the *Exxon Valdez* ran aground, at the time, causing 'the largest oil spill in US history'.[91] The waters of Prince William Sound are relatively calm and ice free, in contrast to the Bering, Beaufort or Chukchi Sea, making it all the more hazardous to explore for and develop this non-renewable resource. The risks are essentially incalculable.

The matters of ship design, construction, and operation for northern waters has been an outstanding matter for decades, especially when one considers the intent of a number of Arctic-rim States and their pursuit of oil and gas development in the Arctic. The recent accidents, such as the grounding of the *Diskos II* (2007), the *Clipper Adventurer* (2010), and the *Kulluk* (2013),[92] demonstrate precisely how dangerous Arctic navigation can be and how important rigourous shipping standards are for safe operations.[93]

For this reason and many others, Arctic Indigenous peoples are concerned about offshore oil and gas exploration and development and ultimately, the risk of spills and contamination of the Arctic Ocean environment.[94] As noted in the volume *Sea Ice Never Stops*, Inuit have identified the fact that 'a

---

incomprehensible amount of force'. 'Standing On the Beaufort Sea' (2 December 2015) accessed 21 March 2017 at http://frontierscientists.com/projects/ocean-sea-ice-science/sea-ice.

89 *Sea Ice Never Stops, supra* note 1 at 42.

90 Indigenous Knowledge and Use of Bering Strait Region: Ocean Currents, *supra* note 69 at 7: 'Experts expressed concern about increased vessel traffic through the Bering Strait, and the possibility of not only trash but also other discharges such as grey water or spills of hazardous materials, being transported to their communities by ocean currents'.

91 Samuel K Skinner and William K Reilly, prepared by the National Response Team 'The Exxon Valdez Oil Spill: A Report to the President' (May 1989) accessed 21 March 2017 at http://www.uscg.mil/history/webshipwrecks/ExxonValdezNRT1989Report.pdf.

92 James Stotts, 'Shell's Great Arctic Adventure' DRUM, Newsletter of ICC Alaska, President's Message (December 2012).

93 *Sea Ice Never Stops, supra* note 1 at 40.

94 *Sea Ice Never Stops, supra* note 1 at 46. See also Diana Haecker, 'Village Consortium Discusses Regional Impacts of Development' *Nome Nugget* (28 June 2013) republished at

catastrophic event such as an oil spill could prove devastating to the marine environment'.[95] Even a small, limited form of contamination resulting from an accidental spill can alter marine mammal habitat and behaviour as 'marine mammal are known to avoid gasoline fumes, even moderate pollution could displace them from habitat areas'.[96]

To date, Inuit are uncertain about the total number of spills that have already taken place, but do not make the headline news. Indeed, in December 2015 a grounded Russian oil tanker spilled 200,000 gallons of oil in the Sea of Okhotsk, in the North Pacific,[97] which has had the devastating impacts upon shore birds and marine mammals that the Inuit have always feared.

3.8 *Militarisation and Sustainable Security in the Arctic*

In the Arctic alone, the ongoing threats to peace and security due to militarisation has been the focus of the ICC since its inception in 1977.[98] The persistent presence of nuclear-powered ballistic missile submarines, bombers, long-range cruise missiles, air launched cruise missiles, military bases, and other armed marine vessels and aircraft all pose serious threats to Arctic indigenous peoples and their lands, territories and resources. These concerns are not unfounded; there have been very real and serious threats to Indigenous peace and security.[99] Therefore, the Indigenous human rights standards concerning not

---

http://www.alaskapublic.org/2013/06/28/village-consortium-discusses-regional-impacts-of-development/, accessed 21 March 2017.

95 *Sea Ice Never Stops, supra* note 1 at 35, reprinting of Kawerak, Inc, Case Study: Ice Seal and Walrus Project.

96 *Ibid.*

97 Emily Russell, 'Grounded Russian oil tanker leaks into North Pacific' *KNOM, Nome, Alaska* (2 December 2015) accessed 21 March 2017 at http://www.alaskapublic.org/2015/12/02/grounded-russian-oil-tanker-leaks-into-bering-strait/.

98 For example, see the 1977 Inuit Circumpolar Conference Resolution calling for the Arctic to be established as a 'nuclear free zone'. In addition, the ICC adopted a chapter concerning 'Principles and Elements on Peaceful and Safe Uses of the Arctic' and 'Principles and Elements on the Emerging Rights of Peace and Development' contained in their 1992 document 'Principles and Elements for a Comprehensive Arctic Policy', on file with author.

99 Incidents such as the US B-52 bomber accident near Thule, Greenland, in 1968, involved four hydrogen bombs. There have also been numerous nuclear disasters at sea. Nuclear weapons are routinely present on all US and Russian aircraft carriers, logistics support ships, submarines, and surface warships. In April 1989, a nuclear-powered attack vessel carrying two nuclear torpedoes sank in the Norwegian Sea. From the period of 1945 to 1989, 50 nuclear weapons and 11 nuclear reactors have been lost at sea. During this same period, 212 confirmed accidents worldwide involving nuclear-powered vessels took place. For more detailed accounts, see generally Dalee Dorough Sambo, 'Sustainable Security:

only peace and security but also militarisation of Indigenous peoples' homelands are highly relevant to Arctic shipping and marine traffic. For Indigenous peoples, peace is not merely the absence of war but rather it includes a fair and inclusive system of international relations, based on principles of mutual cooperation in order to achieve commonly shared goals.

In this regard, there is an important relationship between human rights, peace and development. None of these objectives are truly realisable in isolation from one another. Peaceful co-existence and peace are generally vital factors in striving towards social progress and development. In addition, the UN Declaration on the Right to Development makes the linkage between peace and security 'as essential elements for the realization of the right to development'.[100] Furthermore, severe economic disparities and human rights violations can pose a threat to world peace.[101] Though both the right to development and the right to peace have not been fully recognised[102] or implemented, they may eventually gain international acceptance by usage. Like other forms of customary international law, the absence of binding instruments does not keep States from undertaking positive actions or behaviour in regard to observing human rights or achieving the ultimate objectives of a particular human right.

Similar to State reluctance elsewhere, including within the framework of the Arctic Council,[103] it is highly likely that States have not fully advanced the rights to peace and development because of the corresponding duties that

---

An Inuit Perspective,' in Jyrki Käkönen (ed) *Politics and Sustainable Growth in the Arctic* (Dartmouth Publishing Co, 1993) 51; William M Arkin and Joshua M Handler, 'Nuclear Disasters at Sea, Then and Now' *Bulletin of the Atomic Scientists* (July/August 1989).

100 Declaration on the Right to Development, adopted 4 December 1986, UN Doc A/RES/41/128, Preamble.

101 M C Lam, *At the Edge of the State: Indigenous Peoples and Self-Determination* (Transnational Publishers, 2000), where the author makes the linkage between self-determination as a pre-condition of peace and not a cause of disruption or violence: 'The animating impulse behind the principle of self-determination is the free realization by a people of its sense of self. While the principles sometimes provoke the disruption of peace, it more often than not also constitutes its pre-condition'. See also Rodolfo Stavenhagen, 'Self-Determination: Right or Demon?' in Donald Clark and Robert Williamson (eds) *Self-Determination: International Perspectives* (St Martin's Press, 1996) at 8: 'The violence we see around us is not generated by the drive for self-determination, but by its negation'.

102 Henry J Steiner and Philip Alston, *International Human Rights in Context: Law, Politics, Morals*, 2d ed (Oxford University Press, 1996) at 57, wherein the authors discuss the human rights movement following World War II and the emergence of the international human rights declarations, conventions and institutions for monitoring human rights.

103 Ottawa Declaration, *supra* note 28, footnote 1: The Arctic Council should not deal with matters related to military security.

States should bear in regard to these rights, as well as the need to ensure the direct participation of the beneficiaries of such rights in decision-making concerning peace and development.[104]

To this day, Inuit remain concerned about increased militarisation of the Arctic Ocean and fear the return of Cold War conditions, which separated their blood related families throughout the Bering Straits region. At the March 2016 Senior Arctic Officials meeting in Anchorage, Alaska, some of the delegates proposed future discussion on the role of militarisation and security and the Arctic environment. However, many were careful to ensure that any future Arctic Council agenda item did not touch upon respective national security dialogues and that potential discussions would be confined to environmental impact.[105] In this regard, it is interesting to note the following information prominently displayed on the current opening page of the Arctic Council:

> The Arctic Council has also helped to maintain the Arctic as a zone of peace and stability. In the 2013 "Vision for the Arctic", Ministers of the Arctic States wrote: "We are confident that there is no problem that we cannot solve together through our cooperative relationships on the basis of existing international law and good will." This commitment is also affirmed by the Ministerial Declarations from Nuuk (2011), Kiruna (2013) and Iqaluit (2015), in each of which Ministers of Arctic States recognized "the importance of maintaining peace, stability, and constructive cooperation in the Arctic."

104 One example is the United States, who had opposition to the drafting of the ICESCR and had general opposition to the creation of any state obligations in the context of the drafting of the Declaration on the Rights of Indigenous Peoples.

105 Arctic Council Senior Arctic Officials meeting, 20–22 October 2015, Anchorage, Alaska. Author present as Observer, ICC delegation. See also Valur Ingimundarson, *supra* note 66 at 9: 'Another constraining factor is the taboo on discussing military security within the Arctic Council, which dates back to its establishment in the mid-1990s. The absence of a formal intergovernmental or institutional venue to discuss Arctic security raises questions of long-term management. The development of an "Arctic security community" is highly unlikely in the absence of shared political identities and values. NATO is not set to assume such a role. This raises the question of another external driver—namely, the spillover effect of global disputes into the Arctic. A revival of Great Power rivalry would have wide-ranging effects on Arctic politics and security. The Ukrainian crisis affected Arctic cooperation as was demonstrated by the boycott of some Arctic states of meetings and by the refusal of Russia to accept the EU Commission as an Arctic Council Observer. The will of the major powers to keep this Arctic venue intact has ensured its continuity. But again there is a gap here that needs to be addressed'.

Because of the reality of Arctic militarisation, the past course of the Arctic Council representatives and their collective future desire, Arctic militarisation and associated shipping activity should take into account the potentially severe adverse impacts upon Indigenous food security, cultural security, and environmental security. Because of Inuit reliance on Arctic waters and as 'a well-established maritime culture' that has sustained their communities for millennia, the Inuit insist upon sustainable and equitable development as well as their overall security to be safeguarded in the context of Arctic shipping.[106]

3.9 *Participation of Arctic Indigenous Peoples in PAME*

The Permanent Participants have been able to voice these and other concerns within the context of the Arctic Council Protection of Arctic Marine Environment (PAME) working group and its Arctic Marine Shipping Assessment (AMSA) specifically.[107] During the launch of this assessment, members of the Arctic Council recognised the fundamental role of 'local residents' in emphasising the future of Arctic shipping:

> Marine shipping is one of many factors impacting Arctic communities. There may be some positive economic impacts to increased shipping. However, Arctic residents express concern for the social, cultural and environmental effects of such expansion. The possibility of oil spills is a major concern and hunters are especially concerned about the disruption of marine species and their hunting practices. The costs and benefit of Arctic shipping will likely be unevenly distributed among and within communities and regions. Constructive and early engagement of local residents in planned Arctic marine development projects can help to reduce negative impacts and to increase positive benefits. Importantly, many local Arctic residents today depend heavily on marine resources for subsistence and the local economy; over-the-ice travel and boat transport allow the use of large marine areas during much of the year. Such life in

---

106 *Sea Ice Never Stops, supra* note 1 at 52–54, accessed 21 March 2017 at http://www.inuitcircumpolar.com/uploads/3/0/5/4/30542564/sea_ice_never_stops_-_final.pdf. See also Affidavit of Senator Charlie Watt, *supra* note 1 at 129, para 25, wherein he speaks in detail about food security: 'The Arctic Ocean is a uniquely vulnerable environment to climate change and resource development. Food security is always a concern in the Arctic. Marine mammals provide that security'.

107 See their specific web site at http://www.pame.is/index.php/shortcode/about-us, accessed 21 March 2017. As a result of AMSA recommendations being referred to other Arctic Council working groups, the ICC has been engaged in the numerous, related initiatives of these working groups.

> the Arctic is dependent on movement over the ice and ocean and sea ice is integral to this movement.[108]

The AMSA project has focused specifically on use of the Arctic Ocean by vessels and their impact on both the human and marine environment and has been characterised as one of the most successful working group initiatives[109] of the Arctic Council, with a mandate to: 'conduct a comprehensive Arctic marine shipping assessment as outlined under the Arctic Marine Strategic Plan (AMSP) under the guidance of Canada, Finland and the United States as lead countries and in collaboration with the Emergency Prevention, Preparedness and Response (EPPR) working group and the Permanent Participants as relevant'.[110] PAME has managed to prepare a series of reports, updating their activities specifically, in relation to Arctic shipping through collection of data, early 'work packages', town hall meetings, scenario building and communications that allowed for a snapshot of marine uses and impacts of shipping in the Arctic region generally and the Arctic Ocean specifically. Significantly, the 2009 AMSA report drew attention to Arctic Indigenous peoples' uses of marine resources by recommending that 'the Arctic states should consider conducting surveys on Arctic marine use by indigenous communities where gaps are identified to collect information for establishing up-to-date baseline data to assess the impacts from Arctic shipping activities' in the context of the focus on human dimensions.[111] In addition, the interrelated, interconnected, indivisible and interdependent areas of Arctic marine governance and infrastructure as well as safety and environmental protection were and have been consistently addressed within the framework of the AMSA.

Steadily, PAME and the AMSA in particular, have worked to emphasise the impacts of heavy fuel, shipping impacts, cruise ships and tourism, and offshore oil and gas through the development and documentation of various best practices, guidelines, reports, data collection, a strategic plan and the launching of new and specific projects, such as the Arctic Marine Tourism Project. In addition, they have developed plans for Marine Protected Areas and also taken action in follow up to the 17 recommendations of the 2009 AMSA report as well as prepared an Ecosystem Approach Progress Report. Their various reports

---

108 Decision of the November 2004 Ministerial meeting in Reykjavik, Iceland.

109 Interview with James Stotts, ICC President for Alaska, 1 March 2016.

110 See Arctic Council web site at https://oaarchive.arctic-council.org/handle/11374/53, accessed 21 March 2017.

111 Arctic Council, *Arctic Marine Shipping Assessment 2009 Report*, (Arctic Council, 2009), Executive Summary with Recommendations, at 6.

indicate that most, if not all of this work, has been done in coordination with the other Arctic Council working groups.[112]

This important, collective and cooperative work is applauded and welcomed by Arctic Indigenous peoples and the Permanent Participants of the Arctic Council. However, the real question, in practical terms, is how will these various best practices, guidelines, and plans actually be implemented and possibly more important, how will they be crystalised into stringent standards that compel adherence to by all interests concerned and in particular, Arctic rim nations and other flag States?

3.10 *Participation of Arctic Indigenous Peoples in the IMO*

Though it is highly significant that the Polar Code has been recently adopted by the IMO and will enter into force in 2017,[113] in sum, Inuit had limited input through the Arctic Council or any other entity into the drafting of this new instrument. It appears that few other Arctic Indigenous peoples or representatives of the Arctic Council Permanent Participants had any sustained or direct role in this important work either.[114] However, it must be noted that some individuals at the IMO did identify and make reference to 'risks posed by shipping to Arctic indigenous and other local communities' as well as Indigenous use of various marine resources.[115] As argued by at least one scholar,[116] more effort

112 PAME Summary Report, 2013–2015 Activities, April 2015, accessed 21 March 2017 at http://pame.is/images/02_Document?Library/Reports.

113 'IMO has adopted the International Code for Ships Operating in Polar Waters (Polar Code) and related amendments to make it mandatory under both the International Convention for the Safety of Life at Sea (SOLAS) and the International Convention for the Prevention of Pollution from Ships (MARPOL). The Polar Code entered into force on 1 January 2017. This marks a historic milestone in the Organization's work to protect ships and people aboard them, both seafarers and passengers, in the harsh environment of the waters surrounding the two poles. The Polar Code and SOLAS amendments were adopted during the 94th session of IMO's Maritime Safety Committee (MSC), in November 2014; the environmental provisions and MARPOL amendments were adopted during the 68th session of the Marine Environment Protection Committee (MEPC) in May 2015'. See http://www.imo.org/en/MediaCentre/HotTopics/polar/Pages/default.aspx, accessed 21 March 2017.

114 For further discussion of this matter, see Chapter 5 of this Volume.

115 Heike Deggim, 'Development of a Mandatory Polar Code—Update on Progress' (IMO, Marine Technology Section, 2011) accessed 21 March 2017 at http://www.imo.org/en/MediaCentre/HotTopics/polar/Documents/polarcodePPT2011.pdf#search=Indigenous.

116 Aldo Chircop, 'The Growth of International Shipping in the Arctic: Is a Regulatory Review Timely?', *The International Journal of Marine and Coastal Law* 24 (2009) 355–380, at 380: 'Finally, in the unfolding regulatory drama, the interests of the peoples of the North must be profiled more than ever before as the large governmental and industry players jostle

should have been made to engage Arctic Indigenous peoples and in particular, those of a strong maritime background and who have sustained their coastal communities by having a direct relationship with the Arctic environment through their own 'polar code' so to speak.

Specifically in regard to the ICC, their leadership made an executive decision to not become engaged for a range of reasons: limited time and resources within the organisation; the procedural rules that center on a heavily state- or party-driven process creating limited ability for Indigenous peoples' representatives to influence the subject matter; environmental NGOs that attempted to capitalise on the concerns and agenda of Indigenous peoples in the context of marine environmental protection, etc. The non-governmental organisation, Pacific Environment, had involvement of one or two Indigenous women from Alaska, but with inconsistent attendance at IMO sessions where the Polar Code was under discussion. And, Aleut International Association, as a Permanent Participant, may have had some minimal engagement in the work.

In addition, one of the two members of the Danish Parliament for Greenland was invited by the IMO to present at a workshop to discuss international collaboration, but this was following completion of substantial drafting of the Polar Code by others. At that workshop, Member of Parliament Sara Olsvig, welcomed the Polar Code and looked forward to it coming into force, acknowledged that the role of the Arctic Council is central to collaborative work and that common or uniform Arctic regulations should be adopted and they 'must be balanced and allow for responsible development'.[117]

Following dialogue and limited input through the Arctic Council into the drafting and finalisation of the Polar Code,[118] to a large extent, for the reasons noted above and otherwise, Inuit and other Permanent Participant representatives placed their trust in the hands of the Arctic States to negotiate a constructive and meaningful Polar Code. A cursory search of the terms 'Inuit' and 'indigenous peoples polar' yields some interesting results. For example,

---

for positions of influence on the future of the region. There is a real danger that their vital interests will retract into the background as Arctic shipping regulation moves onto the global stage. Arctic States should consider including representatives of their Arctic communities on their IMO delegations, and Permanent Participants at the Arctic Council should consider obtaining NGO consultative status at the IMO'.

117 Sara Olsvig, MP, Member of Inatsisartut and Folketinget (Greenlandic and Danish Parliaments), IMO Workshop on Safe Ship Operations in the Arctic Ocean, 28 February 2014, London, United Kingdom, accessed 21 March 2017 at http://www.imo.org/en/MediaCentre/HotTopics/polar/Documents/Arctic2014/10.%20Hon.%20S.%20Olsvig.pdf#search=Indigenous.

118 Interview with James Stotts, ICC Alaska President, 1 March 2016.

the term 'Inuit' appeared only twice, one with reference to the *Ljubov Orlova*, a ship that attracted negative attention. The string on 'Indigenous peoples polar' returned 24 documents, not all of which related to discussions on the Polar Code. Variations, e.g., 'Indigenous peoples Arctic' returned 31 documents. However, none of the documents in the searches were submissions by Canada and the United States, all were by Norway. This begs the question as to how the delegations of these Arctic rim countries were, if at all, advancing the interests, concerns or perspectives of Inuit specifically or Arctic Indigenous peoples generally.

A 2011 report of a workshop on the environmental aspects of the Polar Code, did not appear to have Indigenous institutions or Indigenous persons and many of the references to Indigenous peoples were in communications from NGOs, which confirms an earlier point about others potentially appropriating Indigenous issues without consultation.

In order to respond to this lack of direct engagement as well as the lack of recognition of the rights and interests of Indigenous peoples in this context, the Arctic Council Permanent Participants should consider seeking observer status at the IMO, which is an option available to them. In the latest Strategic Plan, the IMO appears committed to an inclusive approach.[119] Also, the rules for observer status[120] appear general enough to accommodate Indigenous Peoples' NGOs. Without a direct voice in the IMO (and observers could be that direct voice) or inclusion in Member State Delegations to sessions discussing polar-related issues, the IMO will not have Indigenous Peoples on the radar screen. The IMO's Strategic Plan, to some extent, is evidence of this: there is an emphasis on pollution, environment and other shipping matters, but the words 'Arctic', 'polar' or 'Indigenous' do not appear even once.

Clearly, there was a lack of extensive, consistent, comprehensive or direct involvement of Arctic Indigenous peoples and in particular, the leadership of

---

119 See International Maritime Organization, Assembly Resolution A.1097(29), adopted 25 November 2015 (Agenda item 8—Strategic Plan for the Organization for the Six-Year Period 2016 to 2021) and in particular, Strategic Decisions 1, 3(1), 5, and 11 that speak to other stakeholders, partnerships and capacity building, environmental protection, and enhancing its public outreach program, accessed 21 March 2017 at http://www.imo.org/en/About/strategy/Documents/A%2029-Res.1097%20-%20Strategic%20Plan%20for%20 2016-2021.pdf.

120 International Maritime Organization, Rules and Guidelines for Consultative Status of Non-Governmental International Organizations with the International Maritime Organization, accessed 21 March 2017 at http://www.imo.org/en/About/Membership/Documents/RULES%20AND%20GUIDELINES%20FOR%20CONSULTATIVE%20STATUS.pdf#search=non%20governmental%20organization%20status.

the Permanent Participants. Potentially, for this reason and others the United States is keen to revisit the Polar Code to ensure that issues that did not gain attention in the first go around, e.g., safety and black carbon, are addressed in the future. And, more important, now that the Polar Code has been concluded, who will effectively ensure compliance throughout the Arctic Ocean? How will Arctic coastal States, with limited on-site, coastal resources and infrastructure, provide timely enforcement and monitoring? What are the rights, roles and responsibilities of the Arctic Indigenous coastal communities that have maintained human habitation of the region for centuries and more recently have had rights affirmed in both national and international law?

4 Conclusion

In response to the recent announcement by Prime Minister Justin Trudeau and President Barack Obama about a partnership for action on climate change, Mary Simon, an Inuk and former Canadian Ambassador for Circumpolar Affairs stated:

> These areas should be at the top of the government's list for protection. The best way to ensure this happens is to create a place for Inuit leaders during the selection of candidate areas—instead of asking our opinion afterwards. Together, we can define the most important *ocean places and policies to safeguard our Arctic home and our future.*
>
> There needs to be a balance struck between sustained economic growth and climate change mitigation and adaptation measures. *Inuit can help achieve this balance by being included in discussions about where and how Arctic shipping, offshore oil and gas exploration and commercial fishing should proceed.* Arctic-specific standards are still needed in many cases and should be built on the best available science and our traditional knowledge of what works in the Arctic.[121]

In regard to the key concerns of the Permanent Participants and the issue of Arctic shipping, Arctic Indigenous leaders have highlighted the role of the

121 Mary Simon, 'Arctic deal a path for full Inuit participation in the northern economy' *The Globe and Mail* (11 March 2016) [emphasis added] accessed 21 March 2017 at http://www.theglobeandmail.com/opinion/arctic-deal-a-path-for-full-inuit-participation-in-the-northern-economy/article29174599/. Mary Simon is a former Canadian ambassador for circumpolar affairs and represented Canada on the Arctic Council.

Arctic Council Permanent Participants in sustaining their homelands—the unique Arctic environment. All States concerned, and in particular Arctic States and non-Arctic States with observer status with the Arctic Council, must respect and recognise the Indigenous peoples' right to self-determination, including the right to free, prior and informed consent (FPIC)[122] as custodians of their homelands. They must also ensure the integration of Inuit and other Indigenous knowledge[123] and local monitoring into environmental impact assessments; the need to support the participation of Inuit in the monitoring and policing of shipping regulations as well as other ongoing or emerging monitoring programs at local, national, regional and international levels;[124] recognise the fundamental human right of Arctic Indigenous peoples to a safe and healthy environment;[125] and to acknowledge the important role of the

122 UN Declaration, *supra* note 3, Arts 10, 11, 19, 28, 29 and 32. See also Affidavit of Peter Ittinuar, *supra* note 1 at 113, para 12, wherein he describes the results of the lack of operationalising FPIC in relation to Inuit rights and interests: 'There is the feeling of quite inadequate consultation in this case. There is the feeling that representation of Inuit interests has been haphazard at best. There is the feeling that the food essential to a community's very survival will be irrevocably lost. There is the feeling that decisions were taken in a context of insufficient knowledge regarding the impacts of marine related activity in Arctic waters; There is the feeling that, since there appears to have been no attempt to settle based on equal and mutual respect, one must resort to the hard road of litigation. There is the feeling that reconciliation was not achieved, and that the decisions in this context will be short lived.'

123 Andy Mahoney, *supra* note 88, further describes that 'There's a lot to be learned by sharing time on the ice with the people who live here in Barrow.... We have a very integrated system of observations with technological moorings and radars but also very fundamental knowledge from people out there living their lives.... I have never failed to learn something new when I go onto the ice and talk to people who depend on this ice for their living and their livelihood'.

124 UN Declaration, *supra* note 3, Art 18: 'Indigenous peoples have the right to participate in decision-making in matters which would affect their rights, through representatives chosen by themselves in accordance with their own procedures, as well as to maintain and develop their own indigenous decision-making institutions'.

125 UN Declaration, *supra* note 3, Art 29: '1. Indigenous peoples have the right to the conservation and protection of the environment and the productive capacity of their lands or territories and resources. States shall establish and implement assistance programmes for indigenous peoples for such conservation and protection, without discrimination. 2. States shall take effective measures to ensure that no storage or disposal of hazardous materials shall take place in the lands or territories of indigenous peoples without their free, prior and informed consent. 3. States shall also take effective measures to ensure, as needed, that programmes for monitoring, maintaining and restoring the health of indigenous peoples, as developed and implemented by the peoples affected by such materials, are duly implemented'.

Arctic Council as a model for cooperation and collaboration between States and Indigenous peoples.

In conclusion, recognising States and their future actions specifically related to Arctic Ocean shipping activity, there is a greater urgency to integrate and institutionalise the status and rights of Arctic Indigenous peoples into all existing and future regimes concerned and an even greater urgency to fully implement robust standards to fully and effectively implement such standards, including those affirmed in the UN Declaration. Though the Arctic Council has now been complemented by the Arctic Economic Council, it is difficult to address all political, economic, social, cultural, and environmental and security matters in a comprehensive and interrelated fashion. The risk of creating 'silos' or segregating fundamental issues facing all Arctic stakeholders is a reality and may potentially create new and different problems that no single intergovernmental and Indigenous partnership can effectively deal with.

To positively construct such Arctic-specific standards, either through the Arctic Council or a potential new regime that comprehensively takes into account Indigenous specific concerns, the direct participation of Arctic Indigenous peoples must be recognised and respected. In this way, the Arctic Council and all other interested States will contribute to the collective effort to safeguard the Arctic and the distinct ways of life and homelands of Arctic Indigenous peoples, not only for their benefit but for the benefit of all of humankind.

PART 2

The Role of the IMO

CHAPTER 4

The IMO, Its Role under UNCLOS and Its Polar Shipping Regulation

Aldo Chircop

1 Introduction

As a specialised agency of the United Nations dedicated to international shipping matters, the International Maritime Organization (IMO) is critical to navigation and seaborne trade, and for this purpose performs vital roles in the law of the sea and maritime law. The United Nations Convention on the Law of the Sea (UNCLOS)[1] provides, among other, a legal and institutional framework aimed at maintaining a delicate balance between coastal State rights and duties, and international community navigation rights and duties in its maritime zones and on the high seas. The exercise of rights and performance of duties as they impact on international navigation and shipping is frequently referenced to or benchmarked against international maritime rules, standards and procedures. UNCLOS contains numerous references to 'the competent international organization' as the lead institution or forum to address maritime matters, and such references have been interpreted to mean the IMO.[2] The IMO is the leading international organisation tasked with the development of maritime rules, standards and procedures to facilitate shipping and trade.

The IMO was established by treaty in 1948 as the Inter-governmental Maritime Consultative Organization (IMCO).[3] Although initial steps were taken towards the end of the Second World War with the establishment of

1 United Nations Convention on the Law of the Sea, adopted 10 December 1982, 1833 UNTS 3 (entered into force 16 November 1994) (UNCLOS).

2 'Competent or Relevant International Organizations' under the United Nations Convention on the Law of the Sea, (1996) *Law of the Sea Bulletin* No. 31, 79–95, accessed 15 March 2017 at http://www.un.org/depts/los/doalos_publications/LOSBulletins/bulletinpdf/bulletinE31.pdf (Competent International Organizations). Implications of the United Nations Convention on the Law of the Sea for the International Maritime Organization, Study by the Secretariat of the IMO, IMO Doc LEG/MISC.6, 19 January 2012 (UNCLOS Implications for IMO).

3 Convention on the Inter-Governmental Maritime Consultative Organization, adopted 6 March 1948, ATS 1958 No 5 (entered into force 17 March 1958), as amended (IMO Convention). The decision to establish the IMO was UN Economic and Social Council Resolution

 | DOI 10.1163/9789004339385_005

the United Maritime Authority, the original idea for an international organisation dedicated to maritime matters was launched by the Comité Maritime International at the International Maritime Conference in 1889.[4] The League of Nations anticipated the establishment of an international organisation dedicated to shipping and communications, but failed to undertake such task as a result of the outbreak of the War.[5] Following its formal establishment by the now renamed Convention on the International Maritime Organization (IMO Convention),[6] the Organization's structure and mandate evolved significantly to encompass a suite of new areas of regulation and facilitation.[7] Since its establishment, the Organization has exercised its competence through over fifty conventions and protocols,[8] as well as numerous other instruments.

The IMO's regulatory reach includes Arctic waters. However, and despite its large portfolio of conventions, codes, resolutions and guidelines on general shipping matters dating back over six decades, polar shipping-specific regulation is of much more recent vintage. Indeed, the Organization's first consideration of specific rules for polar environments, and most especially the Arctic, was in the 1990s. As with all new regulatory initiatives, the IMO's polar regulatory work, most especially the International Code for Ships Operating in Polar Waters (Polar Code)[9] (discussed in Chapter 4 of this Volume) is a 'first generation' regulation that will be further developed in response to new proposals, implementation experience and technological development.

35, Fourth Session. Resolutions adopted by the Economic and Social Council, 4th Session (28 February to 29 March 1947), UN Doc E/437, 22 May 1947.

4 Eula McDonald, 'Toward a World Maritime Organization: A Half-Century of Developments in Ocean Shipping,' *Department of State Bulletin* (1 April 1948) 1–16, at 1 *et seq*, accessed 15 March 2017 at https://archive.org/stream/departmentofstat181948unit#page/98/mode/2up/search/eula.

5 *Ibid.* at 3–5. See also K R Simmonds, *The International Maritime Organization* (Simmonds & Hill Publishing Ltd, 1994) 1.

6 IMO Assembly Resolutions A.358(IX), IMO Doc A.358(IX) 14 November 1975 and A.371(X), IMO Doc A.371(X) 9 November 1977.

7 Aldo Chircop, 'The International Maritime Organization' in Donald R Rothwell, Alex G Oude Elferink, Karen N Scott and Tim Stephens (eds), *The Oxford Handbook of the Law of the Sea* (Oxford University Press, 2015) 416–438.

8 See IMO Conventions, accessed 15 March 2017 at http://www.imo.org/About/Conventions/ListOfConventions/Pages/Default.aspx.

9 For a consolidated online edition of the Polar Code, see International Code for Ships Operating in Polar Waters (Polar Code), accessed 15 March 2017 at http://www.imo.org/en/MediaCentre/HotTopics/polar/Documents/POLAR%20CODE%20TEXT%20AS%20ADOPTED.pdf.

The purpose of this Chapter is to present the IMO's contemporary mandate within the international law of the sea, with particular reference to the regulation of shipping, while assessing constraints and opportunities. The Chapter starts with consideration of the Organization's mandate, structure and decision-making processes, followed by an analysis of its functions as a competent international organisation in UNCLOS. Next, the Chapter surveys and assesses the IMO's role in the regulation of polar shipping, before concluding with general reflections on the role of the Organization in the international law of the sea and its regulatory efforts with regard to polar shipping.

2 Mandate, Structure and Decision-making

2.1 *Mandate*

The IMO's contemporary mandate and related powers arise from (a) its terms of reference under the IMO Convention, (b) tasks assigned by international maritime conventions, and (c) functions in UNCLOS wherever references to 'competent international organization' apply to the Organization. The latter will be discussed separately later below.

2.1.1 Terms of Reference under the IMO Convention

The opening purpose of the IMO Convention sets out an objective, which in many ways defines what the Organization stands for:

> To provide machinery for co-operation among Governments in the field of governmental regulation and practices relating to technical matters of all kinds affecting shipping engaged in international trade; to encourage and facilitate the general adoption of the highest practicable standards in matters concerning the maritime safety, efficiency of navigation and prevention and control of marine pollution from ships; and to deal with administrative and legal matters related to the purposes set out in this Article.[10]

This purpose underscores the instrumental and facilitative role the IMO plays as a medium of international cooperation for shipping and trade in accordance with international rules and standards for safety, shipping efficiency and

---

10 IMO Convention, *supra* note 3, Art 1(a).

pollution prevention.[11] Other purposes include working against discrimination of shipping engaged in international trade in the interests of world commerce and unfair restrictive purposes, consideration of shipping impacts on the environment referred to it by other UN agencies, and to provide for the exchange of information among Member States.[12]

The IMO's contemporary mandate is a far cry from its original purpose. Its original name reflected the expectation that it would be essentially a consultative and technical organisation, without regulatory authority, and functioning in the domains of maritime safety and trade facilitation. Member States conceded only limited powers and it was not until after the *Torrey Canyon* casualty in 1967 that fundamental rethinking of its purposes and structure occurred. That casualty highlighted the need for the Organization to develop a capability to deal with complex legal matters and to expand its traditional mandate to include marine environmental matters, initially understood as vessel-source pollution. The technical assistance function followed in the mid-1970s, motivated by the need to assist developing countries with the implementation of IMO conventions. Following the *Achille Lauro* incident in 1985, the Organization first expanded its portfolio to include maritime security, and then further strengthened this function after the 9/11 2001 terrorist attacks on the World Trade Towers in New York. More recently, the environmental mandate has been expanded to include a broader range of impacts of ships in addition to vessel-source pollution, such as ocean noise, transport of exotic species and pathogens in ballast waters, protection of particularly sensitive sea areas and greenhouse gas emissions, among other.

The substantive areas of the IMO's mandate today encompass, in no particular order, maritime safety, environmental protection, maritime security,

11 The IMO's Strategic Plan further elaborates on this purpose '… to promote safe, secure, environmentally sound, efficient and sustainable shipping through cooperation. This will be accomplished by adopting the highest practicable standards of maritime safety and security, efficiency of navigation and prevention and control of pollution from ships, as well as through consideration of the related legal matters and effective implementation of IMO instruments, with a view to their universal and uniform application.' Strategic Plan for the Organization (2016–2021), Assembly Resolution A.1097(29), 1 December 2015, IMO Doc A 29/Res.1097, 1 December 2015, at 3.

12 IMO Convention, *supra* note 3, Art 1(b) to (e). The IMO's work on non-discrimination of shipping and restrictive practices has focused on safety, environmental and security regulation. Non-discrimination and facilitation of seaborne trade have been largely addressed by UNCTAD and the World Trade Organization. See UNCTAD, accessed 15 March 2017 at http://unctad.org/en/pages/home.aspx and WTO, accessed 15 March 2017 at https://www.wto.org/english/tratop_e/serv_e/transport_e/transport_maritime_e.htm.

facilitation of international maritime trade and technical assistance. Particular IMO actions have also explicitly or implicitly concerned occupational health and safety of seafarers and other workers[13] as well as more broadly the protection of public health.[14] While much of this work is in the public law and regulation field, the Organization's work also spans private law, most especially with regard to civil liability regimes (limitation of liability, carriage of nuclear material, oil pollution, carriage of passengers, hazardous and noxious substances, bunker oil, wreck removal) and particular areas of maritime contracting (e.g., salvage). Its work on carriage of passengers and salvage has provided the basis for standard contractual terms for industry.

In pursuing its mandate, the IMO promotes international uniformity of rules, standards, procedures and practices for international shipping. Guided by its constitutive instrument,[15] perhaps the most visible outputs in this regard are conventions and protocols the development of which has been facilitated by the IMO and the numerous resolutions, codes and guidelines designed to facilitate the national implementation of international instruments. In addition, the IMO has promoted frameworks and practices for cooperation between maritime administrations and industry.

2.1.2 Tasks Assigned by International Maritime Conventions

While the IMO has enabled the adoption of numerous maritime conventions, it also secured for itself a key role in many of those instruments as convention secretariat and to facilitate amendments.[16] An important innovation in international treaty law was the development of the tacit acceptance of amendments procedure (hereafter tacit acceptance procedure) to replace the traditional procedure of treaty amendment requiring the convening of an international

---

13 For example, the Hong Kong International Convention for the Safe and Environmentally Sound Recycling of Ships, adopted 15 May 2009 (IMO Doc SR/CONF/45, 19 May 2009) (not in force) (Hong Kong Convention).

14 For example, Canada and the United States justified in part the designation of the North American Emission Control Area and amendment of MARPOL Annex VI by the necessity 'to protect public health and the environment in the United States and Canada by reducing exposure to harmful levels of air pollution resulting from these emissions.' See Proposal to Designate an Emission Control Area for Nitrogen Oxides, Sulphur Oxides and Particulate Matter Submitted by the United States and Canada, IMO Doc MEPC 59/6/5, 2 April 2009.

15 'Provide for the drafting of conventions, agreements, or other suitable instruments, and recommend these to Governments and to intergovernmental organizations, and convene such conferences as may be necessary'. IMO Convention, *supra* note 3, Art 2(b).

16 *Ibid.*, Art 2(d).

diplomatic conference.[17] This practice has led some commentators to observe that the IMO enjoys a quasi-prescriptive or quasi-legislative function.[18]

Many IMO conventions contain technical annexes whose rules and standards are sensitive to ongoing technological and other change, thus requiring relatively frequent amendment to ensure they remain up to date. For treaty amendment purposes, the traditional diplomatic conference, while appropriate for change that addresses the principles, treaty text and main structures of a convention that can be expected to remain constant for lengthy periods, is not well suited for frequent technical amendments and development of new rules contained in convention annexes. Hence, the tacit acceptance procedure embedded in several IMO conventions, and responsibility for the administration of which is delegated by the convention concerned to one of the IMO main committees, usually the Maritime Safety Committee (MSC) or Marine Environment Protection Committee (MEPC). These committees rely on Member State delegations to provide the necessary technical expertise to guide the negotiation of amendments. The actual adoption of amendments is through a resolution of the committee concerned, on the basis of a specified majority (e.g., two-thirds) of voting Parties to the convention concerned in the Committee. In practice, this process tends to be characterised by consensus. Entry into force of the amendments occurs after the expiry of a designated period, unless a specified minority (e.g., one-third of Parties to the convention concerned) objects within the period open for tacit acceptance of amendments.[19] Examples of the tacit acceptance procedure are to be found in the International Convention for the Safety of Life at Sea (SOLAS),[20] International Convention on Load Lines,[21] and International Convention

17 A O Adede, 'Amendment Procedures for Conventions with Technical Annexes: The IMCO Experience,' (1976–1977) 17 *Virginia Journal of International Law* 201–215.

18 Rüdiger Wolfrum, 'IMO Interface with the Law of the Sea Convention' in Myron H Nordquist and John N Moore (eds), *Current Maritime Issues and the International Maritime Organization* (Martinus Nijhoff Publishers, 1999) 223–236, at 225; Craig H Allen, 'Revisiting the Thames Formula: The Evolving Role of the International Maritime Organization and its Member States in Implementing the 1982 Law of the Sea Convention' (2009) 10 *San Diego International Law Journal* 265–333, at 271.

19 Adede, *supra* note 17 at 206.

20 International Convention for the Safety of Life at Sea, adopted 1 November 1974, 1184 UNTS 2 (entered into force 25 May 1980), as amended (SOLAS), Art 8.

21 International Convention on Load Lines, adopted 5 April 1966, 640 UNTS 133 (entered into force 21 July 1968), as amended by Protocol of 1988, adopted 11 November 1988, 2 UST 102 (entered into force 3 February 2000), as amended, Art 29.

for the Prevention of Pollution from Ships (MARPOL).[22] More recently, the procedure has been used for Polar Code purposes through the adoption of amendments to SOLAS and MARPOL (see 'SOLAS-related initiatives' below and Chapter 4 of this Volume).

2.2 *Structure*

The IMO's institutional structure consists of the Assembly, Council, Secretariat and specialised committees. The Assembly is the plenary forum for Member States and the highest level of decision-making. It is composed of all Member States. Its functions include making recommendations regarding the adoption of regulations and guidelines, promotion of technical cooperation and adoption and amendment of conventions through international conferences or any other procedure.[23] The Council is the executive organ, filling in for the Assembly when the latter is not in session,[24] and coordinating the Organization's complex committee structure. The Council is composed of forty Members elected under a formula designed to ensure representation of States (10) having the largest interest in providing international shipping services, States (10) having the largest interest in international seaborne trade, and States (20) with special interests in maritime transport or navigation and to ensure global representation on the Council. At the time of writing, the Council's membership reflects strong representation of States having interests in the Arctic, effectively ensuring that the regulation of international navigation and shipping in that region will receive appropriate scrutiny. These include the Arctic Ocean coastal States who are also Arctic Council Members.[25] However, not all Arctic Council Members are represented on the IMO Council.[26] Several major non-Arctic States (in particular those having observer status in the Arctic Council) are Members of the IMO Council.[27] Several of the Arctic and non-Arctic States operate some of the largest closed registers, but Council membership also

22 International Convention for the Prevention of Pollution from Ships, adopted 2 November 1973, 1340 UNTS 184 as amended by Protocol of 1978 Relating to the International Convention for the Prevention of Pollution from Ships of 1973, 17 February 1978, 1340 UNTS 61 (both entered into force 2 October 1983), as further amended (MARPOL), Art 16.

23 IMO Convention, *supra* note 3, Art 15(j), (k) and (l). The other functions are listed in this provision.

24 *Ibid.*, Arts 21 and 26.

25 Canada, Denmark, Norway, the Russian Federation and the United States.

26 At this time, Sweden is a member of the IMO Council, whereas Finland and Iceland are not.

27 Brazil, China, France, Germany, Japan, India, Italy, the Netherlands, Singapore, South Korea, Spain and the United Kingdom.

includes major open register flag States.[28] Headed by the Secretary-General, the Secretariat ensures the functionality of the Organization's machinery and also serves as secretariat to various international maritime conventions. In practice, the conduct of the Organization's business is undertaken by Member Delegations, most especially through the committee structure.

The main committees are (a) MSC, (b) MEPC, (c) Legal Committee (LEG), (d) Facilitation Committee (FAL) and (e) Technical Cooperation Committee (TCC). These committees have open membership for all IMO Member States. The first committee to be established was the MSC with a mandate covering a broad scope of maritime safety topics, including navigation aids, construction and equipping of ships, dangerous cargoes, maritime safety procedures and requirements, hydrographical matters, log books and navigational records, marine casualty investigations, salvage, search and rescue.[29] The MSC may also make recommendations to the Council, *inter alia* regarding safety regulations, amendments and guidelines.[30] Importantly, the MSC is delegated by particular maritime conventions to amend those instruments through the tacit acceptance procedure. The other committees were established in response to the evolving mandate of the Organization. The LEG and MEPC committees were created on the realisation, prompted by the *Torrey Canyon* casualty in 1967, that the Organization needed expertise on maritime legal and jurisdictional matters and marine environment protection. The LEG committee was established in 1967 to strengthen the Organization's arm in the development and drafting of conventions and to consider other legal issues arising from time to time.[31] The MEPC's birth was in 1973, initially with a focus on vessel-source pollution, but which today considers a broader range of impacts on the marine environment from ships and reduction of greenhouse gas emissions.[32] Like the MSC, it may recommend the development of regulations and guidelines within its remit to the Council. It is also tasked by particular maritime conventions with tacit acceptance of instruments assigned to it and to facilitate their implementation.[33] The TCC has been in existence since 1977 and, as its

---

28 In particular, The Bahamas, Cyprus, Liberia, Malta and Panama.

29 IMO Convention, *supra* note 3, Art 28(a).

30 *Ibid.*, Art 29(a) and (b).

31 *Ibid.*, Art 34.

32 For a brief description of the IMO's work on greenhouse emissions reduction, see IMO, Greenhouse Gas Emissions, accessed 15 March 2017 at http://www.imo.org/en/OurWork/Environment/PollutionPrevention/AirPollution/Pages/GHG-Emissions.aspx.

33 IMO Convention, *supra* note 3, Arts 38(a) and (b), and 39(a) and (b). See Simmonds, *supra* note 5 at 32.

name suggests, it is responsible for performing the Organization's technical assistance function.[34] After years of functioning as an informal committee, the FAL committee was institutionalised in the IMO Convention with an amendment in 1991,[35] which entered into force in 2008.[36] This committee's functions concern maritime documentation[37] and amendments to the Convention on Facilitation of International Maritime Traffic.[38] The MSC and MEPC are the two major committees principally responsible for the development of polar shipping regulation.

Several sub-committees further support the MSC and MEPC committees. They conduct their work on a sessional and inter-sessional basis. Recently the sub-committees were re-organised into seven as follows: Human Element, Training and Watchkeeping (HTW); Implementation of IMO Instruments (III); Navigation, Communications and Search and Rescue (NCSR); Pollution Prevention and Response (PPR); Ship Design and Construction (SDC); Ship Systems and Equipment (SSE); and Carriage of Cargoes and Containers (CCC). The sub-committees play critical roles with regard to the 'nitty-gritty' work of international rules, standards, codes and guidelines under development or in need of updating. For example, the SDC sub-committee (previously the Sub-Committee on Ship Design and Equipment) played a central role in the conversion of the prior voluntary polar guidelines into a basis for the development of the Polar Code, as discussed further below.

2.3 *Decision-making*

Authoritative decision-making in the IMO is not concentrated exclusively at the top (Assembly and Council), but rather is further distributed throughout its committee structure. The IMO Convention makes provision for decision-making on the basis of absolute or qualified majority voting (as the case may be),[39] but, as noted earlier, in practice consensus is usually the norm. This is important to underscore because broadly-supported decisions tend to carry

34 *Ibid.*, Art 43(a).

35 Amendments to the Convention on the International Maritime Organization (institutionalisation of the Facilitation Committee), IMO Doc A.724(17), 7 November 1991, accessed on 15 March 2017 at http://www.imo.org/blast/blastDataHelper.asp?data_id=22582&filename=A724(17).pdf.

36 The amendment required instruments of acceptance from at least two-thirds of the membership within 12 months of the Resolution. IMO Convention, *supra* note 3, Art 66.

37 *Ibid.*, Art 48.

38 Convention on Facilitation of International Maritime Traffic, adopted 9 April 1965, 591 UNTS 265 (entered into force 5 March 1967).

39 IMO Convention, *supra* note 3, Art 57.

greater weight and better reflect the 'general acceptance' of rules, standards and procedures when the membership lends its full weight. The medium of the decision is the resolution, which may concern a range of recommendations, including new rules and standards not incorporated in existing maritime conventions. The Assembly has power to convene international conferences or decide on any other procedure for the adoption of international conventions and amendments developed by the committees or other organs.[40] As noted earlier, the MSC and MEPC undertake technical amendments to specific maritime conventions through resolutions utilising the tacit acceptance procedure. The instruments used by the IMO in performance of its functions include recommendations, mandatory and voluntary codes, guidelines and information circulars.

While national delegations drive committee work and formally decide, other intergovernmental and non-governmental organisations (NGOs) also play important roles in their capacity of observers. Intergovernmental organisations maintain a special status and relationship with the IMO. On occasion, there is close collaboration on particular regulatory initiatives, such as with the development of the Hong Kong International Convention for the Safe and Environmentally Sound Recycling of Ships.[41] The Council grants consultative status to NGOs that are able to participate in meetings as observers and thereby make substantial contributions to the work of the Organization.[42] The granting of this status is intended to enable the provision of information and expert advice on specific issue areas (including submission of documents on matters under consideration) and to enable representation of the views of stakeholders whose activities bear directly on the work of the Organization.[43] The NGOs encompass a wide range of associations for industry (e.g., shipowners, particular tonnage such as tanker owners, cargo handlers, classification societies, insurers, salvors, etc.), maritime labour (unions, seafarer organisations,

40 *Ibid.*, Art 15(l).

41 See *supra* note 13. The IMO worked closely with the International Labour Organization, Parties to the Basel Convention on the Control of Transboundary Movements of Hazardous Wastes and their Disposal, 1989 and non-governmental organisations. For a study of this relationship and ensuing convention, see Tony George Puthucherril, *From Shipbreaking to Sustainable Ship Recycling: Evolution of a Legal Regime* (Leiden: Martinus Nijhoff, 2010).

42 IMO, Rules and Guidelines for Consultative Status of Non-Governmental Organizations with the International Maritime Organization (2013), accessed 15 March 2017 at http://www.imo.org/en/About/Membership/Documents/RULES%20AND%20GUIDELINES%20FOR%20CONSULTATIVE%20STATUS.pdf.

43 *Ibid.* at 1–2.

etc.), environmental protection (e.g., environmental activists), education and training (e.g., nautical institutes, training organisations, etc.), and professions (e.g., maritime legal practitioners, master mariners, etc.). By way of example, a former LEG committee chairperson acknowledged that success of the treaty-making work was due in part to 'the well-established practice of the IMO' in encouraging 'industry participation in the elaboration of draft treaties under consideration in the Committee'.[44] These and other organisations enjoying consultative status are given 'wide latitude to intervene and contribute to the work of the Committee.'[45] The same can be said of other committees. During the SDC deliberations on the Polar Code, followed by further consideration in the MSC and MEPC committees, NGOs from industry and others representing environmental interests were very active and frequently shaped the discourse. A particularly salient example was the role played by the International Association of Classification Societies (IACS), which adopted the Requirements Concerning Polar Class (also known as Unified Requirements), now forming the basis for the Polar Code's mandatory provisions concerning polar class.[46] While clearly enhancing the level of awareness and providing helpful scientific inputs, environmental NGOs appear to have been less successful in influencing negotiation outcomes.[47]

---

44 Alfred Popp, 'The Treaty-Making Work of the Legal Committee of the International Maritime Organization' in Aldo Chircop, Norman Letalik, Ted L McDorman and Susan Rolston (eds), *The International Regulation of Shipping: Essays in Honour of Edgar Gold* (Martinus Nijhoff Publishers, 2012) 209–225, at 223.

45 *Ibid.* at 224.

46 International Association of Classification Societies, Requirements Concerning Polar Class (2016), accessed 20 June 2017 at http://www.iacs.org.uk/media/3780/ur_i_pdf410.pdf. The IACS polar class requirements are implicitly adopted in the Polar Code, Part IA Reg 1.2.10, *supra* note 9.

47 M N Tsimplis, 'Shipping and the Marine Environment in the 21st Century' in M Clarke (ed), *Maritime Law Evolving: Thirty Years at Southampton* (Hart Publishing, 2013) 95, at 107. Environmental NGOs expressed disappointment with the Polar Code's environmental provisions for which they laboured hard. The environmental provisions of the Code are significantly fewer and narrower than what the NGOs supported. See Environmental Protection in the Polar Code, Submitted by Friends of the Earth International (FOEI), World Wide Fund for Nature (WWF), Pacific Environment and Clean Shipping Coalition (CSC), IMO Doc MEPC 68/INF.37, 6 March 2015.

3 The IMO as a Competent International Organization under UNCLOS

3.1 *'Competence' in Navigation and Shipping Matters*

UNCLOS places heavy reliance on intergovernmental organisations as mechanisms of international cooperation and to facilitate implementation of many of its provisions. In the international navigation and shipping field, both within and outside the UNCLOS framework, the IMO plays a central role as a 'competent international organization'. Although it is mentioned expressly by name only once,[48] UNCLOS implicitly allocates functions to the IMO as a 'competent international organization' in numerous provisions (see Appendix). The Organization has principal competence on the regulation of international shipping and navigation for safety, vessel-source pollution and maritime security purposes.[49] Whenever the definite article 'the' is used in front of 'competent international organization' with regards to specific functions in navigation and shipping, such text has been interpreted to be a reference to the IMO.[50]

However, the IMO does not enjoy exclusive competence with regards to navigation and shipping. Several other agencies and organisations of the UN system have overlapping competence with regards to particular aspects of their mandate and expertise. Established by a UN General Assembly resolution, the United Nations Environment Programme (UNEP) is responsible to 'promote international cooperation in the field of the environment and to recommend, as appropriate, policies to this end; and to provide general policy guidance for the direction and coordination of environmental programmes within the UN system'.[51] In the exercise of its mandate, it has worked with the IMO on several initiatives that overlap with navigation and shipping.[52] The International Labour Organization (ILO) is a UN specialised agency and competent international organisation dedicated to social justice and humane working conditions in all industries,[53] and specifically for the purposes of this

48 UNCLOS, *supra* note 1, Annex VIII, Art 2.

49 Competent International Organizations, *supra* note 2 at 79–95.

50 UNCLOS Implications for IMO, *supra* note 2 at 7.

51 Institutional and Financial Arrangements for International Environmental Cooperation, UN General Assembly Resolution, UN Doc A/RES/2997 (XXVII), 15 December 1972, accessed 15 March 2017 at http://www.un-documents.net/a27r2997.htm.

52 For example, with regard to the establishment and administration of the Regional Marine Pollution Emergency Response Centre for the Mediterranean (REMPEC). See REMPEC, accessed 15 March 2017 at http://www.rempec.org/rempec.asp?pgeVisit=New&theID=6.

53 Constitution of the International Labour Organization, in Part XIII, Treaty of Versailles, adopted 1 April 1919, 15 UNTS 40 (entered into force 28 June 1919), as amended, Preamble,

Chapter also with regard to seafarers. It facilitates the adoption and implementation of international regulations, procedures and practices on such matters to enable flag States to comply with their UNCLOS duties,[54] and cooperates with the IMO for this purpose. The most significant instrument in this regard is the Maritime Labour Convention.[55] The World Meteorological Organization (WMO) is also a UN specialised agency, but with a mandate relating to world weather, climate, hydrology and water resources and related environmental matters. The WMO's work is relevant to shipping with regard to the standards for the reporting of weather information and the division of marine areas into meteorological reporting areas (METAREAS, coinciding with the IMO's navigation areas, NAVAREAS) with lead country responsibilities to facilitate coordination of transmission of meteorological information to international shipping.[56] This work is performed jointly with the Intergovernmental Oceanographic Commission (IOC) of the United Nations Educational, Scientific and Cultural Organization (UNESCO), a UN body having competence in ocean science.[57] The International Atomic Energy Agency (IAEA) has competence, among other, to adopt standards of safety for protection of health and minimisation of danger to life and property from the use of atomic energy and to provide for the application of those standards.[58] The IAEA's role is clearly in evidence in Article 23 of UNCLOS where nuclear-powered ships and ships carrying nuclear substances, while exercising innocent passage in the territorial sea, are required to carry documents and observe special precautionary measures established for such ships by international agreements.[59] The latter include standards adopted by the IMO under SOLAS[60] in cooperation with the IAEA. Also a competent

accessed 15 March 2017 at http://www.ilo.org/dyn/normlex/en/f?p=1000:62:0::NO:62:P62_LIST_ENTRIE_ID:2453907:NO#A1.

54 UNCLOS, *supra* note 1, Art 94(3)(b) and (5).

55 Maritime Labour Convention, adopted 23 February 2006, 45 ILM 792 (entered into force 23 August 2013), as amended 11 June 2014, accessed 15 March 2017 at http://www.ilo.org/dyn/normlex/en/f?p=NORMLEXPUB:12100:0::NO::P12100_ILO_CODE:C186.

56 Global Maritime Distress and Safety System (GMDSS), Report on the Arctic MSI Services, IMO Doc COMSAR 15/3/9, 23 December 2010.

57 See Intergovernmental Oceanographic Commission, accessed 15 March 2017 at http://www.ioc-unesco.org/.

58 Statute of the International Atomic Energy Agency, adopted 23 October 1956, 276 UNTS 3 (entered into force 29 July 1957, as amended, Art 3(6)).

59 UNCLOS, *supra* note 1, Art 23.

60 For example, SOLAS, *supra* note 20, Chapter VII IMDG Code. The provisions of Class 7 nuclear materials are based on the IAEA Regulations for the Safe Transport of Radioactive Material (2012 Edition), accessed 15 March 2017 at http://www-pub.iaea.org/MTCD/

organisation on navigation-related matters, the International Hydrographic Organisation (IHO), an intergovernmental organisation established by treaty for the purpose of 'making navigation easier and safer throughout the world by improving nautical charts and documents' and its objects include realisation of the 'greatest possible uniformity in nautical charts and documents'.[61] The International Civil Aviation Organization (ICAO) is a competent international organisation with regards to air navigation and its safety rules and standards apply to aircraft in transit over straits used for international navigation.[62]

From a maritime trade and private maritime law perspective, the United Nations Conference on Trade and Development (UNCTAD) and the United Nations Commission on International Trade Law (UNCITRAL) may also be described as international bodies having competence in maritime trade and shipping matters, although not strictly within the framework of the international law of the sea. The UNCTAD has played an important role in maritime trade, including by promoting equitable access to the benefits of shipping services, such as through liner conferencing.[63] The UNCITRAL was established by a UN General Assembly resolution as a body within the UN system dedicated to the progressive harmonisation and unification of international trade law.[64] It has played an instrumental role in the development of model rules for the carriage of goods by sea.[65] Further, from a trade law perspective, the World Trade Organization (WTO) and the World Customs Organization (WCO) have

---

publications/PDF/Pub1570_web.pdf. The IMO adopted the Code for the Safe Carriage of Irradiated Nuclear Fuel, Plutonium and High-Level Radioactive Waste in Flasks on Board Ships (INF Code), IMO Doc MSC.88(71), 27 May 1999, as a mandatory SOLAS code to complement the IAEA regulations.

61 Convention on the International Hydrographic Organisation, adopted 3 May 1967, 751 UNTS 41 (entered into force 22 September 1970), as amended, Preamble and Art II(b). The Organization was originally established in 1921 as the International Hydrographic Bureau (IHB). IHB is now the title of the Secretariat of the Organization.

62 UNCLOS, *supra* note 1, Art 39(3)(a).

63 Convention on a Code of Conduct for Liner Conferences, adopted 6 April 1974, 1334 UNTS 15 (entered into force 6 October 1983).

64 Establishment of the United Nations Commission on International Trade Law, UN General Assembly Resolution 2205 (XXI), 17 December 1966, accessed 15 March 2017 at http://www.un.org/en/ga/search/view_doc.asp?symbol=A/RES/2205(XXI).

65 United Nations Convention on the Carriage of Goods by Sea, adopted 31 March 1978, 17 ILM 608 (entered into force 1 November 1992) (known as Hamburg Rules); United Nations Convention on Contracts for the International Carrying of Goods Wholly or Partly by Sea, adopted 11 December 2008, UN General Assembly Resolution, UN Doc. A/RES/63/122 (not in force) (known as Rotterdam Rules), accessed 15 March 2017 at http://www.un.org/en/ga/search/view_doc.asp?symbol=A/RES/63/122.

functions related to shipping. The WTO mandate includes maritime transport services, the negotiation of which is guided by the principles of the General Agreement on Trade in Services.[66] The WCO has developed supply chain security standards that include maritime shipments and is also concerned with port security matters.[67]

UNCLOS contains numerous other provisions referring to 'competent international organizations', which have been interpreted to include roles for multiple intergovernmental organisations, including the IMO. In Part XII on the protection and preservation of the marine environment, several provisions engage clusters of other organisations. For example, cooperation concerning pollution by dumping 'through competent international organizations' for the purpose of establishing rules, standards and recommended practices is understood as referring to the IAEA, ICAO, IMO, IOC, UNEP and the World Health Organization.[68] With regard to contingency plans against pollution, the duty of States in the area affected to cooperate with 'the competent international organizations' refers to the Food and Agricultural Organization, IAEA, IHO, IMO, IOC, International Seabed Authority, UNEP and WMO.[69]

From an UNCLOS perspective, what distinguishes the IMO from other competent international organisations are: (1) its general mandate exclusively dedicated to navigation and shipping without being restricted to a particular issue, and specifically to give content to the protection of international navigation rights; and (2) its key role in the development of international maritime public law and regulation for safe, secure and environmentally responsible shipping.

3.2 *Roles of the IMO under UNCLOS*

The IMO has a broad range of responsibilities in UNCLOS that this author has discussed elsewhere.[70] For the purposes of this book, and specifically because

66 WTO, *supra* note 12.

67 World Customs Organization, SAFE Framework of Standards to Secure and Facilitate Global Trade (June 2015), accessed 15 March 2017 at http://www.wcoomd.org/en/topics/facilitation/instrument-and-tools/tools/~/media/55F00628A9F94827B58ECA90C0F84F7F.ashx. See also Memorandum of Understanding on Cooperation between the World Customs Organization (WCO) and the International Maritime Organization (IMO), 23 July 2002, accessed 15 March 2017 at http://www.wcoomd.org/en/about-us/partners/~/media/887D44574CB0487582155BDE5E42388E.ashx.

68 UNCLOS, *supra* note 1, Art 210(4); Competent International Organizations, *supra* note 2 at 87.

69 UNCLOS, *supra* note 1, Art 199; Competent International Organizations, *supra* note 2 at 85.

70 Chircop, *supra* note 7.

of their relevance for polar shipping, it is worth highlighting the Organization's (a) prescriptive function, (b) facilitation of implementation and compliance, (c) facilitation of management of marine spaces, and (d) facilitation of regional cooperation.

3.2.1 Prescriptive Function

UNCLOS contains numerous references to the rule and standard-making function of the IMO, such as the expectation of Parties to comply with 'generally accepted international regulations, procedures and practices' for safety at sea,[71] vessel-source pollution,[72] and with regard to a wide range of flag State maritime safety responsibilities.[73] The IMO plays a critical role in generating the international maritime regulations, rules, standards, procedures and recommended practices referred to in UNCLOS. Their purpose is to set out expectations of flag States, frame parameters for the exercise of coastal State jurisdiction over international shipping in their maritime zones, and promote international cooperation.

The Appendix lays out provisions where UNCLOS refers to the IMO's prescriptive function either in express or implied terms. Express terms are, for example, where States are to adopt international rules and standards through the IMO, and implied terms are where State conduct in performance of a duty is benchmarked against international rules and standards adopted by the IMO. The pertinent provisions are concentrated in the Parts of UNCLOS concerning coastal State jurisdiction, high seas and marine environment protection. The textual references variously describe the content, type and process of IMO prescriptions using formulations such as: 'applicable international rules and standards', 'internationally agreed rules, standards, and recommended practices and procedures', 'generally accepted international rules and standards', 'generally accepted international regulations', 'applicable international instruments', and 'generally accepted international regulations, procedures and practices'.[74] As a study by the IMO Secretariat explains, the extent of the duty of Parties to UNCLOS to apply or observe IMO prescriptions depends on the interpretation Parties to UNCLOS adopt for the expressions 'take account of', 'conform to', 'give effect to' or 'implement' in individual provisions.[75]

---

71 UNCLOS, *supra* note 1, Art 39(2)(a).

72 *Ibid.*, Art 39(2)(b).

73 For example, construction, equipping, seaworthiness, crewing training and qualifications, use of signals and communications to prevent collisions, surveying and required onboard documentation, etc. *Ibid.*, Art 94(3) and (5).

74 UNCLOS Implications for IMO, *supra* note 2 at 8.

75 *Ibid.* at 10.

3.2.2 Facilitation of Implementation and Compliance

In its earlier years, a criticism of IMO conventions was that its adopted instruments took a long time to secure the necessary number of ratifications and associated tonnage volume to bring them into force, and even when in force, Parties did not necessarily implement those instruments as intended. In other and related situations, most especially MARPOL, the designation of particular marine regions as special areas under an annex of that convention has not always been accompanied by the required designation of reception facilities in the region concerned to enable the MARPOL special area status to become effective.[76] The IMO acknowledged this problem and established the sub-committee on Flag State Implementation (FSI) (recently renamed the sub-committee on Implementation of IMO Instruments (III)) to address the implementation record.

Even in a contemporary setting, there continue to be issues with the implementation of maritime conventions. The difficulty can be explained in part by lack of capacity at the national level to administer the highly technical and complex requirements of maritime conventions. In other instances, the problem is the economic decision of States to enter the open registry business of shipping, but without establishing an effective maritime administration and accompanying legal framework, thereby placing them in the situation of being unable to comply with their commitments under IMO conventions. This situation has led the UN General Assembly to call on such States to not open or even to suspend their ship registries until such capacity is built.[77]

Efforts in the IMO to address ongoing implementation concerns occur at various levels, including: the work of the III sub-committee;[78] the adoption in 2011 of the Code for the Implementation of Mandatory IMO Instruments,[79] followed by the adoption in 2013 of the substitute IMO Instruments Implementation

---

76 Aldo Chircop, 'The Designation of Particularly Sensitive Sea Areas: A New Layer in the Regime for Marine Environmental Protection from International Shipping,' in Aldo Chircop, Ted L McDorman and Susan Rolston (eds), *The Future of Ocean Regime-Building: Essays in Tribute to Douglas M. Johnston* (Martinus Nijhoff Publishers, 2009) 573–608, at 583.

77 Oceans and the Law of the Sea, UN General Assembly Resolution, UN Doc A/RES/68/70, 9 December 2013, para 146, accessed 15 March 2017 at http://www.un.org/en/ga/search/view_doc.asp?symbol=A/RES/68/70.

78 IMO, Implementation, Control and Coordination, accessed 15 March 2017 at http://www.imo.org/en/OurWork/MSAS/Pages/ImplementationOfIMOInstruments.aspx.

79 Code for the Implementation of Mandatory IMO Instruments, adopted by Assembly Resolution A.1054(27), 30 November 2011, IMO Doc A 27/Res.1054(27), 20 December 2011.

Code (III Code),[80] introducing a mandatory audit scheme and specifying responsibilities for flag, port and coastal States; and the provision of technical assistance. The major maritime conventions have been amended to provide a legal basis for the conduct of mandatory audits, with effect as of 2016.[81] Among other, the III sub-committee is guided by the III Code and assesses, monitors and reviews implementation of IMO conventions by flag, port and coastal States. It consults port State control and casualty investigation reports, among others, as these are telling with regards to the quality of registered tonnage and its oversight. In doing so, it identifies difficulties or issues concerning the major maritime conventions, and formulates proposals to the main IMO committees regarding mandatory or voluntary measures to assist such Member States. An important factor in promoting compliance is the role played by technical assistance provided by the IMO. The IMO operates the Integrated Technical Cooperation Programme focusing on the development of institutional capacity, human resources and, more recently, maritime policy capability to enable Member States, especially developing countries, to manage a shipping industry and meet their obligations under the IMO conventions.[82]

The Port State Control (PSC) system has also played an instrumental role in promoting the implementation and enforcement of international maritime standards and weeding out sub-standard shipping.[83] Several IMO conventions contain provisions for port State control inspections. The flag State always retains primary responsibility for maintaining oversight over its registered tonnage, but the PSC system provides a secondary and standard-insuring role played by the ports of call. The system encompasses a series of regional memoranda of understanding (MoU) among national maritime administrations designed to enforce the major maritime conventions through spot checks on international shipping voluntarily calling into the ports of member

80 IMO Instruments Implementation Code (III Code), Assembly Resolution A.1070(28), 4 December 2013, IMO Doc A 28/Res.1070, 10 December 2013.

81 IMO Member State Audit Scheme, accessed 15 March 2017 at http://www.imo.org/en/OurWork/MSAS/Pages/AuditScheme.aspx.

82 IMO, Technical Cooperation, accessed 15 March 2017 at http://www.imo.org/en/OurWork/TechnicalCooperation/Pages/Default.aspx.

83 The IMO Assembly called on Member States to consider establishing regional port State control systems in cooperation with the Organization. Regional Co-operation in the Control of Ships and Discharges, Assembly Resolution, IMO Doc A.682(17), 6 November 1991, accessed 15 March 2017 at http://www.imo.org/blast/blastDataHelper.asp?data_id=24510&filename=A682(17).pdf.

administrations.[84] Inspections may identify deficiencies that require corrective action prior to permitting the inspected ship to leave port. The inspection applies the conventions designated by the respective MoU without discrimination, and effectively with no more favourable treatment to the ships of flag States that might not be parties to the conventions that are the object of the inspection. The system includes the maintenance of databases of ship inspections, enabling inspectors to check the history of non-compliance of particular ships.

3.2.3 Facilitation of Management of Marine Spaces

The IMO is in a position to facilitate coastal State management of navigable waters. As a major ocean user, international shipping interacts with other ocean uses in complex and potentially conflicting ways, most especially in inshore waters (internal waters of ports and harbours, archipelagic waters, territorial seas) and semi-enclosed ocean spaces, including the exclusive economic zone (EEZ). Coastal States undertaking marine spatial planning, which may impact on international shipping, are in a position to seek routeing measures from the IMO to use as tools to manage navigation.[85] The classical example of a routeing measure is the traffic separation scheme, frequently adopted as a collision avoidance measure to enhance maritime safety.

UNCLOS recognises the IMO's technical competence with regards to routeing measures for maritime safety and environmental protection. Routeing systems aimed at minimising the threat of accidents that might cause pollution of the marine environment and impact on the interests of coastal States may be adopted through the IMO.[86] More specifically, the coastal State's designation of sea lanes and traffic separation schemes for ships exercising innocent passage through the territorial sea where the coastal State shall take into account the recommendations of the IMO.[87] There are analogous provisions with regard to the adoption of proposals for sea lanes and traffic separation schemes in straits

84 Current Memoranda of Understanding (MoU) cover the following trading regions: Europe and the North Atlantic (Paris MoU); Asia and the Pacific (Tokyo MoU); Latin America (Acuerdo de Viña del Mar); Caribbean (Caribbean MoU); West and Central Africa (Abuja MoU); the Black Sea region (Black Sea MoU); the Mediterranean (Mediterranean MoU); the Indian Ocean (Indian Ocean MoU) and the Persian Gulf (Riyadh MoU). For links to each MoU, see IMO, Port State Control, accessed 15 March 2017 at http://www.imo.org/blast/mainframe.asp?topic_id=159.

85 Convention on the International Regulations for Preventing Collisions at Sea, adopted 20 October 1972, 1050 UNTS 16 (entered into force 15 July 1977), as amended, Reg 10.

86 UNCLOS, *supra* note 1, Art 211(1).

87 *Ibid.*, Art 22(3)(a).

used for international navigation. Strait States have a duty to refer proposals to designate or change sea lanes and traffic separation schemes to the IMO. Sea lanes and traffic separation schemes may be adopted by the IMO in agreement with the strait States, following which they may be applied by those States.[88] There is a similar duty and procedure for archipelagic States who intend to designate or change archipelagic sea lanes and traffic separation schemes.[89]

The IMO has exclusive competence for the development of rules for ships' routeing systems[90] and has developed guidelines for this purpose, namely the General Provisions on Ships' Routeing and related guidance notes.[91] A routeing system is defined as '[A]ny system of one or more routes or routeing measures aimed at reducing the risk of casualties; it includes traffic separation schemes, two-way routes, recommended tracks, areas to be avoided, no anchoring areas, inshore traffic zones, roundabouts, precautionary areas and deep water routes'.[92] There are also ship reporting and weather routeing measures.[93] The purpose is to improve navigation safety in areas where there is dense or converging traffic and where navigational freedom is constrained by restricted sea-room, obstructions, bathymetry and meteorological conditions.[94] The objective of the 'routeing system will depend upon the particular hazardous circumstances which it is intended to alleviate'.[95] Proposals by States for the adoption of such measures are expected to comply with the Organization's guidelines.

UNCLOS permits archipelagic States to designate archipelagic sea lanes for the continuous and expeditious passage of foreign ships through archipelagic

---

88 *Ibid.*, Art 41(4) and (5).

89 *Ibid.*, Art 53(9). The IMO guidelines on ships' routeing were amended to provide for adoption, designation and substitution of archipelagic sea lanes. See Adoption of Amendments to the General Provisions on Ships' Routeing, IMO Doc MSC.71(69), 19 May 1998.

90 SOLAS, *supra* note 20, Chap V, Reg 10(2).

91 General Provisions on Ships' Routeing, Assembly Resolution, IMO Doc A.572(14), 20 November 1985 (General Routeing Provisions), as amended. Adopted measures are published by the IMO in the loose-leaf *Ships' Routeing* (London: IMO, 2015), updated periodically. See also Guidance Note on the Preparation of Proposals on Ships Routeing Systems and Ship Reporting Systems, IMO Doc MSC/Circ.1060, 6 January 2003.

92 General Routeing Provisions, *supra* note 91, Reg 2.1.1. Specific methods are set out in Part 4 of the General Provisions.

93 Recommendation on Weather Routeing, Assembly Resolution, IMO Doc A.528(13), 17 November 1983.

94 General Routeing Provisions, *supra* note 91, Reg 1.1.

95 *Ibid.*, Reg 1.2.

waters, in accordance with generally accepted international regulations.[96] Such States are expected to submit proposals for designation or substitution of sea lanes to the IMO for adoption and the Organization may adopt them with the agreement of the archipelagic State.[97] The IMO has developed guidelines to assist archipelagic States in preparing submissions.[98] In 1998, the MSC adopted a resolution with a partial system of archipelagic sea lanes in Indonesian waters,[99] followed by guidelines for ships traversing archipelagic waters.[100]

Reporting and routeing measures have also been adopted for conservation purposes, such as protection of the North Atlantic right whale in the Bay of Fundy and off Southeast Nova Scotia.[101] In other situations, routeing measures have been adopted as associated protective measures (APMs) accompanying the designation of particularly sensitive sea areas (PSSAs). The authority to designate PSSAs does not stem from UNCLOS or a maritime convention, but rather from the IMO's general mandate in its constitutive instrument. A PSSA is a marine area 'that needs special protection through action by the IMO because of its significance for recognized ecological, socio-economic, or scientific attributes where such attributes may be vulnerable to damage by international shipping activities'.[102] PSSAs are versatile tools whose spatial scope may overlap with existing marine protected areas (e.g., Great Barrier Reef, Sabana-Camaguey Archipelago, around the Galapagos Islands and Malpelo Island), or even extend to encompass large parts of regional seas (e.g., Baltic

96 UNCLOS, *supra* note 1, Art 53(8).

97 *Ibid.*, Art 53(9).

98 Adoption of Amendments to the General Provisions on Ships' Routeing (A.572(14) as amended), IMO Doc MSC.71(69), 19 May 1998. The MSC resolution included Annex 2 on General Provisions for the Adoption, Designation and Substitution of Archipelagic Sea Lanes.

99 Adoption, Designation and Substitution of Archipelagic Sea Lanes, MSC.72(69), in Report of the Maritime Safety Committee on its Sixty-ninth Session, IMO Doc MSC 69/22/Add.1, Annex 9, 1 June 1998.

100 Guidance for Ships Transiting Archipelagic Waters, IMO Doc SN/Circ.206, 8 January 1999.

101 For example, see Description of the Mandatory Ship Reporting Systems for Protection of Endangered North Atlantic Right Whales in Sea Areas Off the Northeastern Coasts of the United States, IMO Doc MSC.85(70), 7 December 1998; Establishment of New Recommended Seasonal Area To Be Avoided in Roseway Basin, South of Nova Scotia, IMO Doc MSC 83/28/Add.3, 2 November 2007, Annex 25.

102 Revised Guidelines for the Identification and Designation of Particularly Sensitive Sea Areas, Assembly Resolution A.982(24), 1 December 2005, IMO Doc A 24/Res.982, 6 February 2006, as amended by MEPC resolution, Amendments to the Revised Guidelines for the Identification and Designation of Particularly Sensitive Sea Areas (RES A.982(24)), IMO Doc MEPC.267(68), 15 May 2015.

Sea and Western European waters). The IMO has designated thirteen PSSAs to date, as well as two extensions (Table 1),[103] and new areas can be expected to be designated in due course, such as recent initiatives by Malaysia,[104] the Philippines,[105] Mauritania,[106] Papua New Guinea[107] and Viet Nam.[108] The IMO-approved APMs include a broad range of routeing measures to facilitate management of navigational spaces affected (see Table 4.1).

---

103 Chronologically: Great Barrier Reef (Australia), IMO Doc MEPC.44(30), September 1990, with extensions to include the Torres Strait (with Papua New Guinea), IMO Doc MEPC.133(53), July 2003, and the southwest part of the Coral Sea, IMO Doc MEPC.268(68), 15 May 2015; The Sabana-Camagüey Archipelago (Cuba), IMO Doc MEPC.74(40), September 1997; Malpelo Island (Colombia), IMO Doc MEPC.97(47), March 2002; Florida Keys waters (United States), IMO Doc MEPC.98(47), March 2002; The Wadden Sea (Denmark, Germany, Netherlands), IMO Doc MEPC.101(48)), October 2002; Paracas National Reserve (Peru), IMO Doc MEPC.106(49)), July 2003; Western European Waters (Belgium, France, Ireland, Portugal, Spain, United Kingdom), IMO Doc MEPC.121(52), September 2004; Canary Islands (Spain), IMO MEPC.134(53), March 2004; The Galapagos Archipelago (Ecuador), IMO Doc MEPC.135(53), March 2004; Baltic Sea (Denmark, Estonia, Finland, Germany, Latvia, Lithuania, Poland, Sweden; excluding Russian Federation waters), IMO Doc MEPC.136(53), March 2004; The Papahānaumokuākea Marine National Monument (Hawaii, United States), IMO Doc MEPC.171(57), March 2007; Strait of Bonifacio (France and Italy), IMO MEPC.204(62), July 2011; Saba Bank (North-eastern Caribbean area, Kingdom of the Netherlands), IMO Doc MEPC.226(64), October 2012.

104 Protection of Pulau Kukup (Kukup Island) and Tanjung Piai (Cape Piai), Submitted by Malaysia, IMO Doc MEPC 68/INF.22, 6 March 2015.

105 Protection of the Tubbataha Reefs Natural Park and World Heritage Site, Proposed by the Philippines and UNESCO, IMO Doc MEPC 67/INF.25, 8 August 2014, followed by Designation of the Tubbataha Reefs Natural Park as a Particularly Sensitive Sea Area, Submitted by the Philippines, IMO Doc MEPC 69/10/1 15 January 2016. The proposal was approved in principle and with suggested changes. The proposed APM will be reviewed by the NCSR sub-committee. Report of the Technical Group on PSSAs, IMO Doc MEPC 69/WP.11, 21 April 2016.

106 Concerning an area in EEZ waters adjacent to the Banc d'Arguin National Park of Mauritania. If adopted, this would be the first PSSA off the coast of Africa. Report of the Marine Environment Protection Committee on its Sixty-eighth Session, IMO Doc MEPC 68/21, 29 May 2015. The actual submission was made in 2016. Protection of Banc d'Arguin National Park World Heritage Site and an Adjacent Sea Area, Submitted by Mauritania, IMO Doc MEPC 69/INF.19, 11 February 2016.

107 Protection of Jomard Entrance, Louisiade Archipelago, Submitted by Papua New Guinea, IMO Doc MEPC 69/INF.14, 4 February 2016. The proposal is under development.

108 Protection of Ha Long Bay (Quang Ninh)—Cat Ba (Hai Phong) Marine Protected Area, Submitted by Viet Nam, IMO Doc MEPC 69/INF.12, 29 January 2016. This proposal is under development.

TABLE 4.1 *PSSAs and APMs designated by the IMO*

PSSA	Year adopted	Proponent state(s)	Associated protective measures adopted
Great Barrier Reef	1990	Australia	IMO-recommended Australian system of pilotage (includes compulsory pilotage) Mandatory reporting
Sabana-Camaguey Archipelago	1997	Cuba	Area to be avoided
Wadden Sea	2002	Denmark, Germany, Netherlands	Mandatory deep water route
Florida Keys sea area	2002	United States	Areas to be avoided (new and amendment of existing) Mandatory no anchoring areas
Malpelo Island	2002	Colombia	Area to be avoided
Paracas National Reserve	2003	Peru	Area to be avoided
Western European Area	2004	Belgium, France, Ireland, Portugal, Spain and United Kingdom	Mandatory ship-reporting system
Torres Strait (GBR PSSA extension)	2005	Australia and Papua New Guinea	IMO-recommended Australian system of pilotage Two-way shipping route
Canary Islands	2005	Spain	Traffic separation schemes (including inshore traffic zones and precautionary areas) Areas to be avoided Mandatory ship reporting
Galapagos Archipelago	2005	Ecuador	Area to be avoided Mandatory ship reporting system Recommended tracks

TABLE 4.1 *PSSAs and APMs designated by the IMO* (cont.)

PSSA	Year adopted	Proponent state(s)	Associated protective measures adopted
Baltic Sea (less Russian waters)	2005	Denmark, Estonia, Finland, Germany, Latvia, Lithuania, Poland and Sweden	Traffic separation schemes (including inshore traffic zones, precautionary areas) in three areas Deepwater route Areas to be avoided Mandatory ship reporting system
Papahānaumokuākea Marine National Monument (Hawaii)	2008	United States	Areas to be avoided Ship reporting system (mandatory for ships passing through PSSA to or from a US port; voluntary for all others)
The Strait of Bonifacio	2011	France, Italy	Recommendation on navigation
Saba Bank, North-eastern Caribbean	2012	The Netherlands	Area to be avoided Mandatory no anchoring area
Southwest part of Coral Sea (extension to GBR PSSA)	2015	Australia	Two-way routes Areas to be avoided

SOURCE: Adapted from IMO Doc. MEPC.1/Circ.778/Rev.1, 16 November 2012.

3.2.4 Facilitation of Regional Cooperation

In addition to enabling States to fulfil their general duty to protect and preserve the marine environment at the global level,[109] the IMO has facilitated cooperation among Parties to UNCLOS in pursuit of their duties to cooperate, as appropriate, at the regional level with regard to vessel-source pollution matters,[110] navigation safety matters in particular areas[111] and maritime search

109 UNCLOS, *supra* note 1, Art 192.

110 *Ibid.*, Art 197.

111 *Ibid.*, Art 43.

and rescue, among other.[112] The IMO has been instrumental, in association with UNEP's Regional Seas Programme, in promoting regional cooperation with regard to the UNCLOS duty to develop contingency plans to respond to pollution incidents[113] and parallel responsibilities under the International Convention on Oil Pollution Preparedness, Response and Co-operation.[114] The IMO has assisted the establishment of regional centres to coordinate regional responses and build capacity, as in the case of the Mediterranean[115] and Northwest Pacific.[116]

In addition to pollution of the marine environment, the IMO has assisted States bordering a strait used for international navigation and user States to cooperate with regard to navigational and safety aids and prevention, reduction and control of pollution from ships in accordance with Article 43 of UNCLOS.[117] The groundbreaking precedent is the Cooperative Mechanism for the Straits of Malacca and Singapore, the first international strait where bordering States led a collaborative initiative for the implementation of Article 43 with participation from user States and with IMO assistance (further discussed in Chapter 12 of this Volume).[118] As chokepoints on a major navigation route, the two straits serve global and regional interests, and yet the risk of accidents and cost for maintaining navigation aids and services are borne primarily by the straits States of Indonesia, Malaysia and Singapore. UNCLOS places restrictions on charges that may be levied on foreign ships during innocent or transit passage.[119] If a regime of equitable cost sharing is to be developed in compliance with UNCLOS, it must be based on the consent of participating strait and

112 *Ibid.*, Art 98(2).

113 *Ibid.*, Art 199.

114 International Convention on Oil Pollution Preparedness, Response and Co-operation, adopted 30 November 1990, 30 ILM 733 (entered into force 13 May 1995).

115 REMPEC, *supra* note 52.

116 NOWPAP, Marine Environmental Emergency Preparedness and Response Regional Activity Centre (MERRAC), accessed 15 March 2017 at http://merrac.nowpap.org/.

117 UNCLOS, *supra* note 1, Art 43.

118 Cooperative Mechanism between the Littoral States and User States on Safety of Navigation and Environmental Protection in the Straits of Malacca and Singapore, Submitted by Indonesia, Malaysia and Singapore, IMO Doc IMO/SGP 2.1/1, 16 August 2007 (Cooperative Mechanism). For detailed analysis of this initiative, see Robert Beckman, 'The Establishment of a Cooperative Mechanism for the Straits of Malacca and Singapore under Article 43 of the United Nations Convention on the Law of the Sea' in Chircop *et al.*, *supra* note 76, 233–259.

119 UNCLOS, *supra* note 1, Art 26. Charges can only be levied for specific services rendered to the passing or transiting ship, and without discrimination.

user States. A decision by the IMO Council in 2004 opened the door for the Organization to play a higher profile role with regard to straits of particular strategic importance and significance,[120] in turn leading to a series of IMO-sponsored meetings where the straits States would lead the sub-regional co-operation with the Organization's assistance.[121] The agreement includes the Aids to Navigation the Fund, consisting of an IMO-administered Trust Fund to contribute to the renewal and maintenance of navigation aids and including contributions from user States.[122] Ideally, the shipping industry as a key stakeholder and principal user for private gain should be a contributing participant,[123] but in practice it has refrained from participating, possibly because of concern with the establishment of a precedent that could be exported to other straits and effectively raising the cost of shipping.

4 The Role of the IMO in the Regulation of Polar Shipping

4.1 *Context*

In considering the role of the IMO in the regulation of polar shipping, it is essential to contextualise its efforts not only within the framework of UNCLOS, but also in the larger landscape of the governance of international shipping described earlier in this Chapter. In principle, international shipping in the Arctic raises the same issues as it does in other marine regions. Thus, from this perspective, the IMO's role with regard to polar shipping regulation is better understood against the backdrop of the global regulatory regime for international shipping built on international maritime conventions and within the framework of UNCLOS.

However, the global regime is only a starting point, because polar navigation, and in the Arctic for our purposes, is subject to additional safety and environmental risks. Moreover, polar regions are different from other marine regions from a jurisdictional perspective, because in addition to the global regulation under IMO auspices, according to Article 234 of UNCLOS international shipping is potentially subject to a special environmental legislative and enforcement jurisdiction within the limits of the EEZ enjoyed by States bordering ice-covered waters (see Chapter 2 of this Volume). Canada and the

120 Beckman, *supra* note 118 at 246.

121 *Ibid.* at 246–252.

122 Cooperative Mechanism, *supra* note 118, Annex 4 and Appendix. For a list of contributors, see Cooperative Mechanism, accessed 15 March 2017 at http://www.cm-soms.com.

123 Beckman, *supra* note 118 at 256.

Russian Federation have polar shipping legislation that precedes the adoption of UNCLOS and has been further developed while taking into cognisance Article 234 (see Chapters 6 and 7 of this Volume). Norway has legislated polar shipping to a significantly lesser extent (see Chapter 8 of this Volume).

There is a complex relationship between international regulation produced by the IMO as the competent international organisation responsible for international navigation and shipping matters, and the unique Article 234 jurisdiction, including the relationship to international navigation rights protected under other parts of UNCLOS. Unlike in other provisions, in this article UNCLOS does not expressly impose a requirement for States bordering ice-covered areas to act through the IMO in the exercise of this special jurisdiction or to benchmark the exercise of this jurisdiction against generally accepted international rules, standards and procedures. However, the provision does imply that generally applicable international rules, standards and procedures apply as a general and starting base.[124] Otherwise, Article 234 is a *lex specialis* where the terms of the exercise of the power are set out in the provision itself, but not with full clarity or unambiguously. For example, and of particular interest in considering the relationship between global standards and national rules, an interesting question is whether the special jurisdiction with regard to vessel-source pollution prevention inherently includes regulation for maritime safety. Navigation conditions in polar regions are such that environmental and safety matters may be closely intertwined. This is a difficult question to address because the two types of regulation address the ship as a cluster of interrelated technologies, and safety regulation (e.g., ship construction) is central to pollution prevention (e.g., location of bunker spaces). The regulatory purposes of one may not be achievable without addressing the other.

4.2 *IMO Polar Shipping Regulation at Work*

As mentioned earlier, the IMO's incursions into polar shipping regulation are relatively recent. Its regulatory work has primarily focused on amendments to SOLAS (including particular Codes), MARPOL and the International Convention on Standards of Training, Certification and Watchkeeping for Seafarers (STCW).[125]

124 M H Nordquist, Shabtai Rosenne and Alexander Yankov (eds), *United Nations Convention on the Law of the Sea 1982: A Commentary* Vol. IV (Martinus Nijhoff Publishers, 1991) 392–398.

125 International Convention on Standards of Training, Certification and Watchkeeping for Seafarers, adopted 7 July 1978, 1361 UNTS 2 (entered into force 28 April 1984), as amended.

4.2.1 SOLAS-related Initiatives

The SOLAS convention addresses intact stability of ships in Chapter II-1 and in this regard the Intact Stability Code contains 'mandatory and recommendatory stability criteria and other measures for ensuring the safe operation of ships, to minimize the risk to such ships, to the personnel on board and to the environment'.[126] This Code is important as it includes construction standards that ensure a ship is able to maintain stability when loaded, in case of icing on the superstructure, and when the hull suffers damage. The Code was amended in 2008 to include recommendations regarding icing allowances for loading purposes to ensure stability. The Polar Code's specialised stability regulations build on the general requirements of the Intact Stability Code.[127]

Chapter V has also seen pertinent amendments. Ironically, the singularly most important trigger for the first safety of life at sea convention in 1914 was the sinking of the *RMS Titanic* two years earlier after striking an iceberg in non-polar waters off the coast of Newfoundland in the Northwest Atlantic. This loss triggered the launch of the North Atlantic Ice Patrol in 1913, supported by treaty in 1956 and now also addressed by SOLAS Chapter V.[128] The Patrol was intended as a service to monitor and report on the movement of icebergs on the Grand Banks in the North Atlantic and was led by the United States Coast Guard, which continues to lead pursuant to Chapter V.[129] The Patrol and the Canadian Ice Service issue daily reports during the iceberg season. The limits of the Patrol are partially within the geographical scope of the Polar Code.[130] This agreement is also interesting from the perspective of beneficiary maritime states contributing to the cost of the service, a practice that is analogous to the underlying principle behind the Cooperative Mechanism's Aids to Navigation Fund. Other significant safety regulation updates to Chapter V

126 Intact Stability Code, IMO Doc MSC 85/26/Add.1/Annex 2, 4 December 2008, as amended, Chap 6, Reg 1.1. The Code came into force in 2010.

127 Polar Code, *supra* note 9, Chap 4.

128 The agreement gave effect to the Ice Patrol provision in the 1948 SOLAS Convention. See Agreement regarding Financial Support of the North Atlantic Ice Patrol, Washington, adopted 4 January 1956, 256 UNTS 172 (entered into force 5 July 1956). The current SOLAS, *supra* note 20, Chap V, Reg 6 also addresses the funding of the Patrol.

129 SOLAS, *supra* note 20, Chap V, Reg 6 and appendix.

130 Since 2006, the area covered by the Ice Patrol is within 40° N to 65° N and 39° W to 57° W, overlapping with the area of application of the Polar Code, *supra* note 9, Figure 9. Prior to 2006, the geographical area was 40° N to 52° N and 39° W and 57° W.

include meteorological services and warnings, and ice data and danger messages, including for ice conditions.[131]

From a navigational infrastructural perspective, an important development was the change in navigation and meteorological areas in the Arctic. In 2010 the IMO, working with other international organisations and Arctic States, expanded the World-Wide Navigational Warning System (WWNWS) into Arctic waters,[132] thereby extending crucial services for safe navigation and search and rescue. Earlier discussions in the former sub-committee on Communications and Search and Rescue (COMSAR; now restructured as the sub-committee on Navigation, Communications and Search and Rescue (NCSR)), endorsed by the MSC, led to the revision and creation of new NAVAREAS and METAREAS up to 90 degrees north.[133] More recently, the MSC adopted a proposal from the United States to include the Iridium mobile satellite system within the Global Maritime Distress and Safety System (GMDSS) as it enhances communications in polar regions.[134]

Within the framework of Chapter VII, the International Code for the Construction and Equipment of Ships Carrying Liquefied Gases in Bulk (IGC Code), has also been amended to include a procedure for the carriage of cargo at low temperature.[135]

Finally, to present a comprehensive picture of IMO polar regulatory efforts mention of the Polar Code is necessary. The adoption of the Polar Code included the introduction of a new Chapter XIV to SOLAS, amendments to MARPOL Annexes 1, 2, 4 and 5, as well as the Code itself.[136] The Polar Code was preceded by the 2002 Guidelines for Ships Operating in Ice-Covered Arctic Waters,

---

131 SOLAS, *supra* note 20, Chap V, Reg 5 (meteorological services and warnings, ice warnings to be issued twice a day), 31 (danger messages), and 32 (information required in danger messages, including concerning ice).

132 Global Maritime Distress and Safety System (GMDSS), Report on the Arctic MSI Services, IMO Doc COMSAR 15/3/9, 23 December 2010.

133 Global Maritime Distress and Safety System (GMDSS), Report on the Arctic MSI Services, IMO Doc COMSAR 15/3/9, 23 December 2010.

134 Radiocommunications and Search and Rescue, Recognition of the Iridium Mobile-Satellite System, IMO Doc MSC92/9/2, 9 April 2013.

135 International Code for the Construction and Equipment of Ships Carrying Liquefied Gases in Bulk, Reg 18.5, in Amendments to the 1974 SOLAS Convention and Associated Instruments, IMO Doc MSC 93/3, 6 December 2013, Annex 6.

136 International Code for Ships Operating in Polar Waters (Polar Code), MSC Resolution 385(94), 21 November 2014, in Report of the Maritime Safety Committee on its Ninety-Fourth Session, IMO Doc 94/21/Add.1, 27 November 2014, Annex 6; MSC Resolution 386(94), 21 November 2014, Amendments to the International Convention for the Safety

adopted after an initial proposal from Germany in the 1990s and follow up by Canada.[137] The guidelines were voluntary and limited to Arctic waters. The guidelines were amended and renamed in 2009 as the Guidelines for Ships Operating in Polar Waters and were expanded to include Antarctic waters, but remained voluntary.[138] These continued to apply until the Polar Code came into effect on 1 January 2017.

4.2.2 STCW Amendments

With regard to seafarers, IMO Member States used the opportunity of the 2010 Manila Conference review of the STCW Convention and the STCW Code to also include voluntary guidance provisions regarding training for polar seafarers.[139] The Conference adopted a resolution entitled Guidance regarding Training of Masters and Officers for Ships Operating in Polar Waters. The Guidance is valuable for maritime training academies in the preparation of masters, officers in charge of navigational watches and officers in charge of engineering watches on board ships operating in polar waters. The guidance defines the knowledge content and experience for these personnel, such as with regards to ice characteristics, ship performance in ice and cold climates, voyage and passage planning for ships in ice, operating and handling ships in ice, international regulations and local requirements, equipment limitations, safety precautions and emergency procedures, and environmental considerations.

The Polar Code makes cross-reference to STCW, as amended. In meeting the Code's Chapter 12 concerning manning and training, the expectation is that ships operating in polar waters will be properly crewed by qualified and trained personnel in accordance with Chapter V of STCW and the STCW Code.[140] Most recently STCW requirements for polar seafarers were further amended[141] and are discussed in Chapter 5 of this volume.

---

of Life at Sea, 1974, as amended, in Report of the Maritime Safety Committee on its Ninety-Fourth Session, IMO Doc. 94/21/Add.1, 27 November 2014, Annex 7 (SOLAS Chapter XIV).

137 Guidelines for Ships Operating in Arctic Ice-Covered Waters, IMO Doc MSC/Circ.1056 & MEPC/Circ. 399, 23 December 2002.

138 Guidelines for Ships Operating in Polar Waters, Resolution A.1024(26), 2 December 2009, IMO Doc A 26/Res.1024 18 January 2010.

139 Manila Amendments, Final Act of the Conference of the Parties, IMO Doc STCW/CONF.2/33, 1 July 2010), Resolution 11 and Section B-V/g.

140 Polar Code, *supra* note 9, Chap 12.

141 Amendments to the International Convention on Standards of Training, Certification and Watchkeeping for Seafarers (STCW), 1978, as amended, and the Seafarers' Training, Certification and Watchkeeping (STCW) Code, IMO Doc MSC 96/3/2, 4 November 2015, prepared for adoption by MSC 97 to be convened on 21–25 November 2016 in accordance

4.2.3 Other Guidelines

Prior to the Polar Code, IMO anticipated the need for standards for cruise ships operating in polar waters and for this purpose the Assembly adopted a resolution with voluntary Guidelines on Voyage Planning for Passenger Ships in Remote Areas in 2007.[142] The content speaks to appraisal, planning and execution of a list of measures for the voyage and passage plan. The factors to consider are hydrographical data (a major concern most especially in the Arctic), availability and lack of navigation aids, availability of ice navigators, operational limitations in ice covered waters, safe areas and no-go areas, environmental conditions, etc. Over the years, two cruise ships grounded in Canadian waters of the Northwest Passage in areas where charts were either not up to date or the navigation aids relied upon had drifted with ice.[143] Interestingly, and perhaps a significant omission, the Guidelines make no provision for communicating with the closest local authorities to make their position known in case search and rescue, salvage and other assistance are required.

The IMO also adopted a helpful Guide for Cold Water Survival in 2008, revised in 2012, aimed at seafarers for situations where they might fall into cold water, or are compelled to enter it in an emergency situation, or have to use survival craft in cold conditions.[144]

4.2.4 Routeing Measures

At a more localised level, the IMO has responded to specific requests by Arctic coastal States for safety measures in the region. A mandatory ship reporting system for vessels of 5000 tons and over was adopted for the Barents Sea Area (effective on 1 June 2013) on the basis of a proposal to the IMO by Norway and the Russian Federation.[145] More recently, the United States Coast Guard

with STCW Convention, *supra* note 125, Art XII(1)(a)(iv), with an expected entry into force on 1 July 2018.

142 Guidelines on Voyage Planning for Passenger Ships Operating in Remote Areas, IMO Doc A25/Res.999, 3 January 2008.

143 See Marine Occurrence Report, Grounding Passenger Vessel 'Hanseatic', Simson Strait, Northwest territories, 29 August 1996, Transportation Safety Board of Canada Report M96H0016, accessed on 15 March 2017 at http://www.tsb.gc.ca/eng/rapports-reports/marine/1996/m96h0016/m96h0016.pdf; Grounding, Passenger Vessel 'Clipper Adventurer', Coronation Gulf, Nunavut, 27 August 2010, Transportation Safety Board of Canada Report M10H0006, accessed 15 March 2017 at http://www.tsb.gc.ca/eng/rapports-reports/marine/2010/m10h0006/m10h0006.pdf.

144 Guide to Cold Water Survival, IMO Doc MSC.1/Circ.1185/Rev.1, 30 November 2012.

145 Applicable to: all ships with a gross tonnage of 5000 and above; all tankers; all ships carrying hazardous cargoes; a vessel towing when the length of the tow exceeds 200 metres;

launched public consultations regarding proposed fairways, traffic separation schemes and precautionary areas for safe access routes to vessels proceeding to and from its ports in the Aleutian Islands and Bering Sea region, aimed at promoting safer transits and reducing the risk of accidents.[146] The next steps to be expected include the submission of a proposal for new routeing measures to the IMO that will reach deep into the Chukchi Sea.[147]

5 Conclusion

The key message of this Chapter is that the IMO is the competent international organisation for the development and adoption of global rules and standards for maritime safety and environmental protection within the framework of UNCLOS and for facilitating their general acceptance and eventual implementation, including in polar regions. The Organization's role cannot be overstated. During the negotiation of UNCLOS, international navigation rights constituted one of the most sensitive classes of issues requiring delicate balancing between competing interests. The IMO plays a critical role in servicing that balance through its ongoing work of system maintenance. It ensures that international rules and standards continue to evolve in response to commercial, environmental, security and technological forces.

---

any ship not under command, restricted in their ability to manoeuvre or having defective navigational aids. Adoption of a New Mandatory Ship Reporting System in the Barents Area (Barents SRS), Resolution MSC.348(91), 28 November 2012, IMO Doc MSC 91/22/Add.2, Annex 27.

146 USCG, Port Access Route Study: In the Chukchi Sea, Bering Strait and Bering Sea, 12 May 2014, accessed 15 March 2017 at https://www.federalregister.gov/articles/2014/12/05/2014-28672/port-access-route-study-in-the-chukchi-sea-bering-strait-and-bering-sea. Public consultations closed in August 2015. For a discussion of options for routeing measures in the Bering Strait, see Henry P Huntington, Raychelle Daniel, Andrew Hartsig, Kevin Harun, Marilyn Heiman, Rosa Meehan, George Noongwook, Leslie Pearson, Melissa Prior-Parks, Martin Robards and George Stetson, 'Vessels, Risks, and Rules: Planning for Safe Shipping in Bering Strait' (2015) 51 *Marine Policy* 119–127.

147 Earlier, the United States submitted a proposal for routeing measures in part in the same region, but outside Arctic waters. See Establishment of Five Areas to be Avoided in the Region of the Aleutian Islands, Submitted by the United States, IMO Doc NCSR 2/3/X, 4 December 2014. The MSC adopted the NCSR report on the US submission. See Report of the Maritime Safety Committee's Report on its Ninety-fifth Session, IMO Doc MSC 95/22, 19 June 2015, at 50.

Unlike in other marine regions, the IMO's prescriptive role concerning international shipping in the Arctic has to contend with the unique coastal State parallel regulation for the protection of the region's fragile environment. Arctic coastal States, in particular Canada and the Russian Federation, have longstanding shipping regulatory regimes, long before the IMO became active on polar-specific regulation. As seen in this Chapter, the IMO's work on polar shipping regulation is relatively recent, and while it is clear that the prescriptive and facilitative roles it has played for shipping elsewhere apply to Arctic shipping as well, it is yet unclear whether the Organization's recent polar regulation will render unilateral regulatory action unnecessary or even undesirable. Despite the adoption of the Polar Code and other related regulation, Arctic coastal States retain their Article 234 legislative power. While their participation in the development of the Polar Code suggests support for international regulation, the expectation that Arctic coastal States refrain altogether from unilateral regulation is unrealistic. They have vital interests to protect. Whatever stance the Arctic coastal States adopt, it is likely that they will continue to consider the role of the IMO as a vital one and complementary to the Article 234 jurisdiction they enjoy.

Appendix: IMO Prescriptive Functions Referred to in UNCLOS Provisions

Art.	Part	Express or implied prescriptive function
21(2), (4)	II: Territorial Sea and Contiguous Zone	• 'generally accepted international rules or standards' on design, construction, manning or equipment of ships re laws relating to innocent passage • 'generally accepted international regulations' concerning collision avoidance, applicable during innocent passage
22(3)		• 'recommendations of the competent international organization' in designating sea lanes and prescription of traffic separation schemes, and their substitution
23		• Documents and special precautionary measures for nuclear-powered ships and ships carrying nuclear or inherently dangerous or noxious substances established by international agreements
39(2)		• 'generally accepted international regulations, procedures and practices' for safety of life at sea and collision avoidance, applicable during transit passage • 'generally accepted international regulations, procedures and practices' for vessel- source pollution during transit passage
54	IV: Archipelagic States	• 'generally accepted international regulations, procedures and practices' for safety of life at sea and collision avoidance, applicable during archipelagic sea lanes passage • 'generally accepted international regulations, procedures and practices' for vessel- source pollution during archipelagic sea lanes passage
60(3), (5), (6)	V: EEZ	• 'generally accepted international standards established by the competent international organization' for removal of abandoned or disused installations or structures to ensure navigation safety of navigation • 'applicable international standards' in the determination of the breadth of safety zones

Art.	Part	Express or implied prescriptive function
		• where the breadth exceeds 500 metres, as authorized 'generally accepted standards' or recommendations of the 'competent international organization' • 'generally accepted international standards' regarding navigation in the vicinity of artificial islands, installations, structures and safety zones
80	VI: Continental Shelf	• same as 60(3), (5) and (6).
94(3), (4), (5)	VII: High Seas	• 'generally accepted international regulations, procedures and practices' re construction, equipment, seaworthiness of ships, crewing and training of crews, taking into account 'applicable international instruments'
210(4), (6)	XII: Protection and Preservation of the Marine Environment	• establishment 'through competent international organizations or diplomatic conference,' 'global and regional rules, standards and recommended practices and procedures' re pollution from dumping and periodical review • national laws to be no less effective than international standards
211(1), (2), (5), (7)		• establishment of rules and standards re vessel-source pollution 'through the competent international organization or general diplomatic conference' • national pollution laws and regulations shall have the same effect as 'generally accepted international rules and standards established through the competent international organization or diplomatic conference' • laws and regulations to be enforced in the EEZ to conform/give effect to 'generally accepted international rules and standards established through the competent international organization or general diplomatic conference'

(cont.)

Art.	Part	Express or implied prescriptive function
		• where general rules and standards are insufficient and special mandatory measures are required for the protection of special areas in the EEZ, laws and regulations for such areas may only be adopted only after consultations through 'the competent international organization' and 'implementing such international rules and standards or navigational practices as are made applicable, through the organization, for special areas'; national laws and regulations not to require design, construction, equipping and crewing standards other than 'generally accepted international rules and standards' • international rules and standards to include prompt notification to coastal States whose coastlines or interests may be affected
216(1)		• enforcement of laws re pollution from dumping adopted in accordance with 'applicable rules and standards established through competent international organizations or general diplomatic conference'
217(1), (2), (3), (4)		• 'applicable international rules and standards established through the competent international organization or general diplomatic conference' in the context of flag State enforcement • flag State ships to comply with the requirements of 'international rules and standards' • issuance of certificates in accordance with 'international rules and standards' • flag States to investigate violations of international rules and standards established 'through the competent international organization or general diplomatic conference'
218(1)		• port State to investigate and institute proceedings re discharges in violation of 'applicable international rules and standards established through the competent international organization or general diplomatic conference'

Art.	Part	Express or implied prescriptive function
219		• 'applicable international rules and standards' relating to seaworthiness
220(1), (2), (3), (7)		• coastal State enforcement proceedings instituted in accordance with 'applicable international rules and standards' • violation of national pollution laws adopted in accordance with 'international rules and standards' during innocent passage • vessel in the EEZ commits violation of 'applicable international rules and standards' re pollution • procedures re bond and financial security requirements for vessels charged, adopted through 'the competent international organization'
226(1)		• certificates, records, documents carried by a ship as required by 'generally accepted rules and standards' • where investigation reveals violations of 'international rules and standards' • 'applicable international rules and standards' relating to seaworthiness
228		• Suspension and restrictions on institution of proceedings to enforce effectively the 'applicable international rules and standards'

CHAPTER 5

The Polar Code and Its Adequacy

J Ashley Roach[1]

1 Introduction

In an examination of the governance of Arctic shipping that is focused on balancing the rights and interests of Arctic States and user States, it is appropriate to consider whether the International Code for Ships Operating in Polar Waters (Polar Code) as adopted by the International Maritime Organization (IMO) in 2015 is adequate for that task, or whether improvements are in order.

To assess the adequacy of the Polar Code, we must understand its purpose. The first paragraph of the Preamble to the Code states as its purpose:

> The International Code for Ships Operating in Polar Waters has been developed to supplement existing IMO instruments in order to increase the safety of ships' operation and mitigate the impact on the people and environment in the remote, vulnerable and potentially harsh polar waters.

This Chapter therefore addresses the adequacy of the Polar Code, and suggested improvements are assessed, against this stated purpose, including the context in which the Polar Code was prepared.

Although the Polar Code applies both to Arctic waters and the Southern Ocean (i.e., the sea area south of latitude 60°S, defined in the Polar Code as 'the Antarctic area'), this Chapter focuses on the Code's meeting its stated purpose for Arctic waters, the geographic scope of which is illustrated next.

Before beginning an assessment of the adequacy of the Polar Code in meeting its stated objective, we must acknowledge the reality that the Code is in its first edition, that it entered into force on 1 January 2017 and thus has not yet been tested in practice, that changes were anticipated during the negotiations

---

1 Captain, JAGC, USN (retired), Office of the Legal Adviser, US Department of State (retired), Global Associate and Senior Visiting Scholar (2014–2016), Centre for International Law, National University of Singapore. The views expressed in this Chapter are not intended to reflect the position of any government or any of their departments or agencies. The Chapter draws on the author's unpublished *A Guide to Arctic Issues for Arctic Council Observers* prepared for the Centre for International Law.

 | DOI 10.1163/9789004339385_006

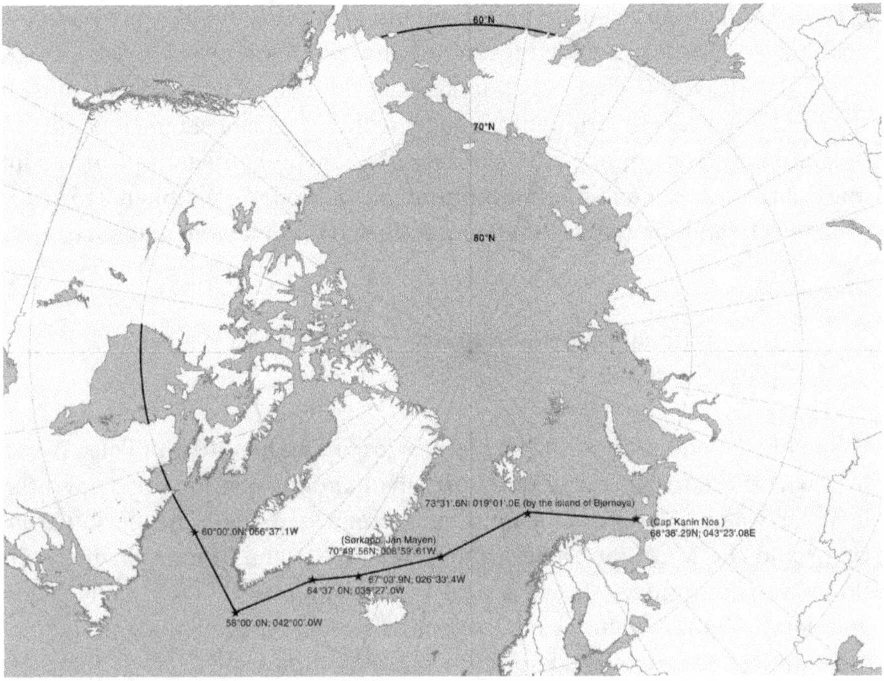

FIGURE 5.1 *Geographic scope of Arctic waters*
SOURCE: POLAR CODE, INTRODUCTION, FIGURE 2, DOC MEPC 68/21/ADD.1 ANNEX 10

of the Code, and that those and other improvements will be made in the future. We must also understand that, as quoted above, the Code is not a stand-alone instrument for ships operating in polar waters. Rather, it supplements existing IMO instruments taking into account the very different conditions in polar waters. The Code must therefore be appreciated in that context.

After a brief summary of the development and content of the Code, this Chapter examines some of the legal and operational shortcomings in the texts of the Code and the amendments to the Safety of Life at Sea Convention (SOLAS),[2] the MARPOL 73/78 Convention (MARPOL)[3] and the 1978 Convention on the Standards of Training, Certification and Watchkeeping for Seafarers

2 International Convention for the Safety of Life at Sea, adopted 1 November 1974, 1184 UNTS 277 (entered into force 25 May 1980) (SOLAS).

3 International Convention for the Prevention of Pollution from Ships, adopted 2 November 1973, as amended by the Protocol of 1978, entered into force 2 October 1983, 1340 UNTS 61 (MARPOL).

(STCW),[4] and proposes some improvements. Thereafter, the Chapter considers possible new measures affecting Arctic shipping that do not involve changes to the Polar Code. The next section assesses the Polar Code in the context of IMO and other legal instruments. A short section then considers implementation and enforcement of the Polar Code. The Chapter concludes with a summary of the recommendations for improving the Code, amendments to SOLAS Chapter XIV and the IMO's implementation and enforcement guidance.

2 International Code for Ships Operating in Polar Waters (Polar Code)

Following the adoption of the Guidelines for Ships Operating in Polar Waters in 2009,[5] the IMO agreed to develop a mandatory Code for ships operating in polar waters. Various subcommittees progressed the work during 2010–2014,[6] and the Maritime Safety Committee (MSC) and Marine Environment Protection Committee (MEPC) considered and adopted the draft Code in 2014 and 2015.[7] The mandatory Code became effective on 1 January 2017 by tacit amendments to SOLAS and four of the MARPOL annexes.[8]

The Polar Code is structured into separate mandatory safety measures (Part I-A) and pollution prevention (Part II-A), with non-mandatory guidance in Parts I-B and II-B for some provisions. We turn first to the safety measures; the pollution prevention measures are dealt with later.

4 International Convention on Standards of Training, Certification and Watchkeeping for Seafarers, adopted 7 July 1978, as amended in 1995 and 2010, entered into force 28 April 1984, 1361 UNTS 1980 (STCW).

5 IMO Resolution A.1024(26), 2 December 2009, Guidelines for Ships Operating in Polar Waters.

6 Initial discussions at the IMO on how to make the Polar Code mandatory are recounted in J Ashley Roach, 'A Note on Making the Polar Code Mandatory' in Suzanne Lalonde and Ted L McDorman (eds), *International Law and Politics of the Arctic Ocean: Essays in Honor of Donat Pharand* (Brill/Nijhoff Publishers, 2015) at 125–140.

7 The text of the Code is appended to IMO document IMO, *Report of the MEPC on its 68th Session*, MEPC 68/21/Add.1 (5 June 2015) Annex 10.

8 The amendments to SOLAS and MARPOL appear in IMO, *Report of the Maritime Safety Committee on its 94th Session*, MSC 94/21/Add.1 Annex 7, at 3–5, and MEPC 68/21/Add.1, *supra* note 7, Annex 11, at 3–10, respectively.

The safety measures are organised into 11 chapters, covering

1. general matters (including definitions, certificates and survey, performance standards, and operational assessment);
2. the Polar Water Operational Manual (to provide the owner, operator, master and crew with sufficient information regarding the ship's operational capabilities and limitations in order to support their decision-making process);
3. ship structure (to provide that the material and scantlings of the structure retain their structural integrity based on global and local response due to environmental loads and conditions);
4. subdivision and stability in both intact and damaged conditions;
5. measures to maintain watertight and weathertight integrity, measures to provide the owner, operator, master and crew with sufficient information regarding the ship's operational capabilities and limitations in order to support their decision-making process;
6. measures to ensure that fire safety systems and appliances are effective and operable, and that means of escape remain available so that persons on board can safely and swiftly escape to the lifeboat and life raft embarkation deck under the expected environmental conditions;
7. life-saving appliances and devices (measures to ensure that fire safety systems and appliances are effective and operable, and that means of escape remain available so that persons on board can safely and swiftly escape to the lifeboat and life raft embarkation deck under the expected environmental conditions;
8. safety of navigation;
9. measures for effective communication for ships and survival craft during normal operation and in emergency situations;
10. voyage planning; and
11. measures to ensure that ships operating in polar waters are appropriately manned by adequately qualified, trained and experienced personnel.

2.1 *Seafarer Training*

In the view of this author, one weakness of Part I-A of the Code as adopted is the minimal requirements for manning and training of crews on ships operating in polar waters. Fortunately, work is underway to improve the situation.

No substantive work on providing Polar area seafarer training requirements had been developed by the end of 2014, either by the Sub-Committee on Human Element, Training and Watchkeeping (HTW 1) or at the earlier 2010

Manila STCW Conference.[9] As the HTW sub-committee meets only once a year, work on the amendments resumed on 5 February 2015 at HTW 2. Acting on the proposals of the United States,[10] HTW 2 endorsed amendments to Chapter V of the Annex to the STCW Convention and Code relating to training requirements for officers and crew on board ships operating in polar waters, and invited MSC 95 to approve them for circulation and adoption at MSC 96 in May 2016, be deemed to be accepted on 1 July 2017 and enter into force on 1 January 2018 through the tacit acceptance procedure.[11]

MSC 95 (June 2015) approved the draft amendments relating to revised training requirements for masters and deck officers onboard ships operating in polar waters, along with the associated draft MSC resolution and STCW Circular for adoption at MSC 96 (May 2016).[12]

However, at MSC 96 the Committee noted that some of the proposed amendments were to provisions of the STCW regulations that were not yet in force, which was legally problematic. Accordingly, the Committee agreed to postpone to MSC 97 in November 2016 adoption of all the STCW amendments as a package.[13] As a result, the entry into force date of these amendments has been delayed six months, until 1 July 2018.

To ameliorate the effect of the delay, the draft MSC 97 resolution:

4 URGES Parties to implement the amendments to regulation I/1.1, regulation I/11 and regulation V/4 at an early stage; [and]

---

9 See http://www.imo.org/en/OurWork/HumanElement/TrainingCertification/Pages/STCW-Convention.aspx, accessed 15 March 2017.

10 IMO, *Training Requirements for* Officers *and Crew on board Ships Operating in Polar Waters*, HTW 2/9 (31 October 2014).

11 IMO, *Report to the Maritime Safety Committee*, HTW 2/19 (6 February 2015) at para 9.10 and Annexes 2 to 4.

12 IMO, *Report of the Maritime Safety Committee on its 95th Session*, MSC 95/22 (19 June 2015), at 18, para.9.5 and MSC 95/22/Add. 2 (22 June 2015), Annexes 8 to 11. The draft amendments were circulated by IMO Circular Letter No 3556, 28 July 2015 and will be considered at MSC 96 as MSC 96/3/2.

13 IMO, *Report of the Maritime Safety Committee on its 96th Session*, MSC 96/25 (31 May 2016), at 15–16, paras 3.52–3.61. The edited proposed amendments were circulated under cover of Circular Letter No 3641 of 20 May 2016, and annexed to MSC 97/3/2 (15 August 2016) (Secretariat). MSC 97 (November 2016) adopted the amendments without change. IMO, *Report of the Maritime Safety Committee on its 97th Session*, MSC 97/22 (22 December 2016), paras 3.49–3.47, 3.90–3.95, and MSC 97/22/Add.1 Annexes 8 (Resolution MSC.416(97) & 9 (Resolution MSC.417(97)).

5 INVITES Parties to recognize seafarers' certificates issued by a Party at an early stage, in accordance with paragraph 4 above, and prior to the entry into force of amendments to regulation V/4[.]

2.1.1 Ice Navigator

One noticeable omission in the Manning and Training Chapter (I-A/12) of the Polar Code is the absence of a provision regarding an experienced ice navigator on the bridge when navigating in Polar Waters. At HTW 1 and MSC 93, Russia and Canada respectively, sought to include in this chapter a provision authorising the use of an ice navigator.[14] The proposals were rebuffed in both cases.[15] This situation has been criticised by experienced ice navigators.[16] The effort appears not to have been renewed at HTW 2, although Russia expressed similar views that practical experience can only be gained through seagoing practice in polar waters and that adopting a sea service equivalent may result in weaker training requirements for masters and chief mates.[17]

The requirements in Chapter I-A/12.2 provide that

> [C]ompanies shall ensure that masters, chief mates and officers in charge of a navigational watch on board ships operating in polar waters shall have completed training to attain the abilities that are appropriate to the capacity to be filled and duties and responsibilities to be taken up, taking into account the provisions of the STCW Convention and the STCW Code, as amended.

Regulation I-A/12.3 then requires basic or advanced training for master, chief mate and officers in charge of a navigational watch on tankers and passenger ships, or other ships, as set out in STCW Convention and Code, depending on ice conditions. There are no requirements for other members of the crew.

14 IMO, *HTW Report to the MSC*, HTW 1/21 (7 March 2014) Annex 12, at 1 (statement of Russia); IMO, *Proposal by Canada*, MSC 93/11/2 (25 March 2014) (Canada), MSC 93/22/Add.3 Annex 32 at 4–5 (statement by Canada). Canada describes the qualifications and requirements for an Ice Navigator, and the situations when an ice navigator is required in Transport Canada, 'User Assistance Package for the Implementation of Arctic Ice Regime Shipping System—AIRSS (1998)—TP 12819 E,' section 6, accessed 15 March 2017 at https://www.tc.gc.ca/eng/marinesafety/tp-tp12819-navigator-2892.htm.

15 HTW 1/21, *supra* note 14 at para 11.16; IMO, *Report of the MSC on its 93rd Session*, MSC 93/22 (30 May 2014) at 45, para 10.38.

16 Sian Prior, 'A New Mandatory Code for Shipping in Polar Waters' (Sept/Oct 2014) 48 *Marine Technology Society Journal* 92 at 94.

17 HTW 2/19, *supra* note 11, Annex 9 at 2.

The amendments to the STCW Code require, i.a., approved seagoing service, performing functions appropriate to the certificate held, for a period of at least two months in total during the preceding five years, or having performed functions considered to be equivalent to the required seagoing service, or passing an approved test, or successfully completing an approved training course or courses. As noted above, the STCW amendments now will likely enter into force 1 July 2018, eighteen months after the Polar Code entered into force. The Russian concerns seem well founded.

2.2 *Application of Part I-A of the Polar Code to International and Domestic Voyages*

SOLAS Regulation 1 Application provides '(a) Unless expressly provided otherwise, the present Regulations apply only to ships engaged on international voyages'. Regulation I/2(d) defines 'international voyage' as 'a voyage from a country to which the present Convention applies to a port outside such country, or conversely'. Regulation XIV/2.1 provides that '[u]nless expressly provided otherwise, this chapter applies to ships operating in polar waters, certified in accordance with chapter I [of SOLAS]', i.e., ships of 500 gross tonnes and greater. MSC 93 understood that the Polar Code applies only to those ships, *whether or not* they are on international voyages.[18] Regulation XIV/2.2 provides that ships constructed before the date of entry into force of the Chapter 'shall meet the relevant requirements of the Polar Code by the first intermediate or renewal survey, whichever occurs first, after one year after the date of entry into force.

In this regard, as noted above the applicability limitations in SOLAS Chapter I, which apply to all of the SOLAS Chapters, are each caveated 'unless expressly provided otherwise'. If that requirement is met by agreeing for the record as MSC 93 did, without including it in the text of the regulation, then the Polar Code applies to SOLAS certificated ships not on international voyages, as specified in SOLAS Regulation I(a). If that requirement is not met, Canada and Russia would be free to apply its domestic regulations to their ships on purely domestic voyages in the NWP and NSR, respectively. That uncertainty should be remedied.[19]

---

18 MSC 93/22, *supra* note 15 at 40, para 10.20.

19 It should be noted that most voyages to the Southern Ocean begin and end in the same port without a stop in another port. Discussed below in the text accompanying note 75 is a similar problem, with the savings clause '*Nothing in this chapter* [*of SOLAS*] *shall prejudice the rights or obligations of States under international law.*'

2.3 *Expansion to Non-SOLAS Ships*

At the 55th session of the Sub-Committee on Ship Design and Equipment (DE 55) in March 2011, the Sub-Committee agreed, in principle, that:

> [A] two step approach should be taken, i.e., the Code should initially apply to SOLAS passenger and cargo ships, taking into account the urgent need for relevant mandatory requirements, and later requirements for non-SOLAS ships, such as fishing vessels, may be developed, after consideration by the Organization.[20]

This agreement was confirmed by DE 56, and repeated by New Zealand at DE 57 and MSC 91.[21]

Thus, when work turns to Phase 2, it would be prudent for any amendment to SOLAS Chapter XIV explicitly to apply the Polar Code to SOLAS vessels on domestic voyages to meet this requirement of SOLAS Regulation I/(a), whether or not the Code is extended to fishing vessels or vessels below 500 gross tonnes.

2.4 *Other Future Work on the Safety Measures of the Polar Code*

Another matter being considered is risk assessment, i.e., judging whether, when and where a particular class of ship may safely operate in the intended voyage in polar waters. This is of particular importance to the ability to obtain maritime insurance for voyages in polar waters.[22]

Paragraph I-A/1.37 of the Polar Code provides that the Polar Ship Certificate 'shall reference a methodology to assess operational capabilities and limitations in ice to the satisfaction of the Administration, taking into account the guidelines developed by the Organization'. At MSC 94, the Committee agreed on the establishment of a correspondence group to prepare draft guidance on a methodology for determining limitations for operation in ice for structural risk assessment, and to exchange information on experience with operations in ice to validate guidance for operations in ice.[23] The correspondence

20 IMO, *DE Report to the MSC*, DE 55/22 (15 April 2011) at 23, para 12.7.1.

21 IMO, *DE Report to the MSC*, DE 56/25 (28 February 2012) at 22, para 10.7; IMO, *DE Report to the MSC and MEPC*, DE 57/25 (5 April 2013) at 23, para 11.7; IMO, *Report of the MSC on its 91st Session*, MSC 91/22 (17 December 2012) at 35, para 8.5.

22 Michael Kingston, 'Implementing the Polar Code; Education about requirements and fostering best practice in operational safety to make it work: Insurance Industry Contributions' (presentation at ShipArc2015, 26 August 2015), accessed 15 March 2017 at http://commons.wmu.se/shiparc/2015/allpresentations/31.

23 IMO, *Report of the Maritime Safety Committee on its 94th Session*, MSC 94/21 (26 November 2014) at para 3.62.

group reported to MSC 95 that it had made some progress on the development of the guidance but recommended the group be reestablished by MSC 95.[24] Taking into account the need to make progress in light of the adoption of the Polar Code by MSC 94 and MEPC 68, MSC 95 decided to re-establish the Correspondence Group on the Development of guidance on a methodology for determining limitations for operation in ice, and associated draft MSC circular, for structural risk assessment and inclusion in the ship's documents, based on the documents previously submitted. MSC 96 approved the report in general and MSC.1/Circ.1519 on *Guidance on methodologies for assessing operational capabilities and limitations in ice.*[25]

The report of the correspondence group to MSC 96 proposed a draft MSC circular on *Guidance on methodologies for assessing operational capabilities and limitations in ice,* as well as additional information and proposals for modifications of the draft MSC circular with regard to the Risk Index of Risk Values (RIVS) for ships under ice-breaking escort for parts of the track that have been reduced to brash ice.[26] After discussion, the Committee, having concurred with the view of the correspondence group that the Guidance should be reviewed four years after the entry into force of the Polar Code, approved MSC.1/Circ.1519 on *Guidance on methodologies for assessing operational capabilities and limitations in ice.* With regard to the future review of the Guidance, which could include discussion on the treatment of brash ice, the Committee agreed that this should be undertaken by the Sub-Committee on Ship Design and Construction (SDC), without a need for a new output, under the existing output 5.2.1.15 (Consequential work related to the new Code for ships operating in polar waters), in due course.[27]

At MSC 95, the Committee also instructed the Sub-committee on Ship Systems and Equipment (SSE 3), in light of the adoption of the Polar Code, to consider whether additional performance or test standards for fire safety/protection and life-saving appliances and arrangements in relation to the Polar Code and necessary, and advise MSC 96 on the best way to proceed.[28] SSE 3 considered one submission, suggesting there is a need to review the Life-Saving

24 IMO, *Report of the Correspondence Group on the Development of guidance on a methodology for determining limitations for operation in ice,* MSC 95/3/7 (6 March 2015) (Norway).

25 MSC 95/22, *supra* note 12 at 22, para 3.91; MSC 96/3/4 (9 February 2016 (Norway); MSC 96/25 paras 3.74–3.78.

26 IMO, *Report of the Correspondence Group on the Development of guidance on a methodology for determining limitations for operation in ice,* MSC 96/3/4 (9 February 2016) (Norway).

27 MSC 96/25, *supra* note 13 at 7–18, paras 3.75–3.78.

28 *Ibid.* at 23, para 3.93.

Appliances (LSA) Code to ensure the relevant requirements of the Polar Code are consistently and globally implemented. SSE 3 agreed and invited MSC 97 (November 2016) to concur. After considering submissions, MSC 97 instructed the Sub-committee on Navigation, Communications and Search and Rescue (NCSR) to consider current communication requirements in SOLAS and the need for any amendments, and to consider the need for a new performance standard for global navigation satellite systems (GNSS) compasses.[29]

As noted above (under Application), the Committee had previously agreed to consider extending the Polar Code to non-SOLAS ships after the Polar Code was adopted.

MSC 95 noted two documents regarding incidents in polar waters involving non-SOLAS vessels[30] and encouraged Member States and international organisations to submit information on incidents in polar waters to assist in assessing the potential scope of the Polar Code to non-Convention vessels operating in polar waters, for consideration at MSC 96.[31] Three papers on this subject were submitted to MSC 96.[32] Various views were expressed at MSC 96 regarding Phase 2 work but no consensus was reached. Accordingly, MSC 96

29 SSE 3/15/5 (Argentina, Marshall Islands, New Zealand, Norway and Vanuatu) (15 December 2015); *Report to the Maritime Safety Committee*, SSE 3/16, paras 15.15–15.16 and 16.2.12 (24 March 2016). MSC 97/22, paras 8.27–8.32, 21.7–21.8.

30 *Request for data on incidents within polar waters*, MSC 95/21/3 (24 March 2015) (Iceland, New Zealand and South Africa) and *Request for data on incidents within polar waters*, MSC 95/21/11 (14 April 2015) (Friends of the Earth International (FOEI) and Pacific Environment).

31 MSC 95/22, *supra* note 12 at 85, para 21.24.

32 *International Code for Ships Operating in Polar Waters (Polar Code)*, MSC 96/24 (14 December 2015) (New Zealand) providing data on non-SOLAS vessels operating in polar waters and SAR incidents involving non-SOLAS vessels within these waters and the New Zealand non-SOLAS vessels which have operated within Antarctica over the last 10 southern hemisphere summer seasons; *International Code for Ships Operating in Polar Waters (Polar Code)*, MSC 96/24/3 (8 March 2016) (Iceland) providing data in relation to non-SOLAS vessels operating in polar waters and SAR incidents involving non-SOLAS vessels north of the Arctic Polar Code demarcation line, within the Icelandic search and rescue region (SRR), and the Icelandic non-SOLAS vessels which have operated in Arctic polar waters during a two-year period (2014–2015); and the information on the parties responsible for coordinating all maritime and aviation search and rescue activities in the Icelandic SRR; *Data on vessels and incidents within polar waters in preparation for work on step 2 of the Polar Code*, MSC 96/24/7 (8 March 2016) *International Code for Ships Operating in Polar Waters (Polar Code)* (FOEI, et al.), informing on incidents involving non-SOLAS vessels operating in polar regions and updating the information previously provided by FOEI and Pacific Environment in document MSC 95/21/11.

invited further views be submitted to MSC 97. MSC 97 considered two papers and noted their information would support the next phase of the Polar Code once it commences.[33]

2.5 *Pollution Prevention Measures*

Part II of the Polar Code on pollution prevention measures is structured differently than Part I on safety measures. The four Chapters of Part II follow the structure of the MARPOL Annexes: prevention of pollution by oil (Annex I), control of pollution by noxious liquid substances in bulk (Annex II), prevention of pollution by sewage from ships (Annex IV), and prevention of pollution by garbage from ships (Annex V).

MEPC 67 stressed that any future amendments to the Polar Code to introduce additional or new environment-related requirements requires approval by the Committee as a new output in accordance with the Committee's Guidelines on the methods of work.[34]

The Polar Code has been criticised for focusing more on prevention of pollution than on environmental protection more broadly, perhaps because of the push to finalise the Code quickly.[35]

3 Possible New Measures Affecting Arctic Shipping not Involving the Polar Code

There are a number of other measures that the IMO could adopt affecting ships operating in the Arctic. Some are under the cognizance of MSC and others of MEPC. In any event, unless a proposal fits under a continuous agenda item, it must first get approval from MSC/MEPC for a new work item/unplanned

---

33 MSC 96/25, *supra* note 13 at 85, para 24.24; MSC 97/22, paras 21.9–21.10. As of March 2017, the second phase had not yet commenced.

34 IMO, *Report of the MEPC on its 67th Session*, MEPC 67/20 (31 October 2014) at 46, para 9.21. On black carbon, *see infra* note 52. The Committee's current *Guidelines on the Organization and Methods of Work of the Maritime Safety Committee and the Marine Environment Protection Committee and their Subsidiary Bodies* are found in MSC-MEPC.1/Circ.4/Rev.4, 22 June 2015.

35 IMO, *Environmental protection in the Polar Code*, MEPC 68/INF.37 (6 March 2015) (FOEI, WWF, CSC); 'Polar Shipping: A 2014 Recap,' *The Maritime Executive* reprinted in *International Shipping News*, 12 January 2015, copy on file with the author, and Bob Weber 'New international shipping rules to protect Arctic are flawed: experts' *The Canadian Press* (13 May 2015), accessed 15 March 2017 at http://www.ctvnews.ca/sci-tech/new-international-shipping-rules-to-protect-arctic-are-flawed-experts-1.2372073.

output. There are two continuous agenda items that can involve new measures affecting Arctic shipping, one for MSC and one for MEPC.

3.1 *Measures under the Cognizance of MSC*

The Sub-committee on NCSR, which reports to MSC, has several continuing agenda items, one of which is 'Routeing measures and mandatory ship reporting systems'. Chapter V of the regulations annexed to SOLAS provides for the establishment of ships' routeing systems and ship reporting systems, which can be made mandatory if the IMO approves them (Regulations V/10 and 11).

Among the types of routeing measures are two-way routes and areas to be avoided (ATBA). The US Coast Guard has considered both in the context of the Bering Strait.

NCSR 2 approved the establishment of five recommendatory ATBAs in the region of the Aleutian Islands, proposed by the United States, and invited MSC 95 to adopt them.[36] MSC 95 did adopt these five ATBAs to be implemented on 1 January 2016.[37]

In its 'Port Access Route Study' the US Coast Guard has proposed in portions of US waters in the Bering Sea north to the Chukchi Sea a voluntary two-way route, as follows:

> (1) A four nautical mile wide, two-way route extending from Unimak Pass in the Aleutian Islands that proceeds Northward through the Bering Sea and Bering Strait before terminating in the Chukchi Sea.
> (2) A four nautical mile wide, two-way route extending from a location North of the Western side of St. Lawrence Island and near the U.S.-Russian Federation maritime border, then proceeding Northeast to a junction with the first two way route located to the West of King Island.
> (3) A total of four precautionary areas, each circular and 8 nautical miles wide in diameter. Three of these precautionary areas will be located at the starting/ending points of the two-way routes, and the fourth will be located at the junction of the recommended two-way routes.

36 IMO, *Establishment of five areas to be avoided in the region of the Aleutian Islands*, NCSR 2/3/5 (5 December 2014 (USA); IMO, *NCSR 2 Report to the Maritime Safety Committee*, NCSR 2/23 (26 March 2015) at 5, para 3.13.3 and Annex 1 at 2–3.

37 MSC 95/22, *supra* note 12 at 50, paras 11.2–11.3 for dissemination by means of SN.1/Circ.331, 13 July 2015.

No decision has yet been made on this proposal. Routeing measures for the Bering Strait are further considered in Chapter 7 of this Volume.

The IMO has approved a number of mandatory ship reporting systems in Arctic waters and elsewhere. Pursuant to a Russian and Norwegian proposal, in 2012 the MSC adopted a new mandatory ship reporting system 'In the Barents Area (BARENTS SRS)' by Resolution MSC.348(91), 28 November 2012, effective 1 June 2013.[38] Reports are to be made to either Vardø VTS center or Murmansk VTS center. The reporting area is between 66°N and 72°N along the northern coast of Norway. Earlier the IMO approved mandatory ship reporting systems in straits used for international navigation for the Straits of Malacca and Singapore (resolution MSC.73(69), Torres Strait (resolution MSC.161(78)), Great Belt (resolution MSC.230(82)), Strait of Gibraltar (resolution MSC.300(87)), and The Sound (resolution MSC.314(88)).[39]

The basic regulations on vessel traffic services (VTS) are contained in SOLAS Regulation V/12. Regulation V/12.3 provides that '[t]he use of VTS may only be made mandatory in sea areas within the territorial seas of a coastal State'. Both Canada and Russia have established VTS for the NWP and NSR respectively, but neither has sought IMO approval for them. If that situation continues, it too raises questions as to the adequacy of the Polar Code to achieve its stated purpose and uniformity of regulation by coastal States.

3.2 *Measures under the Cognizance of MEPC*

MEPC has as one of its continuing agenda items 'Identification and Protection of Special Areas and PSSAs'.

3.2.1 MARPOL Special Areas

In Annexes I (Prevention of pollution by oil), II (Control of pollution by noxious liquid substances) and V (Prevention of pollution by garbage from ships), MARPOL defines certain sea areas as 'special areas' in which, for technical reasons relating to their oceanographical and ecological condition and to their sea traffic, the adoption of special mandatory methods for the prevention of sea pollution is required. Under the Convention, these special areas

38 IMO, *Report of the MSC on its 91st Session,* MSC 91/22/Add.1 (17 December 2012) Annex 27. A list of MSC resolutions may be found at http://www.imo.org/KnowledgeCentre/IndexofIMOResolutions/Maritime-Safety-Committee-%28MSC%29/Pages/default.aspx, accessed 15 March 2017.

39 US Coast Guard, 'IMO MSC Resolutions', accessed 15 March 2017 at http://www.navcen.uscg.gov/?pageName=mscResolutions.

are provided with a higher level of protection than other areas of the sea.[40] Guidelines on designating MARPOL Special Areas are contained in IMO resolution A.1087(28), *2013 Guidelines for the Designation of Special Areas under MARPOL* (21 February 2014).

Annex I to MARPOL 73/78 contains regulations for the prevention of pollution by oil. The Annex provides for the establishment of special sea areas where for recognised technical reasons in relation to its oceanographic and ecological condition and to the particular character of its traffic, the adoption of special mandatory methods for the prevention of sea pollution by oil is required.[41]

In respect of the Arctic Ocean,[42] Part II-A of the Polar Code prohibits any discharge into the sea by oil or oily mixtures from any ship (regulation 1.1.1), and any discharge into the sea of noxious liquid substances or mixtures containing such substances (regulation 2.1.1). With regard to sewage and garbage from ships in Arctic waters, any such discharges are prohibited, except when in accordance with MARPOL Annexes IV and V and the requirements of Regulations 4.2.1–4.2.3 and 5.2.1.

As these prohibitions are more stringent than the normal restrictions in these MARPOL Annexes, it can be said that the Polar Code discharge restrictions in effect make the Arctic Ocean a MARPOL Special Area without saying so.[43]

A prohibition on the use of heavy fuel oil (HFO) in the Southern Ocean was adopted by MEPC 60, effective 1 August 2011,[44] and amended by MEPC 67,

40 For a table listing all MARPOL Special Areas approved by the IMO, see http://www.imo.org/OurWork/Environment/SpecialAreasUnderMARPOL/Pages/Default.aspx, accessed 15 March 2017.

41 MARPOL, *supra* note 3, Annex I, Regulation I/1.11. Resolution A.1087(28). 'Guidelines for the Designation of Special Areas under MARPOL' (2013).

42 The Polar Code uses the term 'Arctic waters' as the geographic scope of the Polar Code in the Arctic includes some ocean areas technically not within the Arctic Ocean. 'Arctic waters' is defined in Regulation 1.3 of SOLAS Chapter XIV and illustrated in Figure 5.1.

43 It should be noted that a MARPOL Special Area may be designated only when there are adequate port waste reception facilities in the area.

44 IMO, *Amendments to the Annex of MARPOL*, Resolution MEPC.189(60) (26 March 2010), MEPC 60/22, Annex 10, adding Chapter 9, Regulation 43, to MARPOL Annex I.

effective 1 March 2016.[45] A similar prohibition for the Arctic Ocean was considered at MEPC 70.[46]

3.2.2 Particularly Sensitive Sea Areas (PSSAs)

A PSSA is an area that needs special protection through action by the IMO because of its significance for recognised ecological, socio-economic or scientific reasons, and which may be vulnerable to damage by international maritime activities.

Guidelines on designating a PSSA are contained in IMO resolution A.982(24) *Revised guidelines for the identification and designation of PSSAs*, as amended.[47] These guidelines include several criteria to allow areas to be designated as a PSSA if they fulfil a number of criteria, including: ecological criteria, such as unique or rare ecosystem, diversity of the ecosystem or vulnerability to degradation by natural events or human activities; social, cultural and economic

---

45 IMO, *Draft Report of the MEPC on its 67th Session*, MEPC 67/WP.1 (16 October 2014) at paras 7–26–7.27; MEPC 67/7 adding the carriage of HFO as ballast to the prohibition.

46 The additional guidance to Chapter I in Part II-B of the Polar Code encourages ships 'to apply regulation 43 of MARPOL Annex I when operating in Arctic waters.' At MEPC 67, several environmental groups proposed in MEPC 67/9/9 (22 August 2014) making this mandatory. MEPC 67 stressed that this would have to be treated as a new work item. See *supra* note 15 and accompanying text. FOEI and others submitted an information paper to MEPC 69 on the harmful effects of the use of HFO in Arctic waters. *Heavy fuel use by vessels in Arctic waters,* MEPC 69/20/1 (12 February 2016) (FOEI and others). After receiving conflicting views on this submission, MEPC 69 noted the contents of the paper and invited interested parties to submit proposals for a new output to address this matter to a future session of the Committee. IMO, *Report of the Marine Environment Protection Committee at its 69th session*, MEPC 69/21 (13 May 2016), at 63, paras 20.3–20.4. MEPC 70 noted the five submissions to MEPC 70, invited Member States and other stakeholders to submit relevant information to future sessions, and noted that further substantive work on these issues would require a new output. MEPC 70/18, para 17.20.

47 The text of IMO, *Revised Guidelines for the Identification and Designation of PSSAs*, Resolution A.982(24) (1 December 2005). The guidelines update IMO, *Guidelines for the Designation of Special Areas under MARPOL 73/78 and Guidelines for the Identification and Designation of Particularly Sensitive Sea Areas*, Resolution A.927(22) (29 November 2001). Consequential amendments to resolution A.982(24) proposed by MEPC 67/10 (22 July 2014) were deferred to MEPC 68, MEPC 67/20, *supra* note 34 at para 10.1. MEPC 68 adopted resolution MEPC.267(68) on Amendments to resolution A.982(24) as set out in Annex 13 to MEPC 68/21/Add.1. MEPC 68/21/Add.1, *supra* note 7 at 48, para 10.3.

criteria, such as significance of the area for recreation or tourism; and scientific and educational criteria, such as biological research or historical value.

An application for PSSA designation should contain a proposal for an associated protective measure (APM), or measures aimed at preventing, reducing or eliminating the threat or identified vulnerability. APMs for PSSAs are limited to actions that are to be, or have been, approved and adopted by the IMO.

When an area is approved as a PSSA, specific measures can be used to control the maritime activities in that area, such as routeing measures; strict application of MARPOL discharge and equipment requirements for ships, such as oil tankers; and installation of VTS. Another routeing measure that can be used in a PSSA is an ATBA (i.e., an area within defined limits in which either navigation is particularly hazardous or it is exceptionally important to avoid casualties and which should be avoided by all ships, or by certain classes of ships).

The guidelines provide advice to IMO Member Governments in the formulation and submission of applications for the designation of PSSAs to ensure that in the process, all interests—those of the coastal State, flag States, and the environmental and shipping communities—are thoroughly considered on the basis of relevant scientific, technical, economic, and environmental information regarding the area at risk of damage from international shipping activities.[48]

An approved PSSA is charted.[49] This serves to warn the mariner of the need for careful navigation. [See Chapter 4 of this Volume for details on approved PSSAs.] A study for the Protection of the Arctic Marine Environment (PAME) Arctic Council Working Group found support for a PSSA for the high seas area of the Arctic Ocean, with APMs of VTS, ship reporting system and ATBA, and establishment of one or more '[c]ore sea ice areas'.[50]

48 The International Chamber of Shipping has publicly stated its desire and willingness to be consulted by States contemplating PSSA submissions, including at ShipArc2015. For a list of IMO approved PSSAs, see Chapter 4, Subsection 3.2.3 of this Volume.

49 IHO Chart Specification B-437.6; MPA Singapore, 'Symbols, Abbreviations, Terms and S-57 Objected used on Singaporean Nautical and Electronic Navigational Charts,' N22, at 37 (2011), accessed 15 March 2017 at http://www.mpa.gov.sg/web/portal/home/publications/chart-symbols-and-abbreviations. See also IMO, *Special Areas and Particularly Sensitive Sea Areas*-- NAV 48/INF.2 (4 April 2002) (IHO).

50 Det Norske Veritas (DNV), 'Report on Specially Designated Marine Areas in the Arctic High Seas', Report No/DNV Reg No: 2013–1442/17JMT1D-26 (11 March 2014) Part I, at 56–60, accessed 15 March 2017 at https://oaarchive.arctic-council.org/handle/11374/1341 (DNV Report).

3.2.3 Emission Control Areas (ECAs)

Another measure the MEPC may consider for the Arctic Ocean is one or more emission control areas. MARPOL Annex VI (Regulations for the Prevention of Air Pollution from Ships (1997)) establishes certain sulphur oxide (SOx) ECAs with more stringent controls on sulphur emissions. Annex VI was revised in 2008 to make the requirements more stringent, including particulate matter, and update the regulations on the establishment of ECAs.[51] This may assist in dealing with the melting caused by the deposit of black carbon on the ice.[52]

4 Compatibility of Coastal State Regulation with the Polar Code[53]

This section considers the adequacy of the Polar Code and associated SOLAS and MARPOL amendments to achieve compatibility with national regulations by coastal States. To assist in understanding the situation, the following briefly describes the relevant national regulations and their compatibility with

---

51 Amendments to MARPOL Annex VI adopted during the October 2008 session of the Marine Environment Protection Committee (by resolution MEPC.176(58)) included a revised regulation 14 on Sulphur Oxides (SOx) and Particulate Matter that permits the establishment of Emission Control Areas. Appendix III provides the criteria and procedures for designation of Emission Control Areas. These amendments entered into force 1 March 2010. The text of the revised Annex VI, IMO, *Report of the Marine Environment Protection Committee on its 53rd Session*, MEPC 53/24/Add.1 (1 August 2005) Annex 13. A list of ECAs may be found at http://www.imo.org/OurWork/Environment/SpecialAreasUnderMARPOL/Pages/Default.aspx, accessed 15 March 2017.

52 For information on the impact of black carbon on the Arctic, see Arctic Monitoring and Assessment Program Working Group (AMAP), 'The Impact of Black Carbon on Arctic Climate', AMAP Technical Report No 4 (2001), accessed 15 March 2017 at http://www.amap.no/documents/doc/the-impact-of-black-carbon-on-arctic-climate/746; the results of PPR 2 consideration in the *Report of the Working Group on Air Pollution from Ships*, PPR 2/WP.5 (22 January 2015) paras 35–47; the *Report to the MEPC*, PPR 2/21 (16 February 2015) paras 8.1–8.7; of PPR 3 in *Report to the Marine Environment Protection Committee*, PPR 3/22 paras 8.1–8.10 and 22.2.6 and .11 (14 March 2016) and the *Report of the Working Group on Air Pollution from Ships*, PPR 3/WP.4 paras 4–9 and Annex 1, *Draft Measurement Reporting Protocol for Black Carbon Determination* (18 February 2016); and the Arctic Council Task Force for Action on Black Carbon and Methane (TFBCM) in *Senior Arctic Officials' Report to Ministers*, Iqaluit, Canada, 24 April 2015, at 8–9 and 118–130, links at http://www.arctic-council.org/index.php/en/task-forces/73-tbcm.

53 The treaty law analysis immediately below is taken from J Ashley Roach and Robert W Smith, *Excessive Maritime Claims*, 3rd ed (Martinus Nijhoff Publishers, 2012) at 493–496.

international law including the Polar Code and associate amendments. As an initial matter, it is clear that domestic legislation that contravenes international law does not justify the deviation.[54]

4.1 *NORDREG*

The action by the Government of Canada to impose the mandatory NORDREG ship reporting unilaterally has been criticised by the United States, other IMO Member States and industry, and was the subject of discussion at the 2010 meetings of the IMO Subcommittee on the Safety of Navigation[55] and the MSC.[56] The criticism is grounded in Canada's failure to follow the requirements of SOLAS to seek IMO approval, particularly Regulation V/11 (Ship-reporting systems) and Regulation V/12 (Vessel traffic services), and the IMO and IALA implementing guidance.[57] See further Chapter 7 of this Volume.

---

54 Vienna Convention on the Law of Treaties, adopted 23 May 1969, entered into force 27 January 1980, 1155 UNTS 331 (VCLT), Art 27: ('[a] party may not invoke the provisions of its internal law as a justification for its failure to perform a treaty'). Canada and Russia are party to the VCLT.

55 IMO, *NAV Report to the MSC*, NAV 56/20 (31 August 2010) at paras 19.21–19.24.

56 IMO, *Safety of Navigation due to Northern Canada Vessel Traffic Services Zone Regulations (Submitted by INTERTANKO and the United States)*, MSC 88/11/2 (22 September 2010), and IMO, *Report of MSC on its 88th session*, MSC 88/26 (15 December 2010) at paras 11.28–11.39 and Annexes 27 (statement of Canada) and 29 (statement of Singapore). At MSC 88, Canada sought but did not receive the Committee's recognition of the mandatory system, MSC 88/26 at para 11.39. See 'Northern Canada Vessel Traffic Service Zone' (2010) *Digest of US Practice in International Law* 514–520, see http://www.state.gov/s/l/c8183.htm and http://www.state.gov/s/l/2010/ch12/index.htm, documents 54a-d for details, both accessed 15 March 2017.

57 IMO, *General Principles for Ship Reporting Systems and Ship Reporting Requirements, including Guidelines for Reporting Incidents involving Dangerous Goods, Harmful Substances and/or Marine Pollutants*, Resolution A.851(20) (27 November 1997); IMO, *Guidance Note on the Preparation of Proposals on Ships' Routeing Systems and Ship Reporting Systems for Submission to the Sub-Committee on Safety of Navigation*, MSC.1/Circ.1060 (6 January 2003); IMO, *Amendment to the Guidance Note on the Preparation of Proposals on Ships' Routeing Systems and Ship Reporting Systems for Submission to the Sub-Committee on Safety of Navigation*, MSC.1/Circ.1060/Add.1 (26 May 2006); IALA, 'Establishment of a Vessel Traffic Service beyond territorial seas', IALA Guideline No 1071 (9 December 2009); and IALA, *Vessel Traffic Services Manual*, 5th ed (IALA, 2012), accessed 15 March 2017 at http://www.pmo.ir/pso_content/media/files/2013/1/22176.pdf. For additional information on VTS, see http://www.imo.org/OurWork/Safety/Navigation/Pages/VesselTrafficServices.aspx, accessed 15 March 2017.

Regardless of the geographic and climatic scope of application of Article 234 discussed in Chapter 7 of this Volume, the assessment would be incomplete without an examination of the relationship between that article and SOLAS Regulations V/8-1 (now V/11) and V/12 under the law of treaties, reflected in the 1969 Vienna Convention on the Law of Treaties (Vienna Convention). Canada is a party to the United Nations Convention on the Law of the Sea (UNCLOS), SOLAS and the Vienna Convention. Under Article 30(3) of the Vienna Convention, 'the earlier treaty applies only to the extent that its provisions are compatible with those of the later treaty'. What constitutes 'incompatibility' is not clear.

A former deputy legal adviser of the UK Foreign and Commonwealth Office, and author of a book on modern treaty law and practice, has written: '[i]n determining which treaty is the earlier and which is the later, the relevant date is the date of adoption, not entry into force.... The obligations under Article 30 [of the Vienna Convention] apply to a state only as from the date it becomes a party to the treaty'.[58]

In this context, UNCLOS is the earlier treaty, as it was adopted on 10 December 1982, while SOLAS Regulation V/8-1 was adopted on 23 May 1994[59] and Regulations V/11 and V/12 were adopted on 5 December 2000.[60] Canada became a party to UNCLOS on 17 November 2003.[61] As the Polar Code has become mandatory, it too is the later treaty.

Since SOLAS Regulations V/8-1, V/11 and V/12, and the Polar Code are setting international rules and standards, and as they are *lex specialis*, 'a specific rule prevails over a general rule',[62] Article 234 of UNCLOS would not permit Canada to enact exceptions to them.

---

58 Anthony Aust, *Modern Treaty Law and Practice*, 3rd ed (Cambridge University Press, 2013) at 204. Accord Ian Sinclair, *The Vienna Convention on the Law of Treaties*, 2nd ed (Manchester University Press, 1984) at 98. Ted L McDorman, 'A Note on the Potential Conflicting Treaty Rights and Obligations between the IMO's Polar Code and Article 234 of the Law of the Sea Convention' in Suzanne Lalonde and Ted L McDorman (eds), *supra* note 6 at 159, opines that this sentence 'makes clear Canada's view that the adopted wording operates as a savings or relationship clause'.

59 IMO, *Adoption of Amendments to the SOLAS Convention*, Resolution MSC.31(63), MSC 63/23/Add.1 Annex 2 (23 May 1994) at 2–3.

60 IMO, *Adoption of Amendments to the SOLAS Convention*, Resolution MSC.99(73), MSC 73/21/Add.2 Annex 7 (5 December 2000) at 128–130.

61 For the status of UNCLOS, see http://www.un.org/Depts/los/reference_files/status2010.pdf, accessed 15 March 2017.

62 Aust, *supra* note 58 at 221.

However, SOLAS Regulations V/8-1(j) (now V/11(9)) and V/12(5) also provide that '[n]othing in this regulation ... shall prejudice the rights and duties of Governments under international law'. Aust states that this provision means that '[t]he treaty is subordinate to an earlier one'.[63] If his analysis is correct, then Article 234 still lives. But then, as discussed in Chapter 7 of this Volume, the geographic and climatic scope of application of Article 234 becomes important to resolve.

4.2 *Northern Sea Route Regulations*

The compatibility of the earlier Russian unilateral actions with international law has similarly been the subject of international attention[64] and need not be repeated here. The evolution of the Russian NSR regulations is discussed in Chapter 6 of this Volume. However, the new Russian Arctic policy has not received much attention and thus needs to be considered in this assessment.

In 2008, then-President Medvedev adopted the 'Basics of the State Policy of the Russian Federation in the Arctic for the period till 2020 and for a further perspective'.[65] Of greatest relevance to this paper is the following provision:

> *Strategic priorities of the state policy of the Russian Federation in the Arctic are ... in the use of the Northern Sea Route for international navigation under the jurisdiction of the Russian Federation and* according to international treaties of the Russian Federation.[66]

63 *Ibid.* at 196, quoting Article 4 of the 1995 UN Fish Stocks Agreement.

64 See J Ashley Roach and Robert W Smith, *Excessive Maritime Claims*, 3rd ed (Martinus Nijhoff Publishers, 2012) at 312–18; James Kraska, 'The New Arctic Geography and US Strategy' in James Kraska (ed), *Arctic Security in an Age of Climate Change* (Cambridge University Press, 2011) at 250 (pilotage fees not related to services rendered); *passim* R Douglas Brubaker, *The Russian Arctic Straits* (Martinus Nijhoff Publishers, 2005); and Erik Franckx, 'The Legal Regime of Navigation in the Russian Arctic' (2009) 18 *Journal of Transnational Law & Policy* 327, www.vliz.be/imisdocs/publications/248348.pdf; and summarised in *The Northern Sea Route: The shortest sea route linking East Asia and Europe* (Ship and Ocean Foundation, 2001) at 85–86, accessed 15 March 2017 at http://www.sof.or.jp/en/report/pdf/200103_rp_ar0103e.pdf.

65 The policy was adopted on 18 September 2008 and promulgated 30 March 2009, the text of which is available online at http://www.arctic-lio.com/docs/nsr/legislation/Policy_of_the_RF_in_the_Arctic.pdf, accessed 15 March 2017.

66 *Ibid.*, para 7(d) (emphasis added).

In 2012, the Russian Duma enacted, and the Council of Federation approved, a 'Federal Law on Amendments to Specific Legislative Acts of the Russian Federation related to Governmental Regulation of Merchant Shipping in the water area of the Northern Sea Route'.[67] In pertinent part, the legislation provided that:

> *Navigation in the water area of the Northern Sea Route, the historically emerged national transportation route of the Russian Federation, shall be performed according to the* commonly accepted principles and norms of the international law, international agreements of the Russian Federation, *this Federal Law, other Federal Laws and other regulatory legal documents issued in relation with the above.*[68]

The relevant international agreements to which Russia is a party are, of course, UNCLOS, the various IMO Conventions and Codes,[69] and the mandatory Polar Code.

The legislation also mandated what the rules on safe navigation of the NSR should contain. It also required that ships desiring to navigate the NSR must receive permits to do so, which are to be issued if the vessel complies with the rules, has adequate insurance and pays for icebreaker support '*based on the amount of services actually delivered*'.[70] As noted above, the regulations are discussed in Chapter 6 of this Volume and need not be repeated here.

However, it may be noted that while payment for ice breaker services is now contingent on the amount of services provided, the requirement to obtain prior permission to transit the NSR is not compatible with the legal regime of straits used for international navigation where the regime of transit passage applies and a notice or permissive requirement is not permitted.[71] In addition,

67 Federal Law No 132-03 (28 July 2012) (Russian Federation), accessed 15 March 2017 at http://www.arctic-lio.com/docs/nsr/legislation/federal_law_nsr.pdf.

68 *Ibid.*, Cl 2, amending Cl 14 of Federal Law No 155-03 (31 July 1998) on Internal Waters, Territorial Sea and Adjacent Zone of the Russian Federation (emphasis added).

69 See Status of IMO Conventions, see http://www.imo.org/About/Conventions/StatusOfConventions/Documents/status-x.xls, accessed 15 March 2017.

70 Act No 132-03, *supra* note 67, Cl 3 (emphasis added). Note that this last provision in quotes, which seems consistent with UNCLOS, *infra* note 71, Art 26, differs from earlier legislation criticised by James Kraska, *supra* note 64 at 250 (pilotage fees not related to services rendered).

71 United Nations Convention on the Law of the Sea, adopted 10 December 1982, 1833 UNTS 397 (entered into force 16 November 1994), (UNCLOS), Art 26 and Part III.

Russia has not obtained IMO approval for its mandatory reporting system, as other States have done for the transit of straits.[72]

Consequently, the next section assesses the relationship of the Polar Code to these national regulations.

5 Legal Effect of Polar Code on National Regulations

In the context of the development of a mandatory Polar Code, Canada and the Russian Federation sought to protect their national regulations regarding foreign shipping in their national Arctic waters from the effects of the Polar Code.[73]

Canada and Russia initially sought explicit exemption for NORDREG and the NSR Regulations, which was not accepted in 2011 after the United States, supported by other delegations, expressed doubt regarding the application of Article 234 of UNCLOS by Canada and Russia, or that the Polar Code in itself would provide the international legal basis for those routeing systems.[74] Although Russia made no further overt efforts in this regard, Canada changed its approach and sought a saving clause in the Polar Code. Ultimately, the MSC decided to put such as clause in the new Chapter XIV of SOLAS, the mechanism by which Part I-A of the Polar Code is to be made mandatory. Regulation 2 of the new SOLAS Chapter XIV provides:

72 See *supra* notes 38 and 39 and accompanying text for details.

73 Michael Byers has reported that on 20 February 2009 the Russian and Canadian Legal Advisers consulted in Moscow on common Arctic concerns: 'Both sides stated a high degree of similarity in their position on the issue of international shipping in the Northwest Passage (Canada) and the **Northern Sea Route** (Russia)—the existing limitations that are being applied to those areas are necessary to preserve the fragile maritime environment and are in sync with the rights that UNCLOS concedes to coastal states in ice-covered areas. Both sides agreed to have more detailed consultations on this topic, including the issue of rights to historical waters in the context of the existing disputes over their status with the US.'—Michael Byers, 'Russia-Canada Consultations on the Legal Status of the Arctic' (*Who Owns the Arctic? Arctic Sovereignty and International Relations*, 20 February 2009)' (emphasis in the original), accessed 15 March 2017 at http://byers.typepad.com/arctic/russiacanada-consultations-on-the-legal-status-of-the-arctic.html.

74 DE 55/22, *supra* note 20 at 24, para 12.7 (2nd para).

5 Nothing in this chapter shall prejudice the rights or obligations of States under international law.[75]

This provision likely protects the Canadian and Russian unilateral national regulations on Arctic shipping from being preempted by the safety provisions of the Polar Code.

Canada proposed a similar statement be included in the amendments to MARPOL Annexes I, II, IV and V by which Part II-A of the Polar Code would be made mandatory. However, the MEPC decided that an existing statement in Article 9(2) of the MARPOL Convention will suffice.[76] Article 9(2) provides:

> Nothing in the present Convention shall prejudice … the present or future claims and legal views of any State concerning the law of the sea and the nature and extent of coastal and flag State jurisdiction.

At MEPC 66, Canada expressed satisfaction with this outcome,[77] presumptively believing this provision likely protects the Canadian (and Russian) unilateral national regulations on Arctic shipping from being preempted by the pollution prevention provisions of the Polar Code.

Nevertheless, the International Chamber of Shipping (ICS) has called for

> *all current national maritime regulatory regimes applicable to Arctic waters, within the jurisdiction of States that are members of the Arctic Council, [to] be harmonized in conformity with the final IMO 'Polar Code', as well as all other relevant IMO Conventions and Codes, consistent with the provisions of the United Nations Convention on the Law of the Sea (UNCLOS). Arctic nations should only apply requirements to foreign flag ships consistent with 'generally accepted international rules and standards' (GAIRAS).*[78]

ICS further stated it 'believes that the UNCLOS regime of transit passage for straits used for international navigation (as codified in Part III of UNCLOS) takes precedence over the rights of coastal States under Article 234'. ICS also urged that relationship between Article 234 and the transit passage regime

75 MSC 94/21/Add.1 Annex 7, *supra* note 8 at 4.

76 IMO, *Report of the MEPC on its 66th Session*, MEPC 66/21 (25 April 2014) at 54, para 11.47.

77 *Ibid.*, Annex 20 at 12.

78 International Chamber of Shipping, *Arctic Shipping Position Paper* (2014), http://www.ics-shipping.org/docs/default-source/Submissions/Other/ics-position-paper-on-arctic-shipping.pdf.

should be clarified, as well as the meaning of the various terms used in Article 234 given the diminution of polar ice.[79] It may be noted that Article 234 requires '[s]uch laws and regulations shall have due regard to navigation…'

Thus, depending on how Canada and the Russian Federation implement the Polar Code, the adequacy of the Polar Code to bring national regulations into conformity with the Polar Code and other rules of international law will be tested.

6 Implementation and Enforcement

UNCLOS and the IMO instruments place primary responsibility for implementation and enforcement of their provisions on the flag State. However, experience has shown that many flag States cannot be relied on to carry out those responsibilities. Hence, it has fallen to port States to do so. Consequently, there are no provisions in the Polar Code for enforcement of its provisions, relying instead on existing provisions in UNCLOS and the IMO instruments.

6.1 *Port State Control*

Port State Control is the inspection of foreign flag ships in national ports to verify the condition of the ship and its equipment comply with the requirements of international regulations and that the ship is manned and operated in compliance with these rules. The basis in codified international law for port State control lies in provisions of UNCLOS[80] and the IMO treaties.[81] Guidance on the conduct of port State control is contained IMO Assembly resolution A.1052(27) (2011). In addition, there are nine regional agreements on port State control to coordinate the inspections to focus on substandard ships and avoid multiple inspections.[82]

It can be expected that the IMO resolution will be revised to include guidance regarding compliance with the Polar Code. The question arises how and whether the Tokyo and Paris MOU port State control maritime authorities,

79 *Ibid.*

80 UNCLOS, *supra* note 71, Arts 94(6) and 219.

81 SOLAS, *supra* note 2, Regs I/19, IX/6.2, XI-1/4, XI-2/9; MARPOL, *supra* note 3, Annex I, Arts 5 and 6 and Reg 11, Annex II Reg 16.9, Annex III Reg 8, Annex IV Reg 13, Annex V Reg 8, Annex VI Reg 10; STCW, *supra* note 4, Art X and Reg I/4; Load Lines Convention, Art 21; Tonnage Convention, Art 121; Anti-Foulants Convention, Art 11.

82 See IMO, 'Port State Control' at http://www.imo.org/en/OurWork/MSAS/Pages/PortStateControl.aspx, accessed 15 March 2017.

Canada and the US Coast Guard will coordinate and cooperate to examine compliance by merchant shipping transiting Arctic waters with the Polar Code and implementing SOLAS, MARPOL and STCW regulations.

Port State control can also be expected to include inspections to verify compliance with anti-fouling requirements and ballast water control (when the latter enters into force in 2017).

6.2 *ISPS Code*

Following September 11, the IMO adopted special measures to enhance maritime security, as amendments to SOLAS (Chapter XI-2) and the International Ship and Port Facility Security (ISPS) Code.[83] These are applicable to commercial ships that could be expected to traverse the Arctic Ocean, and will be applicable to ports on the rim.[84]

7 Summary and Conclusions

It will be recalled that the Polar Code is not a stand-alone instrument, but must be assessed in the context of the related IMO provisions and other instruments of international law.

The Polar Code that entered into force on 1 January 2017 is just the first edition. As experience with it develops improvements will be needed. Some changes are already contemplated. Others are evidently needed.

The contemplated changes include expanding the types of ships to which the Code applies to fishing vessels and ships less than 500 gross tonnes.

This Chapter has identified other amendments that need to be made to ensure the Code is applicable to SOLAS ships on purely domestic voyages. There needs to be a commitment from Canada and Russia to apply the Polar Code to its vessels navigating in Arctic waters, and to conform their domestic regulations to international law including IMO requirements.

In addition, amendments to the STCW Convention and Code are up for adoption by MSC at its meeting in November 2016. There remains the question of the need for ice navigators and not relying solely on obtaining on-the-job experience of masters, chief mates and officers of the watch.

---

83 SOLAS, *supra* note 2, Chapter XI-2 (Special Measures To Enhance Maritime Security) and the International Ship and Port Facility Security Code, adopted 12 December 2002, by the Conference of Contracting Governments to the International Convention for the Safety of Life at Sea, 1974.

84 SOLAS, *supra* note 2, Reg XI-2/2.

The guidelines for the conduct of port State control inspections need to be updated to include the relevant provisions of the Polar Code, beginning with the new certification and ship-specific manual requirements. The Tokyo and Paris MOUs need to be suitably updated as do the US Coast Guard Port State Control rules. Consideration should be given to an Arctic Port State Control MOU as a coordinating instrument.

This Chapter is an initial assessment of the Polar Code. Only in the future will it be seem if the Polar Code and associated and future amendments meet the goal of 'increas[ing] the safety of ships' operation and mitigat[ing] the impact on the people and environment in the remote, vulnerable and potentially harsh polar waters'.

PART 3

Rights, Interests, Positions and Practice of Arctic Coastal States

CHAPTER 6

Russia

Jan J Solski[1]

1 Introduction

Russia's role in the governance of Arctic shipping is difficult to overestimate. It is the key coastal State bordering the Northeast Passage (NEP)—widely believed to be the most practical of Arctic shipping routes—and the only coastal State bordering the Northern Sea Route (NSR) (see Figure 6.1).[2] With respect to the NSR, Russia has committed itself to developing and regulating shipping through it. As Vladimir Putin stated at the International Arctic Forum in 2011, Russia's interest lies in 'turning [the NSR] into a key commercial route of global importance, capable of competing with traditional sea routes in all respects'.[3]

Russia sees a well-functioning NSR as a key feature in its grand plan to reassert its Arctic presence and, among other things, reap the benefits from the Arctic as a 'national strategic resource base'.[4] The Soviet Union,[5] by means of a

1 The author is very grateful for assistance and/or comments received from Alex Oude Elferink, Erik Franckx, Kristine Dalaker Kraabel, Erik J Molenaar, J Ashley Roach, and his colleagues from JCLOS on earlier versions. Mistakes or omissions remain the sole responsibility of the author.

2 The Merchant Shipping Code of the Russian Federation, 30 April 1999, No 81 FZ, (Merchant Shipping Code) includes a definition of the NSR (see *infra* note 45). It forms part of the wider and more generic concept of the NEP—a maritime passage between Atlantic and Pacific ports along the northern coast of Eurasia.

3 Putin, Vladimir, Speech at the International Arctic Forum 'The Arctic—Territory of Dialogue', Arkhangelsk, 22 September 2011, accessed 17 March 2017 at http://archive.government.ru/eng/docs/16536/.

4 The Basics of the State Policy of the Russian Federation in the Arctic for the period till 2020 and for a further perspective, adopted 18 September 2008, promulgated 30 March 2009 (2008 Basics of Arctic Policy). For a recent analysis of Russia's policy regarding Arctic maritime transport, see Katarzyna Zysk, 'Russia turns north, again: interests, policies and the search for coherence' in Leif Christian Jensen, Geir Honneland (eds), *Handbook of the Politics of the Arctic* 437–462, at 442–445.

5 Russia views itself as the continuing State of the Union of Soviet Socialist Republics (USSR or the Soviet Union) and in this Chapter, it is regarded as such.

 | DOI 10.1163/9789004339385_007

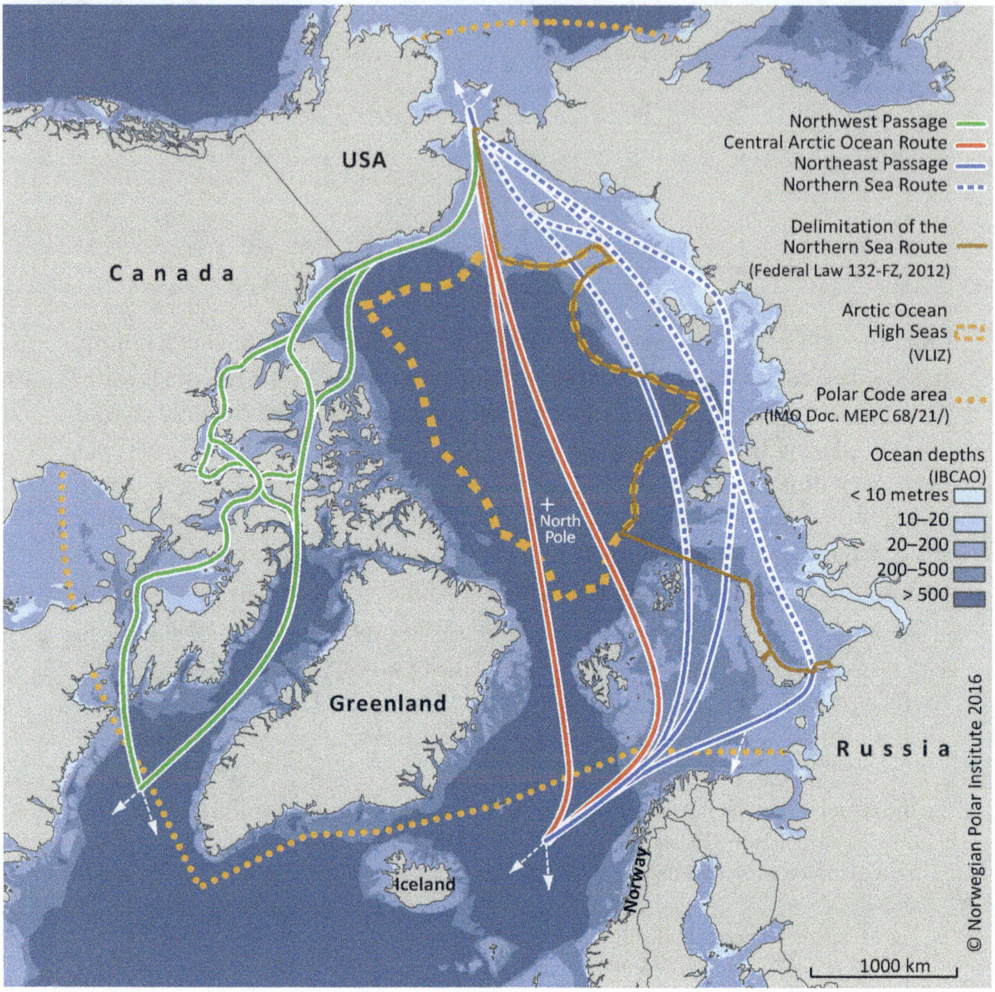

FIGURE 6.1 *Russia and the Northeast Passage and Northern Sea Route*

formidable and concentrated effort, developed the route for military and civil purposes[6] as a domestic transport line to assist exploitation of the resources

6 The official 'development' of the NSR commenced in 1932 with the establishment of a dedicated body—the Chief Directorate of the Northern Sea Route (rus. Glavsevmorput)—essentially a remote prototype of the present Administration of the NSR, see *infra* note 42 and accompanying text. The differences between these or other organisational structures that were formed and disbanded over the history of functioning of the NSR are not covered here. Some insight on this topic can be found in Leonid Tymchenko, 'The Northern Sea

from the Arctic region and link remote Arctic settlements with the rest of the country. Following the dissolution of the USSR[7] in 1991 and the concomitant economic and political transitions, Russia needed to adjust its NSR management system. Notably, the NSR's cargo turnover plummeted approximately fourfold between 1987 and 1998.[8] In recent years, the overall volumes of cargo transport on the NSR have been growing slowly, although mostly due to domestic shipments auxiliary to the construction of a liquid natural gas (LNG) plant on the Yamal Peninsula.[9] Increased traffic on the NSR, including foreign shipping and the revenue generated by it, will be key to funding the costly infrastructure investments critical for the integrated development plan that the Russian government proposed in June 2015.[10] Despite the decline in international interests for the NSR, the Russian authorities remain optimistic about the future development of shipping on the NSR. They seem to acknowledge a larger potential for destination traffic,[11] as well as the need for more

---

Route: Russian Management and Jurisdiction over Navigation in Arctic Seas' in Alex G Oude Elferink and Donald R Rothwell (eds) *The Law of the Sea and Polar Maritime Delimitation and Jurisdiction* (Kluwer Law International, 2001) 269–291, at 272–275; and Alexander I Arikaynen, 'Management of the Northern Sea Route: stages and problems of development' in Lawson W Brigham (ed) *The Soviet Maritime Arctic* (Naval Institute Press, 1991) at 140–149.

7 *Supra* note 5.

8 As reported by Ivan V Bunik and Vladimir V Mikhaylichenko, 'Legal Aspects of Navigation through the Northern Sea Route' in Paul Arthur Berkman, Alexander N Vylegzhanin (eds) *Environmental Security in the Arctic Ocean* (Springer, 2013) 233; there was a drop from 6,579,000 to 1,458,000 tons.

9 According to Trude Pettersen, 'Declining interest in use of Northern Sea Route' *The Independent Barents Observer* (18 March 2016), accessed 17 March 2017 at http://www.thebarentsobserver.com/industry/2016/03/declining-interest-use-northern-sea-route. The total NSR turnover in 2015 was 5,300,000 tons. At the same time, the volumes of cargo moved in transit dropped dramatically from 1,262,000 tons in 2012 to under 40,000 tons in 2015.

10 To address the issue of the less than satisfactory development of shipping on the NSR, Russian Prime Minister Medvedev signed the order on the integrated development plan for the NSR 2015–2030 on 8 June 2015. The order's text is classified, but some information about it has been revealed at the website of the Government, accessed 17 March 2017 at http://m.government.ru/orders/18405/ [in Russian].

11 'Northern Sea Route—focus on domestic projects' *The Barents Observer* (17 October 2015), accessed 17 March 2017 at http://barentsobserver.com/en/arctic/2015/10/northern-sea-route-focus-domestic-projects-17-10.

concentrated efforts to unlock the potential of the NSR.[12] In any event, the increase in international use shall not prejudice the status of the NSR as a 'national transport communication'.[13] As part of its strategy to revive the NSR, Russia adopted the 2012 Federal Law in order to reform its legislation dedicated to the regulation of navigation on the NSR.[14]

Russia has imposed regulatory measures unilaterally, which affect access to and navigation on the NSR that extend beyond coastal State jurisdiction under the *general* law of the sea. Although unilateralism is *in principle* permitted by Article 234 of UNCLOS,[15] the scope and extent of Russia's coastal State jurisdiction in the Arctic are not entirely clear. Russia is, along with Canada, a State that has pioneered the interpretation and application of Article 234. In addition, Russian commentators often attach significant weight to historical circumstances, justifying in their view Russia's authority to regulate shipping on the NSR.[16] Traditionally, this argument dominated the Soviet/Russian scholarly domain, regardless of much more modest official governmental policy, to which other governments filed diplomatic protests.[17] Although the present significance of this argument appears limited, it deserves attention in order to understand Russia's current regulatory practices.

The present Chapter examines how Russia interprets and implements relevant rules of international law of the sea within the context of the regulation of navigation in the Arctic. Section 2 discusses Russia's coastal State jurisdiction in the Arctic, with particular attention to the distinct legal regime for the

---

12 There seems to exist widespread support in Russia to set up a single transport logistics operator of the NSR, as discussed during a meeting of the State Commission for Arctic Development in Arkhangelsk on 24 May 2016, accessed 17 March 2017 at http://arctic.gov.ru/News/733dd4de-b720-e611-80cc-e672fe4e8e4e?nodeId=0778abc6-cd4b-e511-825f-10604b797c23&page=1&pageSize=10 [in Russian]. The Independent Barents Observer reports that this role will be assigned to Oboronlogistika—a company owned by the Russian Ministry of Defence, see Atle Staalesen, 'Ministry of Defense takes charge of Arctic shipping' *The Independent Barents Observer* (7 July 2016), accessed 17 March 2017 at http://thebarentsobserver.com/security/2016/07/ministry-defense-takes-charge-arctic-shipping.

13 The Maritime Doctrine of the Russian Federation signed 26 July 2015 (2015 Maritime Doctrine), accessed 17 March 2017 at http://static.kremlin.ru/media/events/files/ru/uAFi5nvux2twaqjftS5yrIZUVTJan77L.pdf [in Russian], see *infra* note 68 and accompanying text.

14 Federal Law on Amendments to Specific Legislative Acts of the Russian Federation Concerning the State Regulation of Merchant Shipping in the Water Area of the NSR, 28 July 2012, No 132 FZ (2012 Federal Law).

15 United Nations Convention for the Law of the Sea, adopted 10 December 1982, 1833 UNTS 3 (entered into force 16 November 1994) (UNCLOS).

16 See *infra* note 98 and accompanied text.

17 *Infra* note 109.

NSR. Section 3 examines Russia's view on the international legal basis for this regime, and Section 4 is devoted to the analysis of Russia's regulatory practice within this area. The Chapter ends with concluding remarks.

2 Russia's Coastal State Jurisdiction within Arctic Waters

2.1 *Russian Maritime Zones within Arctic Waters*

The International Code for Ships Operating in Polar Waters (Polar Code) provides a useful and convenient definition of Arctic waters in the context of navigation,[18] and for this reason, it serves as the point of departure for the present discussion.[19]

A significant part of the Arctic waters as defined in the Polar Code consists of Russia's maritime zones.[20] They are measured from the baselines established by the USSR Council of Ministers on 15 January 1985 and have not been amended since then.[21] These include normal and straight baselines, but the latter enclose almost all crucial NSR straits.[22] The following straits, presented

18 For the definition and illustrations, see Chapter 5 of this Volume and Figure 6.1 of the present Chapter. The text of the Code is included in IMO Doc MEPC 68/21/Add.1, Annex 10.

19 Although this definition relies on the premise that waters covered by the Polar Code are substantially different from adjacent waters when examined through a 'navigational' lens, it should not be mistaken for the notion of 'ice-covered areas' as used in Article 234 of UNCLOS.

20 The following maritime zones are of relevance: Russia's internal waters, its territorial sea and its exclusive economic zone (EEZ), since they have a bearing on the legal regime of navigation.

21 The USSR Council of Ministers, Decree of 15 January 1985, the English text is available at http://www.un.org/Depts/los/LEGISLATIONANDTREATIES/PDFFILES/RUS_1985_Declaration.pdf, accessed 17 March 2017.

22 The international legal validity of Russian Arctic baselines is not settled, as the baselines, in part, exhibit discrepancies with traditional criteria for the establishment of baselines. See scholarly assessment in William V Dunlap, 'Transit passage in the Russian Arctic straits' Maritime Briefings 1(7), International Boundaries Research Unit, University of Durham 1996 with maps in Appendix 2 at 57–59; and Douglas R Brubaker, 'The Legal Status of the Russian Baselines in the Arctic' (1999) 30 *Ocean Development and International Law* 191–233. Russian scholars also presented critical views on these baselines, see Alexander S Skaridov, *Morskoe Pravo, Uchebnik dlya magistrov*, 2nd ed (Moscow Yurayt, 2012) at 526; Irina Mikhina, *Mezhdunarodno-pravovoi rezhim morskikh prostranstv Arktiki*, A Thesis for a degree of Candidate of Science in Law (Moscow Sojuzmorniiprojekt, 2003) at 141. The United States objects to the characterisation of 'certain straits used for international

in order of their geographical location moving eastwards, lie within baselines: the Matochkin Shar, Kara Gates and Yugorskii Shar—connecting the Barents Sea with the Kara Sea; the Vilkitskii, Shokalskii, Red Army and Yungshturm Straits—connecting the Kara and Laptev Seas; and the Dimitri Laptev and Sannikov Straits—connecting the Laptev and East Siberian Seas. Russia regards waters within these straits as internal waters. Notably, due to their location, these straight baselines only have a limited effect on the location of the 200 nautical mile (nm) limit of the exclusive economic zone (EEZ).

In recent years, the Russian government has turned its attention to investigating a possibility for amending the coordinates of its Arctic baselines. Neither the 2001 Maritime Doctrine of the Russian Federation nor the 2008 Basics of Arctic Policy indicated a need for amending or clarifying the Arctic baselines.[23] In 2010, however, Russia's Ministry of Economic Development, as part of its work under the Federal Program 'World Ocean',[24] announced a tender on, *inter alia*, a scientific contribution to seek legal and historical justification for amendments to Russia's Arctic baselines.[25] Although the coordinates for Russia's Arctic baselines have not been amended, there has been a considerable change in how more recent policy documents address this issue. For instance, the 2013 Arctic Development Strategy calls for hydrographic work to determine the need for amendments to the list of geographical coordinates of the Arctic baselines.[26] In the same vein, the 2015 Maritime Doctrine calls for the clarification of straight baselines along the Arctic coast.[27] As these tasks had not been completed, the issue of Russia's Arctic baselines adjust-

---

navigation' as internal waters, see the Diplomatic Note from the United States to Russia regarding the NSR, 29 May 2015, reproduced in CarrieLyn D Guymon (ed), *Digest Of United States Practice In International Law 2015*, Office of the Legal Adviser US Department of State (2015 US Diplomatic Note to Russia) at 526–528. Formerly, the United States lodged a formal protest against significant parts of the claimed Russian baselines, but not specifically against any of the baselines closing the entrance to NSR straits, see J Ashley Roach and Robert W Smith, *Excessive Maritime Claims*, 3rd ed (Nijhoff, 2012) at 97.

23 The Maritime Doctrine of the Russian Federation, signed 7 June 2001 (2001 Maritime Doctrine); 2008 Basics of Arctic Policy, see *supra* note 4.

24 Purpose-Oriented Federal Program World Ocean, approved by Decree of the President of the Russian Federation No 11, dated 11 January 1997.

25 Order of the Ministry of Economic Development of the Russian Federation No 356, dated 10 August 2010, issue with reference number 2002–07–10.

26 The Development Strategy of the Russian Arctic Zone for the Period until 2020, Items 18 e and 29 в (2013 Arctic Development Strategy), accessed 17 March 2017 at http://government.ru/media/files/2RpSA3sctElhAGn4RN9dHrtzkoA3wZm8.pdf [in Russian].

27 2015 Maritime Doctrine, *supra* note 13, Item 61 щ.

ment was a matter of discussion at a meeting of the State Commission for Arctic Development on 24 May 2016.[28] The Commission's chair—Rogozin[29]—explained that the current coordinates 'did not correspond to the geophysical situation and the fundamental interests of Russia in the Arctic', and asked a representative from the Ministry of Defence (MoD) to inform the Commission about the progress of work.[30] Fedotenkov[31] (MoD) clarified that they expect to 'finalize the draft list of baseline coordinates' by 2020,[32] and added that the MoD had prepared a draft proposal to extend the geographical scope of historic waters.[33]

The regime of Russia's internal waters, territorial sea and contiguous zone is set out in the Federal Law No 155-FZ on the Internal Waters, the Territorial Sea and the Contiguous Zone of the Russian Federation' (1998 Federal Law on the IWTSCZ).[34] This law implements UNCLOS and explicitly recognises the legal regime of innocent passage, but it does not address the legal regime of transit passage related to straits used for international navigation.[35] The legal regime of the EEZ is set out in the 1998 Federal Law on the Exclusive Economic Zone (1998 Federal Law on the EEZ).[36] Article 32 of this act incorporates, *inter alia*, the wording of Article 234 of UNCLOS.[37]

---

28 A protocol from the meeting is available at http://arctic.gov.ru/News/f247f09f-bd33-e611-80cc-e672fe4e8e4e?nodeId=0778abc6-cd4b-e511-825f-10604b797c23&page=1&pageSize=10 [in Russian], accessed 17 March 2017.

29 Deputy Prime Minister of the Russian Federation and the Chairman of the State Commission for Arctic Development.

30 As reported by Ekaterina Zgirovskaya from Gazeta.ru, available at http://m.gazeta.ru/army/2016/05/24/8261825.shtml [in Russian], accessed 17 March 2017.

31 Russian Navy Deputy Commander and a person representing the MoD at the meeting of the State Commission for Arctic Development on 24 May 2016.

32 Zgirovskaya, *supra* note 30.

33 *Ibid.* For the historic waters currently claimed by Russia in the Arctic, see *infra* notes 104–109 and accompanying text. For the relationship between historic waters and the concept of historic rights, see *infra* note 70.

34 Federal Law of the Russian Federation of July 31, 1998 No 155-FZ, 'On the internal sea waters, territorial sea and contiguous zone of the Russian Federation', as amended and supplemented (1998 Federal Law on the IWTSCZ).

35 *Ibid.*, Arts 10–13.

36 The Federal Law of the Russian Federation of December 17, 1998 No 191-FZ, 'On the exclusive economic zone of the Russian Federation', as amended and supplemented (1998 Federal Law on the EEZ).

37 *Ibid.*, Art 32.

2.2 *The Distinct Legal Regime for Navigation on the NSR*

Russia has strictly regulated foreign navigation on the NSR since the 'official opening' of this route for international shipping in 1991.[38] In recent years, Russia revised the legal regime of navigation on the NSR. On 28 July 2012, President Putin signed the 2012 Federal Law,[39] amending the 1998 Federal Law on the IWTSCZ,[40] the Federal Law on Natural Monopolies,[41] and the Merchant Shipping Code. The last enactment serves as the legal basis for the establishment of the Administration of the NSR (ANSR)[42] and a dedicated set of rules of navigation, the 2013 Rules.[43]

The Merchant Shipping Code classifies a part of the Arctic waters under Russian coastal State jurisdiction as the 'area of the NSR'.[44] Article 5.1 defines this notion as:

> [A] water area adjoining the northern coast of the Russian Federation, including internal sea waters, territorial sea, contiguous zone and exclusive

---

38 Suggestions of opening the NSR for foreign shipping had been made earlier by Bekayev in 1967 and later by Gorbachev in 1987, both to no avail for different reasons, see Erik Franckx, 'The Legal Regime of Navigation in the Russian Arctic' (2009) 18 *Journal of Transnational Law & Policy*, 327–342 at 328–329. The 1990 Regulations for Navigation on the Seaways of the Northern Sea Route, approved on 14 September 1990, published on 18 June 1991 in 29 Izvesheniia Moreplavateliam (1990 Regulations) laid out the legal framework for access and navigation on the NSR for vessels of all States. Later they were supplemented with the 1996 Guide to Navigating through the NSR; the 1996 Regulations for Icebreaker and Pilot Guiding of Vessels through the NSR; and the 1996 Requirements for the Design, Equipment, and Supplies of Vessels Navigating the NSR. English texts of the latter two documents are available at http://www.arctic-lio.com/nsr_legislation, accessed 17 March 2017.

39 See *supra* note 14.

40 1998 Federal Law on the IWTSCZ, *supra* note 34.

41 The Federal Law on Natural Monopolies, No 147-FZ, 17 August 1995, as amended.

42 Set up by the Order of the Government of Russian Federation № 358-p, 15 March 2013, adopted on the basis of Article 5.1 (3) of the Merchant Shipping Code.

43 Rules of Navigation in the Water Area of the Northern Sea Route, as approved by the order of the Ministry of Transport of Russia, dated 17 January 2013 № 7, (2013 Rules) are based on Article 5.1.1 of the Merchant Shipping Code.

44 In Russian, the chosen term is 'akvatoria', which can directly translate into 'a water area'. This term denotes a clearly designated area and is not 'normally' used in other contexts than to denote an area of a port. There is no official English translation available for most of the relevant Russian legislation. This Chapter usually relies on the unofficial translations provided by the website of the ANSR. When the translation of different terms is not consistent, the author provides his own translation; see, for instance, *infra* note 200 and accompanying text.

> economic zone of the Russian Federation, and limited in the East by the line delimitating the sea areas with the United States of America and by the parallel of the Dezhnev Cape in the Bering Strait; in the West, by the meridian of the Cape Zhelanie to the Novaya Zemlya archipelago, by the east coastal line of the Novaya Zemlya archipelago and the western limits of the Matochkin Shar, Kara Gates, Yugorski Shar Straits.[45]

This definition determines the geographical scope of the NSR, including its lateral and outer limits.[46] This is quite an important novelty, since the 1990 Regulations defined the NSR in such a way that the northern limits could extend beyond 200 nm from Russia's baselines.[47] The indeterminacy of the NSR's geographical scope under the previous definition made some commentators question whether ships could navigate the NEP without having to comply with the rules of the NSR regime.[48] The 2012 Federal Law resolved this this issue by clarifying that the 2013 Rules do not apply seaward of the outer limits of the Russian EEZ in the Kara, Laptev or East-Siberian Seas. However, due to factors such as ice conditions in high latitudes, limited availability of charts or emergency assistance, it currently does not seem to be practical for ships to navigate through the NEP without entering the NSR.

For the purpose of navigation, the Merchant Shipping Code treats the whole area of the NSR as one distinct area with a uniform legal regime, in spite of the fact that it encompasses different maritime zones.[49] A unique feature of the NSR

45 Merchant Shipping Code, *supra* note 2, Art 5.1.

46 For illustration, see Figure 6.1 Although in the 2015 US Diplomatic Note to Russia, *supra* note 22, the United States seeks confirmation that the NSR does not extend into areas of high seas, as well as clarification of the eastern limits of the NSR.

47 Pursuant to Item 1.2 of the 1990 Regulations, they are applied in Russia's maritime zones and, possibly in addition, on 'seaways suitable for leading in ice'. See, for instance, Jan J Solski, 'New Developments in Russian Regulation of Navigation on the Northern Sea Route' (2013) 4 *Arctic Review on Law and Politics* 90–119 at 95–96; Erik Franckx, 'The "New" Arctic Passages and the "Old" Law of the Sea' in Henrik Ringbom (ed) *Jurisdiction over Ships: Post-UNCLOS Developments in the Law of the Sea* (Brill, 2015) 194–216, at 212.

48 Before the 2012 Federal Law clarified the NSR boundaries, particularly its northward limit, the difference between the two notions was unclear. See, for instance, Erik Franckx and Laura Boone, 'The Northeast Passage and the Northern Sea Route: Unity in Division?' *The 18th International Seminar on Sea Names: Asian and European Perspectives* (Brussels 2012); Solski, *supra* note 47 at 95–96.

49 Irina N Mikhina, 'Sovremennye problemy mezhdunarodno-pravovoi zashity vod Arktiki' in Roman A Kolodkin, Sergey M Punzhin (eds) *Mezhdunarodnoe morskoe pravo. Statii pamyati A. L. Kolodkina* (Statut, 2014) 254–278, at 275; Andrey M Ivanov, 'Severnyi Morskoi Put": Kolizii v Prave i Perspektivy Razvitiya, Istoriya Izucheniya Arktiki—ot proshlogo k budushemu: tr. Nauch. Konf. (Arkhangelsk, 12–13 September 2012) Spb 2013, 107–117, at 113.

is the lack of a single and constant most convenient route used for navigation. The availability of a navigable route can vary depending on the season of navigation or the given conditions, such as the presence and qualities of ice,[50] rapidly changing weather or other factors.[51] Vessels can enter and navigate within the NSR if they obtain a permit from the ANSR.

The ANSR is tasked with administrative and coordinative duties to ensure safe navigation and protect the marine environment in the NSR from vessel-source pollution.[52] Its main functions include: processing applications for permits; monitoring hydro-meteorological, ice and navigation conditions; providing relevant information and recommendations; and providing assistance in emergency response.[53] Russia's authority to coordinate shipping on the NSR is less extensive under the 2013 Rules than it was under the 1990 Regulations. The most significant change in this respect is the abolishment of the Marine Operations Headquarters (MOHs), which operated within the structure of the previous Administration of the NSR.[54] MOHs were located in two Russian Arctic ports—Dikson and Pevek—and were empowered within their respective portions of the NSR to exercise constant and active control over traffic, including prescribing different modes of 'guiding' to individual vessels.[55] The abolishment of these MOHs leaves a larger measure of responsibility for maritime safety to individual vessels, which can plan and execute their voyages without being compelled to follow specific instructions from the shore.

---

50 In particular the location of shore ice and ice massifs.

51 Vladimir Golitsyn, 'The Legal Regime of the Arctic' in David Joseph Attard, Malgosia Fitzmaurice, Norman A Martinez Gutierrez (eds) *The IMLI Manual on International Maritime Law: Volume I: The Law of the Sea* (Oxford University Press, 2014) at 472.

52 After the ANSR website, accessed 17 March 2017 at http://www.nsra.ru/en/celi_funktsii/.

53 Merchant Shipping Code, *supra* note 2, Art 5.1.3.

54 Item 1.7 of the 1990 Regulations defined MOHs as special navigational services of the Murmansk and Far East Shipping Companies, directly performing ice operations on the NSR, under the general coordination by the Administration of the NSR.

55 With a view to ensuring maritime safety and providing favourable navigation conditions, the MOHs were entitled to prescribe one of the following types of guiding: shore-based, aircraft, conventional or icebreaker guiding, or icebreaker assisted pilotage, see Item 1.4 of the 1996 Regulations for Icebreaker and Pilot Guiding of Vessels through the NSR and Item 7.4 of the 1990 Regulations.

2.3 *The Barents Sea and the Bering Sea*

For the sake of completeness, it should be noted that the NSR—as defined in Article 5.1 of the Merchant Shipping Code—does not include any portions of the Barents Sea or the Bering Sea.[56]

Interestingly, the Pechora Sea—a part of the Barents Sea—was considered as a possible area to be included within the NSR. In 2010, Russia's Arctic and Antarctic Research Institute (AARI) recommended that Article 234 of UNCLOS could be applied up to the line linking Cape Kanin Nos and Cape Kostin Nos (which lies west from the current boundaries of the NSR), essentially placing the Pechora Sea within the special legal regime based on Article 234.[57] Among the reasons for not including the Pechora Sea within the NSR was, arguably, the possible detrimental effect to the profitability of economic activity in the Pechora Sea, where the first operating commercial Arctic offshore oil-drilling platform, Prirazlomnaya, is located.[58] Regardless, the Kara Gate—linking the Barents and the Kara Seas—has served as the traditional NSR border for many decades, and maintaining it shows devotion to the history of the development of the NSR.[59]

56 See *supra* note 45 for the geographical scope of the NSR. In the 2015 US Diplomatic Note to Russia, *supra* note 22, the United States requested Russia to clarify whether the NSR extends into the Bering Strait.

57 This essentially relies on Vsevolod Peresypkin, Razvitie Severnogo Morskogo Puti, Морской флот №1–3 (2011), accessed 17 March 2017 at http://www.morvesti.ru/tems/detail.php?ID=28072 [in Russian], where he refers to and cites excerpts from the letter received from AARI.

58 See, for instance, arguments by Denis Selivanov, assistant to the Governor of the Nenets Autonomous Okrug, accessed 17 March 2017 at http://severnash.ru/economics/sevmorput/5623-izmenenie-granic-sevmorputi-grozit-udorozhaniem-severnogo-zavoza.html [in Russian].

59 The Barents Sea was not included in the NSR as it was defined under the 1990 Regulations; however, as noted by Franckx, *supra* note 47 at 212, when the Chief Directorate of the Northern Sea Route was first established on 17 December 1932, its competence extended all the way from the White Sea to the Bering Strait. See The Decree of the Council of Peoples' Commissars of the USSR of December 17, 1932, On the Organization in the Council of Peoples' Commissars of the USSR of the Central Administration of the Northern Sea Route, Sobr. Zak I Rasp SSSR, 1932, I, No 84, para 522, as reprinted in Timothy A Taracouzio, *Soviets in the Arctic: An historical, Economic and Political Study of the Soviet Advance into the Arctic* (Macmillan Company, 1938) at 383.

3 The International Legal Basis for the NSR Legal Regime

3.1 *Introduction*

States are under no obligation to reveal explicitly the international legal basis for specific measures in their national legislation, but it is a fundamental matter that international law is observed.[60] Moreover, a State may not invoke its domestic legislation to justify its non-compliance with international law.[61]

The Russian Constitution allows the incorporation of international law into the Russian domestic legal system.[62] According to paragraph 4 of Article 15 of the Russian Constitution, generally recognised principles and norms of international law and the international treaties of the Russian Federation are an integral part of its legal system. Moreover, as the same provision ensures, the rules of an international treaty take primacy over inconsistent domestic law.[63] Correspondingly and more specifically, Article 14 of the 1998 Federal Law on the IWTSCZ stipulates that navigation in the water area of the NSR 'shall be carried out according to generally recognised principles and norms of international law, international treaties of the Russian Federation, the present Federal Law, other federal laws and other normative legal acts issued in accordance to them'.[64] Russia's relevant international legal rights and obligations follow from the international law of the sea, which includes but is not limited to UNCLOS[65] and instruments adopted by the International Maritime Organization (IMO).

The position of the Russian government regarding the international legal basis for the legal regime of the NSR is not clear. It appears that different parts

---

60 *Pacta sunt servanda*, as reflected in the Vienna Convention on the Law of Treaties, adopted 23 May 1969, 1155 UNTS 331 (entered into force 27 January 1980) (VCLT), Art 26, accessed 17 March 2017 at http://treaties.un.org/doc/Publication/UNTS/Volume%201155/v1155.pdf.

61 *Ibid.*, Art 27.

62 Constitution of the Russian Federation, 23 December 1993, Art 15(4), accessed 17 March 2017 at http://www.rg.ru/2009/01/21/konstitucia-dok.html [in Russian].

63 *Ibid.*

64 1998 Federal Law on the IWTSCZ, *supra* note 34, Art 14, as amended by the 2012 Federal Law.

65 Russia ratified UNCLOS on 26 February 1997, see The Federal Law of 26 February 1997, No 30-FZ On Ratification of the United Nations Convention on the Law of the Sea and the Agreement relating to the implementation of Part XI of the United Nations Convention on the Law of the Sea with a statement, accessed 17 March 2017 at http://www.consultant.ru/document/cons_doc_LAW_15764/ [in Russian].

of the Russian administration have different views on this.[66] Consequently, neither Article 234 nor its domestic implementation—Article 32 of the 1998 Federal Law on the EEZ—have been explicitly referenced in either the 2012 Federal Law or the 2013 Rules. Moreover, Article 14 of the 1998 Federal Law on the IWTSCZ describes the NSR as a 'historically formed national transport communication of the Russian Federation'.[67] Similarly, the most recent version of Russia's Maritime Doctrine lists the 'creation of conditions for preserving the NSR as a national transport communication with a possibility of international use' as one of the long-term targets for policy in the sphere of maritime transport.[68] It is not clear whether this has any bearing on Russia's position regarding the future legal regime of navigation that such international use will rely upon.

It is evident that Article 234 of UNCLOS provides important support for the domestic legislation on the NSR.[69] This provision seems to accommodate Russia's interests sufficiently, as it accords a coastal State with a large measure of unilateral authority to regulate navigation in ice-covered areas. Moreover, as part of a multilateral treaty, invoking Article 234 is arguably less controversial than, for instance, a possible claim based on historic rights.[70]

---

66 Compare the approach taken by the working group under the State Duma Committee for Transport, responsible for drafting the 2012 Federal Law and recent statements coming from the Ministry of Defence. The former did not see the need for describing the NSR as a historically formed national route; see Solski, *supra* note 47 at 108–110. For the latter, see *supra* note 32.

67 1998 Federal Law on the IWTSCZ, *supra* note 34, Art 14, as amended by the 2012 Federal Law.

68 2015 Maritime Doctrine, *supra* note 13, Item 21 и.

69 The language used in the 1990 Regulations and even more evidently in the 2013 Rules reveals that although neither includes explicit reference to Article 234, both were motivated by it.

70 In this respect, some new light on the relation between historic rights and UNCLOS has been shed by the recent Award by the Arbitral Tribunal Constituted under Annex VII to UNCLOS in the matter of the South China Sea Arbitration, 12 July 2016 (South China Sea Award 12 July 2016). Although this decision is only binding for the parties to the dispute, China and the Philippines, it constitutes an authoritative interpretation of international law. The Tribunal in paragraph 225 observed that the term 'historic rights' is general in nature and can describe any rights, including but not limited to sovereignty, that a State may possess due to particular historical circumstances. 'Historic waters', a specific type of a historic right, is a term for historic title over maritime areas, typically exercised as a claim to internal waters or the territorial sea. For a more detailed discussion, see *infra* notes 133–134 and accompanying text.

The parameters for Article 234 were agreed upon multilaterally,[71] and it forms part of the Convention developed out of desire 'to settle ... all issues relating to the law of the sea ...'.[72] There is little doubt that the NSR, or at least of most of it, meets the fundamental conditions for the application of this provision, 'particularly severe climatic conditions and the presence of ice covering [*these*] areas for most of the year'. Under the broad interpretation pursued by Russia and Canada, Article 234 allows them to maintain control of certain waters, in the sense that it requires users to seek coastal State consent for entry and navigation in these waters. In that event, reliance on Article 234 helps these States to circumvent, at least in practice, the controversial issue of the regime of navigation through straits enclosed within straight baselines.

Although a coastal State can apply Article 234 specifically for the purpose of the prevention, reduction and control of marine pollution from vessels, Russia's NSR regulations include maritime safety among their regulatory purposes.[73] The first specific enactment with maritime safety as its purpose in the Soviet Arctic was, arguably, the requirement of mandatory icebreaker assistance and pilotage established for the Vilkitskii and Shokalskii Straits in 1965, which in 1972 was extended to the Laptev and Sannikov Straits.[74] The first document where the USSR asserted special rights to regulate navigation on the NSR was the 1971 Statute on the Administration of the Northern Sea Route Attached to the Ministry of the Maritime Fleet.[75] There is no doubt that the 1971 Statute was motivated by Canada's bold action in 1970 to adopt the Arctic Waters Pollution Prevention Act.[76] Shortly after the adoption of UNCLOS, the USSR took steps to implement it, including Article 234.[77] Since then, this

71 Kristin Bartenstein, 'Navigating the Arctic: The Canadian NORDREG, the International Polar Code and Regional Cooperation' (2011) *German Yearbook of International Law* 54, at 110.

72 UNCLOS, *supra* note 15, Preamble.

73 1990 Regulations, *supra* note 38, Item 2; Merchant Shipping Code, *supra* note 2, Art 5.1.2.

74 The text of the Procedure for Navigation of vessels in the Vilkitskii, Shokalskii, Laptev and Sannikov Straits, Notices to Mariners 1972, Number 20 has been reproduced in William E Butler, *Northeast Arctic Passage* (Sijthoff & Noordhoff, 1978) at 174.

75 Decree of 16 September 1971, 'On the Confirmation of the Statute of the Administration of the Northern Sea Route Attached to the Ministry of the Maritime Fleet', 17 Sobranie Postanovlenii Soveta Ministrov SSSR 124; reproduced in Butler, *supra* note 74 at 177–179.

76 Arctic Waters Pollution Prevention Act, *Revised Statuses of Canada 1985*, c. A-12, as amended.

77 Edict on the Economic Zone of the USSR, 18 February 1984 (1984 Edict on the Economic Zone); Edict On Intensifying Nature Protection in Areas of the Extreme North and Marine Areas Adjacent to the Northern Coast of the USSR, 26 November 1984 (1984 Edict on

provision has provided the USSR and Russia with the international legal basis for imposing specific regulations on foreign vessels transiting the NSR.[78]

Regard for the limitations on coastal State jurisdiction under UNCLOS was observable during both the preparation of the 2012 Federal Law and in its resulting text. An analysis of the preparatory works provides support for the proposition that UNCLOS, in general, and specifically Article 234, served as the international legal basis for the new legislative effort.[79] For example, the explanatory note to the draft 2012 Federal Law refers to Article 234 explicitly.[80] It was evident to the members of the working group who drafted the law that consistency with UNCLOS was one of the most important guiding principles.[81] In addition, this conviction helped to address some of the elements of the prior legal regime that were either controversial or inconsistent with UNCLOS. As a result, and unlike the 1990 Regulations, the 2013 Rules apply only to merchant vessels navigating within the 200 nm limit of the Russian EEZ;[82] and the methodology for the calculation of fees is to correspond with rendered services.[83]

More recently and perhaps most significantly for the determination of Russia's official position, the ANSR provided some clarification when it, for the fourth time, denied a permit to the *Arctic Sunrise*.[84] It stated that the ship was refused a permit on the grounds of 'violation of the rules of navigation in the

---

extreme north). For the analysis, see Erik Franckx, *Maritime Claims in the Arctic: Canadian and Russian Perspectives* (Martinus Nijhoff Publishers, 1993) at 178–179.

78 Primarily, the 1990 Regulations, whose roots can be traced to the 1984 Edict on Extreme North. They remained operative until the adoption of the 2013 Rules.

79 For a more extensive analysis of the preparatory works leading to the adoption of 2012 Federal Law, see Solski, *supra* note 47.

80 English translation, accessed 17 March 2017 at http://www.arctic-lio.com/docs/nsr/legislation/Explanatory_note_to_the_Draft_of_NSR_Federal_Law.pdf.

81 Vitaly Kluev, from Russian Ministry of Transport, emphasised that UNCLOS imposes limits on Russia's jurisdiction on the NSR at a few occasions, for example Round Table Severnyi morskoi put'—magistral' strategicheskoi vazhnosti, 23 March 2012; and the Parliamentary Hearings on 'Legal groundwork of state regulation of development and use of the NSR', at Russia's Council of Federation on 24 April 2012, transcript available at http://region.council.gov.ru/media/files/41d4536b6448d2d89cb3.doc [in Russian], accessed 17 March 2017.

82 Pursuant to Article 1 of the Merchant Shipping Code, which is the legal basis for the 2013 Rules, the Code applies only to relations arising from merchant shipping; Article 3(2) excludes its application to State vessels. For the geographical scope, see *supra* note 45 and accompanying text.

83 See section 4.4 below.

84 Ministry of Transport of the Russian Federation, Federal Agency for Sea and Inland Water Transport, Northern Sea Route Administration, Notification No 77, 20 September 2013, on file with author.

water area of the NSR, adopted and enforced by the Russian Federation in accordance with the article 234 of the United Nations Convention on the Law of the Sea, 1982'.[85]

This statement should be given sufficient weight, as it came from a governmental body responsible for the administration of the NSR. However, it does not necessarily represent the official position of the Russian government, and it is very likely that Russia is yet to adopt a single uniform position on this issue. Article 234 is subject to specific limitations, including the possibility that at some point in time it will not be available due to the effects of climate change.[86] In other words, Article 234 may not give an adequately sound basis for Russia to maintain the *status quo* as regards the national status of the NSR. Currently, however, it is evident that Article 234 takes precedence as the international legal basis for Russia's regulatory practice on the NSR. This does not preclude other arguments in the future, such as those based on historic rights. The next subsection deals with how these issues resonate within Russian academic discussions.

3.2 *Russian Scholarly Views—Past and Present*

For decades in the 20th century, Soviet academics developed different theories regarding the international legal basis, and the scope and extent of Soviet jurisdiction within the so-called 'Soviet Arctic sector'.[87] Rooted in the political realities of their times, these theories emphasised the special character of the Arctic as a factor for the determination of the Soviet Union's special rights. Lakhtin, for example, advocated the assimilation of immovable sea ice

85 *Ibid.*

86 Here it is sufficient to highlight that Article 234 applies in ice-covered areas, so coastal State competence can potentially decrease if ice continues to melt. In addition, the developments at the global level including the adoption of the Polar Code will gradually tighten coastal States' margin of discretion for unilateral regulation. For an analysis of Article 234, see Chapter 2 of this Volume. See also Erik J Molenaar, 'Options for Regional Regulation of Merchant Shipping outside IMO, with Particular Reference to the Arctic Region' (2014) 45 *Ocean Development and International Law* 272–298 at 276; Erik Franckx, 'Should the Law Governing Maritime Areas in the Arctic Adapt to Changing Climatic Circumstances?' in E Carina H Keskitalo, Timo Koivurova, Nigel Bankes (eds), *Climate Governance in the Arctic*, (50 Environment & Policy, Springer 2009) 119–144, at 126.

87 The Soviet Arctic sector refers to a cartographic device used to define the limits of Soviet land territory in the Arctic, as laid down in the Decree on the Proclamation of Lands and Islands Located in the Northern Arctic Ocean as Territory of the USSR of 15 April 1926 (Sobranie Zakonov SSSR 1926, No 32, Item 203) [Russian]; reproduced in Butler, *supra* note 74 at 174.

with land territory and a qualified sovereignty for the remaining parts of the seas within the sector, where even the waters outside the territorial sea should enjoy a territorial sea-like status.[88] Odnopozov and others argued that the Kara, Laptev and East-Siberian Seas had historically belonged to the USSR, and called for an *expressis verbis* recognition of them as internal waters to dispel doubts about their status.[89] Since the USSR, nonetheless, did little to endorse the sector theory's relevance to sea expanses or broad historic claims, other theories emerged, such as Kulebyakin's argument, which pointed to a series of historical, economic, political, geographical, environmental and other factors that played a role in the determination of the legal status of the Arctic marine expanses.[90]

At present, Russian commentators widely accept that the sector theory cannot serve as a source of maritime entitlement under international law,[91] but many still argue that a series of special circumstances relevant for the legal regime of navigation on the NSR exist.[92] Soviet scholarly arguments have largely failed to exert much impact on Soviet/Russian position and practice,[93] but

88 Vladimir Lakhtin, 'Rights over the Arctic' (1930) 10 *American Journal of International Law* 703–17.

89 Petr S Odnopozov, 'Mezhdunarodno-pravovoi rezhim arkticheskih morskih prostranstv' (1973) 4 *Pravovedenie* 78–82. Notably, the topic of Russia's historic waters claim to Arctic seas has resurfaced also in literature published after the determination of baselines in 1985, see Sokolova, *infra* note 98; Igor N Bartsits, 'O pravovom statuse Rossiyskogo Arkticheskogo Sektora', (2000) 12 *Pravo i Polityka* 106–114.

90 Vyacheslav N Kulebyakin, 'Pravovoy rezhim Arktiki' in Igor P Blishchenko (ed) *Mezhdunarodnoe morskoe pravo, Moskwa: Izdatelstvo Universiteta druzhby narodov*, 1988, 134–144, Barsegov Yuriy G, Korzun Vladimir A, Mogilevkin Ilya M (et al) Arktika: Interesy Rossii i mezhdunarodnye uslovya ih realizatsii (Nauka, 2002).

91 Aldo Chircop, Ivan Bunik, Moira L McConnell and Kristoffer Svendsen, 'Course Convergence? Comparative Perspectives on the Governance of Navigation and Shipping in Canadian and Russian Arctic Waters' in Aldo Chircop, Scott Coffen-Smout, and Moira L McConnell (eds), *Ocean Yearbook 28* (Koninklijke Brill, 2014); see also Pavel Gudev 2013 'Rossiya i Kanada v Arktike: novye konkurenty ili staryie soyuzniki?', accessed 17 March 2017 at http://www.regnum.ru/news/1632940.html [in Russian].

92 Alexander A Kovalev, 'Pravovoi Status Severnogo Morskogo Puti—rossiyskoy natsyonalnoy transportnoy arterii', *Ezhegodnik Morskogo Prava 2008, Yublileynoe izdanie k 40-letyu Assotsyatsii Mezhdunarodnogo morskogo prava*, M: Linkor, 2009; Dzhamilya N Dzhunusova, 'Sovremennyi mezhdunarodno-pravovoi rezhim Severnogo Ledovitogo okeana I pribrezhnyh morey arkticheskih gosudarstv, aktualnye problem ekonomiki I prava, Kazan': Poznanie, 2012, No 1(21) 303–311.

93 Alex G Oude Elferink, 'Does Recent Practice of the Russian Federation Point to an Arctic Sunset for the Sector Principle?' in Suzanne Lalonde, Ted McDorman (eds), *International*

the views held in the past provide an important context for current Russian doctrine.[94]

Russian scholars rarely discuss Article 234 to any great extent. It is common for this provision to be addressed alongside a number of other issues,[95] or as a somewhat *a posteriori* international recognition and validation for the priority of national approaches in regulating human activity in the Arctic.[96] Other commentators see Article 234 as a compromise between two fundamentally opposed positions: 1) a sectoral division of the Arctic with a dominant position of each Arctic coastal State in its respective sector; and 2) that, in the Arctic, the freedom of navigation applies beyond the territorial sea.[97] Although this perspective is essentially correct, it does not fully accept Article 234's inherent limitations and its contingency on the presence of ice and other conditions. Consequently, compatibility of Russian practice with Article 234, specifically under the operation of the 1990 Regulations or the 2013 Rules, is rarely subject to critical assessment in domestic academic literature.

Yet, much of the scholarly thought is devoted to the drawbacks related to exclusive reliance on UNCLOS, in general, and Article 234 in particular, in the context of Arctic governance. A number of commentators suggest that Russia's authority to regulate navigation on the NSR could be more extensive or at least exist independently of UNCLOS.[98] Scholars attach varying weight to the

---

Law and Politics of the Arctic Ocean, Essays in Honor of Donat Pharand (Brill Nijhoff 2015) 269–290, at 289–290.

94 A brief systematisation of relevant Russian scholarship is presented in English, for example by Vyatcheslav V Gavrilov, 'Legal Status of the Northern Sea Route and Legislation of the Russian Federation: a Note' (2015) 46 *Ocean Development & International Law*, 256–263. See also Ivan Bunik, Alexander Vylegzhanin, 'International Legal Problems Related to Arctic Exploration' in International Polar Year Information Bulletin—2007/08 News No 5–6 (July-August 2007): 27, accessed 17 March 2017 at http://www.ipyeaso.aari.ru/Documents/MPG_News_5-6_.pdf.

95 For instance, Kovalev *supra* note 92; while the article deals with the legal status of the NSR, Article 234 is mentioned only once. Much more attention is devoted to the similarity and analogy between the NSR, NWP and Indreleia in the sense that they all constitute national communications of respective States.

96 Elvira Pushkareva, 'Concepts of the Legal Status of the Arctic' (2016) 19 *Max Planck Yearbook of United Nations Law Online* 363–385, at 375–376.

97 A O Tulina, 'Aktualnye Voprosy Mezhdunarodno-pravovoi Ohrany Okruzhayushey Sredy Arktiki' in Vyatcheslav V Gavrilov (ed) *Mikhailovskie nauchnye Chtenia: Materialy Mezhdunarodnoy nauchno-prakticheskoy konferentsii* (Vladivostok 23–24 May 2014, Vladivostok Dalnevostochnyi Federalnyi Universitet 2014) 391–397, at 392.

98 For instance, Ivan V Bunik, *Mezhdunarodno-pravovye osnovanya regulirovanya Rossiey sudohodstva po Severnomu Morskomu Puti* (a thesis for a degree of Candidate of Science

recognition of the NSR as national in Russian legislation. Mikhina admits that the future legal status of the NSR can be uncertain,[99] whereas Kripakova or Gudev advocate increased creativity so that Russia 'could follow Canada's example'.[100] The latter group seems to propound an increased reliance on the doctrine of historic title, so that Russia's control (or sovereignty) over the NSR would be less dependent on the presence of ice.[101]

---

in Law, Moscow: MGIMO University 2007) at 91 argues that Russia's jurisdiction is broader under customary international law than under Article 234 of the UNCLOS; Ekaterina Sokolova, *Institut Istoricheskih vod v sovremennom mezhdunarodnom prave* (a thesis for a degree of Candidate of Science in Law, Moscow: MGIMO University 2014) at 47–48 argues that the Kara, Laptev, East-Siberian and Chukchi Seas had in the doctrine been regarded as historic waters and Russia is in full right to claim larger expanses of the marine Arctic based on a historic title. The most prominent representative of Russian academia, consistently suggesting that in the Arctic priority should be given to the rules of customary international law instead of UNCLOS, is Alexander Vylegzhanin. See Alexander N Vylegzhanin, 'Developing International Law Teachings for Preventing Inter-State Disaccords in the Arctic Ocean' in Georg Witschel, Ingo Winkelmann, Kathrin Tiroch, Rüdiger Wolfrum, *New Chances and New Responsibilities in the Arctic Region* (Berliner Wissenschafts-Verlag, 2010) 209–221, at 217, where amongst a number of legal issues supporting, in his view, his claim of predominance of customary international law in the Arctic, he also refers to the longstanding practice of compliance by foreign States, save for one 'persistent objector'—the United States, of Russian legislation on the NSR and Canadian legislation on the NWP. In Alexander N Vylegzhanin, Georgy G Ivanov, Inna P Dudikina, 'The Polar Code (Comments in Foreign Legal Sources)' (2015) 4 *Moscow Journal of International Law* 43–60, at 56, he suggests that the legal regime of the Arctic, as well as the Antarctic, has traditionally been a matter of concern of the general (territorial) international law, rather than the international law of the sea.

99 Mikhina merely highlights this problem, see *supra* note 49 at 269–274.

100 A V Kripakova 'K Voprosu o Pravovom Statuse Severnogo Morskogo Puti' 199–205 at 205, in V V Gavrilov (ed) *Mikhailovskie nauchnye Chtenia: Materialy Mezhdunarodnoy nauchno-prakticheskoy konferentsii* (Vladivostok, 23–24 May 2014, Vladivostok Dalnevostochnyi Federalnyi Universitet 2014), argues that Russia should put its national interests before international, and that the NSR alongside the NWP and Indreleia, are all historic internal seaways of respective States. Pavel Gudev, 'Rossija i Kanada v Arktike: novye konkurenty ili starye soyuzniki?' *Regnum* (6 March 2013), accessed 17 March 2017 at http://regnum.ru/news/polit/1632940.html, advocates increased reliance on historic title as justification for the NSR national legal status. He views the reference to history and national status of the NSR in Article 14 of the 1998 Federal Law on the IWTSCZ as an important step in this direction. However, it is not clear whether these authors argue that Russia should expand its historic waters or rely on 'historic title' in any other way.

101 *Ibid.*

In a recent 'reader' published by the Russian International Affairs Council,[102] Mikhina discusses the issue of the international legal basis for the regulation of foreign navigation on the NSR. She first identifies two factors under which the legal regime of the NSR has been formed: 1) internationally recognised historic entitlements of Russia, economic infrastructure and the interest of the population, together with Russia's historical efforts and achievements in this region over centuries; and 2) the norms of international law, in particular UNCLOS. Mikhina seems to imply that the first factor (historic entitlements) does not belong to the sphere covered by the second factor (international law). Consistent with this reasoning, she places Article 234 at the center of the discussion. Yet, when it comes to the conclusion, she abandons this reasoning and states that the 'historical' classification of the NSR in Article 14 of the 1998 Federal Law on the IWTSCZ is analogous to the status of the NWP and Indreleia—both regarded as internal waters by Canada and Norway, respectively.[103] This recent publication by an established Russian scholar can be viewed as symptomatic of a larger problem that Russia may face in the future, namely, whether it wishes to and can find legal support for historically based arguments to maintain NSR's national status, and what this could possibly entail for the regime of navigation.

3.3 *The Relevance of the Historical Development of the NSR for Its Legal Regime*

As noted above, Russian doctrinal writings and the characterisation of the NSR as a historically formed national transport communication suggest that there might be a role, although an unspecified one, for historical circumstances in the development of the legal regime of navigation on the NSR.

Setting aside the confusing narrative adopted by some Russian scholars, it is clear that there are limited areas within the NSR that have been claimed as historic waters—a claim that has been protested by other States. Article 1(2) of the 1998 Federal Law on IWTSCZ provides that the regime of internal waters also extends to waters of gulfs, bays, inlets, estuaries, seas and straits with a breadth of entrance exceeding 24 nm, which historically belong to the Russian Federation.[104] It further stipulates that the list of internal historic waters shall

---

102 Irina Mikhina, 'Konventsia OON po Morskomu Pravu i razvitie SMP, Vozmozhnosti I Ugrozy dla Rossii' *2015 Russian International Affairs Council*, accessed 17 March 2017 at http://russiancouncil.ru/sevmorput#mikhina [in Russian].

103 *Ibid.*, but the argument of analogy between the three Arctic national routes is often repeated in Russian scholarship on the topic, see Kovalev, *supra* note 92.

104 1998 Federal Law on the IWTSCZ, *supra* note 34, Art 1(2).

be published in Notices to Mariners.[105] However, there seems to be no exhaustive list of Russian Arctic historic waters published anywhere,[106] with the exception of the Decree of 15 January 1985.[107] Apart from the geographical coordinates for baselines, the decree specifies waters proclaimed as historically belonging to the USSR in the Arctic Ocean. These include waters outside the currently defined NSR, such as the White Sea, waters of Cheshskaya Bay, and only one bay located within the NSR—the Baidaratskaya Bay.[108] This list does not include the Laptev and Sannikov Straits, which were in 1964 described by the Soviet Ministry of Foreign Affair as 'historically belonging to the USSR'.[109]

Article 14 of the 1998 Federal Law on the IWTSCZ suggests that historical circumstances may play a wider role in the legal regime of navigation than merely justifying the claims to the Baidaratskaya Bay or the Laptev and Sannikov Straits. Firstly, the language, specifically the adjective 'national', may point to Russia's position that the NSR does not include straits used for international navigation. The question of the applicability of the regime of transit passage to Russian Arctic straits is an unresolved issue.[110] These straits, arguably, do not meet the functional condition of Article 37 of UNCLOS, i.e., they are presently not 'used' for international navigation;[111] but the increase in use will probably deprive Russia of this argument.[112] It is possible that the fear of 'internationalisation' lies behind the strong domestic attachment to the classification of the entire NSR as national. In any case, Article 34(1) of UNCLOS provides that the

105 *Ibid.*

106 This is confirmed by Alexander Vylegzhanin (ed) *Mezhdunarodno-pravovaya Kvalifikatsya Morskih Rayonov v Kachestve Istoricheskih Vod (Teoria i Praktika Gosudarstv)* (Moscow MGIMO, 2012) at 55.

107 See *supra* note 21.

108 *Ibid.*

109 Aide Memoire from the Soviet Ministry of Foreign Affairs to the American Embassy Moscow, dated 21 July 1964, American Embassy Moscow telegram 17002, 21 July 1964, as reproduced in Roach and Smith, *supra* note 22 at 312–313. The United States lodged an official protest, see Roach and Smith, *supra* note 22 at 53; United States Department of State, Bureau of Oceans and International Environmental and Scientific Affairs, Limits in the Seas, No 112, United States Responses to Excessive National Maritime Claims at 20.

110 This has already been raised by the United States, but increased navigation can curtail Russia's counter-arguments.

111 For the sake of argument, it is here assumed that some actual, not merely potential, use of straits is required before transit passage applies. Note that the United States position is different and this issue clearly is not settled.

112 Although one may question whether a strait can be turned into one that is 'used for international navigation' within the context of UNCLOS if all navigation through it is subject to coastal State consent.

legal status of waters forming straits used for international navigation is not affected by the regime of passage.

Secondly, in light of Article 8(2) of UNCLOS, in the NSR chokepoints enclosed within straight baselines that had previously contained territorial sea corridors, the right of innocent passage should still apply after their enclosure. For example, the Vilkitskii Strait was regarded to overlap with the Soviet territorial sea in 1967,[113] but it has never been crossed by a foreign vessel without coastal State authorisation.[114] Prominent Russian scholars explain that before the USSR established straight baselines, its position was that none of these Arctic straits had been used for international navigation;[115] and as a result, no right of innocent passage was preserved. The problem with this reasoning lies in the premise that if straits were 'not used for international navigation', it logically follows that innocent passage did not apply in parts of the Soviet territorial sea. This is manifestly incorrect, since under the 1958 Convention on the Territorial Sea and the Contiguous Zone (TSCZ Convention), the right of innocent passage applies anywhere in the territorial sea, including straits, regardless of whether they are used for international navigation.[116]

However, Article 14 of the 1998 Federal Law on the IWTSCZ refers not only to the seaways passing through straits, but also to the entire water area of the NSR as a 'historically developed national transport communication of the Russian

---

113 Soviet Ministry of Foreign Affairs aide Memoire to American Embassy in Moscow, 24 August 1967, as reprinted in Roach and Smith, *supra* note 22 at 315.

114 In 1967, Soviet legislation required foreign warships to obtain prior authorisation before they could enter Soviet territorial waters. When an American coast guard vessel intended to navigate through the straits without having sought prior authorisation, the Soviets strongly and successfully discouraged the vessel from proceeding. Soviet controversial policy regarding the right of innocent passage for warships was finally addressed by the 1989 United States-USSR Joint Statement with attached Uniform Interpretation of Norms of International Law Governing Innocent Passage, at para 2. For an analysis of the Joint Statement, see Erik Franckx, 'Innocent Passage of Warships: Recent Developments in US-Soviet Relations' 14 *Marine Policy* 484 (1990).

115 Golitsyn, *supra* note 51 at 471–472; Anatolii Kolodkin, Vasilii Gutsuliak, Yulia Bobrova, *The World Ocean: International Legal Regime*, William E Butler (ed) (Eleven International Publishing, 2010) at 19–20.

116 1958 Geneva Convention on the Territorial Sea and the Contiguous Zone, adopted 29 April 1958, 526 UNTS 205 (entered into force 10 September 1964) (TSCZ Convention). The difference between the general right of innocent passage in the territorial sea and the situation of straits used for international navigation under the TSCZ Convention lies in the right of coastal States to suspend innocent passage temporarily in the territorial sea, but not within straits used for international navigation. See Article 16(3) and 16(4) of the TSCZ Convention.

Federation'.[117] It may appear that this provision invokes some sort of historic rights in respect of the entire NSR.[118] Yet, in light of the abovementioned definition of the NSR, it is evident that the NSR covers multiple maritime zones, and most of it is located within the EEZ. Regardless, the 1998 Federal Law on the IWTSCZ does not apply beyond Russia's internal waters, territorial sea or contiguous zone.[119] Moreover, a provision emphasising the national status of the historically developed NSR in Russian law has never served as a legal basis for specific regulations.[120] Finally, when the ANSR felt obliged to clarify the international legal basis for the adoption and enforcement of the 2013 Rules, it did not refer to the NSR's national status, but to Article 234.[121]

The merit of Article 14 of the 1998 Federal Law on the IWTSCZ seems to be reflected in its symbolic recognition of the historical significance of the NSR to the entire nation and the great sacrifices that were made for its development.[122] In 1964, the Soviet Ministry of Foreign Affairs issued a Diplomatic Note to the American Embassy underscoring the same sentiment, but did not refer to it as having any relevance to the legal regime of navigation.[123] The fact that the NSR had been considered as an important national line of communication signified a special interest of the USSR in 'all that dealt with the functioning of the route'.[124] The crux of the note, however, was to emphasise that the NSR also encompassed straits entirely covered by the territorial sea and internal waters, and according to Soviet law of that time, prior authorisation was required.[125] Moreover, when in 1967 the USSR intended to bar the passage of *Edisto* or

---

117 The water are of the NSR is defined in *supra* note 45 and accompanying text.

118 For instance, Pavel Savaskov, 'Pravovoi rezhim Arktiki' in Andriej Zagorskii (ed), *Arktika: Zona Mira i Sotrudnichestva* (IMEMO RAN, 2011) at 38.

119 See 1998 Federal Law on the IWTSCZ, *supra* note 34, Preamble.

120 Article 14 of the 1998 Federal Law on the IWTSCZ in its originally adopted version mandated the Government of the Russian Federation to approve Regulations of navigation on the NSR, but this has never been completed. The 2013 Rules were adopted based on Article 5.1 of the Merchant Shipping Code.

121 *Supra* note 84.

122 This is a recurring argument, as for instance raised by Matveev during the Parliamentary Hearings, see *supra* note 81: 'Yes, we have ratified the UNCLOS and nobody is planning to renounce that. It is just that we have invested so much energy, money and lives into the NSR that turning it into a revolving door ... would not be right.'

123 Aide Memoire from the Soviet Ministry of Foreign Affairs to the American Embassy Moscow, dated 21 July 1964, American Embassy Moscow telegram 17002, 21 July 1964, as reproduced in Roach and Smith, *supra* note 22 at 312–313.

124 *Ibid.*

125 *Ibid.*

East Wind through the Vilkitskii Strait, it did not rely on the concept of a national NSR.[126] The Diplomatic Note of 25 August 1967 does not mention the NSR at all; it merely points out that the legislation on the protection of the USSR border also applies to the 'territorial waters' within the strait.[127] In addition, when the 1998 Federal Law on the IWTSCZ was being drafted, the Russian Ministry of Foreign Affairs objected to the inclusion of Article 14 on the grounds that its initial wording was incompatible with the international law of the sea.[128] Although this provision was eventually still included in the final text, it is clear that the Russian Foreign Ministry had opposed any formulation tantamount to the proclamation of the NSR as part of the Russian internal waters or the territorial sea, since its seaways were located mostly beyond these maritime zones.[129] More recently, Article 14 of the 1998 Federal Law on the IWTSCZ drew the attention of other States. The United States in its 2015 United States Diplomatic Note to Russia[130] related to the characterisation of the NSR as 'a historically established national transport communication route' as a concept 'not established under international law'.[131]

Summing up, it appears that such a vague argument may assuage nationalistic sentiments domestically, and at the same time, it involves little cost when maintained alongside other arguments with a firmer basis in international law.[132] It is unlikely that Russia would be able to make a successful claim to historic rights with respect to vast areas of the NSR. The Arbitral Tribunal in the South China Sea case stated unequivocally that UNCLOS provides for a comprehensive legal regime for the oceans, addressing rights, obligations and jurisdiction of States in maritime zones, including rights deriving from historical processes.[133] UNCLOS defines the scope and extent of maritime entitlements, which may not extend beyond the limits imposed in the Convention, and historic rights short of sovereignty must be compatible with the Convention. If a

126 Soviet Ministry of Foreign Affairs aide memoire to American Embassy in Washington, 25 August 1967, State Dep't File No SCI 31 US, II Cumulative Digest 1816, as reproduced in Roach and Smith, *supra* note 22 at 315.

127 *Ibid.*

128 Bunik, *supra* note 98 at 117.

129 *Ibid.*

130 *Supra* note 22.

131 *Ibid.*

132 See Oude Elferink, *supra* note 93 at 289–290, where he discusses references to the sector theory in the context of maritime delimitation. It appears that there exists a particular analogy in how Russia uses the Arctic sector and the historical development of the NSR as peripheral arguments.

133 South China Sea Award of 12 July 2016, *supra* note 70, paras 230–278.

State enjoyed historic rights before accession to the Convention, they would be superseded if found to be in excess of the limits imposed by the Convention.[134]

Indeed, the Tribunal did not deny that historic waters can provide a State with broader rights than it would be entitled under UNCLOS. However, Russia's current historic waters claims within the NSR are relatively circumspect,[135] and, in light of international protests, not necessarily successful. If Russia ever expands the scope of its historic waters claim,[136] it is conceivable that further protests will follow.

4 Russia's Practice in Regulating Navigation on the NSR

This section discusses specific aspects of Russia's practice in regulating merchant shipping on the NSR. These include the requirements on prior authorisation, prior notification and reporting, icebreaker assistance and ice pilotage, fees, and enforcement. An attempt is made at addressing the compatibility of Russia's regulations with the international law of the sea, but the focus remains on Article 234 only. Such an approach sets aside the complex and disputed issues of the (in)applicability of Article 234 in the territorial sea, the (in)applicability of the regime of transit passage in the NSR and the relationship of the latter with Article 234.

4.1 *Prior Authorisation*

One of the fundamental requirements of the legal regime of the NSR is the requirement imposed on every shipowner or shipmaster to obtain a permit to enter and navigate on the NSR.[137] A permit is issued by the ANSR based on an application transmitted electronically no earlier than 120 and no later than 15 days prior to planned entry.[138] The ANSR is obligated to respond within 10 days of the application and publish the decision on its website together with its reasoning.[139] It is evident that the current regime for obtaining permits has become more streamlined and transparent compared to the regime of the 1990

134 *Ibid.*, para 278.

135 *Supra* notes 108 and 109.

136 See *supra* note 33 and accompanying text.

137 2013 Rules, *supra* note 43, Item 2.

138 *Ibid.*, Item 6.

139 The ANSR keeps records of all the applications, permits and refusals on its website. Decisions regarding foreign vessels are published in English; the rest is published in Russian.

Regulations. Under the latter, the access to the NSR was also subject to the requirement to obtain an official permit, but the process seemed to be more difficult and costly as well as less predictable. Only vessels with an ice class Arc 4 or higher were entitled to navigate the NSR.[140] Every vessel intending to navigate the NSR was required to undergo inspection in a Russian port and the application was required four months in advance.[141]

Under the current rules, the criteria upon which an application for a permit is to be decided are largely incorporated in Annex 2 to the 2013 Rules.[142] According to the applied methodology, the admission to the NSR, subdivided into seven geographically determined zones, depends on the following criteria: navigational period, actual ice conditions (light, medium, heavy), category of ice strengthening,[143] and intended mode of navigation (independent or with icebreaker assistance).[144] In general, there is no minimum requirement regarding the ice class for navigation on the NSR. For example, in the period between July and November, vessels with no ice strengthening can obtain a permit if there are light ice conditions and icebreaker assistance is used.[145] In turn, vessels with an ice class Arc 4 or higher can be allowed to navigate without icebreaker assistance, provided the ice conditions are not heavy.

Applicants are, moreover, required to provide evidence of compliance, and vouch that the vessel in question fulfils the necessary requirements as a condition for the legality of the ship's navigation.[146] The application must include specific information on the vessel's characteristics as well as the planned voyage.[147] In addition, copies of the classification society's certificate, tonnage

---

140 Item 2.2 of the 1996 Requirements for the Design, Equipment and Supplies of Vessels Navigating the Northern Sea Route. Exceptions were allowed.

141 Franckx, *supra* note 38 at 337.

142 Annex No 2 to the 2013 Rules, entitled the 'Criteria for the admission of ships to the NSR in compliance with their category of ice strengthening'.

143 The notations used in the 2013 Rules refer to the Russian Maritime Register of Shipping Rules 2007. See *supra* note 43.

144 *Ibid.*

145 During the second half of the 2015 navigation season (September-October), there were light ice conditions along the entire NSR. Therefore, the whole of the NSR was available for vessels with no ice strengthening whatsoever, provided icebreaker assistance was used.

146 2013 Rules, *supra* note 43, Item 3.

147 Annex No 1 to the 2013 Rules specifies what information is to be submitted; there are 26 positions to fill. The ANSR website provides an application form with 31 positions to fill. The application form seems to correspond with the Annex No 1 list although sometimes the language used differs.

certificate and documents certifying availability of civil liability insurance must be attached.[148]

A refusal can only be issued if the applicant fails to prove that the vessel fulfils requirements concerning safety of navigation and protection of the marine environment from vessel-source pollution.[149] Practice shows that there seems to be no clear procedure to appeal a refusal, and in such case, a new application is required.[150] The burden of proof that a vessel meets the requirements rests on the claimant. If the application is incomplete or misleading, the ANSR can refuse to grant a permit, and has in fact done so on numerous occasions.[151] Over the course of the last few years, it is clear that the ANSR has gradually refused fewer applications.[152] A closer examination of the 15 refusals in 2015 reveals that the ANSR acted in a consistent manner in accordance with Russian law.[153] The higher number of refusals in the first season in which the new rules became effective was probably due in part to the novelty of the rules.

In the few years since the 2013 Rules came into effect, the operators of foreign merchant vessels generally have not challenged these rules. One exception involved the *Arctic Sunrise*, which was operated by Greenpeace International and classified by Det Norske Veritas (DNV) as Icebreaker, and which, according to the DNV Rules (1973 Edition), was the second highest ice-strengthening notation at the time of construction. The ship applied for, and was refused, a permit to enter the NSR four times. After the third refusal, the *Arctic Sunrise* entered the NSR without authorisation.

It was evident that this was no ordinary merchant ship and the primary purpose of its voyage was not merchant shipping. Therefore, the Russian reaction

---

148 2013 Rules, *supra* note 43, Item 4.

149 Merchant Shipping Code, *supra* note 2, Art 5.1.4.

150 For instance, Daniel Simons, the legal counsel of Greenpeace International complained in a letter to the head of the ANSR that instead of accepting some additional information a day after authorisation was refused, the ANSR insisted that a new application needed to be filed. The ANSR has then again 10 working days to decide on the application for consideration.

151 The list of refusals is publicly available, accessed 17 March 2017 at http://www.nsra.ru/en/otkazu/.

152 According to the numbers provided by the ANSR, in 2013 the ANSR refused 83 of 718 applications, accessed 17 March 2017 at http://asmp.morflot.ru/ru/perechen_zayavlenii/. In 2014, 30 of 661 applications were refused, and in 2015, only 15 of 701 applications.

153 Seven of the vessels in question did not have any ice class; others either did not have sufficient ice strengthening for intended voyages, or the applicants did not submit all required documents; two applicants withdrew their own applications, see http://asmp.morflot.ru/ru/otkazu/, accessed 17 March 2017.

to the *Arctic Sunrise* incident should not be taken as representative of its position vis-à-vis 'normal' merchant shipping on the NSR. Yet, in the aftermath, the issue of the repeated refusals by the ANSR in respect of the *Arctic Sunrise*'s intent to navigate the NSR was raised in the Netherlands Parliament and in a diplomatic exchange between the Netherlands and Russia. In the Netherlands Parliament, Frans Timmermans –the Netherlands Minister of Foreign Affairs at the time of the incident, emphasised that Article 234 does not give a coastal State an unfettered right to interfere with the freedom of navigation.[154] This position was, according to Timmermans, presented to the Russian embassy along with the request to provide additional explanation on the reasons for the refusals.[155]

Based on the available material, it seems that in this case the ANSR simply applied Russian legislation, although perhaps in a formalistic manner. The first three refusals were based on the applicant's failure to provide, respectively: 1) information on annual surveys,[156] 2) information on ice strengthening,[157] and 3) information on ice belt breadth.[158] The first two applications were filed on 14 June 2013 and 10 July 2013, respectively. Greenpeace International later published a statement from DNV certifying the class it assigned to the vessel.[159] On the one hand, it is evident that the vessel was certified with the second highest ice class according to the DNV Rules (1973 Edition); on the other hand, the statement was issued on 1 August 2013—*after* the first two applications had already been refused.

154 See Franckx, *supra* note 47 at 209; see Alex G Oude Elferink, 'The Arctic Sunrise Incident: A Multi-faceted Law of the Sea Case with a Human Rights Dimension' (2014) 29/2 *International Journal of Marine and Coastal Law*, at 248.

155 *Vragen gesteld door de leden der Kamer, met de daarop door de regering gegeven antwoorden* Parliamentary Papers 2013–2014, Appendix no 136, accessed 18 November 2016 at https://zoek.officielebekendmakingen.nl/ah-tk-20132014-136.pdf [in Dutch].

156 Ministry of Transport of the Russian Federation, Federal Agency for Sea and Inland Water Transport, Northern Sea Route Administration, Notification No 38, 5 July 2013, on file with author.

157 Ministry of Transport of the Russian Federation, Federal Agency for Sea and Inland Water Transport, Northern Sea Route Administration, Notification No 53, 25 July 2013, on file with author.

158 Ministry of Transport of the Russian Federation, Federal Agency for Sea and Inland Water Transport, Northern Sea Route Administration, Notification No 67, 16 August 2013, on file with author.

159 Det Norske Veritas, Statement, Arctic Sunrise, DNV Id No 09552, 1 August 2013, accessed 17 March 2017 at http://www.greenpeace.org/international/Global/international/briefings/climate/2013/DNV-classification-letter.pdf.

With respect to the third refusal, it is clear that the 2013 Rules require information on the breadth of the vessel's ice belt, as well as on its ice class.[160] There is a proliferation of different standards developed by various classification societies, so it is perhaps reasonable that the ANSR would require some more specific information in this regard. However, one could raise the question of whether the ANSR should have included this issue in its first refusal. Admittedly, in other instances, the ANSR usually provides a complete list of inadequacies of the application in its initial refusal.

While a vessel of such a high ice class (Icebreaker) should be allowed to navigate on the NSR, especially during a period when there is no sea ice, a refusal based on non-compliance with formal requirements appears to have been lawful under Russian law.[161] While the 2013 Rules are complex and elaborate, they are also not overly confusing. Although it is likely that the Russian authorities did not want to allow the *Arctic Sunrise* to enter the NSR, one can only speculate as to how they would have reacted if Greenpeace International had submitted an impeccable application. This incident highlights the crucial issue, namely, whether the Russian requirement to obtain a permit to navigate within the NSR is consistent with the international law of the sea.

A requirement to obtain a permit essentially amounts to a veiled requirement of prior authorisation, which is not a new phenomenon in the law of the sea. The mere fact that a coastal State claims the right to require prior authorisation and thereby to withhold such authorisation for foreign vessels in relation to areas where international rights of navigation apply is highly controversial. A long-standing controversy concerns the right of coastal States to request prior authorisation either for warships or for ships carrying hazardous materials, such as nuclear-powered ships or ships carrying nuclear waste.[162] Commentators generally seem to agree that a requirement of prior authorisation before rights of navigation can be exercised is not compatible with UNCLOS,[163] although a considerable minority of coastal States still request prior authorisation for certain types of ships.[164] Significantly, Russia

160 2013 Rules, *supra* note 43, Annex 1, Item 24; also the application form includes this explicitly.

161 At least at face value, UNCLOS takes precedence in those instances where there is any inconsistency with domestic legislation, see *supra* note 63.

162 Molenaar, *supra* note 86 at 283.

163 Robin R Churchill, 'The impact of state practice on the jurisdictional framework contained in the LOS Convention' in Alex G Oude Elferink (ed), *Stability and Change in the Law of the Sea: The Role of the LOS Convention* (Brill Nijhoff, 2005) 91–143, at 114.

164 Roach and Smith, *supra* note 22 at 239–262.

has presented its position on this issue in a very clear manner. The 1989 Joint Statement by the United States and the USSR dismissed the requirement of prior notification or authorisation for all vessels in innocent passage.[165] The right of innocent passage is substantively narrower than the right of transit passage and the freedom of navigation. It should logically follow that these two States consider the requirement of prior notification or authorisation as not being compatible with the regimes of innocent and transit passage, and of the freedom of navigation. Since Russia requires prior authorisation for ships before they can enter the NSR, the most convincing explanation points to Russia's conviction that Article 234, as a *lex specialis*, allows it. The lingering question is then whether Article 234 authorises a coastal State to impose a requirement of prior authorisation for access to its maritime zones.

In this respect, there exists a clear analogy between the Russian requirement to obtain a permit for navigation on the NSR and the Canadian requirement to obtain clearance prior to entering the NORDREG zone.[166] Canada's decision to render NORDREG mandatory spurred a debate at the IMO and the reaction of some States through diplomatic channels. The United States initially condemned such a requirement as inconsistent with the bedrock principles of the law of the sea and Article 234.[167] Later, a number of States, including the United States, Germany and Singapore, expressed their concerns about the legality of the Canadian decision to make NORDREG mandatory.[168] Although at

165 Joint Statement by the United States of America and the Union of Soviet Socialist Republics, with attached Uniform Interpretation of Norms of International Law Governing Innocent Passage, para 2, adopted 23 September 1989; UN Law of the Sea Bulletin No 14 December 1989, at 12–13.

166 Northern Canada Vessel Traffic Services Zone Regulations (NORDREG), *Canada Gazette* Part II, Vol 144, No 13, 23 June 2010 and Order Amending the Shipping Safety Control Zones Order, *Canada Gazette* Part II, Vol 144, No 13, 23 June 2010. For a more thorough discussion on Canadian regulations, see Chapter 6 of this Volume.

167 A Note from the Embassy of the United States of America to Robert Turner, The Maritime Safety Directorate, Department of Transport, Ottawa, dated 19 March 2010, commenting on Canada Gazette, Part I, Saturday, 27 February 2010; Vol 144, No 9: proposed Northern Canada Vessel Traffic Services Zone Regulations; Diplomatic Note from the US Embassy, Ottawa, Canada to Department of Foreign Affairs and International Trade of Canada, 18 August 2010 (2010 US Diplomatic Note to Canada), accessed 17 March 2017 at http://www.state.gov/documents/organization/179287.pdf.

168 IMO Doc Msc 88/26, Report of the Maritime Safety Committee on its Eighty-Eighth Session, 15 December 2010, paras 11.35 and 11.36. For academic analysis of the NORDREG debate within the IMO, see, for example, James Kraska, 'The Northern Canada Vessel Traffic Services Zone Regulations (NORDREG) and the Law of the Sea' 30 *The International Journal of Marine and Coastal Law* (2015) 225–254, at 243–247; Ted McDorman, 'National

the IMO States generally avoided a debate on Article 234 and focused on the legality of Canada's actions pursuant to IMO instruments, Singapore questioned whether the Canadian requirement to obtain clearance would adequately give 'due regard to navigation'.[169] The debate within the IMO was eventually left unresolved,[170] although the Chairman of the IMO's Maritime Safety Committee (MSC) took the view that the majority of delegations supported the Canadian initiative, while a number believed that Canada should have submitted its proposal to the IMO.[171] It is conceivable that States that were active in the NORDREG debate would also be critical towards similar Russian regulations. In fact, on 29 May 2015, the United States delivered a Diplomatic Note to Russia where it declared the requirement to obtain a Russian permit to enter and transit the EEZ and the territorial sea as inconsistent with international law.[172] Time will show whether other States follow suit.

It is, nonetheless, difficult to assess whether Article 234 allows coastal States to require obtaining its consent prior to entering and navigating in ice-covered areas. So far, the United States and Singapore expressed their concerns regarding the legality of such a requirement. Yet, the complexity and sensitivity of this issue are demonstrated by the stalemate at the NORDREG debate within the IMO, general compliance with NSR regulations,[173] cautious language used by Timmermans (see above) and inconclusive analyses by experts.[174]

Measures for the safety of navigation in Arctic waters: NORDREG, Article 234 and Canada' in Myron H Nordquist, John Norton Moore, Alfred H A Soons, Hak-So Kim (eds) *The Law of the Sea Convention: US Accession and Globalization* (Leiden, 2012) 409–424.

169 Statement by the Delegation of Singapore, IMO Doc MSC 88/26, Report of the Maritime Safety Committee on its Eighty-Eighth Session, 15 December 2010, Annex 28.

170 One should not expect a different outcome since the interpretation of UNCLOS, strictly speaking, does not lie within the purview of the IMO. This debate merely highlighted that there exist different views on this issue.

171 Kraska, *supra* note 168 at 246–247.

172 2015 US Diplomatic Note to Russia, *supra* note 22.

173 The scale of foreign use of the NSR is not yet representative, and compliance with the rules during experimental voyages should not be overestimated. In this regard, the activity of some important shipping organisations, such as INTERTANKO or the International Chamber of Shipping (ICS) can provide insight into the positions taken by the industry. The former sided with the United States during the NORDREG debate, while the latter, in International Chamber of Shipping, 'Arctic Shipping, Position Paper', 2014, Principle 4, accessed 17 March 2017 at http://www.ics-shipping.org/docs/default-source/resources/policy-tools/ics-position-paper-on-arctic-shipping.pdf advocated the precedence of the transit passage regime over Article 234.

174 See, for instance, Bartenstein, *supra* note 71; McDorman, *supra* note 168.

If it is assumed that a coastal State exercising its authority under Article 234 can, in principle, adopt measures other than, or more stringent than, generally accepted rules and standards (GAIRAS), a mechanism needs to exist to verify or ensure compliance with them. It is difficult to expect flag States to do this, as they are only obliged to adopt laws and regulations that have at least the same effect as GAIRAS.[175] It is thus reasonable that the right of coastal States to prescribe other special measures without approval from the IMO be accompanied with the right to enforce them. This factor seems to explain the unprecedented construction of Article 234, which grants both prescriptive and enforcement jurisdiction. A requirement to obtain a permit, if streamlined and contingent on transparent verification of compliance with other rules, appears to rely on both prescriptive and enforcement jurisdiction. Such a requirement helps ensure that specific rules and standards are complied with at an early stage, before a vessel's entry into the NSR.

From a policy perspective, it is preferable that vessels that are not well suited to Arctic conditions are barred from entering the potentially hazardous waters of the NSR. The permit mechanism clearly achieves this objective. In addition, the application procedure gives a better overview of planned shipping activity in different sectors of the NSR. This is a significant factor to consider when decisions are made with respect to the allocation of resources, such as the location of icebreakers ready to offer emergency response.[176] Furthermore, such a requirement in the context of Arctic navigation may be perceived as not affecting the interests of shipping companies as much as prior authorisation does elsewhere in the world.

Normally, ships can change their planned itineraries as and when they wish. Therefore, it is important that they be, in principle, free to navigate without being compelled to familiarise themselves with specific rules applicable to

175 With respect to vessel-source pollution, Article 211(2) requires flag States to adopt laws and regulations that have at least the same effect as GAIRAS. Further, Article 217(1) requires flag States to ensure compliance with applicable international rules and standards and with laws and regulations adopted by the flag State.

176 In light of the Arctic's vastness and the risk of a dramatic deterioration of conditions, icebreakers are often the only reliable way to ensure search and rescue, as well as pollution preparedness and response capability. For example, in 2013, when the tanker *Nordvik* entered waters of the NSR for which it had not obtained authorisation, and was subsequently hit by an ice floe, it had to wait for assistance of icebreakers for a week. This event underscored the importance of prior arrangements with the ANSR and icebreaker operators and was a 'delicate' hint from Atomflot that it is not wise to disregard the rules. See also Northern Sea Route Information Office, 'The tanker "Nordvik" left the NSR water area' (18 September 2013), accessed 17 March 2017 at http://www.arctic-lio.com/node/206.

maritime zones of different coastal States. Arctic navigation, however, requires special planning because vessels are exposed to additional risks. This seems to be reflected in the practice of underwriters, who can require a shipowner to take specific additional measures before engaging in navigation in the NSR. The United Kingdom P&I Club, in general, seems to require shipowners to obtain an appropriate Ice or Polar Class, receive approval from hull underwriters and clarify the intended route with cargo owners.[177] It is possible that, in practice, the requirement to obtain a permit from the ANSR does not necessarily have to constitute an unacceptable burden, but rather that it helps to prepare for the voyage.

Then again, because international standards are in the process of development, it may take quite some time before a truly international and uniform regime for Arctic shipping emerges. Given the traditional tensions surrounding prior authorisation, a unilateral mode of adopting such a requirement does not seem to be acceptable in the long term. The international community never accepted the idea that a coastal State could withhold a right of lateral passage of high-risk vessels even through the territorial sea. A majority of States disagree that a coastal State could possibly interfere with the right of innocent passage in such a way, not to mention the freedom of navigation in the EEZ. In exercising its jurisdiction under Article 234, coastal States are obliged to have due regard to navigation, which should be read together with other more general UNCLOS provisions. Coastal State jurisdiction, with regard to the protection and preservation of the marine environment, shall be exercised with due regard to the rights of other States, including the freedom of navigation in the EEZ.[178] It seems that, in order to show due regard to the rights of navigation, Russia should, as a matter of good faith, consult user States through appropriate channels,[179] with the IMO being the most suitable forum through which Russia could work to add legitimacy to its position, but the cooperative attitude could also be demonstrated elsewhere. If Russia were to develop navigation on the NSR, it needs to be attentive to the rights and positions of

177 'Arctic Shipping: P&I Insurance FAQs' (9 September 2014), accessed 17 March 2017 at https://www.ukpandi.com/knowledge-publications/article/arctic-shipping-p-i-insurance-faqs-130451/.

178 This follows from Articles 56(1)(b)(iii), 56(2), 58(1) and 87 of UNCLOS.

179 A conclusion along similar lines can be found in Robert Beckman, 'UNCLOS Dispute Settlement Regime and Arctic Legal Issues' in Myron H Nordquist, John Norton Moore, Ronán Long (eds), *Challenges of the Changing Arctic, Continental Shelf, Navigation, and Fisheries* (Brill Nijhoff, 2016) 573–592, at 582.

other States. At the end of the day, it seems that it remains for State practice to calibrate the scope and extent of coastal State authority under Article 234.

4.2 *Prior Notification and Reporting*

Russia has unilaterally adopted an extensive system of reporting, including prior notification and a ship reporting system (SRS) within the NSR. Prior to approaching the Western or the Eastern boundary,[180] a shipmaster is obligated to notify the ANSR about its planned time of arrival to the Western or Eastern boundary 72 hours and 24 hours in advance.[181] This first notification must include information regarding, *inter alia*, the ship, its crew, type and amount of cargo, fuel capacity, and destination.[182] Further reports are required upon crossing the Western or the Eastern boundary, entrance into the area of the NSR, and upon leaving the NSR.[183] In addition, after crossing the Eastern or Western boundary, a daily report with information about the ship and the conditions relevant for navigation as observed is required.[184] This allows the ANSR to collect on-site information on navigation on the NSR and disseminate it further to other users via their website.

Although a mandatory SRS and prior notification is to be valued due to its contribution to increased maritime safety and prevention of pollution, its unilateral mode of adoption is clearly controversial under the international law of the sea. Russia did not submit its SRS to the IMO for adoption, which under Regulation V-11.1 of SOLAS[185] is a condition for a SRS to be mandatory. However, SOLAS does not rule out that a State can adopt a SRS without first obtaining IMO approval.[186] Such systems may be submitted to the IMO for recognition,[187] but even then, they will not attain a mandatory status under SOLAS. Yet, Regulation V-11.9 of SOLAS stipulates that it does not prejudice States' rights and duties under international law. In this respect, the principal

---

180 Note that the Western boundary coincides with meridian 33° E, while the Eastern boundary consists of parallel 62° N and meridian 169°W. In effect, for the purpose of notification these boundaries create a wider zone than the area of the NSR.

181 2013 Rules, *supra* note 43, Items 14 and 15.

182 *Ibid.*

183 *Ibid.*, Items 19 and 20.

184 *Ibid.*, Item 42.

185 International Convention for the Safety of Life at Sea, adopted 1 November 1974, entered into force 25 May 1980, 1184 UNTS 277 (SOLAS Convention), Chap V, Reg 11.1.

186 *Ibid.*, Reg 11.4.

187 *Ibid.*

question is whether Article 234 can serve as an independent legal basis for a mandatory SRS.[188]

Prior notification and reporting schemes constitute an additional burden on the master of a vessel, but they do not potentially deny a right or freedom of navigation in a way that prior authorisation does. It is unclear if Article 234 allows any of these, but if one assumes that a requirement of prior permit could possibly fall under the purview of Article 234, the same conclusion, *a fortiori*, applies to the requirement of prior notification and reporting. Again, it is a matter of due regard to the rights of user States that Russia consults them in an appropriate manner. A submission of a SRS to the IMO for adoption, or at least recognition, would add legitimacy, but also perhaps legality, to Russia's practice and would allow it to show good faith.

4.3 *Icebreaker Assistance and Ice Pilotage*

Icebreaker assistance is mandatory only under certain conditions. While the rules for determining if icebreaker assistance is required are generally clear and transparent,[189] there are a few potentially controversial issues.

Only icebreakers registered in Russia are entitled to provide icebreaker assistance.[190] This means that a foreign icebreaker can use the NSR but cannot provide icebreaker assistance to other vessels navigating the NSR behind it. In addition, the 2012 Federal Law amended the Federal Law on Natural Monopolies to include 'icebreaker support, ice pilotage of vessels in the area of the Northern Sea Route' within the sphere of activity of Natural Monopoly Entities.[191] Only a handful of Russian organisations provide icebreaker assistance.[192] In practice, it appears that the main role has been granted to

188 This is precisely the argument of Canada to justify its decision to impose the mandatory NORDREG SRS, but a few States have raised concerns and objections on this at the occasion of the abovementioned debate on Canada's NORDREG within and outside the IMO. See also the US protest as reflected in the 2015 US Diplomatic Note to Russia, *supra* note 22.

189 The ANSR indicates so in its individual decision, it is based on the criteria for the admission of ships to the NSR in compliance with category of their ice strengthening, see 2013 Rules, *supra* note 43, Annex 2.

190 *Ibid.*, Item 22.

191 The Federal Law on Natural Monopolies, 17 August 1995, No 147 FZ.

192 According to the ANSR website, these include Atomflot, Rosmorport, Far Eastern Shipping Company (FESCO), Murmansk Shipping Company, Murmansk Transport Branch of Norilsk Nickel, Lukoil Oil Company, and the Marine Rescue Service of ROSMORRECHFLOT, see http://www.nsra.ru/ru/org_ledokol_provodka/ [in Russian], accessed 17 March 2017. However, the most recent version of the Registry of Natural Monopoly Entities providing

Atomflot, the only organisation operating a fleet of nuclear icebreakers. A possible controversy with respect to this issue is that certain Russian companies, such as Lukoil Oil Company or Norilsk Nickel, are apparently authorised to provide their own icebreaker assistance. This can give these Russian companies a competitive advantage, as foreign companies are not authorised to do the same.

The 2013 Rules provide specific rules for ice pilotage assistance.[193] They fail to clarify under what conditions ice pilotage becomes mandatory, but it is likely that the determinative factor is the shipmaster's experience in ice navigation. Although Article 234 probably allows a coastal State to require icebreaker assistance or ice pilotage under specific circumstances, it is clear that there is little international support for compulsory pilotage schemes to be adopted unilaterally.[194]

4.4 *Fees*

An important novelty of the 2012 Federal Law and subsequent legislation is a different method for the calculation of fees for icebreaker assistances and ice pilotage services. The issue of fees is closely related to services offered for NSR users. As was mentioned above, MOHS had a right to assign one of five types of mandatory guiding;[195] in effect, a vessel was under constant control of the MOHS. This created room for ambiguity regarding the basis for the calculation of fees. Russian courts failed to adjudicate disagreements on the interpretation and application of the relevant rules in a consistent manner, at times stating that it is 'impossible' to navigate the NSR without relying on the services, for which a fee was in order, and at other times stating that a fee can be collected only if icebreaker assistance had been specifically ordered and provided.[196]

---

services in transport, chapter 4 entitled 'icebreaker assistance, ice pilotage in Water Area of the NSR', dated 1 July 2015, accessed 17 March 2017 at http://fas.gov.ru/activity/tariff regulation/reestr-subektov-estestvennyix-monopolij.html [in Russian], includes only FESCO and Atomflot.

193 2013 Rules, *supra* note 43, Items 31–41.

194 See the debate, including strong diplomatic opposition, regarding compulsory pilotage adopted by Australia for the Torres Strait, for example, see Robert C Beckman, 'PSSAs and Transit Passage—Australia's Pilotage System in the Torres Strait Challenges the IMO and UNCLOS' (2007) 38:4 *Ocean Development & International Law*, 325–357. See also the 2015 US Diplomatic Note to Russia, *supra* note 22.

195 *Supra* note 55.

196 Solski, *supra* note 47 at 114; Bunik and Mikhaylichenko, *supra* note 8 at 235–236; I V Maryankova, 'Sudebnaya Praktika primenienia norm kodeksa torgovogo moreplavaniia Rosiyskoy Federatsii' (2015) 1 *Arbitrazhnye spory*; *Ocean Yearbook 28*, *supra* note 91 at 323–324.

This problem clearly required further clarification. The newly adopted approach is based on the premise that fees can only be calculated for specific services provided.[197] This reasoning is in line with Article 26 of UNCLOS, although one cannot preclude that Article 234 could arguably function as a *lex specialis* in this regard.

The amount of the fee for icebreaker assistance and ice pilotage shall be determined 'with due account of the capacity of a vessel, its ice class, the distance of icebreaker assistance and ice pilotage and the period of navigation'.[198] In furtherance of this principle, the Federal Service for Tariffs adopted two Orders on 4 March 2014. The first one sets out the general framework for the calculation of fees.[199] This Order specifies how to determine the key elements for the calculation of fees, such as the 'capacity of a vessel, the 'ice class of a vessel', the 'distance of icebreaker assistance and ice pilotage', and the 'period of navigation'.[200] The second Order establishes a ceiling for fees, expressed in monetary terms, but only for icebreaker assistance rendered by Atomflot.[201]

It is expected that the system will be further refined. The Government has taken action to establish specific and fixed fees, and ceilings for fees for all providers of icebreaker assistance and ice pilotage services, based on the economic reasonableness of costs, and supervised by the Federal Antimonopoly Service.[202] The stated aim of this initiative is to create conditions for

---

197 Under previous rules, the amount of a fee depended on the type and value of the cargo. It thus resembled a tax rather than a fee for a service. During the drafting of the 2012 Federal Law, a tonnage fee was considered but in the end not adopted, see Dmitry Tulupov, 'Russian Services Have a Price' (21 March 2013), accessed 17 March 2017 at http://russiancouncil.ru/en/analytics-and-comments/analytics/russian-services-have-a-price/.

198 Merchant Shipping Code, *supra* note 2, Art 5.1.5.

199 Federal Service for Tariffs, Order of 4 March 2014, No 46-T/2 About The Approval of Rules of the Application of Tariffs for the Icebreaker Escorting of Ships in the Water Area of the Northern Sea Route, Registered in the Ministry of Justice of Russia on 16 April 2014, No 31983.

200 Items 4–7 of this Order, as translated by the author. Note that the difference in wording between Article 5.1.5 of the Merchant Shipping Code and the present Order exists in the English text available at the website of the ANSR, but not in the Russian texts.

201 Federal Service for Tariffs, Order of 4 March 2014, No 45-T/1, About the Approval of Tariffs for the Icebreaker Escorting of Ships Rendered by Fsue 'Atomflot' in the Water Area of the Northern Sea Route, Registered in the Ministry of Justice of Russia on 31 March 2014, No 31774.

202 Decree on 'Adoption of Regulation on State Regulation of Tariffs on Icebreaker Assistance and Ice Pilotage in the Water Area of the Northern Sea Route', 24 April 2015, No 388, later amended by the Decree of the Government adopted on 4 September 2015, No 941.

sustainable and dynamic development of the NSR, based on ensuring a balance of interests between users and service providers.[203]

In total, the shift in fee policy is a major step forward in bringing Russia's legislation in conformity with the international law of the sea. The possibility that Atomflot can offer discounts for its services, however, can diminish the transparency of the system. Some discriminatory practices are possible since there are no clear rules or conditions for when discounts can be applied. If, for instance, Russian companies always obtain discounts, it is likely to amount to a violation of the requirement of non-discrimination included in Articles 26(2) and 234 of UNCLOS.

4.5 *Enforcement*

Among possible actions to ensure compliance with specific rules, a coastal State can resort to interference with navigation, such as boarding, inspection, arrest or expulsion from an area. A coastal State can also impose penalties for non-compliance. The present section will examine Russia's use of such types of enforcement actions against foreign vessels.

A general framework for the enforcement in Russian maritime zones is set out in Chapter VI of the 1998 Federal Law on the IWTSCZ[204] and Chapter VII of the 1998 Federal Law on the EEZ.[205] It is unclear, however, what action can be taken to ensure compliance with specific rules applicable to the area of the NSR. Unlike the 1990 Regulations, including a specific clause explicitly providing for expulsion of a vessel in case of non-compliance with the rules,[206] the 2013 Rules are silent on enforcement actions.

The vast majority of foreign shipmasters navigating the NSR comply with Russian rules. Enforcement of non-compliance so far has related predominantly to Russian vessels, and the relevance of this practice may offer limited insight to clarify the legal framework applicable in cases of foreign non-compliance. Yet, the publicly available information suggests that when the ANSR identifies non-compliance, it publishes the information about the incident on its website,[207] and informs Rostransnadzor, the Federal Service for Supervision of Transport, about the incident. In 2014, this organisation received

---

203 *Ibid.*

204 Article 39 of the 1998 Federal Law on IWTSCZ provides for the protection of internal waters, the territorial sea and their natural resources.

205 1998 Federal Law on the EEZ, *supra* note 36, Art 36.

206 1990 Regulations, *supra* note 38, Item 10.

207 The ANSR website, available at http://www.nsra.ru/ru/non_compliant_vessels/ [in Russian], accessed 17 March 2017.

information on 58 instances of navigation beyond permitted areas, all of which were investigated and 16 of which led to administrative measures being taken against shipowners;[208] relying in this regard on a 'remote control/monitoring principle'.[209] By implication, it does not involve at-sea interference with non-compliant vessels, but rather an administrative investigation combined with the imposition of penalties after non-compliance has been ascertained. The penalties imposed in 2014 were administrative monetary fines based on the Code for Administrative Offences of the Russian Federation (CAO).[210] Rostransnadzor investigated breaches of requirements included in specific technical regulations,[211] much of which applies only to Russian vessels.[212] Non-compliance with the 2013 Rules by a shipmaster of a foreign vessel will likely constitute an administrative offense pursuant to Article 11.7 of the CAO, which entails an imposition of an administrative fine.[213]

Since 2013, the ANSR reported only two instances of foreign vessels' non-compliance. These involved the aforementioned *Arctic Sunrise* flagged to the Netherlands—which defied the ANSR and entered the NSR without authorisation[214]—and a trimaran *Qingdao China* flagged to the United Kingdom.[215] Russia's response to these two events hardly informs its position on the scope and extent of its enforcement jurisdiction vis-à-vis merchant

208 Ministry of Transport of the Russian Federation, '17 Marta sostayalos razshyrennoe zasedanie kollegii Rostransnadzora' (17 March 2015), accessed 17 March 2017 at https://www.mintrans.ru/news/detail.php?ELEMENT_ID=26960 [in Russian].

209 *Ibid.*; note that this contrasts sharply with MOHS' wide competence to interfere with navigation on the NSR under 1990 Regulations, see *supra* note 55.

210 Specifically, Articles 11.7.1, 11.13.1 and 14.43.1 of the Code of Administrative Offences of the Russian Federation, 30 December 2001, No 195 FZ, (CAO).

211 Ministry of Transport of the Russian Federation, Rostransnadzor, novosti (29 August 2014), accessed 17 March 2017 at https://goo.gl/cL7ktW [in Russian].

212 Such as the Technical regulation on the safety of sea transport, approved by Government Decree No 620 of 12.08.2010, pursuant to the Federal Law on Technical Regulation Federal Law On Technical Regulation No 184-Fz, 27 December 2002.

213 The fine seems to be set at a very low level (up to 1000 RUB, which equalled to around 15 USD at the time of writing). Alternatively, a violation of Article 11.7. can lead to a depravation of a right to sail a vessel for up to one year, but it is doubtful that this can be imposed on foreign shipmasters.

214 Greenpeace.org, accessed 17 March 2017, http://www.greenpeace.org/finland/en/media/Press-releases/Greenpeace-defies-Russian-attempt-to-prevent-Arctic-oil-protest-enters-Kara-Sea/.

215 The ANSR reported the vessel for violation of Items 14, 19 and 42 of the 2013 Rules, which generally refer to reporting and notification requirements; see http://asmp.morflot.ru/ru/non_compliant_vessels/, accessed 17 March 2017.

shipping, as neither of the two vessels was a merchant ship. Still, it is interesting to see that Russia's response to both incidents was not consistent.

The *Arctic Sunrise* entered the NSR without a permit on 24 August 2013. Two days later, the vessel was stopped and inspected in the Kara Sea by the Federal Security Service of Russia (FSB). The lack of official permission to navigate the NSR was presented merely as a secondary reason for inspection, the primary being the lack of a raised flag.[216] On 27 August 2013, the vessel left the NSR. The FSB released a statement shortly after the incident where it states that the vessel continued its journey, although it remained under surveillance after the inspection.[217] The FSB statement indicates that, in spite of the breach of, *inter alia*, the 2013 Rules, the vessel was allowed to continue its journey on the NSR.[218] The statement is quite peculiar as it specifically states that 'foreign vessels can navigate the NSR without a permit on the condition that they comply with the rules on the safety of navigation and the protection and preservation of the marine environment'.[219] Greenpeace International, however, presented a starkly different version of the incident. Its press release contends that the vessel was boarded in the Kara Sea without the consent of the flag State and ordered to leave the NSR under threat of gunfire.[220] In support of this view, Greenpeace International released footage of the communication between the vessel's crew and the FSB officers on board of the *Arctic Sunrise*.[221] The aforementioned trimaran *Qingdao China*, however, was reported by the ANSR to have violated the 2013 Rules on account of not providing information required by Items 14, 19 and 42,[222] but the vessel was allowed to continue

216 Commentary of the FSB, available here at http://www.fsb.ru/fsb/press/message/single.htm!id%3D10437474@fsbMessage.html [in Russian], accessed 17 March 2017.

217 *Ibid.*

218 *Ibid.*

219 *Ibid.*

220 Greenpeace International, 'Russian authorities board Greenpeace ship during Arctic oil protest' (26 August 2013), accessed 17 March 2017 at http://www.greenpeace.org/international/en/press/releases/2013/Russian-authorities-board-Greenpeace-ship-during-Arctic-oil-protest/.

221 Greenpeace International, 'Russian Coast Guard threatens Greenpeace with force', accessed 17 March 2017 at http://www.greenpeace.org/international/en/multimedia/videos/Russian-coastguard-threatens-Greenpeace-with-force/. In the footage, the representative of the Russian Coast Guard orders the vessel to 'leave this area', even though it is not entirely clear if the representative is referring to the area of the NSR or any other specified area.

222 The ANSR website, accessed 17 March 2017 at http://www.nsra.ru/en/archive_non_compiant_vessels_2015/.

its journey and even broke a world record of navigating the Arctic Ocean in 13 days, powered by wind alone.[223]

Presently, it appears that the Russian government has taken steps to improve the legislation and ensure better capacity to enforce the 2013 Rules within the NSR. On 23 June 2016, President Putin signed a new law, which authorises the FSB to investigate non-compliance with the rules of navigation pursuant to Article 11.7 of the CAO within the area of the NSR.[224] While it brings more clarity with respect to which governmental body has responsibility for the enforcement of the 2013 Rules, it is still uncertain how far-reaching FSB's authority is in specific instances. It is interesting that the explanatory note to the draft law specifies that the law is aimed at 'ensuring the security of the Russian Federation in the conditions of the increase in transport activity in the area of the NSR'.[225] The focus on security in a law aimed at the enforcement of the rules of navigation on the NSR contrasts somewhat with the official purposes of the 2013 Rules, which were adopted for the purpose of ensuring safety of navigation and the protection of the marine environment.[226] Article 234 clearly does not grant any authority to exercise jurisdiction for the purpose of security.

5 Conclusions

Russia has extensive coastal State jurisdiction within the Arctic. It proclaimed a system of baselines—where straight baselines enclose most of its Arctic straits—and established a 12 nm territorial sea and a 200 nm EEZ. A significant part of these maritime zones is included in the area of the NSR, where a special set of domestic regulations apply.

The NSR plays a crucial role in Russia's grand project to revive, for economic and strategic reasons, the Arctic's potential. Russia promotes the NSR for its usefulness to international shipping, based on the understanding that the

---

223 Crjenglish.com, 'Chinese Skipper Completes Trans-Arctic Journey, Set World Record', accessed 17 March 2017 at http://english.cri.cn/12394/2015/09/16/2941s896289.htm.

224 Federal Law on Amendments to Article 23.10 of the Code for Administrative Offences of the Russian Federation, dated 23 June 2016, No 200-FZ, accessed 17 March 2017 at https://rg.ru/2016/06/28/izmeneniya2-dok.html [in Russian].

225 The explanatory note can be found at the website of the Russian Duma, accessed 17 March 2017 at http://asozd2.duma.gov.ru/main.nsf/(Spravka)?OpenAgent&RN=1008132-6 [in Russian].

226 Merchant Shipping Code, *supra* note 2, Art 5.1.2.

revenue generated by increased traffic will contribute to infrastructure investments. It is, moreover, clear that Russia expects the projected rise of shipping through the NSR not to affect the historically formed national status of this route. These two conflicting rationales and their dialectics seem to inform the overall interest and position of Russia with respect to the NSR. Different parts of the Russian government may be inclined to prioritise one interest over another, but the net result so far has been a clear focus on the usability of the NSR. On the other hand, one cannot ignore the fact that the most recent developments feature an increased role in the management of the NSR given to the FSB[227] and the MoD,[228] both traditionally focused on matters of security.

An analysis of Russia's relevant practice in recent years demonstrates that there has been an improvement in bringing domestic legislation into conformity with the international law of the sea. The practice, at least regarding prescriptive jurisdiction, is more transparent and streamlined under the newly adopted laws and regulations. Article 234 of UNCLOS seems to provide a convenient international legal basis for the legislation applicable to the NSR as, under the interpretation pursued by Russia, it allows for a sufficiently large measure of unilateral authority to adopt specific measures. Nonetheless, it appears that Russia does not have a clear, single and uniform position on whether Article 234 provides the only international legal basis for its legal regime on navigation on the NSR.

Relevant limitations to coastal State jurisdiction, included in Article 234 and other provisions of UNCLOS, are not framed in a particularly clear manner. Therefore, it is difficult to draw conclusions on the consistency of Russia's practice with international law. It is very doubtful that the requirement of prior authorisation—arguably the most controversial of the Russian NSR requirements—will be acceptable to other States in the long term. A requirement of prior notification, although clearly not as controversial as prior authorisation, can also be problematic under international law. Furthermore, Russia did not adopt its SRS, ice pilotage and icebreaker assistance schemes with any participation of the IMO. Although Article 234 in principle allows for unilateral action, seeking international approval or recognition would also have advantages for Russia. In addition, issues that require further clarification still remain; for example, it is unclear what enforcement action can or will be undertaken in case of non-compliance with formal mandatory requirements, such as the

227 The FSB has been granted the authority to investigate non-compliance with the 2013 Rules, see *supra* note 224.

228 The MoD is expected to take the leading role in the effort to establish a single logistic operator of the NSR, see *supra* note 12.

requirement of prior authorisation. Whereas the transparency of the NSR's legal regime has undeniably increased, the consistency and predictability of enforcement needs improvement. One possible explanation for these perceived ambiguities is that the legal regime of navigation on the NSR is still in the process of development.

Some elements will need to be better tailored to the new legal reality created by the Polar Code. During the negotiations, Russia took the view that the Code would not prejudice its rights as a coastal State.[229] A number of documents submitted by Russia reflect its adamant position that the Polar Code cannot impair its Article 234 powers.[230] In light of Regulation XIV-2.5 of SOLAS,[231] and Article 9(2) of MARPOL 73/78,[232] the Polar Code will not prejudice the applicability of Article 234 as such. Yet it may force Russia to amend the NSR legal regime to better correspond with the new international law.[233] It seems, for instance, reasonable to expect the mandatory Polar Code to have an effect on the standard of proof required for reliance on Article 234.[234] Moreover, in its capacity as a flag State, Russia will have to update its legislation to implement the new Polar Code. Russian commentators suggest that the implementation of the Polar Code may require amendments to the regulations of the Russian Maritime Register of Shipping or the 2013 Rules, such as incorporating the

---

229 IMO, Sub-committee on Ship Design and Equipment (DE 55/12/23), Development of a Mandatory Code for Ships Operating in Polar Waters: Procedure of Accounting for National Regulations, Submitted by the Russian Federation, 1 February 2011.

230 See Andrea Scassola, 'An International Polar Code of Navigation: Consequences and Opportunities for the Arctic' (2013) V *Yearbook of Polar Law* 271–297, at 279–280.

231 'Nothing in this chapter shall prejudice the rights or obligations of States under international law'.

232 'Nothing in the present Convention shall prejudice ... the present or future claims and legal views of any State concerning the law of the sea and the nature and extent of coastal and flag State jurisdiction'.

233 The question of the impact of the Polar Code on coastal State jurisdiction pursuant to Article 234 warrants a separate discussion and will not be addressed here. A detailed discussion is included in Chapter 5 of this Volume. As for the opinions expressed in Russian legal literature, Mikhina, *supra* note 49 at 268, argues in an unconvincing manner that the Polar Code will apply only outside the water area of the NSR since the NSR is subject to national regulation, guaranteed by Article 234 of UNCLOS. Vylegzhanin, Ivanov, Dudikina, *supra* note 98 at 55, argue that in case of conflict between the Polar Code and Article 234, the latter overrides the former.

234 Molenaar, *supra* note 86 at 290.

notion of the Polar Ship Certificate and the IACS Unified Requirements for Polar Ships.[235]

Although there remain possible points of disagreement between Russia and other States related to specific aspects of regulation of navigation on the NSR, it is evident that the NSR legal regime has been designed with a view to attract users, including foreigners. Since the interests of maritime mobility and of Russia as an Arctic coastal State coincide to a large extent, there is room for compromise. This generally positive note is to a limited degree affected by the fact that, in individual instances, Russia has acted in a more assertive manner than before. The expulsion of the *Arctic Sunrise* from the Kara Sea contrasted with a more tolerant approach towards vessels navigating in the EEZ in the past.[236] Given the special purpose of the voyage of the *Arctic Sunrise*, and the fact that Russia seemed to be largely unprepared for the challenge posed by it—both within and outside the NSR—it is difficult to conclude to what extent Russia's reaction reflects its actual position on navigational freedom and rights in the Arctic.

---

235 Vladimir Vasiliev, Vladimir Semenov, Lolii Tsoy, 'Mezhdunarodnyi Polyarnyi Kodeks IMO: Aspekty Obespecheniya Sootvetstviya Trebovaniyam Kodeksa v Rossiyskoy Federatsii', Point 3.2, accessed 17 March 2017 at http://www.cniimf.ru/news/22062015/polyarnyi-kodeks-cniimf.pdf [in Russian].

236 In the 1960s, the Soviet authorities were not happy about the presence of American vessels in the same seas but nonetheless tolerated it. For a more recent example, Franckx compares the action taken against the *Arctic Sunrise* in 2013 with the action taken against another Greenpeace vessel—the *Solo*—in 1992. The latter was ordered to stop when navigating through the Kara Gate, but when it had already entered the Russian EEZ, it was allowed to navigate for another two days. It was only detained later, when it wanted to enter the territorial sea around Novaya Zemlya, see Franckx, *supra* note 47 at 214.

CHAPTER 7

Canada and the United States

Donald R Rothwell

1 Introduction

Canada and the United States, two of the larger and politically powerful Arctic States, have had a longstanding interest in Arctic shipping and navigation. For Canada, shipping and navigation were not only critical for the initial exploration and discovery of the Canadian North, but were also pivotal to the development of the region. The Northwest Passage, an iconic Arctic waterway which is deeply ingrained in the Canadian psyche,[1] has also proven to be contentious in Canadian-US relations given differing views as to its status. For the United States, shipping and navigation has likewise been critical to the development of Alaska both economically and strategically, while US strategic interests across the Arctic as a whole have also relied heavily upon the freedom of navigation. When these historical factors are combined with the impacts of climate change and a partially ice free Arctic Ocean,[2] which in turn is attracting significant interest from states that traditionally have not had an interest in Arctic affairs, a range of diplomatic, legal and policy implications are confronting Arctic shipping and navigation.

1 Mieke Coppes and Victoria Herrmann, *First Past the Pole: Harper, Trudeau, and Canada's Arctic Values* (The Arctic Institute: Centre for Circumpolar Security Studies, October 30, 2015) accessed 17 March 2017 at http://www.thearcticinstitute.org/first-past-the-pole-harper-trudeau/; see generally Lee-Anne Broadhead, 'Canadian sovereignty verses northern security: the case for updating our mental map of the Arctic' in Leif Christian Jensen and Geir Hønneland (eds), *Handbook of the Politics of the Arctic* (Edward Elgar, 2015) 281–297.

2 The first time that consistent reports emerged of the Northwest Passage being ice-free was 2007, which coincided with a then record minimum sea ice extent being recorded for Arctic sea ice: John Roach, 'Arctic Melt Opens Northwest Passage' *National Geographic News*, 17 September 2007, accessed 17 March 2017 at http://news.nationalgeographic.com/news/2007/09/070917-northwest-passage.html; John Roach 'Arctic Ice at All-Time Low' *National Geographic News*, 20 August 2007, accessed 17 March 2017 at http://news.nationalgeographic.com/news/2007/08/070820-global-warming.html. See e.g., James Kraska (ed), *Arctic Security in an Age of Climate Change* (Cambridge University Press, 2011); Scott G Borgerson 'Arctic Meltdown: The Economic and Security Implications of Global Warming' (2008) 87 *Foreign Affairs* 63–77.

 | DOI 10.1163/9789004339385_008

One particular dimension of this renewed interest in the Arctic has been the attention given to Arctic shipping in general, and navigational issues in particular.[3] The 2009 *Arctic Maritime Shipping Assessment* (*AMSA*) *Report* highlighted this increased level of interest.[4] The *AMSA Report* indicated that during the 2004 survey year there were nearly 6,000 individual vessels operating in the Arctic region, many making multiple voyages. It was observed that '[n]early all shipping in the Arctic today is destinational, conducted for community re-supply, marine tourism and moving natural resources out of the Arctic'.[5] However, what was also apparent from the *AMSA Report* was the potential for an increase in not only destinational Arctic shipping, but also trans-Arctic shipping, that is, shipping routes that cross the Arctic Ocean from a point of entry to a point of exit. Such shipping routes may operate via the Northeast or Northwest Passage; in either case, the Bering Strait would become pivotal as a point of access or egress, or via other routes, which due to the effects of climate change may become more accessible.[6]

These developments with respect to Arctic Ocean 'chokepoints', that is, those straits and associated waterways, which allow for access to and from the Arctic Ocean, have considerable contemporary ramifications with respect to navigational rights, duties and freedoms generally within the Arctic Ocean, and particularly with respect to Arctic straits.[7] While certain bodies of water provide access to the Arctic, consideration also needs to be given to the 'exit' points. In this respect, Honderich has observed:

> What points there are, are guarded and narrow. Exit from the Arctic can be made from only four points: out the Bering Sea, which is treacherously shallow; out through the thin gap between Greenland and Canada; out through the maze of the Canadian archipelago and the Northwest

3 See e.g., Aldo Chircop 'The Growth of International Shipping in the Arctic: Is a Regulatory Review Timely?' (2009) 24 *International Journal of Marine and Coastal Law* 355–380; Erik J Molenaar 'Arctic Marine Shipping: Overview of the International Legal Framework, Gaps, and Options' (2009) 18 *Journal of Transnational Law and Policy* 289–325.

4 Arctic Council, *Arctic Marine Shipping Assessment 2009 Report* (Arctic Council, 2009) (AMSA Report).

5 *Ibid.* at 4–5.

6 See Molenaar, *supra* note 3 at 292–293.

7 Note the *AMSA Report* specifically refers to the Bering Strait as a 'crucial chokepoint'; AMSA Report, *supra* note 4 at 129; see also 109.

> Passage; and finally out the widest route, the Greenland-Iceland-United Kingdom (GIUK) Gap, which is carefully monitored by NATO.[8]

The Bering Strait and Fram Strait are of particular significance because they allow for access to and between the Pacific and Atlantic Oceans via the Arctic Ocean,[9] diminishing reliance upon routing via the Suez and Panama Canals.[10] In this respect, the Arctic Ocean is distinctive from the world's other oceans in that it is the only ocean surrounded by continents, and where there is only one major high seas point of access to the Atlantic Ocean through the Greenland and Norwegian Seas.[11] The Bering Strait is perhaps the most strategically located of the current Arctic 'chokepoints' given its location at the northern limit of the Pacific Ocean, and the direct access that it provides between the Bering Sea and Chukchi Sea into the Arctic Ocean. Given the rise in Arctic shipping, especially along the Northern Sea Route, the Bering Strait's significance to Arctic navigation will only continue to increase in the future especially due to its proximity to major trading powers, such as China, Japan and South Korea.[12] The Bering Strait will also be important if the Northwest Passage becomes a major Arctic navigation route because of the access that it provides to the Beaufort Sea for ships that are navigating west to east along the Northwest Passage en route to the US east coast and the Atlantic Ocean. The presence of six commercial ports within the Bering Strait region—three American and three Russian—located to the south of the Strait further emphasises the

8 John Honderich, *Arctic Imperative: Is Canada Losing the North?* (University of Toronto Press, 1987) 93–94. For further assessment of the GIUK Gap and its strategic significance, especially during the Cold War, see Hugh Faringdon, *Strategic Geography: NATO, the Warsaw Pact, and the Superpowers* 2nd (Routledge, 1989) 175–179.

9 AMSA Report, *supra* note 4 at 18.

10 Molenaar and Corell distinguish between 'trans-Arctic' and 'intra-Arctic' shipping—the latter being shipping within the confines of the Arctic Ocean along the Northwest Passage and the Northeast Passage/Northern Sea Route. Erik J Molenaar and Robert Corell 'Background Paper: Arctic Shipping' *Arctic Transform* (12 February 2009), accessed 17 March 2017 at http://ecologic.eu/3376.

11 The Greenland Sea is that body of water to the north of Iceland and lies between Greenland and Svalbard and via Fram Strait provides access to the Arctic Ocean; the Norwegian Sea is that body of water off the coast of Norway which between Svalbard and Norway provides access to the Barents Sea and the Northern Sea Route.

12 United States Coast Guard, *Arctic Strategy* (United States Coast Guard, 2013) 5, cites a 118 per cent increase in maritime transit through the Bering Strait from 2008–2012.

current and future commercial capability for shipping through the region.[13] The Bering Strait is also recognised by the US Department of Defense for its strategic importance, with a May 2011 Departmental publication acknowledging that:

> An increase in maritime traffic between Asia and Europe, or Russia, could also raise the prominence of the Bering Strait as a strategic chokepoint and heighten the geostrategic importance of the Arctic region.[14]

This Chapter assesses these issues by first considering the status of the two most significant Canadian and US Arctic waterways—the Northwest Passage and Bering Strait. Brief consideration will also be given to Nares Strait and Davis Strait. An assessment will then be undertaken of Canadian and US rights, duties, interests, positions and practice with respect to Arctic shipping. The dominant framework for the legal assessment is the 1982 United Nations Convention on the Law of the Sea (UNCLOS),[15] which Canada ratified in 2003 and to which the United States has yet to accede.[16]

2 The Canadian and US Arctic Straits

2.1 *Northwest Passage*

The Northwest Passage is a series of connected straits that weave through the islands that make up the Canadian Arctic Archipelago. From the east, it

---

13 AMSA Report, *supra* note 4 at 108; these being the US ports of Nome, Kotzebue and the DeLong Mountain Transportation System port that serves Red Dog Mine; and the Russian ports of Provideniya, Anadyr and Egvekinot.

14 Department of Defense (USA), *Report to Congress on Arctic Operations and the Northwest Passage* (Department of Defense, May 2011) 9; see also United States Coast Guard, *supra* note 12 at 13.

15 United Nations Convention on the Law of the Sea, adopted 10 December 1982, 1833 UNTS 397 (entered into force 16 November 1994) (UNCLOS).

16 As the United States did not sign the UNCLOS during the two-year period that it was open for signature (Article 305), the only option available for the United States to become a party to the convention is by way of accession through the mechanism provided for in Article 307. The United States has indicated its general support for the UNCLOS as per the 'President's Ocean Policy Statement, March 10, 1983' reproduced in J Ashley Roach and Robert W Smith, *Excessive Maritime Claims* 3rd (Martinus Nijhoff, 2012) Appendix One, and 'Presidential Letter of Transmittal of the Law of the Sea Convention, October 6, 1994' reproduced in *ibid.*, Appendix Six.

allows shipping to pass from the North Atlantic up through Davis Strait through the archipelago and into the Beaufort Sea which then provides access to the Chukchi Sea and the Bering Strait. While there are many potential navigation routes that in theory exist within the Canadian Arctic Archipelago, the reality is that historically due to the presence of heavy ice and the shallow draught in some of the straits there have only been a handful of viable combinations of straits that allow for commercial shipping to pass through the Northwest Passage. Pharand has identified seven routes that have been used for transit of the Northwest Passage as follows:[17]

Route 1: M'Clure Strait, Viscount Melville Sound, Barrow Strait and Lancaster Sound.

Route 2: Amundsen Gulf, Prince of Wales Strait, Viscount Melville Sound, Barrow Strait and Lancaster Sound.

Route 3: Amundsen Gulf, coastal waters to Victoria Strait, Larsen Sound, Franklin Strait, Peel Sound, Barrow Strait and Lancaster Sound.

Route 4: Similar to Route 3, but via Simpson, Rae and James Ross Straits.

Route 5: Similar to Route 3, but via Bellot Strait, not Peel Sound, then Price Regent Inlet and Lancaster Sound.

Route 6: Similar to Route 4, Simpson and James Ross Straits, then via Bellot Strait, Prince Regent Inlet and Lancaster Sound.

Route 7: By whichever route from the west, then through the Gulf of Boothia, Fury and Hecla Strait, Foxe Basin, Foxe Channel and Hudson Strait.

2.2 *The Bering Strait*

The Bering Strait is bordered by Russia to the west and the United States to the east and is approximately 51 nautical miles (nm) wide. The northern approach through the Chukchi Sea is relatively wide before it gradually narrows on approach to the strait, while the southern approach has the Aleutian Islands (United States) as a barrier to the east; however high seas equivalent navigation through the central Bering Sea presents no difficulties until St Lawrence Island (United States) is reached immediately to the south of the strait proper. St Lawrence Island straddles the southern entrance to the Bering Strait forcing shipping to route to the east or to the west between the island and the Russian

17 Donat Pharand, 'The Arctic Waters and the Northwest Passage: A Final Revisit' (2007) 38 *Ocean Development and International Law* 3, at 29; see also R K Headland, 'Ten decades of transits of the Northwest Passage' (2010) 33 (1–2) *Polar Geography* 1 at 2, 11.

mainland. The distance between the southeast point of Cape Chukoski (Russia) and Northwest Cape on St Lawrence Island is approximately 38 nm, while the Alaskan mainland is approximately 124 nm at its closest point, allowing for navigation via a high seas equivalent corridor on either side of St Lawrence Island before the Bering Strait is entered.

At the mid-point of the strait there are two islands, Big Diomede (Russia) and Little Diomede (United States), which effectively create three navigational channels:

- Bering Strait—West: which lies between the Russian mainland and Big Diomede Island approximately 22.5 nm wide;
- Bering Strait—East: which lies between the US mainland and Little Diomede Island approximately 22.5 nm wide; and
- The Diomede channel:[18] which is a 2.4 nm channel separating Big Diomede and Little Diomede Islands.[19]

Bering Strait—East and Bering Strait—West are recognised by the US Navy as international straits for the purposes of UNCLOS.[20]

The Bering Strait is the subject of a 1990 maritime boundary delimitation agreement between Russia and the United States, which extends in the south from the Bering Sea through the Strait and into the Chukchi Sea.[21] While the 1990 Agreement makes no express reference to navigational rights and free-

18 There does not appear to be an official name for the body of water that separates the two islands, other than that the waters fall within the Bering Strait; accordingly for this Chapter it is referred to as the 'Diomede channel'.

19 These measurements are taken from Roach and Smith, *supra* note 16 at 479–480.

20 A R Thomas and James C Duncan (eds), 'Annotated Supplement to The Commanders Handbook on the Law of Naval Operations' (1999) 73 *International Legal Studies* 205, Table A2–3. To the south of the Diomede Islands is Fairway Rock which is located within the US EEZ, however given the location of the rock to the south of the Diomede Islands and its small size it would not create a separate shipping channel for navigational purposes in the Bering Strait; cf. Paul Arthur Berkman, Alexander N Vylegzhanin and Oran R Young, 'Governing the Bering Strait: Current Status, Emerging Issues and Future Options' (2016) 47 *Ocean Development and International Law* 186–217, at 189; for the location of Fairway Rock, see National Oceanic and Atmospheric Administration (USA), 'St Lawrence Island to Bering Strait' Chart 16220 (2015).

21 *Agreement between the United States of America and the Union of the Soviet Socialist Republics on the Maritime Boundary*, adopted 1 June 1990, (1990) 29 *International Legal Materials* 941.

doms in the Bering Strait, there is clear recognition that while the maritime boundary places limits upon the extent of coastal State jurisdiction,[22] in all other respects the boundary does not affect or prejudice the rights of either state with respect to 'the exercise of sovereignty, sovereign rights or jurisdiction with respect to the waters' of the area.[23] It is clear therefore that other than the delimitation of the maritime boundary through the Bering Strait, the 1990 Agreement has no direct impact upon the navigational regime which applies within those waters. The 1990 Agreement has not been ratified by Russia, yet has been provisionally applied since 15 June 1990.[24]

2.3 *Canada's Other Significant Arctic Straits*

Canada also has two other significant Arctic Straits: Nares Strait and Davis Strait. Nares Strait is situated between Ellesmere Island (Canada) and Greenland (Denmark) and connects the Lincoln Sea on the fringe of the Arctic Ocean with Baffin Bay eventually leading to Davis Strait, the Labrador Sea and the Atlantic Ocean. Nares Strait comprises a number of smaller interconnecting channels and is the most far northern strait providing direct access to the Arctic Ocean. Shipping coming from Asia via the Bering Strait would, subject to ice, find the Northwest Passage a shorter route, if seeking access to North American ports. Likewise, Fram Strait would be the preferred routing for shipping making its way from the Bering Strait across the Arctic Ocean to Russian, Scandinavian and European ports. Nevertheless, Nares Strait does present an option for some international shipping, though it has traditionally been heavily ice clogged making it impassable for any form of surface shipping other than an ice breaker. The waters of Nares Strait have been delimited as part of the 1973 Agreement between Canada and Denmark relating to the Delimitation of the Continental Shelf Between Greenland and Canada.[25] While predominantly a maritime boundary dealing with the continental shelf in the broad expanses of Baffin Bay and Davis Strait, within Nares Strait the Agreement effectively delimits the territorial sea which in places throughout the strait is only 20 nm in breadth.

Nares Strait and its associated channels is clearly a strait for the purposes of Part III of the UNCLOS as it connects one area of the exclusive economic

---

22 *Ibid.*, Art 1(2).

23 *Ibid.*, Art 4.

24 Jonathan I Charney and Lewis M Alexander (eds), *International Maritime Boundaries* Vol I (Martinus Nijhoff, 1993) 452.

25 (1974) 13 *International Legal Materials* 506.

zone (EEZ)/high seas (Lincoln Sea and Arctic Ocean) with another area of the EEZ/high seas (Baffin Bay). It is a strait which is predominantly, though not exclusively, within the territorial sea of both Canada and Denmark.[26] However, while Nares Strait meets the geographic criteria, some doubt must be raised as to whether the strait at this point in time meets the functional criteria as a strait 'used for international navigation' given the very low level of reported passages of Nares Strait since the region was first subject to exploration. Unlike the Northwest Passage, Northern Sea Route, or the Bering Strait, there have been no significant reports of international maritime traffic using Nares Strait to date.[27] This position may alter over time, but presently it would appear difficult to assert that Nares Strait meets the criteria of a strait used for international navigation consistent with Article 37 of UNCLOS. This would not give to Canada or Denmark a right to bar navigation through Nares Strait subject to Article 25(3) where innocent passage can be temporarily suspended, and there is no evidence to date that either state has sought to do so; however, it does mean that instead of a right of transit passage applying through the strait, the regime of territorial sea innocent passage applies which allows for much closer regulation of the shipping passing through those waters.

Davis Strait is to the south of Nares Strait and is principally located between Baffin Bay and the Labrador Sea and fringed to the west by Baffin Island (Canada) and Greenland (Denmark). The breadth of the strait varies from between 160 nm to 510 nm. In addition to providing an access route to and from Nares Strait, it also provides an access route to and from the Northwest Passage and would therefore be of considerable significance for allowing ease of access to and from the Northwest Passage for shipping en route from east coast Canadian and US ports. Davis Strait is impacted by the 1973 Canada/Denmark Agreement; however, given the width of the strait, this has no implications for delimitation of the territorial sea and there is no area of overlapping territorial sea within the strait.

While the Davis Strait is considered by some international commentators to be an international strait of more than 24 nm in breadth,[28] it is clearly a strait within which there exists a very significant high seas corridor and as

26 Parts of the Kane Basin are beyond the limits of the Greenland territorial sea.

27 Though there remain reports of submerged submarine transits through Nares Strait; see W Harriet Critchley, 'Polar deployment of Soviet submarines' (1984) XXXIX *International Journal* 828–865, at 859–861; see also discussion in Michael Byers, *International Law and the Arctic* (Cambridge University Press, 2013) 161–163, and 167–169 regarding submarine voyages.

28 Thomas and Duncan, *supra* note 20 at 205, Table A2–3.

such is not subject to the transit passage regime, but rather is a strait within which the freedoms of high seas navigation prevail. Given the increased level of international shipping—both traditional commercial traffic and increasing cruise traffic—passing through parts of the strait, there would seem little difficulty in classifying Davis Strait as an international strait, albeit one in which the right of transit passage does not apply because it is the high seas freedom of navigation that prevails. Therefore, other than the application of Canadian and Danish marine environmental measures applicable within their respective territorial sea and EEZs, the legal regulation of navigation within the strait would not appear to be particularly contentious.

3 Canadian and US Arctic Rights and Interests

While Canada and the United States are Arctic States, the way in which they consider their Arctic lands and maritime domain, and the national and international legal and policy framework they pursue with respect to the Arctic, varies considerably. At one level this can simply be reflected in the fact that the Canadian Arctic is geographically proximate to the Canadian metropolitan state, and the Canadian image of the 'True North' is one which encompasses that part of the North American continent that predominantly encompasses polar and sub-polar lands. On the other hand, Arctic issues have historically had a low profile in the United States. While the Alaskan Arctic has certainly been appreciated for its strategic significance, especially during the Cold War,[29] the region has generally attracted disinterest in Washington.[30] Nevertheless, the United States has had a longstanding interest in navigation within the Arctic, which is not only a legacy of the Cold War and the extensive use of nuclear submarines in the region, but also because of the importance of ensuring maritime access to Alaska and its ports for both security and trade, which in turn are pivotal for Alaska's economy given its distance from major North American markets. These differing perspectives of their Arctic territories have also influenced how Canada and the United States have respectively considered their Arctic maritime domain during the era of the modern law of the sea. As a general characterisation, it is suggested that Canada's primary focus is upon sovereignty and environmental protection while for the United States its

29 Shelagh D Grant, *Polar Imperative: A History of Arctic Sovereignty in North America* (Douglas & McIntyre, 2010) 286–288.

30 Borgerson, *supra* note 2 at 71.

primary focus has been upon security and the promotion of the global maritime value of the freedom of navigation.

3.1 *Canada*

An objective assessment of Canadian Arctic sovereignty reaches the conclusion that Canada's territorial claim to the Arctic has been perfected and that it is globally recognised, with the exception of the very minor dispute with Denmark over Hans Island in Nares Strait.[31] With this exception, Canada's claim to the Arctic has either been recognised de jure or de facto by all members of the international community. Again, with the exception of Denmark in the case of Hans Island, no other State has made a competing claim or could make a credible competing claim to any part of the Canadian Arctic. Any suggestion that Canada's Arctic claim is threatened by other States, as reflected in slogans such as 'use it or lose it' as promoted by former Canadian Prime Minister Stephen Harper,[32] would appear to be baseless.[33] How Canada chooses to exercise its Arctic sovereignty is another matter altogether and the Harper government (2006–2015) in particular gave considerable attention to this issue, though not always satisfactorily making the distinction between providing appropriate government resources and developing infrastructure in the Canadian Arctic, as opposed to the very distinctive issues that arise in the context of the Canadian Arctic maritime domain.

The most recent formal statement by the Government of Canada on Arctic Foreign Policy was made in 2013 by the Harper government. That policy was based upon four pillars:

---

31 Discussed in C Stevenson, 'Hans off! The struggle for Hans Island and the potential ramifications for international border dispute resolution' (2007) 30 *Boston College International and Comparative Law Review* 263–275.

32 Stephen Harper, 'Prime Minister Stephen Harper announces new Arctic Offshore Patrol Ships' (9 July 2007), accessed 17 March 2017 at https://www.canada.ca/en/news/archive/2007/07/speech-prime-minister-stephen-harper-announces-new-arctic-offshore-patrol-ships.html.

33 See this author's more extended views on this in Donald R Rothwell, 'Arctic sovereignty and its legal significance for Canada' in Leif Christian Jensen and Geir Hønneland (eds), *Handbook of the Politics of the Arctic* (Edward Elgar, 2015) 247–261; see also Ron Macnab '"Use it or lose it" in Arctic Canada: action agenda or election hype?' (2009) 34 *Vermont Law Review* 3–14.

1. Exercising sovereignty
2. Promoting economic and social development
3. Protecting environmental heritage, and
4. Improving and developing Northern governance.[34]

With respect to the first pillar, which is of most direct relevant to this Chapter, the 2013 statement asserted the following with respect to the maritime domain:

> With regard to Arctic waters, Canada controls all maritime navigation in its waters. Nevertheless, disagreements exist between the United States and Canada regarding the maritime boundary in the Beaufort Sea (approximately 6,250 square nautical miles) and between Canada and Denmark over a small part of the maritime boundary in the Lincoln Sea. All disagreements are well managed, neither posing defence challenges for Canada nor diminishing Canada's ability to collaborate and cooperate with its Arctic neighbours. Canada will continue to manage these discrete boundary issues and will also, as a priority, seek to work with our neighbours to explore the possibility of resolving them in accordance with international law.[35]

The statement also placed emphasis upon UNCLOS and recognised emerging maritime challenges. It was observed as follows:

> Until now, the Arctic Ocean's inaccessibility has meant that the region was largely insulated from the sort of safety and law enforcement challenges present in regions further south. However, decreasing ice cover will lead, over time, to increases in shipping, tourism and economic development in the Arctic Ocean region. While the full extent of the changes will take decades to realize, Canada and other Arctic Ocean coastal states must begin to prepare for greater traffic into the region, with sometimes negative effects.[36]

34 Government of Canada, Statement on Canada's Arctic Foreign Policy (2013), accessed 17 March 2017 at http://www.international.gc.ca/arctic-arctique/assets/pdfs/canada_arctic_foreign_policy-eng.pdf.

35 *Ibid.*

36 *Ibid.* For an assessment of the Harper government's Arctic policy, especially with respect to the promotion of Canadian sovereignty, see Broadhead, *supra* note 1.

The Liberal government of Justin Trudeau, elected in October 2015, has yet to make clear whether Canada's general Arctic policy direction, or its interpretation and reliance upon international law as it applies to the Arctic, will be modified.[37]

3.2 *The United States*

Consistent with the gradual awakening of awareness of the Arctic's importance, US government agencies have in recent years identified the need for appropriate policy responses to be developed as a result of changing circumstances. Two recent initiatives of the Bush and Obama Administrations highlight the increased significance that is attaching to Arctic affairs in the United States, and reinforces the importance of Arctic navigational rights and freedoms to the United States. The joint National Security Presidential Directive (NSPD)/Homeland Security Presidential Directive (HSPD) of 9 January 2009 titled 'Arctic Region Policy'[38] sought to update US Arctic-wide policy for the first time since 1994. The Policy recognises that the United States 'has broad and fundamental national security interests in the Arctic region and is prepared to operate either independently or in conjunction with other states to safe-guard these interests',[39] consistently with US obligations under treaties, customary international law, and the law of the sea.[40] The policy directly asserts with respect to US National Security and Homeland Security Interests in the Arctic that:

> Freedom of the seas is a top national priority. The Northwest Passage is a strait used for international navigation, and the Northern Sea Route includes straits used for international navigation; the regime of transit passage applies to passage through those straits. Preserving the rights and duties relating to navigation and overflight in the Arctic region

---

37 For some initial discussion of the challenges the Trudeau government may face in this area see Coppes and Herrmann, *supra* note 1; and Scott Gilmore, 'Vladimir Putin, Justin Trudeau, and Canada's Arctic problem' *Macleans* (November 4, 2015), accessed 17 March 2017 at http://www.macleans.ca/news/canada/vladimir-putin-justin-trudeau-and-canadas-arctic-problem/.

38 United States of America, 'Arctic Region Policy' National Security Presidential Directive/NSPD—66; Homeland Security Presidential Directive/HSPD—25' (9 January 2009), accessed 17 March 2017 at https://fas.org/irp/offdocs/nspd/nspd-66.htm.

39 *Ibid.*, para III.B.1.

40 *Ibid.*, para I.B.

> supports our ability to exercise these rights throughout the world, including through strategic straits.[41]

The policy goes on to identify further the importance to the United States of maritime transportation in the Arctic, and the need to develop new measures to improve the safety and security of maritime transportation, including ships routing and reporting, traffic separation schemes, and vessel management schemes in what are termed 'Arctic chokepoints'.[42]

More recently, in 2013 the Obama Administration released the *National Strategy for the Arctic Region*,[43] which focuses attention upon advancing US security interests in the Arctic, developing 'Responsible Arctic Region Stewardship', and strengthening international cooperation. The Strategy acknowledges the changing conditions in the Arctic, including that the Arctic Ocean is becoming more navigable, which is increasing interest in the Northwest Passage.[44] Under the general heading of advancing US security interests, it acknowledges that the United States will seek to:

> Preserve Arctic Region Freedom of the Seas—The United States has a national interest in preserving all of the rights, freedoms and uses of the sea and airspace recognized under international law. We will enable prosperity and safe transit by developing and maintaining sea, under-sea, and air assets and necessary infrastructure.... Existing international law provides a comprehensive set of rules governing the rights, freedoms, and uses of the world's oceans and airspace, including the Arctic. The law recognizes these rights, freedoms, and other uses for commercial and military vessels and aircraft.... We will also encourage other nations to adhere to internationally accepted principles.[45]

The Strategy goes on to identify 'Guiding Principles', which are stated to include 'international legal principles of freedom of navigation ... and other uses of the sea related to these freedoms, unimpeded lawful commerce, and the

---

41 *Ibid.*, para III.B.5.

42 *Ibid.*, para III.F.3; these overarching policy considerations for the United States in the Arctic are also reflected in a 2011 Department of Defense publication: Department of Defense, *supra* note 14.

43 President of the United States, *National Strategy for the Arctic Region* (White House, May 2013).

44 *Ibid.* at 5.

45 *Ibid.* at 6–7.

peaceful resolution of disputes'.[46] The 2013 National Strategy for the Arctic Region has now been backed up by a 2015 Presidential Executive Order on 'Enhancing Coordination of National Efforts in the Arctic',[47] which seeks to ensure better coordination of US national efforts in the Arctic.[48] In 2015, President Obama also became the first sitting US President to visit Arctic Alaska.[49]

Freedom of navigation in the Arctic and globally remains a common theme for the United States in its engagement in the region. In September 2015, reports emerged that five Chinese People's Liberation Army Navy vessels had been observed in the Bering Sea off the Alaskan coast. When questioned on the US response, a State Department spokesperson observed that: 'This is certainly the first time we have observed Chinese navy ships in the Bering Sea, but that said, we do certainly respect the freedom of all nations to operate military vessels in international waters in accordance with international law.'[50]

4 Canadian and US Arctic Positions and Practice

4.1 *Northwest Passage: Canadian Practice and US Position*

The status of the Northwest Passage as a shipping route had legally been relatively uncontroversial for much of the 20th century. This was primarily due to the lack of interest that had been shown by commercial navigation in the use of the Passage, and the challenges posed to such navigation by the ice conditions. While the United States took an interest in the Northwest Passage

---

46 *Ibid.* at 10.

47 Government of the United States of America, 'Executive Order: Enhancing Coordination of National Efforts in the Arctic' (21 January 2015), accessed 17 March 2017 at https://obamawhitehouse.archives.gov/the-press-office/2015/01/21/executive-order-enhancing-coordination-national-efforts-arctic.

48 For an assessment of these policy developments in the United States with respect to the Arctic, see Barry Scott Zellen, 'Where East and West converge: the US embrace of collaborative security for the Arctic' in Leif Christian Jensen and Geir Hønneland (eds), *Handbook of the Politics of the Arctic* (Edward Elgar, 2015) 550–572.

49 Julie Hirschfeld Davis, 'Obama, Visiting Arctic, Will Pledge Aid to Alaskans Hit by Climate Change' *The New York Times* (2 September 2015), accessed 17 March 2017 at http://www.nytimes.com/2015/09/03/us/politics/obama-arctic-alaska-climate-change.html?_r=0.

50 'Chinese ships headed home after Bering Sea sighting: U.S. Navy' *Reuters* (4 September 2015), 17 March 2017 at http://www.reuters.com/article/us-usa-china-military-drills-idUSKCN0R30F120150904; see also Helene Cooper, 'In a First, Chinese Navy Sails Off Alaska' *The New York Times* (2 September 2015), accessed 17 March 2017 at https://www.nytimes.com/2015/09/03/world/asia/in-a-first-chinese-navy-sails-off-alaska.html?rref=collection%2Fbyline%2Fhelene-cooper&action=click&contentCollection=undefined&region=stream&module=stream_unit&version=latest&contentPlacement=221&pgtype=collection.

during the early part of the 20th century, this was a lesser order issue compared to Arctic sovereignty more generally and ultimately the threat posed by the Soviet Union across the Arctic Ocean during the Cold War.[51] This all changed in 1969 with the voyage of the *SS Manhattan* from the Beaufort Sea through the Northwest Passage to the Davis Strait. The *Manhattan* was an icebreaking supertanker carrying a small quantity of oil that was intentionally sent through the Northwest Passage by its US owners to demonstrate that such a vessel was capable of year-round sailings between Alaska and the US east coast. The voyage at that time was only the fifth recorded transit of the Northwest Passage, and the first since the end of World War II by a non-government vessel.[52]

Despite the fact that there was a Canadian government official on board during the voyage, and that the *Manhattan* was accompanied by the Canadian Coast Guard vessel *J.A. Macdonald*,[53] the voyage raised multiple issues for the Canadian government.[54] Ultimately, it was the second proposed voyage of the *Manhattan*, scheduled for 1970 and again accompanied by the *J.A. Macdonald*, that raised further public concerns about the status of the Northwest Passage and related fears about Canadian Arctic sovereignty. The United States was perceived, rightly or wrongly, as ignoring Canadian sovereignty by these voyages through 'Canadian waters' and public pressure grew for the Government of Canada to reaffirm Canada's Arctic sovereignty and to ensure that any future voyages did not pose a threat to that sovereignty.[55] In the wake of the *Manhattan* voyage, the government of Liberal Prime Minister Pierre Trudeau[56] adopted a number of measures including enactment of the *Arctic Waters Pollution Prevention Act*,[57] extension of the Canadian territorial sea from 3 to 12 nm, and modification of Canada's acceptance of the compulsory jurisdiction of the International Court of Justice so as to place a bar on any attempt by the United States to challenge Canada's response before the court.

---

51 Grant, *supra* note 29 at 247–338.

52 See discussion of the voyage at T C Pullen, 'What Price Canadian Sovereignty?' (1987) 113 (9) *Proceedings of the US Naval Institute* 66, at 69–71; Pharand, *supra* note 17 at 31 observes that the USCG ships *Storis, Spar* and *Bramble* (all icebreakers) all completed transits in 1957.

53 Pullen, *supra* note 52 at 71.

54 For an initial review, see Donat Pharand, *The Law of the Sea of the Arctic with Special Reference to Canada* (University of Ottawa Press, 1973) 55–57.

55 See discussion in Maxwell Cohen, 'The Arctic and the National Interest' (1970) 26 *International Journal* 52, at 67–68.

56 Trudeau was Prime Minister of Canada from April 1968-June 1979, and March 1980–June 1984; his son, Justin, was elected Prime Minister in 2015.

57 *Arctic Waters Pollution Prevention Act* 1970 (Canada).

Canada's actions, which took place prior to the commencement of the Third United Nations Conference on the Law of the Sea, were not welcomed by the United States. The Department of State asserted that:

> International law provides no basis for these proposed unilateral extensions of jurisdiction on the high seas, and the United States can neither accept nor acquiesce in the assertions of such jurisdiction.[58]

Particular concern was raised as to the impact of these actions upon the freedom of navigation.[59]

4.1.1 *Polar Sea* Transit

Further controversy arose over the status of the Northwest Passage between Canada and the United States in 1985 when it was announced that the *USCGC Polar Sea* would sail through the Passage from east to west as part of a repositioning of the vessel from Greenland to the US west coast. At the time, the US Embassy in Ottawa informed the Canadian Department of External Affairs on 21 May 1985 of the proposed voyage, but did not seek permission for the voyage to take place. It was observed in a *demarche* that:

> The United States considers that this transit by the icebreaker *Polar Sea* will be an exercise of navigational rights and freedoms not requiring prior notification. The United States appreciates that Canada may not share this position.[60]

The US *demarche* was careful to state that an invitation to Canada for its officials to be 'on-board participants' during the transit of the *Polar Sea* was not 'inconsistent with its juridical position' and that Canadian participation in the transit would likewise not be inconsistent with its juridical position.[61]

Following a Canadian response of 11 June 1985 in which Canada made clear that the 'waters of the Arctic Archipelago, including the Northwest Passage, are

---

58 J A Beesley and C B Bourne (eds), 'Canadian Practice in International Law during 1970 as Reflected Mainly in Public Correspondence and Statements of the Department of External Affairs' (1971) 9 *Canadian Yearbook of International Law* 288.

59 *Ibid.* at 287–288; see also Marian Nash, *Cumulative Digest of United States Practice in International Law 1981–1988* vol II (Department of State, 1994) 2043–2052; Roach and Smith, *supra* note 16 at 319.

60 Roach and Smith, *supra* note 16 at 320.

61 *Ibid.* at 321.

internal waters of Canada and fall within Canadian sovereignty',[62] the United States responded on 24 June 1985 by observing that it 'did not share this view' and made clear that while it was pleased to invite Canadian participation in the transit, 'it has not sought the permission of the Government of Canada, nor has it given notification of the fact of the transit'.[63] At the time the Canadian Minister for External Affairs, Joe Clark, commented in the House of Commons that the voyage 'does not compromise in any way the sovereignty of Canada over our northern waters, or affect the quite legitimate differences of views that exist between Canada and the United States on that question'.[64]

The *Polar Sea* completed its transit of the Northwest Passage between 1–11 August 1985. However, in September and following a comprehensive review of Canadian Arctic Policy, Clark announced to the Canadian Parliament a series of six new initiatives that were designed to clarify Canada's legal position with respect to the region. These initiatives included the declaration of straight baselines around the islands that make up the Canadian Arctic Archipelago, new legislation to enforce Canadian civil and criminal law in the waters enclosed within the baselines, and talks with the United States on cooperation over Arctic waters.[65]

4.1.2 Agreement on Arctic Cooperation

The 1988 Agreement on Arctic Cooperation[66] between Canada and the United States is often interpreted as being closely linked to the events of 1985 associated with the *Polar Sea* voyage and Canada's response. The 1988 Agreement focuses on the shared interest of both countries in research conducted during icebreaker navigation off their Arctic coasts and commits both governments to facilitating such navigation and to share research information arising from such voyages. However, the 1988 Agreement also touches upon Northwest Passage issues and directly alludes to this when in Article 3 it provides:

> The Government of the United States pledges that all navigation by U.S. icebreakers within waters claimed by Canada to be internal will be undertaken with the consent of the Government of Canada.

62 *Ibid.*

63 *Ibid.* at 322; see also Nash, *supra* note 59 at 2044–2049.

64 Canada, House of Commons, Debates, vol IV at 6,043 (20 June 1985).

65 Canada, House of Commons, Debates, vol V at 6,463 (10 September 1985).

66 Agreement between the Government of Canada and the Government of the United States of America on Arctic Cooperation, adopted 11 January 1988, 1852 UNTS 59.

In the wake of Canada's 1985 baselines declaration, which enclosed the waters of the Northwest Passage within Canadian proclaimed baselines thereby making all of those waters internal waters, any US icebreaker navigation through the Northwest Passage would pass through Canadian internal waters and so be caught by the apparent obligations to request Canadian consent. However, as both Pharand and McDorman have separately noted, the consent provision needs to be read in the context of how the 1988 Agreement was framed around cooperation for the purposes of research, and that as there is no right under international law for foreign vessels to conduct research within internal waters of another state, the consent provision became necessary so as to acknowledge Canada's core entitlement under international law.[67] Even if the United States had maintained that any transit of the Northwest Passage by its Coast Guard icebreakers was in fact an exercise of transit passage through an international strait, permission would still have been required to conduct research because marine scientific research is not a right that is enjoyed by foreign-flagged vessels in transit passage.[68]

The 1988 Agreement further sought to maintain the essential position of both parties with respect to their prior interpretations of the law of the sea when in Article 4 it was provided that:

> Nothing in this agreement of cooperative endeavour between Arctic neighbours and friends nor any practice thereunder affects the respective positions of the Governments of the United States and of Canada on the Law of the Sea in this or other maritime areas or their respective positions regarding third parties.

At a Press Conference involving Canadian Minister for External Affairs, Joe Clark, and the US Secretary of State, George Shultz, that followed the conclusion of the 1988 Agreement, it was apparent that both governments were of the view that their positions regarding sovereignty over the Northwest Passage, and particularly the US position as to whether consent was required for transit by US military vessels, had not changed as a result of the 1988 Agreement.[69]

---

67 Pharand, *supra* note 17 at 39–40; and Ted L McDorman, *Salt Water Neighbors: International Ocean Law Relations between the United States and Canada* (Oxford University Press, 2009) 250.

68 UNCLOS, Article 40 requires foreign ships seek prior authorisation to conduct marine scientific research during transit passage.

69 Roach and Smith, *supra* note 16 at 325; see also Pharand, *supra* note 17 at 39–40; Nash, *supra* note 59 at 2049–2052.

The first request by the United States for an icebreaker transit conducted consistently with the 1988 Agreement occurred in October 1988 when consent was sought for transit of the *USCGC Polar Star*. In a Note from the US Embassy in Ottawa, the United States expressly sought the consent of the Government of Canada for the transit during which it was made clear that marine scientific research would be conducted. It was also made clear that the *Polar Star* would operate consistently with Canadian law, and a further offer was made that costs incurred from any discharge from the vessel would be the responsibility of the United States in accordance with international law.[70] Canadian consent was given for this transit, which was the first of five transits from 1988–2003.

By the mechanism of the 1988 Agreement, Canada and the United States effectively removed some of the public controversy that had been associated with the 1985 *Polar Sea* Northwest Passage transit and the Canadian government's response. However, as can be seen from a review of the US government's official statements on Arctic policy from 2009 and 2013, the US position on the Northwest Passage remains unchanged. McDorman's 2009 assessment of the situation therefore remains apt:

> The 1988 Agreement, however, was a political fix and not a legal fix to accommodate Canada while not undermining the U.S. legal position. It is an important and instructive example of the cooperative approach that Canada and the United States frequently are able to pursue to circumvent international ocean law disputes.[71]

4.1.3 The Northwest Passage as an International Strait

One of the pivotal legal issues that arises in any analysis of the status of the Northwest Passage is whether it is possible to equate it with a single strait, or whether it is appropriate to characterise it as a series of interconnected straits. In this regard, the Northwest Passage could be considered unique as both customary international law and UNCLOS have focused on the situation of a single strait, and not a series of straits that in sum comprise a navigational route from one area of the high seas/EEZ to another. Nevertheless, it is not contested that the Northwest Passage meets the geographic requirement of a strait or a series of straits as reflected in decisions such as the *Corfu Channel* case, in treaty law

70 American Embassy Ottawa Note. 425 (10 October 1988) reproduced in Roach and Smith, *supra* note 16 at 325.

71 McDorman, *supra* note 67 at 251.

such as in the Convention on the Territorial Sea and the Contiguous Zone or UNCLOS, or in customary international law.[72]

The most significant requirement, and one that has been the principal point of contention between Canada and the United States, is the functional requirement referred to in *Corfu Channel* that the strait actually be used for international navigation. The United States contests this positon and asserts generally with respect to the exercise of transit passage through an international strait that the right can be exercised through any strait capable of being used for international navigation.[73] Pharand's view has been that because of the low number of recorded transits of the strait it would not be possible to classify the Northwest Passage as a 'strait used for international navigation'.[74] This clearly raises issues as to the actual recorded number of transits that have taken place, whether distinctions should be made between historical figures and more contemporary assessments, and the percentage of transits completed by non-Canadian flagged vessels.[75] Pharand identified 15 transits of the Northwest Passage by US flagged vessels in the period to 2005, of which only two were by non-government vessels—the *Manhattan* (1969–1970) and an adventure yacht, the *Belvedere* (1983–1988).[76] More recent figures have indicated 18 transits of the Northwest Passage during the summer of 2010,[77] 30 transits in 2012 and 17 transits in 2014.[78]

Relying upon the actual use of the Northwest Passage since the first successful navigation, Pharand has maintained that the Passage is not an international

72 See Pharand in Donat Pharand, *Canada's Arctic waters in international law* (Cambridge University Press, 1988) 223–224; Donat Pharand, 'Sovereignty in the Arctic: The International Legal Context' in Edgar J Dosman (ed), *Sovereignty and Security in the Arctic* (Routledge, 1989) 145, at 153–154.

73 Roach and Smith, *supra* note 16 at 277–278; 'Senate Executive Report on the Law of the Sea' reproduced in ibid., Appendix Nine, 809 'Understanding 3(D)'.

74 Pharand (1988), *supra* note 72 at 202–214.

75 From the time of the very first transit of the Passage in 1903–1906 by Amundsen until 2005, Pharand identified 69 foreign transits: Pharand, *supra* note 17 at 32–33.

76 *Ibid.* at 31–32.

77 See discussion in Roach and Smith, *supra* note 16 at 478.

78 Environment and Natural Resources (Northwest Territories), '7.3 Trends in shipping in the Northwest Passage and the Beaufort Sea' *State of the Environment* (29 May 2015), accessed 17 March 2017 at http://www.enr.gov.nt.ca/state-environment/73-trends-shipping-northwest-passage-and-beaufort-sea; Headland, *supra* note 17 at 3–9, identified 135 full transits of the Northwest Passage in the period 1903–2009.

strait.[79] He has argued that those who contend otherwise confused potential use with actual use and that mere capacity is not what is required but rather actual use.[80] The United States, however, as recently as May 2013 has reasserted its position that it enjoys the freedom of navigation through the Northwest Passage.[81]

In assessing these differing views, it is important to reflect upon the *Corfu Channel* case formulation where it was observed that: '[I]n the opinion of the Court the decisive criteria is rather its geographical situation as connecting two parts of the high seas and the fact of its being used for international navigation'.[82] The Northwest Passage clearly meets the first element of the test as it is a waterway that geographically connects two bodies of equivalent high seas areas. As to the second element, while prior use of the Northwest Passage for international navigation has been very intermittent, that position has changed in the 21st century as a result of the increase in the regularity of transit by foreign-flagged vessels. While the conclusion must therefore be that the Northwest Passage is an international strait for the purposes of UNCLOS, some caution needs to be exercised with this view because the enclosure of the Passage by Canada's straight baselines, thereby converting them to internal waters, has the result that all transits conducted since 1985 have presumably been undertaken with consent and not by way of exercise of the right of transit passage.

4.2 *NORDREG*

In August 2008, Canada announced that it intended to make what was previously a voluntary Vessel Traffic System (VTS) within Canadian Arctic waters mandatory.[83] The amendments became effective in 2009 and remain operative as the 'Northern Canada Vessel Traffic Services Zone Regulations'

---

79 Donat Pharand, 'Canada's Sovereignty over the Northwest Passage' (1989) 10 *Michigan Journal of International Law* 653 at 669–670; Pharand (1988), *supra* note 72 at 225; Donat Pharand, 'The Northwest Passage in International Law' (1979) 17 *Canadian Yearbook of International Law* 99 at 112–113.

80 Pharand (1988), *supra* note 72 at 225; Pharand (1979), *ibid.* at 113.

81 President of the United States, *supra* note 43 at 9.

82 *Corfu Channel* (United Kingdom v Albania) [1949] ICJ Rep 4, 28.

83 'Archived—Prime Minister Harper Announces Government of Canada Will Extend Jurisdiction over Arctic Waters' Government of Canada News Release—Office of the Prime Minister (27 August 2008), accessed 17 March 2017 at https://www.canada.ca/en/news/archive/2008/08/prime-minister-harper-announces-government-canada-extend-jurisdiction-over-arctic-waters.html.

(NORDREG),[84] made under the framework of the Canada Shipping Act, 2001.[85] NORDREG applies to essentially two types of Canadian Arctic waters: waters prescribed under the Shipping Safety Control Zones Order, which encompass waters that extend to a distance of 200 nm from the territorial sea baseline, and various internal waters within Canada's Arctic baselines, such as the waters of Hudson Bay and James Bay.[86] The relevant waters commence in places as far south as 60°N and encompass the Canadian EEZ as it surrounds the islands of the Canadian Arctic Archipelago to the limits of agreed or respected maritime boundaries with Denmark and the United States.[87] The regulations apply to vessels of 300 gross tonnage, vessels engaged in towing or pushing certain other vessels, and vessels that are carrying or pushing or towing a vessel carrying a pollutant or dangerous goods.[88] Vessels entering the NORDREG controlled area are to provide a sailing plan report, position reports upon entry into the NORDREG area and thereafter on a 24 hour basis, and as soon as feasible once a vessel's master becomes aware of another vessel in difficulty, an obstruction to navigation, hazardous navigational conditions, or a pollutant in the water.[89] Final reports are also to be issued once a vessel has arrived at a berth within the NORDREG Zone, or exited the Zone.[90]

The legitimacy of the NORDREG regulations were the subject of diplomatic exchange between Canada and the United States in 2010, and between Canada, the United States and other States at the International Maritime Organisation (IMO) at the same time.[91] The US critique of NORDREG is framed around the view that they are not supportable under Article 234 of UNCLOS and represent an infringement of the freedom of navigation. Article 234 relevantly provides:

> Coastal States have the right to adopt and enforce non-discriminatory laws and regulations for the prevention, reduction and control of marine pollution from vessels in ice-covered areas within the limits of the

---

84 SOR/2010–127 (10 June 2010) Canada Shipping Act, 2001, SC 2001, c 26.

85 SC 2001, c 26.

86 Northern Canada Vessel Traffic Services Zone Regulations, s 2.

87 Shipping Safety Control Zones Order, CRC, c 356, s 2 and Schedules 1 and 2.

88 Northern Canada Vessel Traffic Services Zone Regulations, s 3.

89 Northern Canada Vessel Traffic Services Zone Regulations, ss 5, 6, 7.

90 Northern Canada Vessel Traffic Services Zone Regulations, s 8. A deviation report is also to be provided if the vessel changes its sailing plan: *ibid.*, s 9.

91 For discussion of the IMO debate, see James Kraska, 'The Northern Canada Vessel Traffic Services Zone Regulations (NORDREG) and the Law of the Sea' (2015) 30 *International Journal of Marine and Coastal Law* 225–254, at 243–247 noting the views also of Germany and Singapore.

> exclusive economic zone, where particularly severe climatic conditions and the presence of ice covering such areas for most of the year create obstructions or exceptional hazards to navigation, and pollution of the marine environment could cause major harm to or irreversible disturbance of the ecological balance. Such laws and regulations shall have due regard to navigation and the protection and preservation of the marine environment based on the best available scientific evidence.[92]

While the United States acknowledged its support for navigational safety and environmental protection objectives in NORDREG and the protection of the marine environment in the Arctic, at the time NORDREG entered into effect the US positon was that they were inconsistent with the freedom of navigation including the rights of innocent passage and transit passage, failed to respect the rights of sovereign immune vessels under Article 236 of UNCLOS, and that Canada had circumvented IMO mechanisms through the adoption of these measures.[93]

Notwithstanding these criticisms, Canada has proceeded to give effect to NORDREG within its declared waters that make up the Canadian Arctic. For commercial shipping, compliance is the 'easiest way to ensure hassle-free transit'[94] and because of the exemptions for sovereign immune vessels no issues to date have arisen with respect to US government vessels operating in the Canadian Arctic beyond the Northwest Passage. Much of the Canadian/US disagreement with respect to NORDREG comes down to Canada's history of unilateral Arctic marine environmental protection measures against continued US assertions of the freedom of navigation via diplomatic channels and

92 Article 234 has been the subject of exhaustive analysis in the scholarly literature, including more recently in Michael Byers, *International Law and the Arctic* (Cambridge University Press, 2013) 185–188; Armand de Mestral, 'Article 234 of the United Nations Convention on the Law of the Sea: Its Origins and Future' in Suzanne Lalonde and Ted L McDorman (eds), *International Law and the Politics of the Arctic Ocean: Essays in Honour of Donat Pharand* (Brill, 2015) 111–124; James Kraska, 'Governance of Ice-Covered Areas: Rule Construction in the Arctic Ocean' (2014) 45 *Ocean Development and International Law* 260–271.

93 See 'U.S. letter to the Canadian Ministry of Transport, commenting on Canada's draft Northern Canada Vessel Traffic Services Zone Regulations ("NORDREG") (March 19, 2010)' *Digest of United States Practice in International Law* 2010, 515; 'U.S. diplomatic note to Canadian Department of Foreign Affairs and International Trade, commenting on Canada's NORDREG (July 2010)' *Digest of United States Practice in International Law* 2010, 518.

94 Kraska, *supra* note 91 at 247.

the actions of the US military. Nevertheless, Canada's reliance upon Article 234 as justification for NORDREG may increasingly be on a weak legal foundation given the need for the waters subject to such measures to be ice-covered for 'most of the year'. As the Arctic sea ice cover therefore recedes from parts of the Canadian EEZ, so too may the legal basis for NORDREG. Canada may therefore have to confront the fact that given its express reliance upon Article 234 as providing an international law foundation for the enactment of NORDREG and given the intent of that provision in providing a coastal State with an exceptional right to adopt certain EEZ marine pollution measures that go beyond the general capacity of a coastal State to adopt equivalent measures in ice-free waters, the right would cease if the waters no longer possessed the relevant ice-covered characteristics. The United States, and other potential user States of Canadian Arctic waters, may therefore be carefully monitoring Canada's position with respect to NORDREG if climate change continues to impact upon the extent of ice in the Canadian EEZ.

4.3 *The United States and the Bering Strait*

The Bering Strait meets all the geographic requirements of a strait for the purposes of Part III of UNCLOS in that it is a body of water that connects one part of the EEZ/high seas (Bering Sea) with another part of the EEZ/high seas (Chukchi Sea). That technically there may exist three geographic straits within the body of water known as the Bering Strait (Bering Strait—East; Bering Strait—West and the Diomede channel) is irrelevant for the purposes of UNCLOS, and there are many other international straits throughout the world that are formed by two opposite land masses within which there may be scattered small islands.[95] Whether the Bering Strait is one used for 'international navigation' in the *Corfu Channel* sense may have been contestable in the past, but it would appear clear on the basis of current usage that the strait is certainly considered useful for international navigation. For example, the 2009 *AMSA Report* noted that at that time '150 large commercial vessels pass through the Bering Strait during the July-October open water period, with transits of these vessels most frequent at the beginning (spring) and end of the period (autumn)'.[96] While some caution needs to be exercised because of the usage of the strait by previously Soviet and currently Russian flagged shipping, it is clear that on current and future projections the strait will be used by many ships other than those which are Russian or US flagged. On that basis,

---

95 The Torres Strait (Australia/Papua New Guinea) and the Singapore Strait (Singapore/Indonesia) are significant examples.

96 AMSA Report, *supra* note 4 at 109.

the Bering Strait meets the requirements for an international strait under Part III of UNCLOS and the regime of transit passage applies.[97]

A somewhat unique feature of the Bering Strait is that international shipping has effectively two viable routes through the Strait: the 'Russian route' to the west of the Diomede Islands and through the Russian territorial sea; and the 'American route' to the east of the Diomede Islands and through the US territorial sea. The Diomede channel, at only 2.4 nm does not appear to be wide enough when compared to the alternate routes to be attractive to commercial shipping. There is also the dimension that the waters between the islands fall within the Russia/US maritime boundary with the effect that shipping would be subject to both Russian and US law at different times as they completed their transit.

In principle, the existence of alternate American and Russian routes through the strait does not raise any significant international law issues given that UNCLOS creates a set of standards that are equally applicable to each route and are not dependent on the strait being a 'one state' or 'two state' strait. It does, however, highlight the fact that the United States has yet to become a party to UNCLOS, and whilst US state practice has been to adhere consistently to the transit passage regime and effectively accept its status as part of customary international law,[98] it still does raise the potential for slight variations in state practice in the interpretation of transit passage on either side of the strait. It also raises the prospect of differing laws and regulations being applicable within either the Russian or US side of the strait, though assuming consistency with Article 42 of UNCLOS such laws are to be non-discriminatory and to not deny, hamper or impair the right of passage. Given the environmental sensitivity associated with all aspects of Arctic shipping, some consideration may in due course be given to the establishment of sea lanes and a

97 The view is also endorsed by the *AMSA Report*, which states that 'The Bering Strait region is an international strait for navigation and a natural chokepoint for marine traffic in and out of the Arctic Ocean from the Pacific Ocean': AMSA Report, *supra* note 4 at 109; for further discussion of maritime traffic in the Bering Strait, see Andrew Hartsig, Ivy Fredrickson, Carmen Yeung, Stan Senner, 'Arctic Bottleneck: Protecting the Bering Strait Region from Increased Vessel Traffic' (2012) 18 *Ocean and Coastal Law Journal* 35, at 46–47, 49–52.

98 See United States Presidential Proclamation 5928 (27 December 1988) in which President Reagan stated that 'In accordance with international law, as reflected in the applicable provisions of the 1982 United Nations Convention on the Law of the Sea, with the territorial sea of the United States, ... the ships and aircraft of all countries enjoy the right of transit passage through international straits'; see generally Roach and Smith, *supra* note 16 at 271–275.

traffic separation scheme through the Bering Strait so as to facilitate 'one way' north-south and south-north traffic on either side of the Diomede Islands. Such measures would be consistent with Article 41 of UNCLOS, but would require cooperation between Russia and the United States in referring such a proposal to the IMO for adoption. The *AMSA Report* noted there were no vessel routing measures within the Bering Strait and few aids to navigation. Given the significant potential of this strait for increased maritime traffic and the difficult navigational conditions, it would be anticipated that in due course such arrangements will be put in place.[99] In response to these developments, in 2010 the US Coast Guard commenced a 'Port Access Route Study' (PARS) in order to assess whether there was a need to create new vessel routing measures in the Bering Strait.[100] While the area under review only encompasses US waters in the strait, the Coast Guard study does have the potential to facilitate appropriate bilateral arrangements with Russia if those are deemed appropriate. In 2015, the US Coast Guard observed that 'A thorough Bering Strait PARS, with input from other Arctic Nations, will provide valuable recommendations for the International Maritime Organization'.[101]

In 2012, the Alaska Legislature in a report into Alaska's Northern Waters recommended that the United States seek to work within the IMO for the establishment of a Bering Strait Vessel Traffic Separation Scheme in which it was commented that:

> The remote, narrow, and hazardous international strait is located in an environmentally sensitive area with little or no search and rescue or maritime-disaster response capability within 800 miles. Increased vessel traffic in the future will make this area particularly vulnerable to maritime disasters. It is only prudent that basic routing measures and vessel monitoring systems be put in place to reduce the risk of calamity in the Bering Strait.[102]

99 AMSA Report, *supra* note 4 at 109.

100 Department of Homeland Security: United States Coast Guard, 'Port Access Route Study: In the Bering Strait', 33 CFR Part 167, *Federal Register*, 75 (No 215), 8 November 2010.

101 Vice Admiral Charles D Michel (Vice-Commandant, US Coast Guard) 'Testimony on "Arctic Operations" before the House Foreign Affairs Committee—Western Hemisphere & Europe, Eurasia, and Emerging Threats Subcommittees' (17 November 2015), accessed 17 March 2017 at http://docs.house.gov/meetings/FA/FA14/20151117/104201/HHRG-114-FA14-Wstate-MichelC-20151117.pdf.

102 Alaska State Legislature, *Findings and Recommendations of the Alaska Northern Waters Task Force* (January 2012) 14–15, accessed 17 March 2017 at http://www.maritime-executive.com/article/coast-guard-defines-bering-strait-shipping-lane.

In November 2015, the United States Coast Guard released details on a proposed four-mile wide commercial shipping lane through the Strait, which would also include vessel traffic services and a traffic separation scheme.[103]

5 Concluding Remarks

Canada and the United States are two of the most significant Arctic maritime powers. They assume this position due to the size of their Arctic lands, length of their Arctic coastlines, the significance of the straits and passages over which they exercise jurisdiction, their historical and contemporary interest in Arctic shipping, their contribution to Arctic governance on maritime matters at both global and regional forums, and in the case of the United States its role as a superpower. Much of the discourse about Canadian and US maritime interests in the Arctic has been dominated by their differing positions with respect to the Northwest Passage. Those differences have been framed around different perspectives on Arctic sovereignty, environmental protection, and the freedom of navigation. While the Northwest Passage has been at the centre of those differences, attention will increasingly turn to how EEZ navigation may be subject to traditional coastal State regulation. Canada has traditionally sought to rely upon measures adopted under the Arctic Waters Pollution Prevention Act post the *Manhattan* incident to provide reassurance that even if foreign vessels seek to pass through its Arctic EEZ it has in place adequate environmental protection measures to be able to regulate strictly those vessels while respecting the freedom of navigation. In this respect, NORDREG is not only an important maritime security initiative but also further assists with Arctic environmental protection.[104] However, while post the conclusion of UNCLOS, Canada has been able to rely upon Article 234 of the Convention to give international legitimacy to these measures, the future capacity of Article 234 to be relied upon may be compromised if the Arctic sea ice continues to melt. An additional point to recall with respect to the Arctic is that while coastal States have

103 Dan Joling, 'US Coast Guard studies shipping lanes for Bering Sea routes' *Alaska Dispatch News* (17 November 2015), accessed 17 March 2017 at https://www.adn.com/arctic/article/coast-guard-studies-shipping-lanes-bering-sea-routes/2015/11/17/; 'Coast Guard Defines Bering Strait Shipping Lane' *The Maritime Executive* (18 November 2015) accessed 17 March 2017 at http://www.maritime-executive.com/article/coast-guard-defines-bering-strait-shipping-lane; for discussion of potential governance options for the Bering Strait, see Berkman, Vylegzhanin and Young, *supra* note 20 at 205–213.

104 Byers, *supra* note 27 at 264.

sovereignty over their internal waters, and also over their territorial sea within which foreign flagged vessels enjoy a right of innocent passage, beyond the limits of the territorial sea and into the EEZ the capacity of the coastal State to be able to regulate navigation substantively is compromised. In this regard, the waters of the EEZ are equivalent to the high seas with respect to navigational rights and freedoms, a right that is emphasised in Article 58 of UNCLOS. While the exercise of those navigational rights and freedoms within the EEZ need to take into account the rights and duties of the coastal State within those waters and to accordingly comply with coastal State laws and regulations to that effect, nonetheless the reality remains that foreign vessels are able to exercise traditional navigational rights through the waters of the EEZ, which includes the Arctic EEZ.

To date, however, it is the Bering Strait that has been the subject of significant international shipping. Through a combination of climate change resulting in melting of the Arctic sea ice cover which in turn will make the Arctic Ocean more accessible to shipping of all types, and the interest of states that traditionally have not had a presence in the Arctic of using Arctic waterways as navigational routes, Arctic shipping is on the brink of very significant activity within the 'North American sector'. This will inevitably create its own tensions for Canada and the United States as they adjust to these changed circumstances and reflect upon their previous practices developed at a time when the demands of maritime traffic were not as great. This Chapter has suggested that there may be different responses emerging from Canada and the United States to these developments. This will partly be the case due to their different maritime domains, different national Arctic political discourses, and different global agendas. Above these debates sits UNCLOS and related international maritime law regarding marine pollution and shipping regulation that creates parameters to regulatory ambition. In this regard, unilateral acts, which have characterised previous national responses in the Arctic, are subject to greater constraints which in turn should give the international community more confidence on how Canada and the United States will respond to the new dynamics of Arctic shipping.

CHAPTER 8

Norway, Denmark (in respect of Greenland) and Iceland

Tore Henriksen

1 Introduction

The challenges to Arctic shipping extend beyond the Central Arctic Ocean. The Polar Code[1] is applicable to *Arctic waters*,[2] which extend to the northern parts of the Barents Sea, the Greenland Sea and the North Atlantic. The geographical proximity of the three Nordic coastal States to these waters—Denmark (in respect of Greenland), Norway and Iceland—obviously makes them relevant actors in the governance of Arctic shipping. The statistics provided by the Arctic Marine Shipping Assessment (AMSA) report commissioned by the Arctic Council suggest that the major volume in present Arctic maritime traffic is in the periphery of the Arctic, along the Norwegian coast, in the Barents Sea northwest of Russia, around Iceland, near the Faroe Islands, southwest Greenland and in the Bering Strait.[3] The three States have different roles in

1 International Code for Ships Operating in Polar Waters (Polar Code), consolidated text of the Polar Code as set out in the annexes to resolutions MSC.385(94) and MEPC.264(68), accessed 17 March 2017 at http://www.imo.org/en/MediaCentre/HotTopics/polar/Pages/default.aspx.

2 Arctic waters are defined in SOLAS 74 (Regulation XIV-1.3) and MARPOL 73/78 (Annex I Regulation 46.2, Annex II Regulation 21.2, Annex IV Regulation 17.3 and Annex V Regulation 13.2.), which makes the Polar Code mandatory in "those waters which are located north of a line from the latitude 58°00′.0 N and longitude 042°00′.0 W to latitude 64°37′.0 N, longitude 035°27′.0 W and thence by a rhumb line to latitude 67°03′.9 N, longitude 026°33′.4 W and thence by a rhumb line to the latitude 70°49′.56 N and longitude 008°59′.61 W (Sørkapp, Jan Mayen) and by the southern shore of Jan Mayen to 73°31′.6 N and 019°01′.0 E by the Island of Bjørnøya, and thence by a great circle line to the latitude 68°38′.29 N and longitude 043°23′.08 E (Cap Kanin Nos) and hence by the northern shore of the Asian Continent eastward to the Bering Strait and thence from the Bering Strait westward to latitude 60° N as far as Il'pyrskiy and following the 60th North parallel eastward as far as and including Etolin Strait and thence by the northern shore of the North American continent as far south as latitude 60° N and thence eastward along parallel of latitude 60° N, to longitude 056°37′.1 W and thence to the latitude 58°00′.0 N, longitude 042°00′.0 W".

3 Arctic Marine Shipping Assessment 2009 Report. Arctic Council, April 2009, second printing (AMSA Report), at 73.

 | DOI 10.1163/9789004339385_009

the governance as coastal States, flag States and Arctic States. Their interests span from ensuring the protection of the fragile Arctic marine environment to promoting economic development of their northern regions through tourism, shipping and fishing.

The objective of this Chapter is to investigate their interests and policies in Arctic shipping governance and how these interests and policies are reflected in their national legislation. Two main questions are addressed: the first is whether the three States have a common interest in the governance of Arctic shipping. Specifically, are they arguing for having international regulations apply to all navigation in Arctic waters or are they satisfied if the national regulations of the Arctic coastal States are applied in a non-discriminatory manner? The investigation will be based on their positions on the Polar Code, the legislation of Canada and the Russian Federation, as well as on the initiatives taken through the Arctic Council. The legislation of Canada and Russia is based on the extended environmental jurisdiction provided under Article 234 of the United Nations Convention on the Law of the Sea (UNCLOS)[4] to coastal States. Is it relevant for any of the three States to adopt national legislation under the authority of Article 234 of UNCLOS? The second main question is whether their national legislation is consistent with international law as set out in UNCLOS and the International Maritime Organization (IMO) conventions. Have any of the States adopted legislation enabling them to apply Article 234 of UNCLOS? Will their legislation be consistent with the Polar Code?

Before these questions are addressed in sections 2 and 3, some background information and data about the three States is set out below.

Norway is located in Northern Europe. It has an area of approximately 385,000 square kilometres (km^2) and a population of 5.2 million.[5] This includes Jan Mayen and the archipelago of Svalbard. Its coastline faces the Arctic waters. Jan Mayen is an island of 377 km^2 in the North Atlantic, 550 kilometres (km) northeast of Iceland and 500 km east of Greenland. The island has no permanent population. It formally became a part of the Kingdom of Norway in 1930.[6] The archipelago of Svalbard consists of Bjørnøya, Spitsbergen, Nordaustlandet, Barentsøya, Edgeøya, Kong Karls Land, Hopen, Prins Karls Forland, Kvitøya and other islands, islets and rocks. The islands cover a total area of 61,020 km^2. The

4 United Nations Convention on the Law of the Sea, adopted 10 December 1982, entered into force 16 November 1994, 1833 UNTS 3.

5 Minifacts about Norway, accessed 17 March 2017 at https://www.ssb.no/en/befolkning/artikler-og-publikasjoner/minifacts-about-norway.

6 Lov av 27.2.1930 nr.2 om Jan Mayen (the Jan Mayen Act), accessed 17 March 2017 at www.lovdata.no [in Norwegian].

sovereignty of Norway over the archipelago was recognised by major States through the adoption of the Spitsbergen Treaty concerning Spitsbergen of 9 February 1920 (also known as the Svalbard Treaty).[7] Svalbard became formally a part of Norway in 1925.[8]

Norway is among the ten largest maritime States.[9] The Norwegian Government has estimated that at present 80 per cent of shipping in the Arctic is taking place in Norwegian waters.[10] The numbers are still small compared to maritime traffic in other parts of Norwegian waters. A substantial part of the sailed distances—58 per cent—is undertaken by fishing vessels.[11] Most of the vessels transiting Norwegian waters are larger tankers and bulk carriers sailing to and from ports in Russia. The estimated cargo equals 200–240 fully loaded ships. The destinational traffic to and around Svalbard includes visits from cruise vessels from ports overseas, cargo vessels, research vessels, fishing vessels, local tourist vessels and vessels transporting coal mined in Svalbard. The Norwegian Government projects a small increase in total traffic in the next decade. Acute vessel-source pollution from oil tankers transiting the coastal waters of mainland Norway from ports in Northwest Russia is the major threat to the marine environment. A series of measures have been taken to mitigate this risk. These measures will be addressed later in the Chapter. The maritime traffic to and around Svalbard and Jan Mayen is dominated by fishing vessels.[12] The major risks are linked to cruise vessels operating closer to the coast that are carrying larger quantities of fuel. Poor chartering and lack of navigational

---

7 Treaty concerning Spitsbergen, adopted 9 February 1920, entered into force 14 August 1925, 2 *League of Nations Treaty Series* 8 (Svalbard Treaty).

8 Lov av 17. juli 1925 nr. 11 om Svalbard, accessed 17 March 2017 at http://app.uio.no/ub/ujur/oversatte-lover/cgi-bin/sok.cgi?dato=&nummer=&tittel=Svalbard&type=LOV&S%F8k=S%F8k.

9 UNCTAD, *Review of Maritime Transport 2015*, Table 2.3 Ownership of the World Fleet, 36, accessed 17 March 2017 at http://unctad.org/en/PublicationsLibrary/rmt2015_en.pdf.

10 Børge Brende, 'The Arctic: Important for Norway, Important for the World' (Spring 2015) 36(3) *Harvard International Review*.

11 Meld. St. 10 (2010–2011) Report to the Storting (white paper), *First update of the Integrated Management Plan for the Marine Environment of the Barents Sea—Lofoten Area*, 60, accessed 17 March 2017 at https://www.Regjeringen.No/En/Dokumenter/Meld.-St.-10–20102011/Id635591/?Ch=1&Q.

12 DN-GL, *Analyse av sannsynligheten for akutt oljeutslipp fra skipstrafikk ved Svalbard og Jan Mayen(translated: Report to the Norwegian Coastal Administration analysing the risks of acute oil pollution from maritime traffic in Svalbard and Jan Mayen)*, accessed 17 March 2017 at http://www.kystverket.no/contentassets/91d373bca4d847d8b4dedc519882587c/rapport-dnvgl_rev3.pdf [in Norwegian].

aids coupled with ice conditions may lead to groundings or other damages to vessels and acute oil pollution.

Denmark (*in respect of Greenland*). Greenland or Kalaallit Nunaat (*Country of the Greenlanders*) is the world's largest island and it is located wholly within the Arctic. It has an area of about 2.2 million km^2 (of which 80 per cent is permanently covered by ice) and more than 44,000 km of coastline.[13] It has a population of approximately 57,000, of whom 88 per cent are Inuit. The Inuits are one of the main indigenous peoples inhabiting the Arctic region.[14] From a geological point of view, it is one of the most interesting areas of the world, with its mineral and natural resources being particularly important.[15] Greenland is a part of the Kingdom of Denmark, but it is not part of the European Union (EU).[16] It enjoys a high degree of autonomy within Denmark.[17] The Self-Government consisting of Inatsisartut (the legislative body) and Naalakkersuisut (executive body) have assumed legislative and executive competence over a wide range of issues.[18] This includes the protection of the environment and resource management. The competence is limited to issues that exclusively concern Greenlandic affairs.[19]

The maritime traffic in Greenlandic waters is similar to that of the waters off Svalbard; it includes a mixture of fishing vessels, domestic cargo supply vessels and cruise ships, particularly centred around the southwestern part of the island.[20] The navigable areas and maritime activities have increased in recent

13 See facts about Greenland, accessed 17 March 2017 at http://www.norden.org/en/fakta-om-norden-1/the-nordic-countries-the-faroe-islands-greenland-and-aaland/facts-about-greenland.

14 According to the webpage of the Government of Greenland, accessed 17 March 2017 at http://naalakkersuisut.gl/en/About-government-of-greenland/About-Greenland/Facts-on-Greenland.

15 US Geological Survey, Circum-Arctic Resource Appraisal: Estimates of Undiscovered Oil and Gas North of the Arctic Circle, accessed 17 March 2017 at http://pubs.usgs.gov/fs/2008/3049/fs2008-3049.pdf.

16 The 1985 Greenland Treaty, accessed 17 March 2017 at http://naalakkersuisut.gl/en/Naalakkersuisut/Greenland-Representation-to-the-EU/European-Union-and-Greenland/The-Greenland-Treaty-of-1985.

17 Danish Constitution of 5 June 1953, Sec 1, accessed 17 March 2017 at http://www.thedanishparliament.dk/Publications/My_Constitutional_Act_with_explanations.aspx; Act No 473 of 12 June 2009 on Greenland Self-Government (Greenland Self-Government Act), accessed 17 March 2017 at http://naalakkersuisut.gl/~/media/Nanoq/Files/Attached%20Files/Engelske-tekster/Act%20on%20Greenland.pdf.

18 Greenland Self-Government Act, *supra* note 17, Sec 2 with Schedules I and II.

19 *Ibid.*, Sec 4.

20 AMSA Report, *supra* note 3 at 75.

years between mid-May and Mid-October due to sea ice melting. Cruise tourism in particular has increased.[21] Many areas of the east coast are still inaccessible most of the year. There are several hazards with navigation in Greenlandic waters.[22] They include unstable communication, non-functioning compasses, poorly charted waters and the presence of sea ice and icebergs. The latter may be in combination with low temperatures and fog. Even during the summer season, there may be the presence of sea ice in the navigable areas.

Iceland is an island republic in the North Atlantic, of approximately 103,000 km^2 with a population of 330,000.[23] The highest concentration of maritime traffic in the Arctic is found in Icelandic waters, together with the waters off Norway, the Barents Sea, the southwest coast of Greenland and the Bering Sea.[24] The traffic in Icelandic waters is a mixture of fishing vessels, cargo supply vessels and cruise vessels. An increased use of the Arctic routes may lead to more transit traffic through Icelandic waters.[25]

2 Interests and Policies of Norway, Iceland and Denmark (in Respect of Greenland) with Respect to the Governance of Arctic Shipping

2.1 *General*

In the following, an overview is given of the interests and policies of each of the three States regarding the Arctic. This includes their positions on the law of the sea and the Arctic. At the end, an assessment and comparison of their policies and interests is offered.

21 Rigsrevisionen, Report to the Public Accounts Committee on Denmark's performance in the Arctic, 2013, at 12, accessed 17 March 2017 at http://uk.rigsrevisionen.dk/publications/2013/162012/.

22 Danish Maritime Authority, *Sikker sejlads i grønlandske farvande* (Working group report on Maritime Safety in Greenlandic waters), accessed 17 March 2017 at http://www.soefartsstyrelsen.dk/SikkerhedTilSoes/Arktis/SejladsGroenland/Documents/sejladssikkerhedgroenland.pdf [in Danish].

23 See information, accessed 17 March 2017 at http://www.iceland.is/the-big-picture.

24 AMSA Report, *supra* note 3 at 73.

25 Icelandic Ministry of Foreign Affairs, A Risk Assessment for Iceland: Global, Societal, and Military Factors, March 2009, accessed 17 March 2017 at https://www.mfa.is/media/Skyrslur/A_Risk_Assessment_for_Iceland_-_English_Summary.pdf.

2.2 *Norway*

The Arctic strategy of Norway identifies the Arctic as Norway's top foreign policy priority.[26] The Norwegian Arctic includes large parts of Norway and important natural resources. The five priority areas of the strategy include: business development, infrastructure, knowledge development, the protection of the environment and international cooperation. The first priority includes further development of the oil and gas resources, mining and mineral resources, fishing activities, biotechnology and bioprospecting. Tourism is a growing industry with increased numbers of cruise vessels visiting ports in mainland Norway and Svalbard. The increased maritime activities, particularly following the increase of extracting industries, may provide opportunities for Norwegian shipowners and ports to provide different types of services. There are also plans to expand the ports e.g., in Longyearbyen on Svalbard, to provide for bases for search and rescue, pollution prevention preparedness and maritime services.[27]

The effects of climate change on the environment and the acidification of the oceans are identified as the priority areas of environmental concern. New activities are subject to strict environmental requirements and particularly valuable and vulnerable areas are protected. A significant part of shipping in the Arctic is located in Norwegian waters. The strategy therefore highlights the need to ensure that vessels operating in these waters are constructed, equipped and manned to operate safely in the region, and in addition that there is adequate search and rescue and oil pollution preparedness. International cooperation is the main measure to achieve maritime safety. The strategy underlines the support to and active participation of Norway in the negotiations of the Polar Code within the IMO and the processes within the Arctic Council to implement the recommendations of the AMSA Report. The latter includes the negotiation and the adoption of the agreements on search

---

26 Norway's Arctic Policy, at 16 and 36, accessed 17 March 2017 at www.regjeringen.no/globalassets/departementene/ud/vedlegg/nord/nordkloden_en.pdf; Denmark, Greenland and the Faroe Islands: Kingdom of Denmark Strategy for the Arctic 2011– 2020, Ministry of Foreign Affairs, 2011, at 13, accessed 17 March 2017 at http://naalakkersuisut.gl/en/Naalakkersuisut/Departments/Selvstaendighed-Udenrigsanlig-Landbrug/Kongerigets-Arktiske-Strategi; A Parliamentary Resolution on Iceland's Arctic Policy (Approved by Althingi at the 139th legislative session March 28 2011), Principles 4 and 7, accessed 17 March 2017 at http://www.mfa.is/media/nordurlandaskrifstofa/A-Parliamentary-Resolution-on-ICE-Arctic-Policy-approved-by-Althingi.pdf.

27 Norway's Arctic Policy, *supra* note 26 at 35.

and rescue[28] and on oil pollution preparedness and response.[29] The strategy recognises that the important interests of Norway in the Arctic are best safeguarded within the international legal framework of law of the sea. It enables Norway to assert its rights and to fulfil its obligations as a coastal State. Respect for the law of the sea and for international cooperation is seen as 'crucial for promoting stability and predictability [in the Arctic]'. Norway is also a major flag and maritime State.[30]

As a flag State, Norway is concerned that the international legal framework for shipping is competitive.[31] Therefore, it has been important to ensure that the Polar Code was developed through the IMO and was based on existing IMO conventions.

The insistence of Norway on the importance of the law of the sea and international cooperation is reflective of the position taken by the five Arctic coastal States in the Ilulissat Declaration. The membership and active participation of Norway in the Arctic Council is seen as important in the strategy. This is further confirmed by Norway being a State Party to UNCLOS since 1996.[32] It is also a member of the IMO.[33] Further, it is a contracting Party to the major IMO conventions, including SOLAS 74,[34] MARPOL 73/78,[35] the STCW Convention,[36]

---

28 The Agreement on Cooperation in Aeronautical and Maritime Search and Rescue in the Arctic, adopted 12 May 2011, entered into force 19 January 2013, accessed 17 March 2017 at www.treaty-accord.gc.ca/text-texte.aspx?id=105240.

29 Agreement on Cooperation on Marine Oil Pollution Preparedness and Response in the Arctic, adopted 15 May 2013 (not in force), accessed 17 March 2017 at https://oaarchive.arctic-council.org/handle/11374/529.

30 UNCTAD, *Review of Maritime Transport 2015*, *supra* note 9 at 42.

31 The Norwegian Maritime Strategy: *Maritime muligheter– blå vekst for grønn fremtid, Regjeringens maritime strategi*, 53, accessed 17 March 2017 at https://www.regjeringen.no/contentassets/05c0e04689cf4fc895398bf8814ab04c/maritim_strategi_engelsk_trykk.pdf.

32 See status of membership of UNCLOS, accessed 17 March 2017 at http://www.un.org/Depts/los/reference_files/status2010.pdf.

33 See overview of IMO membership, accessed 17 March 2017 at http://www.imo.org/en/About/Membership/Pages/MemberStates.aspx.

34 International Convention for the Safety of Life at Sea, adopted 1 November 1974, entered into force 25 May 1980, 1184 UNTS 278 (SOLAS 74).

35 International Convention for the Prevention of Pollution from Ships, as modified by the Protocol of 1978 relating thereto, adopted 2 November 1973 and 17 February 1978, entered into force 2 October 1983, 1340 UNTS 62 (MARPOL 73/78).

36 International Convention on Standards of Training, Certification and Watch-keeping for Seafarers, adopted 1 December 1978, entered into force 28 April 1984, 1361 UNTS I-23001 (STCW Convention). Its annex has been amended, Adoption of Amendments to the Annex to the International Convention on Standards of Training, Certification and

the Anti-fouling Convention[37] and the Ballast Water Management Convention (BWM Convention).[38] [39] Norway was active during the negotiations on the Polar Code, e.g., by chairing the working group under the Maritime Safety Committee of the IMO, which developed most of its text.

In the following, an overview will be given on the jurisdiction assumed by Norway over its Arctic waters and its position on its exercise. The baselines of mainland Norway as well as for Jan Mayen, Bear Island and Svalbard have been revised in recent years with minor changes.[40] There are straight baselines set along the coast of mainland Norway and along the coast of the main islands of Svalbard. Historically, Norway has claimed a four nautical mile (nm) territorial sea.[41] The 2003 Territorial Waters and Contiguous Zone Act establishes the outer limits of the territorial sea at 12 nm measured from the baselines.[42] Territorial waters is a concept still in use in Norwegian legislation that includes internal waters and territorial sea.[43] The extension of the breadth of the territorial sea is applicable to mainland Norway, as well as for Jan Mayen and Svalbard.[44]

Norway established a 200 nm economic zone off its mainland on 1 January 1977.[45] It has a legal basis in national legislation for establishing economic

Watchkeeping for Seafarers, 1978 STCW/CONF.2/DC/1, 24 June 2010 [available in Meeting Documents of IMODOCS at http://docs.imo.org].

37 International Convention on the Control of Harmful Anti-fouling Systems on Ships, adopted 5 October 2001, entered into force 17 September 2008, AFS/CONF/26, 18 October 2001 [available in Meeting Documents of IMODOCS at http://docs.imo.org].

38 International Convention for the Control and Management of Ships' Ballast Water and Sediments, adopted 16 February 2004, entering into force 8 September 2017, BWM/CONF/36 [available in Meeting Documents of IMODOCS at http://docs.imo.org].

39 See status of conventions, accessed 17 March 2017 at http://www.imo.org/en/About/Conventions/StatusOfConventions/Pages/Default.aspx.

40 The geographical coordinates of points for the baselines of Svalbard, Jan Mayen and mainland Norway are available at 'Submission in Compliance with the Deposit Obligations pursuant to the United Nations Convention on the Law of the Sea', accessed 17 March 2017 at www.un.org/Depts/los/LEGISLATIONANDTREATIES/STATEFILES/NOR.htm.

41 Robin R Churchill and A Vaughan Lowe, *The Law of the Sea* (Manchester University Press, 1999) at 77–78.

42 Act No 57 of 27 June 2003 on Norway's Territorial Waters and Contiguous Zone, Sec 2, available in English, Law of the Sea Bulletin No 54 (2004) at 97.

43 *Ibid.*, Sec 1.

44 *Ibid.*, Sec 2 *c.f.* Sec 5. The coordinates of the outer limits of the territorial sea are deposited with the UN Secretary General, see http://www.un.org/Depts/los/LEGISLATIONANDTREATIES/STATEFILES/NOR.htm, accessed 17 March 2017.

45 Act No 91 of 17 December 1976 relating to the Economic Zone of Norway, Sec 1, accessed 17 March 2017 at www.un.org/Depts/los/LEGISLATIONANDTREATIES/PDFFILES/

zones off both Jan Mayen and Svalbard, which has yet to be applied. However, a 200 nm fisheries protection zone has been established for Svalbard and a 200 nm fisheries zone for Jan Mayen.[46] In terms of international shipping, these two 200 nm fisheries zones are equivalent to the high seas. The intention in establishing these zones was to ensure control over the fishing activities and prevent unregulated fishing.[47] Shipping activities in these waters were marginal and most of the shipping was destinational.

The Polar Code will be applicable to vessels operating within the internal waters and territorial sea off Jan Mayen, Bear Island and Svalbard. It might also be applicable to navigation in the northern part of the exclusive economic zone (EEZ) of mainland Norway.

Norway does not have an expressed or public position on the consistency of the legislation and the practice of other Arctic coastal States with the law of the sea. This is the case with the use by Russia and Canada of Article 234 of UNCLOS as a legal basis for regulating shipping within the limits of their EEZs in the Arctic.[48] However, some remarks from an expert group on Arctic shipping established by the Ministry of Foreign Affairs are worth noting. First, the group notes that Norway is not entitled to apply Article 234 since the 200 nm EEZ off mainland Norway is not ice-covered and no EEZ is established off Svalbard.[49] The group notes that the maritime industry of Norway has an interest in the widest possible application of the international legal framework to shipping in the marine Arctic.[50] In the opinion of the expert group, the Polar Code may help provide for more harmonised regulation of Arctic shipping.

NOR_1976_Act.pdf; Regulation No 15 of 17 December 1976 on the Implementation of the Norwegian Economic Zone.

46 Regulation No 6 of 3 June 1977 on the Establishment of a Fisheries Protection Zone around Svalbard; Regulation No 4 of 23 May 1980 on the Establishment of a Fisheries Zone around Jan Mayen. The regulations establishing the two zones operate with different descriptions of the zones, even if they are based on the same act. What distinguishes the Svalbard Fisheries Protection Zone (Svalbard FPZ) from the Jan Mayen Fishery Zone is that the general ban on foreign fishermen is not applicable within the Svalbard FPZ. This is due to the controversy over whether the Spitsbergen Treaty is applicable in the 200 nm zone. But in regard to shipping, the distinction is of no relevance since the zone is regarded as high seas. The coastal State only has jurisdiction with regard to living marine resources.

47 St. Meld. (White Paper) nr 22 (2008–2009) Svalbard, 90–91, accessed 17 March 2017 at https://www.regjeringen.no/en/dokumenter/meld.-st.-22-2008-2009/id554877/?ch=1&q.

48 See e.g., White Paper No 7 (2011–2012) on the High North, 60, accessed 17 March 2017 at www.regjeringen.no/en/dokumenter/meld.-st.-7-20112012/id663433/.

49 Ministry of Foreign Affairs, *Økt skipsfart I Polhavet—muligheter og utfordringer for Norge*, at 16, April 2013, accessed 17 March 2017 at www.regjeringen.no/no/aktuelt/rapport_arktis/id723668/ [in Norwegian].

50 *Ibid.* at 58.

It is recognised that both Russia and Canada may apply additional requirements to vessels transiting their maritime zones. They recommend that initiatives be taken to coordinate the regulations of Canada and Russia with the regulations of the other Arctic coastal States.

2.3 *Denmark (in Respect of Greenland)*

The Arctic strategy of the realm of Denmark (which includes Denmark, the Faroe Islands and Greenland) highlights the commercial opportunities for the industries following the increased access to the Arctic region.[51] Greenland may hold vast deposits of gold, zinc, iron, copper, diamonds, rubies and a number of critical metals, including rare earth elements.[52] The development of the mineral sector may have a significant impact on the Greenlandic economy and its possibility for becoming economically self-supporting. The seabed of the Arctic may also hold vast deposits of oil and gas. Fishing activities may move further northwards. Tourism is a growing industry with increased numbers of cruise vessels visiting ports in Greenland. Ports may provide different types of services. Denmark's Arctic Policy aims at having a peaceful, secure and safe Arctic with self-sustaining growth, with respect for the fragile Arctic climate and environment and close cooperation with international partners.[53] A peaceful, secure and safe Arctic includes maritime safety.[54] Preventing marine vessel accidents is viewed as crucial as vessels will operate under extreme conditions in sparsely populated areas. The strategy therefore highlights the need for constructing and equipping vessels capable of operating under these conditions and which have their own rescue equipment. A series of measures are listed, including the adoption of a mandatory Polar Code, the requirement that vessels cooperate with the emergency services, the improvement of nautical charts, regional cooperation on search and rescue and the possible establishment of ship's routeing measures. Similar to the Norwegian strategy, international cooperation at the global and regional levels is seen as a central tool, recognising that common solutions are needed. This includes Denmark working through the IMO to ensure that Greenlandic and Arctic interests are considered in developing relevant instruments. Even if the strategy

51 *Kingdom of Denmark Strategy for the Arctic 2011–2020, supra* note 26, at 23.

52 Danish Maritime Authority, *Opportunities and Challenges for the Danish Realm's Maritime Industry in the Arctic*, at 11–12, accessed 17 March 2017 at http://www.dma.dk/Vaekst/MaritimErhvervspolitik/Documents/opportunitieschallengesdanishrealmmaritimeindustryarctic.pdf.

53 *Kingdom of Denmark Strategy for the Arctic 2011–2020, supra* note 26 at 10–11.

54 *Ibid.* at 13.

emphasises the need for common and harmonised rules and standards adopted through the IMO, it does not exclude the adoption of national non-discriminatory safety and environmental rules.[55] This could happen if the Polar Code negotiations were unsuccessful. These national regulations would be adopted after consultation with other Arctic States and be consistent with Article 234 of UNCLOS. Denmark also favours strengthening the Arctic Council to develop it into a decision-making organisation. Denmark identifies UNCLOS as the basis for peaceful cooperation in the region and the 'responsibility of the coastal States for managing the development of the Arctic'.[56]

Even if Greenland enjoys extensive autonomy, the competence of entering into treaties and conventions with other States on behalf of the whole realm lies with the Danish Government.[57] This includes UNCLOS and conventions on maritime safety and environmental protection adopted through the IMO. Denmark has been a State Party to UNCLOS since 2004. It is also a member of the IMO and a Contracting Party to the major IMO Conventions, including SOLAS 74, MARPOL 73/78, the STCW Convention, the Anti-fouling Convention and the BWM Convention.[58] Annexes IV (sewage) and VI (air pollution) of MARPOL are not applicable to Greenland.[59] There are procedures established for consulting the Greenlandic Self-Government during the negotiation of such treaties.[60]

The question of whether Denmark has made use of its rights under Article 234 of UNCLOS will be investigated below under section 3. It has not publicly expressed any opinion or position on the consistency of Russian and Canadian legislation with this provision.

In the following, an overview will be given on the jurisdiction assumed by Denmark over its waters off Greenland. The baselines of Greenland have been

---

55 *Ibid.* at 18.

56 *Kingdom of Denmark Strategy for the Arctic 2011– 2020, supra* note 26 at 13.

57 Danish Constitution, *supra* note 17, Sec 19.

58 See Status of Conventions, accessed 17 March 2017 at www.imo.org/en/About/Conventions/StatusOfConventions/Pages/Default.aspx.

59 See IMO, *Status of multilateral Conventions and instruments in respect of which the International Maritime Organization or its Secretary-General performs depositary or other functions*, at 124, on the reservation of Denmark in regard of the obligations of Greenland under Protocol of 1978 relating to the International Convention for the prevention of Pollution from Ships, 1973 (Optional Annex IV) and at 163, regarding the reservation of Denmark in regard of the obligations of Greenland MARPOL Protocol 1997 (Annex VI), accessed 17 March 2017 at http://www.imo.org/en/About/Conventions/StatusOfConventions/Pages/Default.aspx.

60 Greenland Self-Government Act, *supra* note 17, Sec 13.

revised in recent years.[61] The outer limits of the Danish territorial sea were extended to 12 nm in 1999.[62] However, the extension is not applicable to the territorial sea off Greenland.[63] It still has a three nm territorial sea.[64] The reason for not extending the outer limits to 12 nm may be due to a lack of capacity within the Self-Government. It has been conferred the competence to protect the environment within its territory, including the territorial sea.[65] The 200 nm EEZ of Greenland was established in 2004.[66] The Polar Code is applicable to vessels operating within the maritime zones of Greenland.

2.4 *Iceland*

An important part of the Icelandic Arctic Strategy is to establish itself and to be recognised as an Arctic coastal State, a relevant actor in regional and global decision-making. The second of the twelve principles of the strategy is 'Securing Iceland's position as a coastal State within the Arctic region'.[67] It is important for 'influencing its development [the Arctic region] as well as international decisions on regional issues on the basis of legal, economic, ecological and geographical arguments'. The argument is that the northern part of the Icelandic EEZ extends to the Greenland Sea, which is part of the Arctic Ocean.[68] The narrow interpretation of the concept in the 2008 Ilulissat Declaration of 'the coastal States bordering the Arctic Ocean' excluded Iceland.[69] The

---

61 Royal Decree No 1004 of 15 October 2004 on Amendment of Royal Decree on Delimitation of the Territorial Waters of Greenland, accessed 17 March 2017 at http://www.un.org/depts/los/LEGISLATIONANDTREATIES/STATEFILES/DNK.htm.

62 Act No 200 of 7 April 1999 on the Delimitation of the Territorial Sea, accessed 17 March 2017 at http://www.un.org/Depts/los/LEGISLATIONANDTREATIES/PDFFILES/DNK_1999_Act.pdf.

63 *Ibid.*, Sec 6(1).

64 Order N 191 of 27 May 1963 on the Delimitation of the Territorial Sea of Greenland, accessed 17 March 2017 at http://www.un.org/Depts/los/LEGISLATIONANDTREATIES/PDFFILES/DNK_1963_Order.pdf.

65 Lov nr. 921 af 25. november 1992 om ændring af en række miljølove, *c.f.* Lov nr 850 af 21. desember 1988 for Grønland om miljøforhold.

66 Royal Decree No 1005 of 24 October 2004 on the entry into force of Act on Exclusive Economic Zone for Greenland, on the basis of Section 5 of the Act No 411 of 22 May 1996 on Exclusive Economic Zone, Law of the Sea Bulletin No 56 (2004) at 133, accessed 17 March 2017 at www.un.org/Depts/los/doalos_publications/LOSBulletins/bulletinpdf/bulletin56e.pdf.

67 Parliamentary Resolution on Iceland's Arctic Policy, *supra* note 26.

68 *Ibid.*, Principle #3.

69 The Ilulissat Declaration. Arctic Ocean Conference, Ilulissat Greenland, 27–29 May 2008, accessed 17 March 2017 at https://www.regjeringen.no/globalassets/upload/ud/080525_arctic_ocean_conference-_outcome.pdf.

cooperation between the five (self-proclaimed) Arctic coastal States have in recent years concentrated on the governance of living marine resources in the high seas parts of the Central Arctic Ocean. The regional cooperation on shipping is channelled through the Arctic Council, of which Iceland is a member.

Compared with the strategies of the other two Nordic States, the Icelandic strategy is less specific on the commercial opportunities provided by climate change and the melting of the sea. With the exception of tourism, it focuses instead on the need to facilitate opportunities for Icelandic businesses to take part in the development of the industries of the region.[70] Building on and strengthening of cooperation is perhaps the most important element of the strategy, in addition to the protection of the environment. Iceland aims at pursuing cooperation at different levels, with their neighbours on economic development, at the regional level through the Arctic Council and at the global level. An example of the latter is cooperation through the IMO on developing mandatory regulations. UNCLOS, according to Iceland, provides the legal framework for jurisdiction and rights in the Arctic region.

Iceland is a State Party to UNCLOS.[71] It is also a member of the IMO and a Contracting Party to major IMO conventions including: SOLAS 74, MARPOL 73/78 and the Anti-fouling Convention.[72] Iceland has not accepted MARPOL 73/78 Annexes IV (Sewage) and VI (Air Pollution) nor has it ratified the BWM Convention.

The Polar Code is not likely to be applicable to waters under Icelandic jurisdiction. The Arctic waters as defined by Chapter XIV of SOLAS 74 and the amended annexes of MARPOL 73/78 ends north of its EEZ.[73] Iceland's role will be as a flag State and as a port State. The Icelandic Transport Authorities have indicated that legislation to implement the Polar Code has yet to be adopted. The reason given is that there are presently no SOLAS certified vessels in the Icelandic ships' register to which the Polar Code will be applicable.[74]

70 Parliamentary Resolution on Iceland's Arctic Policy, *supra* note 26, Principle #10 with commentaries.

71 See overview of UNCLOS State Parties, accessed 17 March 2017 at http://www.un.org/Depts/los/reference_files/status2010.pdf.

72 See overview of IMO membership, accessed 17 March 2017 at http://www.imo.org/en/About/Membership/Pages/MemberStates.aspx and Status of Conventions, accessed 17 March 2017 at http://www.imo.org/en/About/Conventions/StatusOfConventions/Pages/Default.aspx.

73 SOLAS 74, *supra* note 34, Reg XIV/1(3); MARPOL 73/78, *supra* note 35, Annex I, Reg 46(2).

74 Author's communication with the Icelandic Transport Authority, 21 June 2016.

The Icelandic 12 nm territorial sea and 200 nm EEZ are established under its 1979 Territorial Sea, Economic Zone and Continental Shelf Act.[75] The outer limits of the zones are fixed on the basis of a set of straight baselines.[76] The Act establishes Icelandic jurisdiction within the 200 nm zone regarding the protection of the marine environment and instructs the authorities to exercise the jurisdiction in conformity with its international obligations.[77] Iceland has not issued any public position on the consistency of the practice of Canada and Russia with Article 234 of UNCLOS in regulating Arctic shipping.

2.5 *Summary*

All three States express concern in their policies that increased shipping will heighten the risk of incidents threatening their marine environment and living resources. Their strategies (particularly the strategies of Denmark and Norway) include measures to enhance maritime safety and protection of their marine environment. They emphasise in their Arctic policy documents that the UNCLOS provides the legal framework and basis for regulating shipping and other marine activities in the Arctic. The rule of law and international cooperation are vital principles to these small States. Further, they recognise that the challenges of the Arctic are transboundary and should be managed through international cooperation. The IMO is identified by all as the relevant forum for cooperation on establishing additional Arctic shipping regulations. As members of the Arctic Council, they have accepted the recommendations of the AMSA Report on *inter alia* the mandatory Polar Code, and the negotiation and adoption of agreements on search and rescue and preparedness.[78] They promote general applicable regulations adopted through the IMO. It is only Denmark that is open to the adoption of national non-discriminatory safety and environmental rules. The other Nordic States have not expressed an opinion on this issue.

75 Law No 41 of 1 June 1979 concerning the Territorial Sea, the Economic Zone and the Continental Shelf, accessed 17 March 2017 at http://www.un.org/depts/los/LEGISLATIONANDTREATIES/PDFFILES/ISL_1979_Law.pdf.

76 *Ibid.*, Sec 1.

77 *Ibid.*, Secs 4 and 8.

78 Tromsø Declaration on the occasion of the Sixth Ministerial Meeting of the Arctic Council the 29th of April, 2009, Tromsø, Norway, accessed 17 March 2017 at https://oaarchive.arctic-council.org/handle/11374/91.

3 National Legislation Governing Safety of Navigation and Protection of the Marine Environment from Ship-source Pollution

3.1 *General*

This section provides an overview of the legislation of Norway, Denmark/Greenland and Iceland on the safety of navigation and ship-source pollution relevant for Arctic waters. Further, it will discuss whether their national legislation is consistent with international law as set out in UNCLOS and the IMO Conventions. The section is organised by State: Norway (section 3.2), Denmark/Greenland (section 3.3) and Iceland (section 3.4). Each section will include the presentation of prescriptive and enforcement jurisdiction within the maritime zones and in ports. The prescriptive jurisdiction is thematically organised in presentation of Construction, Design, Equipment and Manning (CDEM) rules and standards, navigational standards and discharge rules and standards.

The jurisdiction of the Nordic coastal States to apply the CDEM and discharge rules and standards of the Polar Code in respect of foreign-flagged vessels exercising the right of innocent passage or/and freedom of navigation are restricted under UNCLOS. Its CDEM rules and standards may not be applied in the territorial sea unless they 'give effect to generally accepted international rules and standards'.[79] The same condition is relevant for the coastal States to apply the CDEM rules and standards and the discharge rules and standards of the Polar Code in their EEZs.[80] The CDEM requirements of the Polar Code may qualify as such rules and standards, but only at the earliest stage when they enter into force. The relevant amendments to SOLAS 74 and the MARPOL 73/78 annexes enter into force in January 2017. The amendments to the STCW Convention to make Chapter 12 (Manning and Training) of Part I-A of the Polar Code mandatory will enter into force in July 2018.[81] Requiring vessels navigating through ice-covered parts of the territorial sea of Svalbard or Greenland to be ice-strengthened and to have a crew adequately manned and trained for such conditions would strengthen the maritime safety. Part I-A of the Polar Code on safety measures includes requirements for vessels operating in Arctic

---

79 UNCLOS, *supra* note 4, Art 21(2).

80 *Ibid.*, Art 211(5).

81 Amendments to the International Convention on Standards of Training, Certification and Watchkeeping for Seafarers (STCW), 1978, as amended, Report of the Maritime Safety Committee on its Ninety-Fifth Session, Annex 8 MSC/95/22/Add.2. The adoption of the amendments was postponed until MSC 97, delaying the entry into force of the amendments.

waters to be ice strengthened.[82] There are three categories of vessels (A, B and C), defined on the basis of their capability to operate in ice and low temperatures.[83] There are no specific requirements for ice strengthening other than that it shall be approved by the flag State or the classification society. The Polar Code includes a reference to the Polar Classes of IACS[84] relevant for each of the categories.[85] The flag State or classification society may decide to use other ice classes. Given that the requirement for ice strengthening may vary dependent on temporal and geographical criteria—is it possible to characterise the norms of the Polar Code as 'generally accepted rules and standards'? In the end, the coastal States may have to accept the Polar Certificate of vessels navigating within ice-covered areas of its territorial sea or EEZ documenting that they have the adequate ice strengthening for operating within those waters. The on-going work within the IMO on guidelines for methodologies for assessing operational capabilities and limitation in ice may be helpful.[86] The guidelines may provide information on the equivalence of the different ice classes.

Chapter 12 on manning and training requires the master, chief mate and officers in charge of navigational watch to have basic training if the vessel is to operate in open waters. There is an additional requirement for the master and chief mate to have advanced training when operating in ice-covered waters.[87] Under the STCW Convention, they are required to hold certificates in basic training and advanced training to document such training.[88] The training requirements are supplemented and specified through amendments to the mandatory parts of the STCW Code.[89] The coastal States are entitled to require the abovementioned members of crews of vessels operating in the territorial sea of their Arctic waters to carry such certificates, dependent on the ice conditions.

It is not only the law of the sea and IMO instruments that affect the national legislation of the Nordic coastal States. EU maritime legislation may affect

82 Polar Code, *supra* note 1, Part I-A, para 3.3.2.

83 *Ibid.*, Introduction, paras 2.1–2.3.

84 International Association of Classification Societies.

85 *Ibid.*, Part I-A, 3.3, nn 6- 8.

86 These guidelines are presupposed in Polar Code, *supra* note 1, I-A, para 1.3.7 and was initiated by the MSC, MSC 94/21, paras 3.28–3.29 and 3.62.

87 Polar Code, *supra* note 1, Part I-A, para 12.3.1.

88 STCW Convention, *supra* note 36, regulation A-V/4, paras 1 and 3.

89 Amendments to Part A of the Seafarers' Training, Certification and Watchkeeping Code (STCW Code), Draft MSC resolution, MSC 95/22/Add.2, Annex 9.

the practice of two of them. Norway and Iceland are parties to the European Economic Area (EEA) Agreement.[90] It is important to note that Svalbard is not included in the EEA Agreement and that Greenland is not a part of the EU. The objective of the EEA Agreement is to integrate non-EU member States (i.e., Norway, Iceland and Lichtenstein) into the internal market of the EU through the establishment of the European Economic Area (which includes the free movement of goods, services, persons and capital).[91] Maritime transport is part of the EEA Agreement.[92] The EU legislation (directives or regulations) adopted to implement regulations adopted through IMO conventions often makes the minimum standards mandatory. These and other relevant EU directives or regulations become international legal obligations of Norway and Iceland when approved by the decision-making body of the EEA Agreement (EEA Joint Committee).[93] Norway and Iceland have implemented more than 70 EU directives and regulations within the maritime sector.[94] They include directives on port State control, flag State compliance, vessel traffic monitoring and information and ship-source pollution.[95]

---

90 Agreement on the European Economic Area, adopted 2 May 1992, entered into force 1 January 1994, 1801 UNTS 3 and 1802 UNTS 3 (EEA Agreement), accessed 17 March 2017 at www.efta.int.

91 *Ibid.*, Art 1.

92 *Ibid.*, Annex XIII.5.

93 *Ibid.*, Art 7, *c.f.* Art 92.

94 An overview of relevant EU maritime legislation, accessed 17 March 2017 at http://europalov.no/omrade/transport [in Norwegian]. As part of the Icelandic application for EU membership there were several screening reports on its implementation of EU legislation, including on transport, including on maritime transport, accessed 17 March 2017 at http://ec.europa.eu/enlargement/pdf/iceland/key-documents/screening_report_14_iceland_internet.pdf. The report provides an overview over relevant EU legislation and its implementation into Icelandic law.

95 Directive 2009/16/EC of the European Parliament and of the Council of 23 April 2009 on port State control; Directive 2009/21/EC of the European Parliament and of the Council of 23 April 2009 on compliance with flag State requirements; Directive 2002/59/EC of the European Parliament and of the Council of 27 June 2002 Establishing a Community Vessel Traffic Monitoring and Information System and Repealing Council Directive 93/75/EEC, Directive 2005/35/EC of the European Parliament and of the Council of 7 September 2005 on Ship-Source Pollution and on the Introduction of Penalties for Infringements.

3.2 *Norway*

3.2.1 General

There are three main acts regulating shipping: First, the Ship Safety and Security Act[96] (SSSA), which has both maritime safety and pollution prevention objectives. It provides a legal basis for establishing CDEM rules and standards and discharge and emission rules and standards. The two others, the Harbours and Fairways Act and the Pilotage Service Act, provide a legal basis for the regulation of navigation within its maritime zones.[97]

All three acts are applicable to the EEZ and territorial waters of mainland Norway and the territorial waters of Svalbard and Jan Mayen. The SSSA is applicable to Norwegian-flagged vessels irrespective of where they operate. In principle, this means that regulations implementing SOLAS 74 and MARPOL 73/78 may be applicable to smaller Norwegian-flagged vessels or Norwegian-flagged vessels in domestic traffic.[98] The SSSA and its regulations are applicable to foreign-flagged vessels while within the territorial waters of Norway, the mainland EEZ and when operating on the continental shelf. The Act and its regulations are applicable so long as they are within the limits of applicable international law.[99] Norway would not introduce CDEM rules and standards unless they are consistent with existing and generally accepted international rules and standards. This reflects the position of Norway to rely on international law.

Regulations are adopted under the Harbour and Fairways Act and the Pilotage Act to specifically make them applicable to the territorial waters of Svalbard.[100] Further, the Svalbard Environmental Protection Act is applicable

---

96 Act No 9 of 16 February 2007 relating to Ship Safety and Security (SSSA), accessed 17 March 2017 at https://www.sjofartsdir.no/en/shipping/legislation/laws/act-of-16-february-2007-no-9-relating-to-ship-safety-and-security/.

97 Act No 19 of 17 April 2009 on Harbour and Fairways (Harbour and Fairways Act), accessed 17 March 2017 at https://lovdata.no/dokument/NL/lov/2009-04-17-19?q=havnelov [in Norwegian]; Act No 61 of 15 August 2014 relating to Pilot Services, accessed 17 March 2017 at http://www.kystverket.no/globalassets/los/regelverk-engelsk/pilotage-act.pdf [in Norwegian].

98 The maritime authorities may adopt regulations where certain types of vessels are exempted or installations or vessels used for non-commercial purposes are included, SSSA, *supra* note 96, Sec 2.

99 *Ibid.*, Sec 3.

100 Regulation No 1846 of 30 December 2009 on Harbours and Fairways of Svalbard, accessed 17 March 2017 at http://lovdata.no/dokument/SF/forskrift/2009-12-30-1846 [in Norwegian]; Regulations No 655 of 25 June 2012 relating to Pilotage Services on Svalbard

within the 12 nm territorial sea of the archipelago (including Bear Island).[101] The latter provides a legal basis for establishing marine protected areas, regulating operational discharges and disposal of wastes from vessels and for regulating the use of particular fuel for vessels visiting the territorial waters of Svalbard.[102] The provisions restricting the navigation of foreign-flagged vessels will be revisited below.

Under the Svalbard Treaty 'the full and absolute sovereignty of Norway over the Archipelago of Spitsbergen' is recognised by its contracting Parties.[103] Norway is competent to exercise sovereignty as a coastal State consistent with the law of the sea within the internal waters and the 12 nm territorial sea. This includes the right to regulate the activities of vessels navigating within these zones. The question is whether the obligations of Norway under the Svalbard Treaty restrict the exercise of this jurisdiction beyond what is provided under the law of the sea. Several of the provisions of the Svalbard Treaty are undoubtedly applicable to the 12 nm territorial sea and internal waters. Norway is *inter alia* obligated to exercise its sovereignty in a manner that provides nationals of the Contracting Parties 'equal liberty of access and entry for any reason or object', to the 'waters, fjords and ports'.[104] Within these areas, they are entitled to carry out 'maritime, industrial, mining or commercial enterprises' on a 'footing of absolute equality'. The rights and corresponding duty of Norway to respect them are explicitly applicable to the territorial waters. This is a right subject to the principle of non-discrimination (directly or indirectly) based on nationality. The corresponding obligation of Norway is not to discriminate between nationals of the Contracting Parties when exercising its jurisdiction (legislative as well as enforcement).

The coastal State has an obligation under UNCLOS not to discriminate based on nationality when exercising environmental jurisdiction over foreign-flagged vessels.[105] Are the obligations (regarding foreign-flagged vessels operating in the territorial waters) of the Svalbard Treaty subsumed by this

(Regulations relating to Pilotage Services on Svalbard), accessed 17 March 2017 at http://www.kystverket.no/globalassets/los/svalbard/regulations-pilotage-and-pec-on-svalbard_as-amended-1.1.2015.pdf.

101 Act of 15 June 2001 No 79 relating to the Protection of the Environment of Svalbard (Svalbard Environmental Protection Act), Sec 2, accessed 17 March 2017 at www.regjeringen.no/en/dokumenter/svalbard-environmental-protection-act/id173945/

102 *Ibid.*, Ch III, Secs 67 and 82a.

103 Svalbard Treaty, *supra* note 7, Art 1.

104 *Ibid.*, Art 3.

105 UNCLOS, *supra* note 4, Arts 227 and 234.

obligation? Norway is under any circumstance obliged to adopt legislation that is equally applicable to its own vessels and to foreign-flagged vessels operating in waters under its jurisdiction, off either Svalbard or mainland Norway. The non-discrimination obligation under the Svalbard Treaty has a separate or additional legal meaning where vessels flying the flags of Contracting Parties are operating within the 12 nm territorial sea, but are not exercising their right of innocent passage. It is in the latter case that the non-discriminatory obligation of UNCLOS is not applicable. Under the Svalbard Treaty, there is an entitlement of nationals of the Contracting Parties to carry out maritime enterprises on an equal footing. A practical example of exercising such rights is the visits of cruise vessels flying the flag of Contracting Parties to coastal areas, the fjords or the sounds of Svalbard and their calling at ports in Svalbard. Since they are not exercising the right of innocent passage under the law of the sea, the vessels are under the full sovereignty of Norway.[106] Norway would be competent to ban these cruise vessels from navigating through marine protected areas, through ice-covered areas or through poorly charted areas. The duty of non-discrimination would require Norway to apply and enforce such bans to all relevant vessels regardless of their nationality.

3.2.2 CDEM Rules and Standards

The SSSA includes a general requirement for the planning, construction and equipment of a vessel that provides it with adequate protection of life, health, environment and material values, according to the purpose of the use of the vessel and its likely areas of operation.[107]

The SSSA is an enabling act that provides the legal basis for adopting regulations implementing CDEM rules and standards binding on Norway under SOLAS 74, MARPOL 73/78 and the STCW Convention.[108] Each chapter of SOLAS 74 is implemented through separate regulations. Examples include regulations on the construction of ships[109] and fire protection.[110] The CDEM requirements

---

106 *Ibid.*, Art 2.

107 SSSA, *supra* note 96, Ch 9.

108 *Ibid.*, Secs 9, 15, 16 and 32.

109 Regulations of 1 July 2014 No 1072 on the Construction of Ships (SOLAS 74 Chapter II-1), accessed 17 March 2017 at https://www.sjofartsdir.no/en/shipping/legislation/regulations/construction-of-ships/.

110 Regulation of 1 July 2014 No 1099 on fire protection on ships (SOLAS 74 Chapter II-2), accessed 17 March 2017 at https://www.sjofartsdir.no/en/shipping/legislation/regulations/fire-protection-on-ships/.

of MARPOL 73/78 are implemented through regulations on environmental safety for ships, which includes operational discharges.[111] Usually, the SOLAS 74 and MARPOL 73/78 regulations are implemented through the use of referencing, giving them direct effect or application in Norwegian law.

The SSSA is applicable to foreign-flagged vessels operating in waters within the 200 nm EEZ and territorial waters of mainland Norway and the territorial waters of Svalbard and Jan Mayen. In practice, the regulations implementing the CDEM requirements of SOLAS and MARPOL apply only to Norwegian-flagged vessels. This is likely to be the case with the CDEM requirements of the Polar Code. The Norwegian Maritime Authority has adopted regulation on the implementation of Part I-A of the Polar Code and of Chapter XIV of SOLAS 74.[112] This regulation will apply to Norwegian-flagged passenger and cargo vessels certified under SOLAS.[113] Both Part I-A and Chapter XIV of SOLAS are incorporated in Norwegian law.[114] The draft regulation does not include the amendments to the STCW Convention and the STCW Code regarding Part I-A, Chapter 12 of the Polar Code.

Consequently, the Norwegian authorities are not planning to introduce CDEM requirements for foreign-flagged vessels exercising innocent passage through or operating within the territorial sea of Svalbard. The control of the compliance of foreign-flagged vessels with the CDEM requirements of SOLAS 74 and MARPOL 73/78 will be undertaken when these vessels are visiting ports in Norway. The use of port State control and other enforcement issues are part of section 3.2.5 below.

3.2.3 Navigational Rules and Standards

The Harbour and Fairways Act provides a legal basis for the Norwegian Coastal Administration to regulate national and international maritime traffic in the territorial waters and EEZ of mainland Norway and in the territorial waters of

111 Regulation of 30 May 2012 No 488 on environmental safety for ships and mobile offshore units, accessed 17 March 2017 at https://www.sjofartsdir.no/en/shipping/legislation/regulations/environmental-safety-for-ships-and-mobile-offshore-units1/.

112 Forskrift av 23 November 2016 nr. 1363. om sikkerhetstiltak for skip som opererer i polare farvann (Regulation on Safety Measures for Vessels operating in Polar Waters), accessed 17 March 2017 at https://www.sjofartsdir.no/en/shipping/legislation/regulations/safety-measures-for-ships-operating-in-polar-waters/.

113 *Ibid.*, Sec 1.

114 *Ibid.*, Secs 2 and 3.

Svalbard.[115] Relevant measures include ships' routeing, restrictions on the use of certain fairways and notification requirements for vessels on their arrival/departure from waters.[116] The act includes a reservation that it is applicable within the limits of general international law and treaties to which Norway is a party.[117] Consequently, the Norwegian Coastal Administration may not adopt a routeing measure that hampers innocent passage in the territorial sea[118] or establishes a routeing measure in the EEZ without applying the procedures under Chapter V of SOLAS 74 and the COLREGS[119] conventions.[120] Chapter V of SOLAS 74 on the Safety of Navigation provides for establishing different types of measures (voluntary as well as mandatory), including ships' routeing and ship reporting systems, for safety as well as for environmental protection purposes.[121] It is assumed that States are required to submit proposals to the IMO for adoption of such measures where they are not competent to establish them unilaterally.[122] Norway has submitted several proposals for such measures to the Maritime Safety Committee of the IMO. The Maritime Safety Committee has approved several mandatory traffic separation schemes as well as recommended routes, which together regulate navigation in the EEZ of mainland Norway.[123] One of the traffic separation schemes is located some 50 nm off the coast between Vardø and Røst in the northern part of Norway. This traffic separation scheme has been supplemented by the mandatory Ship Reporting System in the Barents Area (Barents SRS) that is applicable to the

115 Harbour and Fairways Act, *supra* note 97, Secs 13 and 22, made applicable to the EEZ under Regulation 17 December 2010 No 1607, accessed 17 March 2017 at http://lovdata.no/dokument/SF/forskrift/2010-12-17-1607.

116 *Ibid.*, Secs 13 and 22.

117 *Ibid.*, Sec 3.

118 UNCLOS, *supra* note 4, Art 24.

119 Convention on the International Regulations for Preventing Collisions at Sea, adopted 20 October 1972, entered into force 15 July 1977, 1050 UNTS 18.

120 Under Article 211(5) of UNCLOS, the coastal State is entitled to adopt legislation to prevent ship-source pollution that is consistent with generally accepted international rules and standards. The procedures provided for under the IMO conventions can be categorised as such rules and standards.

121 SOLAS 74, *supra* note 34, Reg V/10 (Ships Routeing and Regulation) and V/11 (Ship Reporting System).

122 *Ibid.*, Reg V/10 (4).

123 COLREG.2/Circ.58 of 11 December 2006 on New and Amended Existing Traffic Separation Schemes (Vardø- Røst) and COLREG.2/Circ.62 of 15 December 2010 on New and Amended Existing Traffic Separation Schemes (off the western coast of Norway and off the southern coast of Norway).

EEZ and territorial seas of Norway and Russia.[124] It provides Norwegian and Russian authorities with improved means of control over and surveillance of maritime transport in the Barents Sea. Norway has adopted regulations to implement these schemes.[125] The regulations are mainly applicable to tankers, vessels carrying hazardous cargoes and vessels above 5,000 gross tonnage (GT). These measures came following concerns over risks of accidents and marine pollution following increased traffic along the coastline of Norway to/from Russia, particularly by oil tankers.

The EU legislation on traffic monitoring and information systems is implemented through the EEA Agreement.[126] Norway and Iceland have introduced regulations requiring vessels to give prior notice of entry into ports (including on Svalbard) when carrying hazardous or polluting cargoes.[127] Vessels above 1000 tonnes carrying bunker oil for its own use are included and they are required to notify the coastal States during their voyage through the EEZ or territorial sea of Norway and Iceland.

There are few regulations on navigation within the territorial waters of Jan Mayen and Svalbard. Passenger vessels and other vessels with a length of more than 24 metres are required to report their positions and sailing route on their entry to or departure from the territorial sea of these islands.[128] The requirement is also applicable to vessels transiting the territorial sea. Tracking maritime traffic navigating in the territorial sea is important because of conditions in the coastal waters, including inadequate charts, changing weather

---

124 Adoption of a New Mandatory Ship Reporting System in the Barents Area, Resolution MSC.348(91) (Barents SRS), available in Annex 27 of the Report of the Maritime Safety Committee on its Ninety-First Session, MSC 91/22/Add.2.

125 Regulation No 1094 of 23 September 2015 relating to the Use of the Vessel Traffic Centre Area of Application and Use of Specific Waters, Ch 4 on Routeing Measures in the Norwegian EEZ, accessed 17 March 2017 at http://www.kystverket.no/globalassets/trafikksentraler/maritime-traffic-regulations_updated-2015.pdf; Regulation No 1790 of 21 December 2015 on Reporting Duties of Vessels under the Harbour and Fairways Act, Secs 19–27, accessed 17 March 2017 at https://lovdata.no/dokument/SF/forskrift/2015-12-21-1790.

126 Directive 59/2002/EC, as amended, establishing a community vessel monitoring and information system.

127 Regulation on vessel duty of notification under the Harbours and Fairways Act, *supra* note 125.

128 Regulation No 1876 of 30 December 2009 on Harbours and Fairways of Svalbard, Secs 22–24, accessed 17 March 2017 at http://lovdata.no/dokument/SF/forskrift/2009-12-30-1846 [in Norwegian].

conditions and ice conditions.[129] Knowing the location of the vessels will enable the authorities to intervene at an early stage in the case of a maritime accident. The reporting requirement does not hamper the right of innocent passage. Vessels carrying or using heavy fuel oil are prohibited from navigating within certain parts of the territorial sea of Svalbard. This regulation will be dealt with below under the section on protection of marine environment. The Regulation under the Pilotage Act on mandatory pilotage is applicable to vessels operating within the territorial waters of Svalbard.[130] Pilotage is particularly important in these waters due to the poor charting of the waters.

3.2.4 Operational Discharge/Environmental Protection Rules and Standards

The SSSA aims at protecting the marine environment from the negative effects of shipping activities. It introduces a general ban on discharges or dumping from vessels or incineration or other activities related to the operation of the vessel.[131] The general ban is specified through regulations. The regulations of Annexes I–VI of MARPOL 73/78 are implemented through the Regulation on Environmental Safety for Vessels and Mobile Offshore Units.[132] The regulations of the MARPOL 73/78 annexes are made directly applicable in Norwegian law by incorporating them through reference The Environmental Safety Regulation is applicable to foreign-flagged vessels operating in waters within the 200 nm EEZ and territorial waters of mainland Norway and territorial waters of Svalbard and Jan Mayen.[133] It is also applicable to foreign-flagged vessels voluntarily in Norwegian ports in respect of discharges in waters outside the maritime zones of Norway. The latter refers to the enforcement jurisdiction enjoyed by port States under Article 218 of UNCLOS.

The Pollution Prevention Measures of the Polar Code (Part II-A) and the relevant amendments of MARPOL 73/78 annexes are implemented in Norwegian law by an amendment the Environmental Safety Regulation, where these

---

129 Report/White Paper to Stortinget No 14 (2004–2005) on the safe side—maritime safety and oil preparedness, at 48–49, accessed 17 March 2017 at www.regjeringen.no/no/dokumenter/stmeld-nr-14-2004-2005-/id406094/ [in Norwegian].

130 Regulations relating to the Pilotage Services on Svalbard, *supra* note 100, Sec 1.

131 SSSA, *supra* note 96, Sec 31.

132 Regulation No 488 of 30 May 2012 on Environmental Safety for Vessels and Mobile Offshore Units (Environmental Safety Regulation), accessed 17 March 2017 at www.sjofartsdir.no/en/legislation/regulations/environmental-safety-for-ships-and-mobile-offshore-units1/.

133 *Ibid.*, Sec 1.

instruments are made directly applicable.[134] These amendments are applicable to Norwegian-flagged vessels operating in polar waters and to foreign-flagged vessels operating in the territorial waters of Jan Mayen and Svalbard.[135] It bans the discharge of oil, oily mixtures and noxious liquid substances at sea by Norwegian-flagged vessels in polar waters and by foreign-flagged vessels when operating in the territorial waters of Jan Mayen and Svalbard.[136] In addition, the discharge regulations for sewage and garbage will apply in the territorial waters of Svalbard and Jan Mayen. The discharge of oil, oily mixtures, noxious liquid substances or other substances in violation of Part II-A of the Polar Code in the waters off the 12 nm zone of Svalbard are subject to enforcement as provided in UNCLOS. Norway is not competent to enforce violations in respect of foreign vessels as these waters are high seas in respect of shipping. The violations may be enforced in respect of foreign vessels if they visit Norwegian ports under Article 218 of UNCLOS.

The BWM Convention is an important contribution by the IMO to prevent the introduction through the exchange of ballast water of alien species that may threaten marine biodiversity, species and their ecosystems. Norway has acceded to the BWM Convention, which entered into force on 8 September 2017.[137] Norway has adopted a regulation on ballast water management in its waters to prevent the introduction of invasive species.[138] The regulation is applicable to all ships constructed for carrying ballast water while within Norwegian territorial waters (including Svalbard and Jan Mayen) and the EEZ of mainland Norway. The regulations are also applicable to foreign vessels transiting Norwegian territorial waters (including Svalbard and Jan Mayen) and the EEZ of mainland Norway while exercising their navigational rights.[139]

---

134 Forskrift om miljømessig sikkerhet for skip og flyttbare innretninger, Section 19 (Regulation on Environmental Safety for Vessels and Mobile Offshore Units), see note 111 for reference.

135 Environmental Safety Regulation, *supra* note 132, Sec 1.

136 Polar Code, *supra* note 1, Part II-A, paras 1.1.1 and 2.1.1.

137 BWM Convention, *supra* note 38, Art 18(1). Information on the status of BWM Convention is regularly updated and available at Summary of Status of Conventions, accessed 17 March 2017 at http://www.imo.org/en/About/Conventions/StatusOfConventions/Pages/Default.aspx.

138 Regulation of 7 July 2009 No 992 concerning the prevention of transfer of alien organisms via ballast water and sediments from ships (Ballast Water Regulation), accessed 17 March 2017 at http://www.sjofartsdir.no/en/legislation/regulations/regulation-of-7-july-2009-no-992-concerning-the-prevention-of-transfer-of-alien-organisms-via-ballast-water-and-sediments-from-ships-the-ballast-water-regulation/.

139 *Ibid.*, Sec 1.

The Polar Code includes a recommendation to apply the ballast-water exchange standard or the ballast-water treatment standard on a voluntary basis until the BWM Convention enters into force.[140] Foreign-flagged vessels visiting ports in Svalbard or in Northern Norway *en route* from areas outside the Barents Sea or the Norwegian Sea are required to manage the ballast water by exchange, treatment or disposal at a reception facility in port.[141] This may be considered as a condition for calling at the port. The port is subject to the sovereignty of Norway and conditions for calling at ports is not necessarily in conflict with the law of the sea. The regulations on the exchange of ballast water beyond coastal areas are more of a recommendatory character.[142] However, the exchange of ballast water must have been done before the vessel enters the territorial waters. The exchange of ballast water within the 12 nm territorial waters of Jan Mayen, Svalbard and mainland Norway is prohibited. Such a ban is consistent with the jurisdiction the coastal State enjoys in these maritime zones.[143]

Another measure to protect marine biodiversity is the establishment of marine protected areas (MPAs) or terrestrial protected areas that include marine space. Within MPAs, navigation and other human activities (such as fishing, marine scientific research and oil exploitation) are restricted. The coastal State is competent under the law of the sea to establish MPAs within their maritime zones if they do not infringe on the rights of other States (e.g., navigational rights). The legislation of Norway provides a legal basis for protecting areas within the territorial waters off mainland Norway[144] and Svalbard.[145] Major parts of terrestrial Svalbard and marine areas are protected by regulations under the Svalbard Environment Protection Act.[146] Following maritime

140 Polar Code, *supra* note 1, Part II-B, para 4.1.

141 Ballast Water Regulation, *supra* note 138, Sec 5.

142 *Ibid.*, Sec 6.

143 UNCLOS, *supra* note 4, Art 21(1)(d) and (f).

144 Act of 19 June 2009 No 100 relating to the Management of Biological, Geological and Landscape Diversity (Nature Diversity Act), Sec 39, accessed 17 March 2017 at www.regjeringen.no/en/dokumenter/nature-diversity-act/id570549/.

145 Svalbard Environmental Protection Act, *supra* note 101, Sec 11.

146 Regulation No 377 of 4 April 2014 on the establishment of bird reserves and larger nature protection areas on Svalbard, accessed 17 March 2017 at http://www.sysselmannen.no/Documents/Sysselmannen_dok/English/Regulations/FOR-2014-04-04-377_Regulations%20relating%20to%20large%20nature%20conservation%20areas%20and%20bird%20reserves%20in%20Svalbard%20as%20established%20in%201973.pdf. For a map, see http://www.sysselmannen.no/en/News/Extended-ban-on-heavy-fuel-oil/, accessed 17 March 2017.

casualties in mainland Norway involving pollution of bunker oil, a ban on carrying and the use of heavy fuel was introduced for vessels operating in the marine parts of the protected areas.[147] Accidental pollution would have particularly serious consequences in these areas because of inadequate oil spill preparedness and prevention capacity. The ban primarily affects the cruise vessels visiting some of the fjords of the archipelago.

The Svalbard Environmental Protection Act has been amended to provide a legal basis for a ban on vessels carrying and using heavy fuel oil while within the 12 nm territorial waters, including areas outside the protected areas.[148] Such a ban may be inconsistent with the right of innocent passage under the law of the sea.[149] A ban on the use or carriage of heavy fuel oil may amount to a CDEM requirement and consequently may hamper the right of innocent passage, an argument that was made by the Norwegian Maritime Authorities when the Bill was introduced.[150] If such ban indeed is a CDEM requirement it can only be lawfully applied to vessels in innocent passage in the territorial sea of Norway if such a measure is first adopted at the international level, e.g., through amendment of Annex I of MARPOL 73/78. The Svalbard Environmental Protection Act provides for the adoption of regulations where heavy fuel oil may be carried or used in designated routes through the territorial sea and internal waters. It is thus doubtful whether such a regulation would be consistent with the right of coastal States to regulate innocent passage through the territorial sea.

3.2.5 Enforcement

The coastal States enjoy limited jurisdiction under the law of the sea to enforce CDEM and navigational rules and standards in respect of the foreign-flagged vessels exercising navigational rights within their territorial sea and EEZ, particularly in the EEZ.[151] Foreign-flagged vessels not exercising their navigational rights under the law of the sea, such as cruise vessels calling at ports and operating both within the territorial sea and within internal waters may be subject to more extensive enforcement jurisdiction.[152]

---

147 *Ibid.*, Sec 4.

148 Svalbard Environment Protection Act, *supra* note 101, Sec 82a.

149 UNCLOS, *supra* note 4, Art 21(2).

150 See Letter from the Norwegian Maritime Authority to the Ministry of Environment of 30.8.2010, accessed 17 March 2017 at https://www.regjeringen.no/contentassets/5363d89659794689a81eb5294bee4871/sjoefartsdirektoratet.pdf.

151 UNCLOS, *supra* note 4, Art 220.

152 As reflected in e.g., UNCLOS, *supra* note 4, Arts 25(2) and 211(3).

One example of the limited enforcement jurisdiction concerns the mandatory ship reporting and traffic separation schemes established by Norway under the SOLAS 74 and COLREG Conventions for the Norwegian EEZ of the Barents Sea. The foreign-flagged vessels are requested to comply with these schemes.[153] The regulation does not provide a legal basis for taking (physical) enforcement measures in respect of vessels violating these schemes. The Norwegian authorities are required to report the incident to the flag State, which is responsible for ensuring compliance with these measures.[154]

The Norwegian SSSA provides a legal basis for refusing foreign-flagged vessels not in compliance with international regulations or Norwegian legislation access to its 12 nm territorial sea.[155] It may be used to ban vessels not adequately constructed or equipped for navigating through sea ice from navigating in the ice-covered parts of the territorial sea of Svalbard. It may be argued that such ban would not be in violation of the right of innocent passage if there is a high probability that the vessel be involved in maritime accident if to proceed into these waters. In practice, this competence is used in the port State control scheme where substandard and blacklisted vessels can be refused access to its ports.[156]

It is enforcement of compliance with operational discharges where the competence of the coastal State is most extensive. Under the Norwegian legislation, a foreign-flagged vessel may be stopped, boarded and inspected while navigating through the 12 nm territorial sea where there are reasonable grounds for suspecting that it has violated international rules on vessel-source pollution or the environmental protection provisions of the SSSA while in Norwegian territorial sea (including off Svalbard and Jan Mayen).[157] The violations may include operational discharges above the limits set by the annexes of MARPOL for these waters, non-compliance with equipment or construction

153 Regulation relating to the Use of the Vessel Traffic Centre Area of Application and Use of Specific Waters, *supra* note 125, Sec 160.

154 UNCLOS, *supra* note 4, Art 220(3) *c.f.* Art 217(6).

155 SSSA, *supra* note 96, Sec 54.

156 Regulation of 24 November 2014 No 1458 concerning Port State Control (Port State Control Regulation), Sec 11, accessed 17 March 2017 at https://www.sjofartsdir.no/en/shipping/legislation/regulations/port-state-control/.

157 SSSA, *supra* note 96, Sec 53, as specified in Regulation No 850 of 2 July 2007 on investigation, stopping and boarding of foreign ships in the event of suspicion of an environmental violation, Sec 3 *c.f.* Secs 1 and 6, accessed 17 March 2017 at www.sjofartsdir.no/en/legislation/regulations/investigation-stopping-and-boarding-of-foreign-ships-in-the-event-of-suspicion-of-an-environmental-violation/.

requirements or lack of valid certificates under these annexes. As part of the investigation, the vessel can be instructed to go to port in Norway.[158]

Where there are reasonable reasons for suspecting that a foreign-flagged vessel has violated the mentioned instruments while in the Norwegian EEZ, the vessel may be asked to provide information on its identity and its next port of call. The vessel may only be stopped and boarded if the violation has caused considerable discharge, which has led to substantial pollution of the marine environment or poses a threat of such pollution.[159] Foreign-flagged vessels in ports may be investigated for violations committed in waters under the jurisdiction of the coastal State.[160] As the application of SSSA and its regulations is subjected to the international legal obligations of Norway, their provisions must be enforced in a manner not violating the navigational rights of foreign-flagged vessels.[161] These regulations are consistent with the (environmental) enforcement jurisdiction of coastal States under Part XII of UNCLOS.

There is a legal basis in Norwegian legislation to enforce the operational discharge standards of Part II-A of the Polar Code (e.g., the ban on discharge of oil and oily mixture to sea). These standards apply to Norwegian-flagged vessels and to foreign-flagged vessels operating within the territorial waters of Svalbard, Jan Mayen and mainland Norway as well as the EEZ to the extent the Polar Code is applicable. This would be consistent with the rights of the coastal State under Article 21 of UNCLOS.

The coastal States may also enforce violations of the Polar Code operational discharge rules and standards committed by foreign-flagged vessels while in Arctic waters beyond their jurisdiction if these call at their ports.[162] This includes discharges in the 200 nm zone off Svalbard and in the high seas area of the Central Arctic Ocean. They may exercise jurisdiction over vessels voluntarily in their ports that have been involved in discharges in violation of applicable international rules and standards. The operational discharge regulations of Part II-A qualify as such rules and standards.[163] These requirements include Annexes I, II, IV and V of MARPOL 73/78, which are applicable to over 90 per cent of the world tonnage.[164] For the coastal States to take enforcement

158 *Ibid.*, Sec 52.

159 Regulation on investigation, stopping and boarding, *supra* note 157, Sec 4.

160 *Ibid.*, Sec 2.

161 SSSA, *supra* note 96, Sec 3.

162 UNCLOS, *supra* note 4, Art 218(1).

163 *Ibid.*, Art 218.

164 See summary of status of Conventions, accessed 17 March 2017 at http://www.imo.org/en/About/Conventions/StatusOfConventions/Pages/Default.aspx.

measures in respect of discharges committed in Arctic waters under the jurisdiction of other coastal States, they need a formal request from the coastal State, flag State in question, or another impacted State.[165] If the illegal discharges have occurred on the high seas or threaten to pollute areas under their jurisdiction, coastal States may take enforcement measures on their own initiative. These provisions of UNCLOS are implemented in Norwegian legislation.[166] The Norwegian authorities are in fact obligated to comply with the requests of flag States or relevant coastal States to assist in the investigation.[167] Under Article 218, the port State has a discretional right to conduct investigations.

Norway is not competent to enforce illegal operational discharges from vessels while within the 200 nm Svalbard fisheries protection zone. As mentioned earlier, the zone is high seas in respect of international shipping. If the vessel visits one of its ports, either on Svalbard or in mainland Norway, the extraterritorial jurisdiction provided by the above-mentioned regulation may be applied.

Port State Control is probably the optimal opportunity for the coastal State to ensure that vessels operating in Arctic waters (within and beyond their jurisdiction) are constructed, designed, equipped, manned and operated consistent with the requirements of the Polar Code. Norway participates in the Paris Memorandum of Understanding on Port State Control (Paris MoU).[168] The Norwegian (including Svalbard) Port State Control Regulation[169] is implementing the EU Port State directive (as part of the EEA Agreement), which is based on the Paris MoU.[170] It means that Norwegian maritime authorities are legally required to apply the regulations of the Paris MOU.

---

165 See Article 218(2) and Article 228 on the rights of coastal States and flag States to stop or suspend the proceedings.

166 SSSA, *supra* note 96, Sec 3 (last paragraph), *c.f.* Regulation on investigation, stopping and boarding of foreign ships, *supra* note 157, Sec 2, para 1 litra e.

167 *Ibid.*

168 Paris Memorandum on Port State Control, accessed 17 March 2017 at https://www.parismou.org/about-us/memorandum.

169 Port State Control Regulation, *supra* note 156.

170 Directive 2009/16/EC (as amended) of the European Parliament and of the Council of 23 April 2009 on Port State Control, *Official Journal of the European Communities: Legislation* 131, at 57. The EU legislation on maritime transport is relevant for the European Economic Area Agreement to which Norway is a party, see EEA Agreement, *supra* note 90, Art 47–52 and Annex XIII/V, 1994 *Official Journal of the European Communities: Legislation* 3. Article 102 of the EEA Agreement provides for the procedures for including new EU legislation into the EEA Agreement.

The objective of the Port State Control Scheme and the Norwegian regulation is to effectively enhance the 'safety, pollution prevention and on-board living and working conditions [...] through a drastic reduction of substandard ships from Community waters, by strictly applying Conventions, international codes and resolutions.' The (Norwegian) Port State Control Regulation makes a wide range of IMO and ILO conventions applicable to foreign-flagged vessels visiting their ports, including SOLAS 74, MARPOL 73/78 and the STCW Convention.[171] As the Polar Code regulations are made mandatory through amendments to the SOLAS 74 and MARPOL 73/78 conventions, they would be part of the Port State Control scheme to be employed by Norway.

The procedures for port inspections are regulated in the EU directive: vessels are selected for inspection based on a risk profile decided on the basis of the vessel (type and age and history), the performance of the flag State (based on detention rate), of the recognised organisation (the detention rate of their certificates) and company performance. The frequency of inspections depends on the level of risk. Other circumstances may override both frequency and the extent of the inspection. If the deficiencies are serious, the vessel may be detained until the deficiencies are addressed.[172] Vessels with a recent history of detention may be refused access to the ports.

The question is how Port State Control may be used to ensure compliance with the additional requirements of the Polar Code by vessels operating in the Arctic waters. The risk profile of a vessel will depend on which areas and in what periods of the year it operates in Arctic waters, as well as how the vessel is constructed, designed and manned.[173] The CDEM rules and standards of the Polar Code that a vessel is required to comply with depend on *inter alia* the sea ice and temperature conditions under which the vessel is planned to operate. In addition, the flag State may approve alternative design or equipment.[174] Consequently, when vessels are making calls at ports outside Arctic waters (particularly when in transit), it may prove difficult for the port State to evaluate its seaworthiness under Arctic conditions. The control of the port State will be limited to determining whether the vessel has a valid Polar Certificate[175] and, if further inspection is necessary, whether the standard of the vessel and the crew is in conformity with the information provided by the certificate.[176]

171 Port State Control Regulation, *supra* note 156, Sec 2.

172 *Ibid.*, Ch 4, on detention and refusal of access.

173 See Polar Code, *supra* note 1, Part I-A, para 1.5.

174 SOLAS 74, *supra* note 34, Ch XIV, Reg 4.

175 Polar Code, *supra* note 1, Part I-A, Sec 1.3, *c.f.* SOLAS 74, *supra* note 34, Ch XIV, Reg 3(2).

176 Directive 2009/16, *supra* note 170, Art 13.

To determine the Arctic seaworthiness of the vessel, the port State would need detailed information on the planned route and the sea ice and temperature conditions the vessel would be subjected to during the voyage. Under the present regime, port States only have information on vessels' port arrival times and final destination or routes.[177] Port States will be in a better position to control foreign-flagged vessels arriving in their ports as part of destinational traffic to/from their Arctic waters, e.g., cruise vessels calling in ports in Svalbard. The reporting requirement for vessels navigating in the territorial sea of Svalbard (which includes providing information on final destination) may prove valuable in the control of vessels visiting ports on the islands.

3.3 *Denmark/Greenland*

3.3.1 General

In Denmark, maritime safety and protection of the marine environment is regulated through the Safety at Sea Act (SSA)[178] and the Marine Environmental Protection Act (MEPA),[179] respectively. The SSA and the MEPA apply to the maritime zones off Greenland through separate and specially adapted regulations (the Greenlandic SSA[180] and the Greenlandic MEPA).[181] The Greenlandic MEPA applies to the 200 nm EEZ, whereas the Greenlandic SSA applies to the territorial waters. The Greenlandic self-governmental authorities have

177 Regulation on vessel duty of notification under the Harbours and Fairways Act, *supra* note 125, Sec 8 (vessels above 300 GT) and Sec 10 (vessels with dangerous or pollutive cargo), accessed 17 March 2017 at https://lovdata.no/dokument/SF/forskrift/2015-12-21-1790#KAPITTEL_2 [in Norwegian].

178 Consolidated Act No 72 of 17 January 2014 on Safety at Sea (Bekendtgørelse af lov nr. 72 af 17/01/2014 om sikkerhed til søs), accessed 17 March 2017 at http://www.dma.dk/Vaekst/Rammevilkaar/Legislation/Acts/Consolidated%20act%20on%20safety%20at%20sea.pdf.

179 Consolidated Act No 963 of 3 July 2013 on the Protection of the Marine Environment (Bekendtgørelse af Low nr. 963 af 3. juli 2013 om beskyttelse af havmiljøet), accessed 17 March 2017 at www.retsinformation.dk/Forms/r0710.aspx?id=145889#Not1 [in Danish].

180 Bekendtgørelse nr. 1674 af 18 december 2015 af anordning om ikrafttræden for Grønland af lov om sikkerhed til søs (Consolidated decree No 1674 of 18 December 2015 on the entry into force for Greenland of the Act on safety at sea), (Greenlandic SSA).

181 Royal Decree No 1035, 22 October 2004, on the Marine Act coming into force for Greenland (Anordning nr 1035 af 22. Oktober 2004 om ikrafttræden for Grønland af lov om beskyttelse af havmiljøet), (Greenlandic MEPA) a draft version of the decree is available in Danish at http://webarkiv.ft.dk/?/samling/20031/udvbilag/fou/almdel_bilag120.htm, accessed 17 March 2017.

adopted a Decree on Protection on the Marine Environment within the three nm territorial sea, consistent with the allocation of powers to them.[182]

A draft Act on Protection of the Marine Environment of the Greenlandic EEZ has been submitted for public consultations.[183] It will eventually replace the Greenlandic MEPA. The act will be applicable to foreign-flagged vessels operating in the 200 nm EEZ of Greenland to the extent consistent with international law.[184] The competence or legislative jurisdiction for protecting the marine environment within the three nm territorial sea still lies with the Self-Government of Greenland. The draft includes a provision providing the Minister of Environment with a legal basis for designating part of the EEZ as an ice-covered area, consistent with international law.[185] The Minister may adopt detailed regulations to protect the marine environment of the designated area. This would provide a legal basis in national legislation for applying the extended environmental jurisdiction under Article 234 of UNCLOS, which provides for the adoption of CDEM and navigational rules and standards to the extent they are necessary to prevent marine pollution.[186] There is separate legislation on maritime safety (Greenlandic SSA), which includes provisions on both CDEM rules and standard and navigational standards, also aimed at preventing marine pollution.[187] It is doubtful if the proposed act will provide a legal basis for such regulations. The proposed act will be addressed further under section 3.3.4 below.

3.3.2 CDEM Rules and Standards

Similar to the Norwegian SSSA, the Greenlandic SSA includes a general CDEM requirement for vessels to operate in Greenlandic waters. Vessels are to be constructed and equipped and operated for their intended use in such a manner that safeguards human lives and the marine environment.[188] The

182 Landtingsforordning nr. 4 af 3.november 1994 om beskyttelse af havmiljøet (Greenland Decree on Marine Environmental Protection), accessed 17 March 2017 at http://lovgivning.gl/lov?rid={7FF13361-5A48-4D05-95B1-D998C96D73BF} [in Danish].

183 Forslag til Lov om beskyttelse af havmiljøet i den eksklusive økonomiske sone ved Grønland (Draft Act on Protection of the Marine Environment of the Greenlandic EEZ), accessed 17 March 2017 at http://www.ft.dk/samling/20151/almdel/mof/bilag/341/1610459.pdf [in Danish].

184 *Ibid.*, Sec 2(1), (4).

185 *Ibid.*, Sec 8(1).

186 For a detailed analysis of Article 234, see Chapter 2 of this Volume.

187 Greenlandic SSA, *supra* note 180, Sec 2(4), *c.f.* Sec 3 (CDEM rules and standards) and Sec 6 (Navigational rules and standards).

188 Greenlandic SSA, *supra* note 180, Sec 2.

requirements for technical safety are relative—dependent on the use of the vessel and its areas of operation. The Greenlandic SSA does not provide detailed technical regulations, but provides a legal basis for the Minister to adopt such regulations, particularly to implement mandatory CDEM rules and standards adopted under SOLAS 74 and MARPOL 73/78.[189] The Minister may also decide to make the Greenlandic SSA and/or its regulations applicable to foreign-flagged vessels while in port, navigating in the territorial sea or the EEZ of Greenland.[190] A regulation has yet to be adopted to make the CDEM rules and standards of SOLAS 74 and MARPOL 73/78 applicable to foreign-flagged vessels while in Greenlandic waters.

The Danish SSA was amended in 2013 to provide a legal basis for adopting enhanced safety requirements for vessels navigating in the maritime zones of Greenland, and which is included in the Greenlandic SSA:

> The Minister for Business and Growth may lay down regulations on stricter safety requirements for ships whose navigation in arctic waters present a special risk to those on board the ship or the arctic environment, including regulations on the use of a pilot certified for navigation in the relevant area.[191]

The amendment entered into force on 1 January 2016.[192] It could be reasonable to assume that this provision is intended to implement Article 234 of UNCLOS in respect of the marine safety legislation. However, there is nothing in the preparatory work to suggest such an interpretation.[193] Also, the wording does not support such reading. The provision uses the 'arctic waters' concept, which may not only include ice-covered waters but also open waters. Therefore, it is more natural to read this provision as being based on the general environmental jurisdiction of the coastal State under Article 211 of UNCLOS.

Three regulations were adopted in December 2016 to implement the provision on both CDEM rules and standards and navigation.[194] The latter will be

---

189 *Ibid.*, Sec 2(4) *c.f.* Sec 3.

190 *Ibid.*, Sec 1(3).

191 Act No 618 of 12 June 2013, amending the merchant shipping act and various other acts, Sec 3(1), accessed 17 March 2017 at https://www.retsinformation.dk/forms/r0710.aspx?id=152132. The provision is included in the Greenlandic SSA, *supra* note 180, Sec 3(2).

192 Consolidated Decree No 1674 of 18 December 2015, *supra* note 180, Sec 33 *c.f.* Section 3(2).

193 Lovforslag L 154 (Folketinget 2012–2013) Forslag til Lov om ændring af søloven og forskellige andre love, at 27–28 and 118.

194 Bekentgørelse nr. 1697 af 11. December 2015 for Grønland om skibes sikre sejlads mv (Regulation on Safe Navigation); Bekentgørelse nr. 1698 af 11. December 2015 om lodsing

addressed in section 3.3.3. The regulations include one regulation on safe navigation and two on pilotage. When circulating the draft regulations for public hearing, the Danish Maritime Authority noted that the regulations were based mainly on the recently adopted Polar Code.[195] Denmark has made the Polar Code applicable to Danish and Greenlandic waters.[196] However, some of the provisions regarding passenger vessels with more than 250 passengers are either not found in the Polar Code or imply stricter requirements than the Polar Code. The intention is to have a higher level of maritime safety for these passenger vessels than provided for in the Polar Code. The proposal to introduce mandatory pilotage would supplement the Polar Code. Under the Polar Code, vessels are required to have an ice class corresponding to the forecasted ice conditions.[197] Under the Danish regulation, a passenger vessel with more than 250 passengers navigating in the northern navigation zone would be required to have a minimum ice class regardless of the presence of ice. The regulations also include more specific requirements than the Polar Code on voyage planning and preparedness of the vessels in case of maritime accidents. Importantly, the requirements under the Danish regulation that are stricter than the Polar Code are not applicable to foreign-flagged vessels exercising navigational rights under the law of the sea.

The regulation on safe navigation is applicable to all cargo vessels of at least 150 GT and vessels carrying more than 12 passengers, operating within the three nm territorial sea of Greenland.[198] The regulation is applicable to foreign-flagged vessels. However, some of its provisions are not applicable to foreign-flagged vessels exercising their right of innocent passage through the territorial sea. These provisions involve CDEM rules and standards, such as

---

mv (Regulation on Pilotage) and Bekentgørelse nr. 1699 af 11. December 2015 om lodseriers virksomhed og pligter (Regulation on the activities of pilotage service providers and the obligations of pilots in Greenland), all accessed 17 March 2017 at http://www.dma.dk/SikkerhedTilSoes/Arktis/SejladsGroenland/Sider/default.aspx.

195 Danish Maritime Directorate, Høring vedrørende udkast til 'Bekendtgørelse for Grønland om skibes sikre sejlads mv. og Bekentgørelse om lodseriers virksomhed og pligter i Grønland, (Consultation papers of October 2015 on draft regulations on Safe Navigation and on the activities of pilotage service providers and the obligations of pilots in Greenland), accessed 17 March 2017 at https://hoeringsportalen.dk/Hearing/Details/58841.

196 Order No 1512 of 8 December 2016 on Notice B from the Danish Maritime Authority, the construction and equipment, etc. of ships, chapters XIV, XV and XXI, available at http://www.dma.dk/Vaekst/Rammevilkaar/Legislation/Notice%20B/Consolidated%20Notice%20B-01012017.pdf.

197 Polar Code, *supra* note 1, Part I-A, para 3.2.2.

198 Regulation on Safe Navigation, *supra* note 194, Sec 1(2).

ice-strengthening requirements and skill requirements for the master of the vessel and deck officers.[199]

Some of these requirements are identical with those of Part I-A of the Polar Code; other requirements are stricter and finally some of the requirements are additional to those set out in the Polar Code. The coastal State may apply CDEM rules and standards to foreign-flagged vessels in innocent passage when they give 'effect to generally accepted international rules or standards'.[200] The CDEM rules and standards of the Polar Code may gain such status at the earliest when Chapter XIV of SOLAS 74 and the Polar Code, as well as the amendments to the Annex of the STCW Convention and STCW Code, which enter into force in 2017 and 2018, respectively. At such time, Denmark/Greenland may make the requirements implementing the Polar Code applicable to foreign-flagged vessels in innocent passage. The other (stricter and additional) requirements of the Danish regulations may first be applied to foreign-flagged vessels in innocent passage when they gain such status.

In the meantime, these CDEM rules and standards may be applied to foreign-flagged vessels during their voyages in internal waters or while operating in the territorial sea when not exercising the right of innocent passage.[201] Examples of such vessels are passenger vessels visiting fjords and other parts of the Greenlandic coast, vessels calling at ports in Greenland or vessels involved in coastal traffic. As these vessels are not merely transiting the territorial sea of Greenland, they are subject to the full sovereignty of the coastal State and are required to comply with these requirements.[202] Denmark is not violating its obligations under SOLAS 74 and the STCW Convention by applying stricter and additional requirements than the safety measures set out in of the Polar Code and the STCW Convention and Code, as neither SOLAS 74 nor the STCW Convention prejudice the rights and obligations of States under international law.[203]

The provisions of the regulation on safe navigation concerning the operation of vessels are applicable to foreign-flagged vessels, regardless of whether they exercise the right of innocent passage. They are addressed in section 3.3.3 on navigation rules and standards.

---

199 Regulation on Pilotage, *supra* note 194, Secs 13 and 16.

200 UNCLOS, *supra* note 4, Art 21(3).

201 Regulation on Safe Navigation, *supra* note 194, Sec 1(4).

202 UNCLOS, *supra* note 4, Art 2(1), *c.f.* Art 25(2).

203 SOLAS 74, *supra* note 34, Ch XIV, Reg 2(5); STCW Convention, *supra* note 36, Art V(4); Regulation on Safe Navigation, *supra* note 194, Sec 7.

Foreign-flagged vessels not exercising the right of innocent passage are required to comply with several CDEM requirements. First, they are required to have a person available on-board with local knowledge of the waters to be navigated.[204] Even if he/she is not necessarily a member of the crew, this may be regarded as a manning requirement. The master of the vessel must document the local knowledge and experience of this person and of her/his knowledge of navigation in Arctic and icy waters. This requirement of local knowledge and experience is an additional requirement to those of Chapter 12 of the Polar Code on manning and training. Vessels operating in Arctic waters are required to have navigational officers (in addition to master and chief mate) with basic or advanced training in operating in polar waters, depending on the ice conditions of the relevant voyage. The second requirement is that vessels may not include open lifeboats as part of their emergency preparedness.[205] According to the survival regulations in Chapter 8 of the Polar Code, only partially or totally enclosed lifeboats are permitted.[206] Whether they are to be partially or totally enclosed depend on the hazards and expected time of rescue.[207] In both instances, the lifeboats will probably comply with the requirement of the regulation on safe navigation. Finally, vessels may only plan for navigation in ice if the vessel is structurally designed for the relevant type and concentration of ice.[208] This is consistent with the functional requirement that vessels shall have ice strengthening adequate for the waters.[209]

As mentioned above, additional safety measures are applicable to passenger vessels with more than 250 passengers operating within the three nm territorial sea (and not in innocent passage). The vessels are to have an ice class that at a minimum corresponds to the prevalent ice conditions.[210] Vessels sailing in the northern navigation zone[211] are required to have minimum Baltic ice class 1 C or equivalent, irrespective of the presence of sea ice. Passenger vessels without ice strengthening may operate in the southern navigational zone when it is classified as open waters or no sea ice.[212]

---

204 Regulation on Safe Navigation, *supra* note 194, Sec 8.

205 *Ibid.*

206 Polar Code, *supra* note 1, Part I-A, para 8.3.3.3.1.

207 *Ibid.*, para 8.2.3.3.

208 Regulation on Safe Navigation, *supra* note 194, Sec 9.

209 Polar Code, *supra* note 1, Part I-A, para 3.2.2.

210 Regulation on Safe Navigation, *supra* note 194, Sec 13(1).

211 The Northern navigation zone includes the internal waters and territorial sea from north of 66N on the east coast to 72N on the west coast, Regulation on Safe Navigation, *supra* note 194, Sec 3(2).

212 Regulation on Safe Navigation, *supra* note 194, Sec 13(3), *c.f.* Sec 3(2).

The owners of these passenger vessels are obligated to ensure that the master and officers on-board are trained in accordance with Part B of the STCW Code regarding training of masters and officers for ships operating in polar waters.[213] The master is required to provide documentation that the crew have completed such programmes. These requirements do not seem to be coordinated with the recent amendments to the STCW Convention and Code discussed above.

3.3.3 Navigational Rules and Standards

The Greenlandic SSA provides a legal basis for regulating maritime traffic in the territorial sea and EEZ of Greenland.[214] The Minister of Business and Growth may adopt regulations establishing routeing measures or prohibiting navigation within specific areas to safeguard navigation and prevent danger. Establishing routeing measures beyond the territorial sea requires the use of the procedures stipulated under the SOLAS 74 and COLREGS conventions, as referred to in section 3.2.3. Denmark/Greenland have had proposals for such measures approved by the Maritime Safety Committee of the IMO under these instruments for areas within the EEZ.

Cargo and passenger vessels on voyage to/from ports in Greenland are to submit a sailing plan and subsequent reports on their positions at regular intervals while navigating into/within/departing the Greenlandic EEZ.[215] The requirement implements a mandatory ship reporting system (GREENPOS) adopted under SOLAS 74.[216] Under the Greenland position reporting system (KYSTKONTROL), vessels of or above 20 GT and fishing vessels on voyages between ports and places of call on Greenland are also required to submit regular reports.[217]

Under the regulation on safe navigation, there is a general duty of due care for all cargo vessels above 150 GT and passenger vessels with more than 12 passengers navigating within the three nm territorial sea, particularly when

---

213 *Ibid.*, Sec 16, *c.f.* STCW Code, *supra* note 89, Sec B-V/g.

214 Greenlandic SSA, *supra* note 180, Sec 6.

215 Order No 170 of 17 March 2003 on Ship Reporting Systems in the Waters off Greenland, Section 2, accessed 17 March 2017 at http://www.dma.dk/Vaekst/Rammevilkaar/Legislation/Orders/Order%20on%20ship%20reporting%20systems%20in%20waters%20off%20Greenland%20(reporting%20service%20in%20Greenland).pdf.

216 Resolution MSC.126(75) adopted on 20 May 2002 on Mandatory Ship Reporting System, SN/Circ.221, accessed 17 March 2017 at http://www.imo.org/blast/blastDataHelper.asp?data_id=5395&filename=221.pdf; the reporting obligations are specified in Order No 170 of 17 March 2003 on ship reporting systems in the waters off Greenland.

217 *Ibid.*, Sec 3.

navigating through poorly charted waters.[218] Specifically, they are to keep ice watch and safe distance from icebergs.[219] When planning the voyage through the territorial sea and internal waters, the master of the vessel shall particularly take into account *inter alia* the presence of sea ice, protected areas near the route, possible places of refuge, the limited search and rescue (SAR) capabilities in the area, and the fact that the waters are inadequately charted.[220] The owners and masters of passenger vessels with more than 250 passengers are required to document that the vessel will be assisted by other vessels during its voyage or that other SAR facilities are available within reasonable time and with reasonable capacity in case of an accident or incident.[221]

Vessels are not permitted to sail in areas containing 'numerous rocks' as indicated by the charts and may only navigate through areas indicated as 'foul' or 'unsurveyed' if the vessel is *inter alia* following recognised routes.[222] These requirements are also applicable to vessels exercising the right of innocent passage. Passenger vessels with more than 250 passengers on a voyage in the territorial sea (and internal waters) are required to use a certified pilot while in the relevant waters.[223] Passenger vessels with less than 250 passengers and cargo vessels operating in the internal waters or in non-innocent passage through the territorial sea are required to have a person on-board with local knowledge of the waters.[224]

The coastal State is competent to regulate vessels in innocent passage for maritime safety and environmental protection purposes.[225] The regulations may, however, not have the practical effect of denying or hampering the right of innocent passage unless they are consistent with UNCLOS.[226] The requirements of the reporting of positions, banning or strictly regulating navigation through dangerous waters, and requiring pilotage and SAR plans can hardly qualify as the illegal hampering of innocent passage. On the contrary, the coastal State has an obligation to give publicity to known dangers to navigation within the territorial sea.[227] These requirements may rather be seen as facilitating safe navigation within and through the territorial sea of Greenland.

218 Regulation on Safe Navigation, *supra* note 194, Sec 4 (1).
219 *Ibid.*, Sec 4 (2) and (3).
220 *Ibid.*, Sec 5(1).
221 *Ibid.*, Sec 15.
222 *Ibid.*, Sec 6 (2).
223 *Ibid.*, Sec 11.
224 *Ibid.*, Sec 7.
225 UNCLOS, *supra* note 4, Art 21(1) (a) and (f).
226 *Ibid.*, Art 24(1).
227 *Ibid.*, Art 24(2).

3.3.4 Operational Discharge/Environmental Protection Rules and Standards

The objectives of the Greenlandic Decree on Marine Environmental Protection[228] and the Greenlandic MEPA are to protect nature and marine environment through the prevention of marine pollution.[229] They are both applicable to foreign-flagged vessels while navigating through these zones.[230] The Greenlandic MEPA also applies to foreign-flagged vessels while operating in areas beyond the EEZ.[231] This refers to the right of the coastal State under international law to intervene on the high seas in cases of maritime accidents.[232]

The Greenland Self-Government has adopted bans under the decree on discharge into the sea of oil or oily mixtures and noxious liquid substances as well as garbage from ships within its three nm territorial sea.[233] The ban on oil is stricter than prescribed by Annex I of MARPOL 73/78 regarding discharges from machinery areas,[234] but is consistent with the jurisdiction of the coastal State within its territorial sea. It is also consistent with the general ban in the Polar Code on the discharge of any oil and oily mixtures from vessels operating in Arctic waters.[235] The Decree of the Self-Government[236] and the Greenlandic MEPA provide a legal basis for regulating discharges or emissions of other pollutants at sea, including implementing international obligations such as MARPOL73/78 regulations.[237] Such regulations have been adopted for the Greenland EEZ. The Self-Government is working on revising the decree applicable to the territorial waters to bring it in accordance with recent year's developments—such as the Polar Code.[238] The Danish Minister of Environ-

228 Greenland Decree on Marine Environmental Protection, *supra* note 182, Sec 1.

229 Greenlandic MEPA, *supra* note 181, Sec 1 (2).

230 Greenland Decree on Marine Environmental Protection, *supra* note 182, Sec 3(1); Greenlandic MEPA, *supra* note 181, Sec 3 (4).

231 Greenlandic MEPA, *supra* note 181, Sec 3(5).

232 See UNCLOS, *supra* note 4, Art 221.

233 Greenland Decree on Marine Environmental Protection, *supra* note 182, Secs 8 and 17.

234 MARPOL Annex I, Reg 15.

235 Polar Code, *supra* note 1, Part II-A, para 1.1.1.

236 Greenlandic Decree on Marine Environmental Protection, *supra* note 182, Secs 14–15 (Annex III: Harmful substances in package form), Art 16 (Annex IV: sewage), Art 17 (Annex V: Garbage);

237 Greenland MEPA, *supra* note 181, Secs 8–9 (Annex I, oil), Secs 10–13 (Annex II: noxious liquid substances in bulk), Secs 14–15 (Annex III: Harmful substances in package form), Sec 16 (Annex IV: sewage) and Sec 17 (Annex V: Garbage).

238 Government of Greenland: Marine Environment. Available at http://naalakkersuisut.gl/en/Naalakkersuisut/Departments/Natur-Miljoe/Miljoe-og-beredskabsafd/Havmiljoe.

ment has adopted regulations under the Greenlandic MEPA to make the operational requirements under Part II-A of the Polar Code applicable to the EEZ.[239] As MARPOL 73/78 Annex IV on sewage is not applicable to Greenland, there is no obligation for Denmark/Greenland to implement Chapter 4 of Part II-A of the Polar Code. The Greenlandic Self-Government would be competent to adopt stricter regulations for the territorial sea. The operational requirements of the above-mentioned Chapter 4 may well qualify as generally accepted international rules and standards under Article 211(5) of UNCLOS. As a contracting Party to UNCLOS, Denmark is competent to apply these requirements in respect of vessels operating within the Greenlandic EEZ (even if it is not obligated by the original instrument).[240]

The Draft Act on the Protection of the Marine Environment of the Greenlandic EEZ will replace the Greenlandic MEPA.[241] The act and its regulations are applicable to foreign-flagged vessels operating in the EEZ to the extent they are consistent with international law.[242] The purpose is to update the legislation as the maritime activities off of Greenland are increasing. The objective of the draft act is to prevent the pollution and other effects of human activities on the marine environment, primarily from shipping.[243] It is also intended to protect natural values as well as cultural values. Similar to the Greenlandic MEPA, the new act will be an enabling act where the Minister of Environment is empowered to adopt regulations to implement international regulations such as those adopted through the MARPOL 73/78 Annexes. This includes regulating the discharge of sewage and emissions into the air even if the MARPOL 73/78 Annexes are not applicable to Greenland.[244] The act provides a legal basis for regulating the use of fuel to reduce air pollution.

The draft act includes two novelties: It provides a legal basis for regulating the exchange and treatment of ballast water, and it provides for extended environmental jurisdiction under Article 234 of UNCLOS.[245] Denmark has acceded

239 Bekendtgørelse nr 539 af 22/05/2017 om udtømning af olie fra skibe (Order No 539 of 22 May 2017 on discharge of oil from vessels) Section 6, available at https://www.retsinformation.dk/Forms/R0710.aspx?id=190205#id36867d5e-3ea9-4971-bcfb-3f0dee49fd57 and Bekendtgørelse nr 537 af 22/05/2017 om udtømning af affald fra skibe og platforme (Order No 537 of 22 May 2017 on discharge of wastes from vessels and platforms), Sections 6, 8 and 9, available at https://www.retsinformation.dk/Forms/R0710.aspx?id=190203.

240 UNCLOS, *supra* note 4, Art 211(5).

241 Draft Act on Protection of the Marine Environment of Greenlandic EEZ, *supra* note 183.

242 *Ibid.*, Sec 2(1)(3).

243 *Ibid.*, Sec 19.

244 *Ibid.*, Secs 19 and 24.

245 *Ibid.*, Ch 6 (Secs 16–18).

to the BWM Convention.[246] Under the act, the Minister of Environment is competent to adopt regulations on *inter alia* the exchange of ballast water.[247] The Minister may also designate part of the EEZ as an ice-covered area to the extent consistent with international law.[248] It is emphasised that the designation of the ice-covered area shall be done consistently with the provisions of Article 234 of UNCLOS. Extensive examination of the factual circumstances of the area is to be undertaken.[249] The area in question must be covered by ice for more than six months to qualify as ice-covered 'most of the year'. Within the designated area, the Minister may take the necessary measures in respect of shipping to protect the marine environment. This may entail stricter requirements than those of the annexes of MARPOL. Since the discharge of oil and oily mixtures is banned under the Polar Code, this provision could potentially be used to adopt stricter regulation of other types of operational discharges not prohibited under the Polar Code. Further, Article 234 of UNCLOS arguably provides a legal basis for adopting CDEM rules and standards and navigational rules and standards to the extent these measures prevent pollution of the marine environment.[250] The text of the provision is wide enough to include such measures. However, as already indicated, these measures to ensure safety objectives are to be regulated through other legislation. This could be used as an argument against using the provision as the basis for such regulations.

Marine protected areas are another measure that can be used to protect the marine environment and its marine biodiversity, through restrictions on navigation and other human activities within a defined area. The legislation of Greenland provides a legal basis for protecting areas within the territorial sea.[251] The world's largest protected area is located in Greenland. The North-east Greenland National Park covers 972,000 km^2 and 18,000 km of coastlines.[252]

246 See overview of the status of the Convention at http://www.imo.org/en/About/Conventions/StatusOfConventions/Pages/Default.aspx, accessed 17 March 2017.

247 Draft Act on Protection of the Marine Environment of Greenlandic EEZ, *supra* note 183, Sec 17 (2).

248 *Ibid.*, Sec 8.

249 *Ibid.*, Comments for Sec 8, at 36.

250 For a detailed analysis of Article 234, see Chapter 2 of this Volume.

251 Decree No 29 of 18 December 2003 on Nature Protection, accessed 17 March 2017 at http://lovgivning.gl/Lov.aspx?rid={B285FE79-D0A5-4C4A-92B4-B93D0C018161} [in Danish].

252 See Information, accessed 17 March 2017 at http://naalakkersuisut.gl/da/Naalakkersuisut/Departementer/Natur-Miljoe-og-Justitsomraadet/Natur_-Energi-og-Klimaafdelingen/Natur/Nationalparken-i-Nord-og-Oestgroenland [in Danish]. For a map, see http://naalakkersuisut.gl/~/media/Nanoq/Files/Attached%20Files/Engelske-tekster/Publications/North-East%20Greenland%20National%20Park.pdf, accessed 17 March 2017.

The three nm territorial sea is included.[253] Within the national park, there is a general ban on travelling.[254] Vessels planning to sail in these waters need to apply for a permit from the Government of Greenland.[255] Further, under the regulation on safe navigation, vessels carrying more than 250 passengers are required to be ice classed when navigating within the territorial sea covered by the national park, irrespective of the presence of sea ice.[256] The draft Act on the Protection of the Marine Environment of the EEZ aims at preventing pollution and other effects on nature and environment, which *inter alia* may harm natural and cultural values of the EEZ. The draft provides for adopting area-based regulations such as 'special areas' under the MARPOL annexes and protection of the marine environment of a designated ice-covered area.[257]

3.3.5 Enforcement

The Greenlandic SSA does not provide for extensive enforcement jurisdiction to ensure compliance with its provisions and regulations in regard of foreign-flagged vessels operating within the EEZ. This is partly because not all provisions are made applicable to these vessels and partly due to the limited jurisdiction coastal States enjoy under the law of the sea in regard to maritime safety. The regulation on safe navigation provides for the use of enforcement measures in the case of violations of its navigational and CDEM rules and standards.[258] One example is the violation of the ban of navigating within areas marked as 'numerous rocks', which is applicable both to vessels in innocent passage and to other foreign-flagged vessels on voyages within the Greenlandic territorial sea. Further, the enforcement of CDEM rules and standards may be conducted when vessels call at ports in Greenland or Denmark (see below).

The Decree on Marine Environment Protection[259] and the Greenlandic MEPA provides for the exercise of more extensive enforcement jurisdiction in the maritime zones.[260] These enforcement measures are consistent with the

253 Landtingslov nr. 11 av 12. november 1980, Sec 15, *c.f.* Hjemmestyrets bekedtgørelse nr. 7 af 17. juni 1992 om nationalparken i Nord- og Østgrønland.

254 Executive Order on Access to and Conditions for Travelling in Certain Parts of Greenland, Sec 1, accessed 17 March 2017 at http://naalakkersuisut.gl/en/About-government-of-greenland/Travel-activities-in-remote-parts-of-Greenland.

255 *Ibid.*, Sec 3(2).

256 Regulation on Safe Navigation, *supra* note 194, Sec 13.

257 Draft Act on Protection of the Marine Environment of Greenlandic EEZ, *supra* note 183, Secs 7 and 8.

258 Regulation on Safe Navigation, *supra* note 194, Sec 17(1).

259 Greenlandic Decree on Marine Environmental Protection, *supra* note 182, Sec 36(1) and (4).

260 Greenlandic MEPA, *supra* note 181, Sec 28(1) and (4).

(environmental) enforcement jurisdiction of coastal States in the territorial sea and EEZ under Part XII of UNCLOS. The marine protection legislation does not provide a legal basis for port State enforcement of illegal discharges by foreign-flagged vessels in areas beyond the jurisdiction of Greenland. Such right is provided under Article 220 of UNCLOS. The reason may be the poorly developed port State control in Greenland. The consequence may be that discharges in violation of Part II-A of the Polar Code in Arctic waters beyond national jurisdiction are not adequately enforced.

The Greenlandic SSA and the Greenlandic MEPA provide for enforcement in regard to vessels calling at ports in Greenland. First, foreign-flagged vessels may be refused entry to the ports.[261] Under the Greenlandic SSA, it is a requirement that any such action must have a legal basis in either EU regulations or other international provisions. This is a reference to the EU Directive on Port State Control and the Paris MoU on Port State Control or similar schemes. If vessels have been blacklisted under either of these schemes, they may be banned from calling at ports in Greenland. The Greenlandic MEPA provides for prohibiting a vessel from calling at port if there is a risk of discharge of pollutants from the vessel in violation of its provisions and the vessel has either violated a ban on sailing or not complied with an instruction to undertake repairs.[262]

Denmark participates in the Paris MoU and is subject to the EU directive.[263] Greenland, however, is not a member of the Paris MoU. Therefore, any deficiencies discovered in Greenlandic ports will not be reported to the Paris MoU. The Greenlandic SSA provides a legal basis for port State control.[264] The Minister of Growth may adopt detailed rules for the control and inspection of vessels in port. Vessels may be detained if they have defects. Importantly, the Greenlandic SSA requires that such rules must specifically be made applicable to foreign-flagged vessels.[265] Such regulations have not been adopted. When the Danish SSA was amended in 2013 to include a special provision on Arctic shipping it was noted that there is limited port State control of vessels visiting Greenland.[266] The reason given was that cruise vessels seldom call at ports in Greenland due to their size. Thus, there is no room for port State control. The Danish Maritime Authorities rely on the control by the flag State or other port States when in Danish ports.

261 Greenlandic SSA, *supra* note 180, Sec 15; Greenlandic MEPA, *supra* note 181, Sec 30.

262 Greenlandic MEPA, *supra* note 181, Sec 30.

263 Paris Memorandum on Port State Control, *supra* note 168.

264 Greenlandic SSA, *supra* note 180, Secs 8a, 14 and 15.

265 Greenlandic SSA, *supra* note 180, Sec 1(3).

266 See L 154 Forslag til lov om ændring af søloven og forskellige andre love.

3.4 *Iceland*

3.4.1 General

The Icelandic legislation on maritime safety and marine environmental protection includes the Ship Survey Act[267] and the Marine and Coastal Antipollution Measures Act.[268] The latter is applicable to any shipping activities, including of foreign-flagged vessels, within the pollution jurisdiction of Iceland.[269] This includes the 200 nm EEZ and 12 nm territorial sea. The Minister may adopt regulations under the Ship Survey Act, which applies to foreign-flagged vessels while in the territorial sea, EEZ and/or calling at ports in Iceland.[270]

3.4.2 CDEM Rules and Standards

The Ship Survey Act includes a general requirement that vessels are to be constructed and equipped in a manner that provide them with safety level adequate for their intended use.[271] The act provides for regulating CDEM requirements primarily aimed at preventing pollution. It is primarily an enabling act, providing a legal basis for adopting regulations implementing mandatory CDEM rules and standards adopted under SOLAS 74 and MARPOL 73/78.[272] One of the purposes of the act is to harmonise Icelandic law with the international legal obligations. Such regulations may be applicable to foreign-flagged vessels operating in waters within the 200 nm EEZ.[273] The CDEM regulations of Part I-A and Part II-A of the Polar Code will apply to Icelandic-flagged vessels through regulations adopted under this act. Since the Polar Code probably is not applicable to areas under Icelandic jurisdiction, the legislation implementing its regulations may be applied to foreign-flagged vessels when calling at its ports on their voyages to/from Arctic waters (see section 3.4.5).

3.4.3 Navigational Rules and Standards

The Maritime Traffic Service Act provides the legal basis for regulating the operation of vessels within the 200 nm EEZ of Iceland.[274] The 2006 Regulation

---

267 Act No 27/2003 on Ship Survey and Safety of Vessels, accessed 17 March 2017 at http://www.lhg.is/media/arsskyrslur/472003.pdf.

268 Act No. 33/84 in Marine and Coastal Antipollution Measures, accessed 17 March 2017 at http://www.lhg.is/media/arsskyrslur/Act_33_2004.pdf.

269 *Ibid.*, Sec 2, *c.f.* Sec 3(10).

270 Ship Survey Act, *supra* note 267, Sec 1.

271 *Ibid.*, Sec 3.

272 *Ibid.*

273 *Ibid.*, Sec 1.

274 The Maritime Traffic Service Act is not available in English translation, this information is inferred from Section 1 of Regulation 672/2006 on the Maritime Traffic Service and vessel

on Maritime Traffic Service includes concrete measures to regulate navigation. Such measures include three areas to be avoided, traffic separation schemes and a mandatory ship reporting system, all of which have been established within the 12 nm territorial sea off the south and southwest coast of Iceland under Chapter V of SOLAS 74.[275]

Further, Iceland has included in the Regulation on Maritime Traffic Service several measures to implement the requirements of the EU legislation on traffic monitoring and information systems as implemented through the EEA Agreement.[276] Vessels are required to give prior notice of entry into ports.[277] There is also a special requirement for the notification of the transport of hazardous goods.[278]

3.4.4 Operational Discharge/Environmental Protection Rules and Standards

The objective of the Marine and Coastal Antipollution Measures Act is to protect beaches and oceans of Iceland from pollution and other activities that could be harmful to human health, natural resources and the environment.[279] It is applicable to foreign-flagged vessels while navigating through their EEZs and within their territorial seas.[280] Similarly to the legislation of Norway and Greenland, the act primarily enables the authorities to adopt regulations implementing the MARPOL 73/78 regulations on operational discharges.[281] It should be noted that Iceland is not a party to MARPOL 73/78 Annex IV on pollution by sewage and Annex VI on air pollution. It would only be required to implement Part II-A of the Polar Code corresponding to the other annexes of MARPOL 73/78, such as the ban on discharge into the sea of oil or oily mixtures from ships. The act includes more specific regulations on discharges of oil liquid substances, refuse and waste within three nm from the baselines that

traffic monitoring and information system, accessed 17 March 2017 at http://www.lhg.is/media/arsskyrslur/Reg_MaritTraffServ.pdf.

275 SN.1/Circ.263 of 23 October 2007 on Routeing measures other than traffic separation schemes; Resolution MSC.250(83) on Mandatory Ship Reporting System off The South and Southwest Coast of Iceland (Transrep), Report of the Maritime Safety Committee on its Eighty-Third session, MSC 83/28/Add.3, Annex 28.

276 Directive 59/2002/EC, *supra* note 126.

277 Regulation on the Maritime Traffic Service, *supra* note 271, Sec 4.

278 *Ibid.*, Secs 13 and 14.

279 Marine and Coastal Antipollution Measures Act, *supra* note 268, Sec 1.

280 *Ibid.*, Sec 2, which stipulates that the act is applicable to 'all kind of activities … related to shipping….'

281 *Ibid.*, Art 6.

are consistent with MARPOL annexes.[282] It also provides a legal basis for regulating the exchange and treatment of ballast water, even if Iceland has yet to become a contracting party to the BWM Convention.[283]

The Nature Conservation Act of Iceland is applicable to its EEZ and continental shelf as well.[284] It provides a legal basis for establishing marine protected areas.[285] Human activities such as traffic and fishing may be restricted within the protected area.[286] Restrictions on international shipping in the EEZ or the territorial sea would need to be based on routeing measures adopted under Chapter V of SOLAS 74.

3.4.5 Enforcement

The Marine and Coastal Antipollution Measures Act provides a general legal basis to undertake inspection of a vessel at sea or in port if there is a risk that it will discharge pollution in violation of the act or is suspected of having committed such a violation.[287] The investigation shall not cause unnecessary disturbance or costs to the vessel. The exercise of the investigation is not explicitly restricted by international law, such as the limited enforcement jurisdiction in the EEZ. Still, the requirement of non-disturbance can be seen as a reflection of such a limitation.

The Ship Survey Act provides a legal basis for the inspection of the compliance by Icelandic- and foreign-flagged vessels with ship safety measures (CDEM requirements and operational requirements) and measures to prevent pollution.[288] Vessels may be instructed to undertake repairs or may be detained.[289] The control of vessels in port is to be undertaken consistently with the Paris MoU.[290] Iceland is a participant in the Paris MoU and is required to apply its provisions by including the relevant EU regulations in the EEA agreement. It means that the mandatory CDEM regulations of the Polar Code will be included as they are part of the SOLAS 74 and MARPOL 73/78.

282 Marine and Coastal Antipollution Measures Act, *supra* note 268, Sec 8.

283 *Ibid.*, Sec 6.m.

284 The Nature Conservation Act No 44/1999, Arts 2 and 54, accessed 17 March 2017 at https://eng.umhverfisraduneyti.is/legislation/nr/389.

285 *Ibid.*, Sec 54.

286 *Ibid.*, Sec 60.

287 Marine and Coastal Antipollution Measures Act, *supra* note 268, Sec 24.

288 Ship Survey Act, *supra* note 267, Sec 12.

289 *Ibid.*, Secs 12 and 20.

290 *Ibid.*, Sec 14.

3.5 *Summary*

The legislation of the three Nordic coastal States regulating shipping in Arctic has been presented in this section. The presentation documents that Norway and Denmark/Greenland have been particularly active in recent years in taking measures to improve the maritime safety and environmental protection in their Arctic coastal waters. These measures are based on risk assessments and on projections of future development of shipping in their waters. The safety legislation of Denmark/Greenland regarding specific Arctic challenges seems to be the most elaborate. It includes CDEM rules and standards, whereas the Norwegian legislation is focusing more on regulating the operation of vessels through pilotage, reporting obligations and routeing measures. The safety and environmental protection legislation of the three coastal States are applicable to foreign-flagged vessels operating in the territorial sea as well as the EEZs. However, it is stipulated that the acts and their regulations be interpreted and applied within international law. This reflects the policies of the States to promote compliance with international law in general and with UNCLOS specifically.

The legislation generally provides a legal basis for adopting regulations to implement the obligations under SOLAS 74 and the Annexes to MARPOL 73/78. Consequently, there is a legal basis for implementing the mandatory elements of the Polar Code. The safety regulations, particularly the CDEM rules and standards, are enforced when vessels are calling at ports. Operational discharges may be enforced at sea, consistent with UNCLOS. Only Norway has legislation providing for the enforcement of discharges in areas beyond national jurisdiction. Norway and Iceland have adopted regulations to implement EU legislation consistent with the Paris MoU on Port State Control. The port State control on Greenland seems to be less developed. Of the three States, Denmark/Greenland may adopt legislation to apply Article 234 of UNCLOS. There is public consultation on a proposal to provide a legal basis for adopting regulations on shipping in ice-covered areas within the Greenlandic EEZ. The proposal does not give any reason for including such a provision, but it will provide Denmark/Greenland with a legal basis to adopt regulations that are stricter than those that are 'generally accepted international rules and standards'.

4 Concluding Remarks

The objective of this Chapter has been to investigate how the three Arctic coastal States, Greenland/Denmark, Iceland and Norway, are addressing Arctic shipping. A general conclusion is that their policy and maritime legislation reflect that as small Arctic States: they aim to pursue the rule of law as reflected in UNCLOS and cooperate through the IMO in establishing common sets of rules. Their active participation in the negotiation and adoption of the Polar Code is a reflection of this commitment.

The maritime safety and marine protection legislation of the three coastal States primarily seeks to implement and apply the rules and standards developed through the IMO. Therefore, it is interesting that the green paper of the Danish Government on a new Act on the Protection of the Marine Environment of the Greenlandic EEZ includes a provision authorising the Ministry to adopt regulations for ice-covered parts of the EEZ consistent with international law. This seems to be at odds with its Arctic Policy where the alternative of taking unilateral measures under Article 234 of UNCLOS was reserved for a situation where the Polar Code negotiations failed. No explanation is offered for this turn in policy. As the provision is included in draft legislation on preventing operational discharges, questions may be raised whether it adds anything beyond the regulations of Part II-A of the Polar Code. Under Article 234, the threshold for exercising enforcement jurisdiction is lower compared with the normal coastal State enforcement jurisdiction within the EEZ.[291] There is no requirement, such as that under Article 220, which provides that a coastal State cannot take enforcement measures unless there is a substantial discharge or serious effects on the environment. A violation of a regulation adopted under Article 234 of UNCLOS may be enforced even if it does not cause or threaten to cause serious pollution. Even violations of operational discharge requirements of Part II-A of the Polar Code may be enforced under Article 234. However, the enforcement will be subject to the safeguards of section 7 of Part XII.

Even if the legislation of the three coastal States is quite elaborate, it has an enabling character. There are a limited number of regulations adopted specifically applicable to their Arctic waters. This is obviously due to the relative limited numbers of vessels visiting these waters. The regulations and infrastructure discussed in this Chapter have primarily been developed to address the risks created by local or destinational traffic. As already noted, the flag States have the primary responsibility for implementing the mandatory requirements and recommendations of the Polar Code. Their role as coastal States will primarily be relevant where vessels are violating the operational discharge requirements of Part II-A of the Polar Code.

As amendments to SOLAS 74, MARPOL 73/78 Annexes and the STCW Convention and Code, the mandatory requirements of the Polar Code will be included in the relevant regional port State control, such as the Paris MoU and

291 UNCLOS, *supra* note 4, Art 220(5) and (6).

Tokyo MoU.[292] Vessels operating in Arctic waters will be subjected to control in ports of their member States, which will include compliance with CDEM requirements of the Polar Code. The port States may control whether the vessel and relevant crewmembers have adequate and valid certificates for operating in Arctic waters under the procedures of the MoU in question. However, they will not be in a position to control whether a vessel is constructed, equipped, designed or manned adequately in accordance with the prevailing conditions under which it will sail. They would then need information on the subsequent route of the vessels and the sea ice and weather and other relevant conditions throughout the route to take such a decision. Such information is not readily available. The task of the port State may not go beyond controlling whether relevant certificates (including the Polar Certificate) are valid. It will be easier controlling vessels that are involved in destinational traffic, such as cruise vessels, vessels shipping natural resources from their Arctic ports or research vessels. The lack of information with the port State may be the rationale for setting up an Arctic MoU on Port State Control.[293] The Arctic port States are in a better position to assess the seaworthiness of the vessels. As pointed out by Molenaar, Article 211(3) of UNCLOS provides a legal basis for cooperation between port States.[294] The argument against establishing an Arctic MoU is that it would not include vessels transiting the Arctic waters without visiting local ports. Further, the destinational (international) shipping is adequately covered. The port States may decide, such as provided by the Greenlandic SSA, to ban vessels from leaving port when there are unfavourable weather and sea ice conditions.[295] Perhaps the better solution is for the existing MoU to develop specific guidelines for controlling compliance with the Polar Code.[296] The Paris MoU is developing Guidelines for the inspection of ships based on the Polar Code, which will enter into force on 1 January 2017.[297] The database will be updated to record deficiencies against the Polar Code.

---

292 Erik J Molenaar, 'Options for Regional Regulation of Merchant Shipping Outside IMO, with Particular Reference to the Arctic Region' (2014) *Ocean Development & International Law* 45:3, 272–298 (285). The Tokyo MoU on Port State Control in the Asia-Pacific Region is one of several regional Port State control mechanisms. Its membership includes 20 States such as Russian Federation, Japan, China, Canada, Republic of Korea, Singapore, Australia and Chile. More information on the Tokyo MoU is available at http://www.tokyo-mou.org/.

293 *Ibid.*

294 *Ibid.* at 284.

295 Greenlandic SSA, *supra* note 180, Sec 14(3).

296 Molenaar, *supra* note 292 at 286.

297 Author's communication with the Paris MoU Secretariat, 21 June 2016.

The possibility of intervening in respect of vessels navigating at sea into areas of danger is more limited as it may infringe on navigational rights. There has to be an imminent danger of pollution for the coastal States to intervene, such as the legal basis provided for in the Greenlandic MEPA applicable within the EEZ. The Norwegian Regulation on Intervention in the EEZ and on the high seas seems to require a maritime accident involving physical damage before measures may be taken. Pre-emptive measures seem to be excluded.

PART 4

Rights, Interests, Positions and Practice of User States

CHAPTER 9

Rights, Interests, Positions and Practices of Asian Flag States, with Special Reference to the Republic of Korea

Deukhoon (Peter) Han and Sung-Woo Lee

1 Introduction

Since the end of the Second World War and the thawing of relations between the United States and the Soviet Union following the Cold War, globalisation has brought about monumental changes in the logistics field, such as containerisation and intermodalism, which presently serve as the basis for the movement of goods. Containerisation has resulted in the rapid growth of international trade, with the global Gross Domestic Product (GDP) increasing from 1.5 to 3 times from 1985 to 2005.[1] Since the first emergence of containerisation, the world maritime container transport network has had to adapt as containerisation proliferated across the globe, spreading from Europe and the United States to Asia and Third World countries.[2] The remarkable aspect is that the field of maritime transport has grown very fast, handling more than 80 per cent of international trade.[3] Due to the rapid and sustained growth of international trade that utilises maritime transport, the port and back-up logistics facilities have had to develop quickly, necessitating changes in the spatial structure of port hinterlands.[4] However, although the port hinterland network connected to maritime transportation has changed dramatically, maritime transportation connected to the ocean has remained the same in terms of its geographic

1 World Bank Databank, accessed 16 February 2017 at http://databank.worldbank.org/data/reports.aspx?Code=NY.GDP.MKTP.CD&id=af3ce82b&report_name=Popular_indicators&populartype=series&ispopular=y.

2 Jean-Paul Rodrigue and Theo Notteboom, 'Foreland-based regionalization: Integrating intermediate hubs with port hinterlands', *Research in Transportation Economics*, 27 (2010) 19–29, at 20.

3 Statista, accessed 16 February 2017 at https://www.statista.com/statistics/267604/capacity-of-general-cargo-vessels-in-seaborne-trade-since-1980. See also World Trade Organization, 'World Trade Organization International Trade Statistics 2015, at 14–15.

4 Sung-Woo Lee, Dong-Wook Song, Cesar Ducruet, 'A Tale of Asia's world ports: the spatial evolution in global hub port cities', *Geoforum* Vol 39(1) (2008) 372–385, at 380.

 | DOI 10.1163/9789004339385_010

aspects for the last several decades. Since the discovery of the sea routes from Europe to Asia, including the route around the Cape of Good Hope in the 16th century and the opening of the Panama Canal in the 20th century, there have been no significant changes in the shipping routes that connect the Atlantic and Pacific Oceans.

While there has been little change in terms of geography, a commercial revolution has taken place recently in the field of sea transport. The thawing of the ice in the Arctic region due to the effects of global warming has provided a shortcut between Europe and Asia. The emergence of the Arctic waters creates a new trade and shipping route between Asia and Europe.[5] For this reason, East Asian countries such as Korea,[6] China and Japan are taking a profound interest in the Arctic waters. Because of this environmental development, there is an increasing need for a user State, such as Korea, to examine the necessary requisites for the use of the Arctic waters in sea transport. This Chapter wishes to examine the elements required and actions needed to be taken in order for Korea to make economical use of the Arctic waters. Specifically, Section 2 of this Chapter will focus on the opportunities, interests and possibilities for Korea's utilisation of the Northern Sea Route (NSR) and other Arctic waters shipping routes. In addition, Section 2 will examine the challenges that are likely to be encountered by East Asian States (especially Korea) in commercialising Arctic shipping. Section 3 of the Chapter will then describe the rights and interests Korea has as a flag State to navigate the NSR. Section 4 will close by drawing some conclusions regarding Korea's position on the balance of flag State and coastal State's interests and rights on Arctic shipping.

2 Opportunities, Interests and Challenges for Navigating the NSR

2.1 *Arctic Shipping Data for the NSR*

As aforementioned, the Arctic waters' shipping routes have contributed to a revolutionary change to the map of international logistics in the 21st century. When going to Europe from Asia, the NSR could reduce in time and distance more than 10 days and 7,000 kilometres (km) from the existing route of passing through the Suez Canal. Although estimates vary, it is reported that approximately 25 per cent of the ocean freight charge could be reduced in terms of

5 Sung-Woo Lee, 'The Change in the port logistics system in East Asia and the commercialization of the Northern Sea Routes' (KMI Press, 2014) at 77.

6 In this chapter, Korea refers to the Republic of Korea.

expense.[7] However, there are many barriers to using the NSR. These include harsh climatic conditions, poor logistics infrastructure and threats to the marine environment through pollution. Despite these barriers, the NSR is already being used, as seen in Figure 9.1. The number of vessels passing through the NSR increased from 2011 until 2013; there were 34 transits in 2011, 46 transits in 2012, and 72 transits in 2013. However, the use of the NSR has decreased to 55 transits in 2014 and 18 transits in 2015. This decline could be the result of political sanctions that have been imposed against Russia due to the Ukraine crisis. Yet, the Russian government continues to control the majority of the management of the NSR and appears to remain committed to its importance. The use of the NSR in the long term may provide opportunities for Korea and other East Asian countries.

As shown in Table 9.1, the main cargo passing through the NSR is mostly liquid cargo, such as crude oil, refined oil, gas, etc. Moreover, of the total cargo volume approximately 60 per cent is shipped from Europe to Asia, while 40

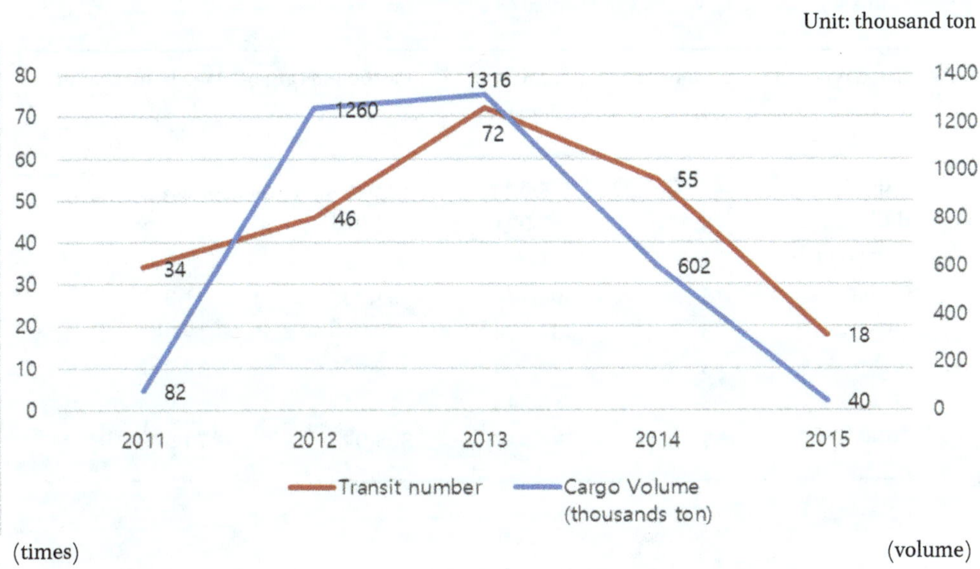

FIGURE 9.1 *Arctic shipping data for the NSR*[8]

7 Sung-Woo Lee, 'Shipping & Port Condition Changes and Throughput Prospects with Opening of the Northern Sea Route' (KMI Press, 2011) at 100.

8 Northern Sea Route Information Office, Transit Statistics 2011–2015, accessed 26 January 2017 at http://www.arctic-lio.com/nsr_transits.

percent is shipped from Asia to Europe. Most of the traffic is done within Russia.[9]

2.2 *Traffic Forecasts for the NSR (2015–2030)*

The Russian Government estimated the total volume of cargo that will pass through the NSR from 2015 to 2030 to be approximately 1.2 billion tons as shown in Table 9.2. The Korean Research Institute has estimated the amount of cargo passing through the NSR located along the Russian coast, as shown in Table 9.3.[10] In addition, the Korean Maritime Institute analysed the price condition of cargo limited to container by comparing the NSR route with that of the Suez Canal route and approximated the volume of cargo transported to be 12 million twenty-foot equivalent units (TEU) by 2030 based on the assumption that the cost of using the NSR is equal to that of the existing route (see Table 9.3).

TABLE 9.1 *Shipping via the NSR by cargo type*[11]

Cargo type	Number of vessels	Cargo volume (t)	Eastbound cargo	Westbound cargo
Liquid	27	434,584	231,207	203,377
Bulk	2	67,961	67,961	–
Frozen Fish	1	1,895	–	1,895
General	15	93,186	51,838	41,348
Passenger	3	32,954	20,666	12,288
Icebreaker	3	22,592	9,605	12,987
Others	2	15,345	12,711	2,634
Total	53	668,517	393,988	274,529

9 Northern Sea Route Information Office, Transit Statistics 2014, accessed 26 January 2017 at http://www.arctic-lio.com/nsr_transits.

10 Sung-Woo Lee, 'Benefit of NSR to North Pacific' in Robert W Corell, James Seong-Cheol Kang, Yoon Hyung Kim (eds) *2011 North Pacific Arctic Conference Proceedings: The Arctic in World Affairs* (The Korea Transport Institute and East-West Center, 2013) at 109.

11 *Ibid.*

TABLE 9.2 *Traffic forecast* via the NSR in bulk*[12]

Unit: o'ooo ton

Category	2015	2020	2030
Liquid	4,140	6,300	6,530
Dry	2,430	3,100	5,550
Port throughput in the NSR	6,570	9,400	12,080

* This traffic forecast includes coastal traffic, transit, import and export.

TABLE 9.3 *Traffic forecast via the NSR in con'*[13]

Unit: 'ooo ton

NSR Cost	2015	2020	2025	2030
120%	54	425	1,402	3,015
110%	**128**	**1,017**	**3,138**	**6,452**
100%	**305**	**2,168**	**6,081**	**12,047**
80%	1,311	6,357	15,193	27,975
70%	2,185	8,746	19,420	34,731

2.3 *East Asian States' Involvement in the NSR*

The forecasted increase in the volume of cargo passing through the NSR can be explained by the high demand of East Asian countries, such as Korea, China and Japan, as well as the trade volume between Europe and the United States. As shown in Table 9.4, given the amount of oil consumed by Korea, China and Japan, East Asian countries are leading the resources market in the world to such an extent that their consumption comprises 18 per cent of global resources, 45 per cent of the world's iron ore resources[14] and 55 per cent of world's coal

12 Russian Government (Rosmorport), 'Strategy of Development of Sea Port Infrastructure of Russia up to 2030' at 93, accessed 16 February 2017 at http://www.rosmorport.ru/uploadify/988-f11a995b44861c9c2b1c7e0f502b433e.pdf [in Russian].

13 Sung-Woo Lee, *supra* note 11 at 109.

14 World Steel Association, 'Steel Statistical Yearbook 2016' at 6, accessed 16 February 2017 at http://www.worldsteel.org/steel-by-topic/statistics/steel-statistical-yearbook-.html.

TABLE 9.4 *Comparative approach of involvement among Korea, China and Japan*

Initiatives	Korea	China	Japan
Status on the Arctic Council	Observer	Observer	Observer
Establishment of Research Institute	• Dasan Science Research Station • Joint research centers with Arctic States • Shipbuilding technology R&D		• Arctic Science Station • JAMSTEC • JCAR
Parties to MOUs	• Russia • Norway • China	• Korea • Finland	• Norway
Arctic Domestic Policy	• Guidelines for Polar Policy Advancement • Arctic Policy Master Plan	• China's Arctic Policy	• Japan's Arctic Policy

resources.[15] Given their levels of resource consumption, East Asian countries are consequently investing efforts into the commercialisation of the NSR, including the implementation of various policies and investments in businesses related to the Arctic.

Korea has been active in the Arctic for several years. Examples include the establishment of the Dasan Science Research Station, which was established in Ny-Ålesund on Svalbard, Norway[16] in 2012 and the building of the first icebreaker named *Araon*, which was built in 2009. Also, Korea became a party to the Spitsbergen Treaty on 7 September 2012 in an effort to participate and

15 US Energy Information Administration, 'International Energy Statistics', accessed 16 February 2017 at http://www.eia.gov/beta/international/rankings/#?prodact=7-2&cy=2014.

16 See also Korea Polar Research Institute (KOPRI) 'Dasan Station', accessed 10 February 2017 at http://eng.kopri.re.kr/home_e/contents/e_3210000/view.cms.

promote scientific research.[17] As an additional example of Korea's involvement in the Arctic, it applied for Observer status on the Arctic Council in 2009 and was granted such status in 2013, with among others, China, Japan and Singapore at the Kiruna Ministerial meeting.[18] In 2013, the Korean Ministry of Oceans and Fisheries announced the Arctic policy framework plan.[19] Moreover, Korea has concluded a Memorandum of Understanding (MOU) on port development in Far East Asia and the Arctic Ocean with Russia in 2014 and an MOU on shipping and Arctic utilisation with Norway in 2012.

The Korean Government expressed its policy regarding Arctic shipping in the Arctic Policy of the Republic of Korea.[20] Under the title of pursuing sustainable Arctic businesses, it emphasises the accumulation of Arctic sea route navigation experience and the provision of incentives to encourage the use of the Arctic sea route. This could be accomplished through (i) conducting international joint research and hosting seminars to promote the use of the Arctic sea routes, (ii) developing Arctic sea operators' capacity, and (iv) revamping Korean ports connected to Arctic sea routes, in addition to cooperating with Russia, Canada and Norway to develop Arctic coastal ports.[21]

2.4 *Challenges of Commercialising Arctic Shipping for East Asian States*

Korea, as a user State, is currently investing significantly in the commercialisation of the NSR. Yet, many obstacles still exist before the NSR can be fully commercialised. The first obstacle is the limitation on the operation of icebreakers in the NSR. At present, only 7 out of 10 existing icebreakers can be operated in the NSR, and among the 7 operable icebreakers, only 3 of them can support the Russian coastline, which constitutes the majority of the NSR.[22] As shipping

17 'Treaty Concerning the Archipelago of Spitsbergen', accessed 10 February 2017 at https://verdragenbank.overheid.nl/en/Verdrag/Details/004293.

18 See also Arctic Council 'Observers' (28 July 2016), accessed 10 February 2017 at http://www.arctic-council.org/index.php/en/about-us/arctic-council/observers.

19 This document is available in Korean only, accessed 28 January 2017 at http://www.koreapolarportal.or.kr/rest/view?no=16. Also, Han argued for a more organised approach to the preparation of legislation for the Arctic study. Deukhoon Han, 'Korean Government should prepare related legislations for Arctic study' (13 July 2013), accessed 27 January 2017 at http://www.kookje.co.kr/news2011/asp/newsbody.asp?code=elec&key=20130704.22020195107 [in Korean].

20 Arctic Policy of the Republic of Korea, at 14, accessed 31 January 2017 at http://www.koreapolarportal.or.kr/rest/view?no=1635 [in Korean].

21 *Ibid.*

22 Three icebreakers are still operating in the NSR in 2015. See 'Vessels Transited NSR in 2015', *supra* note 8, accessed 17 February 2017 at http://www.arctic-lio.com/docs/nsr/transits/Transits_in_2015.pdf.

TABLE 9.5 *Present Allocation of Icebreakers*[23]

Country	In the world	In arctic available (total)
Russia	37	3(5)
Sweden	7	1(1)
Finland	7	1
Canada	6	1
USA	5	1(2)
Denmark	4	–
Others	2	–
Total	78	7(10)

in the NSR increases, the demand for icebreakers will also increase. If there is not a sufficient number of icebreakers to meet the increased demand, any time savings gained from using the NSR may be lost. For instance, the Korean shipping company, Glovis, when conducting a demonstration of shipping in the NSR in 2014 spent more than three days waiting to be escorted by icebreakers. Even though the length of the Arctic shipping route may be comparatively shorter than a traditional shipping route, it does not necessarily guarantee that it will take less time. It might actually cause a decrease in profitability in some economic aspects. Table 9.5 indicates the present allocation of icebreakers operating in the world and in the Arctic.

The second obstacle is the cargo imbalance. As aforementioned in Section 2, the amount of cargo transported from Europe to Asia is greater than the cargo transported from Asia to Europe. In terms of logistics, the fundamental condition for the optimisation of costs is when the size of the cargo transported is the same in both directions. If a vessel is full of cargo in one direction and empty in the other, the shipper will be paying twice the logistics cost, which is uneconomical. Therefore, to improve the economics of the use of the NSR, the cargo imbalance will need to be rectified.

The third obstacle is the poor infrastructure around the NSR. The most urgent priority is to secure the port infrastructure, as well as the logistics complex connecting the relevant ports and the traffic network. It is essential to secure the port infrastructure by providing facilities for cargo and shelter in

23 The US Naval Institute, Allocation of Icebreakers, accessed 15 February 2017 at https://news.usni.org/2013/07/23/u-s-coast-guards-2013-reivew-of-major-ice-breakers-of-the-world.

order to furnish supplies, in addition to ensuring that rescue vessels are on hand because of the various problems that can occur while navigating the long distance routes. Currently, there are several ports located along the NSR coastline; however, most of the ports are in poor condition as they were constructed during the years of the former Soviet Union. Moreover, these ports do not serve as a supply base for the export of resources from the port hinterland or for supply support due to the lack of a transport and logistics network connecting them to the port hinterland. In addition, the shortage of information and communications infrastructure is becoming a serious problem. Better real time communication on information on the operational environment should be established. Also, support of information on the current status of navigation routes and waterways is insufficient. In particular, extensive hydrographical surveys near the coastal areas are necessary.[24]

The fourth obstacle is the issue of securing the punctuality of navigation. The punctuality issue is the comprehensive outcome of the problems of the lack of adequate icebreaker assistance, presence of small icebergs and poor port infrastructure. Due to the lack of information and infrastructure, cargo that requires punctuality, such as containers, cannot pass through the NSR if the port of call cannot be predicted, or the exact time at which a vessel is passing through a particular region can be determined. Due to the irregularity and lack of punctuality, the commercialisation of the NSR will not be fully realised.

The fifth obstacle is the insufficiency of the disaster and safety system. The Search and Rescue (SAR) facilities and services available in the Arctic are limited due to the remoteness and long distances that are involved in responding to emergencies, as well as cold temperatures and sea ice conditions.[25] Also, there is a lack of adequate shore-side infrastructure and communication to support an adequate SAR response. These include shortage of food, lodging and medical facilities. Therefore, the Arctic Council adopted an agreement in 2011 on developing a joint SAR framework.[26] The eight Arctic States have committed to giving assistance to those in distress and to cooperate with each other in times of crisis. The Arctic States have agreed to establish, operate and maintain adequate and effective SAR capabilities within their areas of responsibility. Arctic

24 Basic Plan of Arctic Policy, Ministry of Oceans and Fisheries (December 2013) at 4, accessed 31 January 2017 at http://www.koreapolarportal.or.kr/rest/view?no=16 [in Korean].

25 'Search and Rescue in Arctic', accessed 17 February 2017 at http://www.arctic-council.org/index.php/en/our-work2/8-news-and-events/328-search-and-rescue-in-the-arctic.

26 See also Map of Arctic SAR Areas in the Arctic Search and Rescue Agreement, accessed 10 February 2017 at http://www.arctic-council.org/images/PDF_attachments/SAR/FINAL_ArcticSAR_Pamphlet_4.pdf.

coastal States can allow other foreign States to participate in SAR activities in Arctic waters. This can help develop a more effective SAR system.

The sixth obstacle is possible damage to the environment, which can include oil pollution and damage to coastal areas. The NSR is a very sensitive region with respect to the environment. If a crisis occurs in the region, it will not only seriously affect the larger environment but it will be almost impossible to ameliorate the immediate effects of the pollution once it happens or to act to prevent greater damage to the environment. Therefore, environmentalists have expressed their concerns regarding the commercialisation of the NSR. Prevention is the best way to reduce the likelihood of the occurrence of a serious environmental crisis, yet there are no active prevention plans in place. The implementation of the Polar Code will be helpful and beneficial in this regard.[27]

The seventh obstacle is consideration for the lives of the indigenous people in the Arctic area.[28] Consideration must be given to the indigenous people when developing navigational routes in Arctic waters prior to the commercialisation of the NSR. Although there are benefits associated with the development of the Arctic navigational route, indigenous communities can be negatively affected by the development of the NSR due to pollution and changes to their social environment. In such cases, financial support can be considered as a type of guarantee for the stability of their communities.

The final obstacle is the legal issue. Arctic coastal States' domestic legislation based upon Article 234 of UNCLOS should be formulated and enforced to promote the commercialisation of Arctic shipping. In this regard, user States and coastal States should cooperate more closely.

Many obstacles still exist in commercialising the NSR in addition to those discussed in this Chapter. The full potential of the commercialisation of the NSR will not be realised until these obstacles are overcome. This will take a significant investment of time, expense and joint cooperation by the user States and the Arctic coastal States.

27 Polar Code, Part II-A Pollution Prevention Measures, Chapter 1 Prevention of Pollution by Oil, accessed 31 January 2017 at http://www.imo.org/en/MediaCentre/HotTopics/polar/Documents/POLAR%20CODE%20TEXT%20AS%20ADOPTED.pdf. See *infra* note 59 for full citation to the Polar Code.

28 See the 'Map of Indigenous People and Non-Indigenous People in Arctic' in Laura Arbour, Alan Parkinson, Judith Kulig, 'Human Health at the Ends of the Earth', *Rural and Remote Health* (2010), accessed 23 February 2017 at http://www.rrh.org.au/articles/subviewnthamer.asp?ArticleID=1534.

3 Rights and Interests of Korea in the NSR

3.1 *Korea's Navigational Rights in the Arctic Waters*

Foreign-flagged vessels, including Korean vessels, have a right of innocent passage throughout the territorial waters of Arctic coastal States.[29] Korean vessels are obligated to comply with a coastal State's laws and regulations on innocent passage and all generally accepted international regulations relating to the prevention of collision at sea.[30] In addition, Article 58(1) and (3) of the United Nations Convention on the Law of the Sea (UNCLOS) provides that Korean vessels enjoy the freedom of navigation in the EEZ. Based on Article 38 of UNCLOS, Korean vessels also enjoy the right of transit passage in international straits. However, the extended right of Arctic coastal States under Article 234 to regulate international navigation in ice-covered areas within the exclusive economic zone (EEZ) may restrict navigational rights.

There have been many discussions on navigational rights in the Arctic waters among international law scholars. Korean scholars have also reviewed and discussed this issue, including Canadian and Russian straight baseline claims, the applicability of the international straits regime to the Canadian and Russian straits, and the scope of coastal State powers under Article 234 of UNCLOS.

3.2 *Status of Arctic Shipping Routes: Internal Waters or International Straits*

The legal status of the Northwest Passage (NWP) and the NSR is disputed. Canada claims that the NWP constitutes its 'historic internal waters' and is subject to its own jurisdiction and control,[31] whereas Russia claims that part of the NSR constitutes its internal waters based upon an historic waters argument.[32] The United States regards the entire NWP and the straits in the NSR

29 United Nations Convention on the Law of the Sea, adopted 10 December 1982, 1833 UNTS 3 (entered into force 16 November 1994), Art 17.

30 *Ibid.*, Art 21(4).

31 Statement by Secretary of State for External Affairs Joe Clark in the House of Commons, reproduced in 'Canadian Practice in International Law during 1985—Parliamentary Declarations' (1986) 24 *Canadian Yearbook of International Law* 404 at 418. See also Donat Pharand, *Canada's Arctic Waters in International Law* (Cambridge University Press, 2009) at 111–112.

32 Wen-Jin Piao and Min-Su Kim, 'A Legal Study on the Northern Sea Route' (2010), *The Society of Marine Environment and Safety*, at 256 [in Korean], Statute on the State Boundary of the USSR (1960), The Naval International Law Manual of Russia (1965).

as international straits.[33] Even though the Korean Government did not express its official position regarding Canada's claims to straight baselines on the NWP and Russia's claim to straight baselines on the NSR, Korean international law scholars have raised reservations about their claims.[34] A Korean scholar has argued that the Canadian claim is not well grounded because it is not clear what the straight baseline claim is based upon.[35] According to Article 7 of UNCLOS, straight baselines can be drawn in circumstances where the islands are located in the immediate vicinity of the coast. However, Canada's most remote islands in the NWP region are located 1900 km from the coastline.[36] At the time of writing, however, it seems that most Korean scholars have not drawn specific conclusions regarding whether the straight baseline claims in the NWP and NSR are acceptable.[37] Meanwhile, the United States and the European Union (EU) filed diplomatic protests immediately following Canada's claim to 'historic internal waters'. This could imply that both Russia and Canada's arguments have not received acquiescence from other countries.[38]

With regard to international straits claims, Korean authors are of the view that the NWP strait and the Russian straits in the NSR meet the geographical situation requirement under Article 37 of UNCLOS, of connecting two parts of the high seas or the EEZ.[39] With regard to the functional requirement of

---

33 For more information, see Chapters 6 and 7 of this Volume. See also the National Security Presidential Directive and Homeland Security Presidential Directive (NSPD-66/HSPD-25) (9 January 2009), Section B, para 5: 'Freedom of the seas is a top national priority. The Northwest Passage is a strait used for international navigation, and the Northern Sea Route includes straits used for international navigation; the regime of transit passage applies to passage through those straits. Preserving the rights and duties relating to navigation and overflight in the Arctic region supports our ability to exercise these rights throughout the world, including through strategic straits'.

34 Lee Yong-Hee, 'International Legal Status of the Arctic Northwest Passage' (2012) *Kyunghee Law Review*, 47–4, at 98–99 and 115–117 [in Korean].

35 *Ibid.*

36 *Ibid.* at 116. Lee argues that for this reason it is difficult to agree that the geographical requirements under Article 7 of UNCLOS are fully satisfied in the Canadian case. In addition, several States have established a number of different types of straight baselines in practice. This makes it more difficult to assess whether a specific geographical situation meets the requirements.

37 For more information, see Wen-Jin Piao and Min-Su Kim, *supra* note 32 at 258 [in Korean]; Jong-Man Han, 'The Potential of Russian Arctic Circle: Possibilities and Problems' *Journal of Korea and International Politics*, 27–2 (2011) at 206 [in Korean].

38 Lee Yong-Hee, *supra* note 34 at 116.

39 *Ibid.* at 116–117.

the straits being used for international navigation,[40] even though the number of navigating ships through the NWP and NSR is presently low, given the likelihood that the number will increase in the future, Korean scholars argue that this requirement needs to be interpreted in such a way as to accommodate future potential usage of the Arctic routes. Korean scholars are most likely to interpret that the requirements under Article 37 of UNCLOS are fulfilled.[41] Therefore, Korean scholars tend to emphasise the user State's navigational rights of transit passage in the NWP and NSR as international straits.[42] However, at the same time, Korean scholars emphasise that cooperation with Canada, Russia and other Arctic coastal States is important in order to find the balance between coastal States' interests and possible user States' navigational interests.[43]

3.3 *Coastal State Legislative and Enforcement Powers under Article 234 of UNCLOS*

In accordance with Article 234 of UNCLOS, coastal States of ice-covered areas, such as Russia and Canada, can adopt and enforce laws and regulations in order to protect and preserve the marine environment in ice-covered areas within the limits of the EEZ. In other words, Article 234 provides coastal States with extensive powers to regulate shipping in their EEZ and possibly also within their territorial sea area.[44] Consequently, Russian and Canadian Governments

---

40 Corfu Channel (*United Kingdom v Albania*), [1949] ICJ Rep 4 at 28–29; UNCLOS, *supra* note 29, Art 37.

41 Lee Yong-Hee, *supra* note 34 at 116–117; Yun, Jiwon, 'Changing Environment of Arctic Region and Korea's Arctic Policy: Restriction and Prospect' (2016) *East Asia Review* 31–1 [in Korean]; Sungwon Hong, 'The Northern Sea Route: Current State and feasibility for its Commercial Use' (2014) *International Regional Studies Review* 13–4, at 579–580 [in Korean].

42 *Ibid.*

43 *Ibid.* Wen-Jin Piao and Min-Su Kim, *supra* note 32 at 258; Yeong-Don Loh and Won Park, 'An Analysis of Russia's Legislation of Federal Law on the Water Areas of Northern Sea Route' (2011) *Seoul International Law Review* 18–2, at 119–120 [in Korean].

44 There are different views on the interpretation on the wording of 'within the limits of the exclusive economic zone' in Article 234 of UNCLOS. See Kristin Bartenstein, 'The "Arctic Exception in the Law of the Sea Convention: A Contribution to Safer Navigation in the Northwest Passage?' (2011) 42 *Ocean Development and International Law* 22–52, at 23–24; Donald M McRae and DJ Goundrey, 'Environmental Jurisdiction in Arctic Waters: The Extent of Article 234' (1982) 16 *University of British Colombia Law Review* 197–228, at 221.

have established and enforced their own independent ice-covered area voyage rules based on Article 234 of UNCLOS.[45]

Certain Russian requirements can be controversial under UNCLOS, including prior authorisation from the Russian Administration of the NSR (ANSR) before entry into the boundary of the NSR, reporting on vessels' positions to the related administration, and the payment of fees.[46] If fees are levied in relation to icebreaker services delivered by a coastal State,[47] it would be in accordance with Article 234 of UNCLOS. In other words, if the fees are for services provided for preventing, reducing and controlling pollution from vessels and are collected in a non-discriminatory way, and if the related regulation has due regard for navigation and the protection of the marine environment, such fees would be consistent with Article 234 of UNCLOS.

Icebreaker pilotage fees are collected in the EEZ as well as in territorial waters in accordance with Russian Rules.[48] In accordance with Article 26 of UNCLOS, fees may be levied in territorial waters provided they are levied as payment for specific services and not solely for passing through a coastal State's territorial sea. The icebreaker assistance service can be interpreted as a special service under Article 26 of UNCLOS. Likewise, such fees levied in the EEZ can also be in accordance with Article 234 of UNCLOS because the use of icebreakers may prevent, reduce and control of marine pollution from vessels in ice-covered areas.

---

45 For example, Russian Rules of Navigation on the Water Area of the Northern Sea Route approved by the order of the Ministry of Transport of Russia, dated 17 January 2013, No 7 and Canada's Northern Canada Vessel Traffic Services Zone Regulations (NORDREG).

46 See Chapter 6 of this Volume.

47 For example, The Russian Federation Law on Amendments to Specific Legislative Acts of the Russian Federation related to Governmental Regulation of Merchant Shipping in the Water Area of the Northern Sea Route, adopted by the State Duma on 3 July 2012, approved by the Council of Federation on 18 July 2012, NSR administration, Clause 5.1(5) to the Merchant Marine Code of the Russian Federation. The language is as follows: '5. The amount of payment for icebreaker support and ice pilotage channeling in the water area of the Northern Sea Route shall be determined according to the Natural Monopolies Law of the Russian Federation considering the vessels' tonnage, the vessel's ice class, the distance of channeling, and navigation period. The payment for icebreaker support and ice pilotage channeling in the water area of the Northern Sea Route shall be effected based on the amount of services actually delivered'.

48 Rules of the Icebreaker Assistance of Ships in the Water Area of the Northern Sea Route 24 & 32, Russian Rules of Navigation on the Water Area of the Northern Sea Route, approved by the Order of the Ministry of Transport of Russia No 7, 17 January 2013, accessed 31 January 2017 at http://www.nsra.ru/en/pravila_plavaniya/ or www.arctic-lio.com/nsr_legislation.

However, if these fees are imposed only for the approval of transit and vessels' presence in or passage through ice-covered areas within the limits of EEZ, such fees could conflict with navigational rights under Articles 58 and 234 of UNCLOS.[49] In addition, if the collection of fees would not in practice be imposed and enforced upon its domestic flag ship, then it might violate the non-discrimination clause under Articles 227 and 234 of UNCLOS[50] with respect to foreign vessels, which states that States may not discriminate against the vessels of other countries either legally or practically. In this respect, the current Russian Rules do not appear to be discriminatory in relation to the nationality of the vessel.[51] However, if the fees are applied in a discriminatory way in practice, such fees could violate the non-discriminatory provision under Article 234 of UNCLOS.

To promote Arctic shipping and the development of international rules and standards, the majority of Korean scholars suggest that more frequent dialogue in the form of bilateral or multilateral meetings between coastal States and user States is needed.[52] To establish Arctic shipping governance in particular, more consultation is necessary between coastal States and user States regarding the establishment and implementation of a reasonable fee system regarding Arctic shipping.[53] Korean scholars also emphasise that co-operation regarding the development of port infrastructure near the Arctic coast and close monitoring of domestic navigation legislation on the Arctic is equally important.[54]

Considering the purpose of the International Maritime Organization (IMO), this organisation can also play a leading role in facilitating the balancing of the rights and obligations of coastal States and user States in the region.[55] The

---

49 In the case of navigation in the territorial sea, such fees can be a violation of Article 26 (Charges which may be levied upon foreign ships) of UNCLOS.

50 UNCLOS, *supra* note 29, Art 227 (Non-discrimination with respect to foreign vessels): 'In exercising their rights and performing their duties under this Part, States shall not discriminate in form or in fact against vessels of any other State'.

51 Rules of the Icebreaker Assistance of Ships in the Water Area of the Northern Sea Route, *supra* note 48 at 21–41.

52 Lee Yong-Hee, *supra* note 34 at 117; Yeong-Don Loh and Won Park, *supra* note 43 at 119–120; Hyun-Pyo Hong, Deukhoon Han, Hong-Seok Chang, 'A Study on Arctic Fisheries and its Regulations' *KMI and Ministry of Ocean and Fisheries* (2013.11) at 190–201 [in Korean].

53 Jumi Song, 'Current State of Utilization of the Northern Sea Route and Russia's Commercialization Policy' (2012) *KyeKan Ocean and Fishery (KMI)* at 120–121 [in Korean].

54 *Ibid.* Yun, *supra* note 41; Hong, *supra* note 41 at 579–580 [in Korean]; Han, *supra* note 19.

55 Convention on the International Maritime Organization, adopted 6 March 1948 289 UNTS 48 (entered into force 17 March 1958). Article 1 lists the purposes of the IMO to

prior negotiation of the Polar Code in the IMO serves as one of example of this kind of cooperation, even though it was not that successful in this regard.[56] Once the Polar Code is established as a uniform supplemental international regulation on Arctic shipping, and if a coastal State's stricter regulations have a tendency to discourage international navigation, a coastal State could restrict its own regulations and policies, for example, in the case of Russia, to promote international navigation in Arctic waters. In this circumstance, the coastal States might have another incentive to participate more actively in finding a balance between the activities of coastal States and user States in the Arctic.

3.4 *The Polar Code: Towards More Uniform Arctic Shipping Rules*

As the Polar Code will be part of SOLAS[57] and MARPOL,[58] flag States that are already parties to those Conventions have the obligation to abide by the Polar Code. The Polar Code provides additional mandatory requirements for ships operating in polar waters.[59] Korea is a State Party to both SOLAS and MARPOL. Korea is implementing the Polar Code and its related regulations starting in January 2017.[60] [61] In addition, Korea has incorporated the main provisions of the Polar Code in its preexisting regulations.[62] SOLAS and MARPOL each have

---

encourage and facilitate the general adoption of the highest practicable standards in matters concerning the maritime safety, efficiency of navigation and prevention and control of marine pollution from ships ...

56 See Dorottya Bognar, 'Russian Proposals on the Polar Code: Contributing to Common Rules or Furthering State Interests?' *Arctic Review on Law and Politics* (2016) Vol 7, No 2, 111–135, accessed 18 February 2017 at http://dx.doi.org/10.17585/arctic.v7.415.

57 International Convention for the Safety of Life at Sea, adopted 1 November 1974, 1184 UNTS 277 (entered into force 25 May 1980) with protocols and regularly amended (SOLAS).

58 International Convention for the Prevention of Pollution from Ships, adopted 2 November 1973 (as modified by the 1978 Protocol adopted on 1 June 1978 and the 1997 Protocol adopted on 26 September 1997), 1340 UNTS 61, and as regularly amended (MARPOL).

59 International Code for Ships Operating in Polar Waters, Res. MSC.385 (94) (21 November 2014), IMO Doc. MSC 94/21/Add.1, Annex 6; Res. MEPC.264(68) (15 May 2015), IMO Doc. MEPC 68/21/Add.1, Annex 10, accessed 15 February 2017 at http://www.imo.org/en/MediaCentre/HotTopics/polar/Documents/POLAR%20CODE%20TEXT%20AS%20ADOPTED.pdf.

60 'Korea Ministry of Ocean and Fisheries, Proceeds with Legislation on Standard for Safe Navigation in Arctic waters' *PBC News*, 4 January 2016, accessed 31 January 2017 at http://www.pbc.co.kr/CMS/news/view_body.php?cid=612437&path=201601 [in Korean].

61 Korea's Portal Website for the information on Polar policy and efforts (operated by Korean Ministry of Ocean and Fisheries and Korea Maritime Institute) accessed 31 January 2017 at http://www.koreapolarportal.or.kr/rest/main [in Korean].

62 To cope with the Polar Code, it is necessary to prepare for navigation technology in Arctic waters and educate seafarers and deck officers. Won-Ouk Kim, 'Research on Navigation

a safeguard clause to allow Arctic coastal States to enact and enforce stricter national regulations than set out in the Polar Code.[63] This gives greater opportunity to the coastal States to justify their national measures pursuant to Article 234. However, flag States have a strong interest in the freedom of navigation in these areas. Therefore, more clarification is necessary regarding the extent and level to which coastal States can legislate and enforce regulations in this respect. The determination of the balance of interests between Arctic coastal States and flag States on this matter is necessary.[64] It is desirable that Arctic coastal States and flag States should start close consultations on this issue in multilateral talks, in the Arctic Council or in the IMO. The legality of restrictions on navigation rights in the NSR and other Arctic waters will likely depend upon the progress of any such consultations.

3.5 *The Korean Government's Position on Arctic Shipping*

The Korean Government did not express its official position on Canada's claims to historic internal waters, Russia's claims to internal waters, or on any of the Arctic coastal States' legislation on Arctic shipping. Essentially, the Korean Government promotes the user States' rights and interests to navigate in Arctic waters, but it also emphasises the importance of cooperation with Arctic coastal States. As an Observer on the Arctic Council, the Korean Government wishes to maintain good relationships with other Arctic coastal States. In addition, as a practical matter, because the Arctic Council does not deal with industry and business issues, the Korean Government promotes its Arctic shipping interests through continuing to develop bilateral cooperation with coastal States.[65]

---

of the Northern Sea Route Considering the Safety of Vessel and Crews' (2015) *Journal of Korean Society of Marine Environment and Safety* at 40–46 [in Korean].

63 Chapter XIV of SOLAS (*supra* note 57) provides that '[n]othing in this chapter shall prejudice the rights or obligations of states under international law'. See also MARPOL, *supra* note 58, Art 9(2).

64 Arctic Council Status on Implementation of the AMSA 2009 Report Recommendations, Status of Progress on Recommendations APRIL 2015, Theme I(A). 'That the Arctic states should explore the possible harmonization of Arctic marine shipping regulatory regimes within their own jurisdiction and uniform Arctic safety and environmental protection regulatory regimes, consistent with UNCLOS, that could provide a basis for protection measures in regions of the central Arctic Ocean beyond coastal state jurisdiction for consideration by the IMO'. *Ibid.*, Theme I(C).

65 Korean Ministry of Oceans and Fisheries Official Blog, Establishment and Implementation of Arctic Policy in 2015, accessed 10 January 2017 at http://blog.naver.com/koreamof/220325776198 [in Korean].

4 Conclusion

A step-by-step approach is urgently needed in order for Korea, together with the other East Asian countries and the Arctic States, to make proper use of the NSR. This Chapter has examined the obstacles that should be examined in the course of commercialising the NSR. In order to overcome and mitigate these obstacles, the following measures must be taken.

First, a close examination of the ports and their infrastructure around the Arctic Ocean is required for the commercialisation of the NSR. The support of various services and the securing of cargo passing through the ports are required for the operation of the NSR, regardless of whether it is a liner or steamer. In this regard, the examination should be made based on the available information regarding ports surrounding the NSR. It will most likely be necessary to cooperate with Russia in the joint development of main ports and select hub ports.[66]

Second, the infrastructure necessary for the NSR should be clearly identified. The ports in the Russian Arctic are different from other ports. Many special facilities are required in order for ports to operate in such extreme conditions. These special facilities are different from those in the general ports and include, for example, nuclear power generation for the supply of energy, and winterised port cranes and buildings. Russia is planning to construct an 'ice city' along the coastline of the Arctic Ocean to reinforce its territorial claims in that area.[67] Due to the special facilities that will be required for the port and logistics areas, consideration should be given to securing the relevant technologies.[68]

Third, a large amount of investment will be required to construct port and logistics infrastructure in these areas. In order to promote this development and encourage active participation by the companies of the Arctic coastal States and user States, these governments and their public institutions will need to procure sufficient funding and investment. It is expected that the International Bank for Reconstruction and Development (IBRD), the Arctic Council and the Government-run banks of user States will participate in these

66 Arctic Shipping Traffic Data (ASTD) Project is one of the works implemented by the PAME working group, accessed 31 January 2017 at https://oaarchive.arctic-council.org/bitstream/handle/11374/1828/6-5_PAME_ASTD.pdf?sequence=8&isAllowed=y.

67 Russia has plans to construct a city 1,000 miles from the North Pole on Kotelniy in the Novosibirsk archipelago to solidify territorial claims within the Arctic Circle, *The ArchDaily*, accessed 10 February 2017 at http://www.archdaily.com/186334/russia-plans-ice-city-in-arctic-circle.

68 *Ibid.*

efforts. In addition, the Asian Infrastructure Investment Bank (AIIB)[69] and other multilateral cooperative banks may be good alternatives. Other private banks and investment vehicles will also likely be required to support these immense projects.

Fourth, although there is an urgent requirement for securing the ports and logistics infrastructure in order to commercialise the NSR, logistics can only be efficient when they are well connected to a land logistics network. Therefore, only through the connection of ports around the Arctic Ocean and to the logistics network coming from Fast East Russia, Northern Mongolia, and Harbin of China, will it be possible for the logistics to perform properly and efficiently.

Furthermore, in order to effect the commercialisation of the NSR as soon as possible, several of the actions suggested in this Chapter need to be implemented in parallel. These include (i) establishment of an information support center for the NSR, (ii) formulation and implementation of policies regarding the preservation of the environment and disaster prevention measures, and (iii) provision of guarantees and financial support for indigenous people in the Arctic whose lives and communities are affected by the commercialisation of the NSR.

Last, the NSR and other Arctic waters comprise some of the few last ocean frontiers. Therefore, the Arctic coastal States, user States and other States should all be concerned with establishing a responsible governance regime for both the protection and commercialisation of these areas.

---

69 The Asian Infrastructure Investment Bank (AIIB) is an international financial institution proposed by the government of China. The purpose of the multilateral development bank is to provide finance to infrastructure projects in the Asia region, accessed 31 January 2017 at http://en.wikipedia.org/wiki/Asian_Infrastructure_Investment_Bank.

CHAPTER 10

Equal Treatment and Non-discrimination for User States

Guifang (Julia) Xue and Yu Long

1 Introduction

With global warming bringing about the melting of sea ice, large areas of the Arctic region are expected to be ice-free during the summer months in the coming years. This has improved prospects for the use of Arctic navigation routes by international shipping companies with the potential for significant savings in time and cost.[1] To respond to the increase of risks to the environment by transiting ships, the Arctic coastal States have enhanced national regulatory frameworks for the Arctic waters and strengthened requirements for navigation safety and environmental protection. While the coastal States' grants of transit permits to foreign-flagged ships emphasise measures to prevent, reduce and control of pollution to the marine environment from vessels, this raises the issue of whether the principles of equal treatment and non-discrimination should be applied to the transiting ships of user States. Specifically, the issue that arises is the extent to which coastal States in ice-covered areas can exercise jurisdictional power in a manner that safeguards the rights of user States.

To answer these questions, this Chapter starts with a brief review of the conceptual development of the equal treatment and non-discrimination principle to determine its essence, scope and application in international law. This is followed by a review of the specific provisions with respect to the non-discrimination principle for the navigation regime under the United Nations Convention on the Law of the Sea (UNCLOS).[2] This includes the provisions governing the regulation of passage through the various maritime zones, including the extent to which passage is based upon the principle of non-discrimination. This Chapter then examines the extent to which the national laws and regulations of Russia and Canada governing Arctic shipping are consistent with the

1 See 'Strategic Assessment of Development of the Arctic' at 38, accessed 17 March 2017 at http://www.arcticinfo.eu/images/pdf/SADA_report.pdf.

2 United Nations Convention on the Law of the Sea, adopted 10 December 1982, entered into force 16 November 1994, 1833 UNTS 3.

 | DOI 10.1163/9789004339385_011

principle of non-discrimination. This Chapter will next examine whether the non-discrimination principle has been implemented in the national laws of Canada and Russia governing the prevention, reduction and control of vessel-source pollution in their respective Arctic waters. To date, the user States of the Arctic shipping routes have been cautious in expressing their position with regard to these issues and have sought means to collaborate with the Arctic coastal States. Finally, this Chapter then discusses the procedural safeguards in Section 7 of Part XII of UNCLOS that are designed to ensure the principle of equal treatment and non-discrimination, and examines how these safeguards apply to regulations adopted by coastal States under Article 234 on ice-covered areas.

This Chapter suggests that the equal treatment and non-discrimination rule has generally been observed by the Arctic States in their national legislation. However, when it comes to the implementation and enforcement of their national regulations, it may be difficult for coastal States to ensure equal treatment for foreign ships. Asian user States have legitimate rights and interests in accessing the Arctic shipping routes, and it is essential that when transiting Arctic waters they not be discriminated against by coastal States. If user States exercise their rights of navigation responsibly, they have the option to exercise procedural safeguards against national regulations that are discriminatory, whether in form or in fact.

2 The Non-discrimination Rule and Its Application in International Law

The word 'discrimination', according to the Cambridge Dictionary, means treatment or consideration of, or making a distinction in favour of or against, a person or thing with an unreasonable or disproportionate impact, because of a particular characteristic, e.g., of the group, class, or category, etc. Linked to the essential dignity of the individual and the notion of equality, the development of the non-discrimination principle that has been accepted as customary international law bears a close relationship to equal treatment clauses at the national level.[3] The underlying basis of the equality concept, its philosophical

3 See Raúl Emilio Vinuesa, 'National Treatment, Principle' in Rüdiger Wolfrum (ed), *Max Planck Encyclopedia of Public International Law: Online Edition* (Oxford University Press, 2006) at para 8, accessed 17 March 2017 at http://opil.ouplaw.com/home/EPIL. Important UN documents addressing discrimination include: the Universal Declaration of Human Rights, a declaration adopted by the United Nations General Assembly on 10 December 1948;

content and critical justification relating to the rights to which people are entitled made non-discrimination a decisive principle.[4] When States exercise their sovereign rights to enforce national legislation and jurisdiction over all persons within their territory, including foreign individuals, it has become a universal expectation that such persons will not be subject to differences in treatment.[5]

Along with these developments, the non-discrimination rule received widespread acceptance by the international community. It became an important element in dealing with rights and freedoms in soft-law instruments, such as declarations, statements and programmes of action, and this led to it being included in legally binding treaties and conventions.[6] In addition, international law has established criteria for determining when a distinction in treatment constitutes discrimination contrary to the non-discrimination principle.[7]

International Convention on the Elimination of All Forms of Racial Discrimination (ICERD), adopted by the United Nations General Assembly (UNGA) on 21 December 1965, and entered into force on 4 January 1969; Convention on the Elimination of All Forms of Discrimination against Women (CEDAW), adopted in 1979 by UNGA, entered into force on 3 September 1981; Convention on the Rights of Persons with Disabilities, adopted by the UNGA on 13 December 2006, came into force on 3 May 2008. Under public international law, both the 'principle of non-discrimination' and 'non-discrimination rule' have been used without obvious distinction, in this chapter, 'principle' refers to general requirement, whereas, 'rule' refer to the specific regulations.

4 Among the American States, the Contracting Parties to the Montevideo Convention on the Nationality of Women of December 26, 1933 declared in Article 1 of that treaty that 'There shall be no distinction based on sex as regards nationality, in their legislation or in their practice.' The Convention was adopted at the Seventh International Conference of American States, Montevideo, December 3–26, 1933. The Convention is reproduced in *International Conferences of American States—Supplement 1933–1940* (Carnegie Endowment for International Peace, 1940) at 106.

5 Vinuesa, *supra* note 3 at para 4.

6 The American Declaration declares in Article II that 'All persons are equal before the law and have the rights and duties established in this declaration, without distinction as to race, sex, language, creed or any other factor.' These same principles have been embodied in Article 1(3) of the United Nations Charter and in Article 3(j) of the OAS Charter.

7 One of the first judgements at the international level determining the scope of the principle of non-discrimination was handed down by the European Court in the decision on the Belgian Linguistic case. In this judgement, the European Court agreed that not all types of differential treatment in the provision of rights and freedoms constitute prohibited discrimination under the Convention. In this judgement, the Court set forth its analytical scheme for determining when prohibited discrimination has occurred (para 10). When differential treatment is proposed, three criteria have to be observed: objective and reasonable justification for the aim; and proportionality, an additional element, whether the situation of the

Over decades, international treaty bodies and general State practice have established non-discrimination as a robust principle that is widely implemented under international law, being adopted by numerous resolutions, conventions and declarations.[8] Its application has been the subject matter of various legal instruments, including the General Agreement on Tariffs and Trade (GATT 1947 and 1994).[9] Since 1947, the GATT has attempted to promote trade liberalisation based on the non-discrimination principle, using national origin and most favourable national treatment.[10] Article III of GATT sets forth the general principle on national treatment for a Member State not to treat foreign products less favourably than domestic products. Similarly, the WTO uses the same principle, requiring a WTO member not to discriminate on the basis of the national origin of products, unless an exception can be justified under Article XX of GATT.[11]

In addition to these general provisions on non-discrimination, the GATT 1947 contains a provision on the free transit of goods that prohibits discrimination based on a vessel's flag.[12] Article V(5) requires Contracting States to accord to traffic in transit to or from the territory of any other Contracting State treatment no less favourable than that accorded to traffic in transit to or from any third country.[13] National treatment clauses are found in most trade

application is sufficiently analogous to that of individuals enjoying better protection of the contested right. See: The case 'Relating to Certain Aspects of the Laws on the Use of Languages in Education in Belgium, Application Nos 1474/62, 1677/62, 1691/62, 1769/63, 1994/63, 2126/64, Judgements of 23 July 1968).

8 See Kristin Bartenstein, 'The "Arctic Exception" in the Law of the Sea Convention: A Contribution to Safer Navigation in the Northwest Passage?' (2011) 42 *Ocean Development and International Law* 22 at 41.

9 For example, in UNCLOS, the non-discrimination phrase are found at Article 119(3), Article 140(2), Article 141, Article 151(1(c)), Article 152(1), these provisions cover conservation of the living resources of the high seas and activities in the Area.

10 Vinuesa, *supra* note 3 at para 36.

11 *Ibid.* at para 40.

12 General Agreement on Tariffs and Trade, Art V, para 2, 'There shall be freedom of transit through the territory of each contracting party, via the routes most convenient for international transit, for traffic in transit to or from the territory of other contracting parties. No distinction shall be made based on the flag of vessels, the place of origin, departure, entry, exit or destination, or any circumstances relating to the ownership of goods, of vessels or of other means of transport.' See Henrik Ringbom (ed), *Jurisdiction over Ships: Post-UNCLOS Developments in the Law of the Sea* (Brill/Nijhoff, 2015) at 122.

13 Talia Einhorn, 'Transit of Goods over Foreign Territory' in Rüdiger Wolfrum (ed), *Max Planck Encyclopedia of Public International Law: Online Edition* (Oxford University Press, 2006) at para 31, accessed 17 March 2017 at http://opil.ouplaw.com/home/EPIL.

agreements and they have been construed to ban any discriminatory internal measures, including internal measures that indirectly imply non-justified discrimination including alleged de facto discrimination.[14]

Non-discrimination related provisions are also found in the International Convention for the Prevention of Pollution from Ships (MARPOL 73/78). Article 4.4 of MARPOL 73/78 stipulates that the penalties specified under the law of a party shall be sufficiently severe to discourage violations and shall be of equal severity irrespective of where the violations occur.[15] This provision gives 'teeth' in this Convention against violations of the non-discrimination rule.[16]

Port State control measures are also notable for frequent operation on the basis of 'priority inspection', where vessels are targeted on a variety of objective factors (e.g., vessel age and type or detention record of the states of registry) and not selected randomly. As methods of 'priority inspection' differ among various Memorandum of Understanding (MOU) regimes, both flag States and the shipping industry have questioned whether the targeting systems drifting away from the non-discrimination principle.[17]

3 The Non-discrimination Rule under UNCLOS

UNCLOS is a legal regime based on maritime zones. According to this zone-based regime, coastal States may exercise jurisdiction over foreign merchant ships on the basis of international agreements and/or established international standards and practices. With regard to navigation, one of the most notable features of UNCLOS is the freedom of navigation of ships in various maritime zones, among which, subject to coastal State sovereignty or sovereign rights, include innocent passage in the territorial sea and archipelagic waters, archipelagic sea lanes passage through archipelagic waters, transit passage in straits used for international navigation and freedom of navigation in the exclusive

14 Vinuesa, *supra* note 3 at para 41.

15 International Convention for the Prevention of Pollution from Ships, as Modified by the Protocol of 1978 Relating Thereto, 1340 UNTS 62 (entered into force 2 October 1983) (MARPOL 73/78), Art 4.4, 'The penalties specified under the law of a Party pursuant to the present article shall be adequate in severity to discourage violations of the present Convention and shall be equally severe irrespective of where the violations occur'.

16 D J Devine, 'Garbage Jurisdiction in Maritime Zones: Annex V to MARPOL Examined' (1992–1993) 18 *South African Yearbook of International Law* 24 at 26.

17 Michael A Becker, 'The Shifting Public Order of the Oceans: Freedom of Navigation and the Interdiction of Ships at Sea' (2005) 46 *Harvard International Law Journal* 131 at 189.

economic zone (EEZ).[18] Each passage regime serves the same function in ensuring the navigation of ships while balancing the different influences coastal States may have on the exercise of navigation. This section will examine the jurisdiction coastal States may exercise under the UNCLOS regime over transiting ships, with particular reference to the provisions promoting adherence to the non-discrimination principle.

3.1 *Innocent Passage in the Territorial Sea and Archipelagic Waters*

The innocent passage regime allows vessels to pass through the territorial seas of another State, subject to certain restrictions including the prevention, reduction and control of pollution.[19] It is the most well respected and developed regime dealing with the passage of ships, aside from freedom of navigation on the high seas. Innocent passage concedes that the coastal State has sovereignty in the territorial sea, and acknowledges that a ship exercising freedom of passage is transiting through a country's 12 nautical mile (nm) territorial sea. The law was codified in 1958 and affirmed in 1982 under the UNCLOS regime.

With regard to national legislation on the territorial sea, some States have closely followed Article 21(1) of UNCLOS, which allows coastal States to adopt regulations relating to innocent passage. There are States that claim prescriptive competences over a series of matters that deviate from Article 21(1) or address their claims in a general way by stressing that foreign vessels shall observe promulgated laws and regulations. Still, there are States that either have made no mention of legislative jurisdiction in their legislation on the territorial sea or have not as yet enacted any special laws and regulations.

Innocent passage in the territorial sea and through archipelagic waters is specified in Articles 17 to 26, 45 and 52 of UNCLOS. Essentially, the non-discrimination principle is an integral part of the provisions governing what laws and regulations coastal States may adopt to regulate innocent passage, including Article 24(1)(b), Article 25(3) and Article 26(2).

18 The provisions that establish the navigational regimes include Article 24(1)(b), Article 25(3), Article 26(2), Article 42(2), Article 52(2), Article 227 and Article 234. For relevant discussions, see Rüdiger Wolfrum, *Freedom of Navigation: New Challenges, in Freedom of Seas, Passage Rights and the 1982 Law of the Sea Convention* (Brill, 2008) 79–102.

19 UNCLOS, *supra* note 2, Art 21(1)(f). According to UNCLOS, Articles 54, 39, 40, 42 and 44 apply *mutatis mutandis* to archipelagic sea lanes passage, and the rest of the archipelagic sea applies the innocent passage regime within the territorial sea. See Erik J Molenaar, *Coastal State Jurisdiction over Vessel-Source Pollution* (Kluwer Law International, 1998) at 342–344.

While defining the concept of innocent passage and its application, Article 19 of UNCLOS excludes certain actions from the protection accorded by the notion of innocent passage. Article 19(1) specifies that coastal States may pass laws and regulations on specified matters that apply to foreign ships exercising innnocent passage through their territorial sea. Article 19(2) stipulates restrictions for the passage by stating that passage is not innocent if it is 'prejudicial to the peace, good order or security of the coastal State'. To provide further explanation on what 'prejudicial' could mean, Article 19(2) lists some specific actions by ships that are not protected by the right of innocent passage. Among the listed activities, Article 19(2)(h) includes 'any act of wilful and serious pollution'. The problem is how to determine the 'wilfulness' and 'seriousness' of the pollution.

Article 21 opens the possibility for coastal States to place limits on the right of innocent passage by allowing them to adopt laws and regulations to regulate innocent passage in its territorial sea. The coastal State may regulate innocent passage in a wide range of matters under Article 21(1), in conformity with UNCLOS and other rules of international law. Paragraphs 1(a) and (b) of Article 21 in particular refer to the safety of navigation, the regulation of maritime traffic, and the protection of navigational aids, while paragraph 1(f) relates to the preservation of the marine environment and the prevention, reduction and control of pollution thereof.

However, Article 21(2) sets out a limitation on a coastal State's power to regulate innocent passage in its territorial sea by not permitting laws or regulations with regard to 'the design, construction, manning or equipment of foreign ships unless they are giving effect to generally accepted international rules or standards (GAIRS)'. As such, it clarifies the ambiguity relating to coastal States' legislative competence as regards innocent passage, and tries to establish a delicate balance between the interests of foreign ships and the right of coastal States in regulating the passage in the territorial sea. The GAIRS refers to specified requirements set forth in MARPOL 73/78 and the International Convention for the Safety of Life at Sea, 1974 (1974 SOLAS). In addition, Article 21(3) stresses that all such laws and regulations shall be given due publicity and not hamper innocent passage of foreign vessels.[20] This is a significant restriction concerning the prescriptive power of coastal States. It reflects a basic concept incorporated throughout UNCLOS, namely to protect the integrity of global maritime navigation and to minimise interference from coastal State jurisdiction. Nonetheless, it leaves the question open in reality to balance the two objectives, particularly in some sensitive areas, such as the Arctic waters.

---

20 UNCLOS, *supra* note 2, Arts 24(1) and 211(4).

Article 24 lays down a principle that is essential to the spirit of UNCLOS. Paragraph 1(b) states that when applying UNCLOS or any laws or regulations adopted in conformity with it, the coastal State shall not 'discriminate in form or in fact against the ships of any State or against ships carrying cargoes to, from or on behalf of any State'. This important requirement, emphasising the necessity in eradicating discrimination in all its guises, has its origin from Article 16(3) of 1958 Geneva Convention on the Territorial Sea and the Contiguous Zone. The term of 'in form or in fact' may be interpreted as an unambiguous prohibition on non-equal treatment against foreign ships carrying cargoes to, from or on behalf of any State. Such a prohibition is intended to protect ships from acts in a manner of being overtly discriminatory (discrimination 'in form'), similarly, acts that are not overtly discriminatory, but have the same effect (discrimination 'in fact') shall also be prohibited.[21]

Article 25(3) of UNCLOS deals with enforcement issues under the coastal States' jurisdiction.[22] This provision allows a coastal State to suspend temporarily the innocent passage of foreign ships for security considerations in specified areas, but not for definite closure. The suspension must be 'without discrimination in form or in fact' and 'essential for the protection of its security'. It is worth noting that this requirement addressing non-discrimination 'among foreign ships' only, and such suspension shall take effect only when it is duly publicised. The only difference between the suspension of innocent passage in archipelagic waters and territorial sea is that suspension of the right in archipelagic waters under Article 52(2) does not mention 'weapons exercises', whereas suspension of the right in the territorial sea under Article 25(3) does.[23] With respect to the obligation of investigation under Article 220(2) of UNCLOS, any physical inspection on documents carried by foreign vessels is limited to the regulation under the GAIRS.

---

21 Satya N Nandan and Shabtai Rosenne (eds), *United Nations Convention on the Law of the Sea 1982: A Commentary, Vol* II (Martinus Nijhoff Publishers, 1993) at 226.

22 UNCLOS, *supra* note 2, Art 25(3), 'The coastal State may, without discrimination in form or in fact among foreign ships, suspend temporarily in specified areas of its territorial sea the innocent passage of foreign ships if such suspension is essential for the protection of its security, including weapons exercises. Such suspension shall take effect only after having been duly published'.

23 UNCLOS, *supra* note 2, Art 52(2), 'The archipelagic State may, without discrimination in form or in fact among foreign ships, suspend temporarily in specified areas of its archipelagic waters the innocent passage of foreign ships if such suspension is essential for the protection of its security. Such suspension shall take effect only after having been duly published'.

Article 26(1) of UNCLOS prohibits coastal States from levying charges upon foreign ships simply for their passage through the territorial sea. However, paragraph 2 allows a coastal State to levy charges without discrimination for specific services rendered to foreign ships. Clearly, a service rendered to a given ship, such as pilotage (even if compulsory), will be 'specific'; however, it remains unclear from the text whether general service, such as the maintenance of navigational aids comes within the scope of the expression 'specific services' insofar as concerns the territorial sea itself.[24] It is also generally agreed that the provision of ice-breaking services for specific ships is a specific service for which a charge may be levied.

3.2 *Transit Passage and Archipelagic Sea Lanes Passage*

Transit passage in Part III of UNCLOS is accepted by most countries. As a special regime applies for major international shipping routes through straits used for international navigation even if such straits are within the territorial sea of the coastal State, it allows a vessel or aircraft the freedom of navigation or overflight solely for the purpose of continuous and expeditious transit of a strait between one part of the high seas or EEZ and another.[25] This regime implies a more liberal particular regime described as ranging between the freedom of navigation and innocent passage.[26]

The legal regime of transit passage exists in the most important straits for the international trade exchange and security. All ships and aircraft enjoy the right of unimpeded transit passage through such straits, that is, the freedom of navigation and the right of overflight exist for vessels and aircraft operating in their normal mode.[27] The requirement of continuous and expeditious transit does not preclude passage through a strait for the purpose of entering, leaving or returning from a State bordering the strait, subject to the conditions of entry to that State.

While the coastal States' jurisdictional powers concerning navigation through international straits are limited, they may still impose controls on

---

24 Nandan and Rosenne, *supra* note 21 at 236.

25 UNCLOS, *supra* note 2, Art 38. For discussions, see Molenaar, *supra* note 19.

26 'Transit passage is a neologism, lying somewhere between "free navigation" and "innocent passage". In its definition, transit passage does not depart significantly from the definition of innocent passage. Transit passage must be exercised in accordance with Part III and should be both 'continuous and expeditious' although this does not 'preclude passage through the strait for the purpose of entering, leaving or returning from a State bordering the strait, subject to the conditions of entry to that State'. Molenaar, *supra* note 19 at 287.

27 UNCLOS, *supra* note 2, Art 38(1) and (2).

such navigation. Article 42 of UNCLOS prescribes the limits for such coastal State jurisdiction. States bordering straits may adopt laws and regulations relating to transit passage in respect of the safety of navigation, the regulation of maritime traffic and the prevention, reduction and control of pollution.[28] Article 41 allows States bordering straits to prescribe sea lanes and traffic separation schemes, provided they conform to international regulations and are submitted to the International Maritime Organization (IMO) for adoption.[29] The rules concerning passage through archipelagic sea lanes are similar but not completely identical, and it also requires IMO involvement.[30]

This can be seen to constitute the concrete application of these general principles to protect the marine environment. However, such laws and regulations cannot be effective, unless they comply with 'applicable international regulations regarding the discharge of oil, oily wastes and other noxious substances in the strait'.[31] In addition, the application of such laws and regulations shall not have the effect of inhibiting the right of transit passage.[32]

As an application of the generally applicable rule that laws and regulations shall not discriminate 'in form or in fact among foreign ships', Malta had proposed that this phrase be included in the 'non-discrimination' provision in Article 42(2).[33] In a later proposal submitted by four straits States holding that transit passage shall be the same as innocent passage, and the clause attempted to mention non-discrimination phrase for 'ships carrying cargoes or passengers'.[34] But the proposal was not accepted in either Article 41 in the Informal Single Negotiating Text or the final Article 42 of UNCLOS.[35] The expression 'in form of in fact' corresponds to the terminology of the other non-discrimination provisions in UNCLOS. In applying this provision it is understood that 'by implication, article 42(2), allows discrimination against all foreign ships provided there is no discrimination *among* them, but this would appear to be of little relevance in practice'.[36]

28 *Ibid.*, Art 42(1)(a) and (b).
29 *Ibid.*, Art 41(3) and (4).
30 *Ibid.*, Art 53(9).
31 *Ibid.*, Art 42(1)(b).
32 *Ibid.*, Art 42(2).
33 A/AC/.138/SC. II/ L.28, Art 37, para 3, reproduced in III SBC Report 1973, at 35, 50 (Malta).
34 A/CONF.62/C. 2/L.16 (1974), Art 22, para 3, III Off. Rec. 192 (Malaysia, Morocco, Oman and Yemen).
35 A/CONF.62/WP.8/Part II (ISNT, 1975), Art 41, IV Off Rec 152, 158 (Chairman, Second Committee).
36 Nandan and Rosenne, *supra* note 21 at 377.

From the perspective of the non-discrimination principle, the limit of the laws and regulations by coastal States on transit passage is consistent with innocent passage.[37] From the perspective of suspension, there is a difference. Article 25(1) of UNCLOS allows a coastal State to take necessary steps in its territorial sea to prevent non-innocent passage, but according to Article 44, there shall be no suspension of transit passage in straits used for international navigation.[38] A proposal submitted by Malta concerning Article 43 required user States to provide compensation to States bordering straits without discrimination.[39] This, however, was regarded as a voluntary choice rather than a compulsory duty. In addition, archipelagic sea lanes passage is very similar to transit passage given that Article 54 sets out that most of the provisions on transit passage apply to archipelagic sea lanes passage, including Article 42(2) on non-discrimination.

3.3 *Freedom of Navigation on the High Seas and in the EEZ*

Freedom of navigation is one of the oldest and most recognised principles in the legal regime governing ocean space, upon which the modern international law of the sea has been built. As a principle of customary international law, ships flying the flag of any sovereign State shall not suffer interference from other States. This principle constitutes the origin and one of the pillars of the law of the sea;[40] however, the advent of the EEZ regime has complicated the situation in some cases. Embodied in UNCLOS, the principle of freedom of navigation was codified in Article 38 (freedom of navigation in straits used for international navigation), Article 53 (archipelagic sea lanes passage through archipelagic waters), Article 58 (freedom of navigation in the EEZ), and Article 87 (freedom of navigation on the high seas) and together became part of the broader body of laws of the sea with ample reference.

According to Article 86, the scope of high seas means all parts of the sea that are not included in the EEZ, in the territorial sea or in the internal waters of a State, or in the archipelagic waters of an archipelagic State. Article 87

37 UNCLOS, *supra* note 2, Art 42(2), 'such laws and regulations shall not discriminate in form or in fact among foreign ships or in their application have the practical effect of denying, hampering or impairing the right of transit passage as defined in this section'.

38 Nandan and Rosenne, *supra* note 21 at 377.

39 '[S]tate or States may request the international ocean space institutions to establish an equitable charge payable without discrimination by all vessels or by all vessel of the relevant class or type, as the case may be, using the strait'. See A/AC/138/SC.II/L.28, Art 39(1) and Art 40(2)-(4), reproduced in III SBC Report 1973, at 35, 51 (Malta).

40 For the principle of freedom of navigation, see Becker, *supra* note 17 at 131–230.

stipulates that freedom of navigation on the high seas is listed on the first among six types of freedoms. Freedom of navigation shall be exercised 'under the conditions laid down by this Convention and by other rules of international law' by all States, whether coastal or land-locked, and their performance shall have due regard for the interests of other States' activities on the high seas and rights with regard to activities in the Area. Consequently, all States enjoy freedom of navigation on the high seas, but such freedom is subject to the general responsibility under international law, which requires the flag State to act in conformity with its international obligations. Those obligations include responsibilities relating to the prevention, reduction and control of pollution of the marine environment (set out in Part XII).

Articles 56 and 58 of UNCLOS established the substantive regime of the EEZ. As a newly created extended maritime zone under the international law of the sea, the EEZ connects the rights and duties of both coastal States and other States. Article 58 outlines the rights and duties of other States in the EEZ and mandates a similar obligation upon maritime States to have 'due regard' to the rights and duties of the coastal State. Articles 56 and 58 strike a balance between the interests of the coastal States and the right to the freedom of navigation of all other States. The two provisions mandate that coastal and maritime States shall mutually respect each other's rights and duties in the EEZ. However, differences in interpretation are not surprising.

The cross-reference to Articles 88 to 115 in Article 58 applies certain high seas provisions to the EEZ, so long as they are compatible with the regime. Flag States enjoy the freedom of navigation referred to in Article 87 of UNCLOS in the EEZ and shall comply with the laws and regulations concerning prevention, reduction and control of pollution adopted by the coastal State in accordance with UNCLOS.[41] The following part will discuss provisions in the regime of Part XII with regard to vessel-source pollution, with emphasis added to their application by coastal States in the EEZ.

3.4 *Part XII on Vessel-source Pollution and Article 234*

Part XII contains detailed provisions on legislative and enforcement jurisdiction of flag States, port States and coastal States with regard to vessel-source pollution.

Flag States enjoy legislative jurisdiction for controlling vessel-source pollution. According to Articles 194(3) and 211(2) of UNCLOS, flag States are obligated to adopt laws and regulations for preventing vessel-source pollution, and such laws and regulations shall at least have the same effect as the GAIRS.

41 UNCLOS, *supra* note 2, Art 211(5).

In addition, Article 217 of UNCLOS reaffirms the rule that flag States have primary responsibility for the effective enforcement of vessel-source pollution regulations.

As for port States, their legislative jurisdiction is 'subject to the basic rules for the innocent passage of foreign ships in the territorial sea',[42] and they are entitled to exercise enforcement jurisdiction for supplementing the jurisdiction of flag States. Article 211(3) of UNCLOS stipulates that port States in the exercise of their legislative jurisdiction are subject to several conditions, as follows: any regulation shall be given due publicity and such communication must be made to the 'competent international organization'; and when two or more coastal States enter into a cooperative arrangement in an endeavour to harmonise their identical policy, the communication shall indicate which States are engaging in such cooperative arrangements. In addition, according to Article 218 of UNCLOS, port States are entitled to exercise enforcement jurisdiction over foreign vessels for violations of 'applicable international rules and standards established through the competent international organization or general diplomatic conference'. To enhance port State jurisdiction in Article 218, Article 219 further confers port States, subject to section 7, to take administrative measures based on international rules and standards with regard to the seaworthiness of vessels as a means of avoiding damage to the marine environment.

Coastal States are entitled by Article 211(4), (5), (6) of UNCLOS to exercise prescriptive jurisdiction on vessel-source pollution in order to implement the GAIRS. Foreign-flagged vessels are obliged to comply with such laws, which may be enforced by the coastal States under the conditions specified in Article 220 and subject to the safeguards in section 7 of Part XII of UNCLOS.

Article 211(4) stipulates that coastal States are entitled to adopt laws and regulations for preventing marine pollution from foreign vessels exercising innocent passage in their territorial sea. Such laws and regulations shall be given due publicity, without discrimination in form or in fact and not hamper innocent passage of foreign vessels.

In contrast to innocent passage in the territorial sea, the rest of Article 211 of UNCLOS clearly reflects a system entailing primacy of international rules and standards, with provision for regional and local variations from the global regime.[43] Article 211(1) stresses the priority of international rules and standards for the control of vessel-source pollution. Article 211(5) reiterates the requirement of the laws and regulations adopted by the coastal State to give

42 Nandan and Rosenne, *supra* note 21 at 203.

43 *Ibid.* at 200.

effect to the GAIRS applicable in the EEZ.[44] Article 211(6) authorises coastal States to adopt more stringent 'mandatory measures' for clearly-defined particular areas in their EEZ if required 'for recognized technical reasons in relation to the coastal State's oceanographical and ecological conditions, as well as the utilization or protection of the resources of that zone and the particular character of its traffic'.[45] These laws and regulations have special procedural requirements, including that coastal States shall publicise the limits of any such clearly defined particular area, coastal States shall take appropriate consultations with other States concerned and get agreement from the competent international organisation (refers to the IMO), and these laws and regulations shall become applicable 15 months after the submission.[46] In addition, such additional laws and regulations 'shall not require foreign vessels to observe design, construction, manning or equipment standards other than the GAIRS'.[47]

On the other hand, if a foreign vessel violates the laws and regulations adopted by a coastal State for preventing vessel-source pollution in its territorial seas, the coastal State may conduct a physical inspection, and may, where the evidence so warrants, institute proceedings, including detention of the vessel, based on its laws, subject to the provisions of section 7.[48]

If a foreign vessel violates any of the laws and regulations adopted by a coastal State for preventing vessel-source pollution in its EEZ, the coastal State is provided with a set of choices concerning enforcement. If there exists 'clear grounds for believing' such a violation has occurred, the coastal State is entitled to require the foreign vessel to provide relevant information to establish whether a violation has occurred.[49] If there exists a substantial discharge causing or threatening significant pollution of the marine environment, the coastal State is entitled to undertake physical inspection of the vessel (Article 220(5)). Only when there is clear objective evidence that a foreign vessel has committed a violation resulting in a discharge causing major damage or threat of major damage to the coastline or related interests of the coastal State, a coastal State may, subject to section 7, provided that the evidence so warrants, institute proceedings, including detention of the vessel, in accordance with its laws.

44 *Ibid.* at 204.

45 UNCLOS, *supra* note 2, Art 211(6)(a).

46 *Ibid.*, Art 211(6)(a), (b) and (c).

47 *Ibid.*, Art 211(6)(c).

48 *Ibid.*, Art 220(2).

49 *Ibid.*, Art 220(3).

Article 234 of UNCLOS was negotiated to grant Arctic coastal States broader environment jurisdiction. According to Article 234, a coastal State is entitled to adopt and enforce within the limits of its EEZ its own non-discriminatory laws and regulations for prevention, reduction and control of marine pollution. It constitutes a *lex specialis* regarding the coastal State's jurisdiction to protect the marine environment in the polar areas, overriding paragraphs 5 and 6 of Article 211.[50]

Furthermore, both legislative and enforcement jurisdiction shall be exercised in a non-discriminatory manner that is set out in Article 227, including the special jurisdiction conferred by Article 234.

In the legislative history of Article 227, the draft convention incorporated a principle that standards adopted by States concerning pollution from vessels 'must not be discriminatory in their application'.[51] The Drafting Committee even recommended the wording change of Article 227 from 'of' to 'with respect to' foreign vessels.[52] This would eliminate any ambiguity and clarify that States should apply this provision against foreign vessels in a non-discriminatory manner, and *vise versa*.[53] The phrase 'against vessels of any other state' should be interpreted as 'either forms of discrimination—between foreign and flag state's vessels and among different foreign vessels'.[54] The phrase 'in form or in fact' is consistent with the terminology of other non-discrimination provisions in UNCLOS.

The 'in fact or in form' requirement is the most important expression to emphasise the quality of non-discrimination as to whether the laws and regulations comply with or are not consistent with the GAIRS. The non-discrimination rule does not restrict the creeping jurisdiction of coastal States but requires that their considerations are objective and applied in the same way between domestic and foreign vessels or among foreign vessels. Furthermore, the provisions explicitly prohibit discrimination 'in form or in fact' require a coastal State not to discriminate, either directly or indirectly. If such discrimination is the consequence of a prescription based solely on reasons related to the prevention, reduction, and control of marine pollution and without differentiation of the nationality of the vessels, then the indirect discrimination

50 Shabtai Rosenne and Alexander Yankov (eds), *United Nations Convention on the Law of the Sea 1982: A Commentary, Vol IV* (Martinus Nijhoff Publishers, 1990) at 393.

51 A/AC. 138/SC.III/L. 52/Add. 1, Annex 1 (WG. 2/Paper No.15, Section IV, Alternatives A, para 2, and C, para 2), reproduced in I SBC Report 1973, at 91, 98, 100 (Chairman, WG.2).

52 A/CONF.62/L.152/Add.25 (1982, mimeo.) at 24.

53 Rosenne and Yankov, *supra* note 50 at 347.

54 Bartenstein, *supra* note 8 at 41.

is arguably justified. The State adopting such laws and regulations should bear the burden of proof showing that the discrimination is a non-intended side effect when an indirect discrimination measure is challenged by a State suggesting violation of the non-discrimination rule.[55] Consequently, Article 234 on ice-covered areas confers coastal States with special legislative and enforcement jurisdiction on vessel-source pollution, which are still subject to the general principle on non-discrimination that is set out in Article 227.

As can be seen, UNCLOS is designed to strike a balance between the coastal States' jurisdictional power and free movement of ships in various maritime zones. With respect to the exercise of jurisdictional power, the non-discrimination rule needs to be observed. Considering the delicate balance between various navigational regimes and environment protection requirements under UNCLOS, it is vital to interpret the relevant provisions and to maintain the free flow of international transportation through the world oceans without causing pollution to the marine environment. This is particularly significant with regard to the Arctic shipping. Within this context, the next section will look at the application of the non-discrimination rule by the Arctic coastal States.

4 National Legislation and the Non-discrimination Rule

With their legislative and enforcement jurisdictional competence, coastal States show an increased interest in enforcing laws and regulations to regulate navigation safety and vessel-source pollution in their maritime zones. Similarly, the Arctic States have paid much greater attention than before to the increasing geopolitical importance of the Arctic with a comprehensive view on the challenges and opportunities in developing and managing this unique environment. Essentially, their control over the Arctic waters and navigation of foreign ships are not significantly different than those that are applied elsewhere in the world. Following or deviating from the relevant provisions of the UNCLOS international framework, they allow foreign ships to enjoy the right of innocent passage in the territorial sea. Under the transit passage regime, their jurisdictional powers are limited, but they may still impose controls on transiting ships to control navigation safety and pollution risks to protect the fragile Arctic environment.[56]

---

55 *Ibid.*

56 This raises the issue of whether there are any straits used for international navigation in either the Northern Sea Route or the Northwest Passage. USA has argued there is, but

Nevertheless, with regard to Arctic shipping, the five Arctic coastal States vary in their national stance and State practice. Denmark announced its strategy in 2011 to promote a peaceful, secure and safe Arctic through close international cooperation, not only to deal with global challenges, but also to safeguard Denmark's interests.[57] Norway adopted its Arctic Policy in 2005 and a specific one for 2014 and beyond.[58] The United States adopted two initiatives to highlight the importance of rights and freedoms for the free movement of ships through the Arctic waters. One is the 2009 'Arctic Region Policy', which asserts that: '[f]reedom of the seas is a top national priority. The Northwest Passage is a strait used for international navigation, and the Northern Sea Route includes straits used for international navigation; the regime of transit passage applies to passage through those straits….'[59] This policy directive also stresses the need to develop new measures to improve the safety and security of maritime transportation, such as ships routing and reporting.[60] Another initiative is the 2013 'National Strategy for the Arctic Region', which confirms its priority and approach to freedom of navigation in the Arctic Ocean and interests in seeking to 'Preserve Arctic Region Freedom of the Seas'.[61] It claims that 'the United States has a national interest in preserving all of the rights, freedoms and uses of the sea and airspace recognized under international law…. Existing international law provides a comprehensive set of rules governing the rights, freedoms, and uses of the world's oceans and airspace, including the Arctic…. We will also encourage other nations to adhere to internationally accepted principles'.[62]

As the only two States that have adopted specific legislation to control the Arctic shipping routes, Russia and Canada have utilised their broad and far-reaching jurisdiction to specify prescriptive competences over a series of

---

Russians and Canadians disagree. See J Ashley Roach and Robert W Smith (eds), *Excessive Maritime Claims* 3rd ed, (Martinus Nijhoff Publishers, 2012) 312–328.

57 Denmark, Greenland and the Faroe Islands (2011): Kingdom of Denmark Strategy for the Arctic 2011–2020, accessed 17 March 2017 at http://naalakkersuisut.gl/~/media/Nanoq/Images/Udenrigsdirektoratet/100295_Arktis_Rapport_UK_210x270_Final_Web.pdf.

58 'Norway's Arctic Policy for 2014 and beyond—a Summary, accessed 17 March 2017 at https://www.regjeringen.no/en/dokumenter/report_summary/id2076191/.

59 United States, Arctic Region Policy, National Security Presidential Directive (NSPD)—66; Homeland Security Presidential Directive (HSPD)—25 (9 January 2009) at para III.B.5, accessed 17 March 2017 at http://www.fas.org/irp/offdocs/nspd/nspd-66.htm.

60 *Ibid.* at para III.F.3.

61 *Ibid.* at 6–7.

62 Donald R Rothwell, 'The United States and Arctic Straits: The Northwest Passage and the Bering Strait' in Suzanne Lalonde and Ted L McDorman (eds), *International Law and Politics of the Arctic Ocean: Essays in Honor of Donat Pharand* (Brill Nijhoff, 2015) 160–179.

matters with special laws and regulations to take stringent control over the available Northern Sea Route (NSR) and Northwest Passage (NWP).[63] Both Russia and Canada claim that their special rights are conferred from Article 234 of UNCLOS in regulating the access system, waste discharge standards, reporting, icebreaking and piloting assistance etc., but the question is whether their claims operate within the parameters of Article 234, and how the non-discrimination rule is reflected or limited in their national legislation. This part will focus on the governing regime of Russia and Canada for their Arctic waters, especially within the context of the recent changes.

4.1 *Russia's National Legislation and Application of the Non-discrimination Rule*

In the late 1980s, the Russian Federation adopted regulations to stipulate safety and pollution-prevention requirements for shipping vessels using the NSR.[64]

---

63 The Northern Sea Route is a shipping lane officially defined by Russian legislation from the Kara Sea to the Pacific Ocean specifically running along the Russian Arctic coast from Kara Gates strait between the Barents Sea and the Kara Sea, along Siberia, to the Bering Strait. The entire route lies in Arctic waters and within Russia's EEZ. Parts are free of ice for only two months per year. Before the beginning of the 20th century it was called the Northeast Passage, and is still sometimes referred to by that name. The Northwest Passage is a sea route connecting the northern Atlantic and Pacific Oceans through the Arctic Ocean, along the northern coast of North America via waterways through the Canadian Arctic Archipelago. The various islands of the archipelago are separated from one another and from the Canadian mainland by a series of Arctic waterways collectively known as the Northwest Passages or Northwestern Passages. The Parliament of Canada renamed these waterways the 'Canadian Northwest Passage' in a motion that was passed unanimously in December 2009. On the other hand, the United States has consistently held the position that the Northwest Passage is an international strait in its entirety. See the Note Verbale of the US Embassy to Canada (19 March 2010) 'Subject: *Canada Gazette*, Part I, Saturday, February 27th, 2010, Vol. 144, No. 9: proposed Northern Canada Vessel Traffic Services Zone Regulations'. For discussions, see R Douglas Brubaker, 'The Arctic—Navigational Issues under International Law of the Sea' (2010) 2 *The Yearbook of Polar Law* 7; Peter Luttmann, 'Ice-Covered Areas under the Law of the Sea Convention: How Extensive Are Canada's Coastal State Powers in the Arctic?' (2015) 29 *Ocean Yearbook* 85–124; Donat Pharand, 'The Arctic Waters and the Northwest Passage: A Final Revisit' (2007) 38 *Ocean Development and International Law*; Bartenstein, *supra* note 8.

64 The major regulations include: 1990 Rules for Navigation on the Seaways of the Northern Sea Route (1990 Rules); 1996 Guide for Navigation on the Seaways of the Northern Sea Route; 1996 Regulations for Icebreaking and Pilot Guiding of vessels; 1996 Requirements for the Design, Equipment and Supply of Vessels Navigating the Northern Sea Route. For the text of these regulations, see http://www.arctic-lio.com/nsr_legislation, accessed 17 March 2017.

The initiative signified the development of the NSR as a domestic waterway to allow foreign ships to navigate the route and application of its jurisdictional competence over the subset of Northeast Passage. Since then, Russia has maintained the management under this legislation to regulate navigation safety and pollution prevention from the transiting ships. These regulations largely remain the same except for the ever-increasing fees levied for icebreaker assistance.

Since July 2012, Russia has developed a new regime governing Arctic shipping. First, they adopted Amendments relating to regulations of merchant shipping in the water area of the northern sea route (2012 Amendments).[65]

In January 2013, the Rules of Navigation on the Water Area of the Northern Sea Route (2013 NSR Rules) were enacted to provide detailed regulations for matters concerning permitting, reporting and icebreaking assistance.[66] It is worth mentioning that a differentiated fee for icebreaker assistance between foreign and Russian vessels was removed by the 2014 Order of Federal Tariff Service (2014 Order).[67] These new regulations clarify the scope of the Russian Arctic waters and its jurisdiction,[68] introduce the permits for navigation with certain requirements,[69] and implement the limited mandatory

65 Clause 5.1(1) Navigation in the water area of the Northern Sea Route. See the Russian Federal Law on Amendments to Specific Legislation Acts of the Russian Federation Related to Governmental Regulation of Merchant Shipping in the Water Area of the Northern Sea Route (2012) (2012 Amendments), accessed 17 March 2017 at http://www.arctic-lio.com/nsr_legislation.

66 2013 NSR Rules, accessed 17 March 2017 at http://www.arctic-lio.com/nsr_legislation.

67 2014 Order, accessed 17 March 2017 at http://www.arctic-lio.com/nsr_legislation.

68 2012 Amendments, *supra* note 65, Clause 5.1, Item 1, 'The water area of the Northern Sea Route shall be considered as the water area adjacent to the Northern coast of the Russian Federation, comprising the internal sea waters, the territorial sea, the adjacent zone and the exclusive economic zone of the Russian Federation and confined in the East with the Line of Maritime Demarcation with the United States of America and Cape Dezhnev parallel in Bering Strait, with the meridian of Cape Mys Zhelania to the Novaya Zemlya Archipelago in the West, with the eastern coastline of the Novaya Zemlya Archipelago and the western borders of Matochkin Strait, Kara Strait and Yugorski Shar'.

69 *Ibid.*, Clause 5.1, Item 4, 'Permits for navigation in the water area of the Northern Sea Route as provided for by Subitem 1, Item 3 of this Clause are issued if the vessel complies with the requirements related to navigation safety and marine environment protection from pollution by vessels (associated with the water area of the Northern Sea Route) and the rules of navigation in the water area of the Northern Sea Route as established by international agreements of the Russian Federation, the law of the Russian Federation, the Regulations for navigation in the water area of the Northern Sea Route specified in Item 2 of this Clause and submits the documents to confirm insurance required by international

icebreaking pilotage services.[70] In addition, Russia has also established a new 'Administration of the Northern Sea Route' to oversee the implementation matters along the shipping route.[71]

The 2014 Order introduced three major changes governing Russian's Arctic waters. First, the scope of Russian Arctic waters is clarified according to paragraph 1 of Clause 5.1 of the 2012 Amendments.[72] It clearly excludes its application to the high seas with specific marks for the individual directional boundary. Second, it introduces a new permit regime for navigation with certain requirements.[73] Third, the most important change is the implementation of limited mandatory icebreaking pilotage services. That is, the provision of icebreaking pilotage services will depend on the ice conditions rather than be mandatory, and the payment will be charged according to the actual amount of service hours delivered.[74] In practical terms, the payment should take into account 'the capacity of ship, ice class of ship, distance of the escorting and

agreements of the Russian Federation, the law of the Russian Federation, or other financial security of civil liability against damage caused by pollution or other damage caused by the vessel.' 2013 NSR Rules, *supra* note 66, Art (2)(2), 'In the water area of the Northern Sea Route the authorization-based order of the navigation of ships is in force'.

70 2012 Amendments, *supra* note 65, Clause 5.1, Item 5.

71 Northern Sea Route Administration, accessed 17 March 2017 at http://www.arctic-lio.com/nsr_nsra.

72 2012 Amendments, *supra* note 65, Clause 5.1, Item 1, 'The water area of the Northern Sea Route shall be considered as the water area adjacent to the Northern coast of the Russian Federation, comprising the internal sea waters, the territorial sea, the adjacent zone and the exclusive economic zone of the Russian Federation and confined in the East with the Line of Maritime Demarcation with the United States of America and Cape Dezhnev parallel in Bering Strait, with the meridian of Cape Mys Zhelania to the Novaya Zemlya Archipelago in the West, with the eastern coastline of the Novaya Zemlya Archipelago and the western borders of Matochkin Strait, Kara Strait and Yugorski Shar'.

73 *Ibid.*, Clause 5.1, Item 4, 'Permits for navigation in the water area of the Northern Sea Route as provided for by Subitem 1, Item 3 of this Clause are issued if the vessel complies with the requirements related to navigation safety and marine environment protection from pollution by vessels (associated with the water area of the Northern Sea Route) and the rules of navigation in the water area of the Northern Sea Route as established by international agreements of the Russian Federation, the law of the Russian Federation, the Regulations for navigation in the water area of the Northern Sea Route specified in Item 2 of this Clause and submits the documents to confirm insurance required by international agreements of the Russian Federation, the law of the Russian Federation, or other financial security of civil liability against damage caused by pollution or other damage caused by the vessel.' 2013 NSR Rules, *supra* note 66, Art (2)(2), 'In the water area of the Northern Sea Route the authorization-based order of the navigation of ships is in force'.

74 2012 Amendments, *supra* note 65, Clause 5.1, Item 5.

period of navigation'.[75] The administrative authority will publicise information on the necessity of icebreaking pilotage services based on the required 'sections' and 'period' of navigation when it issues the permits of navigation.[76] In comparison with the previous vague regulations for icebreaking pilotage services, the 2014 Order specifies four classes of ships that can conduct independent navigation on the NSR according to their respective criteria.[77]

The 2013 NSR Rules allow for special regimes applicable for the Arctic shipping routes, even though the entire route lies in its EEZ where all foreign vessels enjoy freedom of navigation. While Russia's jurisdictional powers are limited by UNCLOS, Russia may still impose controls on navigation under Article 234 due to the special conditions of the Arctic waters and environmental concerns in case of incidents.

The 2013 NSR Rules stipulate that icebreaking pilotage services have to be rendered by Russian icebreakers. The requirements indicate that this will be applicable to any transiting foreign ships. If judged within the context of the non-discrimination rule, the introduction of a mandatory pilotage system may become a controversial issue arguably as a requirement of discrimination in form, and may open for further legal reasoning.[78]

Moreover, the 1990 Rules include a requirement that the commanding personnel of the vessel shall be experienced in operating a vessel in ice. If these persons have no such experience, the Administration may assign a State Pilot

75 2013 NSR Rules, *supra* note 66, Art 24, 'In compliance with item 5 of article 51 of CCN the fee rate of the icebreaker assistance of ship in the water area of the Northern Sea Route is determined according to the legislation of the Russian Federation about natural monopolies taking into account the capacity of ship, ice class of ship, distance of the escorting and period of navigation.' *Ibid.*, Art 32, 'In compliance with item 5 of article 51 of CCN fee rate for the pilot ice assistance in the water area of the Northern Sea Route is determined in accordance with legislation of the Russian Federation about natural monopolies taking into account the capacity of ship, ice class of ship, distance of the escorting and period of navigation'.

76 *Ibid.*, Art 10(6), '[I]nformation on the need of icebreaker assistance of ship under heavy, medium and light ice conditions with the indication of sections of the water area of the Northern Sea Route (south-western part of the Kara Sea, north-eastern part of the Kara Sea, western part of the East Siberian Sea, eastern part of the East Siberian Sea, western part of the Laptev Sea, eastern part of the Laptev Sea, Chukchi Sea) and period of navigation indicated in annex 2 to the present Rules, when ship is to navigate under the icebreaker assistance'.

77 *Ibid.*, Criteria for independent navigation on the NSR (July–November, Summer) Annex No 2.

78 2013 NSR Rules, *supra* note 66, Art 21, 'Icebreaker assistance is rendered by the icebreakers authorized to navigate under the State flag of the Russian Federation.'

to guide the navigation.[79] This requirement was not included in the 2013 NSR Rules, and it raises the question of whether this change means that as a practical matter the Russian government has not given up its mandatory icebreaking pilotage.

In order to answer the question, the purpose of the icebreaking pilotage services needs to be examined. Article 31 of the 2013 NSR Rules states its objectives as 'ensuring safety of the navigation of ships and prevention of accidents as well as protection of the marine environment'.[80] Annex 1 also requires the vessels to apply the navigation permits by providing 'information on length of experience with ship master of navigation in ice in the water area of the NSR as a master or chief'.[81] Such information is crucial for the Administrative authority to make the decision.[82] Furthermore, regulations on the qualifications of the pilot indicate that there is a direct relation between the master's or chief's navigation experience and the assignment of pilot ice assistance.[83]

When judged by these specifications, the new regime aims to provide broader discretion over whether a particular vessel requires the icebreaking pilotage services rather than simply make the services mandatory. The Russian administration will determine whether to render the service and assign a state pilot. These requirements raise the potential for discrimination in fact to exist, and they could be open to challenge.

A situation could raise the question on how to properly balance the rights of coastal States and user States, so as to ensure the application of coastal States' legislative and enforcement jurisdiction consistent with the spirit of UNCLOS. Other factors that may be considered contrary to the non-discrimination rule include the provision stipulating preferential treatment in the acquisition of

79 1990 Rules, *supra* note 64, Art 4.

80 2013 NSR Rules, *supra* note 66, Art 31, 'Pilot ice assistance of ships is carried out with the purpose of ensuring safety of the navigation of ships and prevention of accidents as well as protection of the marine environment in the water area of the Northern Sea Route.'

81 *Ibid.*, Annex I, Item 13.

82 *Ibid.*, Art 3.

83 *Ibid.*, Art 33, 'Person carrying out the pilot ice assistance of ships authorized for the pilot ice assistance in the water area of the Northern Sea Route with a service record not less than for three years as ship master or chief mate on sea ships with a capacity of 3000 t and more out of which at least six months of the navigation of ship under ice conditions and being worker of the organization rendering services of the pilot ice assistance of ships in the water area of the Northern Sea Route (hereinafter referred to as ice pilot) gives recommendations to ship master during the navigation of ship under ice conditions in the water area of the Northern Sea Route'.

the master's or chief's experiences, as it makes no distinction on the 'legitimate' requirements that may constitute discrimination contrary to the UNCLOS.

The UNCLOS navigation regime is based on the principle of equality between the coastal and user States. However, taking into account the safety and environmental concerns, UNCLOS allows coastal States exceptions for legislative and enforcement jurisdiction in maritime zones, including the EEZ where foreign ships enjoy freedom of navigation under Articles 58 and 87. There is potential for coastal States to abuse their rights in implementing preferential provisions and differential treatment when considering objective and reasonable applications, but it would be rather difficult to identify when different treatment constitutes discrimination or violates the non-discrimination principle. The difficulty lies in fact that a distinction is discriminatory if it 'has no objective and reasonable justification', that is, if it does not pursue a 'legitimate aim' or if there is not a 'reasonable relationship of proportionality between the means employed and the aim sought to be realized'. It remains to be determined whether the experience requirements in the legislation have legitimate aims or whether they are discriminatory.

4.2 *Canada's National Legislation and Application of the Non-discrimination Rule*

Similar to Russia, Canada has also adopted a series of national laws with regard to navigation matters within the NWP. These national laws consist of regulatory regimes directly governing Arctic shipping and vessel-source pollution and associated regulations, which includes the Arctic Waters Pollution Prevention Act (AWPPA). This act has been the most important piece of national legislation for the prevention of pollution from vessels in Canadian Arctic waters; it was enhanced in 2014 through implementation regulations.[84] A number of pieces of legislation at the national level bear indirect implications for different aspects of the Arctic shipping, such as the Shipping Act of Canada (CSA), 2001, Marine Liability Act, Marine Transportation Security Act, Coastal Trade Act, Labour Code, and the updated NORDREG Regulations.[85]

The AWPPA was first adopted in 1970 and applied up to 100 nm from the Canadian coast.[86] The legislation served in fact as the driving force for the

84 For AWPPA, see https://www.tc.gc.ca/eng/marinesafety/debs-arctic-acts-regulations-awppa-494.htm, accessed 17 March 2017.

85 For Arctic shipping, see https://www.tc.gc.ca/eng/marinesafety/debs-arctic-menu-303.htm, accessed 17 March 2017.

86 AWPPA (RSC, 1985, c A-12), Art 3(1), accessed 17 March 2017 at https://www.tc.gc.ca/eng/acts-regulations/acts-1985ca-12.htm.

introduction of Article 234, but it has been modified to be in conformity with Article 234.[87] In 2009, Canada expanded the geographical scope of AWPPA to cover the Arctic waters up to 200 nm as the outermost limits of its EEZ.[88] It is worth noting that under the AWPPA, the Arctic waters include three types of maritime zones, including internal waters, territorial sea, and EEZ. As such, this Act is regarded as applicable to the water areas entirely under Canadian jurisdiction.

To implement the AWPPA, Canada adopted two major sets of regulations that merit a fuller discussion. The first is the Arctic Shipping Pollution Prevention Regulations (ASPPR); the second is the Arctic Waters Pollution Prevention Regulations (AWPPR). The AWPPA and the AWPPR ensure the right of Canada to enforce pollution control regulations on ships passing through the Canadian Arctic waters. The former in particular, adopts a stringent vessel deposit standard for waste control in the Arctic waters.[89] Vessel owners carrying cargoes are required to provide evidence of financial responsibility (insurance, indemnity bond) when the vessels approach or navigate through any shipping safety

87 Canada has expressly conditioned its acceptance of MARPOL as being without prejudice to the standards it adopts in respect of its Arctic waters. For the Declaration of Canada made on accession to MARPOL (16 November 1992) accessed 17 March 2017 at http://www.imo.org/About/Conventions/StatusOfConventions/Pages/Default.aspx.

88 An Act to Amend the Arctic Waters Pollution Prevention Act (SC 2009, c 11) accessed 17 March 2017 at http://www.laws.justice.gc.ca/eng/AnnualStatutes/2009_11/page-1.html.

89 AWPPA, *supra* note 86, Art 4:

(1) Except as authorized by regulations made under this section, no person or ship shall deposit or permit the deposit of waste of any type in the arctic waters or in any place on the mainland or islands of the Canadian arctic under any conditions where the waste or any other waste that results from the deposit of the waste may enter the arctic waters.

(2) Subsection (1) does not apply to the deposit of waste in waters that form part of a water quality management area designated pursuant to the Canada Water Act if the waste so deposited is of a type and quantity and is deposited under conditions authorized by regulations made under paragraph 18(2)(a) of that Act with respect to that water quality management area.

(3) The Governor in Council may make regulations for the purposes of this section prescribing.

(a) the type and quantity of waste, if any, that may be deposited by any person or ship in the arctic waters or in any place on the mainland or islands of the Canadian arctic under any conditions where that waste or any other waste that results from the deposit of that waste may enter the arctic waters; and.

(b) the conditions under which any such waste may be so deposited.

control zone.[90] With regard to Arctic shipping, both the AWPPA and ASPPR provide for the prescription of shipping safety control zones.[91] Ships have to meet certain requirements relating to the designated standards and icebreaker assistance depending on conditions, if they seek to operate in the specified waters.[92] Currently, the regulations and standards concerning vessel construction incorporate a mix of unique Canadian Arctic Categories (AC&CAC), and Types of Vessel classes in their operation.[93] Vessels designed to any other ice class are only considered for equivalency on a case-by-case basis.[94]

Among the national regulations indirectly applicable to navigating the Canadian part of the Arctic waters, the Canada Shipping Act 2001 (CSA) is the

---

90 *Ibid.*, Art 8:

(1) The Governor in Council may require.

...

(d) the owner of any ship that proposes to navigate or that navigates within any shipping safety control zone specified by the Governor in Council and, subject to subsection 7(4), the owners of the cargo of any such ship, to provide evidence of financial responsibility, in the form of insurance or an indemnity bond satisfactory to the Governor in Council, or in any other form satisfactory to the Governor in Council, in an amount determined in the manner prescribed by regulations made under section 9.

(2) Evidence of financial responsibility in the form of insurance or an indemnity bond shall be in a form that will enable recovery, directly from the proceeds of the insurance or bond, by any person entitled pursuant to section 6 to claim against the person or persons giving that evidence.

91 *Ibid.*, Art 11:

(1) Subject to subsection (2), the Governor in Council may, by order, prescribe as a shipping safety control zone any area of the arctic waters that is specified in the order, and may, as the Governor in Council deems necessary, amend any such area.

(2) A copy of each order that the Governor in Council proposes to make under subsection (1) shall be published in the *Canada Gazette* and no order may be made under that subsection, based on any such proposal, except after the expiration of sixty days following publication of the proposal in the *Canada Gazette*.

92 *Ibid.*, Art 12.

93 ASPPR (CRC, C 353), Annexes V, VI and VII.

94 *Ibid.*, Art 11, 'Where these Regulations require that a particular construction, machinery fitting, appliance, apparatus or material be fitted or carried in a ship or any particular provision to be made in a ship, a pollution prevention officer may allow any other construction, machinery fitting, appliance, apparatus or material to be fitted or carried, or any other provision to be made, if he is satisfied that such other construction, machinery, fitting, appliance, apparatus, material or provision is at least equivalent to that required by these Regulations.'

most important.[95] The CSA applies its pollution prevention regulations and traffic service regulations to vessels within the limits of Canadian jurisdictional waters. The CSA has the same scope of application and legislative authority as the AWPPA, and the two regulations share their function for mutual complementation. The CSA also includes other regulations for the protection of environment from navigation, such as Vessel Pollution and Dangerous Chemicals Regulations and Ballast Water Control and Management Regulations.[96]

In 2010, Canada enacted the Northern Canada Vessel Traffic Services Zone Regulations, 2010 (NORDREG) based on Article 126 of the CSA and made them applicable to the Canadian Arctic waters.[97] When Canada enacted this new mandatory NORDREG to replace its former Regulations[98] in which vessel reporting for the Arctic region was voluntary, it provoked fierce controversy in the Maritime Safety Committee, the highest technical body of the IMO.[99] Some States, including the United States and Singapore, expressed concern that the NORDREG proposed requirements for clearance would hamper the freedom of navigation.[100] In contrast, the Canadian government held that clearance is necessary for prevention of pollution from vessels, because Article 234 of UNCLOS empowers coastal States with ice-covered areas to adopt stricter domestic laws and regulations than those accepted by the international community without referring them to the competent international organisation (the IMO).[101]

95 For more details, see https://www.tc.gc.ca/eng/marinesafety/debs-arctic-acts-regulations-csa-1782.htm, accessed 17 March 2017.

96 For Canadian acts and regulations, see https://www.tc.gc.ca/eng/acts-regulations/menu.htm, accessed 17 March 2017.

97 North Canada Vessel Traffic Service Zone Regulations and 'Order Amending the Shipping Safety Control Zones Order, *Canada Gazette*, Part II, Vol 144, No 13, 23 June 2010'; for more details, see http://www.gazette.gc.ca/archives/p2/2010/index-eng.html, accessed 17 March 2017.

98 These regulations include: *Canada Annual Notice to Mariners 2008*, section 6.1, accessed 17 March 2017 at http://publications.gc.ca/site/eng/9.651093/publication.html; Canadian Coast Guard, Radio Aids to Marine Navigation (Atlantic, St. Lawrence, Great Lakes, Lake Winnipeg and Eastern Arctic), 'Annual Edition 2006,' Part 3, accessed 17 March 2017 at http://www.publications.gc.ca/collections/Collection/T51-4-2006E-0.pdf; *Arctic Ice Regime Shipping System Standards*, Transport Canada publication TP12259E (1988), accessed 17 March 2017 at https://www.tc.gc.ca/eng/marinesafety/tp-tp12259-arctic-ice-regime-2871.htm.

99 IMO Doc MSC 88/26 at 53–56.

100 *Ibid.* at 55.

101 Article 234 of UNCLOS provided for the right of coastal States to adopt and enforce non-discriminatory laws and regulations for the prevention, reduction and control of marine pollution from vessels in ice-covered areas within the limits of the Exclusive Economic

NORDREG applies to vessels over 300 gross tonnage (GT), vessels engaged in towing or pushing other vessels where the combined gross tonnage is 500 GT or more, and vessels carrying or towing vessels carrying cargo pollutants or dangerous goods.[102] This legislation requires ships to provide a detailed sailing plan and report relevant information before entering the NORDREG zone.[103] Under circumstances of safety or environmental concerns, clearance may be granted, or refused, subject to specific conditions. NORDREG requires all prescribed classes of vessels (both Canadian and foreign) to register and report specific information when entering into or transiting through the NORDREG Zone.[104] A severe fine or imprisonment and possible detention of the vessel could be imposed in case of failure to comply with the regulations.

Overall, the regulations implemented by the Canadian authority have been quite domineering, though with clear and specific objectives to 'facilitate the safe and efficient movement of marine traffic'.[105] However, controversies may arise with their practical operation due to undefined terms, etc. In AWPPA, the term 'ship' is loosely defined to include any description of vessel or boat used for navigation, and does not distinguish between government vessels and commercial vessels.[106] The only exception is that those vessels 'owned or operated by a sovereign power' can be exempted from the application of the Shipping Safety Control Zones if the Governor in Council is satisfied that they comply with the relevant conditions in the regulations.[107] Therefore, State-owned

---

Zone, permitting these States to enact these laws and regulations without seeking prior IMO approval—even where IMO had related regulations. See IMO Doc MSC 88/26 at 54 and IMO Doc MSC/88/11/3 at para 5.

102 NORDREG (SOR/2010–127), Art 3.

103 For the specific required information, see http://laws-lois.justice.gc.ca/eng/regulations/SOR-2010-127/FullText.html, accessed 17 March 2017.

104 Canada Shipping Act (SC 2001, c 26), accessed 17 March 2017 at http://laws-lois.justice.gc.ca/eng/acts/C-10.15/page-1.html.

105 See NORDREG objectives, accessed 17 March 2017 at http://laws-lois.justice.gc.ca/eng/regulations/SOR-2010-127/FullText.html.

106 AWPPA, *supra* note 86, Art 2, 'ship' includes any description of vessel or boat used or designed for use in navigation without regard to method or lack of propulsion.

107 *Ibid.*, Art 12:

(2) The Governor in Council may by order exempt from the application of any regulations made under subsection (1) any ship or class of ship that is owned or operated by a sovereign power, other than Canada, where the Governor in Council is satisfied that.

(a) appropriate measures have been taken by or under the authority of that sovereign power to ensure the compliance of the ship with, or with standards substantially equivalent to, standards prescribed by regulations made under paragraph (1)(a) that would otherwise be applicable to it within any shipping safety control zone; and.

vessels may not enjoy sovereign immunity automatically. This may have resulted in discriminatory treatment of foreign-flagged vessels. This issue was later resolved with a positive response from the Canadian government during the debate of NORDREG.[108] The government stated that provisions of the NORDREG do not apply to any warship, naval auxiliary, other vessels or aircraft owned or operated by a State and used, for the time being, only on government non-commercial service.

Another issue that may raise issues of discrimination is the requirement concerning vessel ice classes. Vessels designed for different ice classes may only be considered for equivalency on a case-by-case basis. These regulations and standards have the potential to result in disadvantageous treatment or discrimination in fact against foreign fleets that do not have any vessels qualifying as equivalent to the Canadian classes. If such discrimination is the consequence of prescriptions based solely on reasons related to the prevention, reduction, and control of marine pollution, rather than considerations related to the nationality of the vessels, the indirect discrimination is arguably justified. Yet, if an indirectly discriminating measure was challenged by a State suggesting violation of the non-discrimination rule, Canada would bear the burden of showing that the discrimination is an unintended consequence. Canada could perhaps avoid this issue altogether by modifying its laws and regulations to adopt the prescriptions relating to ships found in the International Association of Classification Societies (IACS) Unified Requirements (UR) for Polar Class ships[109] or the IMO Guidelines for Polar Shipping.[110] However, as the URs and Guidelines for Polar Shipping are only voluntary, it may be worthwhile for Canada to consider modifying its regulations to reflect the forthcoming Polar Code, which contains mandatory construction standards for ships operating in the polar region.[111]

(b) in all other respects all reasonable precautions have been or will be taken to reduce the danger of any deposit of waste resulting from the navigation of the ship within that shipping safety control zone.

108 IMO Doc MSC88/11/3 and IMO Doc MSC 88/11/2.

109 For ISCS URs, see http://www.iacs.org.uk/publications/publications.aspx?pageid=4&sectionid=3, accessed 17 March 2017.

110 For more details on this account, see Guidelines for Ships Operating in Polar Waters (2010 Edition), accessed 17 March 2017 at http://www.imo.org/en/Publications/Documents/Attachments/Pages%20from%20E190E.pdf.

111 Seamus Ryder, 'Breaking Point: A legal analysis of Canadian practice in relation to ice breaking in the Northwest Passage' at 43, accessed 17 March 2017 at http://munin.uit.no/bitstream/handle/10037/6174/thesis.pdf?sequence=1&isAllowed=y.

From the above, it may be seen that the Arctic coastal States, such as Canada and Russia, have tried to strike a balance when dealing with jurisdictional issues regarding Arctic shipping. On the one hand, they are keen to enhance their jurisdiction over Arctic shipping under the 'Arctic provision' in Article 234. Meanwhile, they endeavour to follow reasonably the UNCLOS requirements, at least at the legislative level. The respective adjustment of the geographical scope of their Arctic waters legislation may be seen as indicating that their laws only apply to vessels navigating in the limit of the EEZ.[112] The Russian Federation excludes the application of its regulations on the high seas by marking the boundary in each direction with a specific landmark.[113]

5 The UNCLOS Procedural 'Safeguards' and National Application

To safeguard free movement of ships and ensure non-discrimination, Section 7 of Part XII of UNCLOS provides procedural 'safeguards' to protect the rights of foreign States and their vessels against the abuse of rights by coastal States or port States in the process of exercising their enforcement powers.[114]

5.1 *The UNCLOS Procedural 'Safeguards'*

The UNCLOS 'procedural safeguards' are specified based on various situations. Article 227 clearly underscores that States are not permitted to discriminate in form or in fact in exercising their rights or performing their duties. This prescription incorporates Articles 223 (measures to facilitate proceedings) and 224 (exercise of powers of enforcement), which broadens the scope of the obligations.[115] Article 224 restricts the authorised agency and enforcement ships that can be utilised in exercising enforcement powers against foreign vessels.

Both Articles 228 and 230 are applicable to violations of 'laws and regulations' or 'applicable international rules and standards'. They could also apply

112 AWPPA, *supra* note 86, Art 3(1), accessed 17 March 2017 at http://laws-lois.justice.gc.ca/eng/acts/A-12/page-1.html.

113 It was done by the Russian Federation through amending the rule of navigation for the area, which added Clause 5.1 'Navigation in the water area of the Northern Sea Route'. See the Russian Federation Federal Law on Amendments to Specific Legislation Acts of the Russian Federation Related to Governmental Regulation of Merchant Shipping in the Water Area of the Northern Sea Route, 2012, accessed 17 March 2017 at http://www.arctic-lio.com/nsr_legislation.

114 Rosenne and Yankov, *supra* note 50 at 321.

115 *Ibid.* at 323–324.

to breach of laws and regulations adopted pursuant to Article 234. Article 228 integrates the concept of port State jurisdiction in Article 218 and recognises the primacy of flag State jurisdiction.[116] Throughout Article 218, the violations contemplated are that of 'applicable international rules and standards'. This may be seen as a limitation to the discretion of port State jurisdiction when it transforms the international rules and standards into norms of internal law for procedural purposes (including Article 230 with regard to the penalties), and the same would be true while it takes substantive actions within the scope of Article 218, as they must be directed towards violations of the applicable international rules and standards.[117]

Similar 'safeguards' intention is reflected in Article 226 in two parts: investigation and prompt release procedure (PRP). Article 226(1)(a) requires States not to delay a foreign vessel beyond the period needed for investigation purposes provided for in Articles 216, 218 and 220. Several safeguards in these provisions would apply by analogy to investigations under Article 234. Besides, the basis of physical investigation is the GAIRS. With regard to the PRP, UNCLOS requires the release of detained vessels upon the posting of reasonable bond or other security, provided the vessels have been detained for violation of laws relating to the protection of the marine environment (Articles 220(6) and 226(1)(b)).[118] That means the applicability of PRP could be extended like Article 233 by respecting *mutatis mutandis* the provisions of Section 7 of Part XII of UNCLOS. It may be argued that the PRP also applies to foreign vessels arrested under the laws and regulations adopted under Article 234.

Article 231 requires notification to the flag State of enforcement measures taken against a foreign vessel, and reflects the primacy of the flag State over enforcement jurisdiction, as well as the responsibility of the flag State for the actions of all ships and vessels of their registry of flags and crews. The first sentence of Article 232 restates the general international law of State responsibility.[119] Flag States can apply both by analogy under Article 234.

116 *Ibid.* at 350.

117 *Ibid.* at 272.

118 The Case of the Arctic Sunrise, accessed 17 March 2017 at http://cilj.co.uk/2013/10/31/case-arctic-sunrise/; for comments on prompt release, see Tullio Treves, 'The Proceedings Concerning Prompt Release of Vessels and Crews before the International Tribunal for the Law of the Sea' (1995) 11 *International Journal of Marine and Coastal Law* 179 at 186.

119 Rosenne and Yankov, *supra* note 50 at 380.

5.2 *National Application of the Procedural 'Safeguards'*

Given that the regulations concerning enforcement measures of the Russian Federation are not unclear, this part will focus on the national application of the legal regime of Canada. With regard to procedural safeguards, three situations within the AWPPA provisions may be challenged as being inconsistent with provisions in Part XII of UNCLOS.

First, the Canadian regulations do not distinguish between the different phases of an inspection. A pollution prevention officer may board a foreign vessel within a shipping safety control zone and conduct an inspection for compliance with the standards prescribed by Article 12 of AWPPA.[120] Such enforcement actions can be conducted without any specific requirements on boarding and inspection, and without distinguishing 'physical inspection' and 'further physical inspection' as set out in Article 226 of UNCLOS. Therefore, the inspections could be problematic.

Second, the Canadian regulations do not distinguish between the applicable extent of enforcement. If the officer has a suspicion based on reasonable grounds that there has been a violation of regulations under Article 12(1)(b)(c) of the AWPPA, or that an enforcement action is 'justified in the interests of safety', the officer may order a foreign ship to proceed in such manner as the officer may direct or remain outside the zone when it is near a shipping safety control zone or the officer may order a foreign ship to anchor in a place selected by the officer when it is in a shipping safety control zone.[121] Such classification by 'in or near a shipping safety control zone' and corresponding enforcement measures may be contrary to the stipulations under Articles 220 and 230 of UNCLOS, which provide that enforcement measures should depend upon the location of vessels and the levels of pollution. Moreover, Article 200(6) of UNCLOS requires 'clear objective evidence', whereas the Canadian regulations provide that such enforcement measures largely rely on the officer's subjective judgement.

Finally, the Canadian regulations extend beyond the scope of national jurisdiction. The enforcement officer has the power to 'order any ship to take part in the clean-up of the waste or in any action to control or contain the waste'.[122] The enforcement actions include the imposition of a fine, seizure and forfeiture, but forfeiture will be decided by the court.[123] Such regulations may be contrary to the stipulations under Article 220 of UNCLOS, which provides that

120 AWPPA, *supra* note 86, Art 15(4)(a).

121 *Ibid.*, Art 15(4)(b).

122 *Ibid.*, Art 15(4)(c).

123 *Ibid.*, Art 24.

enforcement measures should be limited to physical inspection and the institution of proceedings, even including detention of the vessel.

6 Interests and Positions of the User States and Safeguards for Equal Treatment

Transit through the Arctic waters did not generate significant attention until 2010, but it has increased steadily since then. Although the newly developed usage of the Arctic passages was not envisaged by the UNCLOS III negotiators, the balance established during the 1970s and codified in UNCLOS is being tested in practice.[124]

6.1 *Interests and Positions of the User States*

With the speedy increase of usage, the Arctic coastal States, especially Canada and the Russian Federation, have adopted more stringent measures to regulate transiting ships. Meanwhile, the States that are interested in the transit of the Arctic shipping routes (user States), particularly the Asian States of China, Japan, Korea, India and Singapore, have started to take a greater interest in the national legislation of the Arctic States.

The Asian user States share common interests in Arctic shipping, but with different emphasis. Since May 2013, China, Japan, Korea, Singapore and India have obtained observer status in the Arctic Council, and have shown an increased interest in the Arctic, especially Japan and Republic of Korea (Korea), who have adopted clear and explicit Arctic Policies.

Korea announced its Arctic Policy (the Master Plan) in December 2013. Its goal is 'to contribute to sustainable future of the Arctic from building a co-operative partnership, enhancing scientific research activities and exploring new business opportunities in the Arctic'.[125] The Master Plan reflects two areas of interest of the Korean government. The first is resource exploration in the Arctic region, and the second is the eventual shipping of these resources via the Arctic Sea Route.[126]

124 Erik Franckx, 'The "New" Arctic Passages and the "Old" Law of the Sea' in Henrik Ringbom (ed), *Jurisdiction over Ships* (Brill Publisher, 2015) 194 at 216.

125 Arctic Policy of the Republic of Korea, accessed 17 March 2017 at http://arcticportal.org/arctic-governance/arctic-policies-database.

126 Aki Tonami, 'Arctic Policies of Japan, South Korea, and Singapore' at 3, accessed 17 March 2017 at https://www.wilsoncenter.org/publication/arctic-policies-japan-south-korea-and-singapore.

Japan presented its first comprehensive Arctic policy in a provisional English version in Tokyo and in Reykjavik at the Arctic Circle Assembly in October 2015.[127] The main objective of the policy is to engage the international community through its actions on Arctic issues. Based on this overall goal, Japan will seek possible economic opportunities to use the Arctic Sea Route for resource development.[128] The Japanese Arctic policy also emphasises active participation in the formulation process of international rules for the Arctic.[129]

The rest of the Asian user States have yet to adopt any official Arctic policies, but their main opinions have been expressed through articles. For example, China, as an important stakeholder in the Arctic, has attracted great attention about its interest in the Arctic. Although, it has not issued any formal national policy document, China follows three principles to guide its Arctic affairs: respect, cooperation and win-win.[130] Singapore stresses that it shares common concerns in the Arctic region on climate change and global warming, and is

127 Japan's Arctic Policy, accessed 17 March 2017 at http://www.kantei.go.jp/jp/singi/kaiyou/arcticpolicy/jpn_arcticpolicy/Japans_Arctic_Policy[ENG].pdf.

128 *Ibid.*, Background and Purpose of Basic Policy, at 2.

129 'As shipping opportunities expand, increasingly active discussions are underway regarding the effect of shipping on the marine environment and on securing the safety of navigation. Japan should participate actively in the international debates regarding the drafting of new rules.' See *ibid.*, Background and Purpose of Basic Policy in 'Japan's Arctic Policy' at 5; 'The International Maritime Organization (IMO) has developed the "Polar Code" … Continue to be an active participant in the discussions based on opinions from related industries.' See *ibid.*, Background and Purpose of Basic Policy in 'Japan's Arctic Policy' at 8.

130 A detailed description about content of the three principles: 'Respect provides the important basis for China's participation in Arctic affairs. China respects Arctic countries' sovereignty, sovereign rights and jurisdiction in the Arctic, and the traditions and culture of Arctic indigenous people. China also believes that the legitimate concerns of non-Arctic countries and the rights they enjoy under international law in the Arctic and the collective interests of the international community should be respected; Cooperation is the fundamental approach China follows in participating in Arctic affairs. China is ready to step up exchanges and cooperation with Arctic countries, non-Arctic countries and other stakeholders and work for concrete outcomes in a wide range of areas including climate change, scientific research, environmental protection, shipping, sustainable development and people-to-people exchanges; Win-win results are the ultimate goals for China's participation in Arctic affairs. The future development of the Arctic bears on the common destiny of mankind. An Arctic that enjoys peace, security and sustainable development serves the interest of the Arctic region and people and the overall interest of the international community. China is ready to work with all parties to share opportunities, jointly meet challenges and strive for win-win results', accessed 17 March 2017 at http://www.gov.cn/guowuyuan/2015-10/19/content_2950053.htm [in Chinese].

interested in technical cooperation and scientific cooperation.[131] Compared with other Asian States that would benefit from the Arctic passage, Singapore's appeal as a port may diminish over time. Given that Singapore is highly dependent on maritime trade, its interests in the Arctic may in some respects be different from that of other Asian countries. India also claims its right of participation in Arctic affairs and shares concerns about the threat of global warming.[132] India expresses its interests in the Arctic region as in 'scientific, environmental, commercial as well as strategic' areas.[133]

Compared with Singapore and India, the three northeast Asian States—China, Japan, and South Korea—show stronger economic expectations to feed their heavy demand for imported mineral and hydrocarbon resources, especially China. In 2015, China started its One Belt One Road (OBOR) initiative that includes the Arctic route as one of its priorities. The Korean government has tried to combine its interests in two areas: resource exploration in the Arctic region, and the eventual shipping of these resources via the Arctic shipping route.[134] Korea proposes to strengthen regional connectivity and to build networks with States along the route named, 'Eurasia-Arctic Route Connectivity'.[135] Japan emphasises issues regarding the safety and environment of Arctic shipping,[136] and seeks possible economic opportunities in Arctic shipping routes and resource development.[137] Japan further stresses its active participation in the process of formulating international rules for the Arctic.[138]

---

131 'What is the connection between Singapore and the Arctic region?', accessed 17 March 2017 at http://www.todayonline.com/commentary/what-connection-between-singapore-and-arctic-region.

132 Government of India Ministry of External Affairs, *India and the Arctic* (New Delhi, 10 June 2013), accessed 17 March 2017 at http://mea.gov.in/in-focus-article.htm?21812/India+and+the+Arctic.

133 *Ibid.*

134 Tonami, *supra* note 126 at 3.

135 Foreign Ministry to Hold an Event on 'Eurasia-Arctic Route Connectivity', accessed 17 March 2017 at http://www.mofa.go.kr/ENG/press/pressreleases/index.jsp?menu=m_10_20&sp=/webmodule/htsboard/template/read/engreadboard.jsp%3FtypeID=12%26boardid=302%26seqno=316630.

136 'Charting Japan's Arctic Strategy', accessed 17 March 2017 at http://www.brookings.edu/~/media/events/2015/10/19-charting-japans-arctic-strategy/taisaku-ikeshima-presentation.pdf.

137 Japan's Arctic Policy, *supra* note 128 at 2.

138 'As shipping opportunities expand, increasingly active discussions are underway regarding the effect of shipping on the marine environment and on securing the safety of navigation. Japan should participate actively in the international debates regarding the drafting of new rules.' See Background and Purpose of Basic Policy in 'Japan's Arctic

6.2 *Procedural Safeguards as a Remedy for the User States*

In general, the Asian user States have not been actively involved in Arctic shipping governance, and none of them have objected to the unilateral environmental measures taken by Russia or Canada in Arctic waters.[139] The user States voiced their views on a few exceptional issues regarding NORDREG[140] and Certification.[141] On the question of whether the NWP is through the internal waters of Canada or an international waterway, China's Foreign Ministry Spokesperson Hua Chunying expressed cautiously that:

> China noted that Canada considers this route as internal waters, while some countries believe it was open for international navigation. We also noted that Canada has imposed some restrictions on the use of the northwest passage, asking foreign vessels to inform the Canadian side and get permission before entering or crossing its exclusive economic zone and territorial waters. The Chinese side will make appropriate decisions by taking into account various factors.[142]

Such an attitude indicates that it is a challenging task for the user States to safeguard their interests in equal treatment in the enforcement procedures of the coastal States.

Policy' at 5; 'The International Maritime Organization (IMO) has developed the "Polar Code" … Continue to be an active participant in the discussions based on opinions from related industries'. See Japan's Arctic Policy, *supra* note 128 at 8.

139 Olav Schram Stokke, 'Asian Stakes and Arctic Governance', 38 *Strategic Analysis* 770 (2014) at 775–777.

140 The delegation of Singapore was of the view that 'Member Governments should follow IMO's guidelines on the preparation and submission of proposals on ship reporting systems for adoption, and encouraged Canada to do the same. The delegation further stated that it was important to ensure that any measures taken did not compromise the freedom of navigation and that it was not clear how the NORDREG's proposed requirement for clearance would adequately give "due regard to navigation", as provided for in UNCLOS.' See MSC 88/26, at 55. And the full text of the statement of the delegation of Singapore is set out in Annex 28.

141 China and Republic of Korea proposed that 'amendments related to certification for existing ships engaged on a single voyage in polar waters and that a short-term Polar Ship Certificate be permitted to be issued by the Administration, in order to reduce the certification burden imposed on the Administrations.' See MSC 94/21, at 12.

142 Foreign Ministry Spokesperson Hua Chunying's Regular Press Conference on 20 April 2016, accessed 17 March 2017 at http://www.fmprc.gov.cn/mfa_eng/xwfw_665399/s2510_665401/2511_665403/t1357177.shtml.

With regard to navigational safety and vessel-source pollution control in the Arctic waters, the UNCLOS safeguards measures in Articles 231 and 232 may be available for the user States as a remedy to ensure the non-discriminatory treatment. As for enforcement measures, user States may apply Article 232 by analogy under Article 234 if they suffer damage or loss due to the enforcement of coastal States. Article 232 provides if the scope of coastal States' enforcement exceeds the 'reasonably required' threshold, they may be liable if their actions are challenged.[143] Article 232 requires States to provide for recourse in their courts for actions in respect of such damage or loss arising from measures that are unlawful or exceed those reasonably required. An action under this article may trigger the application of Article 295 on the exhaustion of local remedies.[144]

In addition to seeking a remedy in a domestic court, Article 292 provides an option for user States if a coastal State has detained a foreign-flagged vessel and has not complied with the prompt release provisions of UNCLOS.[145] In the case of the *Arctic Sunrise*, the Russian Federation did not exercise enforcement measures under Article 234 of UNCLOS.[146] Although in Russia's diplomatic note of 18 September 2013 it explained the reasons leading to the seizure of

143 See Wolfrum, *supra* note 18 at 79–102.

144 Franckx, *supra* note 124 at 216.

145 For discussions, see Heiki Lindpere, 'Prompt Release of Detained Foreign Vessels and Crews in Matters of Marine Environment Protection' (2005) *International Journal of Legal Information*: No 2, Vol 33, accessed 17 March 2017 at http://scholarship.law.cornell.edu/ijli/vol33/iss2/8.

146 The Russian Coast Guard initially justified its order to the master of the *Arctic Sunrise* to stop and allow an inspection by referring to the fact that the actions of the vessel and its boats constituted terrorism. A Russian diplomatic note of 18 September 2013 relied on the same grounds while a court order of 7 October 2013 of a Russian district court concerning the seizure of the *Arctic Sunrise* referred to the provision on piracy contained in the 1958 Convention on the High Seas to which the Russian Federation and the Netherlands are parties. The court order concluded that the Russian Coast Guard took control of the *Arctic Sunrise* in accordance with the Convention on the High Seas 'since there was a reasonable suspicion that the ship was engaged in piracy.' The court order also pointed out that the submitted documents noted that the crew of the *Arctic Sunrise* had attacked the Prirazlomnaya, using threats of violence and using objects as weapons, with the aim of taking possession of property belonging to another person. Finally, the judgment of 8 October by a Coast Guard official and a Russian diplomatic note of 1 October 2013 invoked articles 56 and 60 of the UNCLOS as a basis for the Russian action. See Alex Oude Elferink, 'The Arctic Sunrise Incident and the International Law of the Sea', accessed 17 March 2017 at https://uit.no/Content/361427/The%20Arctic%20Sunrise%20Incident%20and%20ITLOS_final.pdf.

the vessel, including 'possible risk of environmental damage',[147] the Russian Federation did not refer to the provisions under Articles 73 or 220/226 in its later diplomatic notes or the court order or the judgment, nor did it respond to the Netherlands' inquiry for the prompt release of the vessel and its crew by the posting of a bond or other financial security, which would have allowed the Netherlands from having to pursue the prompt release procedure.[148] This situation may be caused by the lack of clear enforcement measures against violation of foreign vessels under its current laws and regulations governing Russian Arctic waters.[149] But if Russia had justified its detention of the *Arctic Sunrise* based on the violation of its laws and regulations under Article 234 of UNCLOS, what would have been the result?

According to the discussion above, some aspects of the approaches of Russia and Canada may lead to violations by coastal States of their obligations under UNCLOS, and because the PRP is subject to the compulsory procedures entailing binding decisions in Section 2, Part XV of UNCLOS, flag States could institute judicial or arbitral proceedings before the International Tribunal of the Law of the Sea (ITLOS) or an arbitral tribunal. It should be noted that under Article 295 of UNCLOS, the exhaustion of local remedies is not a prerequisite for the institution of proceedings for prompt release. The impact of this provision would be softened by the provision that remedies should be exhausted 'as required by international law'. However, any local proceedings would not stand in the way of recourse to the competent international court or tribunal after the peremptory period of 10 days has expired.[150]

147 In the diplomatic note, Russian stated that, 'the actions of the Arctic Sunrise can only be interpreted as a provocation, and exposed the Arctic region to the threat of an ecological disaster with unimaginable consequences'. See Request for Provisional Measures Submitted by the Netherlands, para 23, accessed 17 March 2017 at https://www.itlos.org/fileadmin/itlos/documents/cases/case_no.22/Order/C22_Ord_22_11_2013_orig_Eng.pdf.

148 *Ibid.*, paras 30 and 31.

149 Foreign vessels generally comply with the rules, but it is not clear what will happen when any violation of foreign vessels. See Chapter 6 of this Volume.

150 For a detailed discussion about the '10 days from the time of detention', see Shabtai Rosenne and Louis B Sohn (eds), *United Nations Convention on the Law of the Sea 1982: A Commentary, Vol V* (Martinus Nijhoff Publishers, 1989) at 69.

7 Concluding Remarks

When a legal norm is expressed, it is articulated in a particular manner for a particular purpose. In the context of the non-discrimination rule in ensuring the equal treatment of a foreign ships' navigational rights, it is expressed with certain restrictions (exceptions) for safety concerns and environmental protection needs in direct or indirect ways. The UNCLOS provisions provide ample guidance and establish a set of rules to reduce potential discrimination. It is not difficult to reach a consistent legal interpretation of 'equal treatment' or 'on an equal basis', and coastal States in general, adhere to the non-discrimination rule. However, in the case of jurisdictional and enforcement operations in the maritime zones of ice-covered areas, States have differing, and at times conflicting, interests, and State practice becomes diverse. In light of the ambiguity of the provisions in UNCLOS, and the interests of coastal States in regulating shipping in their Arctic waters, there exists the risk in practice that the equal treatment requirement may become the vehicle for subjective and arbitrary judgments as well as instruments for the effectuation of discriminatory policies which, although not directly apparent on the face of the law, could well be the consequence in their application.

Consistent with its restrictive approach, UNCLOS provides that ships must comply with certain conditions while transiting through sensitive areas such as the Arctic waters. The unique environment in ice-covered areas certainly deserves special considerations, but restrictions on shipping through these areas should not be viewed as the approval of practices that result in an unjustified degree enforcement powers by the coastal States.

In general, the Arctic coastal States have observed the non-discrimination rule, at least in form. But when it comes to the establishment of requirements for foreign ships and determinations on whether they have complied with the laws and procedures of coastal States, such as when a State goes through the formal procedure with the introduction of a compulsory pilotage regime etc., it becomes complicated, and the equal treatment standard may be compromised. The ensuing limitations or attempted restrictions on transiting foreign ships may be problematic. Also, it is not easy to assess the cumulative impact of limitations on the freedom of navigation, right of innocent passage, or transit passage.

User States may adopt a pragmatic approach and follow the laws and regulations of the coastal States. However, in some situations this may involve clear instances of discrimination on the basis of a ships' flag. For example, in permit granting, it is up to the coastal State to determine whether and to what extent a foreign ship has complied with the conditions deemed to ensure effective control of potential pollution in the Arctic waters. It cannot be denied that a given factual context may make it difficult to determine whether a ship has encountered discrimination in conducting the passage according to the national laws.

UNCLOS establishes procedural requirements to balance the legislative and jurisdictional power of the coastal States. The procedural safeguards play an important role in enhancing the transit rights of ships who rely on equal treatment. In interpreting and applying the safeguards procedures, the user States may have to rely on appropriate and relevant international instruments, principles and standards to challenge any discrimination they may encounter in order to secure the quality and quantity of Arctic transit.

In dealing in actual practice with the regulatory requirements of coastal States, it may not be in the long-term interests of user States to formally challenge regulations they believe are in practice discriminatory. It may be wiser for user States to make a good faith effort to comply with the national regulations and to enter into discussions with the authorities when they perceive that the regulations may be discriminatory. If user States can demonstrate in discussions that they are sympathetic to the concerns of the coastal States and the rationale for the regulations, and that they are making a good faith effort to comply with the regulations, they may gain more in the long run than they would by threatening to challenge the regulations. In some cases it may even be in their long-term interests to simply comply with the regulations and pay any fees that are imposed.

As long as the non-discrimination requirement exists in the form of a treaty, it may never be free from a State's will. Equal treatment will be a political tug-of-war involving the Arctic States and user States with different interests, relative rights and privileges in a dynamic system. Negotiations should not be viewed through the lens of a zero-sum perspective, but through the interaction of competing interests, common interests and cooperation.

CHAPTER 11

The Rights and Interests of Japan in regard to Arctic Shipping

Kentaro Nishimoto

1 Introduction

The opening of the Arctic Ocean for shipping due to melting of ice has generated expectations about its use as a shortcut connecting the Pacific and Atlantic Oceans. Because of its geographic location, Japan is considered to be one of the States which would benefit most from Arctic shipping.[1] Indeed, one of the figures often cited to illustrate the benefits of navigation through the Arctic is the distance of travel between Rotterdam and Yokohama: whereas the sailing distance using the current route through the Suez Canal is 11,200 nautical miles (nm), traveling through the Northern Sea Route (NSR) along the Russian coastline would reduce the distance by more than 40 percent, to only 6,500 nm.[2]

The possibility of such benefits from Arctic shipping is now widely recognised in Japan, not only within the shipping industry but also in the popular media. Some parts of the media have voiced the need to accelerate responses towards Arctic issues and have raised alarm against falling behind other States (namely, China and South Korea).[3] On a closer look, however, the attitude of Japan towards Arctic shipping is not a story of yet another non-Arctic State participating in the 'race to the North'. This Chapter discusses the nuances in the attitude of Japan towards Arctic shipping and its implications on Japan's position regarding the discussions on the balance of rights between coastal and user States in the Arctic. It will further place Arctic issues within the

---

1 Gunnar Sander, Johan Gille; Adam Stępień; Timo Koivurova; Jennie Thomas; Jean-Claude Gascard and Debra Justus, 'Changes in Arctic Maritime Transport' in Adam Stępień, Timo Koivurova and Paula Kankaanpää (eds), *The Changing Arctic and the European Union* (Brill, 2015) 81–114, at 95 (showing in Figure 3.7 that Japan has a larger savings in distance to Rotterdam as compared to other parts of East Asia).

2 Scott G Borgerson, 'Arctic Meltdown: The Economic and Security Implications of Global Warming' (2008) 87 *Foreign Affairs* 63 at 69.

3 'The Ice-Melting Arctic: We must Catch-up and Swiftly Formulate a National Strategy' *Sankei Shimbun*, 26 May 2013, accessed 21 March 2017 at http://www.sankei.com/politics/news/130526/plt1305260012-n2.html [in Japanese].

 | DOI 10.1163/9789004339385_012

broader context of Japan's ocean policy, to draw some conclusions on Japan's most likely form of involvement in issues relating to Arctic shipping.

2 Japan's Interests in Arctic Navigation

2.1 *Introduction*

Discussions on Arctic shipping in Japan have mostly focused on the possibilities for commercial navigation through the NSR. The Northwest Passage (NWP) has attracted less attention, with the exception of international law literature discussing Canadian claims regarding the NWP. This is due to the fact that, in addition to its unfavourable ice conditions as compared to the NSR, the NWP is less useful to Japan as a route to Europe. There has also been little discussion on the use of the Arctic Ocean by naval vessels, although some experts have written on the implication of the opening of the Arctic for Japan's sea-lane security.

Japan started to consider seriously possibilities for Arctic shipping from a relatively early period, well before Arctic issues began to attract global attention. An interest in Arctic shipping materialised soon after Mikhail Gorbachev announced his intention to open the NSR for international navigation in 1987. Early efforts were driven by the Nippon Foundation and the Ship and Ocean Foundation (SOF),[4] private foundations with a strong focus on shipping and ocean-related issues. Starting in June 1993, the SOF collaborated with the Central Marine Research and Design Institute (CNIIMF) of Russia and the Fridtjof Nansen Institute (FNI) of Norway and launched the International Northern Sea Route Programme (INSROP). INSROP was a multi-disciplinary research programme aimed at building knowledge necessary for shipping along the NSR.[5] The programme was divided into four subprogrammes (natural conditions and navigation, environmental factors, trade and commercial shipping aspects, and political, legal and strategic factors), and was successful in accumulating knowledge on various aspects of Arctic shipping.[6] The SOF

4 The Ship and Ocean Foundation is currently the Ocean Policy Research Institute of the Sasakawa Peace Foundation.

5 Jan M Markussen, 'International Northern Sea Route Programme (INSROP)' (1994) 11(1) *Ocean Yearbook* 484 at 484.

6 R Douglas Brubaker and Claes L Ragner, 'A Review of the International Northern Sea Route Program (INSROP)—10 Years On' (2010) 33(1–2) *Polar Geography* 15; Willy Østreng, 'The International Northern Sea Route Programme (INSROP): Applicable Lessons Learned' (2006) 42(1) *Polar Record* 71 at 72–77.

also conducted a successful experimental voyage from Yokohama to Kirkenes, Norway, acquiring practical knowledge about navigating through the NSR.[7] The conclusion from INSROP was that commercial use of the NSR for international shipping was now feasible in economic, technological and environmental terms.[8] However, the overall results were somewhat discouraging for the shipping industry, revealing that there were considerable issues that would have to be overcome before commercial shipping could take place in the short or medium-term.[9]

2.2 *Commercial Interests in Arctic Shipping*

The findings from INSROP are believed to have had a negative impact on the attitude of the Japanese shipping sector towards Arctic shipping, causing scepticism as to whether navigation through the NSR could be a commercially viable option.[10] It is somewhat ironic that early efforts towards Arctic shipping in Japan had led to cautious attitudes at the turn of the century, while efforts by China and South Korea began to accelerate around the same time.[11] Various factors, such as ice conditions and the Russian regulations on the NSR have now changed since the 1990s. The ice conditions have become more favourable to shipping—albeit with some fluctuation between years and seasons—and the drastic changes that are occurring in the Arctic are now coming to be more fully realised.[12] The Russian laws and regulations on the NSR were amended in 2012–2013, resulting in a more accommodating environment for shipping to take place.[13] Despite these developments, the Japanese shipping industry still appears to maintain a cautious attitude whether Arctic shipping would bring real economic profit in the near future.

---

7 Hiromitsu Kitagawa (ed), *The Northern Sea Route: The Shortest Sea Route Linking East Asia and Europe* (The Ship and Ocean Foundation, 2001) 135–146.

8 Michael Byers, *International Law and the Arctic* (Cambridge University Press, 2013) at 147; Edgar Gold, 'Northern Sea Route Navigation: The Last Frontier?' in Aldo Chircop, Ted L McDorman and Susan J Rolston (eds), *The Future of Ocean Regime Building: Essays in Tribute to Douglas M. Johnston* (Martinus Nijhoff, 2009) 287–315, at 298–301.

9 Brubaker and Ragner, *supra* note 6 at 33.

10 Aki Tonami, Asian Foreign Policy in a Changing Arctic: The Diplomacy of Economy and Science at New Frontiers (Palgrave Macmillan, 2016) at 58.

11 On China and South Korea's Arctic Policy in this period, see *ibid.*. at 21 and 74.

12 Arctic Council, Arctic Marine Shipping Assessment 2009 Report (2009) at 25–35.

13 See Chapter 5 of this Volume and Erik Franckx, 'The "New" Arctic Passages and the "Old" Law of the Sea' in Henrik Ringbom (ed), *Jurisdiction over Ships: Post-UNCLOS Developments in the Law of the Sea* (Brill, 2015) 194–216, at 201–205.

Experts from major Japanese shipping firms have explained their reluctant attitudes based on the simple fact that shipping companies are driven strictly by profit-making motives.[14] They point out that reduction in sailing distance does not automatically translate into profits for shipping companies. For container shipping, which accounts for a large percentage of shipping between Japan and Europe, the limitation on vessel size due to the shallow waters in some of the straits along the NSR is estimated to result in more costs per volume of cargo.[15] It is further suggested that, due to the nature of the goods shipped between Japan and Europe, the reliability of arrival time is more important for cargo owners than reducing the time required for shipping.[16] The limited ability to deliver 'just-in-time' is suggested to be one of the weaknesses of shipping through the NSR, where shipping time will necessary vary depending on ice conditions.

However, experts also point out that circumstances are different for bulk carriers and liquefied natural gas (LNG) carriers carrying raw material and energy resources.[17] This may explain the growth of trans-Arctic voyages by these types of vessels to East Asia in recent years.[18] Despite the general reluctance of Japanese shipping companies to engage in Arctic shipping, they are looking to Arctic destination shipping as a growing area of opportunity. For example, Mitsui O.S.K. Lines—a major shipping firm in Japan—has announced that it will start operating LNG carriers with icebreaking capacity in 2018, to transport LNG from the Yamal LNG project in Russia to East Asia during the summer.[19] It must be pointed out, however, that the use of the NSR by these vessels is different in nature than the transit of the route as a shortcut between East Asia and Europe. Statistics for the NSR show that even voyages categorised as 'transits' through the NSR (in the sense of passing through both ends of the NSR) largely

14 Hiroshi Ueta and Hiroyuki Goda, 'Commercial Perspective of the Northern Sea Route' in Japan Institute of International Affairs (ed), *Arctic Governance and Japan's Diplomatic Strategy* (Japan Institute of International Affairs, 2013) 1–22, at 10–11, translation into English, accessed 21 March 2017 at https://www2.jiia.or.jp/en/research/2012_arctic_governance.php.

15 *Ibid.* at 14–15.

16 Hiroyuki Goda, 'The Arctic Shipping Route: Review of 2014 and Prospects for the Future' (2015) 1049 *Kaiun* [Maritime Shipping] 16 at 18–19 [in Japanese].

17 *Ibid.* at 17–18; Ueta and Goda, *supra* note 14 at 15–17.

18 Tadeusz Pastusiak, *The Northern Sea Route as a Shipping Lane: Expectations and Reality* (Springer, 2016) at 34–35.

19 'MOL signs Ship Building Contracts with DSME for ice class carriers' *Mitsui O S K Lines*, accessed 21 March 2017 at http://www.mol.co.jp/en/pr/2014/14036.html.

consist of shipping to and from a port within the Arctic, such as in Russia or Norway.[20]

The fact that the Japanese shipping industry is starting to become involved in Arctic destination shipping—while regarding the use of the Arctic Ocean as a shortcut as a more distant possibility in the future—has implications for the position of Japan on Arctic shipping. In short, there is at present more economic incentive for Japan to prioritise cooperation with Russia on the use of the NSR, rather than safeguard its navigational rights and interests under international law for commercial transit shipping that has not yet taken place.

2.3 *Security Interests in Arctic Navigation*

The security implications of the opening of the Arctic for navigation are less discussed in Japan. Experts have only recently started to discuss a variety of issues, such as a possible rise in military activities in the Arctic which may lead to instability in the region, new opportunities for projection of naval power resulting in a change in the military balance in the region and its adjacent areas, and the more long-term non-traditional security challenges which may emerge as a result of a melting Arctic.[21] However, experts do not see any security interests for Japan in using the Arctic for navigational purposes, and are sceptical whether a situation would arise where Japanese naval vessels would navigate in the Arctic Ocean.[22] As of the present, Japan's capabilities are limited in this regard,[23] and discussions on the need for investments in the construction of

---

20 A list of permissions granted to vessels for navigation through the NSR is available at the website of the Northern Sea Route Administration. The Northern Sea Route Administration, 'Permissions for Navigation on the Water Area of the Northern sea route', accessed 21 March 2017 at http://www.nsra.ru/en/razresheniya/. For an analysis of voyages for the years 2007–2012, see Frédéric Lasserre and Olga Alexeeva, 'Analysis of Maritime Transit Trends in the Arctic Passages' in Suzanne Lalonde and Ted L McDorman (eds), *International Law and Politics of the Arctic Ocean* (Brill, 2015) 180–193, at 188.

21 Takahiro Ishihara, 'Security Architecture and Multilateral Institutions at the Arctic' (2014) 4(1) *Japan Maritime Self-Defense Force Staff College Review* 44 [in Japanese]; Hideaki Kaneda, 'The Arctic Ocean and Japan's Defense' in Japan Institute of International Affairs (ed), *supra* note 14, 1–15 at 1–9.

22 National Institute for Defense Studies, *East Asian Strategic Review 2011* (National Institute for Defense Studies, 2011) at 85.

23 Japan currently owns three icebreakers, the *Shirase*, *Soya* and *Teshio*. The *Shirase* is registered with the Japan Self-Defense Force, and is used exclusively for supporting routine scientific expeditions to Antarctica. The *Soya* and *Teshio* are Japan Coast Guard patrol vessels with the capacity to operate in the coastal areas to the north of Hokkaido, which are covered with drift ice in the winter.

new icebreakers have been limited to those to be used as platforms for scientific research.[24] The focus has been on the possibility of increased traffic in the Sea of Japan and the Tsugaru and Soya Straits (which lie between the Sea of Japan and the Pacific Ocean and the Sea of Okhotsk, respectively), which may be used a route by East Asian States and Russia to the Arctic.[25]

2.4 *Development of Japan's Arctic Policy*

Despite the early focus on Arctic shipping by its private sector, Japan was late in formulating responses to promote its interests within the more recent developments in Arctic governance. Japan was one of the five non-Arctic States and the only Asian State to be present at the Ottawa Conference which founded the Arctic Council in 1996. Whereas the four other non-Arctic States eventually became Observers,[26] Japan only applied for (permanent) Observer status in September 2009—after its neighbours China and South Korea—and had to wait until May 2013 for approval by the Council.[27] In the meantime, some efforts to respond to Arctic issues emerged within the government. In 2010, the Ministry of Foreign Affairs established an 'Arctic Taskforce' to deal with Arctic issues in a cross-cutting manner within the Ministry.[28] The Ministry of Land, Transport and Infrastructure also established a committee within the ministry in 2012 to investigate the possibility of utilising the 'Arctic Sea Route',[29]

---

24 An 'Investigative Commission on an Arctic Research Ship' was established in October 2016 within the Ministry of Education, Culture, Sports, Science and Technology (MEXT) to discuss the necessary qualifications for a future research vessel capable of operating in the Arctic. MEXT, 'Investigative Commission on an Arctic Research Ship', accessed 21 March 2017 at http://www.mext.go.jp/b_menu/shingi/chousa/kaihatu/021/index.htm [in Japanese].

25 Takahiro Ishihara, 'The Arctic Ocean and Security' (2013) 629 *Kokusai Mondai* [International Affairs] 49, at 56 [in Japanese].

26 Akiho Shibata, 'Japan and 100 Years of Antarctic Legal Order: Any Lessons for the Arctic?' (2015) 7 *Yearbook of Polar Law* 1 at 5.

27 See the list of Arctic Council Observers, accessed 21 March 2017 at http://www.arctic-council.org/index.php/en/about-us/arctic-council/observers, and in Chapter 2, Section 5.2 of this Volume.

28 Ministry of Foreign Affairs of Japan, 'Launching of the "Arctic Taskforce', press release of 2 September 2010, accessed 21 March 2017 at http://www.mofa.go.jp/announce/announce/2010/9/0902_01.html.

29 Ministry of Land, Infrastructure, Transport and Tourism, 'On the Establishment of an Investigative Committee on the Arctic Sea Route', accessed 21 March 2017 at http://www.mlit.go.jp/common/000219788.pdf [in Japanese].

and further launched a 'Public-Private Partnership Conference Related to the Northern Sea Route' in 2014 to discuss issues with the relevant industries.[30]

One of the first policy documents in Japan to refer to Arctic issues was the second 'Basic Plan on Ocean Policy', which was approved by the Cabinet in April 2013.[31] The Basic Plan on Ocean Policy lists responding to changes in the Arctic Ocean as one of the priority areas within Japan's overall ocean policy, and provides that measures should be taken to address issues such as securing maritime transport, securing the safety of navigation, promotion of research and survey activities, conservation of the environment, and promotion of international coordination and cooperation.[32] Specifically with respect to Arctic shipping, the Basic Plan refers to conducting scientific research in the Arctic to assess its future potential,[33] promoting talks with the coastal States on the utilisation of the Arctic Sea Route,[34] and conducting research and development on the creation of sea ice flash charts for safe navigation by using satellite technology.[35]

In July 2013, after Japan's Observer status at the Arctic Council was approved, a 'Liaison Conference of Relevant Ministries and Agencies for Arctic Issues' was established.[36] The Committee held periodic meetings to share information on Arctic issues and to draft Japan's Arctic Policy. These efforts culminated in the adoption of Japan's Arctic Policy in November 2015.[37] Although this policy document would seem to be more of a comprehensive list of policy issues in the Arctic rather than a document identifying priority areas for Japan, it may be seen that the central theme in Japan's Arctic Policy is to promote

---

30 Ministry of Land, Infrastructure, Transport and Tourism, 'Public-Private Partnership Conference Related to the Northern Sea Route', accessed 21 March 2017 at http://www.mlit.go.jp/sogoseisaku/ocean_policy/sosei_ocean_tk_000021.html [in Japanese].

31 Basic Plan on Ocean Policy (provisional translation), accessed 21 March 2017 at http://www.kantei.go.jp/jp/singi/kaiyou/kihonkeikaku/130426kihonkeikaku_e.pdf. Article 16 of the Basic Act on Ocean Policy (Act No. 33 of 2007), which establishes the basic legal framework for Japan's ocean policy, requires the government to formulate a basic plan with regard to the oceans. The Basic Plan is reviewed around every five years. The first Basic Plan approved in 2008 did not contain any reference to the Arctic.

32 *Ibid.* at 8.

33 *Ibid.* at 11.

34 *Ibid.* at 26.

35 *Ibid.* at 34.

36 Headquarters for Ocean Policy, 'Outline of Japan's Arctic Policy', accessed 21 March 2017 at http://www.kantei.go.jp/jp/singi/kaiyou/arcticpolicy/jpn_arcticpolicy/Outline_Japans_Arctic_Policy[ENG].pdf.

37 Japan's Arctic Policy (provisional translation), accessed 21 March 2017 at http://www.kantei.go.jp/jp/singi/kaiyou/arcticpolicy/jpn_arcticpolicy/Japans_Arctic_Policy[ENG].pdf.

cooperation with the Arctic States and to contribute to resolving Arctic issues through its capabilities in science and technology.[38] Its interests in Arctic shipping are featured among the other Arctic issues to be addressed, which are environmental issues, sustainable development for indigenous peoples, promoting development of science and technology, ensuring the rule of law, and promoting international cooperation.

The basic view of the government of Japan on Arctic shipping expressed in its Arctic Policy is that 'the Arctic Sea Route is not ready yet for safe and reliable use', when factors such as sea ice conditions, the use of ports and other infrastructure along the route, and the status of services and regulations of coastal States are taken into account.[39] It is stated, however, that in light of the importance of having alternative transport routes, the private sector and the government should work together to give the future potential of this route serious consideration.[40] Further, Japan's Arctic Policy instructs the government to participate actively in the drafting of new rules for the Arctic such as through the International Maritime Organization (IMO), and to make contributions towards a suitable environment for Arctic shipping through the development of systems such as for prediction of sea ice distribution and weather forecasts.[41] In sum, corresponding to the views of the shipping sector, the government also regards the current state of Arctic shipping as still in the stage of research and development for its potential to be fully realised in the future.

3 Japan and Navigational Rights in the Arctic

For non-Arctic user States, the legal environment within which Arctic shipping can be realised is provided by the United Nations Convention on the Law of the Sea (UNCLOS).[42] The rules of UNCLOS reflect the balance between navigational rights and freedoms and coastal States' powers. There has already been a thorough discussion of issues concerning navigational rights in the Arctic in the vast amount of international law literature on the subject. Based on a

38 Tonami, *supra* note 10 at 64. There has been some discussion on whether Japan's contributions should be limited to such roles, envisioning the possibility of a more proactive role for Japan in Arctic governance. See Taisaku Ikeshima, 'Should Japan's Arctic Policy be Based on the Assumption that the Arctic Ocean is a Global Commons?' (2015) 12 *Waseda Global Forum* 109 at 125.

39 Japan's Arctic Policy, *supra* note 37 at 5.

40 *Ibid.* at 5.

41 *Ibid.* at 7 and 9.

42 United Nations Convention on the Law of the Sea, adopted 10 December 1982, 1833 UNTS 3 (entered into force 16 November 1994).

close study of these works, Japanese authors have also discussed issues such as the validity of Canadian and Russian straight baselines, the applicability of the transit passage regime to Arctic straits, and the extent and scope of coastal State powers under Article 234 of UNCLOS.

3.1 *Straight Baselines Claims*

The routes through the NSR and NWP both include waters enclosed by straight baselines drawn by the coastal State. Canada has drawn straight baselines enclosing the Canadian Arctic Archipelago, and Russia has done the same for a number of straits in the NSR.[43] These claims are important for user States, since the status of the enclosed waters as internal waters would deny them any navigational rights under international law, unless they could invoke the right of innocent or transit passage under Articles 8(2) and 35(a) of UNCLOS. The Canadian claim to internal waters status for the waters within its straight baselines is further reinforced by a claim to the waters as historic internal waters.[44]

The Canadian position has been thoroughly discussed in the vast amount of literature on the subject, especially by Canadian scholars.[45] Referring to these works, Japanese authors have raised some reservations about whether Canadian straight baselines meet the requirements under Article 7 of UNCLOS.[46] Similar views have also been raised in regard to the Russian straight baselines, although they have been discussed less than those of Canada.[47] However, the

43 Territorial Sea Geographic Coordinates (Area 7) Order, Canada Gazette, Part II, Vol 119, SOR/85-872, 10 September 1985, 3996–4002; USSR Council of Ministers Declaration 4450 (15 January 1985), accessed 21 March 2017 at http://www.un.org/Depts/los/LEGISLATIONANDTREATIES/PDFFILES/RUS_1985_Declaration.pdf.

44 Statement by Secretary of State for External Affairs Joe Clark in the House of Commons, reproduced in 'Canadian Practice in International Law during 1985—Parliamentary Declarations' (1986) 24 *Canadian Yearbook of International Law* 404 at 418.

45 See generally, Donat Pharand, *Canada's Arctic Waters in International Law* (Cambridge University Press, 2009) at 89–183; Michael Byers and Suzanne Lalonde, 'Who Controls the Northwest Passage?' (2009) 42 *Vanderbilt Journal of Transnational Law* 1133 at 1161–1169; and Ted L McDorman, *Salt Water Neighbors: International Ocean Law Relations between the United States and Canada* (Oxford University Press, 2009) at 211–239.

46 Hitoshi Nishitani, 'The Legal Status of the Northwest Passage in International Law: A Crossroad between Ice-covered Areas and International Straits' (2007) 54(4) *Kinki Daigaku Hogaku* [Kindai University Law Review] 209 at 223–224 [in Japanese]; and Kentaro Nishimoto, 'Coastal State Regulation on Arctic Sea Routes and the Regime of International Straits' in Shigeki Sakamoto (ed), *Kokusai Kaikyo* [International Straits] (Toshindo, 2015) 77–103, at 85–87 [in Japanese].

47 Nishimoto, *supra* note 46 at 88. For a discussion of Russian baselines, see R Douglas Brubaker, 'The Legal Status of the Russian Baselines in the Arctic' (1999) 30(3) *Ocean Development and International Law* 191.

conditions and requirements under UNCLOS for drawing straight baselines are somewhat loosely worded, with little further guidance as to its application.[48] In practice, it has been suggested that a number of States have established straight baselines that go beyond the spirit and wording of the rules.[49] Under these circumstances, it is obviously difficult to assess whether a particular geographical situation fulfils the conditions and requirements under UNCLOS, and presumably for this reason authors in Japan have not reached any specific conclusion with respect to the baselines in the NSR and NWP.

3.2 *Application of the UNCLOS Transit Passage Regime*

The application of the UNCLOS transit passage regime to the NWP and the NSR is another contested issue that is of major importance to user States. It is well known that the United States regards the entire NWP as consisting of a series of international straits, and the straits in the NSR as also international straits.[50] According to this position, all States are entitled to the right of transit passage, which affords greater navigational rights to user States and places restrictions on the exercise of jurisdiction by coastal States. Both Canada and Russia regard the transit passage regime to be inapplicable to the straits within their Arctic waters, and there has been a considerable amount of discussion on the contrasting positions by international lawyers.[51]

The transit passage regime applies to straits that connect one part of the high seas or an exclusive economic zone (EEZ) and another part of the high seas or an EEZ, and is 'used for international navigation'.[52] Since the

---

48 See, however, the work of the Committee on Baselines under the International Law of the Sea of the International Law Association, accessed 21 March 2017 at http://www.ila-hq.org/en/committees/index.cfm/cid/1028.

49 Robin R Churchill and A Vaughan Lowe, *The Law of the Sea* (3rd ed) (Manchester University Press, 1999) at 39.

50 J Ashley Roach and Robert W Smith, *Excessive Maritime Claims* (3rd ed) (Martinus Nijhoff, 2012) at 312–328.

51 See for example, Donat Pharand, 'The Arctic Waters and the Northwest Passage: A Final Revisit,' (2007) 38 *Ocean Development and International Law* 3 at 28–45; James Kraska, 'The Law of the Sea Convention and the Northwest Passage,' (2007) 22(2) *International Journal of Marine and Coastal Law* 257 at 275–279; and R Douglas Brubaker, 'Straits in the Russian Arctic,' (2001) 32 *Ocean Development and International Law* 263.

52 Satya N Nandan and David H Anderson, 'Straits Used for International Navigation: A Commentary on Part III of the United Nations Convention on the Law of the Sea 1982' (1989) 60 *British Yearbook of International Law* 159 at 166–169. The language of Article 37 of UNCLOS reflects the decision of the International Court of Justice (ICJ) in the *Corfu Channel* case where the Court stated that the decisive criterion for an international strait is its geographical situation as connecting two parts of the high seas and the fact of its

geographical situation of the NWP and the Russian Arctic straits in the NSR appear to meet the geographical requirement of connecting two parts of the high seas or the EEZ, the focus has been on the functional requirement of being 'used for international navigation'.[53] Discussions in Japan have also focused on the functional criterion, in light of the fact that the straits in the NSR and NWP were seldom used for international navigation before the melting of the ice. Due to the novelty of the situation in which a sea route hitherto unsuitable for international navigation has become a useful route, there have been suggestions that the functional requirement should be relaxed taking into account future potential use,[54] or that the requirement should be interpreted in light of the balance between coastal State interests and the interests of the international community in navigation.[55]

3.3 *Extent of Coastal State Powers under Article 234 of UNCLOS*

Under Article 234 of UNCLOS, which applies to ice-covered areas, coastal States may adopt and enforce laws and regulations which would otherwise exceed their jurisdiction under UNCLOS.[56] However, the impreciseness of the language of Article 234 has raised a number of questions concerning its interpretation. For example, the terms 'within the limits of the exclusive economic zone' has led to discussions on whether the article is intended to apply only to the EEZ or also to the territorial sea. The expression 'presence of ice covering such areas for most of the year' has also raised questions regarding its

being used for international navigation. *Corfu Channel (United Kingdom v Albania)*, [1949] ICJ Rep 4 at 28–29.

53 The United States, however, takes the position that the geographical criterion is decisive, with the understanding that all straits *capable of* being used for international navigation qualifies as an international strait. Roach and Smith, *supra* note 50 at 277–278.

54 Atsuko Kanehara, 'International Law Issues Concerning the Development of the Arctic' in Japan Energy Law Institute (ed), *Umi No Kaihatsu Riyou Ni Kakaru Houteki Mondai No Kentou* [Legal Issues relating to the Development and Use of the Oceans] (Japan Energy Law Institute, 2014) 105–125, at 118 [in Japanese].

55 Kae Oyama, 'The Legal Status of the Northwest Passage in the Arctic Ocean,' (2015) 10 *Sogo Seisaku Foramu* [Multidisciplinary Policy Forum] 23 at 29–30 [in Japanese].

56 For discussion on coastal State powers under Article 234, see Don M McRae and D John Goundrey, 'Environmental Jurisdiction in Arctic Waters: The Extent of Article 234,' (1982) 16 *University of British Colombia Law Review* 197; Tullio Scovazzi, 'Legal Issues Relating to Navigation through Arctic Waters,' (2009) 1 *Yearbook of Polar Law* 371 at 372–347; Kristin Bartenstein, 'The "Arctic Exception" in the Law of the Sea Convention: A Contribution to Safer Navigation in the Northwest Passage?' (2011) 42 *Ocean Development and International Law* 22; and Armand de Mestral, 'Article 234 of the United Nations Convention on the Law of the Sea: Its Origins and Its Future' in Lalonde and McDorman (eds), *supra* note 20 at 111–124.

actual application when areas covered with ice further decrease. The reference generally to 'laws and regulations for the prevention, reduction and control of marine pollution from vessels', even with some qualifications attached, has generated discussions on the types of measures that may be adopted under the coastal States' laws and regulations. Not surprisingly, international lawyers in Japan have not reached clear conclusions on such issues.

A further question is whether Article 234 of UNCLOS applies to international straits.[57] If the answer is in the affirmative, it may still be possible for coastal States argue that Article 234 allows them to exercise jurisdiction beyond the limitations in Article 42 of UNCLOS which would otherwise apply to international straits subject to the regime of transit passage. Views in Japan are also divided on this point. The fact that Article 234 is placed in a separate section (Section 8 of Part XII) and is not referred to in Article 233, which states that '[n]othing in sections 5, 6 and 7 affects the legal regime of straits used for international navigation' has been referred to as supporting the conclusion that Article 234 applies to international straits.[58] However, it has also been suggested that there is room for a contrary interpretation since the lack of reference to Section 8 in Article 233 would only be natural if Article 234 only applied within the EEZ.[59]

Notwithstanding the discussions on its interpretation and application, it is clear that Article 234 gives coastal States' broad powers to unilaterally regulate shipping in their EEZ and possibly also within their territorial sea. While some authors in Japan take a somewhat cautious stance on whether the current laws and regulations of Russia and Canada are entirely consistent with Article 234,[60] the issues have been discussed in terms of a lack of clarity in the law and not as involving a clear violation of UNCLOS. Moreover, the suggested means for the resolution of issues are engaging in a 'dialogue' with the coastal States and promoting the move towards international rules and standards.[61] In the works of Japanese international lawyers, the use of the dispute settlement mechanism

---

57 On this point, see discussions in Bartenstein, *supra* note 56 at 28–30; Brubaker, *supra* note 51 at 269.

58 Kanehara, *supra* note 54 at 117.

59 Nishimoto, *supra* note 46 at 96–97.

60 Shingo Horii, 'The Sea Route Issue in the Arctic Ocean: The Northwest Passage and the Northern Sea Route' (2013) 8 *Hokkyokukai Kiho* [Seasonal Report on the Arctic Ocean] 14 at 16 [in Japanese]; Nishimoto, *supra* note 46 at 97–101.

61 Kanehara, *supra* note 54 at 121–122; Horii, *supra* note 60 at 25; and Kazuhiro Nakatani 'Arctic Issues (An Overview)' in Japan Institute of International Affairs, *supra* note 14 at 7–8 [in Japanese].

under Part XV of UNCLOS to resolve issues in the future is either not discussed or dismissed as an unrealistic option within the context of the Arctic.[62]

3.4 *Adoption of the Polar Code*

In 2015, the IMO completed its work on the safety and environment provisions of the so-called Polar Code.[63] Based on the recognition that polar waters are vulnerable to shipping activities and may impose additional demands on ships, their systems and operation—due to the potentially harsh conditions in polar waters—the Polar Code places additional requirements on ships operating in polar waters, which would not otherwise apply.[64] Amendments were made to SOLAS[65] and MARPOL[66] Annexes I, II, IV and V to require States to comply with the mandatory parts of the Polar Code.[67] The adoption of the Polar Code is a major achievement in the establishment of uniform international rules and standards for Arctic shipping, and may be regarded as an important element of Arctic governance more generally. As such, it is obviously of significance to user States, and is viewed in Japan as an important development in the regulatory framework applicable to Arctic shipping.[68]

The Polar Code raises some questions on its effects on the powers of coastal States in regard to regulation of shipping. The crucial question is whether the Polar Code limits coastal States' powers under Article 234 of UNCLOS. International rules and standards are adopted at the IMO to ensure uniformity

62 Horii, *supra* note 60 at 24–25.

63 International Code for Ships Operating in Polar Waters, Res MSC.385 (94) (21 November 2014), IMO Doc MSC 94/21/Add.1, Annex 6; Res MEPC.264(68) (15 May 2015), IMO Doc MEPC 68/21/Add.1, Annex 10.

64 For a discussion of additional requirements under the Polar Code, see Øystein Jensen, 'The International Code for Ships Operating in Polar Waters: Finalization, Adoption and Law of the Sea Implications' (2016) 7 *Arctic Review on Law and Politics* 60 at 67–70; and David Leary, 'The IMO Mandatory International Code of Safety for Ships: Charting a Sustainable Course for Shipping in the Polar Regions?' (2015) 7 *Yearbook of Polar Law* 426.

65 International Convention for the Safety of Life at Sea, adopted 1 November 1974, 1184 UNTS 277 (entered into force 25 May 1980), with protocols and as regularly amended.

66 International Convention for the Prevention of Pollution from Ships, adopted 2 November 1973 (as modified by the 1978 Protocol adopted on 1 June 1978 and the 1997 Protocol adopted on 26 September 1997), 1340 UNTS 61, and as regularly amended. Entry into force varies for each Annex. At the time of writing, Annexes I–VI were all in force.

67 Res MSC.386(94) (21 November 2014), IMO Doc MSC 94/21/Add.1, Annex 7; Res MEPC.265(68) (15 May 2015), IMO Doc MEPC 68/21/Add.1, Annex 11.

68 Japan's Arctic Policy contains an explicit reference to the Polar Code, and states that Japan should continue to be an active participant in further discussions. Japan's Arctic Policy, *supra* note 37 at 8.

in shipping regulations, and have the effect of creating limits to the jurisdiction of coastal States under the various provisions of UNCLOS when they are regarded as generally accepted international rules and standards (GAIRS).[69] However, Article 234 lacks a reference to GAIRS, and may be considered as giving coastal States unilateral legislative and enforcement jurisdiction regardless of the existence of relevant international rules or standards. This interpretation is supported by the non-prejudice provisions included in SOLAS and MARPOL.[70]

It has nevertheless been observed by some authors in Japan that adoption of the Polar Code may influence discussions on the scope of unilateral measures that can be adopted by coastal States under Article 234.[71] Under Article 234, the laws and regulations of coastal States must have 'due regard to navigation and the protection and preservation of the marine environment based on the best available scientific evidence'. Because the Polar Code could be seen as reflecting international consensus on the appropriate balance between navigational rights and the protection and preservation of the marine environment, it is suggested that the Polar Code could provide an objective criterion to facilitate discussions on that particular requirement under Article 234.[72] Under this view, although coastal States are not necessarily precluded from adopting measures that are more stringent than those in the Polar Code as a matter of law, justification of such measures under Article 234 could be regarded as less persuasive if coastal States cannot show the specific necessity of such requirements based on best available evidence.

---

69 On the role of standard-setting by the IMO in the law of the sea generally, see James Harrison, *Making the Law of the Sea: A Study in the Development of International Law* (Cambridge University Press, 2011) at 154–199; and Rüdiger Wolfrum, 'IMO Interface with the Law of the Sea Convention' in Myron H Nordquist and John N Moore (eds), *Current Maritime Issues and the International Maritime Organization* (Martinus Nijhoff, 1999) 223–234.

70 Regulation 2.5 in the new Chapter XIV of SOLAS, which was adopted to implement the Polar Code, provides that '[n]othing in this chapter shall prejudice the rights or obligations of States under international law'. MARPOL contains a general provision concerning the relationship between the Convention and the law of the sea (Art. 9(2)).

71 Hiroko Sasaki, 'Ensuring the Safety of Navigation and Prevention of Marine Pollution in the Arctic Ocean: the Polar Code' (2016) 45(3) *Kankyo to Kogai* [The Environment and Pollution] 29 at 33 [in Japanese]; and Kentaro Nishimoto, 'Regulation of Arctic Shipping After the Polar Code' (2016) 24(1) *Kokusai Kyoryoku Ronsyu* [Review of International Cooperation] 57 at 61 [in Japanese].

72 Nishimoto, *supra* note 71 at 61 [in Japanese].

4 Japan's Position on Arctic Shipping

Although there has been increased attention on Arctic shipping in Japan in recent years, the government of Japan has not been very vocal about its position on Arctic shipping, and especially on its navigational rights as a user State vis-à-vis the coastal States. Even though international lawyers in Japan have started to engage in discussions on the appropriate balance between the rights and freedoms of user States and the jurisdiction of coastal States, the government has not sent out clear messages in policy documents or in practice. The reason for this would seem to be that it has so far been unnecessary and also undesirable for Japan to engage actively in discussions with coastal States on Japan's navigational rights and freedoms under UNCLOS.

4.1 *Government Position on Arctic Shipping*

Japan's Arctic Policy contains a reference to its navigational rights as a user State in the Arctic Ocean. The document states that:

> The Arctic Ocean and other oceans are subject to international laws, including the United Nations Convention on the Law of the Sea. Freedom of navigation and other principles of international law must be respected. Especially in the 'ice covered areas' of the Arctic Ocean, it is necessary to cooperate with coastal states to ensure appropriate balance between the freedom and safety of navigation, and the protection and preservation of the marine environment under the principle of international law.[73]

The position is admittedly very general, as it only reaffirms the general applicability of UNCLOS—which has also been recognised by the Arctic Ocean coastal States[74]—and refers to the freedom of navigation and other unspecified principles of international law. The reference to 'ice-covered areas' provides some detail, especially since the term is explicitly linked to Article 234. However, the view of the government of Japan on how precisely it sees the 'appropriate balance' between the freedom of navigation and the protection and preservation of the marine environment is unstated, and the reference is in any event within the context of the need to cooperate with coastal States. In fact, the passage itself is contained in a section entitled 'Ensuring the Rule of Law and Promoting

---

73 Japan's Arctic Policy, *supra* note 37 at 4–5. A footnote is added to the phrase 'ice covered areas' in the above passage, which refers to the definition of that term in Article 234 of UNCLOS.

74 Ilulissat Declaration (28 May 2008), 48 ILM 382 (2009).

International Cooperation'. The emphasis is on maintaining the legal order under UNCLOS, which reflects the balance between navigational rights and the rights of coastal States, and not directly on upholding Japan's navigational rights in furtherance of its own immediate interests in Arctic shipping.

The emphasis on the rule of law for the oceans has increasingly become an important component of Japan's ocean policy in recent years. A number of references to establishing and maintaining the rule of law at sea can be found in the Basic Plan on Ocean Policy.[75] Prime Minister Shinzo Abe has also advocated the 'three principles for the rule of law at sea'.[76] Moreover, the respect for navigational rights and freedoms has been a longstanding priority for Japan, which regards seaborne trade as vital to its survival. Apart from a general reference to these principles, however, the government of Japan has not expressed its position on a particular aspect of its navigational rights in the Arctic, or on specific legislative or other measures adopted by the Arctic coastal States.[77]

However, the absence of any objection does not necessarily imply that Japan regards the Arctic coastal States' positions as entirely legitimate, or has acquiesced to their current laws and regulations on Arctic shipping. For a State to be regarded as having acquiesced to a claim, it must have kept silent in circumstances that would have required positive action.[78] In light of the fact that Japanese-flagged vessels have not made transits through the Arctic in recent years,[79] it is arguably the case that an occasion has not yet arisen where Japan was required to express its position as a flag State vis-à-vis certain specific measures taken by coastal States pursuant to their laws and regulations.[80] This

75 *Supra* note 31 at 1, 2 and 7.

76 Keynote address by Shinzo Abe, Prime Minister of Japan at the 13th IISS Shangri-La Dialogue (30 May 2014) accessed 21 March 2017 at http://www.mofa.go.jp/fp/nsp/page4e_000086.html.

77 One caveat that needs to be taken into account in this regard is that there may be unpublished occasions where the government has indicated its position on certain matters in its bilateral exchanges with Arctic coastal States or other States.

78 Iain C MacGibbon, 'The Scope of Acquiescence in International Law' (1954) 31 *British Yearbook of International Law* 133 at 133.

79 See the figure 'Flags of Ships Transiting the Northern Sea Route 2011–2015' in PAME, 'Northern Sea Route Shipping Statistics', accessed 21 March 2017 at https://pame.is/index.php/projects/arctic-marine-shipping/older-projects/northern-sea-route-shipping-statistics. It appears that the only transit by a Japanese-flagged vessel in both the NSR and NWP is the voyage of the Japanese adventurer Kenichi Horie in 1979–82 on his yacht, the *Mermaid*.

80 In the *Fisheries* case, the ICJ listed the following elements in establishing the United Kingdom's acquiescence: the notoriety of facts, general toleration of international community, and prolonged abstention of a State with special interests in the question.

seems to be how the government has perceived the situation. In an article in the *Kokusaiho Gaiko Zasshi* issued by the Japanese Society of International Law, Kikuko Kato—then-director of the Oceans Division of the Ministry of Foreign Affairs in charge of Arctic issues—identified the different views of States with respect to Article 234 as one of the issues regarding the Arctic. The examples given in this regard were Canada's Northern Canada Vessel Traffic Services Zone Regulations (NORDREG) and Russia's Regulations for Navigation on the NSR. While writing in her personal capacity and carefully avoiding taking a position on the matter, she observed that issues concerning the interpretation of Article 234 'will likely be considered in more realistic terms, as the possibility of opening and utilization of the navigational routes in the Arctic increase'.[81]

4.2 *Economic and Political Considerations as a User State*

As a practical matter, it is unlikely for Japan to challenge laws and regulations on Arctic shipping adopted by coastal States, at least in the near future. In terms of the minimal economic interests of Japan at present, it is unnecessary for it to make an outright objection to current coastal State laws and regulations. As described earlier in this Chapter, the focus on Arctic shipping by the Japanese shipping industry is on utilising the NSR for destination shipping to locations within the Arctic, rather than for trans-Arctic shipping to the North Atlantic. Commercial interests in shipping energy resources from projects in the Russian Arctic make it necessary to cooperate with Russia. Even for transit voyages through the NSR, the shipping industry mostly envisages utilising support from Russian icebreakers, and relying on support from Russia in case of an emergency. Since it is in the foreseeable future unrealistic to utilise the Arctic Ocean for shipping without cooperation from a coastal State, it is not in the interest of Japan to become engaged in disputes with coastal States on the interpretation or application of UNCLOS.

Political considerations also make it undesirable for Japan—or for any non-Arctic State—to lodge objections to coastal States' claims unless it is considered necessary for the protection of its rights and interests. Prior to approval of Japan's Observer status with the Arctic Council in 2013—along with China,

---

Fisheries (*UK v Norway*) [1951] ICJ Rep 116 at 138–139. The notoriety of the claims by Canada and Russia raise some questions as to whether they could be regarded as generally tolerated by the international community. A further question is whether user States could be considered as having special interests and whether their silence could be regarded as a prolonged abstention in the current circumstances of Arctic shipping.

81 Kikuko Kato, 'Emerging Challenges regarding the Changing Arctic,' (2011) 110 (3) *Kokusaiho Gaiko Zasshi* [Journal of International Law and Diplomacy] 71 at 79–80 [in Japanese].

Italy, South Korea, Singapore and India—the Arctic Council adopted detailed criteria for admitting Observers.[82] It was agreed that the Arctic Council will take into account, *inter alia*, the extent to which Observers recognise 'Arctic States' sovereignty, sovereign rights and jurisdiction in the Arctic' and that 'an extensive legal framework applies to the Arctic Ocean including, notably, the Law of the Sea, and that this framework provides a solid foundation for responsible management of this ocean'. While objecting to a certain interpretation of UNCLOS by an Arctic coastal State should not necessarily be regarded as in violation of those criteria, the Arctic Council Rules of Procedure provide that '[o]bserver status shall continue for such time as consensus exists at the Ministerial meeting'.[83] The prospect of losing support for its Observer status at the Arctic Council from an Arctic coastal State raises the political cost of challenging the powers of that State under international law to regulate Arctic shipping, even if the asserted jurisdiction is not regarded as consistent with international law.

4.3 *Other Constraints on Japan's Position on Arctic Shipping*

The legal issues regarding navigational rights and freedoms of user States in the Arctic have wider implications for interpretation of UNCLOS outside the Arctic context. Although Japan has placed importance on navigational rights and freedoms for maritime commerce, it is also a coastal State with concerns about safeguarding its interests in waters under its jurisdiction.[84] Thus, Japan's ocean policy is based on a delicate balance between the navigational rights and freedoms of all States and the jurisdiction of coastal States as reflected in UNCLOS. Raising certain issues such as those on the regime of straight baselines, historic waters or international straits within the Arctic context may have repercussions for a number of delicate issues concerning the interpretation of UNCLOS provisions. This situation will work as a disincentive for Japan to discuss actively Arctic coastal States' positions on the regulation of Arctic shipping.

---

82 Nuuk Declaration on the occasion of the Seventh Ministerial Meeting of the Arctic Council (12 May 2011) accessed 21 March 2017 at https://oaarchive.arctic-council.org/handle/11374/92; and Senior Arctic Officials (SAO) Report to Ministers, Nuuk, Greenland, May 2011 at 50, accessed 21 March 2017 at https://oaarchive.arctic-council.org/handle/11374/1535.

83 Arctic Council Rules of Procedure, Rule 37, accessed 21 March 2017 at https://oaarchive.arctic-council.org/handle/11374/940.

84 For an overview of agendas in Japan's ocean policy, see Naoya Okuwaki, 'The Basic Act on Ocean Policy and Japan's Agendas for Legislative Improvement' (2008) 51 *Japanese Yearbook of International Law* 164.

4.3.1 Straight Baselines and Historic Waters

It is possible to point out that certain similarities exist between the position of Canada on the NWP and the position of Japan on the Seto Naikai (Seto Inland Sea). The Seto Naikai is a narrow body of water between the main island of Honshu and the smaller islands of Shikoku and Kyushu. Japan maintains a historic waters claim to the Seto Naikai, and regards this body of water as internal waters.[85] In 1977, when Japan established its straight baselines system under the newly enacted Law on the Territorial Sea, straight baselines were drawn so that the entire area would be encompassed by the baselines.[86] In its *Limits in the Seas*, the United States expressed its position that such baselines are inconsistent with the requirements under UNCLOS,[87] and further commented that the body of waters between the Strait of Shimonoseki and the Bungo Passage in the Seto Naikai is a strait used for international navigation.[88] Although it is not clear whether the United States' position is to deny the status of the Seto Naikai as historic waters, the reference to international straits would seem to imply that this is the case.[89]

Therefore, it may be said that Japan and Canada share a common situation where both States maintain a claim to historic waters that is enclosed by a straight baselines system, to which the United States has objected. Although the historical circumstances are quite different for the two bodies of waters,[90] it may not be in the interest of Japan to respond negatively to a claim to

85 In a case involving a collision of vessels beyond Japan's territorial sea (then three nm), the Osaka High Court in the so-called *Texada* case, held that the relevant area fulfils the requirements of internal waters in light of its geographic situation and historical circumstances. Osaka High Court, 19 November 1976, translation into English in (1976) 22 *Japanese Annual of International Law* 131.

86 Shigeru Oda and Hisashi Owada, 'Annual Review of Japanese Practice in International Law XV (1976–1977),' (1985) 28 *Japanese Annual of International Law* 59 at 94–98.

87 United States Department of State, Limits in the Seas, No 120, Straight Baseline and Territorial Sea Claims: Japan (1998) at 6–13.

88 *Ibid.* at 9.

89 Article 35(a) of UNCLOS provides that 'nothing in this Part affects any areas of internal waters within a strait,' which has been interpreted as meaning that the status of internal waters precludes the application of Part III to that part of a strait. Satya N Nandan and Shabtai Rosenne (eds), *United Nations Convention on the Law of the Sea 1982: A Commentary* Vol II (Martinus Nijhoff, 1993) at 306–307.

90 The Seto Naikai would seem to be an exceptional case where a narrow body of waters have been exclusively used for internal navigation for a long period of time. For a discussion of the legal status of the Seto Naikai in connection with the Texada case, see Hideo Takabayashi, 'Legal Status of the Kii Channel-Limits of the Seto Inland Sea' (1977) 21 *Japanese Annual of International Law* 1.

historic waters by another State, since it could have some repercussions for its own claim. Unless the coastal State intends to completely prevent navigation through the relevant area, the incentives for raising any objections to a straight baselines claim or a historic waters claim in the Arctic are further reduced by the fact that certain measures could in any case be justified by Article 234.

4.3.2 International Straits

As a State consisting of a group of islands, there is a large number of passages between islands that may be considered as straits in geographical terms. As is the case with the straits in the NSR and NWP, the question is whether the straits may be considered to fulfil the functional criterion, that it is 'used for international navigation'. In practice, Japan has not acknowledged the right of transit passage to be applicable within its waters. When the territorial sea of Japan was extended to 12 nm by enactment of the Law on the Territorial Sea in 1977, the extent of the territorial sea for five 'designated areas' was limited to three nm 'for the time being'.[91] This measure was designed to avoid the regime of transit passage from being applied to straits, by leaving a high seas corridor suitable for navigation and thereby making the exception in Article 36 of UNCLOS applicable.[92] Debates in the National Diet reveal that the selection of five straits was based on their use for international navigation.[93]

The practice of Japan regarding its straits seems to have provided a satisfactory regime in guaranteeing navigational rights and freedoms for other States, and until recently no State had challenged Japan's position, with the exception of the United States.[94] However, in June 2016, a Chinese naval vessel for the first time passed through the Tokara strait, which lies between the Island

91 Law on the Territorial Sea (Law No 30 of 2 May 1977), supplementary provisions, para 2. An unofficial English translation of the law appears in Shunji Yanai and Kuniaki Asomura, 'Japan and the Emerging Order of the Sea—Two Maritime Laws of Japan' (1977) 21 *Japanese Annual of International Law* 48 at 92–93. The five areas are the Soya Strait, Tsugaru Strait, eastern channel of the Tsushima Strait, western channel of the Tsushima Strait, and the Osumi Strait, including areas which are adjacent to the waters and which are recognised as forming integral parts of those straits in terms of routes normally used for navigation by vessels. A map showing the location of the straits appears in *ibid.* at 59.

92 Article 36 of UNCLOS provides that Part III on international straits does not apply if there exists through the strait a route through the high seas or through an EEZ of similar convenience with respect to navigational and hydrographical characteristics. See Nandan and Anderson, *supra* note 52 at 176–178.

93 Minutes of the Committee on Agriculture, Forestry and Fishery, House of Representatives, 20 April 1977 at 4 [in Japanese].

94 United States Department of State, *supra* note 87 at 9.

of Yakushima and Kuchinoshima. The Chinese government explicitly claimed that the passage was in exercise of the right of transit passage.[95] In response, the Japanese government protested that the Tokara strait is not an international strait, relying on the fact that the strait is not used for international navigation.[96] Reliance on the right of transit passage by China may increase in the future, since it would allow China to assert navigational rights against other States while remaining consistent with its position on requiring prior authorisation for passage of warships in its territorial sea.[97]

Therefore, Japan may find itself in a position close to Canada and Russia with regard to international straits.[98] Since the meaning of a strait 'used for international navigation' has been the subject of considerable debate, it may be desirable for Japan to refrain from asserting the right of transit passage where there are differences of views on whether a particular strait meets the functional criterion of being used for international navigation.

5 Conclusions

Through the formulation of its Arctic policy, Japan has shown its desire to participate in the ongoing process of building and maintaining an international regime for the sustainable governance of the Arctic. Its main motives for participation in Arctic issues are in relation to the global implications of the various aspects of the changing Arctic. With respect to utilisation of the Arctic for shipping, Japan has adopted a cautious attitude on the direct economic benefits to be gained, especially from the use of the NSR as a shortcut between East Asia and Europe. While fully recognising the long-term future potential

---

95 Ministry of Foreign Affairs of the People's Republic of China, Foreign Ministry Spokesperson Hua Chunying's Regular Press Conference (17 June 2016) accessed 21 March 2017 at http://www.fmprc.gov.cn/mfa_eng/xwfw_665399/s2510_665401/t1373233.shtml.

96 'China says it does not need Japanese permission to sail ships through Tokara Strait' *The Japan Times*, 18 June 2016, accessed 21 March 2017 at http://www.japantimes.co.jp/news/2016/06/18/national/china-says-not-need-japanese-permission-sail-ships-tokara-strait.

97 The Law on the Territorial Sea and the Contiguous Zone of the People's Republic of China (25 February 1992), Art 6, translation into English, accessed 21 March 2017 at http://www.un.org/Depts/los/LEGISLATIONANDTREATIES/PDFFILES/CHN_1992_Law.pdf.

98 For a discussion on the relevance of practice regarding the straits of Japan for debates on the NWP, see Suzanne Lalonde and Frédéric Lasserre, 'The Position of the United States on the Northwest Passage: Is the Fear of Creating a Precedent Warranted?' (2013) 44 *Ocean Development and International Law* 28 at 39–42.

for Arctic shipping, Japan's current policy is to make contributions towards the fulfilment of the prerequisites for commercial shipping to be realised, in cooperation with the Arctic coastal States, and especially Russia.

Japan has not yet expressed its views on the provisions of UNCLOS relevant to the limits of coastal State powers in the Arctic, and appears to have kept quiet in practice. While it would seem unwarranted to assume that Japan agrees with or has acquiesced in the views of Canada and Russia on their powers under UNCLOS, the issue of acquiescence is a somewhat moot point as a practical matter. Practical, political and legal considerations make it unnecessary and undesirable for Japan to lodge objections to the current regulation of Arctic shipping by coastal States, and in particular the regulation of the NSR by Russia. Furthermore, the issues Japan faces at home regarding the balance between navigational rights and freedoms and coastal State powers make it unlikely that Japan would play an active role in the legal discussions on the extent of coastal States' powers in the Arctic. Given these circumstances, it may safely be suggested that the emphasis on cooperation with coastal States in Japan's Arctic Policy can be taken at face value and not as mere political rhetoric.

PART 5

Cooperative Mechanisms for the Governance of Shipping

CHAPTER 12

The Cooperative Mechanism for the Straits of Malacca and Singapore

Robert C Beckman and Sun Zhen

1 Introduction

The Straits of Malacca and Singapore (SOMS) is one of the most important shipping lanes in the world from both an economic and a strategic perspective. It is the main shipping channel linking the East-West trade for oil, natural gas, and raw and manufactured goods. It is also one of the most congested shipping chokepoints with various shallow and narrow sections within the Singapore Strait. The SOMS is a strait used for international navigation as defined in the 1982 United Nations Convention on the Law of Sea (UNCLOS) and therefore all States have the right of transit passage through the SOMS.[1] There are, however, a number of challenges to international shipping in the SOMS, including the lack of aids to navigation, the presence of shipwrecks and shallow reefs, potential marine pollution from ships and the lack of reception facilities and emergency response facilities.

The three littoral States—Indonesia, Malaysia and Singapore—have been cooperating to facilitate the safety of navigation and the prevention of ship-source pollution in the SOMS since the 1970s.[2] In 2007, after three years of discussions and negotiations, the three littoral States, with the assistance from the International Maritime Organization (IMO), formally launched the Cooperative Mechanism on Safety of Navigation and Environment Protection in the Straits of Malacca and Singapore (Cooperative Mechanism).[3] The Cooperative Mechanism enables user States and other stakeholders to

1 United Nations Convention on the Law of the Sea, adopted 10 December 1982 (entered into force 16 November 1994), 1833 UNTS 3 (UNCLOS), Art 38.

2 Joint Statement of Indonesia, Malaysia and Singapore on the Straits of Malacca, announced on 16 November 1971 (1971 Joint Statement), in (1972) 5 *New York University Journal of International Law and Politics* 425 at 425–426.

3 Cooperative Mechanism on Safety of Navigation and Environment Protection in the Straits of Malacca and Singapore (Cooperative Mechanism), Establishment, accessed 21 March 2017 at http://www.cm-soms.com/index.php?p=td&id=6.

 | DOI 10.1163/9789004339385_013

cooperate with the States bordering the SOMS by sharing the responsibility to maintain and enhance navigational safety and to protect the marine environment in the SOMS from the impacts of international shipping.

This Chapter will examine how the three States bordering the SOMS have worked with each other and the IMO to enhance the safety of navigation and minimise the risk of ship-source pollution in the SOMS. It first reviews the strategic importance of the SOMS and its legal status under UNCLOS, and discusses the initiatives taken by the three littoral States to cooperate in managing the SOMS, including by making proposals to the IMO and engaging users of the SOMS. It then examines the legal basis for establishing the Cooperative Mechanism. This is followed by a detailed analysis of the components of the Cooperative Mechanism and the reasons for its success. It concludes with lessons learnt from the Cooperative Mechanism and raises the issue of whether any of the features in the Cooperative Mechanism could be used as a model for cooperation between the coastal States and the user States in the management of shipping lanes in the Arctic.

2 The Straits of Malacca and Singapore

2.1 *The Importance of the SOMS*

The SOMS is the shortest watercourse that connects the Indian Ocean with the South China Sea. The entire Malacca Strait is approximately 520 nautical miles (nm) in length with a width of 10 nm in the south that broadens northward to about 174 nm between the Indonesian island of Sumatra and Thailand's Phuket Island.[4] The length of the Singapore Strait is about 52 nm, its breadth is about 8.6 nm at the west entrance and 17.3 nm at the east entrance, but it narrows to about 2.1 nm at Phillips Channel south of Singapore.[5] The Malacca Strait and the Singapore Strait are connected and managed as a single strait by the three littoral States and by the IMO.[6]

---

4 'Protection of Vital Shipping Lanes Note by the Secretary-General', Annex 'Profile of the Straits of Malacca and Singapore', 7 October 2004, International Maritime Organization (IMO), C 93/15.

5 Robert Beckman, 'Singapore Strives to Enhance Safety, Security, and Environmental Protection in Its Port and in the Straits of Malacca and Singapore' (2009) 14 *Ocean and Coastal Law Journal* 167 at 168. 'Strait of Malacca and Sumatera' in National Geospatial-Intelligence Agency, Pub No 174, Sailing Directions (Enroute) (2016, 14th ed), accessed 21 March 2017 at http://msi.nga.mil/MSISiteContent/StaticFiles/NAV_PUBS/SD/Pub174/Pub174bk.pdf.

6 1971 Joint Statement, *supra* note 2. Efthimios Mitropoulos, Secretary-General of the IMO, 'Opening Remarks at the Jakarta Meeting on Straits of Malacca and Singapore: Enhancing

The SOMS is one of the busiest and most important international straits in the world. It is the vital link for the carriage of oil from the Persian Gulf to the burgeoning Southeast and East Asian States. China, Japan, South Korea and Singapore all have considerable oil refining capacities that require a continuous stream of tankers to feed their refineries with crude oil.[7] It is also the main shipping lane for raw and manufactured goods to be transported from Asia to Europe. Currently, more than 60,000 vessels pass through the SOMS annually, carrying half of the world's oil flows and one-third of the world's seaborne trade.[8]

The safety and security of the SOMS are crucial to both the littoral States and the user States. Because of the narrowness and shallowness of the SOMS and the density of the traffic, navigation through SOMS is a challenge, and there is an ever-present concern about the risk of collisions, groundings or oil spills.

2.2 *Legal Status of the SOMS*

The three littoral States played an active part in the negotiations at the Third United Nations Conference on the Law of the Sea (UNCLOS III), which began in 1973 and concluded with the adoption of UNCLOS in 1982.[9] The establishment of the new regime on Straits Used for International Navigation that was included in Part III also reflects certain specific concerns of the SOMS.

It was agreed early in the negotiations at UNCLOS III that the breadth of the territorial sea should extend up to a limit not exceeding 12 nm.[10] This means

---

Safety, Security and Environmental Protection', 7 September 2005, accessed 21 March 2017 at http://www.imo.org/blast/mainframe.asp?topic_id=1028&doc_id=5269.

7 BP Statistical Review of World Energy, June 2016, 16–19, accessed 21 March 2017 at https://www.bp.com/content/dam/bp/pdf/energy-economics/statistical-review-2016/bp-statistical-review-of-world-energy-2016-full-report.pdf.

8 Sam Bateman, Catherine Zara Raymond and Joshua Ho, 'Safety and Security in the Malacca and Singapore Straits: An Agenda for Action' (Institute of Defence & Strategic Studies Policy Paper, May 2006) at 8, accessed 21 March 2017 at https://www.rsis.edu.sg/wp-content/uploads/2014/07/PR060501_Safety_and_Security_in_Malacca_Singapore.pdf; United States Energy Information Administration, 'World Oil Transit Chokepoints', 10 November 2014, accessed 21 March 2017 at http://www.eia.gov/beta/international/analysis_includes/special_topics/World_Oil_Transit_Chokepoints/wotc.pdf.

9 United Nations Diplomatic Conferences, Third United Nations Conference on the Law of the Sea, 1973–1982, accessed 21 March 2017 at http://legal.un.org/diplomaticconferences/1973_los/.

10 Satya N Nandan and Shabtai Rosenne (eds), *United Nations Convention on the Law of the Sea 1982: A Commentary Vol II* (Martinus Nijhoff Publishers, 1993) (Virginia Commentary Vol II) at 80–81. Kheng Lian Koh, *Straits in International Navigation* (Oceana Publications, 1982) at 3–4.

that ships transiting the SOMS (and many other straits used for international navigation) would pass through the territorial sea of one or the other of the littoral States and would be subject to their sovereignty.[11] It was essential that a carefully crafted regime be established for straits used for international navigation, including the SOMS, to provide a balance between the safety and security of the littoral States and their interests in protecting the marine environment, and the right of unhindered international navigation for all States through the straits.[12]

Under the regime of straits used for international navigation established by UNCLOS, all ships and aircraft enjoy the right of transit passage in the SOMS, which shall not be impeded.[13] The passage has to be solely for the purpose of continuous and expeditious transit of the strait, without threat to the sovereignty, territorial integrity or political independence of States bordering the strait, and in compliance with international regulations.[14] The littoral States retain their sovereignty over the waters forming such straits, but their sovereignty is subject to the provisions in Part III of UNCLOS. The littoral States may not hamper or suspend transit passage, and their right to regulate foreign vessels transiting through the SOMS is limited to matters on the safety of navigation and vessel-source pollution by giving effect to applicable international regulations established by the IMO.[15] In order to promote the safe passage of ships, the littoral States may designate sea lanes and prescribe traffic separation schemes for navigation in the SOMS, but these schemes must first be proposed by the three littoral States and then adopted by the IMO.[16]

Nonetheless, the transit passage regime applicable in the SOMS does not in other respects affect the legal status of the waters forming such straits, as territorial sea or exclusive economic zone, or the exercise by the littoral States of their sovereignty or jurisdiction over such waters. This carefully crafted balance between the rights and interests of the littoral States and the user States on the transit passage regime has become one of the most critical components of the overall 'package deal' in UNCLOS.

---

11 United States Department of State (USDOS), Limits in the Seas, No. 50, Territorial Sea Boundary: Indonesia-Malaysia, signed 17 March 1970 (entered into force 10 march 1971) (1970 Territorial Sea Boundary: Indonesia-Malaysia), accessed 21 March 2017 at http://www.state.gov/e/oes/ocns/opa/c16065.htm.

12 Virginia Commentary Vol II, *supra* note 10 at 279–293.

13 UNCLOS, *supra* note 1, Art 38(1).

14 *Ibid.*, Arts 38(2) and 39.

15 *Ibid.*, Arts 42 and 44.

16 *Ibid.*, Art 41.

3 Cooperation Prior to the Cooperative Mechanism

3.1 *Trilateral Cooperation*

The economic and strategic importance of the SOMS has long been recognised by the three littoral States and user States. Issues relating to navigation in the SOMS arose from the interaction of several factors that materialised in the 1960s. Each of the three littoral States had won their independence and were eager to solidify their achievement, both domestically and internationally. The immediate task in front of them was to establish a relationship of trust with their neighbouring States given the complicated history between them and the uncertain challenges from other States.

Indonesia's interests in the maritime domain date back to before independence. It was well aware of its maritime vulnerability because its land territory is divided by seas. The Indonesian government issued a two-point announcement in 1957 to declare an archipelagic State regime for Indonesia and to extend its territorial sea limit to 12 nm.[17] Indonesia's efforts to develop the law of the sea in the following decades had been centred on these two issues. After its confrontation with Malaysia ended in 1966, the two governments assumed a common position towards the status of the SOMS and to oppose any attempt to internationalise the straits. Singapore, on the other hand, had a stronger interest in maintaining the freedom of navigation through the straits, given the fact that it is geographically restricted by the two neighbouring States and its economy is dependent on international commerce. But the three littoral States shared common interests on the safety of navigation and the prevention, reduction and control of pollution in the SOMS.[18]

World trade surged after the Second World War and the shipping industry also grew as an important industry worldwide. Ships built with modern technology were more sophisticated in design and structure, and much bigger in size and capacity. During this period, the most dynamic trading routes were between European countries and Japan for merchandise exports, and between Middle East countries and Japan for energy supplies.[19] Japan's development

17 Hasjim Djalal, *Indonesia and the Law of the Sea* (Centre for Strategic and International Studies, 1995) at 298–300.

18 Michael Leifer, *Malacca, Singapore, and Indonesia* (Sijthoff & Noordhoff, 1978) at 31–35; Djalal, *supra* note 17 at 55–57.

19 World Trade Organization (WTO), 'World Trade Report 2008: Trade in a Globalizing World' at 15–16, accessed 21 March 2017 at https://www.wto.org/english/res_e/reser_e/wtr08_e.htm.

heavily depended on safe and efficient transportation in water ways through the SOMS. To this end, Japan was active in conducting hydrographic surveys to obtain accurate navigation data and in advancing the proposal to the IMO (then IMCO) to establish sea lanes in the SOMS.[20] Another factor that complicated the situation in the SOMS was that the British government withdrew its military presence from Southeast Asia in 1971, raising concerns whether Russia, Japan or any other maritime powers would attempt to assume the maritime security role previously undertaken by the British.[21]

The political environment among the three littoral States became more amicable with the establishment of the Association of Southeast Asian Nations (ASEAN) and the signing of the ASEAN Declaration in 1967 by Indonesia, Malaysia, Philippines, Singapore and Thailand.[22] It was explicitly stated in the ASEAN Declaration that:

> the countries of South East Asia share a primary responsibility for strengthening the economic and social stability of the region and ensuring their peacefull and progressive national development, and that they are determined to ensure their stability and security from external interference in any form or manifestation in order to preserve their national identities in accordance with the ideals and aspirations of their peoples.[23]

The convergence of political attitudes by the three littoral States provided an opportunity to resolve some of their maritime disputes. Indonesia and Malaysia entered into an agreement to delimit the continental shelf between them in the Strait of Malacca and in the South China Sea in 1969, and signed a treaty to delimit the territorial sea boundary in the Strait of Malacca, south of One Fathom Bank, in 1970.[24] Indonesia and Singapore negotiated and signed

---

20 Leifer, *supra* note 18 at 42–45; Koh, *supra* note 10 at 71. The IMO was known as the Inter-Governmental Maritime Consultative Organization (IMCO) until 1982 as a result of the entry into force of the amendments to the 1948 Convention by Res A.358 (IX) of 14 November 1975 and A.371 (X) of 9 November 1977, accessed 21 March 2017 at https://treaties.un.org/Pages/ViewDetails.aspx?src=TREATY&mtdsg_no=XII-1&chapter=12&lang=en.

21 Leifer, *supra* note 18 at 39.

22 Association of Southeast Asian Nations (ASEAN), About ASEAN, accessed 21 March 2017 at http://www.asean.org/asean/about-asean/.

23 The ASEAN Declaration (Bangkok Declaration) Bangkok, 8 August 1967, Preamble, accessed 21 March 2017 at http://www.asean.org/the-asean-declaration-bangkok-declaration-bangkok-8-august-1967/.

24 USDOS, Limits in the Seas, No. 1, Continental Shelf Boundary: Indonesia-Malaysia, signed 27 October 1969 (entered into force 7 November 1969), *supra* note 11; 1970 Territorial Sea

a treaty to delimit part of the territorial sea boundary between them in the Singapore Strait in 1973.[25]

These factors enabled the three littoral States to establish the political will necessary to cooperate in managing the SOMS despite their different positions on the legal status of the strait. In 1971, the three States signed a Joint Statement on the Straits of Malacca (1971 Joint Statement) 'with a view to adopting a common position on matters relating to the Straits of Malacca and Singapore'. The 1971 Joint Statement reads as follows:

(i) the three governments agreed that the safety of navigation in the Straits of Malacca and Singapore is the responsibility of the coastal states concerned;
(ii) the three governments agreed on the need for a tripartite cooperation on the safety of navigation in the two straits;
(ii) the three governments agreed that a body for cooperation to coordinate efforts for the safety of navigation in the Straits of Malacca and Singapore be established as soon as possible and that such body should be composed of only the three coastal states concerned;
(iv) the three governments also agreed that the problem of the safety of navigation and the question of internationalisation of the straits are two separate issues;
(v) the governments of the Republic of Indonesia and of Malaysia agreed that the Straits of Malacca and Singapore are not international straits, while fully recognising their use for international shipping in accordance with the principle of innocent passage. The Government of Singapore takes note of the position of the Governments of the Republic of Indonesia and of Malaysia on this point;
(vi) on the basis of this understanding, the three governments approved the continuation of the hydrographic survey.[26]

In this statement the three littoral States agreed that the safety of navigation in the SOMS should be the responsibility of the coastal States concerned, and that issues concerning the safety of navigation in the SOMS could be separated from the issue of internationalisation of the straits. It is apparent from the statement that there was lack of agreement on the legal status of the SOMS and

Boundary: Indonesia-Malaysia, *supra* note 11.

25 USDOS, Limits in the Seas, No 60, Territorial Sea Boundary: Indonesia-Singapore, signed 25 May 1973 (entered into force 29 August 1974), *supra* note 11.

26 1971 Joint Statement, *supra* note 2.

on the issue of internationalisation. Indonesia and Malaysia maintained that the SOMS were not international straits and that passage through the SOMS should be governed by the regime of innocent passage, and they sought to deny any attempt to internationalise the SOMS. Singapore, on the other hand, merely took note of their position. These differences continued when negotiations at UNCLOS III began in 1973. Indonesia and Malaysia maintained that innocent passage should apply in the SOMS, whereas Singapore supported a regime closer to freedom of navigation on the high seas.[27] These differences were finally resolved when agreement was reached on a new Part III on Straits Used for International Navigation.

In 1977, the littoral States established the Tripartite Technical Expert Group on Safety of Navigation in the Straits of Malacca and Singapore (TTEG) to set guidelines for senior officials and technical experts to further their cooperation in managing the SOMS.[28] The TTEG is comprised of experts from the maritime administrations of the three littoral States and meets annually to discuss and collaborate on measures to enhance navigational safety and to promote cooperation and coordination on anti-pollution policy and measures in the SOMS. Under the TTEG, the three littoral States have worked with the IMO to adopt routeing measures, navigational rules and a ship reporting system for ships transiting the SOMS. In addition, the TTEG established cooperation with a major user State—Japan—on several projects aimed at improving the safety of navigation in the SOMS. The TTEG remains an important platform for relevant States and other stakeholders to discuss and coordinate their efforts to manage issues relating to the SOMS. The annual meeting of the TTEG is now attended not only by the three littoral States, but also by observers from user States, for instance Australia, China, Germany, India, Japan and Norway, and other stakeholders, such as the IMO, the Malacca Strait Council, the Nippon Foundation, the Japan International Cooperation Agency (JICA), and shipping industry associations, such as the International Association of Independent Tanker Owners (INTERTANKO), the International Chamber of Shipping (ICS), the Baltic and International Maritime Council (BIMCO), and OMC International.[29]

---

27 Virginia Commentary Vol II, *supra* note 10 at 284–289.

28 Cooperative Mechanism on Safety of Navigation and Environment Protection in the Straits of Malacca and Singapore (Cooperative Mechanism), Tripartite Technical Experts Group (TTEG), accessed 21 March 2017 at http://www.cm-soms.com/index.php?p=component-info&id=1.

29 Cooperative Mechanism, Tripartite Technical Experts Group—Meeting Series, accessed 21 March 2017 at http://www.cm-soms.com/index.php?p=meeting-series&id=1.

3.2 *Ships' Routeing and Ship Reporting Systems*

The three littoral States have been cooperating with the IMO by proposing measures to enhance the safety of navigation and to minimise the risk of ship-source pollution from incidents in the SOMS. This cooperation began during the negotiations at UNCLOS III and the procedures are now set out in Part III of UNCLOS.

Both Indonesia[30] and Malaysia[31] established a 12 nm territorial sea in the 1960s and concluded a boundary agreement between them in delimiting the territorial sea in the SOMS in 1970.[32] Under the then international law, most importantly the 1958 Territorial Sea Convention, foreign ships exercising the right of innocent passage in the territorial sea were required to comply with the applicable laws and regulations of the coastal States on the safety of navigation.[33] The IMO, a specialised agency of the United Nations with the mandate for standard-setting for the safety, security and environmental performance of international shipping,[34] was recognised as the only body for establishing and adopting ships' routeing measures on the international level.[35]

With the increase in the numbers of large oil tankers transiting through the SOMS in the 1960s, the safety of navigation in these chokepoints became a topic of discussion at the Sub-Committee on Safety of Navigation of the

30 Government Regulation No. 4 of 1960 on Indonesian Waters, Art 1(2), accessed 21 March 2017 at https://portal.mahkamahkonstitusi.go.id/eLaw/mg58ufsc89hrsg/4_1960.pdf [in Indonesian]; Act No 6 of 8 August 1996 regarding Indonesian Waters, Art 3(2), accessed 21 March 2017 at http://www.un.org/Depts/los/LEGISLATIONANDTREATIES/PDFFILES/IDN_1996_Act.pdf; USDOS, Limits in the Sea, No 141, Indonesia: Archipelagic and other Maritime Claims and Boundaries, 15 September 2014, *supra* note 11.

31 Emergency (Essential Powers) Ordinance, No 7, 1969, as amended in 1969, Art 3(1), accessed 21 March 2017 at http://www.un.org/Depts/los/LEGISLATIONANDTREATIES/PDFFILES/MYS_1969_Ordinance.pdf.

32 1970 Territorial Sea Boundary: Indonesia-Malaysia, *supra* note 11.

33 Convention on the Territorial Sea and the Contiguous Zone, adopted 29 April 1958 (entered into force 10 September 1964) (1958 Territorial Sea Convention), Art 17, accessed 21 March 2017 at http://legal.un.org/ilc/texts/instruments/english/conventions/8_1_1958_territorial_sea.pdf. Malaysia became a party in 1960 but Indonesia is not a party, see Status of Treaties, accessed 21 March 2017 at https://treaties.un.org/pages/ParticipationStatus.aspx?clang=_en.

34 Introduction to the IMO, accessed 21 March 2017 at http://www.imo.org/en/About/Pages/Default.aspx.

35 'General Provisions on Ships' Routeing', IMCO, Res.A.378(X), adopted 14 November 1977, Preamble.

IMO.[36] Because the three littoral States had different views on the legal status of the SOMS, cooperation could not be strengthened until the rules governing passage through international straits were resolved at UNCLOS III. Once agreement was reached on the new legal regime governing straits used for international navigation, the three littoral States agreed to submit a joint proposal to the IMO to establish a traffic separation scheme (TSS) and standards for under-keel clearance in the SOMS. These measures were adopted by the IMO in 1977 in Resolution A.375(X) on Navigation through the Straits of Malacca and Singapore.[37] This new routeing system included a number of TSSs and deep water routes in areas at One Fathom Bank (off Port Klang—the main port for Kuala Lumpur), in the Singapore Strait and at the Horsburgh Lighthouse Area at the entrance to the South China Sea. In addition, special rules were adopted for deep draught vessels and very large crude carriers (VLCC) transiting the SOMS, including a requirement for an under-keel clearance of at least 3.5 metres at all times during the entire passage. In the same proposal, the three littoral States also included a list of navigational aids to be installed or improved in the SOMS for ships using the new routeing system. These routeing measures were amended in 1981 upon the recommendation of the three littoral States.[38]

The procedure for adopting a ships' routeing system is set out in Article 41 of UNCLOS, which provides that the States bordering straits may designate sea lanes and prescribe TSSs for promoting the safety of navigation. The littoral States are required to refer such proposals to the IMO with a view to adopt these measures that will subsequently be designated, prescribed or substituted by the littoral States. Ships in transit passage are obliged to respect applicable sea lanes and TSSs established in accordance with this procedure. The enforcement of such measures is primarily the responsibility of flag States. However, littoral States are given enforcement jurisdiction over these ships' routeing measures if a violation poses a threat of major damage to the marine environment. Article 233 provides that, if a foreign ship has committed a violation of the laws and regulations in respect of the safety of navigation and the regulation of maritime traffic, causing or threatening major damage to the marine

36 Leifer, *supra* note 18 at 35–42.

37 'Navigation through the Straits of Malacca and Singapore', IMCO, Res.A.375(X), adopted 14 November 1977.

38 'Navigation through the Straits of Malacca and Singapore', IMCO, Res.A.476(XII), adopted 19 November 1981.

environment of the straits, the littoral States may take appropriate enforcement measures.[39] It was the understanding of the three littoral States and a number of major user States of the SOMS that a violation of the provision of Resolution A.375(X) shall be deemed to be a violation within the meaning of Article 233, and the littoral States may take appropriate enforcement measures for such violation, including preventing a vessel violating the required under keel clearance from proceeding.[40]

In 1998, the three littoral States proposed to the Maritime Safety Committee (MSC) of the IMO that the TSS for the SOMS should be amended to facilitate the safe and efficient flow of traffic.[41] The MSC approved the proposal to amend the TSS so that the operation areas extended for more than 260 nm, from One Fathom Bank through the southern half of the Malacca Strait and the entire Singapore Strait, to the Horsburgh Lighthouse area in the South China Sea.[42] Along with these new and amended TSS and deep water routes, the MSC adopted a number of precautionary areas and inshore traffic zones, and amended the rules for vessels navigating through the SOMS. These measures have subsequently been amended to further enhance the safety of navigation in the SOMS.[43]

In addition, the littoral States proposed to the MSC that a mandatory ship reporting system be established in the SOMS. It was adopted by Resolution MSC.73(69) and entered into force on 1 December 1998, and is known as STRAITREP.[44] The operational area of STRAITREP overlaps with the TSS from One Fathom Bank in the west to the Horsburgh Lighthouse area in the east.

39 UNCLOS, *supra* note 1, Arts 41, 42(1)(a) and 233; J Ashley Roach and Robert W Smith, *Excessive Maritime Claims*, 3rd ed (Martinus Nijhoff, 2012) at 305–306.

40 Shabtai Rosenne and Alexander Yankov (eds), *United Nations Convention on the Law of the Sea 1982: A Commentary Vol IV* (Martinus Nijhoff Publishers, 1990) (Virginia Commentary Vol IV), Art 233, at 388–389.

41 'Procedures for the Adoption and Amendment of Traffic Separation Schemes, Routeing Measures other than Traffic Separation Schemes, Including Designation and Substitution of Archipelagic Sea Lanes, and Ship Reporting Systems', IMO Res.A.858(20), adopted 27 November 1997, authorises the Maritime Safety Committee (MSC) to act on behalf of the IMO in adopting and amending such measures.

42 'Report of the Maritime Safety Committee on Its Sixty-Ninth Session, Annex 6, "New and Amended Existing Traffic Separation Schemes"', IMO, MSC.69/22/Add.1, 1 June 1998.

43 IMO, *Ships' Routeing* (IMO Publication Sales Number: IE927E, 11th edition, 2013), Part B—Traffic Separation Schemes and Inshore Traffic Zones, Section V—South-East Asia, V1–V9.

44 'Mandatory Ship Reporting Systems', IMO, Res.MSC.73(69), adopted 19 May 1998.

It is divided into nine sectors each with an assigned very high frequency (VHF) channel for participating vessels to communicate with the vessel traffic service (VTS) authorities in Malaysia and Singapore. The primary objectives of STRAITREP are to improve navigational safety, prevent marine pollution, facilitate the movements of vessels, and support search and rescue and oil pollution response operations.[45]

3.3 *Voluntary Contributions by Japan to Safety of Navigation in the SOMS*

The safety of navigation in the SOMS is also a major concern for the international shipping community and the user States who rely on the sea lane for facilitating the shipment of their energy supplies and commercial goods. Sufficient and effective deployment and maintenance of lighthouses, light beacons, buoys and other aids to navigation are crucial to the safe passage of ships. Traditionally, it has been the coastal States that provide and maintain these facilities for navigation in waters under their sovereignty. But the coastal State's legal obligation regarding the safety of navigation is limited to giving 'appropriate publicity to any dangers to navigation, of which it has knowledge, within its territorial sea'.[46] In the SOMS, both Indonesia and Malaysia had voiced their concern over the burden of the financial costs, particularly with regard to the additional aids to navigation to be installed or improved for the use of TSSs and other routeing systems.[47]

Japan has been a major user State of the SOMS since the 1950s when its imports and exports increased as its economy grew. Japan's concern over the safety of navigation through the SOMS increased after the grounding of the supertanker *Tokyo Maru* in the Malacca Strait in April 1967.[48] In the same year, Japan submitted a proposal to the Sub-Committee on Safety of Navigation of the IMO, in which it proposed that the IMO consult with the littoral States to establish sea lanes in the SOMS. To this end, Japan also proposed that it be permitted to conduct hydrographic surveys in three areas in the SOMS in order to place additional aids to navigation and to remove navigational obstacles.[49]

45 Maritime and Port Authority Singapore (MPA), Vessel Traffic Information System: STRAITREP, accessed 21 March 2017 at http://www.mpa.gov.sg/web/portal/home/port-of-singapore/port-operations/vessel-traffic-information-system-vtis/straitrep.

46 1958 Territorial Sea Convention, *supra* note 33, Art 15(2); UNCLOS, *supra* note 1, Art 24(2).

47 Leifer, *supra* note 18 at 38–39.

48 Euan Graham, *Japan's Sea Lane Security 1940–2004: A Matter of Life and Death?* (Routledge, 2006) at 156–157.

49 Leifer, *supra* note 18 at 37.

Japan's proposal did not directly lead to the establishment of the sea lanes in the SOMS, but Japan did secure permission from the three littoral States to conduct a preliminary survey. Meanwhile, with the support from the Japanese government, the Malacca Strait Council was established in 1968 with financial support from the Japanese maritime community, primarily the Nippon Foundation, in order to conduct cooperative activities to enhance safe navigation in the SOMS.[50] In early 1969, the *Koyo Maru*, chartered by the Malacca Strait Council, conducted hydrographic surveys in areas from Eastern Bank to One Fathom Bank that provided data for identifying the critical areas for further survey.[51] Since then, Japan has made major contributions to enhance the safety of navigation in the SOMS by providing funding for hydrographic surveys and the establishment and maintenance of aids to navigation, and by providing buoy tender vessels and removing shipwrecks and dredging shallows of the seabed in certain areas.[52]

Japan also assisted the littoral States in addressing issues relating to ship-source pollution. In 1981, the Malacca Strait Council signed a Memorandum of Understanding with the three littoral States to establish a Revolving Fund under which the three littoral States can draw funds to combat oil spills from ships, and then repay the fund once the State recovers the clean-up costs from the responsible parties.[53] Japan, through the Malacca Strait Council, has been the sole country contributing to this fund, which amounts to SGD 6.18 million as of 2010 and is managed by the Revolving Fund Committee.[54] To date, the littoral States have drawn on the fund on several occasions: Indonesia and Malaysia in October 1992 to clean up the *Nagasaki Spirit* incident in the north Malacca Strait; Indonesia in October 2000 to clean up the *Natuna Sea* incident near Tanjung Pinang; and all three littoral States in May 2010 to deal with the collision between the *MT Bunga Kelana 3* and the *MV Waily*.[55]

---

50 Leifer, *supra* note 18 at 40; Nazery Khalid, *Yen and the Art of Malacca Strait Maintenance*, June 2007, accessed 21 March 2017 at http://www.mima.gov.my/mima/wp-content/uploads/Japanese%20contribution%20in%20SOM%20_26June07_.pdf.

51 Leifer, *supra* note 18 at 40–41.

52 Kiyoshi Saishoji, 'Japan's Contribution to Safe Navigation in the Straits of Malacca and Singapore' (1998) 2 *Singapore Journal of International and Comparative Law* 511 at 511–512.

53 *Ibid.* at 513.

54 MPA, *Factsheet on the Revolving Fund Committee* (*RFC*), accessed 21 March 2017 at http://www.mpa.gov.sg/web/wcm/connect/www/374402e3-20b7-421b-b177-2a27af1e965e/annexa_270510.pdf?MOD=AJPERES.

55 *Ibid.*, MPA, *Factsheet on the RFC*. MPA, 31st Meeting of the Straits of Malacca and Singapore Revolving Fund Committee, 27 May 2010, accessed 21 March 2017 at http://www.mpa.gov.sg/web/portal/home/media-centre/news-releases/detail/60cd2977-2908-4818-a891-790009od3823.

Core elements of these cooperative arrangements between the littoral States and user States have been incorporated into the Cooperative Mechanism established under Article 43 of UNCLOS.

4 The Cooperative Mechanism

4.1 *Article 43 of UNCLOS and the Duty to Cooperate*

The rules governing the innocent passage of ships in the territorial sea that were set out in the 1958 Territorial Sea Convention provided that no charge could be levied on foreign ships by reason only of their passage through the territorial sea, but that charges could be levied for specific services rendered to the ship such as pilotage, towage or ice-breaking services.[56] This understanding continued at the negotiations of UNCLOS III and is now set out in Article 26 of UNCLOS.[57] Since the maintenance of aids to navigation and vessel traffic services are not specific services rendered to a ship, the coastal States are not permitted to charge a toll or levy on ships benefiting from such services.[58]

In the negotiations on the regime for straits used for international navigation, some States recognised that it would be unfair if States bordering a strait were required to bear the entire burden of maintaining navigational and safety aids in the straits when user States were the major beneficiaries of safe passage through the straits.[59] The result was the inclusion of Article 43 in Part III of UNCLOS. Article 43 is designed to address the financial concerns of the States bordering straits in facilitating the safety of navigation and environmental protection. It supplements the regulatory regime governing transit passage by calling for the establishment of cooperative arrangements between the littoral States and the user States. In this regard, there are two primary reasons for such cooperative arrangements: first, it provides a mechanism for user States to assist the littoral States with expertise and other resources, and secondly, it

---

56 1958 Territorial Sea Convention, *supra* note 33, Art 18.

57 Virginia Commentary Vol II, *supra* note 10 at 235–236.

58 'Report of the International Law Commission covering the work of its eighth session', Doc A/3159, Commentary to the Articles Concerning the Law of the Sea, Art 19 Commentary para (1), (1956) II *Yearbook of the International Law Commission* at 274.

59 Virginia Commentary Vol II, *supra* note 10 at 383. 'Malaysia, Morocco, Oman and Yemen: Draft Articles on Navigation through the Territorial Sea, including Straits used for International Navigation', Art 23, A/CONF.62/C.2/L.16, (1974) *Official Records of the Third United Nations Conference on the Law of the Sea Vol* III, at 195.

ensures that the views and interests of the user States are taken into account in dealing with aids to navigation and pollution matters.[60] Article 43 reads as follows:

> User States and States bordering a strait should by agreement cooperate:
> (a) in the establishment and maintenance in a strait of necessary navigational and safety aids or other improvements in aid of international navigation; and
> (b) for the prevention, reduction and control of pollution from ships.[61]

Article 43 was carefully crafted in order to encourage cooperation between user States and States bordering the straits. Its language is deliberately hortatory in nature in order to balance the rights and interests of the littoral States and user States with regard to the safety of navigation and environmental protection. The use of the word 'should' rather than 'shall' in the chapeau indicates that any cooperative mechanisms must be agreed on by both the user States and States bordering the strait. Hence, the littoral States may not unilaterally impose charges on passing vessels based on Article 43. This approach was consistent with the principle that vessels should not be subject to tolls by reason of their passage alone through important arteries of the world.[62]

Article 43 does not define 'user States'. In the context of international merchant shipping, this presumably refers at any rate to the flag States of the vessels navigating through the straits. This is also reflected in the provisions of UNCLOS in relation to the regulation of navigation and pollution. But in a broader context of beneficial use of international shipping lanes, both the exporting and importing States could also be considered as user States. In the hypothetical case, for example, if a privately owned tanker flying a Panamanian flag regularly transport oil from Saudi Arabia to Japan through the SOMS, Panama is a user State because it enjoys the relevant rights and duties of the flag State with respect to the administration and regulation of the tanker, but it is equally clear that both Saudi Arabia and Japan have economic interests that might justify considering them user States for the purposes of Article 43.

60 Bernard H Oxman, 'Observations on the Interpretation and Application of Article 43 of UNCLOS with Particular Reference to the Straits of Malacca and Singapore' (1998) 2 *Singapore Journal of International and Comparative Law* 408 at 416.

61 UNCLOS, *supra* note 1, Art 43.

62 Satya N Nandan, 'The Provisions on Straits Used for International Navigation in the 1982 United Nations Convention on the Law of the Sea' (1998) 2 *Singapore Journal of International and Comparative Law* 393 at 397.

Despite the vague language in Article 43, cooperation between littoral States and user States may in fact be necessary. On the one hand, the littoral States have no independent duty to establish or maintain a system of navigational and safety aids in the straits.[63] Their duty with respect to the safety of navigation is limited to giving 'appropriate publicity to any danger to navigation or overflight within or over the strait of which they have knowledge'.[64] On the other hand, even if user States are willing to fund the establishment of aids to navigation to enhance safety, they are not able to do so without the consent and cooperation of the littoral States, since the waters forming the straits are under the sovereignty and jurisdiction of the littoral States.

Article 43 leaves it to the littoral States and interested user States to determine the precise procedures and specific measures to be adopted for specific straits used for international navigation. The legal significance of Article 43 is that it mandates cooperation and agreement.[65] Article 43 was drafted in response to specific concerns expressed by Malaysia, in particular, relating to the financial burden it would have to bear in ensuring the safety of navigation and the protection of the marine environment through the Malacca Strait without receiving any direct corresponding benefit.[66] It was therefore not surprising that the SOMS became the first strait to implement Article 43.

4.2 *Establishment of the Cooperative Mechanism*

After UNCLOS entered into force in 1994, Indonesia, Malaysia and Singapore initiated a series of conferences and workshops to discuss the prospect of establishing a cooperative arrangement to improve navigational safety and prevent pollution in the SOMS.[67] It was also around the same time period when the littoral States prepared and proposed to the IMO to amend ships' routeing measures and establish a mandatory ship reporting system in the SOMS. These new systems were intended to benefit all vessels navigating through the SOMS but it was the responsibility of the littoral States to provide and improve a large number of aids to navigation in the SOMS and to establish a shore-based vessel traffic service. Both Malaysia and Indonesia believed that it would be an unfair burden on them to enhance the safety of navigation and bear the risk of ship-source pollution in the SOMS, and they were not satisfied with the fact

63 *Ibid.*, at 397; Virginia Commentary Vol II, *supra* note 10 at 383.

64 UNCLOS, *supra* note 1, Art 44.

65 Oxman, *supra* note 60 at 409–410.

66 Nandan, *supra* note 62 at 396–397.

67 Beckman, *supra* note 5 at 241–242.

that there was only one user State—Japan—that was willing to cooperate to share such burden.

The IMO co-organised two conferences in Singapore with the Institute of Policy Studies on 'Navigational Safety and the Control of Pollution in the Straits of Malacca and Singapore: Modalities of International Cooperation' in 1996, and on 'Towards Implementation of Article 43 of the Law of the Sea Convention for the Straits of Malacca and Singapore' in 1999.[68] Although no agreement could be reached on the implementation of Article 43, the two conferences made significant progress toward reaching a consensus on the establishment of a cooperative arrangement.[69] The 1999 conference revealed a common understanding on a number of core issues: (a) the littoral States are in good faith seeking to find a mechanism to implement Article 43; (b) the potential mechanism should be designed in a way to respect and recognise both the sovereignty of the littoral States and the legitimate interests of the user States; and (c) the littoral States should take the initiative to establish such a mechanism in cooperation with the IMO.[70] One crucial issue that remained unresolved was how to design and manage a funding system that would meet the interests of both the user States and the littoral States.[71]

Discussion on the implementation of Article 43 faded after the two conferences. Nonetheless, in the early 2000s new developments at both the international and regional levels triggered a renewed interest in cooperating to implement Article 43 in the SOMS. After the 9–11 terrorist attack in the United States in 2001, there was an increased concern in the international shipping community about the potential of maritime terrorism, particularly in strategic chokepoints in major shipping lanes, such as the SOMS. As a result, the IMO introduced a number of measures to enhance the security of international shipping and port areas, including adopting the International Ship and

68 Tommy Koh, 'Keeping the Straits of Malacca and Singapore Safe and Clean: A Triumph for Cooperation', Keynote Speech at the 8th Cooperation Forum, Cooperative Mechanism on Safety of Navigation and Environmental Protection in the Straits of Malacca and Singapore, 5–6 October 2015, Resorts World Convention Centre, Singapore, accessed 21 March 2017 at http://www.cm-soms.com/index.php?p=meeting-series&id=2.

69 Beckman, *supra* note 5 at 242–243.

70 Robert Beckman, 'Towards Implementation of UNCLOS Article 43 for the Straits of Malacca and Singapore—Rapporteur's Report on the 1999 IPS/IMO Conference on the Straits of Malacca and Singapore' (1999) 3 *Singapore Journal of International and Comparative Law* 253 at 285–287, 290–291.

71 *Ibid.* at 291–292.

Port Facility Security Code (ISPS Code) in 2002.[72] Another factor that raised the concern over the safety and security of shipping in the SOMS was the upsurge in the number of incidents of piracy and armed robbery against ships in Southeast Asia in the early 2000s.[73] Alarm bells rang in Southeast Asia when Lloyds declared the Malacca Strait a war-risk zone, raising the prospect of increased costs of shipping.[74] Several major maritime States—including China, Japan, India and the United States—indicated their intention to take unilateral measures to improve the safety of navigation through important international shipping lanes if necessary, including for shipping in the SOMS.[75] In addition, in 2004, Japan, the only user State that had been voluntarily contributing to the navigation safety in the SOMS, communicated to the littoral States that it could no longer bear this burden alone.[76] These developments created pressure on the littoral States to reconsider establishing a cooperative arrangement under Article 43.

The decisive impetus for action to establish a new cooperative mechanism for the SOMS came from the Secretary-General of the IMO with the support of the IMO Council. As part of the IMO's Protection of Vital Shipping Lanes Initiative, the Secretary-General accepted an offer by the delegation of Indonesia to initiate an IMO-sponsored meeting to be hosted in Jakarta in September 2005 (Jakarta Meeting).[77] The purpose of the meeting was to provide an opportunity for the littoral States, user States and other stakeholders to agree to work together to enhance the safety of navigation, environmental protection, and overall security in the SOMS.

In order to set the framework for the discussions, the Foreign Ministers of the three littoral States met in Batam, Indonesia at the 4th Tripartite Ministerial

---

72 IMO, Maritime Security, accessed 21 March 2017 at http://www.imo.org/en/OurWork/Security/Guide_to_Maritime_Security/Pages/Default.aspx.

73 Karsten von Hoesslin, 'Piracy and Armed Robbery against Ships in the ASEAN Region: Incidents and Trends', in Robert C Beckman and J Ashley Roach (eds), *Piracy and International Maritime Crimes in ASEAN: Prospects for Cooperation* (Edward Elgar, 2012) at 119–138.

74 Nazery Khalid, 'Security in the Straits of Malacca' (2006) 4 *The Asia-Pacific Journal* 1 at 4–6, accessed 21 March 2017 at http://apjjf.org/-Nazery-Khalid/2042/article.pdf.

75 Beckman, *supra* note 5 at 244–245.

76 Beckman, *supra* note 70 at 245; Koh, *supra* note 68.

77 'Protection of Vital Shipping Lanes: The Jakarta Meeting, Note by the Secretary-General', IMO, C/ES.23/8, 16 September 2005; MPA, 'Background Information on the IMO and the Protection of Vital Shipping Lanes Initiative', accessed 21 March 2017 at http://www.mpa.gov.sg/web/wcm/connect/www/5b88f6d5-8b89-48dd-8420-6fb67631a117/background-info-imo-pvsl-070904.pdf?MOD=AJPERES.

Meeting one month before the meeting called by the IMO Secretary-General. The three Foreign Ministers issued a joint statement—which came to be known as the Batam Joint Statement—setting out the basic principles that the three littoral States would be guided by in the subsequent Jakarta Meeting. Among the most important paragraphs in the statement were the following:

> 4. The Ministers reaffirmed the sovereignty and the sovereign rights of the littoral States over the Straits of Malacca and Singapore, defined under UNCLOS 1982 as straits used for international navigation. As such, the primary responsibility over the safety of navigation, environmental protection, and maritime security in the Straits of Malacca and Singapore lies with the littoral States;
>
> 5. The Ministers emphasized that whatever measures undertaken in the Straits should be in accordance with international law including UNCLOS 1982. In this regard they acknowledged the interest of user States and relevant international agencies and the role they could play in respect of the Straits.
>
> [....]
>
> 13. Bearing in mind the responsibility and burden of littoral States and the interests of user States in maintaining the safety of navigation, environmental protection and maritime security, the Ministers welcomed the assistance of the user States, relevant international agencies, and the shipping community in the areas of capacity building, training and technology transfer, and other forms of assistance in accordance with UNCLOS 1982. In this regard they also welcomed closer collaboration between littoral States and the international community.[78]

The Batam Joint Statement represented the common position of the three littoral States on several important points. First, they emphasised that the littoral States have sovereignty and sovereign rights in the SOMS subject to Part III of UNCLOS, and thus their primary responsibility for the safety of navigation, environmental protection and maritime security in the SOMS must be recognised. Second, they acknowledged the interests of user States and the relevant international agencies (IMO) in these issues. Third, they welcomed assistance

78 The Batam Joint Statement of the 4th Tripartite Ministerial Meeting of the Littoral States on the Straits of Malacca and Singapore (Batam Joint Statement), Batam, Indonesia, 1–2 August 2005, accessed 21 March 2017 at https://www.mfa.gov.sg/content/mfa/media_centre/press_room/if/2005/200508/infocus_20050802_02.html.

from user States, the IMO and the shipping community in specific areas and forms in accordance with UNCLOS. In short, they signaled that because they have the primary responsibility under UNCLOS with regard to the safety of the SOMS, they must take the lead, but they would welcome assistance from user States, the IMO and the shipping industry, as long as it was consistent with UNCLOS. In other words, the three littoral States would not enter into any cooperative arrangement that would compromise their sovereignty or that would otherwise not be consistent with the UNCLOS.

The Jakarta Meeting, named the Meeting on the Straits of Malacca and Singapore: Enhancing Safety, Security and Environmental Protection, was held in September 2005 and attended by representatives of 34 States, two intergovernmental and seven non-governmental organisations.[79] The Jakarta Statement that was unanimously adopted by all of the participants reaffirmed the main points agreed on by the three littoral States in the Batam Joint Statement, and recognised the strategic importance of the SOMS and the need to ensure that it remain safe and open to shipping at all times. In particular, it agreed to establish a mechanism for the littoral States to meet regularly with the user States and other stakeholders to discuss issues relating to safety, security and environmental protection, and to explore the possible options for burden sharing.[80]

The second IMO-sponsored meeting took place in Kuala Lumpur in September in 2006, and was attended by representatives from a total of 31 States and one intergovernmental and nine non-governmental organisations.[81] The Kuala Lumpur Meeting reaffirmed the previous statements and made significant progress on the framework for establishing a cooperative mechanism between the littoral States, the user States and other stakeholders in the SOMS. Moreover, the littoral States had identified and prioritised six projects that would enable user States and other stakeholders to cooperate with the littoral States by providing technical and financial assistance to enhance

79 Protection of Vital Shipping Lanes, The Jakarta Meeting, Note by the Secretary-General, *supra* note 77.

80 'Jakarta Statement on Enhancement of Safety, Security and Environmental Protection in the Straits of Malacca and Singapore', IMO/JKT 1/2, Jakarta, Indonesia on 8 September 2005, in 'Protection of Vital Shipping Lanes: The Jakarta Meeting', IMO, C/ES.23/8, *supra* note 77.

81 'Protection of Vital Shipping Lanes: The Kuala Lumpur Meeting, Note by the Secretary-General', IMO, C.97/12, 25 September 2006.

navigational safety and environmental protection.[82] Issues related to maritime security were also discussed at the meeting. It was noted that progress had been made by the littoral States in enhancing maritime security and that the Regional Co-operation Agreement on Combating Piracy and Armed Robbery against Ships in Asia (ReCAAP) had been adopted.[83] It was agreed that the littoral States should continue trilateral efforts to enhance maritime security in the SOMS, but that issues relating to maritime security should not be included in the Cooperative Mechanism.[84]

The final meeting was held in Singapore in September 2007 with attendees from a total of 38 States, one United Nations specialised agency, one intergovernmental and 14 non-governmental organisations.[85] The Singapore Meeting welcomed and endorsed the newly established Cooperative Mechanism between the littoral States, the user States and other stakeholders on safety of navigation and environmental protection in the SOMS.[86] The Singapore Statement endorsed and upheld the statements and achievements by previous

82 The six proposed projects were: 1) Removal of wrecks in the Traffic Separation Scheme in the Straits of Malacca and Singapore; 2) Co-operation and capacity building on hazardous and noxious substance preparedness and response in the Straits of Malacca and Singapore; 3) Demonstration project of class B Automatic Identification System transponder on small ships; 4) Setting up tide, current and wind measurement systems for the Straits of Malacca and Singapore to enhance navigational safety and marine environment protection; 5) Replacement and maintenance of aids to navigation in the Malacca and Singapore Straits; and 6) Replacement of aids to navigation damaged by the tsunami disaster of December 2004.

83 Regional Cooperation Agreement on Combating Piracy and Armed Robbery against Ships in Asia Information Sharing Centre (ReCAAP ISC), About ReCAAP, adopted 11 November 2004 (entered into force 4 September 2006), accessed 21 March 2017 at http://www.recaap.org/AboutReCAAPISC.aspx.

84 'Kuala Lumpur Statement on Enhancement of Safety, Security and Environmental Protection in the Straits of Malacca and Singapore', IMO/KUL 1/4, Kuala Lumpur, Malaysia on 20 September 2006, in 'Protection of Vital Shipping Lanes: The Kuala Lumpur Meeting', *supra* note 81.

85 'Protection of Vital Shipping Lanes: The Singapore Meeting, Note by the Secretary-General', IMO, C/ES.24/7, 9 September 2007.

86 'The Co-Operative Mechanism between the Littoral States and User States on Safety of Navigation and Environmental Protection in the Straits of Malacca and Singapore (The Co-Operative Mechanism)', IMO/SGP 2.1/1, 16 August 2007, submitted by Indonesia, Malaysia and Singapore, accessed 21 March 2017 at http://www.mpa.gov.sg/web/wcm/connect/www/d87fcd3c-0b64-4f72-a3d9-dfeebd612412/spore-mtg-co-op-mechan-070904.pdf?MOD=AJPERES.

meetings, and invited the IMO to participate in the Cooperative Mechanism, to continue cooperation with the littoral States and to assist in attracting sponsors for projects and the Aids to Navigation Fund.[87] It was also agreed at the Singapore Meeting that the work of the TTEG in enhancing the safety of navigation and in protecting the marine environment in the SOMS should continue to be supported and encouraged. It was further agreed that the efforts by the littoral States to enhance maritime security in the SOMS should be supported and encouraged as well, but outside the scope of the Cooperative Mechanism.

4.3 *Components of the Cooperative Mechanism*

The Cooperative Mechanism was established to promote dialogue and facilitate close cooperation on matters pertaining to the enhancement of navigational safety and the protection of marine environment of the SOMS.[88] It was established based on several fundamental principles. First, it re-affirms the sovereignty, sovereign rights and jurisdiction of the littoral States over the SOMS; secondly, it is consistent with international law and in particular Article 43 of UNCLOS; thirdly, it is established with the agreement that the primary responsibility for maritime safety, security and environmental protection lies with the littoral States; fourthly, it recognises the interests of user States and other stakeholders, and that such cooperation should be on a voluntary basis.[89] The Cooperative Mechanism consists of three main components: the Cooperation Forum, the Project Coordination Committee, and the Aids to Navigation Fund. The TTEG will be the principal coordinating body of the three littoral States in the Cooperative Mechanism. An illustration chart of the structure is attached as Appendix 1.

4.3.1 Cooperation Forum

The Cooperation Forum (Forum) is the main avenue for user States, the shipping industry and other stakeholders to meet and hold discussions with the littoral States.[90] It is intended to promote open dialogue and an exchange of views among participants on issues relating to the safety of navigation and

87 'Singapore Statement on Enhancement of Safety, Security and Environmental Protection in the Straits of Malacca and Singapore', IMO/SGP 1/4, Singapore on 6 September 2007, in 'Protection of Vital Shipping Lanes: The Singapore Meeting', *supra* note 85.

88 *Ibid.*, Singapore Statement, IMO/SGP 1/4.

89 'The Co-Operative Mechanism', IMO/SGP 2.1/1, *supra* note 86.

90 Cooperative Mechanism, Cooperation Forum, accessed 21 March 2017 at http://www.cm-soms.com/index.php?p=component-info&id=2.

environmental protection in the SOMS.[91] The littoral States host, chair and provide the secretariat for the Forum on a rotation basis. The Forum will normally be held in conjunction with TTEG meetings and report its outcome to the TTEG for its further consideration and approval, where necessary; the TTEG, through any of the littoral States, may communicate the outcome to the IMO for its information and assistance.[92]

In addition to the littoral States, participation in the Forum includes representatives from user States, the shipping industry and other stakeholders, and is by invitation and on a voluntary basis.[93] Participation in the Forum has increased. For example, the 8th Cooperation Forum in 2015 was attended by over 150 participants from over 40 States and organisations (including 13 user States), compared to over 50 participants from 28 States and organisations (including 17 user States) when the Forum was first convened in 2008.[94]

4.3.2 Project Coordination Committee

The Project Coordination Committee (PCC), comprising representatives from the littoral States and project sponsors, is established to oversee the coordination of the implementation of the projects that have been identified and agreed to jointly by the littoral States and the contributing parties under the ambit of the Cooperative Mechanism.[95] The implementation of straits projects is a concrete demonstration of cooperation and burden sharing between littoral States, user States and other stakeholders, and is a key element in the success of the Cooperative Mechanism.[96]

The user States, the shipping industry and other stakeholders may voluntarily contribute to the implementation of specific projects either by financing support or by providing in-kind resources such as technical assistance and

---

91 Cooperative Mechanism, Cooperation Forum Rules of Procedure, Art 1, accessed 21 March 2017 at http://www.cm-soms.com/uploads/cmportal2014/Rules_of_Procedure/Cooperation_Forum.pdf.

92 *Ibid.*, Arts 3–4 and 8–9.

93 *Ibid.*, Art 5.

94 Cooperative Mechanism, Cooperation Forum—Meeting Series, accessed 21 March 2017 at http://www.cm-soms.com/index.php?p=meeting-series&id=2.

95 Cooperative Mechanism, Project Co-Ordination Committee Rules of Procedure, Arts 1–3, accessed 21 March 2017 at http://www.cm-soms.com/uploads/cmportal2014/Rules_of_Procedure/Project_Coordination_Committee.pdf.

96 Cooperative Mechanism, Project Coordination Committee (PCC), accessed 21 March 2017 at http://www.cm-soms.com/index.php?p=component-info&id=8.

equipment to specific aspects of a project.[97] The PCC enables the sponsors of projects to have a role in the overall project planning and implementation. In particular, the littoral States directly involved and the sponsors of a specific project may form a joint Project Implementation Team for the technical management and implementation of the project, and—to ensure equal involvement of the sponsors—all decisions must be made by consensus.[98] The PCC meetings are hosted by the littoral States on the basis of rotation, and are held in conjunction with the TTEG meeting or as decided otherwise by the TTEG.[99] All decisions of the PCC must be made by consensus with full participation of all representatives, and the outcome is reported to the TTEG for its further consideration and guidance, and if appropriate, through any of the littoral States, to the IMO and the Cooperation Forum for their information and further assistance.[100]

The first six projects were proposed at the Kuala Lumpur Meeting in 2006 and officially introduced at the Singapore Meeting in 2007. To date, thirteen projects have been identified and agreed upon under the Cooperative Mechanism. The user States that have participated in and/or contributed to projects include: Australia, China, Germany, India, Japan, Republic of Korea, Norway, Saudi Arabia, the United Arab Emirates and the United States; while other contributors include the European Commission, the IMO, the Malacca Strait Council and the Nippon Foundation.[101] A list of the projects, together with the contributing parties and the lead littoral State, are listed in Appendix 2.

4.3.3 Aids to Navigation Fund

The Aids to Navigation Fund (Fund) is intended to enable user States and other stakeholders to make voluntary, direct financial contributions for the provision and maintenance of aids to navigation and thereby improve navigational

97 *Ibid.*

98 Project Co-Ordination Committee Rules of Procedure, *supra* note 95, Art 6.

99 *Ibid.*, Art 7.

100 *Ibid.*, Arts 7 and 11, and Appendix.

101 Cooperative Mechanism, Contribution, accessed 21 March 2017 at http://www.cm-soms.com/index.php?p=td&id=9. 8th Project Co-Ordination Committee Meeting under the Co-operative Mechanism on Safety on Navigation and Environmental Protection in the Straits of Malacca and Singapore, Official Meeting Report, 8 October 2015, accessed 21 March 2017 at http://www.cm-soms.com/index.php?p=meeting-series&id=8.

safety and environmental protection in the SOMS.[102] The Fund is used mainly for the purpose of establishing and maintaining aids to navigation in the SOMS that are identified and agreed to by the three littoral States through the TTEG, in consultation with the contributing user States or other parties.[103]

The Fund is administrated and operated by an Authority appointed by the littoral States on a three-year rotational basis.[104] The Authority reports to the Aids to Navigation Fund Committee (Fund Committee), which is comprised of representatives from littoral States as well as invited contributors to manage the Fund in accordance with the best international financial practices of transparency and accountability.[105] All decisions of the Fund Committee must be made by consensus with full participation of all representatives, to ensure equal involvement.[106] The mechanics of administering the Fund include a clearly defined scope of the Fund, an annual audit by a qualified and independent third party auditor, an annual report to the TTEG and the disbursement of funds based on an approved work plan.[107]

Contributions to the Fund can be made on voluntary basis by States, industries, private benefactors, non-governmental organisations and intergovernmental organisations, including the IMO.[108] The following user States contribute directly to the Fund: China, India, Japan, Republic of Korea, Saudi Arabia, and the United Arab Emirates.[109] Moreover, some States and entities, such as China, Germany, Greece, Norway and the European Commission, also contribute to the Fund through an IMO Malacca and Singapore Straits Trust Fund that was established by the IMO in 2009 for the purpose of supporting

102 Cooperative Mechanism, Aids to Navigation Fund Rules of Procedure, Arts 1 and 3, accessed 21 March 2017 at http://www.cm-soms.com/cmportal%202014/Rules_of_Procedure/Aids_to_Navigation_Fund.pdf.

103 *Ibid.*, Art 2.

104 *Ibid.*, Art 8.

105 *Ibid.*, Art 6.

106 *Ibid.*, Art 7.

107 *Ibid.*, Appendix Rules and Regulations Relating to the Functions, Responsibilities and Management of the Aids to Navigation Fund.

108 Cooperative Mechanism, Aids to Navigation Fund, accessed 21 March 2017 at http://www.cm-soms.com/index.php?p=component-info&id=4.

109 *Ibid.* MPA, 'Cooperative Mechanism on Safety of Navigation and Environmental Protection in the Straits of Malacca and Singapore', accessed 21 March 2017 at http://www.mpa.gov.sg/web/wcm/connect/www/ce096504-e546-4710-af36-052bcf3418c0/annex_a_factsheet_on_co-operative_mechanism.pdf?MOD=AJPERES.

projects under the Cooperative Mechanism.[110] Furthermore, several non-governmental organisations with an interest in shipping contribute to the Fund, including the Nippon Foundation, the Malacca Strait Council, the International Foundation for Aids to Navigation (IFAN)[111] and the Whitherby Publishing Group.[112] As of 20 October 2015, the total contributions received by the Fund since its inception was approximately US$21.4 million.[113]

Placing and maintaining sufficient aids to navigation is a crucial element for the safety of ships navigating through the SOMS. There are currently more than 51 aids to navigation installed to assist mariners within the TSS, such as lighthouses, beacons, and navigational and mooring buoys.[114] The aids to navigation are primarily installed and maintained by the littoral States in whose waters they are located. Each littoral State will propose the work programmes on the basis of an annual plan to the Fund Committee and the TTEG, and, upon approval, the littoral State will receive disbursements from the Fund to meet the approved work plan.[115] Each littoral State will prepare an annual report of expenditures and work performance that is submitted to the Authority and subsequently presented to the Aids to Navigation Committee.[116]

---

110 MPA, 'IMO Fund Raises Straits Co-operation to a New High', 14 October 2009, accessed 21 March 2017 at http://www.mpa.gov.sg/web/portal/home/media-centre/news-releases/detail/b4e25fb0-b11c-44fd-add2-99221efeb35a; Ashok Mahapatra, 'Update on IMO Malacca and Singapore Straits Fund', CF7-3-1, 1 September 2014, at the 7th Cooperation Forum, accessed 21 March 2017, http://www.cm-soms.com/index.php?p=meeting-series&id=2.

111 IFAN is constituted as an English company limited by guarantee and is registered with the UK Charity Commission as a charity. It started in the Persian Gulf to provide navigational services. Until 2011, it was known as the Middle East Navigation Aids Service (MENAS). International Foundation for Aids to Navigation, IFAN About US, accessed 21 March 2017 at http://www.ifan-maritime.org/.

112 Witherby Publishing Group Ltd is a specialist publisher of regulatory, technical and operational marine and insurance publications. The company was established in January 2008 through the merger of Seamanship International and Witherbys Publishing. See Witherby, accessed 21 March 2017 at http://witherbypublishinggroup.com/Home.

113 'Protection of Vital Shipping Lanes: Recent Development of the Cooperative Mechanism for the Straits of Malacca and Singapore', IMO, C/ES.28/INF.2, 22 October 2015, submitted by Indonesia, Malaysia and Singapore, 3.

114 Aids to Navigation Fund, *supra* note 108.

115 Aids to Navigation Fund Rules of Procedure, *supra* note 102, Art 8.

116 *Ibid.*, Appendix Rules and Regulations Relating to the Functions, Responsibilities and Management of the Aids to Navigation Fund, para 2.

4.4 *Lessons Learnt from the Cooperative Mechanism*

The Cooperative Mechanism devised by the three littoral States, in consultation with the IMO, user States and other stakeholders, is a historic breakthrough.[117] It was the first example of the implementation of Article 43 of UNCLOS, which encourages rather than obligates user States and States bordering a strait to, by agreement, cooperate on the establishment and maintenance of aids to navigation, and on the prevention, reduction and control of vessel-source pollution. The Cooperative Mechanism goes beyond Article 43 in two ways. First, although Article 43 does not mention the IMO, the Cooperative Mechanism recognises that the IMO has a role as a facilitator. Second, Article 43 only calls for an agreement between the littoral States and user States, while the Cooperative Mechanism also provides for participation by non-State entities and international organisations, the shipping industry and other stakeholders.

The Forum provides an avenue for the user States and representatives of the shipping industry to meet with government officials from the littoral States to discuss issues concerning the safety of navigation and environmental protection in the SOMS. The users are given the opportunity to identify measures that can be taken, including proposing new projects which will enhance safety and environmental protection in the SOMS. The PCC provides a vehicle whereby the major user States and other stakeholders can demonstrate their interests by working with the littoral States on specific projects whereby they can provide not only direct financial support but also technical expertise. The Fund addresses the concern of the littoral States that the burden of providing aids to navigation should be shared between littoral States and users. In return, user States and other stakeholders who contribute to the Fund are invited to contribute to discussions on the management and operation of the Fund.

In sum, among the reasons that have contributed to the success of the Cooperative Mechanism are as follows:

1. The littoral States have had the political will since the 1970s to work closely together to advance their common interests through the technical working group known as the TTEG, and the Cooperative Mechanism allows the TTEG to continue to play its critically important role of enhancing cooperation among the three littoral States;

117 Joshua Ho, 'Enhancing Safety, Security, and Environmental Protection of the Straits of Malacca and Singapore: The Cooperative Mechanism' (2009) 40 *Ocean Development and International Law* 233 at 242.

2. The littoral States have demonstrated that they are willing to cooperate with the user States as long as the Cooperative Mechanism recognises their sovereignty, sovereign rights and jurisdiction over the waters of the SOMS and is consistent with Part III of UNCLOS on straits used for international navigation;
3. The substantive scope of the Cooperative Mechanism is limited to issues relating to the safety of navigation and environment protection in the SOMS only;
4. The littoral States share the view that the Cooperative Mechanism should be open and inclusive and should acknowledge the legitimate interests of the user States and other stakeholders in enhancing the safety of navigation and promoting environmental protection in the SOMS;
5. The littoral States recognised that the IMO could play an indispensable role as a facilitator for the Cooperative Mechanism;
6. The Cooperative Mechanism provides user States and other stakeholders with a platform to meet on a regular basis with officials from the littoral States to discuss the safety of navigation and environmental protection in the SOMS;
7. The Cooperative Mechanisms provides a vehicle whereby the major user States and other stakeholders can make financial and in-kind contributions to enhance navigational safety and environmental protection in the SOMS while at the same time having a voice in the management and implementation of their contributions; and
8. The Cooperative Mechanisms allows the littoral States to receive assistance in covering the costs related to discharging their obligations on safety of navigation and environmental protection in the SOMS.

5 Conclusions

The Cooperative Mechanism was developed for a specific strait used for international navigation in order to implement a particular provision in UNCLOS. While respecting and acknowledging the sovereignty, sovereign rights and jurisdiction of the littoral States, it encourages user States to fulfil their general obligation to cooperate with the littoral States to enhance the safety of navigation and to prevent, reduce and control ship-source pollution. The Cooperation Mechanism also provides user States and other stakeholders with a forum whereby they can engage with government officials from the littoral States, and with a structure that enables them to cooperate with the littoral

States in maintaining aids to navigation and in developing projects that will further enhance safety and environmental protection.

The issue which arises is whether the Cooperative Mechanism could serve as a model to enhance the safety of navigation and minimise the risk of ship-source pollution in the Arctic. The diminishing geographical extent and thickness of sea ice in the marine Arctic have a profound effect on the accessibility of shipping routes and natural resources, which in turn has attracted great attention from potential user States and the international shipping industry. One major concern for ships navigating through the marine Arctic is that the harsh, remote and vulnerable marine environment presents a number of unique risks. The lack of modern charts and infrastructure, communication systems and other aids to navigation pose great challenges for mariners. In addition, the remoteness of the marine Arctic makes rescue or clean-up operations difficult and costly, if not impossible.[118] It is both financially costly and technologically challenging to build and maintain sufficient aids to navigation and other infrastructure to assist international shipping in the Arctic.

It is noteworthy that major parts of both the Northwest Passage and the Northern Sea Route are within internal waters or territorial seas and thereby under the sovereignty and jurisdiction of the respective coastal States. If the major littoral States, Russia and Canada, take the lead in engaging the user States and other stakeholders to design a mechanism for cooperation, they may be able to safeguard their sovereignty and at the same time secure assistance from interested users States and other stakeholders to share the burden of enhancing the safety of navigation and protecting the marine environment in the marine Arctic. Under such circumstances, some elements of the Cooperative Mechanism for the SOMS could prove to be a useful model for the Arctic.[119]

118 Arctic Council, Protection of the Arctic Marine Environment (PAME), The Arctic Marine Shipping Assessment (AMSA) 2009 Report, at 186–187, accessed 21 March 2017 at http://www.pame.is/index.php/projects/arctic-marine-shipping/amsa.

119 For further discussion on the implementation of a cooperative mechanism in the Arctic, see Chapter 14 of this Volume.

Appendices

Appendix 1: Structure of the Cooperative Mechanism:[120]

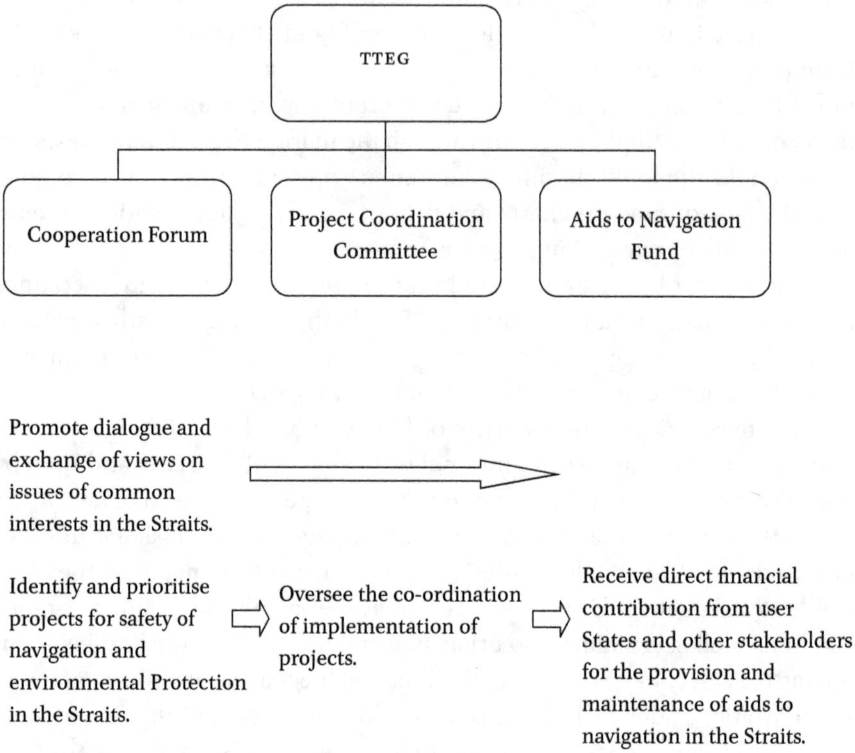

120 Cooperative Mechanism, Rules of Procedure, accessed 21 March 2017 at http://www.cm-soms.com/index.php?p=td&id=7.

Appendix 2: Projects under the Project Coordination Committee 2007–2016[121]

1—**Removal of Wrecks in the Traffic Separation Scheme in the Straits** Adopted in 2007 expected to be completed in 2016 Leading Littoral State: Malaysia Contributors: India, Germany, IMO
2—**Cooperation and Capacity Building on Hazardous and Noxious Substance (HNS) Preparedness and Response in the Straits** Adopted in 2007, completed in 2015 Leading Littoral State: Malaysia Contributors: Australia, China, European Commission, IMO Malacca and Singapore Straits Trust Fund and United States
3—**Demonstration Project of Class B Automatic Identification System (AIS) Transponders on Small Ships** Adopted in 2007, completed in 2011 Leading Littoral State: Singapore Contributors: Australia, Japan, IMO
4—**Setting Up of a Tide, Current and Wind Measurement System for the Straits** Adopted in 2007, completed in 2012 Leading Littoral State: Singapore Contributors: China, India
5—**Replacement and Maintenance of Aids to Navigation in the Straits** Adopted in 2007, on going Leading Littoral State: Indonesia Contributors: China, India, Japan, Korea, Saudi Arabia, UAE, IFAN, IMO, Malacca Strait Council, Nippon Foundation
6—**Replacement of Aids to Navigation Destroyed or Damaged by the Tsunami in December 2004** Adopted in 2007, subsequently withdrawn (after completion of the first phase with a contribution from China, Indonesia financed the second phase alone. Both countries agreed to withdraw the project from the list) Leading Littoral State: Indonesia Contributor: China

121 Cooperative Mechanism, Project Coordination Committee (PCC)—Meeting Series, http://www.cm-soms.com/?p=meeting-series&id=8, accessed 21 March 2017.

(cont.)

7—**Feasibility Study on Emergency Towing Vessel (ETV) Service in SOMS** Adopted in 2009 at the 34th TTEG Meeting, completed in 2011 Leading Littoral State: Singapore Contributor: IMO
8—**Concept Study on Real-time Monitoring of Under-Keel Clearance in the SOMS** Adopted in 2012 at the 37th TTEG Meeting. Completed in 2013 Leading Littoral State: Singapore Contributor: IMO
9—**Ship Traffic Management System in the SOMS** Adopted in 2014 at the 39th TTEG Meeting. Expected to be completed in 2016 Leading Littoral State: Singapore Contributor: Norway
10—**Study of the Blueprint for the Future Development of Safety of Navigation and Marine Environment Protection in the SOMS** Adopted in 2014 at the 39th TTEG Meeting. Expected to be completed within five years Leading Littoral State: Indonesia
11—**Development of Guidelines on Places of Refuge for Ships in Need of Assistance in the SOMS** Adopted in 2015 at the 40th TTEG Meeting Leading Littoral State: Malaysia Contributor: IMO
12—**Marine Oil Spill Monitoring System in the SOMS** Adopted in 2015 at the 40th TTEG Meeting Leading Littoral State: Malaysia Contributor: China
13—**New Study for the Enhancement of Safety of Navigation in the SOMS** Adopted in 2015 at the 40th TTEG Meeting Leading Littoral State: Singapore Contributor: Malacca Strait Council

CHAPTER 13

Oil Spill Preparedness and Response—The Singapore Experience

Captain M Segar

1 Introduction

The Straits of Malacca and Singapore is presently one of the shortest shipping routes linking West Asia to Europe. Incidentally, it is also the shortest sea route between the Persian Gulf oil suppliers and the Asian markets. As such, more than 50,000 vessels and around 90 per cent of the world's crude oil trade pass through the Straits of Malacca and Singapore each year,[1] making it one of the busiest shipping lanes in the world.

The Port of Singapore itself is one of the world's busiest ports with more than 140,000 ships calling annually and more than 1,000 vessels in her waters at any one time.[2] Singapore is also one of the major oil-refining centres and petrochemical hubs in the world,[3] which in turn has been a catalyst for developing Singapore into the world's busiest marine bunkering hub. In 2014, close to 42 million tons of bunker were lifted from Singapore.[4] The heavy marine

* The author wishes to thank Mr Gary Chew and Ms Denise Cheong for their assistance in this paper as well as Ms Angela Png, Mr Samuel Soo and Ms Shen Wanling for their valuable comments and inputs.

1 *National Ocean Environment Contingency Plan in Asian Pacific States: The Singapore Perspective*, Denise Cheong, Research Fellow, Centre for International Law, 3rd Asia Pacific Ocean Law Institutions Alliance (APOLIA) Conference Busan, Korea 26–28 April 2015, accessed 21 March 2017 at http://cil.nus.edu.sg/wp/wp-content/uploads/2015/05/APOLIA-Singapore-DeniseCheong.pdf.

2 SG Press Centre, 'Singapore Hosts Regional Oil Spill Contingency Workshop', *Maritime and Port Authority of Singapore (MPA)* (29 September 2015) accessed 21 March 2017 at http://www.gov.sg/resources/sgpc/media_releases/MPA/press_release/P-20150929-1.

3 Singapore Economic Development Board (EDB), 'Energy—Industry Background', *EDB* (16 September 2015) accessed 21 March 2017 at https://www.edb.gov.sg/content/edb/en/industries/industries/energy.html.

4 Adrian Lim, 'From a small port in Boat Quay to a world leader: 10 Facts about Singapore's port', *Straits Times* (26 June 2015) accessed 21 March 2017 at http://www.straitstimes.com/singapore/from-a-small-port-in-boat-quay-to-a-world-leader-10-facts-about-singapores-port.

 | DOI 10.1163/9789004339385_014

traffic and high volume of oil moving in and out of the port makes Singapore especially vulnerable to oil spills.

Comprising one main island and over 60 significantly smaller islets and with barely 270 kilometres (km) of coastline,[5] it is also not surprising that Singapore's coastal and marine environment is subject to dense use for an array of diverse coastal and marine activities, ranging from industrial uses such as anchorages, fairways, offshore installations, port facilities, oil refineries, petrochemical facilities, passenger cruise terminals and even an offshore landfill site; recreational uses such as sea-sports and beach resorts; to military use in the form of live firing areas. Oil pollution can easily disrupt many of these activities with economic and social consequences.

Notwithstanding such dense use of Singapore's limited coastline and sea space, our waters are abundant and rich in marine biodiversity. The five-year Comprehensive Marine Biodiversity Survey conducted by the National Parks Board of Singapore in 2010[6] discovered possibly 100 species of organisms new to science, 200 records new to Singapore and 10 rediscoveries, i.e., not recorded for more than 50 years in Singapore waters, many of which are sensitive to oil spills.

These factors make Singapore not only vulnerable to oil spills, but also sensitive to oil pollution. Vulnerability is the probability that Singapore will be exposed to oil pollution.[7] Sensitivity in this context refers to the economic, social and ecological sensitivity; sensitivity being the degree to which economic activity, society and the marine environment are affected by an oil spill.

Recognising the vulnerability and sensitivity of Singapore to oil pollution in our waters, the Maritime and Port Authority of Singapore (MPA) has put in place a comprehensive system to promote navigational safety in the port of Singapore and so minimising marine accidents and any consequent oil pollution. In addition, Singapore has an oil spill contingency plan, which helps to ensure that the relevant parties are operationally ready to respond to any marine emergency or accident (Oil Spill Contingency Plan).

---

5 A T K Yee, W F Ang, S Teo, S C Liew and H T W Tan, 'The Present Extent of Mangrove Forests in Singapore' (2010) 3 *Nature in Singapore* 139–45.

6 The Technical Committee on the Coastal and Marine Environment, 'Singapore's Integrated Urban Coastal Management', *Comprehensive Marine Biodiveristy Survey of Singapore*, accessed 21 March 2017 at https://www.nparks.gov.sg/cmbs/about-this-survey.

7 John A Matthews, *Encyclopaedia of Environmental Change* (Sage Publishing, 2014). See also Mark A Zacharias and Edward J Gregr, 'Sensitivity and Vulnerability in Marine Environments: an Approach to Identifying Vulnerable Marine Areas' (2005) 19 *Conservation Biology* 86–97.

This Chapter will focus on Singapore's strategies and experience in oil pollution preparedness and response, and will briefly discuss the lessons learnt from one of Singapore's major oil spills—the collision between oil tanker *Bunga Kelana 3* and bulk carrier *MV Waily* in May 2010. The Chapter will also discuss the various cooperative mechanisms that Singapore has with her neighbouring States, as well as with ASEAN member States, and will offer some observations for cross-learning and exchange of best practices with the Arctic States on oil spill preparedness and response.

2 International Convention on Oil Pollution Preparedness, Response and Co-operation

Following the *Exxon Valdez* incident in 1989, one of the worst oil spills of the last century, the International Maritime Organization (IMO) adopted the International Convention on Oil Pollution Preparedness, Response and Co-operation in 1990[8] (OPRC). The OPRC came into force on 13 May 1995. The Convention recognises the serious threat posed to the marine environment by oil pollution incidents involving ships, seaports and oil handling facilities[9] and is designed to facilitate international cooperation and mutual assistance in preparing for and responding to a major oil pollution incident and to encourage States to develop and maintain an adequate capability to deal with oil pollution emergencies.[10]

Parties to the OPRC are required to establish a national system for responding promptly and effectively to oil pollution incidents.[11] The basic minimum is the creation of a national contingency plan.[12] In addition, seaports and oil handling facilities have to maintain Oil Pollution Emergency Plans (OPEPs) if there are risks of oil pollution.[13] Masters of ships have to report to the relevant authorities any observed event involving a discharge of oil at sea or the presence of oil in the sea.[14]

8 International Convention on Oil Pollution Preparedness, Response and Co-Operation, adopted 30 November 1990, 1891 UNTS 51 (entered into force 13 May 1995) (OPRC).

9 *Ibid.*, Preamble.

10 *Ibid.*

11 *Ibid.*, Art 6(1).

12 *Ibid.*, Art 6(1)(b).

13 *Ibid.*, Art 3.

14 *Ibid.*, Art 4(1)(b).

Being a major oil refining centre and the world's top bunkering port, Singapore has to be prepared at all times to deal with pollution incidents that may arise. Recognising its responsibility to ensure that it has the capability and the resources to respond promptly and effectively to oil pollution incidents in order to minimise damage that may result from such incidents, Singapore welcomes the OPRC and acceded to the convention on 10 March 1999.[15] Our accession to the OPRC also demonstrates Singapore's commitment to cooperate with and to render assistance to requests for help from fellow OPRC parties to deal with pollution incidents and vice versa.[16]

To give effect to the OPRC in Singapore, Singapore amended its Prevention of Pollution of the Sea Act[17] (PPSA). The PPSA was originally enacted for Singapore's accession to the 1973 International Convention for the Prevention of Pollution from Ships as modified by the 1978 Protocol[18] (together, MARPOL Convention). The amendments allow Singapore to adopt and implement the many technical treaties and requirements for the prevention, reduction or control of pollution—this is done by giving MPA the power to make regulations to give effect to the OPRC and other international agreements relating to the prevention, reduction or control of pollution of the sea or pollution from ships (and any agreements that modify these international agreements).[19]

Pursuant to this power in the PPSA, the Prevention of Pollution of the Sea (Oil Pollution Preparedness, Response and Co-operation) Regulations[20] (OPRC Regulations) was passed and came into force on 10 June 1999. The OPRC Regulations have provisions that deal with emergency plans,[21] dispersants and equipment,[22] reporting of pollution incidents[23] and the right of MPA

15 MPA, 'Singapore Accedes To the International Convention on Oil Pollution Preparedness, Response and Co-Operation, 1990 (OPRC)', *MPA* (12 March 1999) accessed 21 March 2017 at http://www.mpa.gov.sg/web/portal/home/media-centre/news-releases/detail/caedoc46-504b-4964-8ecd-883495f9a67f.

16 *Ibid.*

17 Cap 243, 1999 Rev Ed Sing.

18 1978 Protocol Relating to the 1973 International Convention for the Prevention of Pollution from Ships (including Annexes, Final Act and 1973 International Convention), adopted 17 February 1978, 1340 UNTS 61 (entered into force 2 October 1983).

19 Chan Leng Sun, 'Singapore Legislation on Oil Pollution' (2005) 9 *Singapore Year Book of International Law* 147 at 154.

20 Cap 243, Reg 5 (OPRC Regulations).

21 *Ibid.*, Part II.

22 *Ibid.*, Part I.

23 *Ibid.*, Reg 9.

to carry out inspections for compliance with the requirements of the OPRC Regulations.[24]

3 Singapore's Response Strategies and Experience

The *Evoikos* (Oct 1997), *Natuna Sea* (Oct 2000) and *MT Bunga Kelana 3* (May 2010) were three of the largest oil spills in Singapore's history. The largest oil spill in Singapore waters resulted from the collision between two oil tankers *Evoikos* and *Orapin Global* on 15 October 1997. The collision resulted in a spill by *Evoikos* of 28,500 tons of marine fuel oil.[25] On 3 October 2000, the oil tanker *Natuna Sea* went aground in Indonesian waters and spilled some 7,000 tons of Nile Blend crude oil into the sea.[26] As the oil had also spilled into Singapore's waters, Singapore activated resources to clean up the oil spill. More recently, on 25 May 2010, oil tanker *MT Bunga Kelana 3* collided with a bulk carrier in the Traffic Separation Scheme of the Singapore Strait and spilled 2,500 tons of Bintulu crude oil into the sea.[27] These incidents highlight the importance of a comprehensive oil spill contingency plan and more importantly, the need to be prepared at all times to deal with emergencies.

MPA is the responsible national authority and lead agency for oil spill response in Singapore's waters. In all three incidents mentioned above, MPA played a critical role in coordinating seaward clean-up efforts, ensuring the continuity of safe operations in port, managing crisis communication efforts and conducting investigations into the collisions. MPA adopts a strategy of Prevention, Preparedness, Response, Recovery and Review, or the 2P-3R model, to respond to and combat oil pollution in Singapore's waters.

---

24 *Ibid.*, Reg 10.

25 Captain Mark Heah Eng Siang, 'Prevention and Combat of Oil Pollution in Singapore and the "Evoikos" Oil Spill Incident on 15 October 1997', *PAJ Oil Spill Symposium '98* (7–8 October 1998) accessed 21 March 2017 at http://www.pcs.gr.jp/doc/esymposium/12172/98_mark-heau-e.pdf.

26 Captain Mark Heah Eng Siang, 'Natuna Sea Incident—Singapore's Experience', *PAJ Oil Spill Symposium '01* (2001) accessed 21 March 2017 at http://www.pcs.gr.jp/doc/esymposium/2001/2001_mark_heah_e.pdf.

27 The International Tanker Owners Pollution Federation Limited (ITOPF), 'Bunga Kelana 3, Singapore/Malaysia, 2010', *ITOPF* (25 May 2010) accessed 21 March 2017 at http://www.itopf.com/in-action/case-studies/case-study/bunga-kelana-3-singaporemalaysia-may-2010.

3.1 *Prevention*

MPA works to prevent the occurrence of incidents through a series of measures, which include (i) enhancing navigational safety in our port waters, (ii) enforcing port regulations, and (iii) conducting regular checks to ensure shipboard safety. For example, Singapore's Vessel Traffic Information System is a multi-radar tracking system which can track some 10,000 targets.[28] With its monitoring and prediction system, the vessel traffic operators will be alerted by the system of any impending collision and this information would be relayed to the ship masters.[29] At least six enforcement patrol craft are deployed in the port at any one time to ensure that all ships and craft are in compliance with the port regulations.[30] MPA's inspectors and surveyors also conduct regular checks and inspections to ensure that safety measures on board vessels are observed and complied with.

3.2 *Preparedness*

Despite having the measures to prevent the occurrence of incidents in our waters, Singapore must still be prepared for the worst. MPA has the Marine Emergency Action Plan (MEAP) which is a national contingency plan for all marine emergencies such as collision, groundings, fire, search and rescue, oil and chemical pollution, where the primary objectives are to save lives, protect and minimise damage to properties, safeguard the marine environment, and restore normality of affected port operations as quickly as possible.[31] The MEAP contains detailed procedures on reporting, control, communication and co-ordination and rescue in a marine emergency and establishes channels of authority for the marshalling of resources.[32]

---

28 MPA, 'A Vessel Traffic Information System for the Future', *MPA* (25 July 2011) accessed 21 March 2017 at http://www.mpa.gov.sg/web/portal/home/media-centre/news-releases/detail/52cd3a9f-3dcd-4e29-9376-6ec4cb496537.

29 *Ibid.*

30 MPA, 'Inauguration of New MPA Patrol Craft', *MPA* (2 February 2012) accessed 21 March 2017 at http://www.nas.gov.sg/archivesonline/speeches/view-html?filename=20120209003.htm.

31 MPA, 'Welcome Address by Capt M Segar, Assistant Chief Executive (Operations), Maritime and Port Authority of Singapore, at the Salvage and Wreck Asia Conference, Salve & Emergency Response in Singapore: Meeting the Needs of a Global Maritime Hub', *MPA* (13 September 2012) accessed 21 March 2017 at http://www.mpa.gov.sg/web/portal/home/media-centre/news-releases/speeches/detail/43456580-f606-4c50-914e-619b32b732b1.

32 MPA, 'Towards A Future Ready Maritime Singapore—Annual Report 2014', *MPA* (2014) at 32, accessed 21 March 2017 at http://www.mpa.gov.sg/web/wcm/connect/www/6ddbdf35

The Oil Spill Contingency Plan supplements the MEAP and enables MPA to call upon resources from the oil industry and response companies during an oil spill. The Oil Spill Contingency Plan defines the roles of all stakeholders, identifies and prioritises sensitive areas, requires that regular exercises and training be conducted and periodic reviews of the plan to determine if any revisions are needed. It also includes standard operating procedures for various aspects of oil spill clean up, including notification, evaluation, response requirements, clean-up operations and termination of operations. As all relevant stakeholders from both government and private entities (e.g., oil spill response companies, various oil terminals) are parties to the plan, this ensures a common understanding between all parties and thus a more coordinated and efficient response in the event of an oil spill emergency.[33]

To prepare our officers and ensure that they are properly trained, MPA sends our officers for oil spill response courses which have been developed in line with the International Maritime Organization's (IMO) OPRC Model Courses.[34] There are three levels of competency for these courses, namely Level 1 (operational staff), Level 2 (supervisors and on-scene commanders) and Level 3 (senior management personnel).

To test and demonstrate Singapore's readiness to respond effectively to marine incidents, MPA organises annually a multi-agency joint oil spill exercise codenamed 'Ex JOSE' to test and demonstrate Singapore's readiness to tackle oil spills. These exercises are conducted to ensure the effective implementation of the Oil Spill Contingency Plan and the readiness of personnel to respond to incidents should prevention fail. The recent Ex JOSE in April 2015 comprised a table-top management exercise at MPA's Port Operations Control Centre Vista and a full-scale oil and chemical spill response equipment deployment. Over 180 personnel from various agencies participated in the table-top exercise and seaward exercise. The spill response teams deployed equipment such as oil containment booms, harbour busters and specialised skimmers. In addition to 22 anti-pollution craft, MPA also deployed an aircraft fitted with aerial dispersant spraying system and an unmanned aerial vehicle (UAV) that

-93d0-4a1d-9ee4-4a997d8c241c/mpa-intergrated-report-2014.pdf?MOD=AJPERES &CACHEID=6ddbdf35-93d0-4a1d-9ee4-4a997d8c241c.

33 *Ibid.*

34 International Maritime Organization (IMO), 'IMO Model Courses', *IMO* (2016) accessed 21 March 2017 at http://www.imo.org/en/OurWork/Environment/PollutionResponse/IMOOPRCModelCourses/Pages/IMO-OPRC-Model-Courses.aspx.

had the capability to provide aerial footages for better situational awareness on the ground and to monitor the effectiveness of the clean-up operations.[35]

3.3 *Response*

Under the Oil Spill Contingency Plan, MPA employs the use of a three-tiered response system in the event of an oil spill emergency, which is in line with international best practices. The concept of tiered response links the oil spill scenarios to attainable scales of response and enables escalation from one-tiered response to another should the need arise. In addition, it provides a practical basis for planning of an oil spill response in terms of required resources and likely environmental impact.

In the event of large-scale oil pollution, specifically Tier-Two and Tier-Three incidents, the Emergency Operations Committee (EOC) is activated to oversee operations relating to the mitigation and combat of such large-scale oil spills. The EOC is chaired by MPA and comprises representatives from other government agencies and commercial service providers who will be activated as required to support MPA in various aspects of spill response operations. For example, the Police Coast Guard (PCG) may be activated to support in seaward traffic management, while the National Environmental Agency (NEA) may be activated to coordinate shoreline clean-up if the oil spill reaches shore.[36] Commercial service providers such as terminal operators, oil spill response companies, salvage companies, P&I clubs, technical experts and vessel owners may also be activated to provide assistance and resources as required.

The following categorisation of responses would be used to determine the resources to be mobilised and deployed:

---

35 MPA, 'Singapore showcases response capabilities at multi-agency oil spill exercise', *MPA* (24 April 2015) accessed 21 March 2017 at http://www.mpa.gov.sg/web/portal/home/media-centre/news-releases/detail/68bcbfb3-bde2-4d00-ab13-d561e81f9604.

36 Other government agencies include Public Utilities Board (PUB), Immigration Checkpoint Authority (ICA), Singapore Civil Defense Force (SCDF), Singapore Police Force (SPF), Republic of Singapore Navy (RSN), Republic of Singapore Air Force (RSAF), Army, Ministry of Health (MOH), Ministry of Communications and Information (MCI), Ministry of Foreign Affairs (MFA), Civil Aviation Authority of Singapore (CAAS), Singapore Land Authority (SLA), Jurong Town Council (JTC), Sentosa Development Corporation (SDC), Singapore Tourism Board (STB), Customs, Housing Development Board (HDB), National Parks Board (NParks), Agri-Food & Veterinary Authority of Singapore (AVA), Building Construction Authority (BCA), and People's Association (PA).

Tier-One Incident

A tier-one incident is a minor oil spill where the situation can be managed effectively using the vessel's or oil handling facility's own resources. The OPRC Regulations require all operators of oil handling facilities and owners of licensed tug boats to maintain anti-pollution resources such as dispersants, booms, pumps etc. at their facilities and on board the tug boats (as applicable).[37] The operators of these oil terminals and owners of licensed tug boats are to render their anti-pollution resources and such other assistance to MPA as may be required.[38]

Tier-Two Incident

A tier-two incident is an oil spill where the extent of pollution is wider than it is for a tier-one incident but the situation is contained at sea and does not extend to land. Such an incident typically draws on not only a vessel's or terminal's resources but also MPA's resources. In a tier-two incident, the EOC will be activated. MPA will be the lead agency coordinating resources from government and commercial providers as needed and directing seaward operations through the EOC.

TABLE 13.1 *EOC set-up*

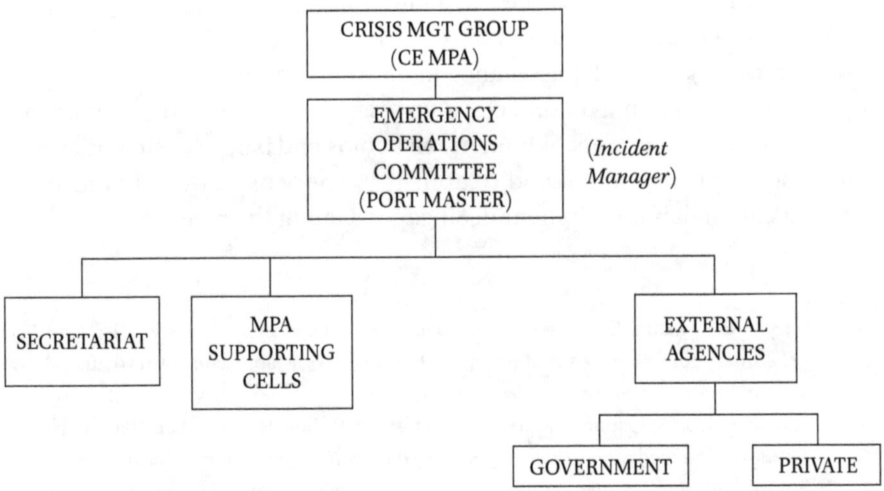

37 OPRC Regulations, *supra* note 20, Regs 4 and 5.

38 *Ibid.*, Reg 6.

Tier-Three Incident

A tier-three incident is a large-scale oil spill with the potential to cause significant economic and environmental damage. Such an incident requires an extensive multi-agency emergency response and potentially even resources from overseas if national resources prove insufficient. As with tier-two incidents, MPA will be the lead agency coordinating resources from government and commercial providers as needed and all seaward operations will be directed by MPA through the EOC.

Response actions are prioritised based on the circumstances of the spill and prevailing conditions such as weather and water current, type of oil and time needed to deploy resources to the scene. The circumstances of each incident will be evaluated before mobilising equipment or other resources. Depending on the circumstances, the typical response actions include (i) preventing or reducing further spillage, (ii) containment and recovery, (iii) applying dispersants, (iv) protection of sensitive resources, e.g., water-intake points, and (v) shoreline clean up.

MPA is usually the first responder to an oil spill incident; hence we have also built up our own first-response capability by equipping our patrol craft with approved oil spill dispersants. When deployed, these patrol craft will be able to spray dispersants to mitigate the impact of an oil spill if appropriate.[39] In the case of tier-two and tier-three incidents, apart from involving other government agencies, MPA may also activate the oil terminals and oil spill clean-up agencies, such as Oil Spill Response Ltd (OSRL) and Singapore Oil Spill Response Centre (SOSRC), to render assistance in oil spill clean up. The resources used by the oil terminals and oil spill clean-up agencies include anti-pollution craft with approved dispersants, skimmers, oil booms and barges to store recovered oil for subsequent disposal and treatment.[40] The MEAP also contains up-to-date lists of available equipment in Singapore and in the region.[41]

---

39 Daryll Nanayakara, 'New MPA patrol boats can tackle oil spills faster', *AsiaOne News* (3 February 2012) accessed 21 March 2017 at http://news.asiaone.com/News/Latest+News/Singapore/Story/A1Story20120203-325543.html.

40 Joshua H Ho, 'Singapore's Maritime Interest' in Joshua H Ho & Sam Bateman (eds), *Maritime Challenges and Priorities in Asia: Implications for Regional Security* (Routledge Publishing, 2012) at 132; International Tanker Owners Pollution Federation Limited (ITOPF), 'Country Profiles—A Summary of Oil Spill Response Arrangements & Resources Worldwide—Singapore', *ITOPF* (December 2009) accessed 21 March 2017 at http://www.itopf.com/fileadmin/data/Documents/Country_Profiles/singapore.pdf.

41 MPA, 'Welcome Address by Mr Cheong Keng Soon, Director Port Division, Maritime and Port Authority of Singapore, at the Salvage and Wreck Asia Conference', *MPA*

As the lead agency for marine incidents, it is critical for MPA to optimise its situational awareness so that it has as much information as is available to assist in the decision-making process. Besides having our on-scene commander and port inspectors at the incident site to report on the situation, MPA also leverages technology to enhance our situational awareness. At the onset of an oil spill, MPA uses the oil spill modelling tool, OILMAP, to predict the movement of the oil slick based on the forecasted weather and tide conditions. This will allow MPA better to deploy resources to areas that might be affected by the oil spill and prioritise their actions with the aim of minimising damage and loss. MPA also works with Republic of Singapore Air Force (RSAF) and private contractors to conduct aerial reconnaissance. At times, satellite imaging is also used to complement the aerial reconnaissance. To reduce reliance on other agencies and the unreliability of satellite imaging due to cloud cover, MPA has equipped our patrol boats with Closed-Circuit Television (CCTV) and UAVs that provide video links back to the EOC based at MPA's Port Operations Control Centre (POCC) for real-time coverage of the incident.[42] With their ability to fly at higher altitudes, the UAVs are able to enhance the EOC's situational awareness by providing greater line of sight.

3.4 *Recovery*

After the initial spill response, steps must be taken to ensure the return to normalcy. There are procedures in place to ensure a smooth recovery process. Oil that is recovered from the sea by skimmers is collected in storage tanks and brought to our approved reception facilities for proper treatment and disposal. If the oil slicks reach shore, the NEA will be activated to coordinate shoreline clean up. This involves the removal of final traces of oil and oily stains on the beach and shore facilities.

Recovery also includes the settlement of claims, which is usually a difficult and long-drawn process that might take months and even years to settle. To avoid such a scenario, MPA has signed a Memorandum of Understanding (MOU) with the International Tanker Owners Pollution Federation (ITOPF) to pre-set the rates for vessels and equipment deployment.[43] This will reduce disagreements and expedite claims settlement for oil pollution incidents occurring in Singapore's waters, involving vessels covered by any of the International

(12 September 2013) accessed 21 March 2017 at http://www.mpa.gov.sg/web/portal/home/media-centre/news-releases/speeches/detail/5c174094-a182-4f68-a372-133dd33e6fc5.

42 MPA, *supra* note 35.

43 ITOPF, *supra* note 40.

Group of P&I Clubs.[44] MPA gazettes its rates for the provision of its oil spill response services, which include hydrographic, garbage collection and patrol craft used for anti-oil pollution purposes.[45] Where the oil spill response services are provided by participating oil spill response agencies other than MPA, the charges payable will be computed according to the applicable rates set out in the MOU.

3.5 *Review*

MPA regularly (annually and after every oil spill incident) reviews its oil spill contingency plan to ensure that it remains relevant and effective and will consult with other government agencies where appropriate.[46] MPA has in the past also engaged experts, such as ITOPF and the Centre of Documentation, Research and Experimentation on Accidental Water Pollution (CEDRE), to conduct an independent review of our Oil Spill Contingency Plan, resources and response strategy.[47] As the Oil Spill Contingency Plan is tested annually through exercises, these exercises also serve as an important platform where various documents of the Plan, including the standard operating procedures and contact lists, are updated. Valuable lessons learnt from past oil spill incidents are also taken into consideration when updating our Oil Spill Contingency Plan.

4 Case Study: MT Bunga Kelana 3

The oil spill incident resulting from a collision between the *MT Bunga Kelana 3* and *MV Waily* illustrates how the elements of preparedness and response in MPA's 2P-3R model were critical. It also illustrates the importance of

44 MPA, 'MPA and ITOPF renew pioneering agreement to expedite oil spill compensation claims', *MPA* (10 April 2013) accessed 21 March 2017 at http://www.mpa.gov.sg/web/portal/home/media-centre/news-releases/detail/37fecaod-a6bd-46be-bf22-ecedd929885c.

45 Cap 170A, 2000 Rev Ed Sing, N 2, Section 9.

46 For example, reviews were conducted following the *Evoikos* and *Natuna Sea* incidents where the MPA reflected on the lessons they had learnt and identified areas of strength as well as those for further improvement. See Heah, *supra* notes 25 and 26.

47 Brian Dicks, Tosh Moller and Richard Santner, 'The *Evoikos* and *Pontoon 300* Incidents—The Technical Adviser's Perspective', *ITOPF* (7–8 October 1998) accessed 21 March 2017 at http://www.itopf.com/fileadmin/data/Documents/Papers/paj_98.pdf.

conducting a review—very much a part of the 2P-3R model—which yielded several valuable lessons.

4.1 *Background*

On 25 May 2010, MPA received a report that a Malaysian-registered tanker, *MT Bunga Kelana 3*, and a St Vincent and The Grenadines-registered bulk carrier, *MV Waily*, had collided in the Traffic Separation Scheme of the Straits of Malacca and Singapore. The incident location is about 13 km southeast of Changi East, in the eastern part of Singapore. The collision resulted in the rupture of four cargo tanks on board *MT Bunga Kelana 3* and 2,500 tons of crude oil were spilled. MPA activated the Oil Spill Contingency Plan and convened the EOC to respond to the incident.

4.2 *How MPA Used Its 2P–3R Model*

As the first responder, MPA deployed four patrol craft to survey the situation. The EOC, oil spill response companies, and salvage companies were then activated and resources were deployed to combat the oil spill. The resources deployed included anti-pollution craft with dispersant, containment booms and skimmers. The response strategies adopted by MPA were as follows: (1) isolate the spill source by transferring the remaining oil in the breached tanks of the tanker to other tanks while laying of oil booms around the tanker; (2) protect sensitive areas by booming areas such as recreational beaches and water in-take points; (3) disperse the oil using dispersants during the 'window period' when the spilled oil can still be dispersed; and (4) contain and recover the spilled oil using skimmers and flotsam-retrieving craft, especially when the dispersants were no longer effective. Response decisions were aided by information from OILMAP as well as from aerial reconnaissance and satellite imaging.

4.3 *Lessons Learnt*

Having a contingency plan in place as well as an annual oil spill exercise enabled MPA and all the government agencies to respond quickly and take steps to minimise marine environmental damage and economic losses. A review following the termination of clean-up operations yielded the following lessons:

1. Inter-agency Coordination and Communication

   One of the lessons we learnt was the value of strong inter-agency coordination and communication. There was some initial confusion about the roles of each government agency in the area of shoreline protection and clean up. However, the agencies were quick to come to a consensus and worked expeditiously to clean up the oil spill. Having all relevant agencies represented at the EOC facilitated the coordination and communication process between all parties. Meetings were also held to update the tanker managers, P&I Club and ITOPF representatives on the progress of clean-up operations and to discuss the next steps. The EOC also kept our Indonesian and Malaysian counterparts informed of the situation. In addition, being able to communicate with our assets at sea allowed the EOC to have better situational awareness and control of the situation. To facilitate the flow of information exchange, MPA's response craft were fitted with communication equipment that had direct access to the EOC and other response agencies.

2. Risk-based Approach

We learnt the importance of prioritising the sensitive areas. As the extent of the oil spill was large, it was difficult to protect all the sensitive areas at once. Hence, we had to do a risk analysis of the sensitive areas and determine which ones were the most vulnerable, taking into consideration predictions from OILMAP. Resources were then deployed to various sensitive areas, such as East Coast Park, Changi Naval Base, Tanah Merah Ferry Terminal, for protection.

3. Multi-prong Action Plan

Implementation of a multi-prong action plan, which used a combination of clean-up strategies to locate and clean up the oil, was very effective. For example, MPA used its OILMAP prediction tool with hourly updated wind direction as well as aerial and ground reconnaissance efforts to track the movement of oil. Based on such predictions and surveillance reports, anti-pollution craft and personnel were deployed effectively round the clock to expedite clean-up operations. We also learnt that instead of just relying solely on the air force for air surveillance, we could complement it using commercial helicopter operators.

4. Guidelines for Dispersants Used

We also learnt that it was important to have guidelines on the use of dispersants to facilitate decisions on operational strategies to employ, as well as to ensure the prudent use of, dispersants. This, in turn, will help reduce disagreements from owners and P&I Clubs on the appropriate use of dispersants, thus expediting claims settlement for oil pollution incidents occurring in Singapore's waters. The guidelines serve to provide general guidance on the effectiveness of dispersants with reference to time, weather and oil viscosity and pour point.

5. Keeping the Public Informed

We learnt the importance of keeping the public informed. The public demographic has become more informed and tech-savvy and it has become increasingly important for the government to be transparent in their actions and provide prompt response to local and foreign media queries, as well as timely and regular updates to the public and media. These actions by government and public agencies serve to minimise both media and public speculation.

5 Cooperative Mechanisms with Neighbouring Countries

Oil spills can sometimes be transboundary in nature and when this happens, cooperation amongst all countries affected by an oil spill is an essential step for effective management of such spill. Singapore is a party to two such regional cooperation arrangements, namely, the Revolving Fund and the ASEAN Regional Oil Spill Contingency Plan.

5.1 *Revolving Fund*

The Revolving Fund was established on 11 February 1981 through a Memorandum of Understanding signed by Indonesia, Malaysia, Singapore and the Malacca Strait Council (Revolving Fund MOU). Although the Revolving Fund's main purpose is to allow for any of the three littoral States of the Straits of Malacca and Singapore (i.e., Indonesia, Malaysia and Singapore) to draw a cash advance for use in combating oil pollution caused by ships, the Revolving Fund Committee also meets annually to discuss issues relating to oil spills and to update the Standard Operating Procedure for Joint Oil Spill Combat in the Straits of Malacca and Singapore (SOP).[48] The SOP was drawn up following

48 MPA, 'Factsheet on the Revolving Fund Committee (RFC)', *MPA* (27 May 2010) accessed 21 March 2017 at http://www.mpa.gov.sg/web/wcm/connect/www/374402e3-20b7-421b-b177-2a27af1e965e/annexa_270510.pdf?MOD=AJPERES. The most recent RFC meeting was held on 26 February 2015 in Jakarta.

the establishment of the Revolving Fund; it covers areas such as the response areas and division of responsibility among the littoral states, contact points, communication and information sharing procedures, inter-state assistance, reimbursement procedures and provides a list of available resources.[49] The SOP's objectives are to facilitate early information sharing and prompt and co-ordinated response to any oil spill incident.

The three littoral States also conduct regular joint communication exercises to test the procedures. Any lessons learnt are used to further improve and up-date these procedures.

The size of the Fund is 400 million yen (approximately USD 1.82 million) and any amount drawn will need to be repaid to the Fund when the State recovers the clean-up costs from the parties responsible.[50] In its history of almost 30 years, the Revolving Fund has only been used twice:

- In October 1992, both Indonesia and Malaysia tapped into the Revolving Fund to combat the oil spill from the *Nagasaki Spirit*.[51] The incident occurred in the northern part of the Straits of Malacca and Singapore.
- In October 2000, Indonesia used the Revolving Fund to clean up the oil spill from the *Natuna Sea*.[52] The incident occurred near Tanjung Pinang, Indonesia.

Under the Revolving Fund MOU, management of the Revolving Fund is rotated between Indonesia, Malaysia and Singapore for a period of five years each.

5.2 *ASEAN Regional Oil Spill Contingency Plan*

In 1994, under the auspices of the 'Project on Oil Spill Preparedness and Response in the ASEAN Seas Area' (ASEAN-OSPAR Project) and with the support of the Japanese Government,[53] the ASEAN Oil Spill Response Action Plan

49 *Ibid.*

50 MPA, 'Opening Address by BG(NS) Choi Shing Kwok, Permanent Secretary, Ministry of Transport at the Revolving Fund Hand-over Ceremony', *MPA* (26 April 2006) accessed 21 March 2017 at http://www.mpa.gov.sg/web/portal/home/media-centre/news-releases/speeches/detail/e20704e9-7df8-41f2-b806-05a97db35044.

51 MPA, *supra* note 48.

52 *Ibid.*

53 Under the ASEAN-OSPAR Project, Japan donated a sum of one billion Yen (approximately USD 10 million based on 1994 average rate of 1 USD to 99.72 JPY, data from FXTop Currency Converter, 'Historical exchange rates from 1953 with graph and charts', *FXTop*, accessed 21 March 2017 at http://fxtop.com/en/historical-exchange-rates.php) to purchase oil spill equipment to reinforce national stockpiles in the ASEAN region.

(ASEAN OSRAP) was established with the signing of an MOU by six ASEAN Member States—Brunei Darussalam, Indonesia, Malaysia, the Philippines, Thailand and Singapore.[54] The ASEAN OSRAP formed the basis for cooperation among the ASEAN member States at the operational level and sets out the standard operating procedures for mutual cooperation and information exchange on oil pollution incidents in the event of a major oil spill that exceeds the response capability of the national government.

However, the implementation of the ASEAN OSRAP was met with challenges. For example, Cambodia, Laos, Myanmar and Viet Nam became ASEAN Member States only after 1994 and were not party to the ASEAN OSRAP. There was also no mechanism linking the ASEAN OSRAP with the ASEAN Maritime Transport Working Group, which had the competency to discuss the technical and operational aspects of oil spill preparedness and response. In 2012, it was agreed that a new regional cooperation mechanism for oil spill preparedness would be developed to include all ten ASEAN Member States. On 28 November 2014, the ASEAN Member States signed the Memorandum of Understanding on ASEAN Cooperation Mechanism for Joint Oil Spill Preparedness and Response (OSRAP MOU).[55] In accordance to the OSRAP MOU, each party shall cooperate to develop a Regional Oil Spill Contingency Plan, to coordinate and integrate response to oil spill incidents affecting the marine and coastal environment of one or more parties or exceeding the response capacity of any one party.

The ASEAN Regional Oil Spill Contingency Plan, which will replace the ASEAN OSRAP, is currently being drafted. The ASEAN Regional Oil Spill Contingency Plan will address the requirement to develop a regional plan of cooperation and represents the key operational framework for achieving the objectives of the OSRAP MOU. It will provide a mechanism for ASEAN Member States to request and provide support in response to oil spills, to the extent that their resources allow. This draft plan, when put into operation, will implement a regional cooperative mechanism for oil spill preparedness and response that is in line with the OPRC.

---

54 Joselito Guevarra, 'Global Initiative for Southeast Asia: The Journey Towards Regional Cooperation in Oil Spill Preparedness and Response in ASEAN', *Interspill* (2015) accessed 21 March 2017 at http://interspill.org/previous-events/2015/WhitePapers/Interspill2015ConferenceProceedings/25%20MARCH%202015/IMO-IPIECA%20Global%20Initiative/Global-Initiative-for-Southeast-Asia.pdf.

55 Association of Southeast Asian Nations (ASEAN), 'Memorandum of Understanding On ASEAN Cooperation Mechanism for Joint Oil Spill Preparedness and Response', *ASEAN* (28 November 2014) at Table 13.1, accessed 21 March 2017 at http://www.asean.org/wp-content/uploads/images/pdf/2014_upload/MOU%20on%20ASEAN%20OSRAP.pdf.

The coordination framework that is being contemplated by the draft ASEAN Regional Oil Spill Contingency Plan neither alters nor replaces the existing national response systems of ASEAN Member States. In practice, the affected State will continue to execute its response operations based on its own national contingency plan and incident management system.

6 Opportunities for Sharing Experiences and Best Practices

Given the similarities between the cooperative mechanisms to which Singapore is a party (i.e., the Revolving Fund and the ASEAN Regional Oil Spill Contingency Plan) and the Agreement on Cooperation on Marine Oil Pollution Preparedness and Response in the Arctic (Arctic MOSPA),[56] there could be opportunities for cross-learning. For example, we could learn from the Arctic MOSPA's Operating Guidelines[57] to include an overview of each Member State's current national response system. This will allow the Member States to have a better understanding on each other's response framework, thus facilitating effective cooperation on oil pollution incident response. On the other hand, the Arctic MOSPA could consider including a list of available resources in its Operating Guidelines so that other State Parties would know where the relevant resources are located in the event of an emergency. Besides cross-learning opportunities, it would be beneficial for all parties to share our experiences and best practices in implementing these cooperative mechanisms.

Since Singapore was accorded observer status in the Arctic Council in 2013, MPA has been a member of the Emergency Prevention, Preparedness and Response (EPPR) Working Group. The EPPR Working Group is one of six working groups of the Arctic Council whose role is to address various aspects of prevention, preparedness and response to environmental emergencies in the Arctic, as well as search and rescue. The goal of the EPPR Working Group is to

---

56 Emergency Prevention, Preparedness and Response (EPPR)—Working Group of the Arctic Council, 'Agreement on Cooperation on Marine Oil Pollution Preparedness and Response in the Arctic', *Arctic Council* accessed 21 March 2017 at http://arctic-council.org/eppr/agreement-on-cooperation-on-marine-oil-pollution-preparedness-and-response-in-the-arctic/.

57 EPPR—Working Group of the Arctic Council, 'Agreement on Cooperation on Marine Oil Pollution Preparedness and Response in the Arctic—Appendix IV—Operational Guidelines', *Arctic Council* (28 January 2014) at 23, accessed 21 March 2017 at http://www.arctic-council.org/eppr/wp-content/uploads/2015/04/MOSPA_OPERATIONAL_GUIDELINES_ENGLISH_FINAL.pdf.

contribute to the protection of the Arctic environment from the threat or impact that may result from an accidental release of pollutants or radionuclides.[58] Members of the EPPR Working Group exchange information on best practices and conduct projects to include development of guidance and risk assessment methodologies, response exercises, and training. MPA shared its experience in oil spill preparedness and response at the 12th EPPR Working Group meeting in Tromsø, Norway, in 2013, using the *Evoikos* oil spill as a case study. In December 2014, MPA shared its operational experiences on the use of UAVs for surveillance of oil spills during a workshop hosted by the United States on unmanned aircraft systems (UAS) and their potential applications in the Arctic. In September 2015, Singapore also participated in the MOSPA exercise-planning workshop held in Washington DC that was led by the United States.[59]

7 Conclusion

The risk of a major oil pollution incident in both the Straits of Malacca and Singapore and the Arctic is very real and the importance of being prepared and responding expeditiously and effectively, as well as cooperation between all relevant stakeholders cannot be overemphasised. Our oil pollution risk management approach as encapsulated in our 2P-3R model has served us well and our cooperation with neighbouring States have helped us to minimise the risk of oil pollution in our waters. Through our participation in the EPPR Working Group, we hope, in a small way, to be able to share our experience in oil spill preparedness and response and, although there are significant differences in the weather, sea, traffic and geopolitical conditions between the ASEAN and Arctic regions, there are many similarities in the mechanisms that are used to combat oil spills within these regions and a mutual sharing of experiences and ideas to combat oil spills more effectively would certainly benefit all.

---

58 EPPR—Working Group of the Arctic Council, 'Homepage', *Arctic Council* (2016) accessed 21 March 2017 at http://arctic-council.org/eppr/.

59 Captain M Segar, 'Oil Spill Preparedness and Response: The Singapore Experience', *MPA* (9–11 December 2015) at slide 25, accessed 21 March 2017 at http://cil.nus.edu.sg/wp/wp-content/uploads/2015/10/Session-6-Oil-Spill-Preparedness-and-Response-The-Singapore-Experience-Muhammad-Segar.pdf.

CHAPTER 14

Conclusions on Challenges and Prospects for Enhanced Cooperation on the Governance of Arctic Shipping

Robert C Beckman, Tore Henriksen, Kristine Dalaker Kraabel, Erik J Molenaar and J Ashley Roach

This concluding Chapter focuses on the challenges and prospects for enhanced cooperation on the governance of shipping in the Arctic. It first highlights some of the major findings in the previous Chapters. Then it examines the major challenges to enhanced cooperation on the governance of Arctic shipping and the feasibility of establishing mechanisms that will promote cooperation among all the major stakeholders on matters of common interest. The underlying premise of this Chapter is that shipping in the Arctic is likely to increase, and therefore it is in the interests of all stakeholders to enhance further the safety of navigation, the protection of the marine environment from the impacts of shipping, and protect the culture and way of life of Arctic indigenous peoples.

Major Conclusions from the Previous Chapters

With respect to the future of shipping in the Arctic, the following major conclusions can be drawn from the previous Chapters.

First, the extent and thickness of sea ice in the Arctic is likely to decrease, and as a result, shipping in the Arctic will grow in the future, at least on a seasonal basis for specific types of shipping.

Second, shipping in the Arctic will continue to face many challenges due to the remoteness of the region, the harsh climate, extended periods of darkness and significant shortcomings in the broader marine infrastructure, such as poor port facilities, and lack of accurate navigational charts, communications systems, aids to navigation and emergency response services.

Third, significant financial investments will be required by both the public sector and the private sector to improve the broader marine infrastructure.

Fourth, there is widespread concern among States, Arctic indigenous peoples and non-governmental organisations about the various threats posed by increased shipping to the marine environment.

 | DOI 10.1163/9789004339385_015

Fifth, Arctic indigenous peoples are concerned about the impact of increased shipping on their culture and way of life.

With respect to the governance of shipping in the Arctic, key conclusions of the previous Chapters are set out below.

First, the IMO will continue to be the competent international organisation for the development and adoption of global rules and standards for maritime safety and the environmental impact of shipping within the framework of the United Nations Convention on the Law of the Sea (UNCLOS) and for facilitating their general acceptance and eventual implementation, including in the polar regions.

Second, adoption of the Polar Code by the International Maritime Organization (IMO) was a major achievement toward establishing common global rules and standards to enhance the safety of navigation and protect the marine environment from the impacts of shipping in the Arctic. In addition to keeping the Polar Code under review and amending it when necessary,[1] the IMO will also adopt instruments that are related to the Polar Code, consequential to it, or which complement it.[2]

Third, while Canada and Russia are likely to take steps to bring their national legislation into harmony with the Polar Code, they are also likely to take the position that they have the power under Article 234 of UNCLOS to continue to adopt national laws and regulations that are more stringent than the Polar Code when they determine that such laws and regulations are required to protect the Arctic marine environment from the impacts of shipping.

Fourth, if the Arctic becomes open for international navigation on a seasonal basis, user States and other stakeholders are likely to take the position that foreign ships in transit through the Arctic should be governed by international rules and standards adopted by the IMO and other competent international organisations, rather than the national laws and regulations of the coastal States.

Fifth, the Arctic Council is likely to continue to play an active and important role in the governance of shipping in the Arctic by examining particular issues

---

1 For instance, by making the Polar Code also applicable to non-SOLAS ships (Phase 2). At MSC 97, however, no decision was taken on the commencement of Phase 2, as this was perceived as being premature (MSC 97/22, at 74, para 21.10).

2 E.g., see Amendments to the International Convention on Standards of Training, Certification and Watchkeeping for Seafarers, adopted 7 July 1978, as amended in 1995 and 2010, entered into force 28 April 1984, 1361 UNTS (STCW) and the Seafarers' Training, Certification and Watchkeeping (STCW Code), IMO Doc MSC 96/3/2, 4 November 2015, prepared for adoption by MSC 97 in accordance with the STCW and with an expected entry into force on 1 July 2018, specifically, MSC 97/22, at 13–14, paras 3.49–3.57, and other decisions made at MSC 97, including MSC 97/22, at. 41–43, paras 8.27–8.32, at 50, paras 9.22–9.23, at 61, paras 16.6–16.7, and at 73–74, paras 21.7–21.8.

relating to maritime safety and the impacts of shipping on the marine environment and on the culture and way of life of the Arctic indigenous peoples.

Sixth, the Paris and Tokyo Memoranda of Understanding on Port State Control could become involved in ensuring that vessels engaged in Arctic shipping comply with the Polar Code.

Factors Supporting the Establishment of a Cooperative Mechanism for Arctic Shipping

There are several reasons why it may be feasible to begin discussions on developing one or more cooperative mechanisms in the Arctic similar to that for the Straits of Malacca and Singapore (SOMS).

First, the Arctic States are likely to see the economic advantages of opening up the Arctic to international shipping, if it can be done without posing a threat to their sovereignty or their security interests, and if they can be assured that Arctic shipping will follow the best international rules, standards and practices for safety of navigation and protection of the marine environment.

Second, the Arctic States recognise that they will likely require outside assistance to help fund the necessary improvements to the broader marine infrastructure.

Third, major user States such as China, Japan and South Korea have demonstrated that they have a serious interest in developing Arctic shipping, and that they have the technology and resources necessary to assist in improving the broader marine infrastructure and technology.

Fourth, Arctic indigenous peoples—whether through the Arctic Council or otherwise—will demand a voice in the process to ensure that their interests are taken into account.

Fifth, other stakeholders, such as non-governmental organisations (NGOs) representing the international shipping industry and national and international environmental NGOs, will want to have the opportunity to present their views and positions on the issues.

Any Cooperative Mechanism Must Be 'Without Prejudice' to Sensitive Issues

Any cooperative mechanism on shipping in and through the Arctic is unlikely to succeed if it requires any of the interested States to change their national position on sensitive issues of sovereignty or existing maritime disputes. Therefore, it must be clear that participation in a cooperative mechanism is 'without prejudice' to the position of the cooperating States on the following issues.

First, it is without prejudice to the position of any State on the legal status of Arctic waters.

Second, it is without prejudice to the issue of whether passage through Arctic waters is subject to the regime of transit passage through straits used for international navigation.

Third, it is without prejudice to the positions of the interested States on the geographical and substantive scope of the powers of coastal States under Article 234 of UNCLOS.

Fourth, it is without prejudice to the position of any interested State on any disputes concerning sovereignty claims, maritime boundaries, baselines, or submissions to the Commission on the Limits of the Continental Shelf.

Principles Governing Cooperative Mechanisms for Arctic Shipping

The cooperative mechanism in the Straits of Malacca and Singapore (SOMS Cooperative Mechanism) has several key features that have been responsible for its success.

First, it is consistent with UNCLOS and does not infringe on the primary role of the IMO in the establishment of global rules and standards governing international shipping.

Second, it recognises that the three littoral States bordering the SOMS have sovereignty over their waters in the straits and primary responsibility for the safety of navigation and the protection of the marine environment, and provides that any cooperative measures must be approved by the three littoral States.

Third, it recognises that user States and other stakeholders, such as industry and environmental NGOs, have an interest in the safety of navigation and the protection of the marine environment in the SOMS. It provides a forum where they can meet regularly with officials from the three littoral States to discuss issues relating to safety and ship-source pollution in the SOMS. In return, the user States and other stakeholders provide funds either to the general Aids to Navigation Fund or to support specific projects that will enhance maritime safety or environmental protection in the SOMS.

In many respects the situation in the Arctic is similar to that in the SOMS.

First, the Arctic States, especially Canada and Russia, jealously guard their sovereignty and jurisdiction and are wary of any arrangements that may infringe on their sovereignty and jurisdiction.

Second, the Arctic States are interested in enhancing navigation, but they lack the funding and resources required to enhance safety of navigation, protection of the marine environment and improvement of the broader marine infrastructure.

Third, user States and other stakeholders have a genuine interest in enhancing safety and environmental protection in Arctic shipping, and they may be willing to provide financial and technical assistance if a mechanism is created that gives them a forum to discuss these issues with the coastal States.

There is, however, one critically important difference between shipping in the SOMS and in the Arctic. In the SOMS, the three littoral States have agreed to manage the two straits as a single unit and to make decisions on the basis of consensus. By contrast, in the Arctic, Russia is the sole major State bordering the Northern Sea Route and Canada is the sole major State bordering the Northwest Passage. Therefore, Russia and Canada are likely to take the position that no cooperative mechanism can be created for passage through these routes unless the mechanism recognises their sovereignty and jurisdiction and their primary responsibility for navigational safety and the marine environment.

This important difference means that it is unlikely that a single cooperative mechanism can be established which governs all shipping in the Arctic and which gives all the Arctic coastal States an equal voice. Instead, it may be more feasible to begin by exploring the prospect of establishing a cooperative mechanism for the Northern Sea Route. The mechanism would recognise the sovereignty and jurisdiction of Russia and its primary responsibility for the safety of navigation and the protection of the marine environment in the Northern Sea Route. At the same time, a forum could be established that would enable major user States and other stakeholders, including Arctic indigenous peoples and industry and environmental NGOs, to meet on a regular basis with officials from Russia to explore prospects for improving and developing the necessary broader marine infrastructure. If they had a voice in the planning of such infrastructure, user States may be willing to provide technical and financial assistance to strengthen the broader marine infrastructure in the Northern Sea Route or to encourage their companies to participate in public sector-private sector partnerships to make the necessary investments.

At the same time, discussions could also be expanded among officials from Russia, the United States, user States and other stakeholders in relation to the Bering Strait. Similar discussions could also be initiated with Canadian officials in relation to the Canadian Arctic.

Alternatively, discussions could be initiated between Canadian officials and user States and representatives of industry on the infrastructure required to enhance safe navigation and protect the marine environment in the Canadian

Arctic. Such discussions in Canada should include representatives of indigenous peoples and environmental organisations.

The first phase in such endeavours could consist of workshops convened by one or more of the relevant Arctic coastal States to exchange views among stakeholders, to examine the interests and concerns of all stakeholders, and to develop proposals for concrete cooperative projects. Such projects should above all be aimed at building confidence and experience among the participants. Examples could be aids to navigation, routeing measures and nautical charting.

Consideration should be given to inviting the IMO to play a role in establishing cooperative mechanisms in the Arctic, given the important role it played in facilitating the establishment of the SOMS Cooperative Mechanism. The IMO may be willing to perform a similar role in facilitating the establishment of one or more cooperative mechanisms for Arctic shipping. If the IMO is given such a role, it may increase the chances that major user States and shipping organisations will be willing to be involved.

The SOMS Cooperative Mechanism is nevertheless an autonomous body, which has not been established under the auspices of an overarching intergovernmental organisation or body. This institutional choice may well be the most appropriate solution for the abovementioned cooperative mechanisms for Arctic shipping. However, a possible role for the Arctic Council in establishing cooperative mechanisms in the Arctic should also be considered. Given the extensive activities relating to Arctic shipping that have been and continue to be undertaken within the Arctic Council, with due regard to the primary role of the IMO in the establishment of rules and standards governing international shipping, it may also be possible and desirable to link such mechanisms in one way or another to the Arctic Council. As highlighted in Chapter 2 of this Volume, the last decade has seen the establishment of several new Arctic bodies that are not formally part of the Arctic Council. Some of these were established under legally binding instruments negotiated under the auspices of the Arctic Council, and others build on earlier work of the Arctic Council or even aim to implement and support such earlier work. This institutional diversity and flexibility reflects a willingness to consider tailor-made and innovative solutions that would be of crucial importance to cooperative mechanisms for Arctic shipping.

Index

www.ingramcontent.com/pod-product-compliance
Lightning Source LLC
LaVergne TN
LVHW012053011026
849162LV00018B/192
* 9 7 8 9 0 0 4 3 3 9 3 7 8 *